THE CONCEPT DESIGN OF A TWENTY-FIRST CENTURY PREFERENTIAL TRADE AGREEMENT

The Concept Design of a Twenty-First Century Preferential Trade Agreement describes the current status and possible future evolution of trade agreements. The individual contributions provide fine-grained analyses of the various challenges trade agreements face and how these differ across countries. The book brings together leading researchers from international law and international relations to provide conceptual and empirical insights to inform the ongoing reform debates. By taking stock of scholarly advances, the book further aims at stimulating cross-fertilisation in the study of trade agreements in the field of international economic law. This title is also available as Open Access on Cambridge Core.

Kathleen Claussen is Professor of Law at Georgetown University, Washington, DC. She is the author of more than forty articles and essays concerning trade, investment, and international dispute settlement, among other related research areas. She has also served as counsel or arbitrator in over two dozen international disputes. Among other leadership roles, she has served on the Executive Council and Executive Committee of the American Society of International Law and is Co-Editor-in-Chief of the *Journal of International Economic Law*.

Manfred Elsig is Full Professor of International Relations at the World Trade Institute, University of Bern. His research focuses on international political economy, international organisations, international courts, preferential trade agreements, and European trade policy. He is the Co-Editor of *Governing the WTO: Past, Present and Beyond Doha* (Cambridge University Press, 2011), *Assessing the World Trade Organization: Fit for Purpose?* (Cambridge University Press, 2017), and *The Shifting Landscape of Global Trade Governance* (Cambridge University Press, 2019).

Rodrigo Polanco is a senior researcher, lecturer, and academic coordinator at the World Trade Institute, University of Bern, a legal adviser at the Swiss Institute of Comparative Law, and a visiting professor at the University of Chile. He holds a Bachelor and a Master of Laws (University of Chile), an LLM in International Legal Studies (New York University), and a PhD in Law (University of Bern). He has published extensively as an author and editor in leading international academic publications and journals on investment, trade, tax, and environmental law.

The Concept Design of a Twenty-First Century Preferential Trade Agreement

TRENDS AND FUTURE INNOVATIONS

Edited by

KATHLEEN CLAUSSEN

Georgetown University

MANFRED ELSIG

University of Bern

RODRIGO POLANCO

University of Bern

CAMBRIDGE
UNIVERSITY PRESS

CAMBRIDGE
UNIVERSITY PRESS

Shaftesbury Road, Cambridge CB2 8EA, United Kingdom

One Liberty Plaza, 20th Floor, New York, NY 10006, USA

477 Williamstown Road, Port Melbourne, VIC 3207, Australia

314–321, 3rd Floor, Plot 3, Splendor Forum, Jasola District Centre, New Delhi – 110025, India

103 Penang Road, #05–06/07, Visioncrest Commercial, Singapore 238467

Cambridge University Press is part of Cambridge University Press & Assessment, a department of the University of Cambridge.

We share the University's mission to contribute to society through the pursuit of education, learning and research at the highest international levels of excellence.

www.cambridge.org
Information on this title: www.cambridge.org/9781009484626

DOI: 10.1017/9781009484640

First published 2025

A catalogue record for this publication is available from the British Library

A Cataloging-in-Publication data record for this book is available from the Library of Congress

ISBN 978-1-009-48462-6 Hardback

Contents

Figures

Tables

Contributors

Arthur Appleton Appleton Luff

Harro Van Asselt University of Cambridge

Amrita Bahri Mexico Autonomous Institute of Technology – ITAM

Leopoldo Biffi Graduate Institute of International and Development Studies

Amanda Bisong European Centre for Development Policy Management

Anoush der Boghossian World Trade Organization

Clara Brandi University of Bonn and German Institute of Development and Sustainability

Mira Burri University of Lucerne

María Vásquez Callo-Müller University of Lucerne

Kathleen Claussen Georgetown University

Maria Anna Corvaglia University of Leeds

Thomas Cottier University of Bern – World Trade Institute

Manfred Elsig University of Bern – World Trade Institute

Gregory Felder University of Bern – Institute of European and International Economic Law

Kirthana Ganeson University of Bern – World Trade Institute

Israel Gutiérrez Graduate Institute of International and Development Studies

Selina Hauser University of Bern – World Trade Institute

Kateryna Holzer University of Eastern Finland

Martin Jehli University of Bern – World Trade Institute

Sebastian Klotz PwC Switzerland and World Trade Institute

Yuliia Kucheriava University of Bern – World Trade Institute

Kholofelo Kugler University of Lucerne

Lolita Laperle-Forget World Bank

Yinuo Liu University of Bern – World Trade Institute

Jean-Frédéric Morin Laval University

Nora Neufeld World Trade Organization (***Ms Neufeld passed away in November 2023***)

Federico Ortino King's College London

Marion Panizzon University of Bern – World Trade Institute

Rodrigo Polanco University of Bern – World Trade Institute and Swiss Institute of Comparative Law

Marine Roux University of Bern – World Trade Institute

Martin Roy World Trade Organization

Luca Rubini University of Turin

Pierre Sauvé World Bank

Anirudh Shingal S. P. Jain Institute of Management and Research

Shailja Singh Indian Institute of Foreign Trade

Patrick Wagner University of Konstanz

Christian Winkler Graduate Institute of International and Development Studies

Preface

In early June 2022, the World Trade Institute organised a doctoral retreat in the Swiss Alps in a remote hotel with a view on the Aletsch Glacier. Over three days, many of the ideas found in this edited volume took shape. PhD students from the University of Bern, the Graduate Institute of International and Development Studies, and the University of Lucerne were organised into interdisciplinary groups tackling different themes. Several experts were invited to share their experiences and challenge conventional (and other) wisdoms. The Spirit of 'Belalp' that developed has guided the project ever since. Shortly after, in July 2022, we organised jointly with the Embassy of the United Kingdom (UK) in Switzerland a workshop with additional colleagues and experts to further brainstorm and develop concrete ideas for future preferential trade agreement (PTA) design.

After many more exchanges across teams of authors and the editors, we are very happy to see this collective effort in printed form. We hope that readers will find the various chapters thought-provoking and insightful, in particular for understanding the potential transformation of PTAs going forward and future design options.

This book would not have been possible without the generous support of the UK Embassy in Bern and friends of the World Trade Institute. Special thanks go to Kris Camponi, Joel Plaja, Peter van den Bossche, Victor do Prado, Cédric Dupont, Michael Hahn, Joe Francois, Andrew Lugg, and Sophia Thompson. Finally, we wish to thank Sharon McCann from Cambridge University Press for her excellent guidance throughout the entire process, as well as her support for the World Trade Forum Series.

1

Thinking about the Future Design of Preferential Trade Agreements

Kathleen Claussen, Manfred Elsig, and Rodrigo Polanco

1.1 MOTIVATION

How should future trade agreements address new and upcoming challenges to the international trading system? The inspiration to address this overarching question grew out of discussions with trade experts at the United Kingdom (UK) Embassy in Switzerland and the Swiss State Secretariat for Economic Affairs (SECO). The discussions showed a need from an academic but also trade diplomacy perspective to look beyond the current design features of preferential trade agreements (PTAs) and spearhead new innovative thinking about how future trade agreements could and should look.[1] Many scholarly contributions focus on explaining the current design and various effects of existing trade agreements. They usually take stock of such treaties and evaluate their impact. However, few projects elaborate future concepts that could be advanced through PTAs. This is what this book project aims to achieve.

The analogy of a car show comes to mind, where different leading car producers showcase their concept cars for the future. Many of these innovations will not be directly marketable and it will take time to achieve mass production for these initial concepts. In this same spirit, the contributors have been invited to develop future ideas, explore the known unknowns, and go beyond the status quo.

1.2 PTAS AS A FORUM FOR TALKING TRADE

Trade agreements have a long history. Often, countries secured and strengthened their trade through diverse arrangements ranging from colonial preferences to bilateral treaties or broader regional agreements. From the Romans to the

[1] We define PTAs as reciprocal trade agreements where a limited number of members grant each other preferences in terms of market access and work towards aligning trade-related regulations.

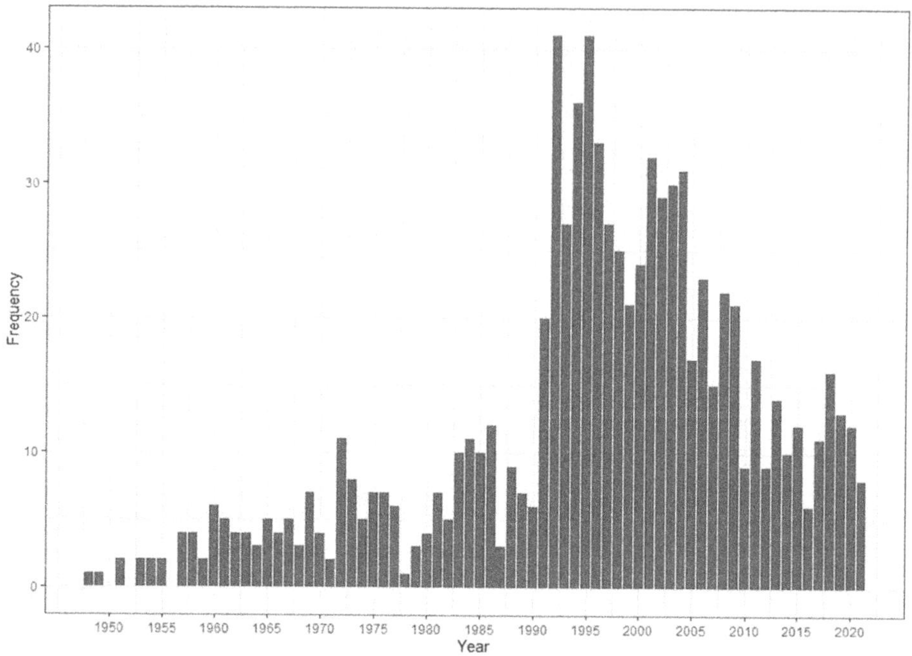

FIGURE 1.1 PTA signing over time.
Source: www.designoftradeagreements.org; Dür et al. (2014).

Ottomans, empires were among the earliest movers in securing trade interests, using their influence and force to give their traders and producers secure access to foreign markets, usually on an exclusive basis. Early trade agreements were concerned less with liberalising trade and opening up new markets than with ensuring that a country's traders and their property received protection from arbitrary measures in foreign countries (World Trade Organization 2011).

The now widespread idea that trade agreements could reciprocally secure trade interests is relatively modern, starting with the Cobden–Chevalier Treaty (1860) between Britain and France, which, for the first time, considered notable reciprocal tariff reductions and a most-favoured-nation (MFN) clause. States slowly rediscovered PTAs after World War II, partly inspired by a number of bilateral agreements the United States had negotiated in the interwar period under the Reciprocal Tariff Act of 1934. While we observe a limited number of initiatives to negotiate PTAs up to the mid-1980s, they have grown in popularity since the 1990s. The rise in the early 1990s was mainly a result of former Soviet satellite states negotiating such agreements, in particular with European states, some in view of a future association with the European Union (EU). In addition, crises in multilateral rulemaking since the end of the 1990s have also led to a sustained high level of trade diplomacy through PTAs (see Figure 1.1).

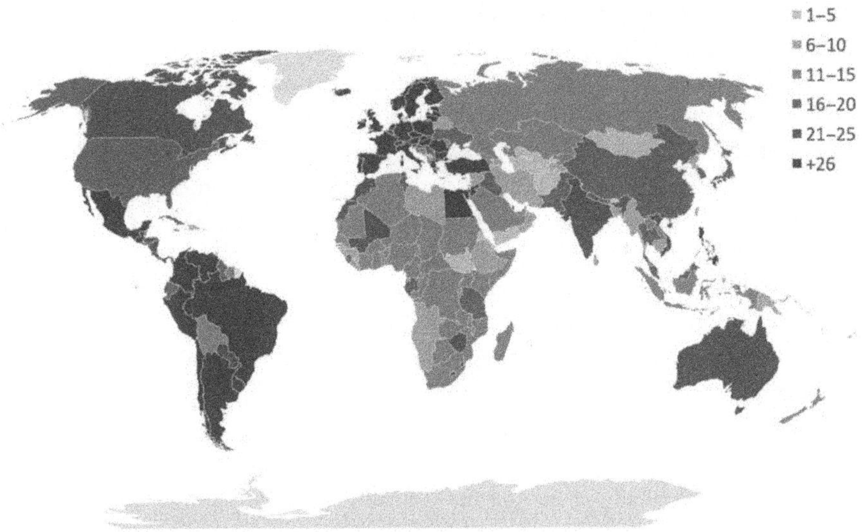

FIGURE 1.2 World map of PTA signing.
Source: www.designoftradeagreements.org

While the increase in the number of new PTAs signed each year demonstrates their continued popularity, there is considerable variation across states in the deployment and reliance on such agreements. Figure 1.2 shows how many PTAs countries have successfully negotiated since the 1950s. Numbers have generally been high in Europe and in Latin America. While many important PTAs have been concluded, it is striking that the United States and the EU do not share a PTA, nor do the EU and China or the United States and China.[2] This is particularly surprising, given the extent of trade and investment flows among these economies, although tariffs are already at generally low levels between the United States and the EU, and trade barriers are rather modest.

In the United States, the Trump Administration withdrew from a concluded but not yet ratified PTA (the Trans-Pacific Partnership, TPP) and has not embarked on any new major preferential engagement except for a reform of the North American Free Trade Agreement (NAFTA), which was replaced by the United States–Mexico–Canada Agreement (USMCA).[3] The Biden Administration has indicated

[2] We do not consider the Trump Administration trade deal with China as a PTA based on reciprocity with a view of extending trade.

[3] The USMCA was negotiated under strong pressure by the Trump Administration. Both Canada and Mexico were reluctant to engage in the negotiations (Bahri and Lugo 2020). This agreement included a number of novel provisions, some of which will be addressed in the different chapters of this book. The USMCA, however, has also a mercantilist undertone that led to provisions that read as quite protectionist.

that it does not favour negotiating new PTAs, at least not in their usual form (Claussen 2022b).[4]

The EU has also struggled with negotiating ambitious treaties and with long-lasting domestic debates to ratify them. For example, the signature of the 2016 Comprehensive Economic and Trade Agreement (CETA) between the EU and Canada was blocked by the Belgian region of Wallonia, forcing the inclusion of a legal interpretative instrument to clarify obligations stated in the investment chapter of the agreement (Paquin 2022). More recently, the Irish Supreme Court precluded the ratification of the CETA absent changes to the Irish domestic legislation governing arbitration (Baker 2022). Likewise, earlier versions of the EU's PTAs with Singapore (2018) and Viet Nam (2019) included an investment chapter. As a consequence of the Court of Justice of the European Union (CJEU) Opinion 2/15 of 16 May 2017, such provisions were segregated into separate investment protection agreements (IPAs). According to the CJEU, all subject matters of those PTAs fall within the scope of the EU's common commercial policy, with the exceptions of non-direct forms of investments and investor–state dispute settlement (ISDS). The segregation of investment issues from the PTAs was aimed at improving the chances of their ratification, but it also negatively affected the EU's ability to use its political weight to shape the standardisation of rules (Hainbach 2018).

Politicisation of PTAs varies by region. We witness continued interest in this form of institutionalised trade liberalisation and cooperation in Latin America, Asia, and Africa. On a regional basis, the 2020 Regional Comprehensive Economic Partnership (RCEP) stands out in Asia; and in Africa, the 2018 African Continental Free Trade Area (AfCFTA) is hailed as a landmark agreement as well. In Latin America, the 2014 Pacific Alliance Additional Protocol between Chile, Colombia, Mexico, and Peru stands out (Sauvé et al. 2018).

In addition, a number of trans-regional agreements have come to the fore, such as the 2018 Comprehensive and Progressive Agreement for Trans-Pacific Partnership (CPTPP) – a slightly modified version of the TPP after the US withdrawal, as well as CETA. Most recently, in 2022, the Pacific Alliance concluded a free trade agreement with Singapore (the Pacific Alliance–Singapore Free Trade Agreement, PASFTA), the first negotiated by that trade bloc. Some of these agreements have also developed novel provisions in various trade and trade-related areas, such as regulatory coherence/cooperation/good regulatory practices, electronic

[4] See, for example, the Indo-Pacific Economic Framework for Prosperity (IPEF), which is designed to be different from a traditional PTA. It includes a trade pillar and three additional pillars on supply chains; clean energy, decarbonisation, and infrastructure; and tax and anti-corruption. The trade pillar seeks to build 'high-standard, inclusive, free, and fair-trade commitments and to develop new and creative approaches to trade and technology cooperation that will support enduring prosperity in the Indo-Pacific region'. Participant countries include Australia, Brunei Darussalam, Fiji, Japan, Indonesia, Republic of Korea, Malaysia, New Zealand, Philippines, Singapore, Thailand, Viet Nam, and the United States (United States Trade Representative (USTR) 2022).

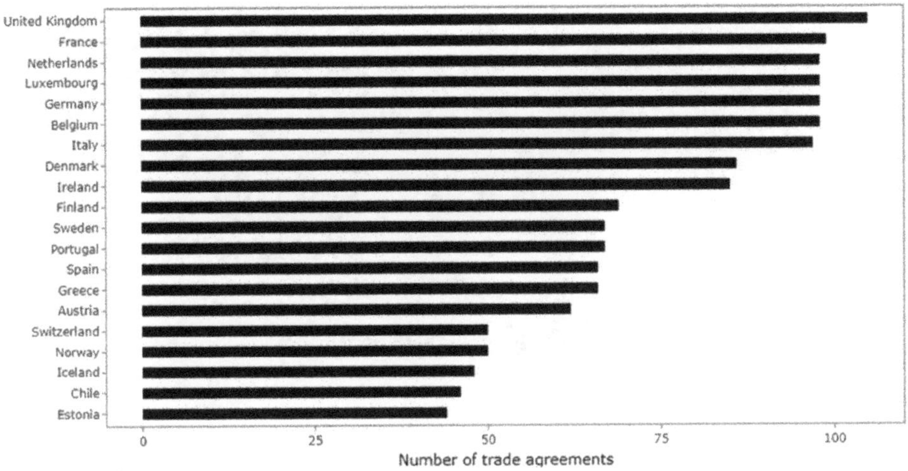

FIGURE 1.3 Countries with the most PTAs.
Note: Older members of the EU have historically signed more agreements, some of which are no longer in force.
Source: www.designoftradeagreements.org

commerce/digital trade, labour, environment and development, transparency and corruption, as well as trade and gender.

One country stands out in its negotiation and conclusion of PTAs in the past few years. Due to Brexit, since 2019, the UK has concluded thirty PTAs starting with agreements that largely allow the UK to keep the same deals that it had when it was an EU Member (e.g. PTAs with Chile, Israel, and Lebanon). Consecutive UK governments have actively sought to replicate existing EU agreements. The UK built up its trade diplomatic machinery to conclude new treaties that included novel chapters on topics not included in EU agreements, like animal welfare, digital trade, and gender, as can be seen in the PTAs with Australia (2021) and New Zealand (2022). Figure 1.3 shows the top twenty countries in terms of overall numbers of PTAs, with the UK leading a group of nearly exclusively European states.

Trade agreements have become substantially deeper over time (see Figure 1.4). In addition to developing more ambitious market access commitments, countries have also extended the scope of PTAs. While PTAs in the 1990s began to focus on behind-the-border issues and regulatory issues (intellectual property rights (IPR), public procurement, services), since the turn of the century, we have seen increasing attention to new issues (e.g. digital trade, global value chains – GVCs) but also to topics formerly called 'non-trade concerns', which have slowly extended the PTA agenda, including labour rights, environmental protection, gender, mobility, and good governance (Claussen 2022a).

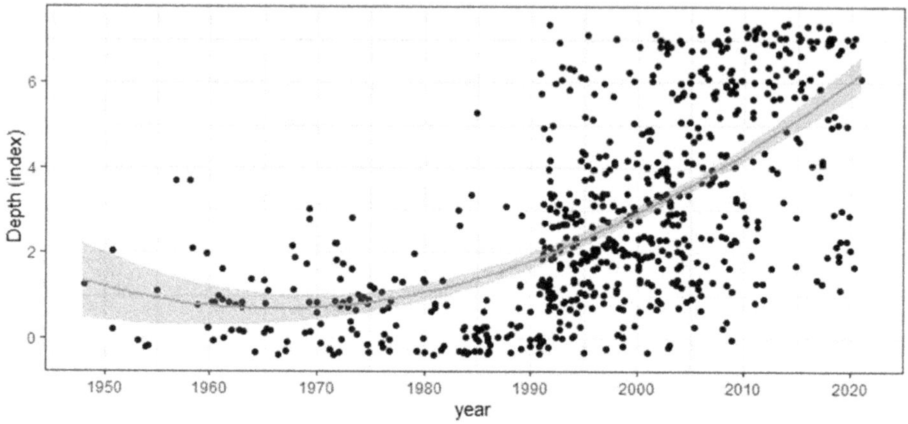

FIGURE 1.4 Deepening of trade agreements over time.
Source: www.designoftradeagreements.org

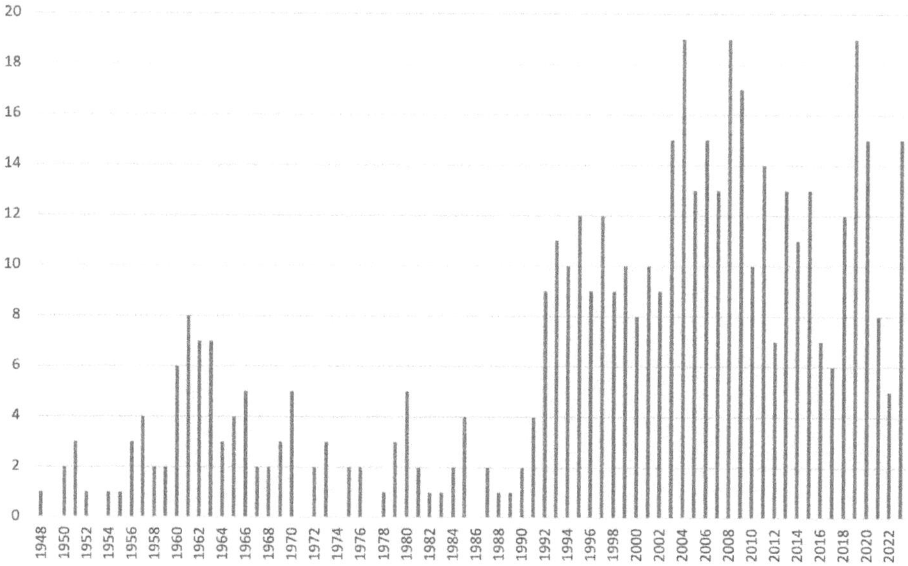

FIGURE 1.5 PTAs with investment provisions over time.
Source: EDIT, https://edit.wti.org/; Alschner et al. (2021)

Most recently, we also observe that investment regulation has entered the universe of PTAs through dedicated chapters. Figure 1.5 shows the number of PTAs per year that include investment provisions.

Preferential trade agreements often replicate provisions from other PTAs. The phenomenon of boilerplating has been well documented (Claussen 2018; Allee and Elsig 2019). Some treaties have more influence over future treaty-making than others. Treaty models and templates travel through the PTA network, and this diffusion also creates unintended effects. Ideas developed in one PTA can inspire future negotiations beyond geographic boundaries. Scholars have also noted the dialectical relationship between the World Trade Organization (WTO) and PTAs (Allee et al. 2017; Elsig and Klotz 2021). In other words, some innovations developed in the context of PTA negotiations can also spill into multilateral negotiations, as the example of the WTO's Joint Statement Initiative on electronic commerce negotiations shows (World Trade Organization 2021).

1.3 DESIGN SCENARIOS FOR THE FUTURE

As outlined above, PTAs have become more prominent over time, but have also led to increased politicisation. Notwithstanding both enthusiasm for and opposition to PTAs, several assumptions have guided the work presented in the following chapters.

First, we generally assume that a country wants to pursue a PTA; in other words, countries are not coerced into treaty-making. A realist approach would certainly lead to a different set of future design features than the ones developed in this edited volume. We see the negotiation of PTAs as a predominantly voluntary exercise with the aim of gradually liberalising markets and aligning regulatory philosophies. We also acknowledge increasing geopolitical tensions but do not develop ideas following a zero-sum game logic or a world of blocs.

Second, and related, while we acknowledge that the issue of national security has come to dominate discourses across the globe, we share the conviction that such clauses should not be used as disguised protection and that states' reliance on them should only be temporary.

Third, while market access is still a primary driving factor in PTA negotiations, there is an increasing need to address concerns or regulatory cooperation, to meet related sustainability goals, and to allow for smart flexibility mechanisms to address societal concerns.

Fourth, while we are aware of political economy forces at home that often tend to limit innovations and ground negotiators' expectations of what is feasible, we aim to look beyond what is possible in the near future and develop ideas that could inspire ambitious future treaty-making initiatives.

1.4 OVERVIEW OF THE BOOK

The project brings together experts on a rich range of topics covered in PTAs. The authors represent different disciplines and research traditions. Some chapters have been developed by academic partners working together with leading practitioners. All chapters start by taking stock of the current advances in PTA design. They then outline forward-looking design ideas. All authors have been asked to discuss novel developments across PTA models as well as the relationship between PTAs and multilateral agreements where applicable. Each group of authors has selected a limited number of issues within its selected topic area to reflect how these issues could be taken up by PTAs in the future. While cognisant of the political challenges of implementing their ideas, the authors have tried to overcome this status quo bias and consider the conditions under which new design features could work.

The book is divided into four parts. After this Introduction, a set of chapters focus on traditional *core trade issues*. Chapter 2 ('Preferential Frontiers in Services Trade Governance') by Martin Roy and Pierre Sauvé reviews the main innovations brought about by preferential agreements in the global governance of services trade and highlights some limits. The contribution of services PTAs is analysed along three key angles: 1) rulemaking, 2) market access commitments, and 3) architecture and liberalisation modalities. The chapter shows how innovations in PTAs have mostly taken place in the context of the last two angles, and highlights some possible avenues in the design of future services PTAs. Building on recent trends, the design of future PTAs should move beyond the traditional dichotomy between positive and negative listing modalities; taking account of particular parties involved, elements of the two approaches can be used and combined so as to provide for maximum transparency of existing market access conditions. These innovations might also provide inspiration for revisiting and reviving certain positive-list PTAs that were concluded one or two decades ago. Noting the relatively limited participation of least developed countries (LDCs) in services PTAs despite the service sector growing importance in the global economy and increasing relevance for development strategies, the chapter also underscores the need for relevant future PTAs to incorporate development assistance components focusing on services trade. These can provide support for implementation, but also assist in taking advantage of opportunities afforded by services provisions by aiding to facilitate exports, as well as by helping to improve the performance of the domestic service sectors and the use of services inputs by different sectors of the economy.

Chapter 3 focuses on technical barriers to trade (TBT) and sanitary and phytosanitary (SPS) measures ('TBT and SPS Measures in PTAs: The Recent Past and the Near Future'). In their contribution Sebastian Klotz and Arthur Appleton discuss the design and evolution of TBT and SPS measures present in four mega-regional PTAs: the EU–Canada CETA, the CPTPP, the USMCA, and the RCEP. Their analysis shows that negotiators rely more heavily on previous PTAs when designing TBT chapters than SPS chapters. Compared to SPS chapters, not only do negotiators incorporate text from a larger number of previous PTAs, they also duplicate a larger share of previous PTAs' TBT chapters. Building on this, they then consider the future design of TBT and SPS chapters with a view towards eventual multilateralisation. From the SPS perspective, they note promising developments in compartmentalisation and zoning. From the TBT perspective, they focus on the growing use of protocols and annexes as a means to further mutual recognition and harmonisation.

Chapter 4, by Nora Neufeld, examines trade facilitation. In her chapter, titled 'Trade Facilitation in Preferential Trade Agreements: The Edge of a New Frontier?', Neufeld looks at how a new generation of PTAs addresses the need to facilitate trade, analysing common approaches, shared characteristics, and recent developments. The chapter compares the envisaged measures with the reforms mandated by the Trade Facilitation (TF) Agreement and discusses novel trends, such as an emphasis on deeper, behind-the-border obstacles, the increased focus on electronic means, and an overall move towards greater regulatory depth. The argument is made that while a renewed regional focus on trade facilitation rulemaking makes sense – especially against the current global backdrop of supply shortages, value-chain disruptions, and illicit trade – much unfinished business remains. The final segment of the chapter discusses TF reforms with particular potential for delivering positive impacts and suggests specific areas where PTAs might focus in the future to take trade facilitation to a new level.

Chapter 5, co-authored by María Vásquez Callo-Müller, Kholofelo Kugler, Marine Roux, Yinuo Liu, and Thomas Cottier, elaborates concepts that could see more prominence in future PTAs in the domain of IPR ('The Future Design of Intellectual Property Provisions in Preferential Trade Agreements: Three Propositions'). The authors introduce the current international IPR framework and trace the main trade-offs for policymaking in this area. They develop specific ideas on how to use PTAs to address, first, the role of trade secrets in the context of the digital economy; second, technology transfer in the context of climate change; and, last, the role of private–public partnerships in providing equitable access to medicines.

Finally, Chapter 6, co-authored by Anirudh Shingal and Maria Anna Corvaglia, focuses on 'Government Procurement in Twenty-First Century PTAs'. The contribution aims at deepening the understanding of the evolution of the design of deep government procurement provisions in PTAs, adopting an interdisciplinary approach, combining economic and legal insights. The following aspects are discussed: the relationship with the WTO Government Procurement Agreement, potential gaps in the public procurement coverage, dispute settlement mechanisms, and new regulatory areas likely to gain prominence as preferential procurement provisions in the near future, such as e-procurement, sustainable procurement, fight against corruption, and the participation of small and medium-sized enterprises (SMEs). Building on the patterns identified, the chapter zooms in on the specific design of procurement clauses in selected PTAs (CETA, CPTPP, and RCEP among others) and it questions the transferability of a model of preferential deep procurement regulation to lower-middle-income countries.

The second group of chapters tackles more recent *regulatory trade issues*. The contribution by Mira Burri (Chapter 7: 'Digital Trade: New Design Elements in

Preferential Trade Agreements') discusses the dynamics of digital trade regulation in the past decade in a complex geopolitical setting. She looks at broad trends, as well as distinct regulatory models (exemplified by the CPTPP, the USMCA, the EU–UK Trade and Cooperation Agreement (TCA), and the RCEP) and the templates of new digital economy agreements (DEAs) that also signal room for regulatory innovation in trade law. The chapter recognises new design elements found in PTAs, traces how these have diffused over time, and identifies their implications for domestic regulatory space. Finally, in view of multilateral discussions on electronic commerce, the chapter tests to what extent PTAs have worked as regulatory laboratories and whether some of the newly emerged digital trade rules can be multilateralised.

Chapter 8 by Federico Ortino ('Recent Trends and Future Developments with regard to Foreign Investment in PTAs') maps the evolution of the last thirty years of PTAs addressing foreign investment. It explains the interactions between PTAs and bilateral investment treaties (BITs), as well as between PTAs and the WTO on the topic of investment. The chapter focuses on key provisions related to investment protection, investment liberalisation, and ISDS, highlighting novel approaches. In addition, the chapter identifies and discusses provisions that go beyond traditional aspects of investment and trade, such as investment facilitation, corporate social responsibility, and regulatory coherence. The chapter concludes by offering suggestions for future design.

Chapter 9, titled 'Subsidies and Future PTAs: From Market Distortions to Legitimate Policy Goals?', explores the potential for innovation on subsidies. Leopoldo Biffi, Yuliia Kucheriava, and Shailja Singh argue that the WTO's Agreement on Subsidies and Countervailing Measures fails to adequately address the role that subsidies can play in addressing twenty-first century challenges. These include policies aimed at delivering public goods, including the green transition, economic-recovery or research and development (R&D) aid, and emerging forms of distortive industrial subsidies. It proposes an approach that balances regulation of the 'good' and 'bad' subsidies, placing emphasis on the former. This chapter concludes that PTAs' built-in flexibilities make them best-suited for future-proof subsidy regulation and have the potential to further international trade cooperation by informing a new WTO agenda on subsidies.

In Chapter 10, titled 'The Concept Design of International Rules on State Intervention in the Economy', Luca Rubini also engages with subsidy rules with a special view on regulating state enterprises. After assessing the multilateral regulatory standards, represented by WTO rules, the chapter takes stock of the chapters on subsidies and state enterprises in the PTAs currently in force. Using the notions of principles, standards, and rules, the author applies these conceptual 'bricks' to subsidies and state enterprises, respectively, to map out future avenues for new rules. The chapter ends with reflections on some necessary conditions for steering the future design process.

Chapter 11 focuses on the recent transformation of the trading system towards increasing reliance on production networks across borders and regions ('Global Value Chains: The Road to Resilience'). Selina Hauser, Israel Gutiérrez, and Christian Winkler emphasise how recent events, such as the financial crisis, the COVID-19 pandemic, and the Russian invasion of Ukraine, have exposed the fragility of GVCs. This chapter discusses the role of PTAs in fostering GVC resilience. Building on a novel data set that covers nearly 700 PTAs and their GVC-related provisions, the authors first discuss the major trends of GVC-related provisions in PTAs and their impact on the development of value-chain complexity. Second, they describe a set of possible instruments that, if included in future PTAs, could make GVCs more resilient and reduce the impact of shocks on trade flows.

In the third group of chapters we focus on what used to be called *trade-related issues*, which have moved to centre stage in the PTA universe, and on newer themes. In their contribution Mode 4 'On the Move' Towards a Migrantification of the Temporary Movement of Persons in Preferential Trade Agreements, Marion Panizzon and Amanda Bisong address the issue of cross-border movement of natural persons for the supply of services. In this chapter, they explore the prevalence of mode 4 in PTAs and uncover why in certain geopolitical contexts, some mega-regionals have been more forthcoming in adding mode 4 General Agreement on Trade in Services (GATS)-plus or GATS-extra advances than in others. In a selective mapping of several key PTAs, including AfCFTA, RCEP, CPTPP and UK accession, EU Deep and Comprehensive Free Trade Areas (DCFTAs), Japan/European Free Trade Association (EFTA)/EU Economic Partnership Agreements (EPAs), and EU-Mercosur Association Agreement, they highlight which annexes and protocols on the movement of natural persons feature GATS-extra/ GATS-plus commitments. These include national treatment limitations to motivate the transfers of skills; unilateral or reciprocal obligation to fast-track visa delivery, extension, and renewal; skill testing alternatives where mutual recognition of credentials is not possible; and measures preventing irregular migration. Finally, they look beyond mode 4 to broader forms of labour migration and suggest ways to systemically link legal pathways in the Global Compacts for Migration and Refugees with PTA obligations and GATS mode 4.

In Chapter 13, an interdisciplinary team consisting of Gregory Felder, Kirthana Ganeson, Martin Jehli, and Patrick Wagner addresses the theme of trade and labour. In their contribution titled 'The Trade and Labour Nexus: Envisioning the Design and Implementation of Future Labour Chapters in PTAs' they first examine trends as to the extent to which PTAs cover labour provisions as well as the levels of success in the implementation of these provisions on the domestic level. Upon evaluating past practices, this chapter recommends a higher level of ambition in labour chapters of trade agreements of the future. By relying on case studies, they prescribe that future labour chapters should i) expand the scope of labour rights, ii) emphasise the involvement of local stakeholders for implementation and enforcement, and iii) reinvent the approach in which labour violations in trade are examined.

The chapter concludes by exploring ways in which PTAs can act as a safeguard for labour rights amid future developments, such as automation and migration.

In Chapter 14, 'Taking Climate Change Seriously in the Design of Trade Agreements', another interdisciplinary group of scholars observes that while environmental provisions are well represented in modern PTAs, specific climate-related ones are still rare. In their contribution, Clara Brandi, Kateryna Holzer, Jean-Frédéric Morin, and Harro van Asselt first introduce a 2x2 typology of environmental provisions that are the most relevant for climate governance. This typology distinguishes positive and negative commitments as well as direct and diffused commitments. The second part builds on a data set of environmental provisions in 774 trade agreements to map the existing distribution of these four types of climate-relevant provisions. The third part zooms in on one important provision per type: restriction on fossil fuel subsidies, liberalisation of environmental goods and services, climate exceptions related to investment protection, and exceptions allowing for carbon border adjustments. The fourth part makes specific suggestions to increase the degree of precision, obligation, and delegation for these four types of provisions. The chapter concludes with a discussion of the legal and political context necessary to have PTAs that take climate change more seriously.

Chapter 15 tackles 'Gender Equality in Trade Agreements: The Old, the New, and the Future' and is co-authored by Anoush der Boghossian, Amrita Bahri, and Lolita Laperle-Forget. The purpose of this chapter is threefold: providing an overview and analysis of gender provisions in PTAs, assessing what gender issues are not covered and why, and showing how PTAs can be used as a policymaking tool to address specific needs and obstacles women face. More specifically, the chapter provides an overview of the inclusion of gender provisions in PTAs and, more precisely, looks at how PTAs can support women's economic empowerment and tackle gender inequalities, mapping out and analysing the gender provisions included in PTAs, in substance (what gender issues they cover and why) and in type (legally binding or best endeavours language, etc.). It explores how they are tied to PTA dispute settlement mechanisms or monitoring and enforcement processes. It also provides an assessment of what gender issues are not covered and addressed in PTAs and links these to women's needs, adding a practical perspective to the analysis. Lastly, the chapter shows how policymakers can use PTAs as a toolbox to identify the adequate approach, methods, and matters when they develop their trade policies pertaining to gender equality in trade.

The last group of chapters focuses on the implementation of trade agreements. Over time, trade commentators have turned increasingly to how to support the implementation process and how to bring about compliance with the commitments. The chapters round up our volume. Kathleen Claussen's contribution, titled 'The Future of Trade Agreement Dispute Settlement Provisions', shows how, in recent years, the role and design of dispute settlement mechanisms have begun to evolve. Chapter 16 begins by reviewing recent innovations and the disputes that have arisen under those mechanisms. Next, it studies how these trends have highlighted additional areas for study in the areas of procedures and institutions. Finally, the chapter turns to the purpose of dispute settlement mechanisms in trade agreements and argues that the future of dispute settlement is multipurpose and multi-optional.

Chapter 17 by Rodrigo Polanco discusses the increasing attention to regulatory convergence as a means to increase the benefits of PTAs. In 'Regulatory Convergence in Preferential Trade Agreements: What Does the Future Hold?', he traces how recent PTAs include chapters dealing with the process of procedural or substantive regulatory convergence under different denominations such as 'regulatory cooperation', 'good regulatory practices', 'regulatory improvement', and 'regulatory coherence', among others. After mapping this discipline, he disaggregates its development into three different categories of approach: substantive regulatory harmonisation (or 'substantive coherence' – the same rule), procedural coherence (the same process), and regulatory cooperation (or 'regulatory compatibility' – equivalent rule/equivalent process). The chapter concludes by presenting possible ways forward for regulatory convergence, considering the use of dispute settlement, regional and sectoral harmonisation, and an increased role for private and mixed actors.

REFERENCES

Allee, T. and M. Elsig 2019. 'Are the Contents of International Treaties Copy-Pasted? Evidence from Preferential Trade Agreements', *International Studies Quarterly* 63(3): 603–613.

Allee, T., M. Elsig and A. Lugg 2017. 'The Ties between the World Trade Organization and Preferential Trade Agreements: A Textual Analysis', *Journal of International Economic Law* 20(2): 333–363.

Alschner, W., M. Elsig and R. Polanco 2021. 'Introducing the Electronic Database of Investment Treaties (EDIT): The Genesis of a New Database and its Use', *World Trade Review* 20(1): 73–94.

Bahri, A. and M. Lugo 2020. 'Trumping Capacity Gap with Negotiation Strategies: The Mexican USMCA Negotiation Experience', *Journal of International Economic Law* 23 (1): 1–23.

Baker, J. 2022. 'Costello v The Government of Ireland, Ireland and the Attorney General (Supreme Court of Ireland 11 November 2022)'. Retrieved from www.courts.ie/view/judgments/d9589327-898e-4d2d-a2f3-1cc17f7105a6/bc918f1c-9730-4c69-acde-a76d256e37b5/2022_IESC_44_(Baker%20J).pdf/pdf.

Claussen, K. 2018. 'Separation of Trade Law Powers', *Yale Journal of International Law* 43(3): 15–54.

2022a. 'Next Generation Agreements and the WTO', *World Trade Review* 21(3): 380–388.

2022b. 'Trade's Mini-Deals', *Virginia Journal of International Law* 62(3): 315–382.

Dür, A., L. Baccini and M. Elsig 2014. 'The Design of International Trade Agreements: Introducing a New Dataset', *The Review of International Organizations* 9(3): 353–375.

Elsig, M. and S. Klotz 2021. 'Digital Trade Rules in Preferential Trade Agreements: Is There a WTO Impact?' *Global Policy* 12: 25–36.

Hainbach, P. 2018. 'The CJEU's Opinion 2/15 and the Future of EU Investment Policy and Law-Making', *Legal Issues of Economic Integration* 45(2): 199–209.

Paquin, S. 2022. 'Trade Paradiplomacy and the Politics of International Economic Law: The Inclusion of Quebec and the Exclusion of Wallonia in the CETA Negotiations', *New Political Economy* 27(4): 597–609.

Sauvé, P., R. Polanco Lazo and J.M. Álvarez Zárate (eds.) 2018. *The Pacific Alliance in a World of Preferential Trade Agreements: Lessons in Comparative Regionalism*. New York: Springer.

United States Trade Representative (USTR) 2022. 'The Indo-Pacific Economic Framework for Prosperity: Biden-Harris Administration's Negotiating Goals for the Connected Economy (Trade) Pillar'. Retrieved 21 November 2022, from http://ustr.gov/about-us/policy-offices/press-office/press-releases/2022/september/indo-pacific-economic-framework-prosperity-biden-harris-administrations-negotiating-goals-connected.

World Trade Organization 2011. *The WTO and Preferential Trade Agreements: From Co-Existence to Coherence*. Geneva: WTO.

2021. 'WTO Electronic Commerce Negotiations. Updated Consolidated Negotiating Text – September 2021'. Revision. INF/ECOM/62/Rev.2. Retrieved 22 November 2022, from www.bilaterals.org/IMG/pdf/wto_plurilateral_ecommerce_draft_consolidated_text_september_2021.pdf.

2

Preferential Frontiers in Services Trade Governance

*Martin Roy and Pierre Sauvé**

2.1 INTRODUCTION

Preferential trade agreements (PTAs) featuring disciplines on trade and investment in services (hitherto referred to as 'services PTAs'[1]) have expanded at breakneck speed since the early 2000s, a trend that shows no sign of abating. Over that period, services PTAs have increased at a faster pace than PTAs without services provisions. While only a few services PTAs chiefly involving a small number of more economically advanced World Trade Organization (WTO) Members had been notified during the first five years of the WTO's existence, services PTAs have increased almost forty-fold from 2000 to 2022 (Figure 2.1). A large majority of Members at all levels of development are today parties to at least one services PTA. A number of deep PTAs featuring services disciplines are furthermore under negotiation or were recently completed but not yet notified under the WTO's General Agreement on Trade in Services (GATS). These include the African Continental Free Trade Area (AfCFTA), the Regional Comprehensive Economic Partnership (RCEP), and the EU–Mercosur PTA.[2] Services provisions have become a standard feature of latest-generation PTAs, including within South–South agreements linking developing and least developed countries.

The sharp recent rise in services agreements conducted along preferential lines stands in stark contrast to the frozen state of multilateral services commitments and

* The authors are, respectively, Counsellor in the WTO's Trade in Services and Investment Division and Senior Trade Specialist in the World Bank's Trade and Regional Integration unit. The views expressed in this chapter are those of the authors and should not be ascribed to the institutions and the Members of the organisations to which they are affiliated. The authors are grateful to Shishira Johny and Ravneek Bhullar for their excellent research assistance and to participants at a seminar held at the University of Bern's World Trade Institute at which the outline of this chapter was first presented and debated.

1 Services PTAs refer to any PTAs with substantive provisions on trade in services, whether these form part of a more comprehensive preferential agreement or not.

2 As of 1 January 2023.

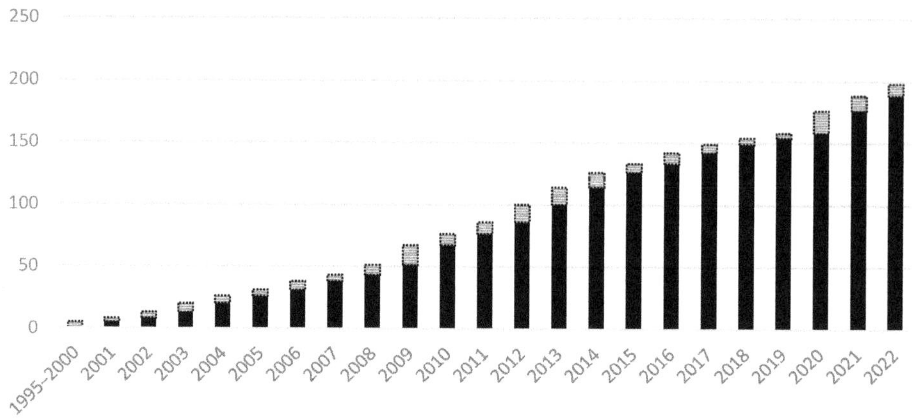

FIGURE 2.1 Number of services PTAs notified under GATS Article V, 1995–2022.
Note: New PTAs notified each year are highlighted in the upper part of the bars, while those notified in previous years are represented in the lower part of the bars, in black.
Source: Computed by authors from: http://rtais.wto.org/UI/PublicMaintainRTAHome.aspx

negotiations at the WTO, where, aside from those supplied by acceding Members, no new market opening commitments have been undertaken by WTO Members since the curtain fell on the Uruguay Round and its extended negotiations.[3]

The growing embrace of services within preferential agreements reflects mounting recognition of the central importance of services to global production, employment, innovation, foreign investment, and trade. Accounting for half of global trade in value-added terms, services present increasing opportunities for developing country exports and global value chain (GVC) insertion, driven in part by the increasing digitalisation of cross-border transactions (WTO 2020; World Bank and WTO 2023).

This chapter reviews the main innovations brought about by preferential agreements in the global governance of services trade while pointing to some limitations. The contribution of services PTAs is assessed against the background of existing multilateral norms across a threefold prism: (1) architecture and liberalisation modalities, (2) rulemaking, and (3) market opening commitments.

Our analysis underscores that, while WTO+ levels of market opening commitments have been an important feature of services PTAs, progress on rulemaking has been more modest overall, though advances in some related cross-cutting areas carry potentially important implications for services trade. This is most notably the case of advances registered in the areas of e-commerce/digital trade, investment, and procurement. As regards the architecture of services agreements, services

[3] In December 2021, a group of WTO Members agreed on a Reference Paper on Domestic Regulation which is being inscribed in their schedules of commitments. The Reference Paper's provisions do not concern matters pertaining to the liberalisation of trade in services via market access or national treatment commitments.

PTAs – including many concluded most recently – have produced major advances, exhibiting the role that PTAs can play as policy laboratories. Such advances are most prominent with regard to liberalisation modalities, with agreements predicated on a negative-list approach to market opening today outnumbering the positive-list approach first pioneered in the GATS, even as the latter tends to be favoured in many South–South services PTAs.[4]

In recent years, services PTAs between larger economies have progressively moved away from the binary choice between the traditional positive versus negative listing models. Overall, this has resulted in the extension of some of the key features of the negative-list approach to a growing number of countries and served to further emphasise, sometimes through innovative means, the importance of sowing greater transparency on the multiplicity of measures governing market access conditions at and behind borders, across sectors and modes of supply.[5] Looking ahead, services PTAs can be expected to further consolidate this trend and move beyond the traditional dichotomy between positive- and negative-list approaches, focusing instead on maximising transparency and predictability, promoting improved regulatory governance, while also taking due account of the policy sensitivities of countries at different levels of service sector development. Ensuring that services PTAs feature scaled-up Aid for Trade provisions and resources will also prove necessary to increase the participation of lower-income countries in services trade and help them reap the full development dividends of an ever more service-centric world economy.

2.2 KEY TRENDS IN SERVICES PTAS

The evolving practice of preferential negotiations in services reveals a range of salient recent trends. For one, an increasing number of new WTO Members have initiated, or intensified, their participation in services PTAs. This includes the United Kingdom (UK), which has not only concluded continuity agreements with trading partners to which it was previously bound through PTAs of the European Union (EU), but has also concluded preferential pacts with new preferential

[4] As explained in more detail in Section 3.1, positive-list agreements are characterised by the fact that liberalisation obligations apply only to sectors expressly listed in each party's schedule of commitments, and subject to limitations listed. In contrast, in negative-list agreements, the liberalisation obligations apply fully to all sectors, unless provided otherwise.

[5] Trade in services is typically categorised, in the GATS and in many PTAs, as involving four modes of services supply: cross-border supply (mode 1), in which services are supplied from the territory of one party into the territory of another party, such as through the Internet; consumption abroad (mode 2), in which services are provided in the territory of one party to a consumer of another party, such as tourism; commercial presence (mode 3), in which services are delivered by a supplier of one party through commercial presence in the territory of another party, such as establishing a branch or affiliate in a foreign country to serve the local market; and presence of natural persons (mode 4), in which a supplier of one party provides services through the presence of natural persons in the territory of another party, such as business consultants.

partners. The UK's exit from the EU accounts for a significant share of the new services PTAs notified since the end of 2020.

Recent years have also seen Türkiye, the Pacific Islands, and countries from Eastern Europe and the Caucasus become involved in services PTAs for the first time, while others, including India, China, and Mauritius, have become more active in recent years. While the heightened involvement of developing countries in services PTAs has reduced cross-regional gaps in participation levels, imbalances nevertheless persist to a greater degree than in goods trade, as some regions, notably the Middle East, Africa, and South Asia (aside from India), are home to few notified services PTAs. Such a situation is expected to change in the coming years, particularly in Africa, where the services Protocol of the Southern African Development Community (SADC) was notified to the WTO in 2022, and where schedules of services commitments have been negotiated among the fifty-four parties to the AfCFTA. Meanwhile, countries of the Gulf region, where far-reaching unilateral reforms have been enacted in services markets, have recently notified new services PTAs, either as a regional grouping (Gulf Cooperation Council with the European Free Trade Association (EFTA) in 2022) or individually (United Arab Emirates with India in 2022).

A major new trend is the increasing involvement of developing and least developed countries (LDCs) in services PTAs. Services agreements among countries long hesitant to make commitments in the sector account today for a significant share (41%) of all notified PTAs. Reflecting a marked shift in policy attitudes among countries, agreements *between* developing countries have, since 2010, accounted for a growing share of services PTAs (49%), compared to developing–developed country PTAs (45%) and developed–developed country agreements (6%) (Figure 2.2).

Despite marked changes in the geography of services PTAs, the fact remains that, other than the AfCFTA negotiations encompassing all thirty-three of the continent's least developed members, lower-income countries are, on the whole, party to few services PTAs in comparison with goods-only PTAs. Currently, LDC participation is mostly through agreements signed by LDCs that are part of the Association of Southeast Asian Nations (ASEAN) (Lao PDR, Cambodia, Myanmar), Pacific Island countries that are parties to the Pacific Agreement on Closer Economic Relations Plus (PACER Plus) Agreement (Kiribati, Solomon Islands, Tuvalu, Vanuatu), the Member States of the East African Community (Burundi, Democratic Republic of Congo, Rwanda, South Sudan, Tanzania, and Uganda) and, more recently, those of the SADC (Lesotho, Malawi, Mozambique).[6]

Recent years have witnessed a continuation of the trend towards multi-party PTAs, sometimes dubbed mega-regional when spanning regional lines. Such agreements tend to consolidate pre-existing bilateral links or can create new links among parties. Examples include the RCEP (fifteen parties), the Comprehensive and

6 Vanuatu graduated from LDC status in December 2020, after conclusion of the PACER Plus negotiations.

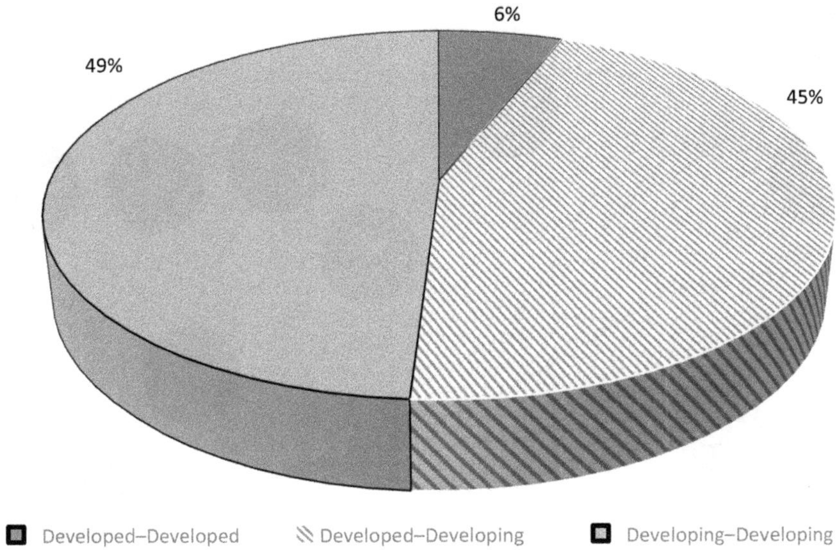

FIGURE 2.2 Services PTAs by development level of parties, 2010–2022.
Note: Not including notifications of agreements to ensure the maintenance of PTAs of the UK that had been earlier notified by the EU.
Source: Computed by authors from: http://rtais.wto.org/UI/PublicMaintainRTAHome.aspx

Progressive Agreement for Trans-Pacific Partnership (CPTPP) (eleven parties), PACER Plus (ten parties), SADC (eleven parties applying the Protocol on Trade in Services), as well as the AfCFTA (fifty-four parties). All of these large-membership PTAs are mostly composed of developing countries.

In the fifteen years that followed the creation of the WTO, the largest economies (developing and developed) had few preferential agreements on services linking them, with the obvious exceptions of the EU and the Members of the North American Free Trade Agreement (NAFTA). Another notable recent trend, with consequential implications for the scope and depth of agreed outcomes, is the greater number of agreements linking large economies and important services exporters. These include the India–Japan and EU–Korea Agreements notified in 2011, the China–Australia Agreement brokered in 2015, the Canada–EU Comprehensive Economic and Trade Agreement (CETA) of 2017, the CPTPP (which includes Canada, Japan, and Australia) in 2018, the EU–Japan Agreement of 2019, the EU–UK Agreement in 2021, the RCEP signed in 2022 (linking, among others, the economies of China, Japan, Korea, and Australia), as well as the Australia–India Agreement also signed in 2022.[7] Figure 2.3 illustrates the marked uptake in preferential services agreements among larger economies since 2010.

7 Though signed, both the RCEP and the India–Australia Agreement have yet to be notified to the WTO under Article V of the GATS.

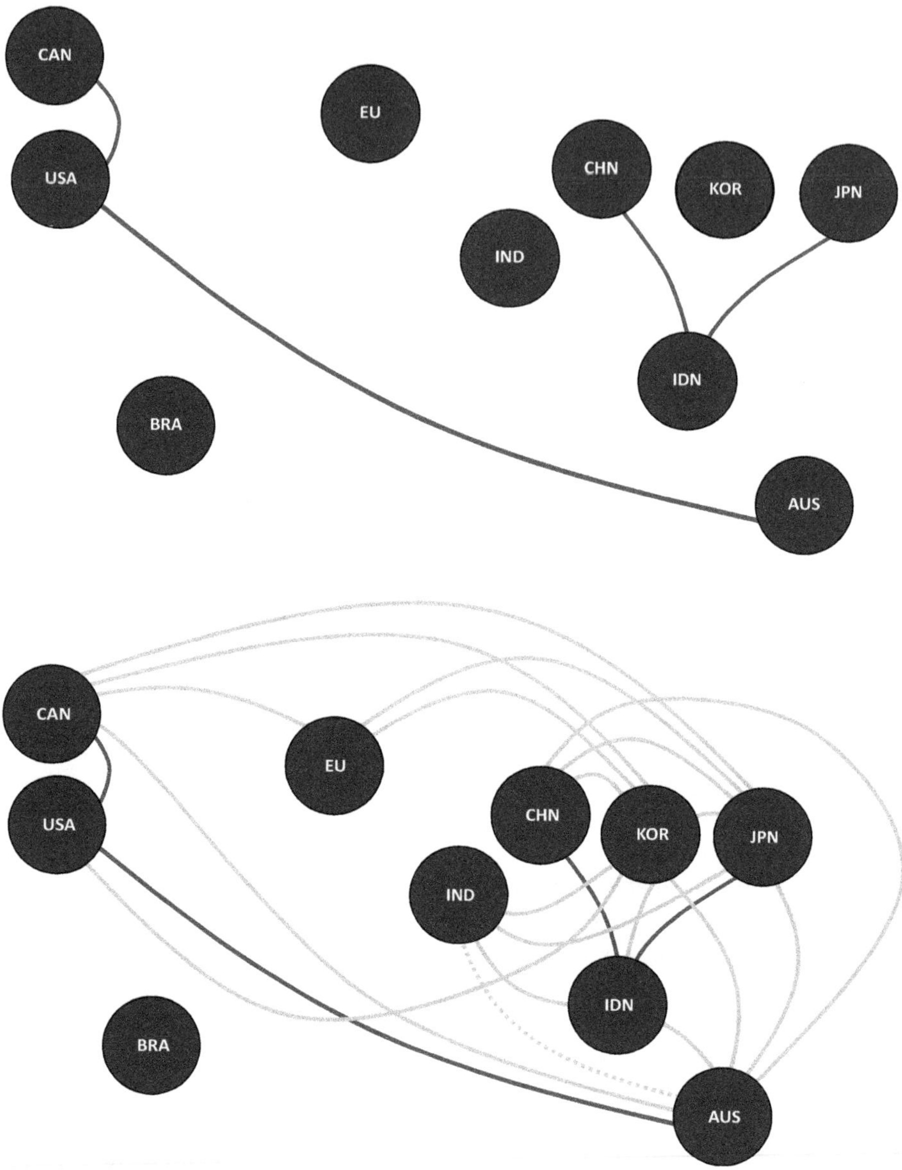

FIGURE 2.3 Notified services PTAs linking large developing and developed countries, before and after 2010.
Source: Computed by authors from: http://rtais.wto.org/UI/PublicMaintainRTAHome.aspx

This latest development holds important implications. As supported by earlier studies (Roy et al. 2007; Marchetti and Roy 2008), larger countries are likely to extract from smaller trading partners greater market access commitments than smaller economies might. Large economies can also be expected to provide greater market access when negotiating with trading partners of similar size. As will be examined in greater detail in the next sections, agreements among larger economies also tend to influence the architecture and liberalisation modalities of subsequent PTAs. Greater balance and the resulting search for compromise have favoured the emergence of innovative negotiating models and approaches.

Even though services trade relations between economies such as the United States, the EU, and China are not governed by PTAs but rather by the GATS, the question arises whether deep preferential arrangements among larger economies may actually lessen their interest in pursuing market opening bargains at the multilateral level. This may occur as the value of WTO commitments from countries with which commitments have already been secured in PTAs is reduced.

In the context of trade in goods, another consideration is the impact of multilateral negotiations on the erosion of preferences granted earlier. Indeed, one may ponder the reactions of Members when seeing their PTA partners dilute hard-fought tariff preferences by extending them on a most-favoured-nation (MFN) basis at the WTO. However, given the far greater administrative burden of maintaining parallel regulatory regimes between preferential and non-preferential trading partners, the market opening commitments that are bound in PTAs tend to be applied in most instances on a de facto MFN basis. Accordingly, the question of preference erosion should not be as significant in services as in goods trade. Seen this way, one may well conclude that the proliferation of WTO+ advances registered by PTAs and the proclivity for implementing such commitments on a non-discriminatory basis should, in principle, facilitate their multilateralisation under the GATS. Important qualitative gains in policy predictability and effective access to markets could be reaped if WTO Members were to inscribe their best PTA commitments in GATS schedules (World Bank and WTO 2023).

A final important recent trend is the progressive disengagement of the United States – the world's leading services exporter along with the EU – from preferential market opening in goods and services trade alike. With the exception of the United States–Mexico–Canada Agreement (USMCA) that replaced the NAFTA in 2020, the last services PTA the United States notified to the WTO dates back to 2012. Since then, the United States, who was an original signatory of the Trans-Pacific Partnership (TPP) Agreement whose substantive provisions it had largely shaped, informed its trading partners in January 2017 that it would not become a party to the agreement (USTR 2017). Around the same time, negotiations on a plurilateral Trade in Services Agreement (TiSA) fizzled out, with the last meeting of participating economies taking place in December 2016 (Global Affairs Canada 2022). Recently, the United States has focused its efforts on soft law approaches to facilitating trade, boosting the resilience of supply chains and promoting regulatory convergence through the Indo-Pacific Economic Framework and the Americas Partnership for Economic Prosperity, among other similar initiatives. These initiatives do not seek to reduce tariff barriers nor pursue enhanced market access opportunities in areas such as trade in services or investment.

2.3 INNOVATIONS AND VALUE ADDED IN SERVICES PTAS

Services PTAs can be analysed by assessing how they differ from – and potentially add value to – the multilateral framework of obligations and market opening commitments found in the WTO's GATS. This can be done along three dimensions: (1) negotiating architecture and liberalisation modalities, (2) rulemaking, and (3) liberalisation commitments.

While this chapter cannot do justice to a full assessment of services PTAs under all three dimensions, the discussion that follows focuses greater attention on the issue of architecture and liberalisation modalities while touching more briefly on the other two dimensions. This chapter's focus on the latest-generation PTAs suggests that the greatest scope for policy innovation in services PTAs rests with the choice of architecture and liberalisation modalities. With few exceptions, services PTAs have not, on the whole, revealed a marked appetite for extending the frontiers of services rulemaking. Meanwhile, continued multilateral stasis favours an ever-increasing gap in the degree of preferential versus GATS-induced market access commitments. However, as noted above, where preferential market opening advances appear possible, their tendency to be implemented on an MFN basis and the limited evidence of policy reversal once services reforms are enacted and commitments made both suggest that the latest generation of services PTAs likely produces less trade distortion than PTAs governing goods trade.

2.3.1 *Architecture and Liberalisation Modalities*

From the outset, services PTAs have followed two main and well-delineated approaches: positive and negative listing approaches to liberalisation commitments. The positive list – or bottom-up approach – is modelled on the GATS and provides, in essence, that market opening obligations – market access and national treatment – only apply to the sectors, subsectors, and modes of supply expressly inscribed in each party's schedule of commitments. As a result, if a sector is not mentioned in a schedule, the obligations of market access and national treatment do not apply, and the Member retains full discretion to introduce new discriminatory or market access-impeding measures.

For sectors and subsectors that are inscribed in schedules, parties can, as under the GATS, list limitations for particular modes of supply, indicating which measures inconsistent with market access or national treatment they wish to retain the right to apply. Parties may also indicate, for a committed sector, that market access or national treatment does not apply to a particular mode of supply (i.e. the inscription 'unbound').

This approach to scheduling liberalisation commitments was initially followed by the EU in its PTAs with non-European partners, in the PTAs signed by EFTA and China, as well as within Mercosur and ASEAN. In traditional positive-list agreements, all elements relating to trade in services, including all modes of supply, are typically addressed in the same chapter in a manner analogous to the GATS.

The main difference between negative- and positive-list approaches is that, in the former, all sectors and subsectors are deemed open unless otherwise stated through the (negative) listing of reservations of non-confirming measures. Reversing the logic of positive listing, measures and sectors not found in reservation lists are deemed open, that is, fully compliant with relevant obligations. Obligations subject to negative listing modalities involve not only national treatment – and, in more recent agreements, market access – obligations, but typically also feature obligations on performance requirements, local presence requirements, nationality of senior management and boards of directors, as well as MFN treatment.

Reservations for non-conforming measures are typically contained in two annexes. The first annex – and default scheduling option – lists reservations for *existing* non-conforming measures, that is, restrictive measures currently applied. A second annex contains reservations listing the sectors or policy areas where parties can maintain and adopt new restrictive measures. The transparent listing of *existing* non-conforming measures under negative-list modalities marks an important departure from the GATS and positive-list PTAs, where limitations inscribed in schedules do not necessarily reflect *existing* measures. Because the starting point is that all sectors are covered, and because it binds and lists the bulk of existing non-conforming measures, negative-list agreements yield commitments that largely bind the regulatory status quo, thereby better ensuring against the introduction of new trade-restrictive measures and providing a higher level of transparency and predictability.

Another distinctive feature of the negative-list approach is the so-called ratchet mechanism, which ensures that any subsequent liberalisation of existing non-conforming measures listed in the first annex of reservations is automatically bound. Through such a mechanism, the PTAs' services commitments can harvest autonomous liberalisation measures enacted after an agreement's entry into force, preventing the kind of situation occurring under the GATS, for example, where the gap between the level of openness bound in commitments negotiated in the 1990s and the level of applied openness has gradually increased over the following decades. The gap between levels of commitments bound in PTAs and future applied levels of openness, which fuelled recourse to a ratchet, is linked to the nature of services liberalisation and services agreements. Indeed, unlike for goods, where PTAs will typically bring down customs duties to zero within agreed timelines for most products, services agreements tend to result in little de novo liberalisation,[8] arguably

8 See Roy et al. (2007) for a discussion of this matter, and for examples of new liberalisation resulting from services PTAs.

because services barriers are behind-the-border measures embedded within broader regulatory frameworks that are most often not the responsibility of trade authorities and whose reform is more complex (e.g. a need for new regulations to accompany liberalisation) and more challenging to implement than a modification of duty rates. In addition, since most services reforms tend to be implemented on an MFN basis, the urge to achieve them through PTAs is more contained.

A negative listing implies important architectural implications. Contrasting positive-list agreements, where all services elements and modes are addressed within the same chapter, negative-list agreements typically address different modes or areas of services trade across multiple complementary chapters dealing with cross-border trade in services, investment, movement of business persons, alongside dedicated chapters on financial services, telecommunication services, and digital trade.

Negative listing was pioneered in the NAFTA and subsequently used in agreements signed by the United States, Canada, and Mexico with various other trading partners. It is commonly found in several agreements brokered by Latin American countries. Nowadays, negative-list agreements account for a majority of notified services PTAs. Studies have highlighted that such agreements show a higher incidence of GATS+ commitments than do positive-list agreements (Roy et al. 2007; Stephenson and Robert 2014; Stephenson 2015). Other studies have found that countries whose PTAs feature a negative-list approach are more likely to engage in agreements with other countries using such a modality (Kim and Manger 2017).

2.3.2 *Recent Innovations in Negotiating Architecture and Modalities*

In recent years, various innovations in negotiating architectures and modalities have been introduced, resulting in variations in the traditional positive- and negative-list approaches and the emergence of models combining elements of the two approaches in novel ways. Some of these innovations have evolved organically through experience with the traditional approaches, while others are more closely associated with the necessities of finding negotiating compromises between parties with differing interests.

Earlier on, one novel departure from the pure negative-list approach was to include in the chapter on cross-border trade in services a market access obligation modelled on Article XVI of the GATS. In other negative-list PTAs, which typically did not cover mode 3 in the services chapter but rather addressed investment in services through a chapter governing investment in goods and services alike, another improvement has been to ensure that relevant obligations of the chapter on cross-border trade in services (e.g. on domestic regulation) also apply to services supplied through foreign-owned/foreign-controlled investments.

More recently, more significant architectural innovations, focusing on liberalisation modalities, have emerged from PTAs among larger economies at the global and regional levels. A chronology of notable advances includes the following examples:

Trade in Services Agreement (TiSA, 2013–2016): The negotiation of the TiSA – a plurilateral and non-WTO-anchored negotiation among twenty-three economies, including many of the top services exporters (e.g. US, EU, Japan) – was suspended in 2016.[9] While some issues in relation to rulemaking and national schedules of commitments remained outstanding when the talks were stopped, participants had agreed on scheduling modalities involving a mix of the elements of positive-list and negative-list elements. A negative listing approach was thus to be used for national treatment commitments (i.e. applying fully to all sectors, unless otherwise indicated). Meanwhile, a positive listing approach was used for commitments on market access. This information was all contained in a schedule format resembling that of the GATS (Fefer 2017). As in most negative-list agreements, a standstill (i.e. binding of existing non-conforming measures) would apply for national treatment purposes, unless otherwise specified, along with a ratchet to capture autonomously decreed liberalisation measures (Villup 2015).

The TiSA scheduling modalities were motivated, in part, by the desire of some participants to use a format that would have similarities to the GATS so as to facilitate subsequent multilateral integration. No other PTA has used such an approach, likely because there was no similar interest in possible future incorporation into the WTO. However, subsequent PTAs have, in different ways, tried to combine elements of positive and negative listing approaches.

Australia–China PTA (2015): An early and significant effort to combine elements of positive and negative listing modalities was found in the Australia–China Agreement. China had until then solely pursued positive listing for trade in services, and Australia, while having used different approaches in different contexts, had more often opted for negative listing.

The agreement's chapter on trade in services innovates by laying out two alternative scheduling approaches, where China opted to follow a positive listing approach while Australia pursued a negative-list approach, with a standstill but without a ratchet. While Australia also uses the negative-list approach for MFN, the MFN obligation for China applies, in a positive-list manner, only to certain services listed in an annex, and, notably, without an exception for preferential treatment granted in future PTAs.

A similarly innovative approach was used for the Agreement's investment chapter. The chapter features a broad, asset-based definition of investment (covering, e.g., portfolio investment and not only ownership/control of enterprises) but does not apply to measures covered by the trade in services chapter, which covers supply through commercial presence. In the investment chapter, both parties use a negative-list approach – with both a standstill and a ratchet – though there is still asymmetry between the two parties in that the scope of the key obligations differ. The national treatment obligation applies to both the pre- and post-establishment

[9] See Sauvé (2014) and Marchetti and Roy (2014).

phases of investment in the case of Australia, but only to post-establishment for China. Meanwhile, unlike in the services chapter, the MFN obligation applies to both parties on a negative-list basis and covers pre-establishment. For both national treatment and MFN, the main difference between the two parties is that Australia has to list its non-conforming measures, while China's existing non-conforming measures are grandfathered (i.e. bound, but not listed).

Canada–EU (2017): The CETA marked the first time that the EU used a negative-list modality for trade in services in a PTA. The chapter on cross-border trade in services, covering modes 1 and 2, uses a negative scheduling technique for the obligations of market access, national treatment, and MFN, with a standstill and a ratchet. The investment chapter, which includes coverage of investment in services,[10] uses the same approach for provisions on market access, performance requirements, national treatment, MFN treatment, and nationality of senior management and boards of directors.

The CETA also marked the first time that Canada listed reservations for non-conforming measures maintained by provincial governments, which have significant responsibilities in various service sectors under the country's federal system of governance. While, in past agreements, including the NAFTA, liberalisation obligations applied to measures at the sub-federal level of government, existing non-conforming measures of provinces did not have to be listed and were simply grandfathered with no information provided on them. In the CETA, existing non-conforming measures of provinces are not only bound, but listed in detail in Annex I.

Comprehensive and Progressive Agreement for Trans-Pacific Partnership (CPTPP, 2018): The CPTPP featured important innovations in services-related areas, notably by including comprehensive disciplines on state-owned enterprises (SOEs), including in services, as well as deep disciplines on digital trade in its e-commerce chapter. It also secured higher levels of market opening commitments relative to what many of the parties had agreed in their earlier agreements (Elms 2018).

In terms of negotiating modalities, the CPTPP, like the TPP on which it was based and which was negotiated earlier, followed negative-list modalities for both cross-border trade in services and investment, as per the PTA practice of various parties. However, an interesting novelty concerns liberalisation commitments on the temporary entry of business persons, as a number of parties undertook commitments on a variable geometry or less than an MFN basis, with commitments for particular categories of business persons extended solely to parties making reciprocal commitments in similar categories.

European Union–Japan PTA (2018), UK–Japan PTA (2020), and EU–UK PTA (2021): The EU's turn to negative listing modalities in the CETA was reiterated in the subsequently concluded EU–Japan PTA through chapters on investment

[10] See Article 8.2 on Scope.

liberalisation (covering service sectors) and on cross-border trade in services (for modes 1 and 2), together with a ratchet and a standstill.

The EU–UK Agreement, of significance given its commercial relevance and the broad scope of disciplines it contains, followed a similar approach, with negative listing modalities for the chapters on cross-border trade in services (modes 1 and 2) and investment. The UK's PTA with Japan, from 2021, also pursues a negative-list approach, with a ratchet and a standstill.

UK and EU PTAs with Armenia, Moldova, and Ukraine (2019–2020): In recent PTAs that the EU and UK each concluded with certain countries of Eastern Europe and the Caucasus, a hybrid model was used, whereby a positive listing approach was followed for modes 1 and 2 (chapter on Cross-Border Trade), while a negative-list was used for mode 3 (chapter on Investment/Establishment).

Australia–Indonesia PTA (2020): The particular relevance of the liberalisation modalities of the Australia–Indonesia PTA stems from the fact that this Agreement was concluded before the RCEP, where discussions surrounding the choice of negotiating modalities had proven difficult, given that various ASEAN Members had so far stuck with a positive listing in their individual PTAs, and that PTAs negotiated by ASEAN as a whole had until then always used GATS-type approaches.

The Agreement's chapter on trade in services, which covers all four modes of supply, uses a negative-list approach, with a standstill and a ratchet. The investment chapter, which applies to investments in services, also uses a negative-list approach but does not feature a ratchet mechanism. These aspects are novel for Indonesia, ASEAN's largest economy.

Even though negative-list modalities are referred to in the chapters and are used for Annex I on existing non-conforming measures, Indonesia's reservations under its Annex II use a positive listing of commitments, where a broad right to maintain and adopt non-conforming measures is spelt out.[11]

Regional Comprehensive Economic Partnership (RCEP, 2022): The RCEP is the largest PTA, as it links ASEAN Members with countries of the region with which ASEAN had already concluded PTAs, namely Australia, China, Japan, Korea (Rep. of), and New Zealand. The Agreement's commercial significance was, however, negatively impacted by India's decision to withdraw from the negotiations prior to their conclusion.

The negotiations pitted countries that had frequently used negative listing in their earlier PTAs (Australia, Japan, Korea, New Zealand), with others that had traditionally favoured positive listing modalities: China, India, and a number of ASEAN Members. While the ASEAN Framework Agreement on Services and the PTAs that ASEAN collectively negotiated with third parties followed a GATS-type approach, Singapore has often used negative lists in its own PTAs, while Malaysia, Viet Nam,

[11] Except for sectors listed in Annex 1 and subject to GATS-type commitments listed in Annex II.

and Brunei Darussalam had used negative lists in the context of the CPTPP. Indonesia, for its part, had, as noted above, experimented with some elements of a negative-list architecture in its PTA with Australia.

For the trade in services chapter, which covered the four modes of supply, the negotiated solution to diverging positions on liberalisation modalities was akin to the approach taken in the Australia–China PTA, where each party can choose between two liberalisation modalities.[12] Those choosing positive-list modalities would make commitments on market access and national treatment (as well as on any additional commitments). Those making commitments in accordance with negative-list modalities would list non-conforming measures in relation to national treatment and market access as well as with regard to local presence requirements.

The modalities for negative listing provided for a standstill (list of existing non-conforming measures in a first annex) and a ratchet. The novelty of the approach taken in the RCEP relates to the conditions attached to the use of the positive listing modality. A first deviation from the traditional, or GATS-type, approach is that a provision provides that parties choosing to schedule on a positive-list basis could identify sectors for future liberalisation through the annotation 'FL'. In these sectors, the limitations scheduled are to relate to existing measures (Article 8.7:3), and a ratchet applies (Article 8.7:4).[13]

Another innovation within the positive-list modality concerns the inclusion of non-binding transparency lists of existing measures that are inconsistent with national treatment and market access. The Agreement (Article 8.3) provides that parties choosing to use the positive-list modalities shall either make commitments on MFN treatment (Article 8.6) or with respect to transparency lists (Article 8.10). parties choosing the 'transparency list' option are to make publicly available a non-binding list of existing measures that are inconsistent with market access and national treatment. The list would cover sectors in which the party had undertaken specific commitments, and the measures listed were limited to those of the central government. As with reservation lists under negative-list agreements, the elements of information in the list are to include the sector and subsector, the obligation with which the measure is inconsistent, the legal source of the measure, and a succinct description. The Agreement specifies that the sole purpose of the lists is to promote regulatory transparency, that the measures can be amended by the relevant party, and that they are not subject to dispute settlement. At the time of writing, no party had made its transparency list publicly available, in lieu of MFN commitments.

The 'transparency list' approach, while non-binding, can be seen as aiming to offset a perceived shortcoming of GATS-type agreements, namely that

[12] According to Article 8.7 (Schedules of Specific Commitments) or to Article 8.8 (Schedules of Non-Conforming Measures).

[13] New Zealand, Thailand, and Viet Nam have made use of this provision in their schedule, though sometimes in relation to commitments without limitations.

commitments undertaken – and limitations inscribed – do not necessarily reflect prevailing levels of openness and therefore that the value added of commitments in terms of transparency is limited. Indeed, even where GATS commitments may well reflect existing conditions of access at the time of entry into force, nothing indicates so.

A further significant architectural innovation of RCEP's trade in services chapter is the binding obligation for those who used positive-list modalities to transition to a negative-list schedule within a specified time frame. A draft negative-list schedule of non-conforming measures has to be submitted to other parties no later than three years after entry into force and adopted no later than six years after entry into force. For Cambodia, Lao PDR, and Myanmar, which are LDCs, longer compliance time frames were agreed upon (up to fifteen years). In addition to the three LDCs, China, New Zealand, the Philippines, Thailand, and Viet Nam used the Agreement's positive-list modalities for trade in services, meaning they will transition to negative listing. The other parties, including Indonesia, used the negative-list scheduling approach. As a result, at the end of the transition period, the top ten countries in the Asia-Pacific (by GDP size), with the exception of India, but with the notable inclusion of China, will all have scheduled commitments on a negative-list basis, with sectoral coverage that could, in theory, far exceed that of the same countries' commitments in positive-list PTAs and in the GATS, and, through increased sector coverage, standstill and ratchet, mark a pivotal shift towards negative listing, given that such a model was already being used by the main developed country economies and was most common in Latin America (with the exception, for the time being, of Mercosur, though the group is now negotiating negative-list PTAs).

The RCEP's investment chapter, which adopts a broad definition of investment but does not apply to measures covered by the chapter on trade in services, also uses negative-list modalities. All parties list non-conforming measures in this way for liberalisation obligations, including national treatment for pre-establishment. One particularity is that the ratchet mechanism for existing non-conforming measures does not apply to some parties (Cambodia, Lao PDR, Myanmar, but also Indonesia and the Philippines). For the other parties, the ratchet starts to apply five years after the Agreement's entry into force.

Australia–India (2022): While India did not, in the end, join the fifteen-country RCEP Agreement, the bilateral PTA that it recently concluded with Australia largely replicates the main liberalisation modalities of the RCEP for services trade, in particular the obligation to transition towards negative listing.

As in the RCEP, each party can choose whether to use the positive-list or the negative-list modalities, the latter with a ratchet. A draft negative-list schedule of non-conforming measures has to be submitted to the other party no later than five years after the PTA's entry into force, and an agreed schedule should be submitted no later than six years after entry into force. This PTA has no investment chapter.

Japan–ASEAN (2022): The Japan–ASEAN PTA was signed in 2019 and entered into force in 2020 before being notified to the WTO in 2022. It contains, along similar lines as in the RCEP, an obligation (Article 50.4) for parties to produce a non-legally binding list (central government only) of measures inconsistent with the obligations of market access and national treatment, as well as MFN treatment. The transparency lists cover sectors where specific commitments are undertaken in the PTA and in other PTAs in force, as well as, where possible, other sectors.

The obligation to produce the transparency lists has a broader scope of application than in the RCEP since it here applies to all eleven parties, which all use a positive-list approach for the listing of specific commitments. In the RCEP, the use of such lists was subject to conditions and did not apply to parties using negative listing modalities. Parties have to exchange the lists and make them public four years after entry into force. The lists are not to form an integral part of the Agreement and shall not be subject to dispute settlement.

2.3.3 *Advances in Services Rulemaking*

2.3.3.1 Progressing the GATS' Unfinished Agenda

Contrasting the changes observed in the architecture and negotiating modalities used to open services markets, PTAs have, on the whole, proven less transformative as rulemaking laboratories in the services field, notably with regard to the GATS' unfinished rulemaking agenda (Adlung 2006). Trade officials involved in PTA talks in services have not moved the needle markedly on key elements that the first generation of GATS negotiators confronted but failed to resolve three decades ago. As a result, and with obvious exceptions noted below, substantive provisions found in the services chapters of PTAs tend to mirror provisions found in the GATS. Thus, PTAs pursuing a GATS-type approach have tended to largely cut and paste the WTO framework into their services instruments and focus negotiations almost exclusively on scheduling matters. Meanwhile, PTAs following the negative-list approach first pioneered in the NAFTA have also revealed a marked degree of path dependency by largely replicating that original template into their different PTAs.

Emergency safeguard measures and subsidy disciplines: Regardless of the architectural choices made, PTA negotiations have for the most part not tackled the key elements of the GATS' unfinished agenda. This is particularly so with regard to emergency safeguard measures (Article X of the GATS), where scepticism over the very need for – and the operational means of – deploying safeguard provisions in services trade has arguably deepened since the end of the Uruguay Round (Gauthier et al. 2000; Sauvé 2002). Much the same can be said of calls to negotiate subsidy disciplines for services trade as mandated by GATS Article XV, where a host of political economy reasons can be adduced to explain the tepid appetite of governments to curtail their ability to lend support to fledgling services industries. This is so even in countries devoid of the fiscal means of lending such support (Sauvé and Soprana 2018).

Disciplines on non-discriminatory domestic regulation: Rather than searching for novel ways to expand the frontiers of GATS rules, a first wave of PTAs concluded after the Uruguay Round relied on hoped-for GATS developments on unfinished rulemaking challenges, with many PTAs affirming the desire of parties to incorporate by reference any advances flowing from multilateral discussions. This was notably the case for disciplines on domestic regulation mandated by GATS Article VI:4. While the latest generation of PTAs shows no progress on the issues of emergency safeguards and subsidies, more notable advances can be observed on disciplining non-discriminatory domestic regulation where the notion that market access and national treatment commitments may not be sufficient to allow service suppliers to operate effectively in foreign services markets has gained increasing currency. This has led services negotiators to use trade agreements not only as a tool to remove quantitative restrictions and discriminatory measures relating to international services trade and investment, but also to address regulatory obstacles and promote improved good governance in services markets.

As a result, significant developments on domestic regulation matters can be observed in the drafting of 'newer generation' PTAs. Such a development offers evidence of a parallel and iterative dialogue between multilateral and preferential attempts at rulemaking. That dialogue accelerated when, faced with a negotiating stalemate in the GATS Working Group on Domestic Regulation, a subset of like-minded WTO Members launched a plurilateral Joint Statement Initiative (JSI) on services domestic regulation (SDR) at the WTO's Eleventh Ministerial meeting held in Buenos Aires in December 2017 with a view to facilitating trade and reducing trade costs through streamlined procedures governing licencing, accreditation and standards-making in services. Mirroring their contentious multilateral and plurilateral nature, services PTAs have, with only a few exceptions, registered little headway in incorporating necessity or proportionality tests in services trade, an area on which the December 2021 JSI outcome on SDR also remained silent.

Assessing the prevalence of disciplines on domestic regulation in a sample of seventy-four services PTAs, a recent WTO study found that the trend towards including SDR provisions in PTAs held broadly across economies at all levels of development and regions, with only low-income economies participating to a more limited extent, as may be expected given the often-weaker state of LDC regulatory regimes. Almost 40 per cent of WTO Members in the study's sample adopted, on average, at least half of the disciplines found in the SDR JSI. The study also shows that economies have already implemented SDR measures in their regulatory frameworks, with only low-income economies having done so to a lesser degree. Averaged across all service sectors and modes of supply, parties to more than half of the PTAs under review implemented at least two-thirds of the JSI-SDR measures (Baiker et al. 2021).

Government procurement: Considerable negotiating headway has been achieved in opening government procurement markets (including in service sectors) within PTAs, though such advances are most notable in PTAs among developed countries already party to the WTO's plurilateral Government Procurement Agreement that covers services. Such advances are also common within PTAs conducted along North–South lines and where procurement liberalisation was often one of the preconditions set by developed countries to launch preferential negotiations with developing country partners (Anderson et al. 2011). A prime example of the latter trend can be found in the NAFTA. It bears recalling, however, that the progress achieved on procurement matters at the PTA level has occurred in standalone dedicated chapters governing state purchases rather than in the services chapters of PTAs.

2.3.3.2 PTA Advances Relevant to Services Trade Governance

If PTAs register uneven progress on the GATS+ rulemaking front, significant progress can be reported in so-called GATS-X terms, that is, in agreeing to services-relevant rules not explicitly included in the GATS. As in the case of government procurement, most such advances have been made outside of the services chapters of PTAs, within dedicated separate chapters, while others relate to generic (i.e. non-services-specific) provisions calling for stepped-up levels of regulatory cooperation and to government-to-government and public–private dialogue on services issues.

Advances on new rules relating to services have often been achieved in policy areas that feature a market access component. This is notably the case for government procurement, investment, the movement of business persons, as well as specific mandates to conclude mutual recognition agreements in selected professional service sectors. New sector-specific rules (recalling GATS annexes) have also been agreed as complements to the market opening commitments some PTAs have secured in novel sectors, such as express delivery, postal, and courier services.[14]

Investment: Far-reaching advances have been made in incorporating comprehensive investment disciplines covering services that span investment promotion, protection, liberalisation, dispute settlement, and, most recently (mirroring WTO-JSI developments), investment facilitation into PTAs. Such a trend started with the NAFTA in 1994, anchoring the investment protection provisions found in bilateral investment treaties into PTAs to which a liberalisation (market access) component was added. Mounting controversy over investment litigation, particularly that

[14] Various services PTAs included distinct chapters or annexes dedicated to telecommunication services. Many of those include provisions going beyond the GATS annex on basic telecommunications and/or the Reference Paper on basic telecommunication services. See Monteiro et al. (2022). On financial services, see Cantore (2020) and Papaconstantinou (2020).

flowing from investor–state arbitration, has either fuelled a major revision of many substantive and procedural features of investment rulemaking or induced significant policy aversion. Both trends have found their way into latest-generation PTAs. For instance, the USMCA that replaced the NAFTA in 2020 limited investor–state dispute settlement to Mexico and the United States, and with a reduced scope and subject to additional conditions triggering its use (Bernasconi-Osterwalder 2018). Meanwhile, the Investment Protocol of the AfCFTA has altogether eschewed questions of investment protection, liberalisation, and investor–state dispute settlement,[15] focusing solely on questions of investment facilitation with market opening commitments limited to mode 3 transactions governed by the Agreement's Protocol on Trade in Services.

Preferential trade agreements brokered along North–North and North–South lines are exhibiting notable adaptability in the investment sphere, with dedicated chapters reflecting a new equilibrium between the rights and obligations of investors and host states while also embracing a greater focus on quality investment aimed at satisfying sustainability aims (OECD 2022). The ability of some PTAs to produce a more balanced set of investment disciplines stands in marked and paradoxical contrast to the repeated inability of WTO Members to take up a more ambitious investment agenda (Echandi and Sauvé 2020).

Movement of business persons: A large number of PTAs also include separate chapters on the temporary entry of business persons featuring entry commitments. Such chapters, which apply to categories of business persons in different sectors, including services, generally go beyond the GATS by including obligations in relation to transparency and procedural matters, including on the processing of applications (Stephenson and Hufbauer 2011).

Digital trade: Unlike investment, where the adoption of multilateral norms rooted in preferential practice has not proven possible, the advent of increasingly prescriptive chapters on digital trade illustrates the important role that PTAs can potentially play as rulemaking laboratories (Monteiro and Teh 2017). While close to two-thirds (64 per cent) of PTAs featuring digital trade rules involve developed countries endowed with greater digital capacities, more than a third (36 per cent) can be found in agreements among developing countries (Figure 2.4). This suggests the heightened interest that some developing countries have begun to show towards the development promise of the unfurling digital transformation, though many of them, particularly in Africa, currently abstain from rulemaking efforts in this area, whether in PTAs or in the ongoing plurilateral negotiations on e-commerce at the WTO.

The question arises of whether the growing corpus of digital rules adopted by countries, both within PTAs and stand alone digital trade agreements, can be replicated multilaterally. The distinctive feature of PTAs, involving as they do

[15] The parties have agreed to revisit in future the case for embedding investor–state dispute settlement provisions into the AfCFTA's Investment Protocol.

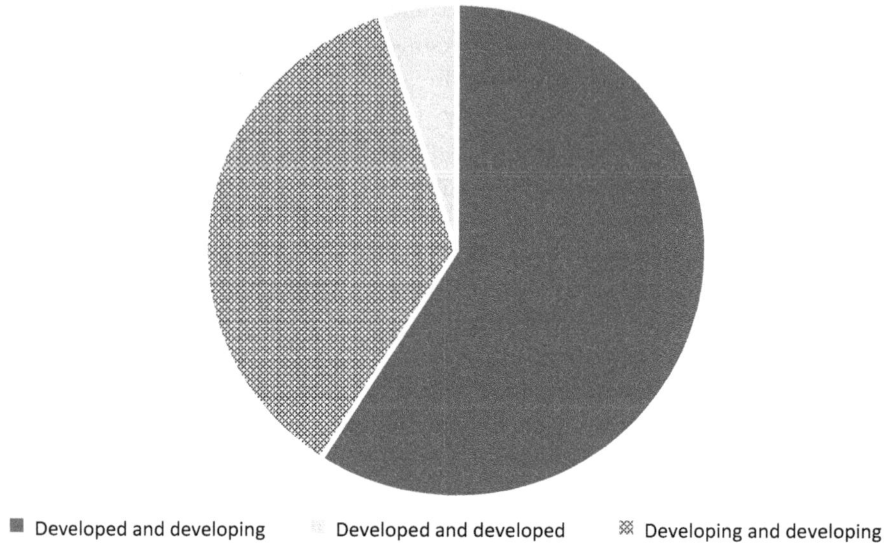

FIGURE 2.4 Parties to PTAs with digital trade provisions, by levels of development.
Source: Burri and Polanco (2020).

partnerships of choice, has allowed significant progress to be registered on matters of digital trade governance. This includes, among other key PTA developments, acceptance of a permanent moratorium on the application of customs duties on electronic transmissions, the prohibition of requirements on the localisation of computing facilities, provisions for the protection of personal data, as well as commitments aimed at freeing cross-border data flows. All are issues at play within ongoing JSI negotiations on e-commerce at the WTO.

Disciplines on SOEs: Disciplines on SOEs represent another new frontier in PTA rulemaking. Though horizontal (i.e. non-services-specific) disciplines on competition policy matters have long been embedded in PTAs, the CPTPP introduced detailed provisions specifically targeting the potential trade-distortive actions of SOEs, including those active in services.

The CPTPP's SOEs and Designated Monopolies chapter (Chapter 17) aims at ensuring that commercial SOEs operate in a transparent manner and in a way that does not put privately owned companies at a competitive disadvantage. More specifically, the chapter aims at ensuring that SOEs act in accordance with commercial considerations in their purchase and sale of services, and that they do not discriminate against services and service suppliers of other parties. In addition, the chapter disciplines non-commercial assistance provided directly or indirectly to SOEs if it causes adverse effects on other parties' interests. For example, parties are prevented from causing adverse effects by providing non-commercial assistance to an SOE that supplies a service into the territory of another party through mode 1 or through an investment in the territory of another party. Adverse effects arise when, for example, the services of SOEs having received non-commercial assistance displace or impede a like service from the market of another party.

Regulatory cooperation: Preferential trade agreements have been argued to offer greater scope for making speedier headway on matters relating to regulatory cooperation in services trade, notably in areas such as services-related standards and the mutual recognition of licenses and professional or educational qualifications (Hoekman and Mattoo 2007; Mattoo 2015). The evidence in this area remains somewhat mixed. Regulatory harmonisation induced by PTAs beyond *de minimis* thresholds remains a rarity, and the conclusion of trade facilitating mutual recognition agreements has proven challenging even within the more comfortable confines of preferential partnerships of choice and within economies characterised by broadly convergent regulatory ecosystems (Sauvé 1995).

The question thus arises of whether PTAs facilitate regulatory convergence. To the limited extent that negotiated convergence occurs, it tends to proceed far more under 'closed' Article V (Economic Integration) agreements than through the open regionalism called for under GATS Article VII (Recognition). Furthermore, with only a few exceptions, progress on regulatory issues tends to be less pronounced in trans-regional PTAs. This suggests stronger returns to geographical proximity in matters of regulatory cooperation (Sauvé and Shingal, 2011). PTAs can, however, play a useful role in promoting dialogue between regulators, business groupings, and civil society organisations, the 'regional public good' benefits of which may be reaped outside of trade agreements but in a manner that nonetheless facilitates and promotes trade and investment, helps to promote improved policy outcomes, and strengthens investment climates.

2.3.4 *Liberalisation Commitments*

As for trade in goods, an obvious motivation for services PTAs is to allow parties to secure deeper and broader commitments on market access and national treatment than those benefiting all WTO Members under GATS schedules. Market opening commitments can liberalise services trade by reducing discriminatory measures or market access impediments to trade and investment in services. But just as importantly, such commitments can also enhance the predictability of policy regimes and the resulting conditions for business operations. By binding existing levels of openness, they will prevent trade-restrictive policy reversals. Various studies have documented the benefits deriving from higher levels of binding commitments in services, pointing to the value of PTA commitments that (merely) bind the status quo.[16]

The levels of market opening secured by services PTAs and, in particular, the extent to which they go beyond GATS commitments, have been well documented

[16] See: Ciuriak and Lysenko (2016), OECD (2017), Lamprecht and Miroudot (2018).

in Roy et al. (2007), Marchetti and Roy (2008), Fink and Molinuevo (2008), Mattoo and Sauvé (2010), Roy (2014), and van der Marel and Miroudot (2014). Overall, services PTAs tend to contain commitments that go well beyond those under the GATS (as well as beyond offers of improvements to GATS commitments made during the Doha Round), even if levels of GATS+ commitments naturally vary across agreements, parties, sectors, and modes of supply.

Van der Marel and Miroudot (2014) found that such factors as the quality of governance, market size, skill endowments, and asymmetries between parties are relevant in accounting for GATS+ commitments in PTAs, while Shingal et al. (2018) emphasised that the coherence and level of restrictiveness of parties' regulatory frameworks, as well as the importance of parties' bilateral merchandise trade had a positive impact. Roy et al. (2007) observed that countries that were parties to negative-list PTAs had undertaken greater commitments than they had under positive-list agreements.

In more recent years, the gap between market opening commitments in PTAs and the WTO has increased further, given that, as noted earlier, a host of new countries are now engaging in preferential services negotiations and in light of WTO Members' continued inability (or absent appetite) to resume market access negotiations under the GATS.

Two other trends are at play in fuelling the gap between preferential and multilateral commitments in services trade. First, PTAs linking larger economies can be expected to yield a richer harvest of commitments compared with similar agreements reached with smaller trading partners. Indeed, as observed by Roy et al. (2007), countries that are parties to multiple PTAs tend to assume greater commitments in their agreements with the United States and, to a lesser degree, with the EU, than they do with other trading partners. Second, the greater number of negative-list agreements, including the adoption of such a negotiating modality by the EU in 2017 and by a growing number of other countries more recently, also shows a proclivity for yielding a qualitative and quantitative upgrade in services commitments over and above those found in GATS schedules.

Figure 2.5 presents a new analysis of PTA commitments in three sectors: environmental services, tourism and travel-related services, and computer services. Using the methodology developed by Roy et al. (2007), we assess the extent of GATS+ commitments in over 140 services PTAs, including some notified up to early 2022. The three sectors have different characteristics and have attracted different types of commitments under the GATS. While environmental services are subject to a relatively low level of commitments in the WTO, tourism is the most committed sector. For its part, the computer service sector, more than the other two, is subject to a relatively low level of market access and national treatment limitations and is highly reliant on cross-border supply (mode 1).

Despite the differing characteristics noted above, PTA commitments in all three sectors largely exceed GATS commitments and Doha Round offers. In travel and

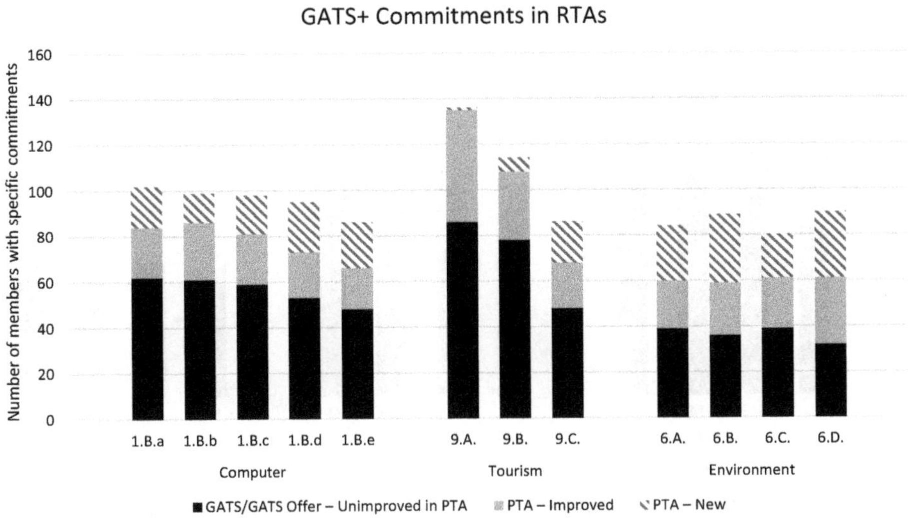

FIGURE 2.5 GATS+ commitments on environmental services, computer services, and tourism services in PTAs.

Note: On the basis of 142 of the 193 regional trade agreements notified under GATS Article V as of 1 March 2022. Counting the EU as one. 'GATS/GATS offer – unimproved in PTA' means the number of Members that have GATS commitments or that have made an offer in the WTO services negotiations in the relevant subsector, and that have not taken better commitments in PTAs. 'PTA – Improved' means the number of Members that have undertaken a commitment in PTAs that improve a GATS commitment or offer. 'PTA – New' means the number of Members that have undertaken a commitment in PTAs, where no commitment or offer had been made under the GATS. For computer services: 1.B.a = consultancy services related to the installation of computer hardware; 1.B.b = software implementation services; 1.B.c. = data processing services; 1.B.d. = data base services; 1.B.e. other computer services. For environmental services: 6.A. = sewage services (CPC 9401); 6.B. = refuse disposal services (CPC 9402); 6.C. = sanitation and similar services (CPC 9403); and 6.D. = other environmental services. For tourism and travel-related services: 9.A. = hotels and restaurants; 9.B. = travel agencies and tour operators services; 9.C. = tourist guides services.

Source: Computed by authors.

tourism services, fifty-nine WTO Members (counting the EU as one) undertook greater commitments than in their GATS schedule or Doha Development Agenda (DDA) offer. Given that a large majority of WTO Members already have some commitments in the sector, PTA improvements have mostly taken the form of binding better levels of treatment in subsectors already committed in GATS schedules. This is particularly the case for the subsectors of hotels and restaurants and of travel agencies/tour operators, which had attracted a much higher level of commitment at the multilateral level than in the case of tourist guide services.

For computer and environmental services, GATS+ commitments have taken the form of better guarantees of access in sectors already committed, as well as

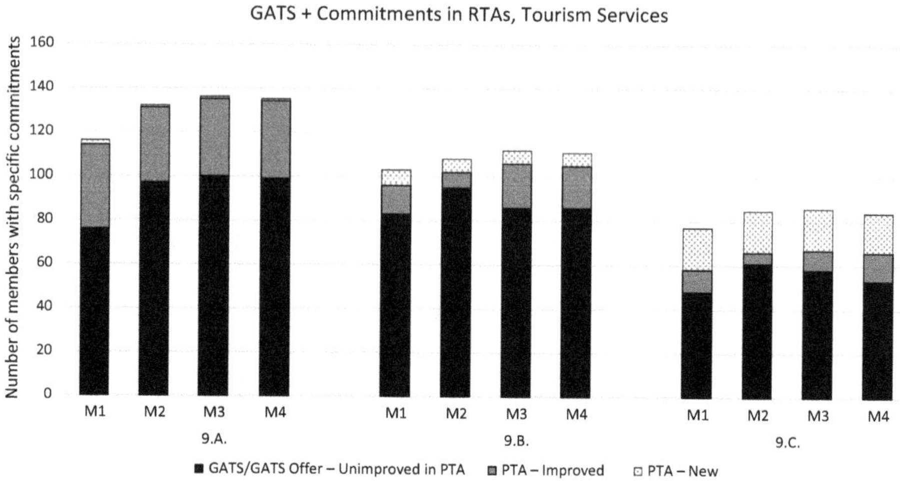

FIGURE 2.6 GATS+ commitments on tourism services in PTAs, by mode of supply.
Note: See information on Figure 2.5.
Source: Computed by authors.

commitments in subsectors that are uncommitted at the multilateral level. Overall, for the sample of agreements considered, fifty Members undertook GATS+ commitments in computer services, while sixty-two did so in environmental services. The rapid growth in digital trade and rising salience of concerns over environmental stewardship given evolving climate change dynamics would appear to explain the propensity for significantly improved commitments relative to when GATS commitments in both sectors were contemplated in the mid- to late 1990s.

Figure 2.6 offers a more detailed view by comparing GATS and PTA commitments in tourism and travel-related services across different modes of supply. It shows that GATS+ commitments were not concentrated in only certain modes of supply. Across the three sectors, a significant number of improvements took place under mode 1, which is of greatest significance for digital trade. For example, while 35% of GATS commitments in hotel and restaurant services were unrestricted (full commitments), the proportion jumped to 56% in the sample of PTAs under review. For travel agencies and tour operator services, full commitments were found in 73% of PTAs reviewed, compared to 62% when looking at GATS commitments/offers, or 56% when considering only existing GATS commitments. For tourist guide services, full commitments were found in 77% of PTAs reviewed, a 15% premium over the GATS.

As noted above, the significant and growing gap in services commitments between the WTO and PTAs does not carry, in principle, the same risks of trade diversion or preference erosion as is in goods trade. Indeed, unlike goods trade, where PTAs aim to eliminate tariffs over time for substantially all trade, services

PTAs chiefly tend to bind the status quo, although examples of agreements bringing about de novo liberalisation in certain areas do exist (Roy et al. 2007). Services PTAs hold lesser negative consequences for non-parties because, again in contrast to goods trade, services trade liberalisation is typically implemented on an MFN basis given the challenge and administrative costs of maintaining differentiated regulatory regimes. However, cases of applied discrimination do exist, including as a result of PTAs, such as in the case of differentiated screening thresholds for foreign investment. The movement of natural persons is another area where the potential for applied preferences exists, though comprehensive information documenting such practices is often lacking.

Given that most PTA commitments bind *existing* levels of openness and that such applied levels do not distinguish across different foreign services and suppliers to the same extent as for goods trade, WTO Members should, in principle, find it easier to formally extend their PTA commitments on an MFN basis under the GATS. The recent broadening and deepening of PTA commitments – new actors engaging in services PTAs, increasing links between larger economies – suggests that the basket of potential services commitments that could be multilateralised is significant and growing. This recalls the urgency of reviving the WTO's market opening machinery in services, if only to consolidate what has been achieved preferentially if appetites for rolling back existing restrictive practices continue to prove deficient (World Bank and WTO 2023).

2.4 CONCLUDING REMARKS: WHAT FUTURE DIRECTIONS FOR SERVICES PTAS?

This chapter highlighted how advances in the services chapters of PTAs have chiefly taken the form of innovations with respect to architecture and negotiating modalities, as well as GATS+ advances in the level of bound commitments. Services PTAs, on the whole, display fewer notable advances regarding the rules governing services trade, though notable PTA progress on issues relevant to the functioning and external competitiveness of services markets has been secured in the latest-generation agreements.

Evidence of GATS+ rulemaking varies considerably across PTAs, with most innovations embedded in dedicated chapters (or annexes) that target specific service sectors (e.g. chapters on telecommunications services that build on the GATS Annex on Telecommunications and/or Reference Paper on Basic Telecommunications) or through dedicated chapters that usually do not distinguish between goods and services trade, such as those dealing with e-commerce/digital trade, the movement of business persons, investment, government procurement, regulatory convergence, or SOEs. The latter shows every sign of becoming more common in future PTAs and can be expected to add value to the obligations and commitments on services embedded in future PTAs.

Advances in services induced by PTAs are on the whole less marked than in other areas of trade and investment governance, a situation that in our view shows little prospect of significant change in the coming years. This is so because services trade negotiations confront much the same challenges and complexities regardless of the settings in which negotiations proceed. Indeed, the sheer diversity of the service economy poses significant challenges to governments as they enact policies aimed at harnessing the potential contribution of services trade to inclusive economic growth and development.

The service sector's heterogeneity implies that, regardless of the setting, whether at the domestic level or in international negotiations, policy reforms in services need to pay close attention to – and be informed by – differences in the nature and roles that various services play, in the multiplicity of ways in which they are traded, in the broad range of public policy aims their supply pursues, and in the political economy forces they put in play. Services further differ in their skill- and capital-intensity, the degree to which they are connected to other sectors, their propensity to be supplied by micro-, small, and medium enterprises (MSMEs) or by large multinational firms, and the degree to which they can be remotely supplied. Such differentiation explains why service sector governance rarely, if ever, proceeds on a one-size-fits-all basis. It also recalls why domestic reforms anchored in trade agreements typically proceed in a progressive manner, including within preferential confines.

A further layer of complexity stems from the high degree of regulatory scrutiny services transactions tend to command, including across borders. Such scrutiny reflects the ubiquity of instances in which services markets can fail to produce socially optimal outcomes in the absence of regulatory measures pursuing legitimate public policy aims, such as consumer protection, the prevention of systemic risks in financial markets, environmental degradation, or undue market concentration in network industries. All are factors that define the realm of what can be negotiated, whether on a preferential or global basis.

Heterogeneity is centrally at play in the conduct of services negotiations, which typically involve a broad and complex set of policies, regulations, lead sectoral ministries, regulatory agencies, and diverse constituencies, domestic and foreign, public and private. For these reasons, and once again regardless of the negotiating setting, care is needed in assessing the nature, pace, and sequencing of regulatory reform and market opening undertakings in services markets if they are to maximise a country's growth and development prospects. For all the above reasons, the process of conducting service sector reforms, whether autonomously or in the context of trade agreements, tends to prove more challenging than in other sectors (Sáez et al. 2014).

Still, despite the limitations noted above, innovations in recent years in relation to architecture and liberalisation modalities highlight some possible avenues in the design of future services PTAs. Building on recent trends, future PTAs can be expected to keep moving beyond the traditional dichotomy between positive and negative listing modalities. Taking account of the particular parties involved, elements of the two approaches can be used and combined so as to provide for maximum transparency of existing market access conditions. These innovations might also provide inspiration for revisiting and reviving certain positive-list PTAs that were concluded one or two decades ago.

Greater use can be made of transition periods to facilitate the shift towards negative listing approaches. Agreements should also incorporate commitments to lend support to developing countries through independent technical advice to facilitate the preparation of these lists, as transition periods and proper sequencing are relevant for those countries with limited or no prior experience with negative listing.

For those agreements and parties that cannot move to negative listing, even with transition periods, certain elements inspired by negative listing agreements could still be incorporated into a positive listing structure. One such element would be to use annotations in schedules to indicate which specific commitments contain limitations that reflect the existing, applied, situation. This feature has been used in a few PTAs but remains underutilised, even in the few positive-list agreements incorporating such features. PTAs could also usefully enshrine a standstill obligation under positive-list agreements with a view to reaping status quo commitments that have greater commercial meaning and stronger signalling effects.

Perhaps most importantly, another element inspired by negative listing approaches that could be used in positive-list agreements concerns the production of non-binding lists of existing non-conforming measures embedded in PTAs for transparency purposes. Such lists may help promote periodic domestic assessments of the trade and investment incidence of prevailing regulatory conditions. An important difference between the two traditional negotiating modalities is that positive-list agreements cannot be counted on to provide information on *applied* restrictions, whether for sectors committed or for sectors not committed to the extent that parties are allowed to commit less than the status quo or eschew commitments altogether (i.e. remain 'unbound') in specific sectors, subsectors, and/or modes of supply. In contrast, negative-list agreements are generally designed to bind the status quo and detail existing non-conforming measures and the measures maintained in sectors where future regulatory immunity is sought. When the transition to negative listing is not achievable, GATS-type approaches could be supplemented by an obligation to parties to prepare, make transparently available, and periodically update non-binding lists detailing their existing non-conforming measures in different modes and sectors, whether those are committed or not.

While such non-binding lists would not prevent the introduction of new restrictions, they would nevertheless reduce uncertainty by allowing for more informed investment and trade decisions, facilitating needed dialogue between government departments and with external stakeholders, promote a better understanding and assessment of any policy changes and their impacts, and help reduce trade costs. Nowadays, it appears increasingly odd to see PTAs aiming to boost trade and investment – most of which without the expectation of seeing liberalisation commitments reopened or supplemented after their entry into force – while providing little or no information on key existing trade measures across many service sectors and modes of supply.

Since such non-binding transparency lists carry no MFN or market access implications, they could also be considered at the multilateral level as a partial remedy to the stasis of WTO services negotiations (without substituting for them nor implying the initiation of new market opening talks) and to the low level of liberalisation but also of transparency provided by existing GATS commitments, where a majority of Members have no commitments in a plurality of sectors.

Another forward-looking element of services PTAs relates to the importance of integrating services-specific development assistance – Aid for Trade – features into services agreements. The growing prevalence of services in world trade and investment – to say nothing of their predominance in production and employment, their gendered gains, and lesser aggregate environmental footprint – points to their central integrating role in the global economy and key contribution to sustainable development strategies. Yet, as highlighted above, LDCs remain much less engaged in services PTAs than are middle- and higher-income developing countries, even if their participation has increased as a result of a few recent negotiations. And such participation is set to grow markedly in the wake of the AfCFTA's implementation, thirty-three of whose fifty-four signatories are LDCs.

This deficit in participation is troubling given the benefits that could accrue to LDCs, in light of the potential for enhancing competition, strengthening regulatory practices, boosting inward direct investment in service sectors, facilitating access to quality and affordable services inputs for their companies in different sectors, and expanding their exports and diversification prospects, notably through digital means. Agreements to which LDCs are parties, especially those that also involve more advanced economies, should feature provisions on the supply of technical assistance focused not only on the implementation of negotiated outcomes, but also on durably strengthening supply capacities with a view to diversifying baskets of competitive service exports.

REFERENCES

Adlung, R. 2006. 'Services Negotiations in the Doha Round: Lost in Flexibility?' *Journal of International Economic Law* 9(4): 865–893.

Anderson, R., A. Muller, K. Osei-Lah, J. De Leon and P. Pelletier 2011. 'Government Procurement Provisions in Regional Trade Agreements: A Stepping Stone to GPA Accession?' in S. Arrowsmith and R. Anderson (eds.), *The WTO Regime on Government Procurement: Challenge and Reform*. Cambridge: Cambridge University Press.

Baiker, L., E. Bertola and M. Jelitto 2021. 'Services Domestic Regulation: Locking in Good Regulatory Practices – Analysing the Prevalence of Services Domestic Regulation

Disciplines and Their Potential Linkages with Economic Performance', WTO Staff Working Paper, ERSD-2021-14 (September). Geneva: World Trade Organization.

Bernasconi-Osterwalder, N. 2018. 'USMCA Curbs How Much Investors Can Sue Countries – Sort of', IISD Insight, Geneva: International Institute for Sustainable Development (2 October), available at www.iisd.org/articles/usmca-investors.

Burri, M. and R. Polanco 2020. 'Digital Trade Provisions in Preferential Trade Agreements: Introducing a New Dataset', *Journal of International Economic Law* 23(1): 187–220.

Cantore, C. 2020. '"Parallel Convergences" in Free Trade Agreements on Financial Services: Select Issues', in R. Hoffmann and M. Krajewski (eds.), *Coherence and Divergence in Services Trade Law, European Yearbook of International Economic Law*. Cham: Springer.

Ciuriak, D. and D. Lysenko 2016. *Quantifying Services-Trade Liberalization: The Impact of Binding Commitments*. Toronto: C. D. Howe Institute.

Echandi, R. and P. Sauvé 2020. 'Investment Facilitation and Mode 3 Trade in Services: Are Current Discussions Addressing the Key Issues?' World Bank Policy Research Working Paper No. 9229 (6 May), available at https://openknowledge.worldbank.org/handle/10986/33711?show = full&locale-attribute = fr.

Elms, D. 2018. 'The Comprehensive and Progressive Trans-Pacific Partnership: Policy Innovations and Impacts', GED Focus Paper, Gütersloh: Bertelsmann Stiftung, available at http://aei.pitt.edu/102526/1/MT_Comprehensive_and_Progressive_Trans-Pacific_Partnership.pdf.

Fefer, R. F. 2017. 'Trade in Services Agreement (TiSA) Negotiations: Overview and Issues for Congress', Washington, DC: US Congressional Research Service.

Fink, C. and M. Molinuevo 2008. 'East Asian Free Trade Agreements in Services: Key Architectural Elements', *Journal of International Economic Law* 11(2): 263–311.

Gauthier, G., E. O'Brien and S. Spencer 2000. 'Déjà Vu, or New Beginning for Safeguards and Subsidies Rules in Services Trade?' in P. Sauvé and R. M. Stern (eds.), *GATS 2000: New Directions in Services Liberalization*. Washington, DC: Brookings Institution Press and Centre for Business and Government, Harvard University.

Global Affairs Canada 2022. 'Trade in Services Agreement (TISA)', Website, www.international.gc.ca/trade-agreements-accords-commerciaux/topics-domaines/services/tisa-acs.aspx?lang = eng#a.

Hoekman, B. and A. Mattoo 2007. 'Regulatory Cooperation, Aid for Trade and the GATS', *Pacific Economic Review* 7(4): 399–418.

Kim, S. Y. and M. S. Manger 2017. 'Hubs of Governance: Path Dependence and Higher-Order Effects of Preferential Trade Agreement Formation', *Political Science Research and Methods* 5(3): 467–488.

Lamprecht, P. and S. Miroudot 2018. 'The Value of Market Access and National Treatment Commitments in Services Trade Agreements', OECD Trade Policy Papers 213, Paris: OECD Publishing.

Marchetti, J. and M. Roy 2008. 'Services Liberalisation in the WTO and in PTAs', in J. Marchetti and M. Roy (eds.), *Opening Markets for Trade in Services: Countries and Sectors in Bilateral and WTO Negotiations*. Cambridge and Geneva: Cambridge University Press and World Trade Organization.

2014. 'The TISA Initiative: An Overview of Market Access Issues', *Journal of World Trade* 48(4): 683–728.

Mattoo, A. 2015. 'Services and Regulatory Cooperation', Think Piece, E15 Expert Group on Services, Geneva: ICTSD and World Economic Forum, available at https://e15initiative.org/wp-content/uploads/2015/09/E15-Services-Mattoo-FINAL.pdf.

Mattoo, A. and P. Sauvé 2010. 'The Preferential Liberalisation of Trade in Services', NCCR Trade Working Paper 2010/13, Bern: World Trade Institute, available at www.wti.org/research/publications/100/the-preferential-liberalization-of-services-trade/.

Monteiro, J. A. and R. Teh 2017. 'Provisions on Electronic Commerce in Regional Trade Agreements', WTO Staff Working Paper ERSD-2017-11, Geneva: World Trade Organization.

Monteiro, J. A., K. Cassehgari Posada and L. Tuthill 2022. 'Communication Breakdown: Typology of Telecommunications Provisions in Regional Trade Agreements', WTO Staff Working Paper, ERSD-2022-02, Geneva: World Trade Organization.

OECD 2017. *Services Trade Policies and the Global Economy*. Paris: OECD Publishing.

2022. *FDI Qualities Indicators 2022*. Paris: OECD Publishing, available at www.oecd.org/investment/investment-policy/OECD-FDI-Qualities-Indicators-2022-update.pdf.

Papaconstantinou, G. A. 2020. 'Financial Services Liberalisation under EU FTAs: The Case of Clearing and Settlement Services', in W. Weiß and C. Furculita (eds.), *Global Politics and EU Trade Policy: Facing the Challenges to a Multilateral Approach*. Cham: Springer.

Roy, M. 2014. 'Services Commitments in Preferential Trade Agreements: Surveying the Empirical Landscape', in P. Sauvé and A. Shingal (eds.), *The Preferential Liberalisation of Trade in Services: Comparative Regionalism*. Cheltenham: Edward Elgar Publishers.

2019. 'Elevating Services: Services Trade Policy, WTO Commitments, and Their Role in Economic Development and Trade Integration', *Journal of World Trade* 53(6): 923–950.

Roy, M., J. Marchetti, and H. Lim 2007. 'Services Liberalisation in the New Generation of Preferential Trade Agreements (PTAs): How Much Further than the GATS?' *World Trade Review* 6(2): 155–192.

Sáez, S., D. Taglioni, E. van der Marel, C. H. Hollweg and V. Zavacka 2014. *Valuing Services in Trade: A Toolkit for Competitiveness Diagnostics*. Washington, DC: World Bank.

Sauvé, P. 1995. 'The Long and Winding Road: NAFTA and the Professions', in OECD (ed.), *Liberalization of Trade in Professional Services*. Paris: Organization for Economic Cooperation and Development.

2002. 'Completing the GATS Framework: Addressing Uruguay Round Leftovers', *Aussenwirtschaft (Swiss International Economic Review)* 57(3): 310–341.

2014. 'A Plurilateral Agenda for Services: Assessing the Case for a Trade in Services Agreement (TISA)', *Journal of International Commerce, Economics and Policy* 5(4): 413–432.

Sauvé, P. and A. Shingal 2011. 'Reflections on the Preferential Liberalisation of Services Trade', *Journal of World Trade* 45(5): 953–963.

(eds.) 2014. *The Preferential Liberalisation of Trade in Services: Comparative Regionalism*. Cheltenham: Edward Elgar Publishers.

Sauvé, P. and M. Soprana 2018. 'Disciplining Service Sector Subsidies: Where Do We Stand and Where Can We (Realistically) Go?' *Journal of International Economic Law* 21(3): 599–619.

Shingal, A., M. Roy and P. Sauvé 2018. 'Do WTO+ Commitments in Services Trade Agreements Reflect a Quest for Optimal Regulatory Convergence? Evidence from Asia', *World Economy* 41(5): 1223–1250.

Stephenson, S. 2015. 'Overview of Various Approaches to Services Liberalisation', UNCTAD-USAID Training Workshop on Trade in Services for EU-AfCFTA Negotiations, Nairobi, Kenya (24–28 August), available at https://unctad.org/system/files/non-official-document/ditc-ted-Nairobi-24082015-USAID-stephenson.pdf.

Stephenson, S. and G. Hufbauer 2011. 'Labour Mobility', in J.-P. Chauffour and J.-C. Maur (eds.), *Preferential Trade Agreement Policies for Development; A Handbook*. Washington, DC: World Bank Group.

Stephenson, S. and M. Robert 2014. 'Innovating Regionalism: The Americas', in P. Sauvé and A. Shingal (eds.), *The Preferential Liberalisation of Trade in Services*. Cheltenham: Edward Elgar.

USTR 2017. 'The United States Officially Withdraws from the Trans-Pacific Partnership', Press Release, https://ustr.gov/about-us/policy-offices/press-office/press-releases/2017/january/US-Withdraws-From-TPP, accessed on 17 April 2023.

Van der Marel, E. and S. Miroudot 2014. 'The Economics and Political Economy of Going beyond the GATS', *Review of International Organizations* 9(2): 205–239.

Villup, E. 2015. 'The Trade in Services Agreement (TISA): An End to Negotiations in Sight?' In Depth Analysis, European Parliament, available at www.europarl.europa.eu/thinktank/en/document/EXPO_IDA(2015)570448.

World Bank and WTO 2023. 'Services Trade for Development: Harnessing Services for Sustainable Growth, Economic Integration and Deepened Integration', Washington, DC and Geneva: World Bank and WTO.

WTO 2020. 'Trade in Services and Economic Diversification', Discussion Paper for the G20 Trade and Investment Working Group (TIWG), Geneva: WTO Secretariat, available at: www.wto.org/english/tratop_e/serv_e/trade_services_economic_diversification_e.pdf.

3

Technical Barriers to Trade and Sanitary and Phytosanitary Measures in Preferential Trade Agreements

The Recent Past and the Near Future

Sebastian Klotz and Arthur Appleton

3.1 INTRODUCTION

The United Nations defines '[n]on-tariff measures (NTMs) [as] policy measures other than tariffs that can potentially have an economic effect on international trade in goods' (UN, 2022).[1] While many NTMs take the form of government regulations, standards, and testing procedures aimed at protecting public health or the environment, they often pose challenges to exporters, importers, and policymakers.

This chapter focuses on two NTMs: technical barriers to trade (TBT) and sanitary and phytosanitary (SPS) measures. The World Trade Organization's (WTO) TBT Agreement aims to ensure that technical regulations, standards, and conformity assessment procedures are non-discriminatory and do not create unnecessary obstacles to trade. The WTO's SPS Agreement seeks to protect human, animal, and plant life or health from pests, and diseases, as well as additives, contaminants, and toxins, and aims to ensure that such measures do not constitute disguised restrictions on international trade. Both Agreements seek to ensure that WTO Members have sufficient policy space to address these important public policy objectives, while at the same time ensuring that NTMs do not result in arbitrary and unjustifiable discrimination and disguised restrictions on international trade.

Since the establishment of the WTO in 1995, the number of TBT and SPS measures notified by WTO Members to the WTO increased gradually by an annual average of around 10 per cent (Figure 3.1). With the steady decline in tariffs since 1947, WTO Members have devoted increasing attention to disciplining the use of NTMs, such as TBT and SPS measures. While fluctuating from year to year, TBT and SPS measures continue to cause WTO Members to raise trade concerns in the relevant WTO committees (Figure 3.2).

[1] The authors express their appreciation to Rodrigo Polanco for his review and comments on the text. All remaining errors are those of the authors.

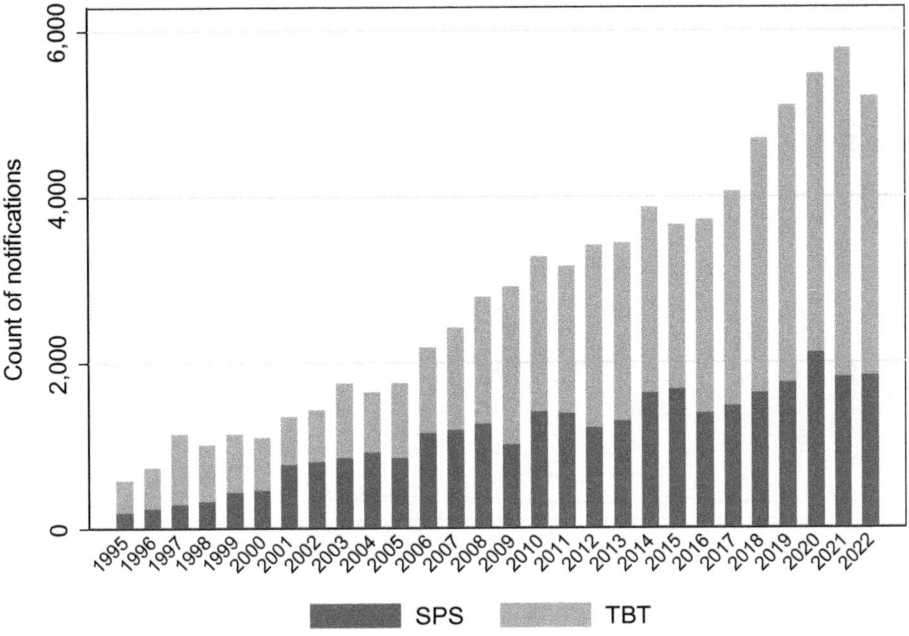

FIGURE 3.1 TBT and SPS notifications to the WTO.
Source: Sebastian Klotz's calculations and illustration based on WTO (2022)

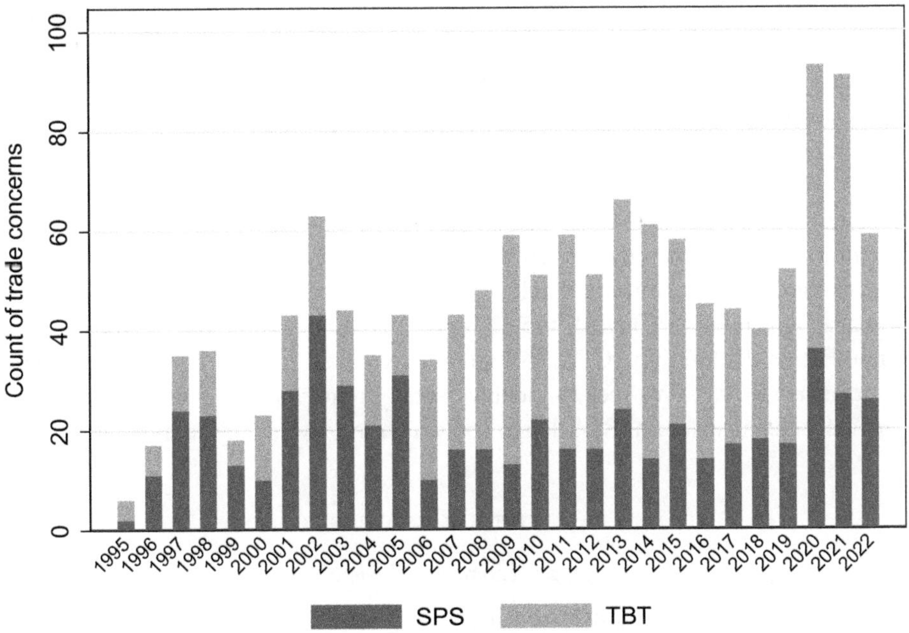

FIGURE 3.2 TBT and SPS trade concerns raised at the WTO.
Source: Sebastian Klotz's calculations and illustration based on WTO (2022)

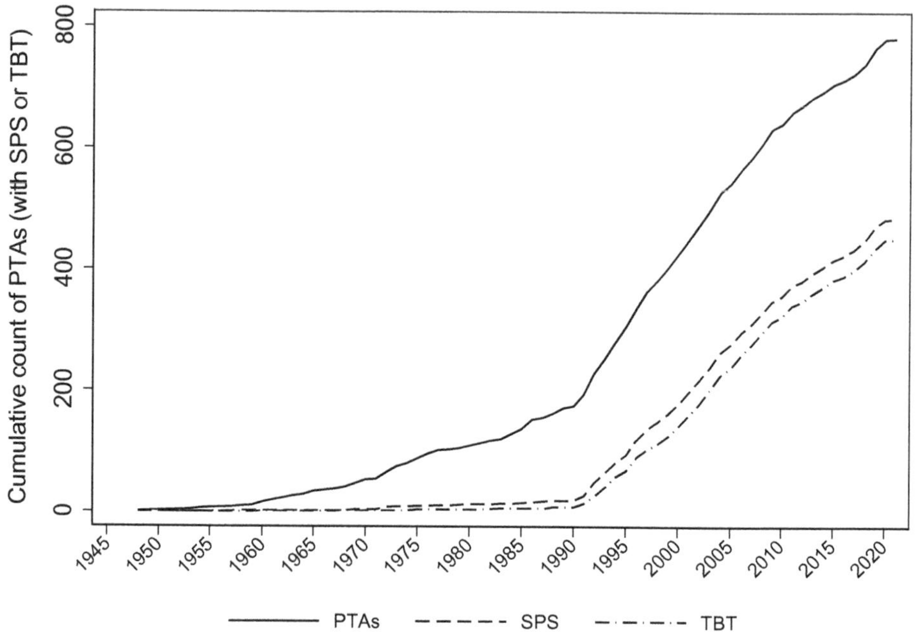

FIGURE 3.3 TBT and SPS chapters in PTAs.
Source: Sebastian Klotz's calculations and illustration based on Dür et al. (2014)

TBT and SPS measures play an important role in the governance of NTMs in the multilateral trade policy regime, but also in preferential trade agreements (PTAs). Indeed, since the entry into force of the WTO TBT and SPS Agreements, on 1 January 1995, an increasing number of PTAs include TBT and SPS chapters and provisions (Figure 3.3).

This chapter is organised as follows. We briefly outline the existing literature on the evolution and design of TBT and SPS chapters in PTAs. We then examine the recent past and assess the extent to which four mega-regional agreements appear to be inspired by previous agreements. Our analysis is focused on the European Union (EU)–Canada Comprehensive Economic and Trade Agreement (CETA), the United States–Mexico–Canada Agreement (USMCA), the Comprehensive and Progressive Agreement for Trans-Pacific Partnership (CPTPP), and the Regional Comprehensive Economic Partnership (RCEP). We seek to identify existing trends and novel development and provisions that may inform PTA design and which may eventually be multilateralised.

3.2 THE RECENT PAST

3.2.1 *Literature Review*

3.2.1.1 Spillovers between the WTO and PTAs

Preferential trade agreements and multilateral trade agreements, such as the WTO TBT and SPS Agreements, are often closely intertwined and build upon one another (Cottier et al. 2015). Approximately 85 per cent of PTAs signed since 1995 include a reference to the WTO or replicate sizeable parts of the relevant legal texts (Allee et al. 2017a). Of the PTAs that include a TBT and/or SPS chapter, around three-quarters include a reference to the WTO. On average, around 11 per cent of these TBT and SPS chapters replicate verbatim from the respective WTO agreements (Allee et al. 2017a). In some instances, particularly in the areas of TBT and SPS measures, PTA parties may agree on deeper cooperation (WTO plus, WTO+). In other areas, such as competition and human rights, PTA partners may agree on cooperation that goes well beyond the WTO mandate (WTO extra, WTO-X) (Horn et al. 2010).

3.2.1.2 Spillovers between PTAs

Preferential trade agreement negotiators rely on multilateral trade agreements and also replicate texts from other PTAs. European Union and United States (US) PTA provisions are found in many other PTAs due to replication by third countries (Horn et al. 2010, 2011; WTO 2011a; Lester and Barbee 2013; Baccini et al. 2015; Egan and Pelkmans 2015; Allee and Elsig 2019; Elsig and Klotz 2019). Forty-five per cent of the Trans-Pacific Partnership (TPP) text, the CPTPP predecessor, is drawn directly from US PTAs signed between 1995 and 2015 (Allee and Lugg 2016). Notably, around 35% of the US–Bahrain Free Trade Agreement (FTA) (2004) TBT chapter and 28% of the US–Australia FTA (2005) SPS chapter are replicated in TPP. Although the US withdrew from TPP in 2017, its TBT and SPS chapters appear to have been influential in the 2018 USMCA. The United States–Mexico–Canada Agreement duplicates 37% and 65% of TPP's TBT and SPS provisions (Elsig and Klotz, 2019).

The EU also reuses its template, albeit less consistently than the US. With respect to TBT provisions, 16% of previous Canadian and EU TBT chapters are replicated in CETA. More than 50% of the TBT chapter in the 2009 Canada–Jordan FTA appears in CETA. Similarly, CETA replicates approximately 17% of the SPS chapter of the 2008 Canada–Colombia FTA (Elsig and Klotz 2019).

The inclusion of specific TBT and SPS provisions in PTAs follows a hub-and-spoke approach (Horn et al. 2010, 2011; WTO 2011a). For example, the type of transparency provisions favoured by the US are also commonly included in other North American, East Asian, South-Central American, and Pacific Ocean PTAs, but are less commonly featured in EU and African PTAs (WTO 2011a; Lejárraga 2013, 2014).

3.2.1.3 The Design of SPS Chapters

An early analysis of fifty-one PTAs signed between 1992 and 2009 finds that more than 80 per cent of these PTAs include SPS provisions on harmonisation, equivalence, regionalisation, risk assessment, transparency, and technical cooperation and joint committees (Fulponi et al. 2011). The authors conclude that approximately one-quarter are WTO+ in the areas of harmonisation, equivalence, regionalisation, and risk assessment. Almost half go beyond WTO rules on transparency. Other early studies with a larger sample size focus on transparency and enforceability (Lejárraga, 2013, 2014). These studies point to a close relationship between multilateral and preferential trade policy regimes, in particular a close relationship between WTO Members' work in the SPS Committee and the design of SPS chapters in PTAs.

3.2.1.4 The Design of TBT Chapters

Early TBT studies (Lesser 2007; Piermartini and Budetta 2009) found that TBT liberalisation is influenced by PTA Members' level of development, the PTA's integration ambition, and EU and US involvement. More recent studies (Molina and Khoroshavina 2015, 2018; Espitia et al. 2020) largely confirm these findings and the importance of the transatlantic divide as a determinant in the design of TBT chapters.

3.2.1.5 Transatlantic Differences in the Design of TBT and SPS Chapters

Transatlantic differences between the EU and the US on TBT- and SPS-related measures have a long history and are well documented (Lesser 2007; Heydon and Woolcock 2009; Piermartini and Budetta 2009; Stoler 2011; Ti-Ting 2012; Molina and Khoroshavina, 2015, 2018; Espitia et al., 2020). The EU favours harmonisation towards EU regulations, standards, and conformity assessment procedures when it signs PTAs with geographically close partner countries, and towards international standards when it signs PTAs with geographically more distant countries. The US emphasises that any international standard developed in line with the 'Six Principles' of transparency, openness, impartiality and consensus, effectiveness and relevance, coherence, and a development dimension is an international standard (McDaniels et al., 2018).

The United States Trade Representative's (USTR) National Trade Estimate Report on Foreign Trade Barriers repeatedly raises TBT- and SPS-related concerns. In its 2020 edition, the Report identifies TBT-related concerns, including transparency and notification, European standardisation, and conformity assessment procedures; chemicals; renewable fuels; sustainability criteria; energy efficiency regulations; transport fuel quality; agriculture quality schemes; wine traditional terms; distilled spirits ageing requirements; and the certification of animal welfare. SPS measures-related concerns included hormones and beta agonists, antimicrobials, agricultural biotechnology, pathogen reduction treatments, certification requirements, somatic cell count, animal by-products, live cattle, agricultural chemicals, and pesticide residues. The USTR Report also notes that '*[t]he EU's approach to standards-related measures, including its conformity assessment framework, and its efforts to encourage governments around the world to adopt its approach, including European regional standards, creates a challenging environment for U.S. exporters*' (USTR, 2020, p. 178).

TABLE 3.1 *Text overlaps between the four mega-regionals and previous PTAs*

	Share of used PTAs (%)		Share of duplicated text (%)	
PTAs	TBT	SPS	TBT	SPS
CETA	34	21	20	9
CPTPP	81	51	20	15
USMCA	70	46	20	18
RCEP	80	58	17	14
Average	66	44	19	14

3.2.2 *Data Analysis*

Building upon the literature outlined above, we apply a text-as-data analysis to explore the TBT and SPS chapters of the four mega-regional PTAs: CETA, CPTPP, USMCA, and RCEP. Before discussing the details of this analysis, we summarise the first set of results in Table 3.1. We find that, in all four mega-regional PTAs, negotiators rely more on previous PTAs when designing the TBT chapter than the SPS chapter. This can be observed in two ways: first, on average, the negotiators copy-pasted 66% of previous TBT chapters but only 44% of prior SPS chapters. Second, the negotiators duplicated, on average, around 19% of previous TBT chapters but only 14% of prior SPS chapters. In other words, the negotiators did not only consult more PTAs but also replicated relatively more text from those PTAs for TBT than for SPS chapters.

The second set of results is summarised in Table 3.2. Here, we analyse the text overlap only among the four mega-regionals. We find that considerable parts of CPTPP are duplicated in USMCA and, to a lesser extent, in RCEP. In contrast to the first set of results, this analysis indicates that relatively more text is duplicated in the area of SPS than in TBT chapters.

3.2.2.1 Data and Methodology

To generate these results, we analysed all PTAs that have been signed since 2000, notified to the WTO, that are currently in force, and include at least one signatory party that is also party to CETA (signed in 2016), CPTPP (2018), USMCA (2018), or RCEP (2020). This sample includes 160 PTAs. Of these PTAs, 124 PTAs (77%) include a TBT chapter, and 118 PTAs (73%) include an SPS chapter. For these PTAs, we extract all texts from the latest version of the Design of Trade Agreements database (DESTA, Dür, Baccini, and Elsig 2014).[2]

To assess the extent to which CETA, CPTPP, USMCA, and RCEP are influenced by previous PTAs, we rely on text-as-data analysis techniques previously

[2] We thank the DESTA team for access to their collection of texts.

TABLE 3.2 *Text overlaps between the four mega-regionals*

	TBT			
	CETA (%)	CPTPP (%)	USMCA (%)	RCEP (%)
CETA	–			
CPTPP	9	–		
USMCA	9	27	–	
RCEP	11	13	13	–
	SPS			
	CETA (%)	**CPTPP (%)**	**USMCA (%)**	**RCEP (%)**
CETA	–			
CPTPP	5	–		
USMCA	5	56	–	
RCEP	4	28	17	–

employed by Allee and Lugg (2016), Allee et al. (2017a, b), and Elsig and Klotz (2019). More precisely, we use the open-source Windows-based program WCopyfind (version 4.1.5) to compare all PTA texts and assess text overlaps. In line with previous research, we define a minimum of six consecutive identical words as a match. Non-words, letter cases, numbers, and punctuation are ignored. Based on the number of matches, WCopyfind calculates a percentage similarity score.

3.2.2.2 Comprehensive Economic and Trade Agreement (CETA)

To assess CETA, we analyse thirty-five PTAs previously signed by the EU or Canada (Figure 3.4). Twenty-six of these PTAs (74%) include a TBT chapter, and 23 PTAs (65%) include an SPS chapter. Of the PTAs that do include a TBT chapter, nine PTAs (34%) are identified as influential for CETA's TBT chapter, and five PTAs (21%) are influential for CETA's SPS chapter. The average text overlap for the TBT chapter is 20%, and for the SPS chapter, 9%. By far, the most influential TBT chapter is Canada–Jordan (2009) (51% overlap). The most influential SPS chapter is Canada–Colombia (2008) (17% overlap).

3.2.2.3 Comprehensive and Progressive Agreement for Trans-Pacific Partnership (CPTPP)

For the analysis of CPTPP, we focus on ninety-nine PTAs signed by Australia, Brunei, Canada, Chile, Japan, Malaysia, Mexico, New Zealand, Peru, Singapore, and Viet Nam (Figure 3.5). Despite the withdrawal of the US from CPTPP, we also include previous US PTAs, as the US participated strongly in the negotiation of TPP (CPTPP's predecessor) (Allee and Lugg 2016). Ninety-one of the ninety-nine PTAs

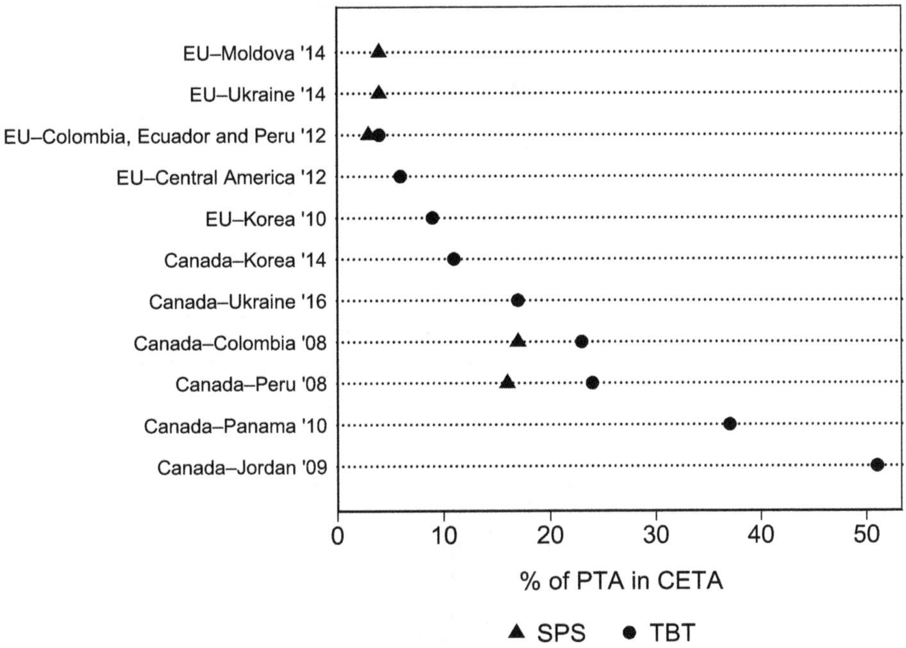

FIGURE 3.4 TBT and SPS chapters in CETA.
Source: Sebastian Klotz's calculations and illustration

(91%) include a TBT chapter, and eighty-eight of the ninety-nine PTAs (88%) include an SPS chapter. Of the PTAs that include a TBT chapter, seventy-four PTAs (81%) are identified as influencing CPTPP. Of the PTAs that include an SPS chapter, fifty-one PTAs (57%) are identified as influential. On average, the text overlap for CPTPP's TBT chapter is 20%, while the average text overlap for the SPS chapter is 15%. The PTA between Peru and Australia (2018) stands out in both areas. The text overlap is 94% for the TBT chapters and 80% for the SPS chapters. USMCA, which was signed in the same year as CPTPP, is also among the most influential PTAs. Thirty-four per cent of its TBT chapter and 45% of its SPS chapter overlap with the respective CPTPP chapters. USMCA is one of the few PTAs where the text overlap is larger for the SPS chapter than for the TBT chapter.

3.2.2.4 United States–Mexico–Canada Agreement (USMCA)

To assess USMCA, we analyse thirty-two PTAs signed by the US, Mexico, and Canada (Figure 3.6). Almost all of these PTAs include TBT chapters (96%) and SPS chapters (93%). Of these, twenty-two PTAs (70%) are influenced by the USMCA TBT chapter. Fourteen PTAs (46%) influenced the USMCA SPS chapter. On average, the text overlap of the USMCA TBT chapter with previous PTAs is

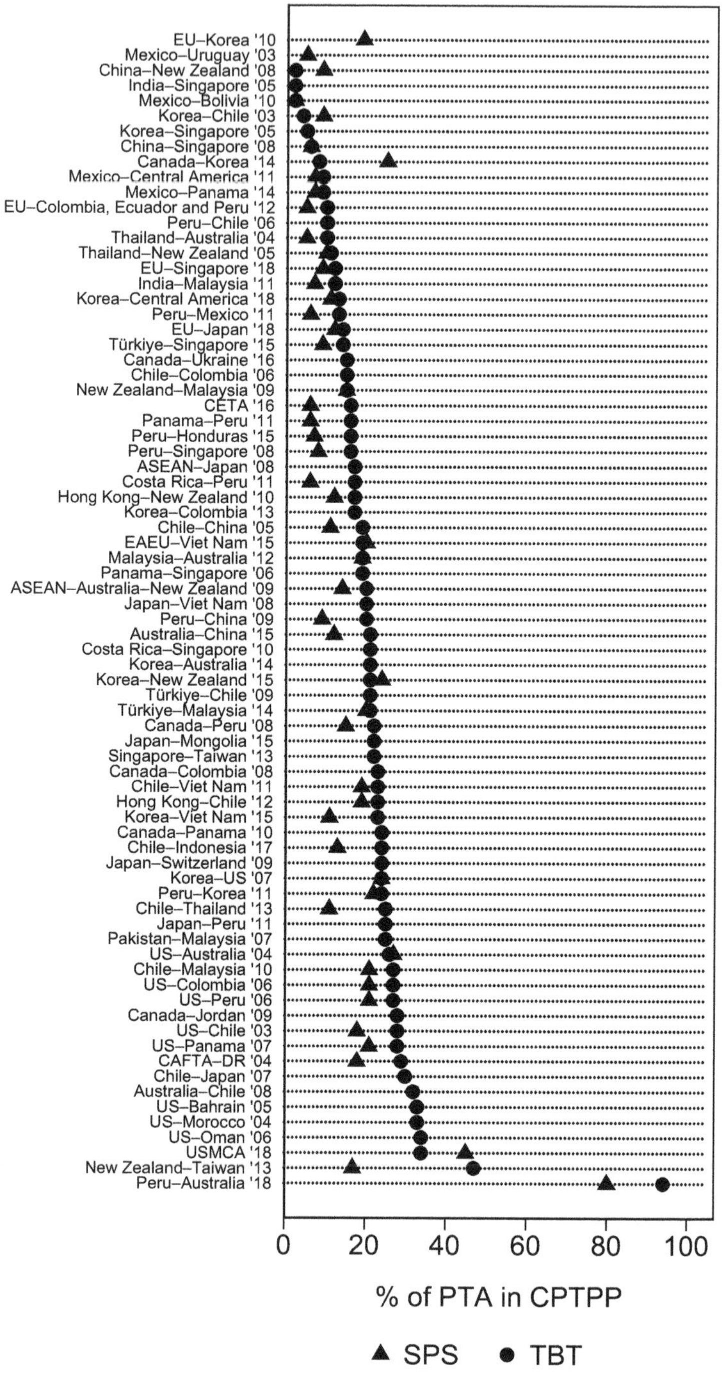

FIGURE 3.5 TBT and SPS chapters in CPTPP.
Source: Sebastian Klotz's calculations and illustration

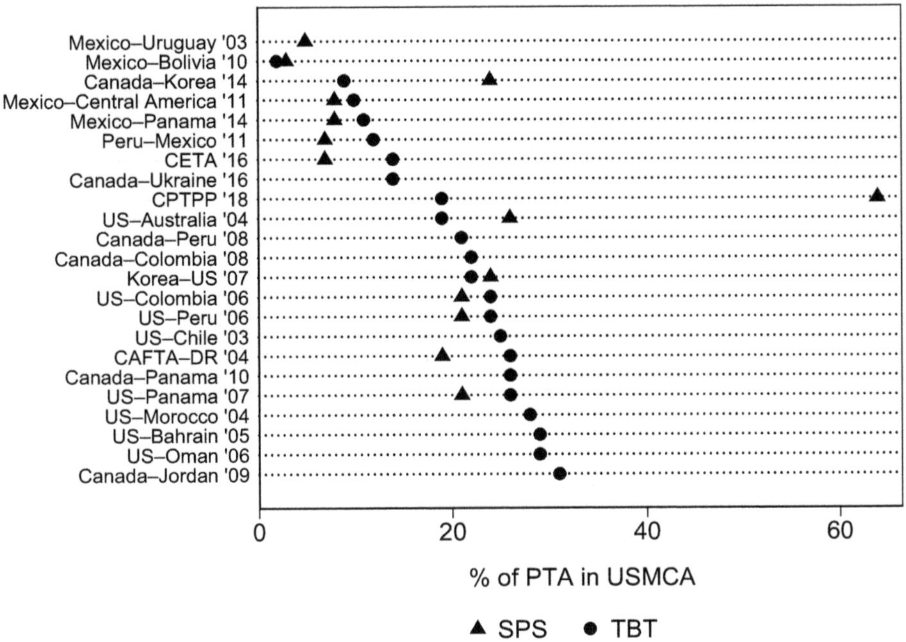

FIGURE 3.6 TBT and SPS chapters in USMCA.
Source: Sebastian Klotz's calculations and illustration

20%; for the USMCA SPS chapter, the average overlap is 18%. For the TBT chapter, Canada–Jordan (2009) is the most influential, with an overlap of 31%. In the area of SPS, CPTPP stands out with an overlap of 64%.

3.2.2.5 Regional Comprehensive Economic Partnership (RCEP)

For the analysis of RCEP, we assess eighty-eight previous PTAs signed by Australia, Brunei, Cambodia, China, Indonesia, Japan, South Korea, Laos, Malaysia, Myanmar, New Zealand, the Philippines, Singapore, Thailand, and Viet Nam (Figure 3.7). Seventy-one of these PTAs (80%) include TBT chapters, and sixty-eight PTAs (77%) include SPS chapters. Of the PTAs that include TBT chapters, fifty-seven PTAs (80%) are influential for the RCEP TBT chapter. Of the PTAs that include SPS chapters, forty PTAs (58%) are influential for the RCEP SPS chapter. The average text overlap of the RCEP TBT chapter with previous PTAs is 17%. The average text overlap for the SPS chapter is 14%. ASEAN–Australia–New Zealand (2009) and Indonesia–Australia (2019) are almost equally influential for the RCEP TBT chapter, with respective overlaps of 37% and 38%. Together with ASEAN–Hong Kong (2018), the PTA between ASEAN–Australia–New Zealand (2009) is also the most influential source for the RCEP SPS chapter (overlap 31%).

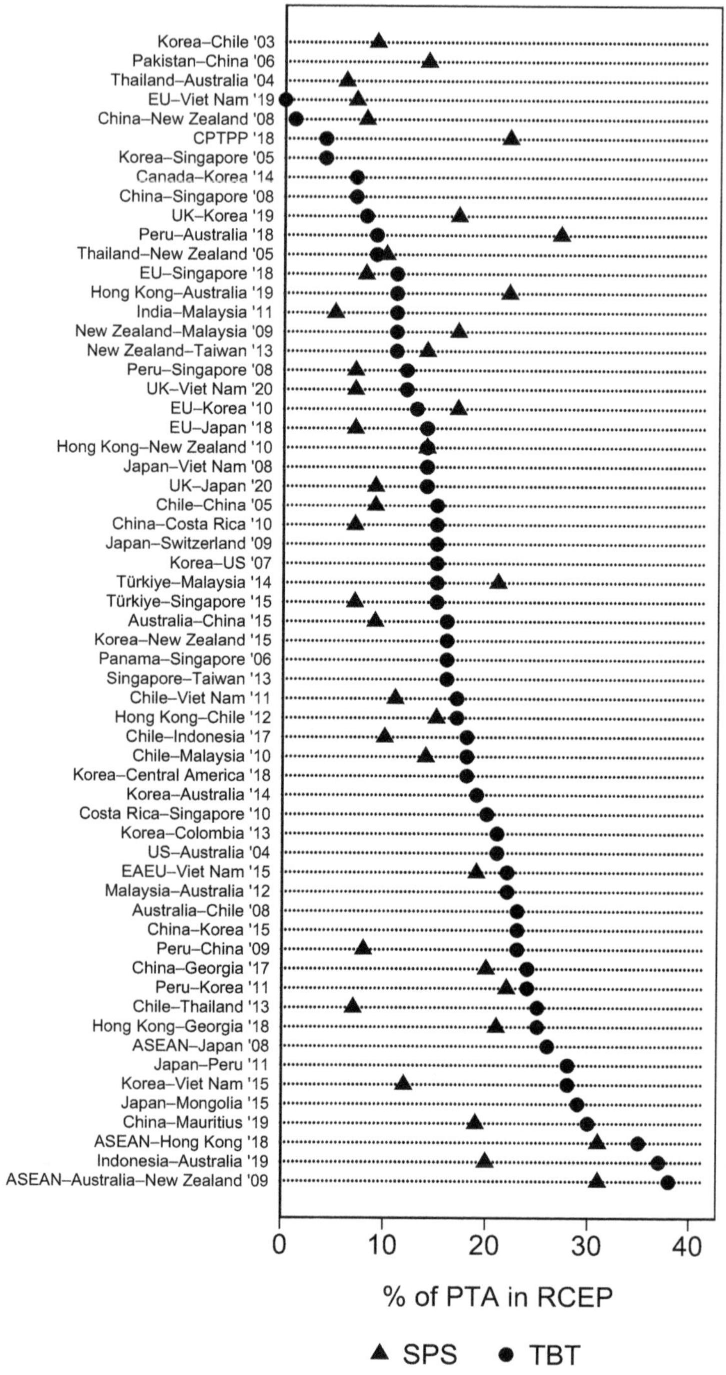

FIGURE 3.7 TBT and SPS chapters in RCEP.
Source: Sebastian Klotz's calculations and illustration

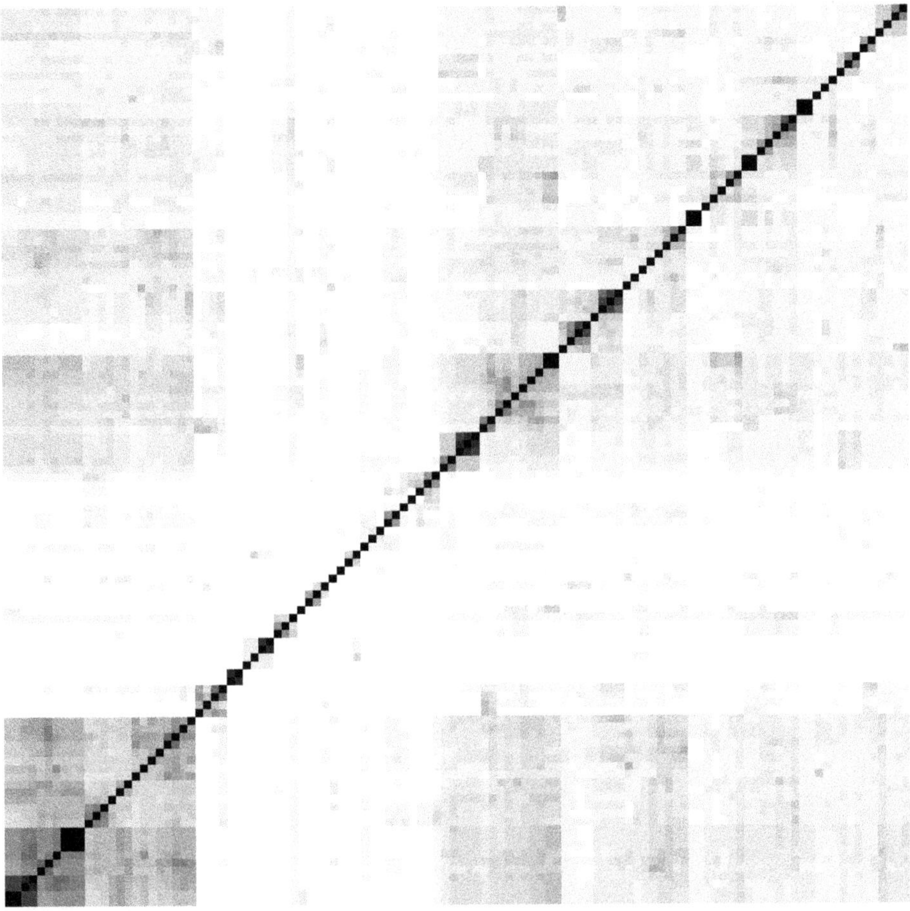

FIGURE 3.8 TBT chapters in CETA, CPTPP, USMCA and RCEP, and previous PTAs.
Source: Sebastian Klotz's calculations and illustration; darker shades indicate greater text overlaps

3.2.2.6 The Full Sample

To conclude this section, we provide a bird's-eye view of all 160 PTAs. Figures 3.8 and 3.9 illustrate the results of the text comparison for the full sample using heatmaps.[3] Essentially, this methodology compares each PTA to one another. The larger the text overlap, the darker the colour. The heatmaps also allow for identifying certain clusters. Two observations stand out. First, the overall shading is darker for TBT than for SPS chapters, indicating again that more text is duplicated between PTAs' TBT chapters than SPS chapters. And indeed, the average overlap for TBT

[3] The X and Y axes are omitted for readability. For more details on the methodology, please see Elsig and Klotz (2021).

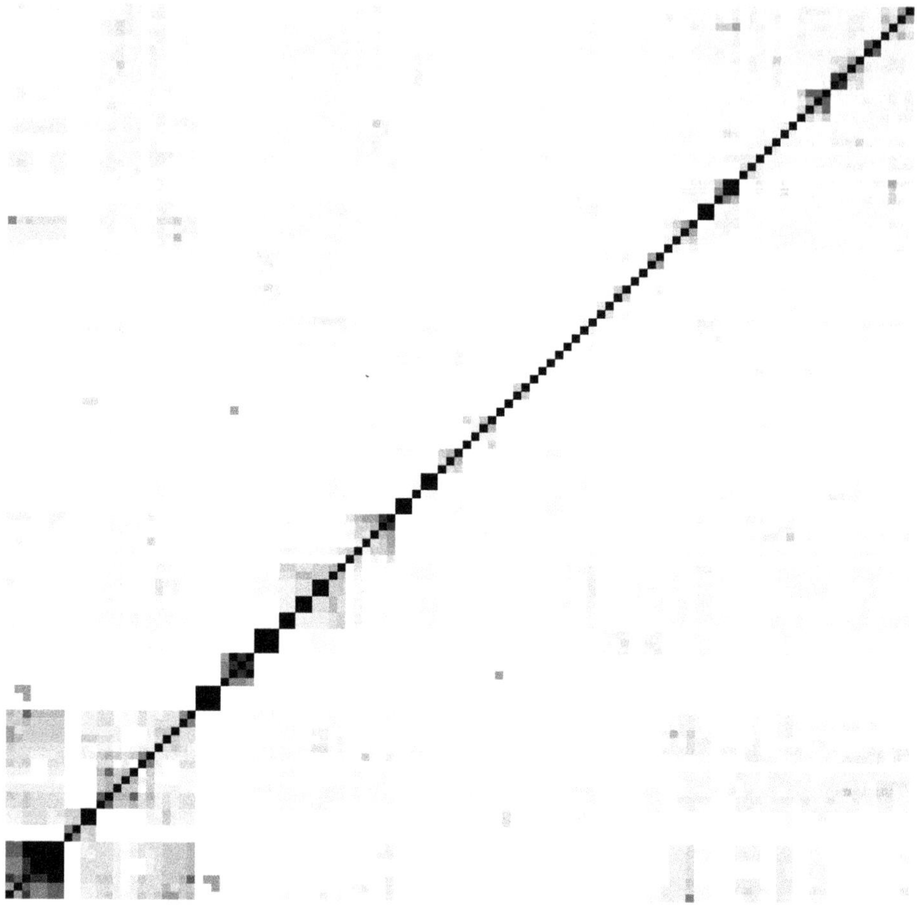

FIGURE 3.9 SPS chapters in CETA, CPTPP, USMCA and RCEP, and previous PTAs.
Source: Sebastian Klotz's calculations and illustration; darker shades indicate greater text overlaps

chapters is 16%, whereas the overlap for SPS chapters is slightly lower at 13%. Second, both figures show a dark cluster in the lower left corner. In the area of TBT, these text overlaps are particularly evident among PTAs to which Chile, Singapore, and the US are parties. US–Peru (2006), US–Colombia (2006), US–Bahrain (2005), and US–Oman (2006) have essentially identical TBT chapters. Similar to TBT, the highest overlaps in SPS chapters can be found in PTAs to which the US and Chile, but also Canada, are parties.

3.3 THE NEAR FUTURE

The failure of the Doha Round of Trade negotiations (Doha Development Agenda) to achieve meaningful results has encouraged WTO Members to seek bilateral and plurilateral solutions to various trade issues. This section examines novel or innovative developments (or lack thereof) in the TBT and SPS provisions of four mega-regional PTAs to ascertain whether certain models are dominating and whether there are areas of contention. It builds upon the first part of this article by adding greater granularity to the analysis – comparing typical and new TBT and SPS provisions across CETA, USMCA, CPTPP, and RCEP.

These four agreements demonstrate varying levels of ambition. This is evident when one compares the treatment of TBT and SPS measures. A comparison reveals that CETA and CPTPP are the most ambitious, followed by USMCA. RCEP is somewhat less ambitious in terms of both TBT and SPS provisions. The difference in the level of ambition in the selected agreements makes the identification of novel or innovative developments a bit easier. As one would expect, the greater the level of ambition, the more likely there will be novel TBT and SPS developments (frequently in the form of ideas and language not repeated in many other agreements). Modest agreements often reflect dominant templates favoured by large trading countries and blocks (demonstrated in the first section of this chapter). Comparing TBT and SPS chapters with high and low levels of ambition may reveal areas of contention.

As most lawyers and diplomats will appreciate, there are many ways to frame similar obligations – an analysis of word patterns found in various agreements scratches the surface – revealing only when drafters subscribe to existing templates. Once a computerised word pattern analysis is complete (see the previous section), it is necessary to undertake a legal analysis of selected provisions to identify novel developments, emerging concepts, and areas of contention. These are likely to be provisions that are not repeated, or infrequently repeated, in existing PTAs.

3.3.1 *TBT Provisions*

The treatment of technical regulations in FTAs is of considerable importance as it can be a major determinant of market access for, primarily, non-agricultural goods. With the decline in tariffs since 1947, and the lack of progress in WTO negotiations, in particular the Doha Development Agenda, it is not surprising that trading countries have taken a bilateral or plurilateral approach towards liberalisation of non-tariff barriers, in particular technical regulations, standards, and conformity assessment procedures. Having said this, the liberalisation of TBT-related NTMs has proven slow, uneven, and not particularly ambitious, as demonstrated by the following analysis.

3.3.1.1 TBT Definitions and General Incorporation of the TBT Agreement

All four of the agreements under review apply the definitions found in the TBT Agreement in their entirety.[4] CETA and RCEP do not go beyond the TBT definitions.

[4] Article 4.2.1 CETA, Article 11.1 USMCA, Article 8.1.1 (TPP), and Article 6.1 RCEP. CPTPP incorporates large portions of TPP. Throughout the chapter, a reference to TPP is therefore a reference to sections of TPP incorporated into CPTPP.

USMCA and TPP, the two agreements that involved the US at the negotiating stage, go beyond the TBT definitions, for example, by adding definitions for a 'mutual recognition agreement' (MRA) and a 'mutual recognition arrangement'.[5] Both agreements provide that MRAs include agreements to implement two Asia Pacific Economic Cooperation (APEC) mutual recognition arrangements.[6]

All four agreements also incorporate certain TBT provisions, but here the analysis becomes more complex. CETA incorporates almost all of the TBT Agreement in its entirety.[7] USMCA and CPTPP include the most important TBT provisions, with the primary exception of the provisions dealing with the equivalence of technical regulations (Article 2.7 TBT), and mutual recognition of conformity assessment procedures (Article 6 TBT). While affirming the obligations of the TBT Agreement,[8] RCEP incorporates a smaller selection of TBT provisions,[9] and specifically excludes the requirement to use international standards as a basis for technical regulations (harmonisation – Article 2.4) and the requirement that WTO Members shall ensure that central government bodies use relevant guides or recommendations issued by international standardising bodies (harmonisation – Article 5.4). RCEP does not strengthen the TBT Agreement's already weak mutual recognition provisions; it only recognises the importance of MRA procedures and encourages cooperation between relevant conformity assessment bodies to accept results.[10]

3.3.1.2 Scope of the Mega-regional Agreements

All four mega-regional agreements follow the TBT Agreement approach with respect to their scope by excluding government procurement and SPS measures

[5] Article 8.1.2 TPP and Article 11.1.2 footnote 1 USMCA. The two agreements are: the APEC Mutual Recognition Arrangement for Conformity Assessment of Telecommunications Equipment of 8 May 1988, and the Electrical Equipment Mutual recognition Arrangement of 7 July 1999.

[6] Article 4.2 CETA incorporates TBT Articles 2, 3, 4, 5, 6, 7, 8, and 9, and Annexes 1 and 3.

[7] Article 11.3 USMCA incorporates in its subparagraphs: (a) Articles 2.1, 2.2, 2.3, 2.4, 2.5, 2.9, 2.10, 2.11, and 2.12; (b) Articles 3.1, 4.1, and 7.1; (c) Articles 5.1, 5.2, 5.3, 5.4, 5.6, 5.7, 5.8, and 5.9; and (d) paras D, E, F, and J of Annex 3.

Article 8.4.1 TPP incorporates in its subparagraphs: (a) Articles 2.1, 2.2, 2.4, 2.5, 2.9, 2.10, 2.11, and 2.12; (b) Articles 5.1, 5.2, 5.3, 5.4, 5.6, 5.7, 5.8, and 5.9; and (c) paras D, E, and F of Annex 3.

[8] Article 6.4.1 RCEP.

[9] Article 6.4.1 RCEP incorporates in its subparagraphs: (a) Article 2, except paras 4, 7, 8, and 12; (b) para 2 of Article 4; (c) Article 5, except para 4; (d) para 3 of Article 6; (e) para 1 of Article 9; and (f) Annex 3, except para A.

[10] Article 6.8.5(a) RCEP recognises the utility of mutual recognition of conformity assessment procedures and Article 6.8.8 encourages cooperation between the parties' conformity assessment bodies to facilitate acceptance of conformity assessment results. Article 6.9.3 endorses cooperation between the parties' conformity assessment bodies.

from their purview.[11] Their scope differs to some degree with respect to how standardisation bodies below the central government level should be treated. Article 1.8.2 CETA makes a party's obligations applicable to all levels of government. At first glance, Article 4.1.5 would seem to limit the scope of Article 1.8 by stating that the 'extent of obligations' provision does not apply to Article 3 TBT (which would have required that parties take 'all necessary measures' to give effect to the Agreement at all levels of government). This is an incorrect conclusion. Instead, Article 4.2.1 CETA incorporates the obligations present in Article 3 TBT with the effect that parties must take 'reasonable measures' to ensure compliance by local governments.

Through its incorporation of Articles 3.1 and 4.1 of the WTO TBT Agreement, Article 11.3.1 USMCA applies a 'reasonable measures' approach to ensure that local government bodies comply with the provisions of the PTA governing technical regulations and standards but is silent with respect to conformity assessment procedures.[12]

The obligation in Article 8.3.2 TPP is weaker. Parties have an obligation to take reasonable measures within their authority 'to encourage observance' by regional and local government bodies with respect to the preparation, adoption, and application of technical regulations, standards, and conformity assessment procedures and extend this obligation to other articles in chapter 8 and its annexes.

Article 6.3.2 RCEP also contains a 'reasonable measures' provision applicable to local government bodies and non-governmental bodies responsible for the preparation, adoption, and application of technical regulations, standards, and conformity assessment procedures.

3.3.1.3 Incorporation of TBT Committee Decisions

Unlike USMCA, CPTPP, and RCEP, CETA does not explicitly incorporate the WTO TBT Committee's 'Decision of the Committee on Principles for the Development of International Standards, Guides and Recommendations with relation to Articles 2, 5 and Annex 3 of the Agreement'.[13] But as CETA incorporates almost all of the TBT Agreement, and as Articles 1.6 (Reference to Other Agreements)[14]

[11] With respect to government procurement see Article 4.1.2(a) CETA, Article 11.2.2(a) USMCA, Article 8.3.4 TPP, and Article 6.3(b) RCEP. With respect to sanitary and phytosanitary measures see Article 4.1.2(b) CETA, Article 11.2.2(b) USMCA, Article 8.3.5 TPP, and Article 6.3(a) RCEP.

[12] Many such measures might nevertheless fall within the purview of Article 7 TBT as the underlying technical regulations and standards are likely to be the same.

[13] WTO Document G/TBT1 with numerous revisions.

[14] Article 1.6 CETA provides: 'When this Agreement refers to or incorporates by reference other agreements or legal instruments in whole or in part, those references include: (a) related annexes, protocols, footnotes, interpretative notes and explanatory notes; and (b) successor

and 4.1.4 CETA[15] contemplate updating CETA based on changes to other agreements (which would include the TBT Agreement), the ambitious nature of CETA is evident. Not only does CETA implicitly incorporate the Decision, and related annexes, protocols, footnotes, interpretative notes, and explanatory notes, it also incorporates successor agreements that bind the parties. Due to its unique language and broad scope, CETA stands in contrast to the narrower scope of the other mega-regionals. Automatic updating of CETA based on WTO developments is a novel approach worthy of recognition.

Article 11.4.2 USMCA requires each party to adopt the Committee Decision on International Standards (as revised) to determine whether there is an international standard, guide, or recommendation within the meaning of Articles 2 and 5 and Annex 3 of the TBT Agreement,[16] and for notification purposes 'to consider, among other things, the relevant guidance in the Decisions and Recommendations Adopted by the WTO Committee on Technical Barriers to Trade Since 1 January 1995 (G/TBT/1/Rev.13), as may be revised'. The TPP uses the same language in Article 8.5.2 with respect to the application of the TBT Committee Decision on International Standards. RCEP uses similar language but contains a weaker obligation. Article 6.5.2 only requires that 'each Party take into account the principles set out in the Decision of the Committee ... and subsequent relevant decisions and recommendations ... adopted by the WTO Committee ...'.

3.3.1.4 Strengthened Use of International Standards

The US, Canada, and the EU apply different approaches to the formulation of standards with the result that one can expect to see somewhat divergent language. The US and Canada take a more private sector approach, while the EU favours standardisation at the regional (governmental) level. Differences in approaches colour provisions related to standardisation. Article 4.3 CETA calls for the parties to strengthen cooperation, including in the area of international standards. Articles 4.6.2 and 4.7.1(d) also encourage the parties to promote cooperation between their standardisation bodies. Article 4.6.2 further encourages the parties to exchange information and harmonise standards based on mutual interest and reciprocity. Article 11.9.5 USMCA encourages cooperation between the parties' respective

agreements to which the Parties are party or amendments that are binding on the Parties, except where the reference affirms existing rights.'

[15] Article 4.1.4 CETA provides: 'References in this Chapter to technical regulations, standards, and conformity assessment procedures include amendments thereto, and additions to the rules or the product coverage thereof, except amendments and additions of an insignificant nature.'

[16] Defined in Article 11.1 USMCA as Annex 2 to Part 1 (Decision of the Committee on Principles for the Development of International Standards, Guides and Recommendations with relation to Articles 2, 5 and Annex 3 of the Agreement) in the Decisions and Recommendations adopted by the WTO Committee on Technical Barriers to Trade since 1 January 1995 (G/TBT/1/Rev.13), as may be revised, issued by the WTO Committee on Technical Barriers to Trade.

standardisation organisations. Article 11.4.3 USMCA makes it clear that only the TBT Committee Decision on International Standards can be relied upon to recognise what is an international standardisation organisation. The result is that the EU's regional standardisation bodies do not qualify. A similar approach is taken in Article 8.5.3 TPP, which supports cooperation, and Article 8.5.2 TPP, which reinforces the application by the parties of the TBT Agreement and the Decisions and Recommendations adopted by the WTO Committee on Technical Barriers to Trade. RCEP Article 6.4.1(f) incorporates the TBT Code of Good Practice (Annex A), and Article 6.6.4 encourages cooperation between standardising bodies, supporting information exchanges regarding procedures and supporting cooperation in international standardising activities in areas of mutual interest. In summary, the distinctive North American approach to standardisation will continue to lead PTA negotiations in divergent directions. This is an area of contention that will be difficult to resolve.

3.3.1.5 Mutual Recognition

By incorporating TBT Article 6.3, CETA encourages the negotiation of MRAs related to the parties' conformity assessment procedures. Likewise, the inclusion of: (i) the Protocol on the mutual acceptance of the results of conformity assessment[17] and (ii) the Protocol on the mutual recognition of the compliance and enforcement programme regarding good manufacturing practices for pharmaceutical products also moves CETA in the direction of mutual recognition.[18] Article 11.1.2 USMCA defines both an MRA and a mutual recognition arrangement.[19] Article 11.9.4 USMCA, which is a novel provision, requires parties to explain reasons for a decision declining to recognise the results from a conformity assessment body that is a signatory to an MRA, and a decision not to continue MRA negotiations. Article 11.6.7 encourages parties to facilitate and encourage mutual recognition arrangements to recognise conformity assessment bodies, and again novelly, 'consider approving or recognizing accredited conformity assessment bodies for its technical regulations or standards, by an accreditation body that is a signatory to a mutual or multilateral recognition arrangement, for example, the International Laboratory Accreditation Cooperation (ILAC) and the International Accreditation Forum (IAF)'. Article 11.9.1 requires parties to consider sector-specific cooperation proposals for mutual recognition of the results of conformity assessment bodies, recognising existing mutual recognition arrangements between or among accreditation bodies of conformity assessment bodies. Likewise, Article 8.1

[17] Council of the European Union (2016a).
[18] Council of the European Union (2016b).
[19] Article 11.1.2 distinguishes between the two – an MRA is an intergovernmental agreement that specifies conditions for the recognition of the results of conformity assessment procedures, while a mutual recognition arrangement is an international or regional arrangement among accreditation bodies in which these bodies accept each other's results.

TPP defines an MRA (with the definition specifically including certain APEC Agreements) and a mutual recognition arrangement. Like USMCA, Article 8.6.8 TPP encourages parties 'adopting measures to approve conformity assessment bodies that have accreditation for the technical regulations or standards of the importing Party, by an accreditation body that is a signatory to an international or regional mutual recognition arrangement'. Again, like USMCA, Article 8.6.12 TPP requires parties to explain decisions to decline the use of a mutual recognition arrangement and to explain reasons for not entering into MRA negotiations. Finally, Article 8.9.1 TPP acknowledges that MRAs are one mechanism that may facilitate the acceptance of conformity assessment proceedings. Section C (Regional Cooperation Activities on Telecommunications Equipment) of TPP Annex 8-B also encourages parties to implement the APEC Mutual Recognition Arrangement for Conformity Assessment of Telecommunications Equipment of 8 May 1998 (MRA-TEL) and the APEC Mutual Recognition Arrangement for Equivalence of Technical Requirements of 31 October 2010 (MRA-ETR).

Article 6.8.5(a) RCEP recognises that MRAs are one of a broad range of mechanisms to facilitate the acceptance of the results of conformity assessment procedures. Article 6.9.3(c) RCEP recognises that enhancing participation in the frameworks for mutual recognition developed by regional and international bodies may be an avenue for cooperation.

3.3.1.6 Equivalence

Although none of the mega-regionals under review mandate equivalence, CETA incorporates the TBT Agreement's provision on equivalence (Article 2.7), and Article 4.4 establishes a cooperative procedure for requesting recognition that a technical regulation is equivalent. The other three agreements take a less ambitious approach. Neither USMCA nor TPP incorporate Article 2.7 TBT; nevertheless, Article 11.9.2(c) USMCA and Article 8.9.2(d) of TPP use almost identical language and recognise that promotion of the acceptance of technical regulations as equivalent is one of a broad range of measures that supports greater regulatory alignment. RCEP Article 6.7.3 simply repeats the language of TBT Article 2.7, thus requiring a party to give positive consideration that technical regulations that differ from their own are equivalent if they 'adequately fulfil the objectives of its own regulations'. The lack of novelty with respect to equivalence in the TBT chapters of the mega-regionals stands in contrast to the more aggressive and somewhat more novel approach taken in the SPS chapters (discussed below).

3.3.1.7 Supplier's Declaration of Conformity

Reference to the use of a Supplier's Declaration of Conformity (SDOC) is notably absent from CETA's TBT chapter. This is in contrast to Article 11.9.1(f) USMCA,

Article 8.9(f) TPP, and Article 6.8.5(f) RCEP, which recognise that a broad range of mechanisms exist to facilitate the acceptance of conformity assessment procedures and note the acceptance of an SDOC is one means to facilitate the acceptance of conformity assessment results. The mention of SDOC is a step forward, and this is a path that could be followed in future PTAs.

3.3.1.8 Strengthened Transparency

All four of the mega-regionals emphasise strengthened transparency. These provisions are detailed, and there is some commonality in their approach. While national treatment provisions feature in each, permitting various degrees of participation in the development of technical regulations and conformity assessment procedures by the central government, these provisions nevertheless differ in subtle ways.

For CETA, the Article 4.6 transparency procedure is limited to technical regulations and conformity assessment procedures and applies to interested persons of the parties. Where a consultation process is open to the public, persons of the other party may participate on terms no less favourable than its own persons (national treatment). Comments from parties must be replied to in writing before the technical regulation or conformity assessment procedure is adopted. Responses or summaries of responses to significant comments must be made public. Except in urgent cases, parties must endeavour to allow sixty days following WTO notification for comments and must give positive consideration to requests to extend the comment period. Each party must give the importer, without undue delay, the reason for the detention of goods that do not meet a technical regulation. Bodies below the central government level are subject to the 'reasonable measures' provisions incorporated from the TBT Agreement.

Article 11.7 of the USMCA national treatment obligation extends to the participation of parties in the development of technical regulations, standards, and conformity assessment procedures by central government bodies. Each party must allow persons from another party to submit written comments during a public consultation on terms no less favourable than it provides its own persons and to make these written comments publicly available. If practicable, a party is to accept written requests from another party to discuss written comments. Each party has an obligation to publish how it has addressed substantive issues raised in these comments. Standardising bodies (which are often private sector bodies in the US and Canada) are encouraged to apply the national treatment provisions set forth in Article 11.7.1. There is no provision dealing with detained goods. Provisions below the central government level are subject to the 'reasonable measures' provisions incorporated from the TBT Agreement. There is an additional obligation to take reasonable measures to ensure that proposed and final technical regulations and conformity assessment procedures of regional governments are published.

In the case of TPP, the Article 8.7.1 national treatment obligation extends to the participation of parties in the development of technical regulations, standards, and conformity assessment procedures by central government bodies. If appropriate, parties are expected to encourage non-governmental bodies to allow for parties' participation. With respect to regional government bodies and local government bodies on the level directly below the central level of government, parties are required to ensure that all new final technical regulations and conformity assessment procedures and amendments to these procedures are accessible through official websites or journals. Except in urgent circumstances, each party should normally allow sixty days from WTO notification of a draft regulation for comment. On or before the date of publication of the technical regulation or conformity assessment procedure, a party is required to make publicly available its response to significant or substantive issues presented in comments received on proposals for technical regulations and conformity assessment procedures. Lastly, a party must provide within sixty days of receipt of a request from another party a description of significant revisions it made to a proposal for a technical regulation or a conformity assessment procedure, including those made in response to comments.

In the case of RCEP Article 6.11, the transparency obligations are weaker. Parties are required to 'take into account relevant decisions and recommendations in the Decisions and Recommendations adopted by the WTO Committee on Technical Barriers to Trade since 1 January 1995 (G/TBT/1/Rev.13) as may be revised ...'. Each party 'should normally allow 60 days' from the date of WTO notification for comments from other Parties, should take into account those comments, and 'endeavour to provide responses ...'. Parties must allow other parties to participate in consultation procedures 'that are available to the general public for the development of technical regulations, national standards and conformity assessment procedures ...', 'subject to its laws and regulations on terms no less favourable than those accorded its own persons'. Like CETA, there is also an obligation to notify an importer as soon as possible, or its representative, when goods are detained at the point of entry for non-compliance with a technical regulation or a conformity assessment procedure and provide the reasons for detention. The foregoing analysis demonstrates widespread agreement that increased transparency is an advantageous direction for future PTAs.

3.3.1.9 Dispute Settlement

CETA offers an important dispute settlement feature. Article 4.7.1(b) designates the CETA Committee on Trade in Goods to address issues that the Parties raise concerning the development, adoption, or application of standards, technical regulations, or conformity assessment procedures. If the parties are unable to resolve a matter arising under the TBT chapter, Article 4.7.2 CETA allows a party to request that the CETA Joint Committee establish an *ad hoc* technical working group to identify solutions to facilitate trade. This consultative approach is novel to the extent that it invokes a technical working group as opposed to trade negotiators. Recourse to a technical working group does not prevent a Party from seeking redress under CETA Article 29 (Dispute Settlement) for violations at the national level of the WTO TBT Agreement or CETA's TBT Chapter.

Moreover, Article 4.2.3 CETA allows recourse to the treaty's dispute settlement mechanism for matters involving standards, technical regulations, and conformity assessment procedures of local government bodies, as well as conformity assessment procedures by non-governmental bodies and international and regional systems if one party has not achieved satisfactory results under these articles and its trade interests are significantly affected.

Article 29.3.3 CETA governs the choice of forum and clarifies that recourse to the CETA dispute settlement mechanism is without prejudice to the WTO dispute settlement system. Article 29.3.4 offers a fork-in-the-road provision whereby parties may choose to resolve equivalent obligations in either the WTO or CETA, but not both.

Dispute settlement under the USMCA follows a similar fork-in-the-road approach. Article 11.3.2 eliminates recourse to Chapter 31 of USMCA (Dispute Settlement) for: (i) claims made under the provisions of the TBT Agreement incorporated into Chapter 11 of the USMCA, or (ii) if a matter was referred, or is subsequently referred by a party to a WTO dispute settlement panel, or is taken to comply with a WTO dispute settlement decision.

Likewise, Article 28.4 TPP contains a fork-in-the-road provision that gives exclusive jurisdiction to the first forum chosen (TPP or WTO dispute settlement). However, Article 8.5 TPP prohibits recourse to that treaty's dispute settlement (Chapter 28) for disputes alleging a violation of TBT provisions incorporated into chapter 8 TPP. Otherwise, Article 28.3.1(c) brings matters arising under Chapter 8 (Technical Barriers to Trade) within the ambit of TPP dispute settlement.

RCEP rejects jurisdiction over TBT disputes that *exclusively* allege a violation of TBT provisions incorporated into RCEP through Article 6.4.1. Somewhat surprisingly, and again possibly emblematic of RCEP's lower level of ambition, Article 6.14 provides that Chapter 19 (Dispute Settlement) is not applicable to disputes arising under the TBT chapter for the first two years after entry into force of RCEP, and only then will the non-application clause be reviewed, with review to be completed within three years. In short, it is unclear from Article 6.14 when the RCEP dispute settlement provisions will apply to RCEP TBT disputes. Also surprisingly, Article 6.4.2 RCEP elevates the provisions of RCEP's TBT chapter above incorporated WTO TBT provisions in the event of inconsistency.

Fork-in-the-road approaches are achieving a consensus, at least in the mega-regionals. Of course, they still lead to uncertainty as it is unclear how a WTO panel would react if charged with resolving a dispute already before a PTA dispute settlement body.

3.3.1.10 Annexes and Protocols

One novel feature of two of the four mega-regional agreements under review, which may pave the way for future TBT alignment, is the creation of topic-specific annexes and protocols dealing with technical regulations and conformity assessment procedures. For example, Annex 4-A CETA mandates cooperation in the field of motor vehicle regulations. Of particular importance, and again demonstrating the ambitious nature of CETA, Article 4.5 CETA mandates observation of two CETA protocols: 1) the Protocol on the mutual acceptance of the results of conformity assessment,[20] and 2) the Protocol on the mutual recognition of the compliance and enforcement programme regarding good manufacturing practices for pharmaceutical products.[21]

TPP also demonstrates a significant level of ambition that suggests the importance of gradual sectoral expansion of the scope of the TBT chapter. Article 8.3.2 TPP requires each party to take reasonable measures to encourage observation of regional and local governmental bodies of the annexes to Chapter 8 (which binds central government bodies). And Article 8.3.3 TPP leaves room for the creation of amendments and additions to technical regulations, standards, and conformity assessment procedures.

Article 8.13(1) TPP provides that the *scope* of the Annexes on Pharmaceuticals, Cosmetics, Medical Devices and Proprietary Formulas for Prepackaged Food products and Food Additives is set out in the respective annexes. The *scope* of other annexes is set out in Article 8.3 (Scope), including: Annex 8-A: Wine and Distilled Spirits, Annex 8-B: Information and Communications Technology Products, Annex 8-C: Pharmaceuticals, Annex 8-D: Cosmetics, Annex 8-E: Medical Devices, Annex 8-F: Proprietary Formulas for Prepackaged Foods and Food Additives, and Annex 8-G: Organic Products.

3.3.1.11 TBT Conclusions

There are not many novel TBT developments in the mega-regionals. Three that stand out are CETA's incorporation of future WTO TBT decisions, the possibility under CETA to create a technical working group to address disagreements before the invocation of CETA dispute settlement, and the use of subject-specific and sector-specific annexes and protocols in CETA and TPP.

Except for the private sector approach that the US and Canada apply with respect to standardisation, and RCEP's postponement of TBT dispute settlement, there are not many differences of note in the agreements reviewed above. Divergences that do exist, such as recognition and implementation of the broad range of mechanisms

[20] Council of the European Union (2016a).
[21] Council of the European Union (2016b).

available to facilitate trade, have more to do with the level of ambition, rather than points of contention. Instead, what is discernible is acceptance of logical solutions that are eventually becoming dominant, such as fork-in-the-road provisions for dispute settlement, and widespread agreement on the gradual expansion of TBT disciplines, such as improved transparency – which is indicative of greater cooperation.

3.3.2 *SPS Provisions*

The treatment of SPS regulations in regional trade agreements is a major determinant of market access for agricultural goods, including processed food and beverages destined for human and animal consumption. With the decline in tariffs since 1947, weaknesses in the WTO Agreement on Agriculture, and the lack of progress in the Doha Development Agenda negotiations, trading countries are increasingly taking a regional approach towards the treatment of non-tariff barriers affecting agricultural trade. Nevertheless, defining the ideal SPS framework and disciplining liberalisation of SPS-related NTMs have proven slow, uneven, and not particularly ambitious, as demonstrated by the following analysis.

As with the TBT discussion, this section examines novel or innovative developments (or lack thereof) in the SPS provisions of the same four mega-regional trade agreements to ascertain whether certain models are dominating and whether there are areas of contention. It builds upon the first part of this chapter by adding greater granularity to the analysis – comparing typical and new SPS provisions across the four selected mega-regional trade agreements.

3.3.2.1 SPS Definitions and General Incorporation of the SPS Agreement

All four of the agreements under review apply the definitions found in Annex A of the SPS Agreement in their entirety,[22] and expressly affirm the parties' obligations under the WTO SPS Agreement.[23] CETA also incorporates definitions adopted by Codex Alimentarius (Codex), the World Organisation for Animal Health (OIE), the International Plant Protection Convention (IPPC), and the EU definition of a 'protected zone for a specified regulated harmful organism'. Annex 5-A CETA defines 'competent authorities' and allocates responsibilities to various EU, Member State, and Canadian competent authorities. In the event of a conflict, the definitions of the WTO SPS Agreement prevail. USMCA and TPP add several additional definitions which take precedence over the WTO definitions. There is considerable overlap in terms of these additional definitions (not surprising as the US participated in both negotiations). As in CETA, in TPP and USMCA a

[22] Article 5.1.1 CETA, Article 11.1 USMCA, Article 7.1.1 TPP, and Article 5.1 RCEP.
[23] Article 5.4 CETA, Article 9.4.1 USMCA, Article 7.4.1 TPP, and Article 5.4 RCEP.

competent authority is defined in terms of government bodies of each party.[24] Finally, in addition to adopting the SPS Agreement definitions, RCEP also defines 'competent authorities' and states that relevant definitions of Codex, OIE, and IPPC shall be taken into account.[25]

3.3.2.2 Scope and Objectives

All four mega-regionals use almost identical language with respect to the scope of their SPS chapters. They apply to SPS measures that may, directly or indirectly, affect trade between the parties.[26] TPP also makes clear that the SPS chapter shall not prevent parties from adopting or maintaining halal food requirements.[27] A similar provision appears in footnote 2 to Article 5.8 of RCEP. While halal labelling would normally fall under the TBT Agreement, this novel development encouraged support for TPP and RCEP from Muslim communities among the parties.

All four agreements list the objectives of their SPS chapters. The CETA objectives simply repeat the objective of the SPS Agreement and seek to further its implementation.[28] The objectives of USMCA, TPP, and RCEP are broader, emphasising transparency, strengthened communication, cooperation, and consultation.[29] The objectives of USMCA also emphasise the development and adoption of science-based international standards, and decision-making, a concept further underscored in Article 9.6 USMCA.

3.3.2.3 Adaptation to Regional Conditions

All four agreements contain provisions dealing with adaptation to regional conditions. The level of ambition varies. CETA, USMCA, and TPP contain novel provisions that one can expect to see in future agreements. Article 5.5.1 CETA recognises the concept of zoning for animals, animal products, and animal by-products, lists the diseases in Annex 5-B covered by zoning, and leaves room in Annex 5-C for the development of principles and guidelines to recognise regional conditions. For plant and plant products, Article 5.5.2 requires that a party imposing an SPS measure take into account the pest status of an area, including pest-free areas, pest-free places of production, pest-free production sites, areas of low pest prevalence, and a protected zone that the exporting party has established.

24 Article 7.1 TPP and Article 9.1.2 USMCA.
25 Article 5.1 RCEP.
26 Article 5.3 CETA, Article 9.2 USMCA, Article 7.3.1 TPP, and Article 5.3 RCEP.
27 Article 7.3.2 TPP.
28 Article 5.2(b) CETA.
29 Article 9.3 USMCA, Article 7.2 TPP, and Article 5.2 RCEP.

Article 9.8.1 USMCA recognises the concepts of regionalisation, zoning, and compartmentalisation as a means to facilitate trade, and calls for the parties to endeavour to cooperate on the recognition of pest- or disease-free areas, and areas of low pest or disease prevalence with the objective of acquiring confidence in the procedures followed by each party. Likewise, Article 7.7.1 TPP also recognises the concepts of regionalisation, zoning, and compartmentalisation to facilitate trade and Article 7.7.3 contains similar confidence-building language.

In comparison, Article 5.6 RCEP is a weaker provision. It only recognises pest-and disease-free areas and areas of low pest or disease prevalence.

3.3.2.4 Equivalence

Equivalence is treated in all four mega-regionals. Article 5.6 CETA contains the shortest equivalence provision, shifting much of the work to annexes, several of which remain to be negotiated. Although Article 5.6.1 CETA repeats the first sentence of Article 4.1 of the WTO SPS Agreement, Article 5.6.2 allows for possible innovation by saving room in Annex 5-D for the eventual negotiation of principles and guidelines to determine, recognise, and maintain equivalence. Annex 5-C CETA, which is also still to be negotiated, sets the stage for developing a process for the recognition of regional conditions concerning animal diseases and plant pests.

Most of Annex 5-E CETA is complete. As noted in Article 5.6, Annex 5-E 'sets out' '(a) the area for which the importing Party recognises that an SPS measure of the exporting Party is equivalent to its own' and '(b) the area for which the importing Party recognises that fulfilment of the specified special conditions, combined with the exporting Party's SPS measure, achieves the importing Party's appropriate level of SPS protection'. While not entirely complete (Appendix B on phytosanitary measures remains to be negotiated), Annex 5-E is an important step towards the advancement of equivalence and provides a possible direction that other countries may wish to apply in equivalence negotiations.

Another example where equivalence can play a role in PTA negotiations is demonstrated by Article 5.9 CETA and Annex 5-I. When an official health certificate is required for the import of live animals and animal products and the importer has accepted the exporter's SPS measures as equivalent to its own, Article 5.9 CETA requires the use of the model health attestation prescribed in Annex 5-I. Document recognition can play an important role in facilitating trade.

Several of the equivalence provisions in Article 9.9 USMCA and Article 7.8 TPP are similar – again, no surprise, as the US participated in each negotiation. Both articles: (i) recognise that a positive determination of equivalence is a means to facilitate trade, (ii) seek to apply equivalence to the extent feasible and appropriate, (iii) call for the parties to take into account the guidance of the WTO SPS Committee and relevant international standards, guidelines, and recommendations,

(iv) require importing parties, upon request of the exporting party, to explain the objectives and rationale behind SPS measures and identify the risk the measure is intended to address, (v) require, upon request, that equivalence assessments begin without undue delay, (vi) require the importing party to explain its process for making an equivalence assessment and if equivalence is found its plan for enabling trade, (vii) call for recognition of equivalence if the exporting party objectively demonstrates that its SPS measure achieves the same level of protection, (viii) provide for enhanced communications between the parties, and (ix) require that the importing party explain the rationale for a determination that two measures are not equivalent. The USMCA goes further in two respects: it establishes a process for streamlining an equivalence assessment, and it establishes a procedure, including a notification and communications procedure, if a party adopts, modifies, or repeals a recognition of equivalence.

Lastly, Article 5.5 RCEP sets forth an equivalence procedure based on strengthened cooperation, taking into account the principles of the WTO SPS Agreement, the decisions of the SPS Committee and international standards, guidelines, and recommendations. Like USMCA and TPP, RCEP calls for recognition of equivalence if a party can objectively demonstrate that an SPS measure achieves the same level of protection. Unlike the other three mega-regional agreements, when making an equivalence assessment RCEP specifically permits parties to take into account 'available knowledge, information, and experience, as well as the regulatory competence, of the exporting Party'. RCEP calls for parties to enter into consultations aimed at achieving 'bilateral recognition arrangements' and sets forth a procedure, somewhat similar to that of USMCA and TPP, for conducting the equivalence recognition consultations and communicating the results.

3.3.2.5 Science and Risk Analysis

Neither CETA nor RCEP deals specifically with science-based risk assessments in their SPS chapters. However, Article 5.7 RCEP aims to improve cooperation in risk analysis and risk management. Both CETA and RCEP deal generally with risk management in their Customs and Trade Facilitation chapters.[30]

Article 9.6 USMCA and Article 7.9 TPP contain extensive and somewhat similar provisions on science-based risk assessments in their SPS chapters – no doubt due to the presence of the US at the negotiation stage. Where not identical to provisions in the WTO SPS Agreement, they complement SPS provisions. With respect to identical provisions, both Articles note the right to apply SPS measures, emphasise the requirement to base SPS measures on scientific principles, note that parties can determine the level of protection deemed appropriate, require that risk assessments be appropriate to the circumstances, and provide measures to ensure transparency in

[30] Article 6.7 CETA and Article 4.14 RCEP.

the risk assessment process. USMCA goes further in its elaboration of precaution, risk assessment, and risk management, though none of the provisions are particularly novel or contestable, and all seem to be consistent with the spirit of the WTO SPS Agreement.

3.3.2.6 Compliance Measures: Audits, Import Checks, and Certifications

Annex C of the SPS Agreement provides for control, inspection, and approval procedures, but these procedures are not fully elaborated in the annex. All four mega-regional agreements deal with similar subjects: audits, import checks, and certifications, and exceed the scope of the SPS Agreement. They can therefore be viewed as novel developments.

Article 5.8.1 CETA allows for an audit or verification to maintain confidence that the provisions of the SPS chapter are being implemented. Article 5.8.2 provides for a placeholder in Annex 5-H if the parties decide to develop principles and guidelines to conduct an audit or verification. Article 5.10 CETA governs import checks (inspections), with the frequency of import checks governed by the table present in Annex 5-J (with fees to be agreed upon later). Import checks are to be based on an assessment of the risk involved and not be more trade-restrictive than necessary. Specifying frequency is a novelty among the four agreements examined.

The audit provisions in Article 9.10 USMCA and Article 7.10 TPP are almost identical. Audits may include an assessment of control programmes, including reviews of inspection and audit programmes and on-site inspection of facilities. Both require system-based audits to check the effectiveness of regulatory controls. Both require the parties to discuss the rationale of the audit and its objectives and scope, and criteria against which the exporting party will be assessed, and base decisions on objective evidence and data. Both require the opportunity to comment, protection of confidential information, and that costs incurred be borne by the auditing party.[31]

Article 9.11 USMCA and Article 7.11 TPP govern import checks to assess compliance with SPS measures and to obtain information to assess risks associated with importation. Again, there are major similarities between the two articles. Both require: (i) parties to make available information on import processes so that the nature and frequency of import checks can be assessed, (ii) the importing party to make available information on the analytical methods, quality controls sampling procedures, and facilities used to test the goods, (iii) that testing be conducted using appropriate and validated methods in a facility operating under a quality assurance programme consistent with international standards, and (iv) that the importing party retain documentation. Final decisions in response to a finding of non-conformity must be limited to what is reasonable and necessary. If prohibitions or restrictions on

[31] Article 9.10.11 USMCA allows the parties to decide otherwise on costs.

importation are imposed, notifications must be provided to the importer, exporter, or manufacturer. Notifications must include the reason for the restriction, the legal basis or authorisation, and information on the status of the affected goods. Article 9.11.9 (a)(iii) USMCA goes further, requiring, if applicable, laboratory methodology and results, pest identification, and information on the disposition of goods. Both agreements require that the importing party imposing restrictions must provide an opportunity for review within a reasonable period of time.

Article 9.12 USMCA and Article 7.12 TPP deal with certification. With one exception, the provisions are almost identical. Both agreements recognise that certificates are not the only way to assure respect for SPS requirements. Both require that certifications be applied only to the extent necessary to achieve the appropriate level of protection, and that the importing party take into account relevant guidance from the SPS Committee and relevant international standards, guidelines, and recommendations. Attestations and information required must be limited to essential SPS information, and the rationale for such requirements must be transmitted to the other party upon request. The parties may work together to develop model certificates to accompany specific goods in trade and shall promote the implementation of electronic certification and other technologies to facilitate trade. The only point of difference is that USMCA requires that certification requirements be based on relevant international standards or that the certification requirement is appropriate to the circumstances, with respect to risks to human, animal, or plant life or health at issue.[32]

RCEP's audit provisions in Article 5.8 are minimal, and those that exist strongly resemble Articles 7.10.2–7.10.5 of TPP. RCEP provisions on import checks, set forth in Article 5.10, are also not novel. They require parties to take into account the relevant decisions of the SPS Committee and international standards, guidelines, and recommendations. Import checks shall be based on SPS risks associated with importation, and final decisions shall be appropriate to the SPS risk. In the event of non-compliance, there shall be notification of non-compliance, and significant and recurring non-compliance shall be subject to discussion between the parties. RCEP treats certification in Article 5.9. But for a requirement in Article 5.9.2 that certification is in English unless otherwise agreed, there is little novel in this RCEP provision. It largely parallels Articles 7.12.1–7.12.3 TPP.

3.3.2.7 Strengthened Transparency

All four of the mega-regionals strengthen transparency. Article 5.11 CETA sets forth additional 'Notification and Information Exchange' requirements. Likewise, Article 9.13 USMCA and Article 7.13 TPP establish very similar 'Transparency' requirements, in particular a sixty-day period for offering comments on most proposed

[32] Article 9.12.2 USMCA.

measures, which are to appear on a publicly available website or in an official journal, with written comments or a summary of written comments. If a proposed measure does not conform to a relevant international standard, the party is to provide upon request to another party the relevant documentation considered when developing the proposed measure. If a final SPS measure is substantially altered from the proposed measure, a party shall include in the notice of the final SPS measure the objective and rationale of the measure, how the measure advances that objective and rationale, and any substantive revisions that it made. The transparency obligations also contain novel provisions requiring the exporting party to notify the importing party in a timely and appropriate manner of any significant SPS risks of which it is aware, and any new scientific findings of importance which affect the regulatory response. In addition, there is a novel provision that obligates parties, upon request, to make available all SPS measures related to the importation of a good into that party's territory.

RCEP also sets forth transparency requirements. While weaker than those of USMCA and TPP, Article 5.12 RCEP does include a sixty-day comment period, a thirty-day period for providing parties with documents or a summary describing in English the requirements of draft SPS measures notified to the WTO and following notification the requirements of adopted SPS measures, and upon reasonable request relevant information regarding SPS requirements that apply to specific products. The same provision also obliges parties to provide timely and appropriate information on significant and recurring SPS non-compliance and provisional SPS measures. Lastly, like USMCA and TPP, exporting parties are, to the extent possible, obligated to provide information to importing parties if an export consignment poses a significant SPS risk.

3.3.2.8 Emergency SPS Measures

All four mega-regional agreements contain provisions dealing with the imposition of emergency SPS measures. Article 5.13 CETA requires notification of emergency measures within twenty-four hours of a Party's decision to implement the measure and, upon request, requires technical consultations within ten days. Article 9.14 USMCA and Article 7.14 TPP require prompt notification and eventual review of the emergency measure. Article 5.11 RCEP requires immediate notification of emergency measures to relevant exporting parties and, upon request, discussion with exporting parties as soon as is practicable. A review of emergency measures is also required within a reasonable period of time or upon request of the exporting party.

3.3.2.9 Cooperation and Cooperative Technical Consultations

All four mega-regional agreements provide for enhanced cooperation and technical consultations. Article 5.14 CETA establishes a Joint Management Committee, which, among many things, is responsible for information exchange and greater bilateral engagement. Furthermore, Article 5.12 CETA allows a party to request technical consultations with the other party. Article 9.16 USMCA calls for the parties to explore opportunities for cooperation and sets forth a list of areas where cooperation is encouraged. Cooperation is also possible through the USMCA's Committee on Sanitary and Phytosanitary Measures (Article 9.17), its Technical Working Groups (Article 9.18), and Technical Consultations (Article 9.19). TPP takes a similar approach requiring the parties to explore opportunities for cooperation, collaboration, and information exchange in Article 7.15, establishing a procedure for information exchange in Article 7.16, and a procedure for cooperative technical consultations in Article 7.17. Article 5.13 RCEP also calls upon the parties to explore further cooperation, and Article 5.14 establishes procedures for technical consultations.

3.3.2.10 Dispute Settlement

Unlike its TBT chapter, CETA's SPS chapter is silent with respect to dispute settlement. As a result, the SPS chapter falls under Chapter 29. As already noted, Article 29.3.1 CETA governs the choice of forum and clarifies that recourse to the CETA dispute settlement mechanism is without prejudice to the WTO dispute settlement system. However, Article 29.3.4 offers a fork-in-the-road provision whereby parties may choose to resolve equivalent obligations in either the WTO or CETA, but not both.

Article 9.19.6 USMCA requires that parties first seek to resolve SPS disputes through technical consultations before having recourse to Chapter 31 (Dispute Settlement). Article 9.20 (Dispute Settlement) provides that if a dispute involves scientific or technical issues, a panel should seek advice from experts chosen by the panel in consultation with the Parties. Otherwise, Article 31.3 follows a fork-in-the-road approach. The complaining party may select the forum for disputes arising under both the WTO Agreement and the SPS chapter of USMCA. Once the forum is selected, the other forum is excluded.

Likewise, Article 28.4 TPP contains a fork-in-the-road provision that gives exclusive jurisdiction to the first forum chosen (TPP or WTO dispute settlement). However, Article 7.17.8 prohibits recourse to dispute settlement under Article 28 for SPS disputes without first seeking to resolve the matter through cooperative technical consultations. The TPP also prohibits recourse to Chapter 28 for matters arising under Article 7.9.2, which deals with whether an SPS measure conforms to an international standard or is based on documented and objective scientific evidence that is rationally related to the measure.[33] Finally, like USMCA, Article 7.18.2 TPP encourages panels to seek advice from technical expert groups for matters involving scientific or technical issues.

[33] This exclusion is contained in footnote 3 to Article 7.9.2.

Pursuant to Article 5.17 RCEP, Chapter 19 (Dispute Settlement) shall not apply at the entry into force of the agreement (1 January 2022). Non-application is to be reviewed two years after the entry into force of the agreement, with the review to be completed within three years. Parties will then have a choice as to whether they are ready to apply Chapter 19.

3.3.2.11 Annexes

CETA has several SPS annexes, not all of which are complete. Some serve as placeholders for the results of future negotiations. Their existence sets the course for further negotiations and may provide insight into how other countries may treat the negotiation of SPS provisions in PTAs:

- ANNEX 5-A *COMPETENT AUTHORITIES*
- ANNEX 5-B *REGIONAL CONDITIONS* Lists diseases for which regionalisation decisions may be taken.
- ANNEX 5-C *PROCESS OF RECOGNITION OF REGIONAL CONDITIONS* To be agreed at a later stage.
- ANNEX 5-D *GUIDELINES TO DETERMINE, RECOGNISE AND MAINTAIN EQUIVALENCE Determination and Recognition of Equivalence* To be agreed at a later stage. *Maintenance of Equivalence* (already agreed)
- ANNEX 5-E *RECOGNITION OF SANITARY AND PHYTOSANITARY MEASURES* Annex 5-E sets out: (a) the area for which the importing party recognises that an SPS measure of the exporting party is equivalent to its own; and (b) the area for which the importing party recognises that the fulfilment of the specified special condition, combined with the exporting party's SPS measure, achieves the importing party's appropriate level of SPS protection.
- ANNEX 5 F *APPROVAL OF ESTABLISHMENTS OR FACILITIES*
- ANNEX 5-G *PROCEDURE RELATED TO SPECIFIC IMPORT REQUIREMENTS FOR PLANT HEALTH*
- ANNEX 5-H *PRINCIPLES AND GUIDELINES TO CONDUCT AN AUDIT OR VERIFICATION* To be agreed at a later stage.
- ANNEX 5-I *EXPORT CERTIFICATION*
- ANNEX 5-J *IMPORT CHECKS AND FEES* (*Fees:* To be agreed at a later stage.)

3.3.2.12 SPS Conclusions

There are several novel SPS developments in the mega-regionals. Those that stand out include the recognition of regionalisation, zoning, and compartmentalisation to facilitate trade in both USMCA and TPP, and calls to cooperate more on the recognition of pest- or disease-free areas, and areas of low pest or disease prevalence with the objective of acquiring confidence in the procedures followed by each party. CETA also recognises zoning for animals, animal products, and animal by-products, and lists diseases covered by zoning. CETA also leaves room to negotiate principles and guidelines to recognise regional conditions.

Equivalence also appears to be an emerging area receiving greater emphasis in mega-regional negotiations. For example, CETA sets out the area for which the importing party recognises that an SPS measure of the exporting party is equivalent to its own and the area for which the importing party recognises that fulfilment of the specified special conditions, combined with the exporting party's SPS measure, achieves the importing party's appropriate level of SPS protection. USMCA and TPP, the two mega-regionals spearheaded by the US, take a less ambitious approach to equivalence, but leave the door open for recognition of equivalent SPS measures. USMCA goes further in two respects: it establishes a process for streamlining an equivalence assessment, and it establishes a procedure, including a notification and communications procedure, if a party adopts, modifies, or repeals a recognition of equivalence.

CETA's use of annexes is also a novel approach. CETA's annexes establish a roadmap for negotiation. Parties can decide to fill in the gaps when practicable.

As with the aforementioned TBT chapters, there are a few major areas of contention. What differences do exist seem to be related to the level of ambition of the parties to various agreements. This is apparent with respect to SPS dispute settlement, where RCEP Members postponed the implementation of RCEP's dispute settlement provisions.

Again, what is discernible is the acceptance of logical solutions that are eventually becoming dominant, such as greater transparency, enhanced cooperation, fork-in-the-road provisions for dispute settlement, and some degree of alignment in USMCA, TPP, and CETA with respect to compliance measures – audit, import checks, and certification procedures.

3.4 CONCLUSIONS ON FUTURE DESIGN

Looking at existing practice, we only found a few novel TBT developments. Three CETA developments stand out: (i) incorporation of future WTO TBT decisions, (ii) requirement that technical working groups address disagreements before the invocation of CETA dispute settlement, and (iii) the use of subject-specific and sector-specific annexes and protocols in CETA (and TPP). Likewise, we found that there are few points of contention. Instead, what is discernible is acceptance of logical solutions that are eventually becoming dominant, such as fork-in-the-road provisions for dispute settlement, and widespread agreement on the gradual expansion of TBT disciplines, such as improved transparency and greater cooperation.

The future design of PTA TBT provisions is likely to be influenced by the soft law provisions in existing PTAs. For example, Article 11.9 USMCA and Article 8.9 TPP acknowledge that a broad range of mechanisms exist to facilitate acceptance of conformity assessment results. Among those mechanisms that might eventually shape the future design of TBT provisions are: greater mutual recognition of technical regulations and the results of conformity assessment procedures by government bodies, mutual recognition arrangements between or among accreditation bodies, accreditation to qualify conformity assessment bodies, unilateral recognition of conformity assessment procedures, and acceptance of supplier's declarations of conformity. In addition, an emphasis on greater cooperation, information sharing, transparency, and trade facilitation discussions between and among PTA parties is likely to be a feature of all future PTAs.

As with the TBT chapters, there are a few major areas of contention in the SPS chapters. What is discernible is the acceptance of logical solutions that are eventually becoming dominant, such as greater transparency, enhanced cooperation, fork-in-the-road provisions for dispute settlement, and some degree of alignment in USMCA, TPP, and CETA with respect to compliance measures – audit, import checks, and certification procedures.

The design of SPS provisions in future PTAs is also indicated by certain features in existing PTAs. Negotiators relied less on provisions from previous SPS chapters when designing the mega-regionals, which suggests they contain several novel developments, for example: (i) recognition of regionalisation, zoning, and compartmentalisation to facilitate trade in both USMCA and TPP, and (ii) general calls to cooperate more on the recognition of pest- or disease-free areas, and areas of low pest or disease prevalence. Equivalence is also receiving greater emphasis, as can be seen in the SPS chapters of the mega-regional agreements. One can expect that equivalence, cooperation, transparency, and trade facilitation will feature prominently in future PTAs. Likewise, CETA's use of annexes is a novel approach that establishes a roadmap for negotiations and is another mechanism that is likely to feature in future PTAs. In summary, any mechanism that can encourage dialogue, information exchange, technical advice and assistance, cooperation including scientific cooperation, and the use of good regulatory practices, is likely to play a prominent role in the development of future SPS chapters.

One problematic area that remains is dispute settlement. Fork-in-the-road provisions that lead to WTO dispute settlement will stymie resolution of many TBT and SPS disputes until the re-emergence of the Appellate Body in some form.[34] One idea suggested in Article 4.7.2 CETA that merits further study is the possibility of resolving disputes in *ad hoc* technical working groups that would identify solutions

[34] With the absence of a functioning Appellate Body, the practice by the losing party in WTO disputes of 'appeals into the void' prevents resolution of many trade disputes.

to facilitate trade. This idea is particularly interesting for disputes of a highly technical nature that require scientific input.

Beyond the analysis conducted for this chapter, we believe there are a number of other trends in TBT and SPS chapters that may become more pronounced, both within and outside PTAs. In the TBT area, there is at least one instance in which governments appear to move beyond PTAs. The Trade and Technology Council, recently established between the EU and the US, provides a platform to develop common standards and potentially overcome some of the TBT-related challenges that contributed to the 2019 failure of the Transatlantic Trade and Investment Partnership (TTIP).

Technology will also play an increasingly important role in SPS chapters. Distributed ledger technology, and blockchain more specifically, is already used by companies around the world to track food supply chains and manage food safety measures. The governance of these technologies may eventually be featured in future SPS chapters that seek to regulate international food trade.

REFERENCES

Allee, T. and M. Elsig 2019. 'Are the Contents of International Treaties Copied and Pasted? Evidence from Preferential Trade Agreements', *International Studies Quarterly* 63(3): 603–613.

Allee, T. and A. Lugg 2016. 'Who Wrote the Rules for the Trans-Pacific Partnership?' *Research and Politics* 3(3): 1–9.

Allee, T., M. Elsig and A. Lugg 2017a. 'The Ties between the World Trade Organization and Preferential Trade Agreements: A Text Analysis', *Journal of International Economic Law* 20(2): 333–363.

2017b. 'Is the European Union Deal with Canada New or Recycled? A Text-as-Data Approach', *Global Policy* 8(2): 246–252.

Baccini, L., A. Dür and Y. Z. Haftel 2015. 'Imitation and Innovation in International Governance: The Diffusion of Trade Agreement Design', in A. Dür and M. Elsig (eds.), *Trade Cooperation: The Purpose, Design and Effects of Preferential Trade Agreements*. Cambridge: Cambridge University Press.

Cottier, T., C. Sieber-Gasser and G. Wermelinger 2015. 'The Dialectical Relationship of Preferential and Multilateral Trade Agreements', in A. Dür and M. Elsig (eds.), *Trade Cooperation: The Purpose, Design and Effects of Preferential Trade Agreements*. Cambridge: Cambridge University Press.

Council of the European Union 2016a. 'CETA: Protocol on the Mutual Acceptance of the Results of Conformity Assessment'. Available at: https://data.consilium.europa.eu/doc/document/ST-10973-2016-ADD-7/en/pdf. Accessed 9 January 2023.

2016b. 'CETA: Protocol on the Mutual Recognition of the Compliance and Enforcement Programme Regarding Good Manufacturing Practices for Pharmaceutical Products'. Available at: https://data.consilium.europa.eu/doc/document/ST-10973–2016-ADD-8/en/pdf. Accessed 9 January 2023.

Dür, A., L. Baccini and M. Elsig 2014. 'The Design of International Trade Agreements: Introducing a New Dataset', *The Review of International Organizations* 9(3): 353–375.

Egan, M. and J. Pelkmans 2015. 'TTIPs Hard Core: Technical Barriers to Trade and Standards', Technical Report 117, Centre for European Policy Studies, Brussels. Special Report.

Elsig, M. and S. Klotz 2019. 'Behind-the-Border Measures and the New Generation of Trade Agreements: Technical Barriers to Trade and Sanitary and Phytosanitary Measures Compared', in J. Francois and B. Hoekman (eds.), *Behind-the-Border Policies: Assessing and Addressing Non-Tariff Measures*. Cambridge: Cambridge University Press.

Elsig. M. and Klotz, S. 2021. 'Data Flow-Related Provisions in Preferential Trade Agreements: Trends and Patterns of Diffusion', in M. Burri (ed.), *Big Data and Global Trade Law*. Cambridge: Cambridge University Press.

Espitia, A., S. Pardo, R. Piermartini and N. Rocha 2020. 'Technical Barriers to Trade', in A. Mattoo, N. Rocha and M. Ruta (eds.), *Handbook of Deep Trade Agreements*. Washington, DC: World Bank Group.

Fulponi, L., M. Shearer and J. Almeida 2011. 'Regional Trade Agreements – Treatment of Agriculture', Organisation for Economic Co-operation and Development (OECD) Food, Agriculture and Fisheries Papers, 44: 1–72.

Heydon, K. and S. Woolcock 2009. *The Rise of Bilateralism, Comparing American, European and Asian Approaches to Preferential Trade Agreements*. Shibuya City: United Nations University Press.

Horn, H., P. C. Mavroidis and A. Sapir 2010. 'Beyond the WTO? An Anatomy of EU and US Preferential Trade Agreements', *The World Economy* 33(11): 1565–1588.

2011. 'EU and US Preferential Trade Agreements: Deepening or Widening of WTO Commitments', in K. W. Bagwell and P. C. Mavroidis (eds.), *Preferential Trade Agreements: A Law and Economics Analysis*. Cambridge: Cambridge University Press.

Lejárraga, I. 2013. 'Multilateralising Regionalism: Strengthening Transparency Disciplines in Trade', Organisation for Economic Co-operation and Development (OECD) Trade Policy Papers, 152: 1–48.

2014. 'Deep Provisions in Regional Trade Agreements: How Multilateral friendly?' Organisation for Economic Co-operation and Development (OECD) Trade Policy Papers, 168: 1–44.

Lesser, C. 2007. 'Do Bilateral and Regional Approaches for Reducing Technical Barriers to Trade Converge Towards the Multilateral Trading System?' Organisation for Economic Co-operation and Development (OECD) Trade Policy Working Papers, 58: 1–75.

Lester, S. and I. Barbee 2013. 'The Challenge of Cooperation: Regulatory Trade Barriers in the Transatlantic Trade and Investment Partnership', *Journal of International Economic Law* 16(4): 847–867.

McDaniels, D., A. C. Molina and E. N. Wijkström 2018. 'A Closer Look At WTO's Third Pillar: How WTO Committees Influence Regional Trade Agreements', *Journal of International Economic Law* 21(4): 815–843.

Molina, A. C. and V. Khoroshavina 2015. 'TBT Provisions in Regional Trade Agreements: To What Extent Do They Go Beyond the WTO TBT Agreement?' World Trade Organisation (WTO) Staff Working Paper 9: 1–24.

2018. 'How Regional Trade Agreements Deal with Disputes Concerning their TBT Provisions?' World Trade Organisation (WTO) Staff Working Paper 9: 1–22.

Piermartini, R. and M. Budetta 2009. 'A Mapping of Regional Rules on Technical Barriers to Trade', in A. Estevadeordal, K. Suominen and R. Teh (eds.), *Regional Rules in the Global Trading System*. Cambridge: Cambridge University Press.

Stoler, A. L. 2011. 'TBT and SPS Measures, in Practice', in: J.-P. Chauffour and J.-C. Maur (eds.), *Preferential Trade Agreement Policies for Development: A Handbook*. Washington, DC: World Bank.

Ti-Ting, L. 2012. 'Technical Barriers to Trade Provisions in Regional Trade Agreements. Society of International Economic Law (SIEL)', Working Paper, 12: 629–682.
United Nations 2022. 'Non-tariff Measures (NTMs)'. Geneva: United Nations Conference on Trade and Development. Available at: https://unctad.org/topic/trade-analysis/non-tariff-measures. Accessed 8 January 2023.
USTR 2020. '2020 National Trade Estimate Report on Foreign Trade Barriers'. Washington, DC: Office of the United States Trade Representative (USTR).
WTO 2011a. 'World Trade Report 2011 – The WTO and Preferential Trade Agreements: From Co-existence to Coherence'. Technical Report, World Trade Organisation, Geneva.
2011b. 'Market Access for Non-agricultural Products – International Standards in Support of Trade and Economic Development: Strengthening the Contribution of the Committee Decision – A proposal from the United States'. Negotiating Group on Market Access, TN/MA/W/141. 29 March 2011.
2011c. 'Market Access for Non-agricultural Products, International Standardisation – Communication from the delegations of the European Union, India, Indonesia, Norway, Philippines, Switzerland and Thailand'. Negotiating Group on Market Access, TN/MA/W/142. 12 April 2011.
2022. 'ePing SPS and TBT Platform'. Geneva: World Trade Organisation. Available at: https://epingalert.org/. Accessed 8 January 2023.

4

Trade Facilitation in Preferential Trade Agreements

The Edge of a New Frontier?

Nora Neufeld[†]

4.1 SETTING THE STAGE

Trade facilitation (TF) – the simplification, modernisation, and harmonisation of cross-border trade processes – is once again moving up the trade policy agenda. When exploratory discussions were first launched in the 1990s, TF was considered little more than the plumbing of the trading system. Its importance has grown steadily as the world economy has become more integrated, supply chains expanded, and technological change reshaped the way goods and services are traded around the planet. Paradoxically, even the major disruptions to the world trading system in the last several years have tended to amplify, not diminish, the need to facilitate trade.

The COVID-19 pandemic served as a massive wake-up call about the importance of TF, underscoring the critical need to deliver essential products, especially medical supplies, to consumers as quickly as possible, highlighting countries' dependency on complex and far-flung supply networks. It increased pressure on governments to find secure sources of supply and to diversify their trade relations, sometimes involving new trade partners and routes that lay beyond the well-beaten paths of traditional United States (US)–European Union (EU)–China trade corridors. Suddenly, pragmatic measures to speed up cross-border transactions, cut unnecessary red tape, harmonise trade processes, and digitalise them wherever possible became critically important. Supply chain disruptions have only increased since the outbreak of war in Ukraine, cutting off traditional sources for key commodities such as energy and grains and accelerating the push to diversify sources of supply. A subsequent series of sanctions added a whole new layer of complexity to already overstretched and overburdened customs procedures.

† After a long illness, Nora Neufeld died on 18 November 2023. She managed to finish her contribution before that date, which is a testament to her professionalism. This book is dedicated to her memory.

Those events have delivered unprecedented shocks to world trade. They also laid bare deeply rooted structural weaknesses in the system that have been hampering the smooth flow of goods long before the pandemic, straining supply chains and causing trade bottlenecks.

The conclusion of the Trade Facilitation Agreement (TFA) in 2013 was a major breakthrough, not just because it marked the first multilateral agreement since the World Trade Organization (WTO) was founded nearly two decades earlier, but because it established baseline global rules for accelerating the movement, release, and clearance of goods across borders, promising to reduce trade transaction costs by an average of over 14 per cent (WTO, 2015).[1]

Even before its conclusion, the TFA was already encouraging regional TF efforts, accumulating policy innovations, widening country engagement, and building momentum in the multilateral arena. The TFA negotiation process helped energise and cross-fertilise parallel regional efforts and spurred a noticeable increase in TF outcomes elsewhere (Neufeld, 2014). After the successful adoption of the TFA, TF rulemaking in preferential trade agreements (PTAs)[2] surged even more, with the aim of building on – and going further than – the multilateral foundation provided by the TFA. Slow progress in other aspects of the WTO's work and growing pessimism about the possibilities of securing consensus for additional reforms among 164 Members reinforced perceptions that TF advances might more likely occur at the regional level in the near future. Over the last few years, most bilateral and regional trade agreements (RTAs) have incorporated TF provisions with varying degrees of ambition, including vast mega-regional agreements such as the Comprehensive and Progressive Agreement for a Trans-Pacific Partnership (CPTPP), the African Continental Free Trade Agreement (AfCFTA), or the Regional Comprehensive Economic Partnership (RCEP). Complementing the TFA, these agreements were widely expected to be delivering new TFA-plus rules for facilitating trade and offering signposts for how the global TF regime might advance.

Yet, an examination of the TF provisions in this newest wave of PTAs suggests that there is often less to these agreements than meets the eye. Few of the PTAs were concluded before the TFA went beyond that multilateral benchmark – and many fell well short. Even regional agreements negotiated in the wake of the TFA are often somewhat uneven and underwhelming when it comes to their TF content, especially when viewed against the backdrop of the massive advances in digitalisation and automation that are dramatically changing the way goods and services move across borders and calling into question old approaches that require pen, paper, and, indeed, even people.

1 A 2017 Organisation for Economic Co-operation and Development (OECD) study even estimated that TFA implementation would generate cost reductions of between 14 and 18 per cent (OECD 2017).

2 This chapter uses the term PTAs for RTAs.

This chapter argues that rapid technological change risks rendering many old TF approaches outdated – or even obsolete – and that a renewed effort to advance and modernise the TF rulebook makes sense. It explores the changes in the world economy since the TFA entered into force in 2017 – including the impact of the COVID-19 pandemic and the war in Ukraine – and suggests how they have amplified, not diminished, the importance of facilitating trade. It then examines how the post-TFA generation of PTAs has approached the need to facilitate trade, analysing common philosophies, shared characteristics, and recent trends. These include the emphasis on addressing deeper, behind-the-border obstacles, the increased focus on electronic means, and the overall move towards greater regulatory depth. A brief look is taken at how regional measures compare with baseline reforms mandated by the TFA, where useful advances have been made and where efforts have fallen short. Lastly, the chapter argues that several TF reforms can potentially deliver positive impacts and suggests specific areas where PTAs might focus in the future to take TF to a new level.

4.2 CHANGING LANDSCAPES

The growing salience of TF is directly related to a broader transformation of the global trade landscape. Thanks to falling tariff barriers, declining transport costs, and the spread of new information and communications technologies, companies have unbundled their production processes and located the various stages in the most cost-efficient or technologically proficient regions around the planet, knitting every part together through complex, just-in-time transnational trade networks. The last century's assembly line has become today's supply chain; the factory floor is now globalised. As a result, modern economies are increasingly dependent on a vast and complex array of global inputs that cannot be supplied by any single country alone. Agricultural production, for instance, requires multiple imports of fertilisers, seeds, pesticides, energy, and advanced machinery to maintain sufficient output. And as production processes become more technologically complex, the supporting supply chains become more complex, too. One of the key manufacturers of the COVID-19 vaccine, for example, depends on sourcing 280 components from nineteen different countries to produce the final product (JDSUPRA, 2021; Bourla, 2023).

Rather than decreasing the importance of TF, today's highly interconnected global production systems are increasing it. Even modest delays or disruptions in the cross-border delivery of key parts, equipment, or resources can have a ripple effect across supply chains that shut down production, cause goods to pile up in storage, and disrupt shipping, rail, or airfreight logistics. This ultimately restricts global trade flows, preventing businesses from importing critical components, and keeping consumer products off store shelves. These trade and production disruptions can drive up prices, fuel inflation and result in critical shortages of food, medicine, and other necessities. Meanwhile, the experience of COVID-19 lockdowns – and the mass requirement to shift economic activity online – has fuelled growing interest in how digitalisation and automation can be harnessed to improve and strengthen TF. All these challenges and opportunities are reinforcing calls to advance new 'TF-plus' initiatives.

How should they advance? On the one hand, many TF issues are inherently global in nature and underscore the logic of trying to reach multilateral solutions. It was one of the factors that allowed WTO Members to adopt the TFA in 2013. Bilateral and regional approaches often did not provide optimal outcomes, as many facilitation measures were of an inherent most-favoured-nation (MFN) nature. It made little sense, for instance, for countries to agree to a single window on that basis – if such a window were built for one trade partner, it would therefore automatically have been built for others as well. It made even less sense to streamline customs procedures or to standardise paperwork bilaterally or regionally, especially for increasingly 'multinational' products. Anything less than a multilateral approach to these issues meant complicating, not facilitating, cross-border transactions, and making them more expensive.

On the other hand, many advanced TF initiatives – especially those involving new technologies – are more readily embraced by more developed economies and often beyond the reach or resources of their less advanced partners. During the WTO's TFA negotiations, several more ambitious facilitation proposals ended up watered down because less developed countries baulked at making binding commitments they feared to entail sizable technological and financial investments. Then there are the related challenges of trying to get 164 countries to agree to multilateral outcomes that may not reflect everyone's specific trade needs or stages of development. In these circumstances, there is a clear logic in pursuing the next generation of TF measures regionally, especially if they build upon the WTO foundation, advance TF innovations, and can be easily multilateralised if and when other countries want to join. While it is still early to assess the extent to which this renewed focus on TF will be reflected in meaningful new rules and commitments in PTAs, one can already identify a series of noteworthy developments. The following section will take a closer look at these trends, focusing on PTAs concluded during the past five years.[3]

4.3 LOVE AT SECOND SIGHT?

A first glance at the PTA landscape seems to suggest intense TF activity. Of the 353 agreements currently[4] recorded in the WTO's RTA database (listing all RTAs notified since 1958), almost seventy entered into force during the past five years.

[3] In doing so, it follows up on an earlier analysis of previous PTAs (Neufeld 2016). An initial version of this study was published as a WTO Working paper (Neufeld 2014).

[4] The study includes all PTAs notified to the WTO's database up until 22 September 2022.

A closer look, however, reveals that more than half of those treaties were primarily concluded to compensate for EU agreements no longer extending to the United Kingdom (UK) post-Brexit. The vast majority of these PTAs incorporate the relevant provisions of an earlier EU Agreement through a mutatis mutandis application – with only minimal adjustments (referred to as 'short form agreements' by the UK government). Only a handful of recent PTAs concluded by the UK fully set out each provision ('long form agreements'). This is not to suggest an absence of meaningful activity, but the substantiveness of recent PTAs requires a more in-depth analysis.

The launch of the TFA negotiations in 2004 had sparked a sharp rise in TF content of PTAs, lifting it from virtual absence in earlier agreements to forming considerable parts of later treaties.[5] The scope and substance of TF chapters continued to increase when WTO rulemaking ended a decade later, and the final content of the resulting agreement had become clear. Few PTAs from that period went beyond the TFA – and some remained well below its scope – but TF had become an inherent part of the PTA landscape. This trend continued after the TFA had entered into force in 2017, with most of the PTAs concluded from this time onward, setting out robust TF reforms. Efforts to elevate facilitation to a new level remained limited, however, with governments often focusing their resources on implementing the TFA. New issues moved into the trade spotlight, such as joined initiatives on investment facilitation, e-commerce, and micro-, small, and medium-sized enterprises launched at the WTO's Buenos Aires Ministerial in 2017.

It was not until a series of events hit the global economy that TF regained a more prominent place on governments' radar screens. While the impact of Brexit was mostly regional in character, it left a particular mark on the PTA front as the UK's efforts to reorient its international trade relations triggered an avalanche of agreements. Before they had even entered into force, a pandemic started to spread around the globe, triggering an unprecedented health crisis and delivering a massive shock to the world economy.

The world was confronted with social and economic challenges unmatched in living memory. And as if a serious health crisis had not been enough, it was quickly followed by war, shortages in energy and other essential products, and a rise in inflation. Initial responses exposed some of the fragilities inherent to global value chains and economic interdependence. Protectionist reflexes put a strain on supply chain patterns and negatively impacted stability and logistics costs. Just-in-time production risked being replaced by 'just-in-case' strategies.

The scale of the supply chain disruptions triggered worldwide restoration efforts and led to a change in approach. Many of the early export bans were repealed, and a significant part of pandemic-related trade restrictions implemented by G20 economies were removed after a few months.[6] Governments introduced measures to

[5] For additional background, see Neufeld (2016).
[6] For additional information, see WTO (2022b).

facilitate the import of key supplies, including lowered tariffs on urgently needed goods, simplified customs procedures and documentation requirements, the establishment of priority channels, and cooperation on regulatory approval.

There was growing awareness that countries that embraced TF had proven more resilient and better equipped to handle the challenges than those that had been slower to do so and were faring less well. Keeping international markets open to trade was increasingly seen as an essential component of the agenda for economic recovery. Initially often considered a mere oiling of the pipes that enable cross-border trade, TF reforms were appreciated as an essential component of the multilateral commercial machinery and the backbone of global supply chains.

Calls for increased facilitation reforms were made on many fronts. Some took the form of advocating the accelerated implementation of the TFA. Recommendations to this end were not only made in various WTO bodies[7] but also within the framework of high-level fora such as G20 summits or Asia-Pacific Economic Cooperation (APEC) Trade Ministers meetings.[8] They focused on advancing full implementation, which the TFA permits the majority of WTO Members to delay.[9] Several aspects of the Agreement were highlighted as priority areas for such expedited action, including measures relating to publication requirements, pre-arrival processing, separation of release from payments, expedited shipments, border agency cooperation, reduced formalities and documentation requirements, and single window implementation.[10] Suggestions were equally made to improve the free transit of goods.[11]

Several proposals went beyond the TFA's scope. In May 2020, for instance, the G20's Trade and Investment Working Groups complemented their call for accelerated TFA implementation with an encouragement to use electronic documentation and processes, where possible and practical, including the use of smart applications.[12] Additional TF measures were equally discussed in various WTO fora. They

[7] A dedicated proposal was first presented to the WTO Committee on Trade Facilitation in October 2020 (WTO Committee on Trade Facilitation 2021a). Initially tabled by the US, Brazil, and Colombia, support quickly expanded with sponsorship now including over fifty WTO Members. The proposal was also discussed in the WTO's Council for Trade in Goods as well as the General Council.

[8] See, for instance, G20 (2020) and WTO General Council (2021).

[9] All developing and least developed countries have the right to self-determine how much time they need for implementing the reforms, and to designate required capacity-building support. For more information, see WTO (n.d. 2023).

[10] See, for instance, a proposal made by a group of WTO Members to the Trade Facilitation Committee on 2 December 2021 (WTO Committee on Trade Facilitation 2021b). A recommendation of the G20's Trade and Investment Working Group – made in May 2020 – focused on similar areas, highlighting pre-arrival processing, separation of release from payments, and expedited shipments. It also called for speeding up and streamlining customs procedures in line with the TFA.

[11] See, for instance, the APEC Declaration on Facilitating the Movement of Essential Goods (APEC 2020).

[12] G20 (2020) annex, section 1.2.

included strengthening pre-arrival procedures, post-release verification and audits to control for compliance, reducing and/or eliminating procedures requiring the physical presence of operators or the submission of physical documents, and, for countries sharing a common border,[13] cooperation on additional working hours (WTO, 2020, 6–7). Proposals were also made to reduce or eliminate penalties for bona fide mistakes in connection with importing certain products (WTO, 2020, 6–7).[14]

Common to these suggestions was the aim of keeping markets open and trade transaction costs in check. They further sought to strengthen supply chain resilience and to combat corruption and illicit trade.[15]

Much of the attention focused on domestic measures, either as calls for national action or by advocating multilateral initiatives. Many suggestions involved the TFA, which was increasingly seen as offering a way of mitigating the impact of trade tensions and providing an undisputed baseline for cross-border clearance when globalisation had come under strain. Trade facilitation initiatives in the regional context received less attention, but merit closer examination, even if their full impact will require more time to be seen.

4.4 STEPPING STONE OR STAGNATION?

A comparison with the WTO's TFA is a natural reference point when assessing the role of TF initiatives under the PTA umbrella. The TFA's impact on earlier regional agreements is well documented (Duval et al., 2016; Neufeld, 2016; Kieck, 2020). It could already be seen when the WTO negotiations were still underway and continued to increase after their conclusion.[16] The influence extended to the scope and depth of reforms and ranged from conceptual inspiration to using almost identical formulations. The closer the WTO negotiations got to their finishing line, the stronger the alignment became.

However, few of the PTAs from the pre-TFA period went beyond the TF Agreement coverage. A previous analysis of earlier PTAs (covering all agreements up until 2016) found only a limited amount of TFA-plus provisions (Neufeld, 2016). Even PTAs concluded during the first years after the TFA's entry into force in 2017 rarely went beyond its scope. TFA implementation seems to have absorbed a

[13] The parties making this suggestion did not offer a particular explanation, but one could assume that they considered it more likely to be feasible in such cases. The TFA also contains a reference to a common border for the measures it mandates for international cooperation (Article 8.2).

[14] For additional information, see World Bank Group and WTO (2022).

[15] For additional information on measures to tackle illicit trade in medical products, see WTO (2022c).

[16] For more detail, see Neufeld (2016).

fair amount of resources, and with most countries already being part of PTAs, the appetite for additional regional action might have been limited.

As far as recent PTAs are concerned, the TFA clearly left a mark on their TF chapters.[17] The degree of influence varies, however. Some agreements contain an explicit reference with parties affirming their rights and obligations under the TFA.[18] There are even cases of the TFA incorporated as a whole and made an integral part of a PTA.[19] The most frequent form of impact is more subtle and of a de facto nature, with PTAs setting out provisions that resemble TFA-mandated reforms.

Despite those differences, one can make out a few broader trends:

1. The first consists of an even further alignment with the TFA. While there are still some PTAs with no reference, this is usually the result of a treaty not containing any TF provisions at all (possibly due to the parties having considered the TFA to offer a sufficient TF framework or due to a narrowly targeted overall scope). Where TF chapters exist, which is the case for most recent PTAs, they almost always show clear signs of having been inspired by the TFA. In some cases, this influence is quite specific and can even take the form of identical or at least very similar language. In others, there is greater adaptation to local circumstances and particular interests, while at the same time showing noticeable traces of inspiration by the TFA.
2. A second tendency is an increased occurrence of TFA-plus measures. While such added ambition remained the exception in earlier PTAs, one finds a significant part of the recent treaties to go beyond the scope of the TFA. In some cases, this is done by introducing an additional level of strength or specificity, such as by using more stringent terms (like 'shall' instead of best endeavour language) or by prescribing specific timelines for the execution of an activity.[20] The more frequent constellation, however, includes entirely new areas, such as provisions on information technology (IT). Thematic focus areas are digitalisation, international standards, and relations with the business community.

[17] Except the ones which essentially limit themselves to repeating earlier agreements from the pre-TFA era, such as the short-form agreements signed by the UK.

[18] See, for instance, the 2021 Free Trade Agreement between the United Kingdom of Great Britain and Northern Ireland and Australia (Chapter 5, Article 5.3, para 2).

[19] See, for example, the Regional Trade Agreement between Turkey and Singapore (Chapter 6, Article 6.1) or the PTA between EFTA and Turkey (Annex VI, Article 1).

[20] See, for instance, the requirement set out in the Trans-Pacific Partnership (TPP), Article 4.9, and the Pacific Agreement on Closer Economic Relations (PACER), Chapter 4, Article 8, for goods to be released within forty-eight hours or the call for advance rulings to be issued no later than 150 days after receipt of the related request set out in the Free Trade Agreement between Peru and Australia, Article 4.10.

3. A related trend consists of a move towards greater technological sophistication, reflecting the availability of new tools. This is hardly surprising considering that most of the TFA disciplines were first introduced almost twenty years ago, with the window for incorporating technical innovation closing at the end of the negotiations nearly a decade ago. Recent PTAs place increased emphasis on digitalisation and electronic means. Unlike the TFA, which often mentions the use of information technologies merely as an option – while equally allowing for less ambitious alternatives[21] – PTAs no longer seek to soften related disciplines. Many reforms adopted in the context of recent agreements explicitly mandate governments to execute them via electronic means (see, for instance, provisions on pre-arrival processing, publication, or exchanges with the business community). Obligations are also strengthened by less frequently qualifying them with formulations such as 'to the extent possible' or 'as practicable'.[22]
4. Growing emphasis is placed on removing deeper, behind-the-border obstacles. While early PTAs concentrated on improving customs clearance and removing related barriers, new-generation agreements extend their focus to include larger segments of the movement, release, and clearance of goods. This is already reflected in how relevant chapters are headed, no longer referring to 'customs' in their titles but opting for the broader 'trade facilitation' instead. Many obligations target a wider range of government authorities, focusing not only on customs but equally including other border agencies. Often, they also explicitly include provisions that seek to enhance their coordination.
5. Several red-flag areas encountered during the TFA negotiations have disappeared. While references to automation, for instance, had been a no-go zone with many least developed countries (LDCs) and some developing countries expressing discomfort with the associated level of ambition, this taboo no longer seems to exist. Many PTAs contain specific disciplines on automation, including agreements involving developing (and even least developed) countries.[23] There are also open references to specific international standards, which had been unacceptable even to some developed countries when the TFA was being

[21] When setting out provisions for the establishment of a single window, for instance, the TFA merely calls for the use of IT 'to the extent possible and practicable', thereby allowing for non-IT-based alternatives (Article 10.4.4 of the TFA).

[22] See, for instance, provisions in the PTA between El Salvador and Ecuador, mandating electronic publication means, or in the PTA between Peru and Honduras on automation, IT, and electronic systems. Various provisions mandating electronic means can also be found in the PTA between the EU and Canada.

[23] See, for instance, the PTAs between El Salvador and Ecuador, Peru and Australia, or the UK and Ghana.

negotiated. And several PTAs now openly target illicit trade and corruption, which had initially been attempted during the TFA negotiations but failed to make it into the Agreement's final draft.[24]

4.5 THIRD TIME CAN BE A CHARM

In addition to these broader trends, one finds several cases of parties using the opportunity to pick up unfinished business from the TFA negotiating days. They are pursued by a limited group of stakeholders – in particular, the EU, the European Free Trade Association (EFTA), and the US – but in a consistent manner and with noticeable rates of success.[25] In all instances, these initiatives follow failed attempts to make the targeted measure part of the TFA. Some envisaged reforms date back to pre-TFA days when WTO Members discussed a possible rulemaking exercise and presented initial ideas.

1. A first example consists of efforts to eliminate the mandatory use of customs brokers. The EU sought to achieve a full ban during the TFA negotiations but had to accept a watered-down outcome due to opposition from a group of (mostly Latin American) countries. The finally adopted provision merely prohibits the introduction of new requirements, combined with an obligation to inform of existing practices.[26] The abandoned goal of outlawing mandatory broker requirements altogether made a comeback in several recent PTAs.[27]
2. A similar objective was pursued in the area of pre-shipment inspection (PSI), which the EU (and other WTO Members) attempted to ban during the TFA talks. The proposal had not been acceptable to the entire membership, however. And as a result, the finally adopted language merely ruled out the practice in relation to tariff classification and customs valuation and encouraged governments not to use other types of PSI.[28] The unachieved goal of a total PSI ban was now included in some of the recently negotiated PTAs.[29]
3. The EU also spearheaded the attempt to outlaw the calculation of import/export fees and charges on an ad valorem basis, which remained

[24] See, for example, the Agreements between the UK, Southern African Customs Union (SACU), and Mozambique or between the UK and Ghana.
[25] The notion of success is defined as showing a high degree of overlap with the proposed measure initially sought to get adopted in the context of the TFA negotiations.
[26] For details, see Article 10.6 of the TFA.
[27] Examples include the PTAs between the EU and Indonesia, EU and SADC, EFTA and Georgia, or the UK and Cameroon.
[28] See Article 10.5 of the TFA.
[29] See, for instance, the PTAs between the EU and Indonesia, EU and Viet Nam, or the EU and Singapore.

unsuccessful when adopting the TFA.[30] It was now included in several recent PTAs, not just by the EU, but also the EFTA.[31]

4. Another example of a revived EU negotiating goal relates to the area of transit of goods. During the TFA negotiations, Brussels sought to introduce a national treatment component when proposing measures to improve free traffic in transit. While this attempt failed to meet the consensus threshold mandated under WTO rules, the EU succeeded in introducing a very similar provision in a PTA recently concluded with Ghana.[32]
5. Efforts to outlaw the requirement of consular transactions for importation processes have a particularly long history, dating back to the General Agreement on Tariffs and Trade (GATT) days. A first recommendation to phase out the practice was already made in 1952.[33] When the TFA negotiations started, the US sought to elevate its status to a mandatory requirement, teaming up with Uganda to launch a joint initiative to this end. Despite the new alliance, and the small number of countries opposing the idea, it ultimately proved impossible to obtain the required consensus to ban the practice. Faced with the choice between watering down the language or dropping the suggestion altogether, the US opted for the latter. The proposal never completely died, however, and made a comeback at the regional level by being incorporated in several recently concluded PTAs.[34] It also resurfaced at the multilateral level when Norway and the US called for revisiting the need for global action to eliminate consularisation requirements in the WTO's Trade Facilitation Committee.[35]
6. The US further continued its pursuit of introducing a firm de minimis threshold for customs duties and taxes on express shipments. An attempt to include a related requirement in the TFA had only been partially successful. WTO Members were called to provide for a de minimis shipment value or dutiable amount for which customs duties and taxes would not be collected, aside from certain prescribed goods.[36] But the obligation was softened by merely asking them to do so 'to the extent possible', and efforts to introduce a fixed exemption limit failed to

30 See PTAs between the EU and Indonesia, EFTA and Georgia, or EFTA and the Philippines.
31 See, for instance, the PTAs between EFTA and Ecuador, EFTA and Georgia, or the UK, Iceland, Liechtenstein, and Norway.
32 EU–Ghana PTA, Chapter 3, Article 29:1.
33 For a full history, see a communication presented by Uganda and the US in 2008, WTO document TF/TF/W/156.
34 See, for instance, the PTA between EFTA and Georgia, Annex III, Article 11.
35 Communication from Norway and the US, circulated in April 2021, WTO document G/TFA/W/38.
36 Article 7:8 of the TFA.

generate consensus. A fresh attempt to create a stronger commitment succeeded a few years later at the regional level in the context of the renegotiated North American Free Trade Agreement (NAFTA). Article 7.8 of the relevant United States of America, United Mexican States, and Canada Trade Agreement (USMCA) chapter (carrying the same article number used in the TFA) calls for the exemption to apply 'under normal circumstances' and sets out a fixed de minimis amount.[37]

7. A final example relates to the coverage of transit disciplines. The EU had long sought to interpret a key GATT provision (Article V) as including the movement of energy goods via pipelines or electricity grids in transit disciplines. Efforts to make this a shared understanding remained unsuccessful during the TFA talks – but Brussels was at least able to preserve that view vis-à-vis its former union member by explicitly including related language in its recent PTA with the UK.

4.6 WHERE NO PTA HAS GONE BEFORE

When negotiating the TFA, proponents of ambitious outcomes faced resistance on multiple fronts. Apart from opposition to a particular measure – usually based on specific domestic interests – reservations were often of a broader, systemic nature and fuelled by concerns from two sides. Wary of the WTO's dispute settlement system, many developing countries and LDCs preferred to keep the scope of new disciplines within (what they considered to be) digestible limits. Developed Members usually wished to aim high(er), both as far as scope and specificity were concerned, but became increasingly mindful of the concessions they were expected to make on the implementation support side. The large range of contracting parties – well over 160 – and their considerable differences in interests and levels of development posed no small challenge to finding an acceptable middle ground. The task was further complicated by the (initially widely unexpected) long duration of the negotiating exercise, not to mention the procedural and political constraints resulting from its embedding in a packing deal setting where progress in one area was contingent on advances on other files.[38] Concessions were often pocketed without that leading to the unblocking of other issues when progress was lacking on external fronts. This made the middle ground a moving target and frequently led to reforms being watered down during the additional negotiating years that followed.

[37] USMCA, Chapter 7, Article 7:8.

[38] As part of the Doha Development Agenda (DDA) with a large number of portfolios, the TF negotiations were subjected to the so-called Single Undertaking principle under which nothing was agreed until everything was agreed. It was not until the Bali Ministerial Conference – well over ten years after the DDA had been launched – that the Trade Facilitation Agreement was allowed to go ahead even in the absence of consensus on other important files (such as agriculture or negotiations on industrial tariffs).

Some measures even had to be dropped altogether as it became clear that they would fail to meet the necessary consensus threshold.[39] The surviving disciplines were frequently phrased in soft terms[40] and coupled with extensive implementation flexibilities. Developing countries and LDCs, which make up the vast majority of the WTO's membership, were allowed to self-determine implementation times and required capacity-building support.

No PTA ever came close to matching such implementation terms. Most of them have no special and different treatment to speak of, and even where certain provisions exist, they tend to be rudimentary and hardly ever exceed aspirational terrain.[41] Some agreements leave the development of a support pillar for later – usually without setting a deadline – and many do not set out any assistance obligations at all. There are also no PTAs with a comparably large membership. Most of them have less than a handful of contracting parties (if they are not bilateral in the first place), and only a very limited number has more than a dozen signatories. In addition, PTAs do not come without an enforcement mechanism comparable to the WTO's dispute settlement – a major limiting factor for several countries when considering their willingness to take on certain reforms. And almost all potential PTA partners are already committed to implementing the TFA reforms, allowing for the consideration of additional measures with the benefit of starting from a higher base level.

This begs the question of what could be achieved in the PTA setting – and whether this potential is currently being reaped – even when recognising different aims and purposes of regional and multilateral treaties. While much of the achievable objectives will depend on the respective parties involved, as well as the circumstances in which they are being pursued, there are a number of factors that play a role in assessing a PTA's potential impact, which will be analysed in the following sections.

4.7 SIZE DOES (NOT) MATTER

The assumption of a positive correlation between size and ambition may seem intuitive, but does not necessarily find corroboration when analysing the actual content of regional TF reforms. Preferential trade agreements involving economic

[39] In one instance, a proposed measure (the ban of a consularisation requirement for import of a merchandise) was abandoned only a few weeks before the end of the negotiations after having been on the table for many years and despite it having won the approval of the vast majority of WTO Members.

[40] In many cases, this implied best endeavour language. But even stronger legal terms were often softened by combining them with built-in flexibilities à la 'whenever practicable' or 'to the extent possible'.

[41] Even the PTAs that make the TFA an integral part of their terms only do so with respect to the TF disciplines without incorporating the implementation architecture with its special and differential treatment for developing and least developed Members.

heavyweights are not always characterised by extensive depth and broad scope – not even when concluded with partners of similar gravitas. And PTAs among smaller players can have impressive reach. Treaties among developing countries do not necessarily lag behind those concluded by more developed partners.

What seems more relevant are points of departure – in the sense of baseline levels of prior engagement in TF. Countries that have already committed to cutting their red tape – be it through domestic, bilateral, or multilateral initiatives – tend to be more open to adding an additional layer of reforms. At the PTA level, governments with a robust facilitation record often follow up on earlier agreements with ambitious successor treaties.[42]

4.8 GEOGRAPHY CONTINUES TO SHAPE OUTCOMES

Old-fashioned as it may sound, geography matters even in the digital age. As much as operations have become increasingly digitalised, ground realities still weigh heavily. Cooperation between border agencies, for instance, clearly is very conducive to facilitating international trade. For countries without a common land border, the actual scope is far more limited than those sharing a joint frontier (which is sometimes also reflected in the absence of related provisions in PTAs).[43] Not having easy access to maritime transport – due to being landlocked or as a result of underdeveloped infrastructure – also continues to have a significant impact on the ability to engage in international trade. Distance between PTA partners is also an important factor, as it tends to impact trade patterns and participation in global supply chains. It can also explain the absence of TF provisions in certain areas – such as transit – which should not rashly be equated with representing a TFA minus. In some cases, the lack of measures in one area can also be the result of there simply not being any sizable obstacles, with geography potentially playing an important role. A PTA between advanced economies with ocean access simply may not require any transit provisions, for instance, due to the absence of relevant barriers.

4.9 VOLUME DOES NOT EQUAL VALUE

First impressions can be misleading. Some PTAs have long facilitation chapters, without size-matching substance. Provisions are phrased in aspirational terms, qualifying the call for action by framing the related commitments in best endeavour terms.[44] To-do lists may seem comprehensive at first glance, but turn out to be set as

42 See, for instance, PTAs concluded by Peru.

43 See, for example, the PTA between EFTA and Georgia. There are also cases of PTAs between countries without a common land border that have only very limited provisions on border agency cooperation – less than the TFA – such as the treaty between EFTA and the Philippines or EFTA and Ecuador.

44 See, for instance, the PTA concluded between the UK and Côte d'Ivoire.

a mere basis for future work in soft legal language. There are also cases of committing parties to 'cooperate' on a broad range of issues – which can be spelt out in quite specific and ambitious-looking terms – but without mandating concrete actions towards this end.

At the same time, one should not hastily judge the value of such arrangements. In some instances, a single phrase can add value to pre-existing obligations, especially requirements set out in the TFA, such as the insertion of a call for carrying out a measure via electronic means, or by specifying the international standards to be used.[45]

4.10 GOOD THINGS CAN COME IN SMALL PACKAGES

Similarly, one should not fall into the trap of rigidly equating brevity with absence of ambition. Some TF chapters might be short, but endowed with a high TFA-plus factor due to their design as an add-on instrument.[46] A small number of provisions can still imply significant reforms if phrased in strong terms. Implementation flexibilities equally play a role, especially when considering the time horizon of actual changes on the ground. Given the widespread lack of possibilities to delay or request capacity-building support, reforms can be relatively quick when set out through the PTA track. There are further cases of interim outcomes with parties agreeing on certain measures while indicating their intention to add additional measures at a later time. An accurate assessment of ambition levels therefore requires careful analysis and a detailed look at the fine print.

4.11 FEARS OF DUPLICATION MAY BE OVERRATED

When considering measures for adoption in a PTA, their inclusion in the TFA should not serve as a deterrent on the grounds of fear of duplication. Apart from the fact that disciplines are rarely phrased in identical terms, the different implementation modalities already ensure a complementary role. The absence of the TFA's extensive flexibilities alone would add an additional layer of commitment, even in the case of matching provisions. Not having the ability to self-determine implementation dates, for instance – without an upper limit – clearly influences when a measure's impact can be expected on the ground.

This becomes all the more relevant when considering that current commitment rates for some of the most impactful TFA measures leave room for upward movement. Only slightly more than half of all WTO Members are currently bound to have established a single window, for instance, even though the TFA sets out the

[45] See, for instance, provisions set out in Chapter 4 of the PTA concluded between the EU and Viet Nam.
[46] See, for example, the PTAs between Turkey and Singapore and between the EU and Canada.

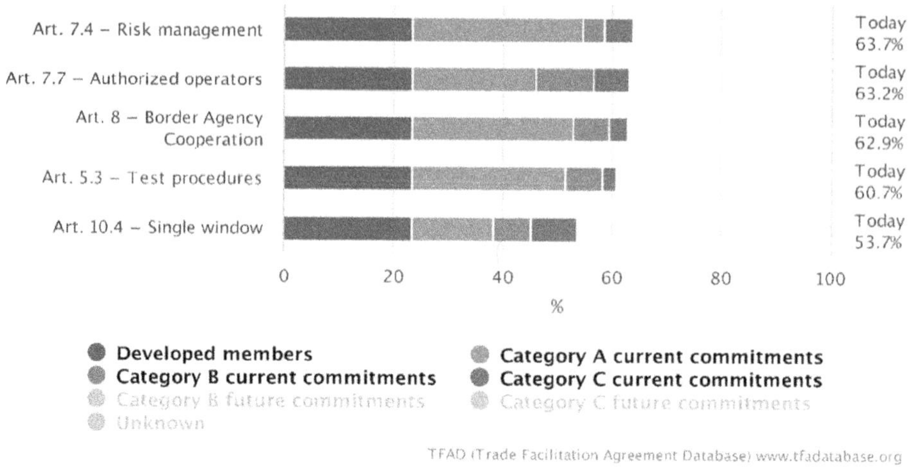

FIGURE 4.1 Bottom five TFA measures with the lowest commitment rate.
Source: WTO (2023), Trade Facilitation Agreement Database (TFAD), www.tfadatabase.org/en

related obligation in best endeavour terms. Little more than 60 per cent are already committed to border agency cooperation, despite its important role in enhancing supply chain resilience and reducing illicit trade (see Figure 4.1).

When seeking to enhance facilitation at the regional level, there are a few lessons to be learned from the COVID-19 crisis. The pandemic clearly underlined the importance of global supply chains, but also exposed their vulnerability. With many of the production and distribution networks currently under review, thought should be given to optimising – and in some cases redrawing – existing trade and supply chain maps with a focus on the areas most affected by the crisis, which continues to be a stress test to the current system.

Trade facilitation initiatives in PTAs can be an important component of such endeavours. Countries seeking to improve their integration into global production networks could use the PTA track as a (complementary) tool in their efforts to remove border bottlenecks and transform them into gateways for their imports and exports. Consistently pursuing improved access to regional production networks could further promote the expansion of global value chains and enhance their resilience.

While substantive focus areas will differ, depending on the parties' circumstances and priorities, certain aspects frequently promise particular gains. Automation is one such area with considerable potential, especially in developing economies. Even in developed countries, there is noticeable room for improvement. The TFA does not once refer to automation when setting out its requirements due to reservations from some WTO Members at the time of its negotiation. And while concerns seem to have eased since then as automated systems have become widely used, it would not be easy to introduce upgraded requirements at the multilateral level – and certainly not a speedy process.

Enhancements are also still to be achieved on the other end of the technology spectrum, such as with respect to access to trade-related information. It may seem surprising, but the publication of that information featured prominently on the list of measures highlighted as meriting particular attention when identifying TFA measures with a special need for fast-track implementation (WTO Committee on Trade Facilitation, 2021a).

The COVID-19 crisis highlighted additional issues with particular relevance for enhancing supply chain resilience and keeping trade flows open, such as measures to facilitate the release and clearance of goods. A look at the TF initiatives taken by many governments at the onset of the pandemic shows that they often included improvements in the areas of electronic payment, separation of release from clearance, and pre-arrival processing. Measures were also taken to improve border agency cooperation and to accelerate the release of perishable goods. The majority of those measures were designed to be temporary in nature – and enacted with little leadup time – but the experience seems to have been positive, and several WTO Members saw merit in continued – and sometimes also accelerated – initiatives in those areas.[47]

4.12 NEW PROGRESS OR UNUSED POTENTIAL?

Some of the recent PTAs appear to already have taken those aspects on board. And while there may not have been seismic shifts when comparing them to their earlier counterparts, one can find a steady evolution towards more modern approaches and the incorporation of recent information technologies. Trade Facilitation Agreement-plus commitments are still largely limited to a few core areas (such as an increased call for the use of electronic means or alignment with specified international standards), but are noticeably more frequent than in PTAs from an earlier period. There are also several cases of added specificity, such as by introducing time limits for the completion of certain actions (like releasing goods or issuing advance rulings).

At the same time, progress remains incremental. Few of the recently concluded PTAs really seek to push facilitation to the next level. There are also still agreements with no or only very limited TF content,[48] as well as cases where substance is left to be defined in future, yet to be negotiated terms.[49]

[47] See WTO Committee on Trade Facilitation (2021a), WTO Committee on Trade Facilitation (2022).

[48] See, for instance, the PTAs between Turkey and Kosovo, Turkey and Moldova, or the EU and Armenia.

[49] See, for instance, the PTA between the UK and Eastern and Southern African countries.

Additional progress could especially be achieved in the area of digitalisation, where technological innovation continues to open up new possibilities – and where the TFA no longer reflects the latest state of play. The benefits of improvements in this area are substantial. A recent study for the Asia-Pacific region found that further acceleration of digital TF could cut average trade costs by more than 13 per cent (UNESCAP, 2021). This potential is increasingly recognised at the highest political levels, as reflected in G20 declarations and Ministerial statements. Calls for additional measures in this area are also repeatedly made by industry groups.[50] Several regional groupings, such as the Association of Southeast Asian Nations (ASEAN) or the Eurasian Economic Union already adopted strategies that include digital initiatives as a priority area.[51]

Introducing such reforms through the PTA channel would come with the benefit of a more flexible framework due to the absence of institutional constraints inherent to the WTO rulemaking machinery. While multilateral rules under the WTO umbrella remain the best option for achieving broad and sustainable advances, they are notoriously hard to agree upon and usually take a long time to become a reality.

Even for measures already included in the TFA, there is often room for taking reforms to the next level, or for at least accelerating their actual application on the ground. The design of the TFA's architecture makes implementation a gradual process, and its full impact will only emerge over time. According to the WTO's Trade Facilitation Agreement Database (WTO, 2023), six years after the TFA's entry into force, the global rate of implementation commitments stands at 76 per cent (see Figure 4.2).[52] Broken down by Members' levels of development, this number is noticeably lower, sometimes barely exceeding 40 per cent.[53]

Current implementation rates for measures that are widely considered to be particularly impactful are even lower. Global commitment to establishing a single window, for instance, only stands at slightly above 50 per cent (see Figure 4.3), even though the obligation is phrased in best endeavour terms (WTO, 2023). For developing countries and LDCs, the number does not even reach 40 per cent (see Figure 4.4) (WTO, 2023), despite the possibility of requesting capacity-building support.

Based on those commitments, it will take at least another twenty-five years until one can expect full single window implementation by all WTO Members. While

[50] Calls to this end were made at a Global Supply Chain Forum held at the WTO in June 2022. The Secretary General of the International Chamber of Commerce, for instance, said that 'More collaboration is needed to build common digital infrastructure that allows private operators to communicate with border agencies.' He advocated 'bold reforms', with more governments allowing instruments like bills of lading to be digitised (WTO 2022a).

[51] See, for instance, the ASEAN Digital Integration Framework (ASEAN 2018) or the EAEU's 'Strategy 2025' (EAEU 2020).

[52] Determined by Members' notifications and existing requirements for immediate application. Developed WTO Members are required to implement the entire TFA from the moment it entered into force (i.e. as of 22 February 2017). Their obligations are added to the calculation to the overall implementation commitment rate.

[53] Commitment rates by LDCs currently stand at slightly above 41 per cent. https://tfadatabase.org/. For additional information, see WTO (2023).

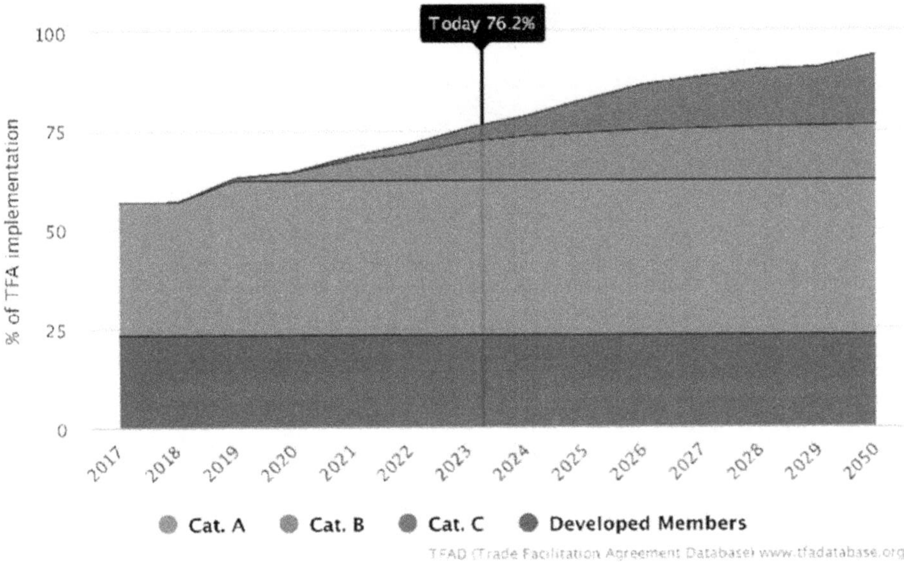

FIGURE 4.2 Timeline of TFA implementation commitments.
Source: WTO (2023), Trade Facilitation Agreement Database (TFAD), www.tfadatabase.org/en

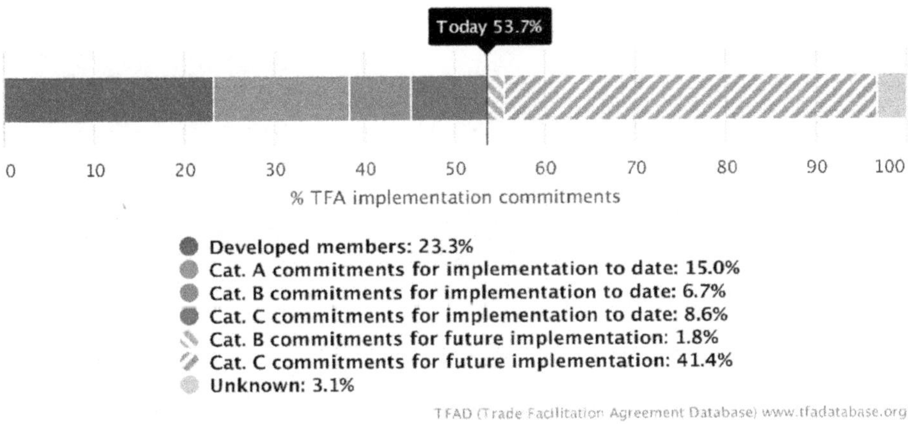

FIGURE 4.3 Implementation commitments for single window implementation – all members.
Source: WTO (2023), Trade Facilitation Agreement Database (TFAD), www.tfadatabase.org/en

the numbers continue to go up as transition periods expire, it will take a while for all reforms to be applied by the entire WTO membership and for all related benefits to fully kick in (see Figure 4.5).

Implementation rates of additional measures with particular relevance for facilitating the global exchange of goods also leave room for improvement. According to

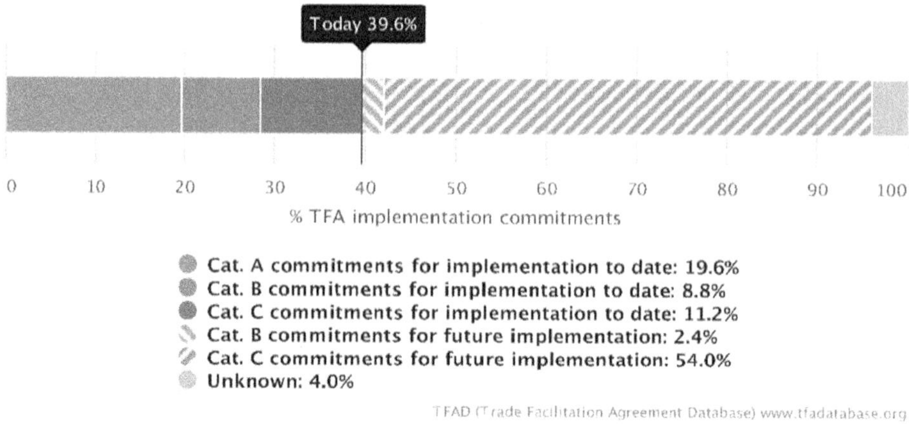

FIGURE 4.4 Single window implementation commitments – developing countries and LDCs.
Source: WTO (2023), Trade Facilitation Agreement Database (TFAD), www.tfadatabase.org/en

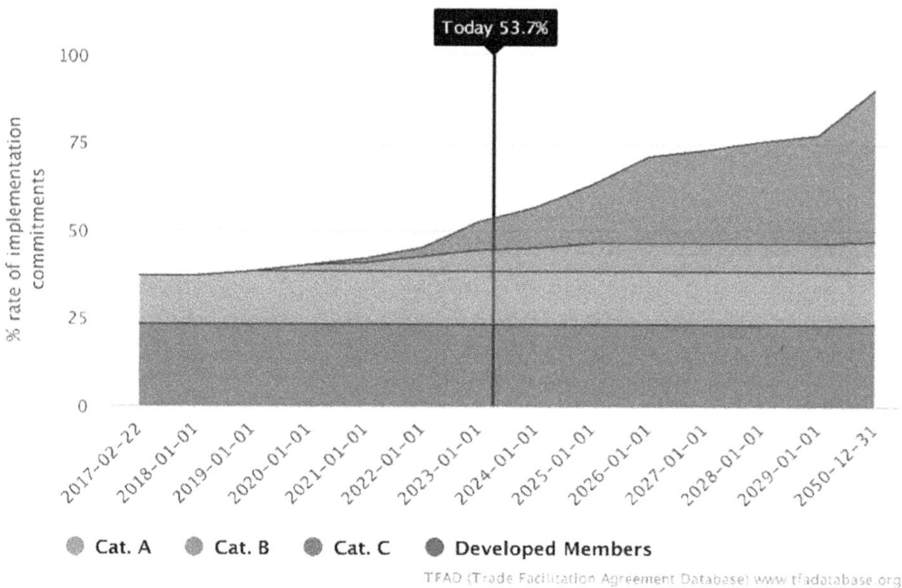

FIGURE 4.5 Global timeline of single window implementation commitments.
Source: WTO (2023), Trade Facilitation Agreement Database (TFAD), www.tfadatabase.org/en

the WTO's Trade Facilitation Agreement Database, little more than 60 per cent[54] of WTO Members have current commitments to implement the TFA's provisions

[54] The current global rate of notified implementation commitments stands at 62.9 per cent (WTO 2023).

regarding border agency cooperation, and this despite a considerable level of built-in flexibility (such as merely mandating collaboration among countries sharing a common border on mutually agreed terms and 'to the extent possible and practicable').[55] Risk management numbers are roughly the same level (63 per cent). Measures to reduce formalities and documentation requirements have currently been committed to by less than three-quarters of the WTO's membership, despite a series of built-in flexibilities.[56]

Many of these measures could be especially impactful when pursued in a consistent manner and with coverage of a large segment of global value chains. The recent COVID-19 crisis has already led to a few cases of concerted action in several PTAs, reducing various barriers to trade (such as simplified customs procedures and the introduction of expedited clearance channels).[57]

Engaging in such reforms would further come with the additional benefit of testing the ground for possible follow-up at the multilateral level, similar to the cross-fertilisation witnessed during the TFA negotiations when negotiators took inspiration from measures successfully applied in a regional setting.

4.13 TOWARDS TRADE FACILITATION 2.0

The increased focus on facilitating trade is happening despite – or perhaps, because of – the major headwinds that trade negotiators face in trying to advance a broader trade liberalisation and integration agenda. Already grappling with the fallout from COVID-19 lockdowns and escalating US–China trade frictions, negotiators are now confronting a host of new challenges arising from the Ukraine war, slowing global growth, and rising inflation. If this were not enough, UK negotiators face the additional task of trying to recast their country's international trade relations in the wake of the 2016 Brexit vote. This confluence of challenges – or 'poly-crises' – risks fuelling new protectionist pressures and undermining political support for further trade opening.

Yet, paradoxically, this unprecedented tsunami of problems has made TF all the more important. Today's increasingly integrated and interdependent global economy places a growing premium on TF – the ability to move resources, components, and finished goods swiftly and seamlessly across national borders. At the same time, digitalisation, automation and other technological innovations provide valuable new tools for making this happen. Although global initiatives in the WTO remain the first-best option for advancing trade facilitation efforts, the reality is that PTAs might offer the most viable pathway ahead in the near term because they involve like-minded countries, are generally easier to negotiate, and can be more easily tailored to reflect countries' technological capacities, financial resources, and trade needs.

[55] Article 8.2 of the TFA.

[56] The current number is 73.5 per cent (WTO 2023).

[57] For additional information, see World Bank Group and WTO (2022).

They can be especially impactful when pursued in a consistent, consolidated manner. As long as TF measures in PTAs are consistent with WTO rules, are non-discriminatory in their application, and aim to build upon its foundation, they can spearhead and advance TF innovations that could ultimately help inspire and guide future multilateral efforts. In doing so, they could also contribute to turning the vast web of regional TF reforms into a more streamlined trading regime that covers all key stakeholders in global supply chains and becomes part of a broader transformation of the global trade landscape.

In analysing how a new generation of PTAs might approach the continued need to facilitate trade, this chapter has suggested that the regional TF reforms with the potential to deliver the greatest positive, real-world impacts are those aimed at harnessing digitalisation, automation, and the use of other electronic means to modernise cross-border transactions and to ensure that national systems are interoperable and seamlessly integrated. Progress in these critical areas would not just elevate existing TFA requirements to a new level. More importantly, they would bring TF rules and disciplines up to date with modern trading realities. These changes are already underway in a growing number of practical cases. But there remains a task for negotiators to codify these practices – and the underlying innovation – and to anchor them in trade agreements so that new 'rules of the road' are transparent, predictable, and secure.

This chapter also argues these various regional efforts should, whenever possible, share common approaches, similar characteristics, and parallel goals – minimising the risk of conflict or confusion and maximising the potential for complementarity and convergence. This is particularly important when the focus is on addressing deeper, behind-the-border obstacles and when efforts to harness digitalisation and automation, almost by definition, need to be non-discriminatory. But while a renewed regional focus on TF rulemaking makes sense – and is clearly needed in a world of disrupted supply chains, rising inflation, and growing economic uncertainty – much work remains to be done. If more steps were to be taken in that direction, TF could be taken to the next level and, indeed, become a new frontier.

REFERENCES

APEC 2020. 'Declaration on Facilitating the Movement of Essential Goods by the APEC Ministers Responsible for Trade (MRT)', www.apec.org/Meeting-Papers/Sectoral-Ministerial-Meetings/Trade/2020_MRT/Annex-A

ASEAN 2018. 'Digital Integration Framework', https://asean.org/wp-content/uploads/2020/12/Adopted-ASEAN-Digital-Integration-Framework.pdf

Bourla, A. 2023. 'An Open Letter from Pfizer Chairman and CEO to Colleagues', www.pfizer.com/news/articles/why_pfizer_opposes_the_trips_intellectual_property_waiver_for_covid_19_vaccines

Duval, Y., Neufeld, N. and Utoktham, C. 2016. 'Do Trade Facilitation Provisions in Regional Trade Agreements Matter? Impact on Trade Costs and Multilateral Spillovers'. Asia-Pacific Research and Training Network on Trade working paper.

EAEU 2020. 'Strategic Directions for Developing the Eurasian Economic Integration until 2025', https://eec.eaeunion.org/en/comission/department/dep_razv_integr/strategicheskie-napravleniya-razvitiya.php
G20 2020. 'G20 Trade and Investment Ministerial Meeting: Ministerial Statement' (14 May 2020), www.g20.utoronto.ca/2020/2020-g20-trade-0514.html
JDSUPRA 2021. 'Pfizer CEO Pens Open Letter on COVID-19 Vaccine IP Waiver' (11 May 2021), www.jdsupra.com/legalnews/pfizer-ceo-pens-open-letter-on-covid-19-9412404/
Kieck, E. 2020. 'Trade Facilitation and Customs', in A. Mattoo, N. Rocha and M. Ruta (eds.), *Handbook of Deep Trade Agreements*. Washington, DC: World Bank.
Neufeld, N. 2014. 'Trade Facilitation Provisions Regional Trade Agreements: Traits and Trends', WTO Working Paper, ERSD-2014-01.
2016. 'Trade Facilitation under the Regional Trade Agreement Umbrella: Origins and Evolution', in R. Acharya (ed.), *Regional Trade Agreements and Multilateral Trading System*. Cambridge: Cambridge University Press.
Nicols, J. 2022. 'Leveraging WTO Rules to Combat Illicit Trade in Medical Products', WTO Working Paper, www.wto.org/english/tratop_e/markacc_e/illicit_trade_working_paper.pdf
OECD, Working Party of the Trade Committee, 2017. 'Trade Facilitation and the Global Economy: State of Play in 2017', TAD/TC/WP(2017)2/FINAL.
United Nations Economic and Social Commission for Asia and the Pacific – UNESCAP 2021. 'Asia-Pacific Trade Facilitation Report 2021: Supply Chains of Critical Goods Amid the COVID-19 Pandemic – Disruptions, Recovery, and Resilience', October 2021, www.unescap.org/kp/2021/APTF#
World Bank Group and WTO 2022. 'Trade Therapy: Deepening Cooperation to Strengthen Pandemic Defenses', https://thedocs.worldbank.org/en/doc/6cc7058e0f37323d7667fbd59fec3c58-0430012022/original/overview-trade-therapy-260622.pdf
WTO (n.d.). 'Trade Facilitation', www.wto.org/english/tratop_e/tradfa_e/tradfa_e.htm
(2008). 'Communication from Uganda and the United States', TN/TF/W/156, July 2008.
(2015). 'World Trade Report 2015. Speeding up Trade: Benefits and Challenges of Implementing the WTO Trade Facilitation Agreement'.
(2020). 'How WTO Members Have Used Trade Measures to Expedite Access to Covid-19 Critical Medical Goods and Services', 18 September 2020.
(2022a). 'Global Supply Chains Forum. Easing Supply Chain Bottlenecks for a Sustainable Future'. Event Report (21 March 2022), www.wto.org/english/news_e/events_e/report-gscforum2022_e.pdf
(2022b). 'Summary of Notified Export Restrictions and Trade Easing Measures Relating to the Covid-19 Pandemic', WTO Document G/MA/W/168/Rev.2, 29 March 2022.
(2022c). 'Tackling Illicit Trade in Medical Products, Better International Cooperation for Better Health' (July 2022), www.wto.org/english/news_e/news22_e/igo_27jul22_e.htm
(2023). 'Trade Facilitation Agreement Database (TFAD)', https://tfadatabase.org/
WTO Committee on Trade Facilitation (2021a). 'First Review of the Operation and Implementation of the Trade Facilitation Agreement (adopted at the meeting of 26 November 2021)', G/TFA/2, 30 November 2021.
(2021b). 'Supporting the Timely and Efficient Release of Global Goods Through Accelerated Implementation of the WTO Trade Facilitation Agreement', G/TFA/W/25/Rev.8, 2 December 2021.
(2022). 'Supporting the Timely and Efficient Release of Global Goods Through Accelerated Implementation of the WTO Trade Facilitation Agreement', G/TFA/W/25/Rev.9, 8 April 2022.
WTO General Council (2021). 'APEC Ministers Responsible for Trade Virtual Meeting'. Joint Statement 2021 (4–5 June 2021), WT/GC/232, 8 June 2021.

5

The Future Design of Intellectual Property Provisions in Preferential Trade Agreements

Three Propositions

María Vásquez Callo-Müller, Kholofelo Kugler, Marine Roux, Yinuo Liu, and Thomas Cottier

5.1 SETTING THE SCENE

The world is facing increasingly pressing challenges. Pandemics, the consequences of climate change, as well as the evolution of digital technologies, which the World Intellectual Property Organization (WIPO) has identified as twenty-first century challenges (WIPO, 2022), require a rapid and coordinated global response. Yet, the interfacing of these issues with intellectual property rights (IPR) protection revives age-old debates about the adequate level of IPR protection vis-à-vis other societal goals.

As the appetite to negotiate IPR rules at the multilateral level has slowed down, preferential trade agreements (PTAs) – long-standing instruments of trade policy – may constitute an opportunity to address these twenty-first century challenges, spearheading solutions that could be multilateralised in the future. In this chapter, we discuss the need to introduce a 'balanced' approach in future IPR PTA policy-making – one that reconciles far-reaching PTA's IPR provisions (TRIPS-plus) with corresponding flexibilities. We do so by structuring this chapter into two parts. Part 1 sets the scene, first providing a brief overview of the history and economics of international IPR. It then addresses the evolution of IPR within PTAs. Finally, it introduces the need to combine higher IPR standards with increased flexibility (what we call a 'balanced approach'). Part 2 delves deeper into the three twenty-first century case study challenges selected for this analysis.

5.1.1 *Overview of the History and Economics of International IPR*

The historical link between the protection of IPR and trade is well documented (Drahos, 1998; Ricketson, 2018; Abbott et al., 2019). It traces its origins back to the nineteenth century and the need to establish minimum standards of IPR protection across borders so that inventors' and authors' intellectual property (IP) could be protected in overseas markets. The 'first globalisation wave' and the Second Industrial Revolution, in the late nineteenth century/early twentieth century, led to enhanced trade and investment worldwide, showcasing the need to establish rules and standards for the protection of IPR at the international level. Such rules and standards were later embedded in international treaties. The Paris Convention for the Protection of Industrial Property (1883) established industrial protection through patents, trademarks, and industrial designs. The Berne Convention for the Protection of Literary and Artistic Works (1886) established the protection of authors' rights. The Madrid Agreement (1891) established an international registration system for trademarks. These agreements further led to the foundation of the United International Bureaux for the Protection of Intellectual Property in Bern, Switzerland, in 1893, which was subsequently replaced in 1970 by the World Intellectual Property Organisation (WIPO), headquartered in Geneva, Switzerland.

The link between IPR protection and trade is further reinforced by the adoption in 1995 of the Trade-Related Aspects of Intellectual Property Rights (TRIPS) Agreement,[1] which incorporates by reference several provisions of these earlier IP treaties. The TRIPS Agreement sets out minimum standards of IPR for all members of the World Trade Organization (WTO). Unlike previous IPR conventions, it has the additional peculiarity of providing most-favoured-nation (MFN) treatment – a cornerstone principle of trade law. The MFN principle in Article 4 of the TRIPS Agreement provides that 'any advantage, favour, privilege or immunity granted by a [WTO] Member to the nationals of any other country shall be accorded immediately and unconditionally to the nationals of all other [WTO] Members'. Few exceptions are envisaged in this rule, one of them being the case of customs unions (Cottier, 2022). However, with regard to all other advantages, favours, privileges, and immunities, including those found in PTAs, the MFN principle is applicable. This means that third-party WTO Members are entitled to MFN treatment in any PTA involving at least one WTO Member. The MFN provision contributes to the common law of international IP protection (Cottier, 2015).

The historical link between IPR and trade law and policy also has underlying economic considerations. IPR, according to the economic literature, contribute to addressing the market failures associated with the nature of public goods (typically, non-rival and non-excludable) and information asymmetry. Patents, one type of IPR, provide quasi-monopoly rights for inventors, granting them incentives to invest in the research and development (R&D) of public goods (Maskus, 2000, 2022). Moreover, IPR can enhance the dissemination of knowledge through technology transfer. Although a specific invention/technology cannot be used during the

[1] Agreement on Trade-Related Aspects of Intellectual Property Rights, 15 April 1994, Marrakesh Agreement Establishing the World Trade Organization, Annex 1C, 1869 U.N.T.S. 299, 33 I.L.M.

protected time, Lall (2003) shows that the disclosure of the patents' full description may lead to innovations 'around' the patented technology (i.e. innovators can still use some of the knowledge enclosed in the patent). In other cases, IPR can reduce asymmetries of information for consumers. For example, geographical indications (GIs) and trademarks, two types of IPR, provide guarantees on products' characteristics and origins.

Despite the positive effects of the creation of knowledge and innovation described above, IPR have also been criticised for their adverse effects. First, higher levels of IPR protection could potentially translate into higher prices as innovators and other patent holders benefit from a temporary or lasting monopoly. The higher prices would affect not only consumers but also producers who depend on the invention as input for the production of other goods. In addition, there is a risk that temporary monopolies can slow down economic activity through the lack of competitors and potentially lead to monopoly abuse (Lall, 2003). The regulation of standard essential patents and the obligation to license such patents under fair, reasonable, and non-discriminatory (FRAND) terms is an example of measures taken to offset the risks of the abuse of patent protection. Second, the spillover effects of IPR on the economy have been debated. According to Maskus (2000), '*[t]he evidence suggests that there are large spillover gains from major inventions, while IPR on smaller inventions generally do not create significant monopoly rents*'. In a more recent study, Kelly et al. (2021) traced technological waves based on patent text similarity and showed that patented breakthrough innovations have a long-lasting impact on technological change. There remains, however, limited evidence of the impact of smaller innovations. Third, opponents of IPR also pointed out its opacity. Trade secrets, by nature, prevent the dissemination of information. Information on patents and trademarks is only accessible once published (often eighteen months after the patent filing, which varies across countries).[2]

However, empirical evidence regarding IPR, innovation, and growth is mixed. Neves et al. (2021) conducted a meta-analysis showing that many studies led to different results when looking at the impact of IPR on innovation and growth. Beyond disparities caused by different data and methods used, IPR have an overall positive impact on innovation and growth. Yet this impact may vary depending on a country's level of development and technology (Lall, 2003; Neves et al., 2021). Countries with high levels of economic development are more likely to have strong IPR. As countries develop, there is increased demand from producers for IPR (as more businesses/inventors engage in innovation) and more capacity from governments to establish and enforce those rights (Shadlen et al., 2005). On the contrary, countries with lower innovative capacity have a higher interest in weak IPR in order to facilitate the imitation of foreign technologies. Developing economies typically

[2] WIPO, 'Frequently Asked Questions: Patents', www.wipo.int/patents/en/faq_patents.html, accessed on 6 June 2023.

have fewer resources to innovate and less government capacity and therefore derive fewer benefits from IPR (Lall, 2003; Shadlen et al., 2005). As countries' level of development increases, they have more interests in raising IPR standards to promote domestic innovations (Chen and Puttitanun, 2005; Chu et al., 2014). Empirically, the positive impact of strengthening IPR on growth and welfare increases as a country's innovative capacity comes closer to the world technology frontier and participation in world trade. IPR will also generate more innovation spillovers across businesses/sectors the higher the current levels of in-country innovation (Lall, 2003). This leads to great variations in countries' levels of domestic IPR and can further generate trade conflicts (Maskus, 2000, 2022).

One might argue that IPR, which establish temporary quasi-monopoly rights, go against the idea of trade liberalism and the progressive decrease in barriers to trade. However, Snorrason (2012) contends there are instances in which trade barriers might be preferable, including when they compensate for market failure. The multilateral and bilateral coordination for setting common IPR standards, be it at the WTO- or PTAs-level, addresses those market failures internationally. Yet, those who benefit are the ones better equipped to take advantage of it. Maskus and Ridley (2021), for instance, find a significant impact of IPR provisions in PTAs involving the United States (US), the European Union (EU), or parties to the European Free Trade Association (EFTA) on exports. Export-competing industries of these countries benefit from protection to produce abroad.

5.1.2 *International IPR Protection within PTAs*

PTAs, as laboratories of higher standards of IPR protection, often go beyond the minimum standards established by the TRIPS Agreement, in part to compensate for tremendous changes in technology and business practices in the past decades (Ezell and Cory, 2019) and in part because these changes, and their implications for IPR protection, have not been reflected in multilateral treaties. The trend to include higher standards of protection for IPR through PTAs, which accelerated during the 1990s–2000s, was mostly led by the US and the EU, followed by other technology-based economies, such as Japan and Switzerland (Cottier 2017b; Cottier et al., 2017). These standards set in these PTAs are known as TRIPS-plus provisions. In the long run, these enhanced standards are likely to facilitate and influence future multilateral developments, in particular in revising the TRIPS Agreement due to the dialectical relationship between bilateral agreements, plurilateral agreements, and multilateral agreements and the pervasive effect of MFN in the areas of IP (Cottier et al., 2015).

Developed and developing countries undertake TRIPS-plus commitments in a different way. The US is one of the most vocal advocates of TRIPS-plus provisions in PTAs. The North American Free Trade Agreement (NAFTA) was the first PTA to include an IPR chapter in 1994, a year before the TRIPS Agreement entered into force. In 2020, NAFTA was replaced by the Agreement between the United States of America, the United Mexican States, and Canada (USMCA), incorporating even more comprehensive TRIPS-plus provisions. The origins of these provisions can be traced back to the Trans-Pacific Partnership Agreement (TPP). Other US PTAs also showcase heightened TRIPS-plus standards of protection in areas such as pharmaceutical patents, amplify governance on digital goods copyrights, and augment penalties for IPR breach (Maskus and Ridley, 2021).

The EU has also acted as a rule-maker by advocating TRIPS-plus provisions. However, unlike the US, the EU has only slowly pushed for TRIPS-plus provisions in its PTAs since 2008 (Erixon et al., 2022). This is partly due to the wider enhancement of the EU's trade policy, which envisages a more active use of PTAs as an economic policy tool. The EU approach favours far-reaching provisions on enforcement and GIs. For example, the 2008 Economic Partnership Agreement (EPA) signed between the EU and the Caribbean Forum (CARIFORUM) includes provisions specifically concentrating on enforcement, which is unprecedented (Spence, 2009). The language adopted here is substantially identical to the EU's original proposal, which was transferred essentially from EU domestic comprehensive instruments on enforcement. The breadth and scope of these obligations raises major concerns over the administrative and judicial systems in CARIFORUM countries (Center for International Environmental, 2008). In the 2012 EU–Colombia/Peru Trade Agreement (which Ecuador joined in 2017), the three Andean parties must amend current or enact new GI legislation to comply with their obligations (Viju et al., 2013).

Since the first comprehensive PTAs (e.g. NAFTA) were concluded, TRIPS-plus provisions permeated into the negotiation of subsequent PTAs. This is an aspect that has been studied by a wealth of literature; nonetheless, there are interesting developments worth highlighting. For example, Australia and Canada's PTA practice, which traditionally followed the US lead on TRIPS-plus provisions, reveals that these countries might be reconsidering their approach to IP provisions negotiated in their PTAs. Australia has shown less ambition to conclude a stringent IP chapter with TRIPS-plus provisions in multiple fields (Townsend et al., 2016). Moreover, Australia previously resisted some of the IPR provisions included in the TPP, which were removed from the Comprehensive and Progressive Agreement for Trans-Pacific Partnership (CPTPP) (Australian Government Department of Foreign Affairs and Trade, 2019). It has also recently started implementing the Regional Comprehensive Economic Partnership (RCEP), which contains less stringent TRIPS-plus provisions, which were mostly proposed and pushed by Japan and Korea. The RCEP incorporates a few critical TRIPS-plus articles regarding public health and none concerning IP enforcement.

On the other hand, Canada has kept pace with negotiating stringent TRIPS-plus provisions, following the path established by the US and EU. The Canada–EU Comprehensive Economic and Trade Agreement (CETA), for instance, contains strong TRIPS-plus provisions for GIs, mostly proposed by the EU (European Union, 2019). In this agreement, Canada has accepted the obligation to protect all types of food products in the EU's proposal at a comparable level to that offered under EU law, thereby raising the standards of protection for GIs in Canada. On Canada's side, even though the CETA essentially changes the current domestic IP protection framework vis-à-vis EU products, domestic companies from different IP-related industries generally support the significant enhancement of IPR. Representatives from Canadian pharmaceutical research companies claim that the CETA would strengthen the IP system and robust industrial innovation, which would help the healthcare sector and the Canadian economy (House of Commons Canada, 2012).

In contrast, developing countries usually tend to accept TRIPS-plus provisions in PTAs because of political or economic concerns (Maskus and Ridley, 2017). China had an early start to concluding IP-only bilateral agreements with the US to counteract the lack of IP protection in China. Over the years, China has joined multilateral agreements on IPR and increased its internal IP legal and administrative capacities, while gradually pursuing stronger IP protection in its PTAs (Yu, 2019; Shaffer and Gao, 2021). Notwithstanding its economic power, China, like other developing countries, has accepted TRIPS-plus provisions as trade-offs. As part of the Economic and Trade Agreement between the Government of the United States of America and the Government of the People's Republic of China, 2020 (US–China Phase One Trade Agreement), China agreed to reform the economic and trade regime in IPR in exchange for the US' modification of its Section 301 tariffs actions (Upreti and Vasquez Callo-Müller, 2020). In comparison, the RCEP, an agreement led by China, adopts a moderate approach to IPR.

India, on the other hand, has only recently taken up substantive IPR obligations in its PTAs. India eventually dropped out of the RCEP negotiations in 2019 for domestic political reasons (Mohamad and Cheng, 2020). The final agreement contains an extensive (but modest in terms of TRIPS-plus standards) IP chapter. Since 2002, India has concluded PTAs with IP chapters with selected trading partners. Of its thirteen fully fledged FTAs[3] only those with the United Arab Emirates (UAE), Japan, and South Korea include these obligations. The UAE Agreement is the most extensive, containing TRIPS-plus provisions, largely modelled after RCEP's IP chapter. The rest of its PTAs, however, which are mainly with other developing countries, do not have IPR chapters. Interestingly, the 2022 agreement with Australia (a developed country), also does not have IPR provisions (Government of India (Ministry of Commerce and Industry), 2023).

The divergent approaches to IPR protection in PTAs showcase that the negotiation of TRIPS-plus protection is not a given and that the shaping of international IP

[3] India signed other trade agreements, more limited in scope, with Afghanistan, Chile, and Mercosur and is also part of the Asia-Pacific Trade Agreement, the Global System of Trade Preferences, and the South Asian Free Trade Area.

norms has evolved, in certain ways, away from traditional US or EU approaches. In the following section, we discuss the need to combine the ever-proliferating TRIPS-plus provisions with flexibility in PTAs to create a more balanced approach to the global IP regulatory framework.

5.1.3 *Combining Higher Standards and Flexibility: Towards a More Balanced Approach*

In raising the standards of IPR protection and by including new obligations, TRIPS-plus agreements have been subject to persistent critique: they are considered to erode policy space to regulate issues such as access to medicines and climate change. Such critiques have been accentuated by the understanding of IP (and TRIPS-plus standards) as protected investments under international investment agreements (IIAs). This opens the possibility of bringing claims against a state under investor–state dispute settlement mechanisms,[4] exposing the complex interaction between the IP and IIA regimes. The '*investmentisation* of intellectual property' carries the risk that the IP sets aside its societal objectives 'so that the sole incentive rationale protection of IP protection becomes investment protection' (Upreti, 2022). In addition, by moving beyond the standards of protection found in multilateral IP treaties, TRIPS-plus agreements are deemed to affect the balance between IP protection and other societal interests (Dinwoodie and Dreyfuss, 2012). This balance is embedded in Article 7 of the TRIPS Agreement, which provides as follows:

> The protection and enforcement of intellectual property rights should contribute to the promotion of technological innovation and to the transfer and dissemination of technology, to the mutual advantage of producers and users of technological knowledge and in a manner conducive to social and economic welfare, and to a *balance of rights and obligations.* (emphasis added)

This perspective finds support in how TRIPS-plus agreements are negotiated, that is, in secrecy and without public scrutiny.

Notwithstanding these critiques, the flexibilities included in recent TRIPS-plus agreements – in the form of limitations and exceptions to certain IP rights – are less explored in the legal academic literature. For example, certain agreements include provisions on 'balance in copyright and related rights systems', which aim to provide

[4] High profile cases include: *Philip Morris Brands Sàrl, Philip Morris Products S.A. and Abal Hermanos S.A. v. Oriental Republic of Uruguay*, ICSID Case No. ARB/10/7, Award (8 July 2016); *Eli Lilly and Company v. The Government of Canada*, UNCITRAL, ICSID Case No. UNCT/14/2, Award (16 March 2017); *Bridgestone Licensing Services, Inc. and Bridgestone Americas, Inc. v. Republic of Panama*, ICSID Case No. ARB/16/34, Award (14 August 2020); *Theodore David Einarsson, Harold Paul Einarsson and Russell John Einarsson v. Canada*, UNCITRAL, Notice of Arbitration (18 April 2019).

more leeway for a country to design its copyright policy in a way that may be more conducive, for example, to innovation in the digital realm (Vásquez Callo-Müller 2023). This is the case of Article 18.66 of the CPTPP, which provides that:

> Each Party shall endeavour to achieve an appropriate balance in its copyright and related rights system, among other things by means of limitations or exceptions that are consistent with Article 18(65), including those for the digital environment, giving due consideration to legitimate purposes such as, but not limited to: criticism; comment; news reporting; teaching, scholarship, research, and other similar purposes; and facilitating access to published works for persons who are blind, visually impaired or otherwise print disabled.

But also, more recent PTAs, such as RCEP, contain innovative provisions not observed before in TRIPS-plus agreements. Namely, Article 11(18) (4) provides that a party may adopt or maintain limitations or exceptions to copyright for fair use, a notion present in domestic US copyright law,[5] but largely absent in other jurisdictions. Fair use is deemed to provide enough flexibility for digital industries to innovate (Sag, 2019), and to some, it has been considered to be one of the factors allowing the development of technology hubs such as Silicon Valley (Chander, 2015).

These examples showcase, as Baccini et al. (2015) have previously argued, that there is a link between the depth of PTAs and the flexibilities included in these same agreements – 'deeper PTAs are more flexible' (Baccini et al., 2015). While we acknowledge that TRIPS-plus agreements include higher standards of protection for IPR, we consider that it is similarly important to observe to what extent new limitations and exceptions to IPR are included in these treaties.

First, PTAs precisely enable leveraging flexibility in IPR provisions (Trimble, 2022), which will be key in tackling these challenges to strike a better balance between reaping a return on investment and societal benefits. Reducing IPR standards as such is unlikely to facilitate better access to medicines or enhance the development of new climate change-mitigating technology across the world. There is a need to promote domestic governments' and businesses' innovative capacity. We suggest technology transfer could be carried out by establishing public–private partnerships (PPPs) to ensure access to medicines in countries with lower levels of technological innovation. This would enable policymakers to strike a balance between ensuring access to medicines in countries with lower levels of technological innovation while incentivising pharmaceutical companies to pursue R&D. Technology transfer could also be enhanced through granting tax rebates to businesses investing in green technologies in low-income countries and redistributive funds to further promote technology dissemination. Additional flexibility in PTAs can also mitigate adverse effects of the increased use of trade secrets. Unlike other

[5] US Copyright Act, Section 107.

types of IPR (e.g. patents, trademarks, GIs), trade secrets hinder information dissemination and technology transfer opportunities. In the context of the digital revolution, the increasing use of trade secrets can lead to fewer innovation spillovers in other sectors, security threats, and information asymmetries with users. We suggest that PTAs could help to harmonise rules on setting limitations and exceptions to trade secrets.

Second, PTAs constitute a better tool than the multilateral fora to negotiate such provisions. Multilateral fora have encountered many barriers to negotiating IPR (although not limited to this area). Since the TRIPS Agreement, no major IPR agreements have been signed or updated as part of the WTO framework. The IPR question was dropped from the WTO's Doha Round agenda. The Anti-Counterfeiting Trade Agreement (ACTA) was signed in 2011 by ten countries outside the WTO (and WIPO) and has still not been ratified by all (Morin and Surbeck, 2019). Since the mid-1990s, the WIPO has been a more active and successful multilateral negotiation forum leading to the signature of six treaties. Most of these treaties expanded the scope of existing international IPR agreements to include digital creations and promote harmonisation across domestic IPR procedures.[6] Nevertheless, countries have increasingly turned to the use of PTAs, allowing them to simultaneously negotiate a wide range of market access issues at a faster pace. Indeed, multilateral negotiations gather countries with many different interests increasing transaction costs and time required to negotiate. The COVID-19 pandemic has shed light on the difficulties for WTO Members to reach an agreement given the time limitations and high divergence in countries' interests. PTAs, in turn, involve low[er] transaction costs with often a limited number of members. Further, Trimble (2022) argues bilateral and plurilateral negotiations of IPR provisions can leave more room for countries to experiment with different types of standards and set the ground for further multilateral agreements. Lastly, as previously mentioned, Article 4 of the TRIPS Agreement includes MFN treatment for all IPR provisions in PTAs, giving the latter a multilateral nature almost by default.

In the following subsections, we analyse how this proposed balanced approach in PTAs could contribute to meeting the needs of 'twenty-first century challenges', namely, global health pandemics, climate change, and digital technologies.

[6] The WIPO Copyright Treaty (WCT) and the WIPO Performances and Phonograms Treaty (WPPT) were both signed in 1996 and established IPR of authors, performers, and producers of phonograms in the context of the digital environment. The Patent Law Treaty (2000) harmonised patenting procedures across national and regional systems. The Singapore Treaty (2006) harmonised procedures for registering trademarks. The Beijing Treaty (2012) established IPR of audiovisual performers. The Marrakesh Treaty (2013) authorised exceptions to copyright rules to facilitate published content access to people with visual disability. The Geneva Act (2015) extended the scope of the Lisbon Agreement to geographical indications.

5.2 THREE MAIN AREAS OFFERING A MORE BALANCED APPROACH

5.2.1 *Access to Essential Medical Products and PPPs*

The COVID-19 pandemic exposed, in a dramatic fashion, the tension between IPR and access to medical products. The world experienced, in real time, confined in our homes, the clear delineation between the haves and have-nots when prioritising access to COVID-19 vaccines and related medical products. The geopolitics of COVID-19 vaccine access spun off a slew of new terms such as 'vaccine inequity' (Tatar et al., 2021), 'vaccine nationalism' (Bollyky and Bown, 2020; Liz, 2022), 'vaccine diplomacy' (Suzuki and Yang, 2022), and 'vaccine apartheid' (Joseph and Dore, 2022), to mention a few.

The challenges in accessing COVID-19 vaccines and medical products occurred notwithstanding the flexibilities granted to WTO Members under the TRIPS Agreement. Articles 31 and 31*bis* of the TRIPS Agreement permit countries to issue compulsory licenses on patented products in times of national health emergencies, both for domestic production and, under specific conditions, also for exports. The issued compulsory licences also cover the importation of these potentially life-saving medical products if the issuing country does not have the domestic capacity to produce them. However, there are practical and legal challenges to using this system to access essential medical products. Among others, the compulsory licence regime only applies to patents and the procedures to access these products, established in the annex of the TRIPS Agreement, are complex (Sucker and Kugler, 2022).

COVID-19 medical products (including vaccines) are not only protected by patents but also by, potentially, copyrights, industrial designs, and trade secrets. Unlike patents (and some copyrights), there is no mechanism for issuing compulsory licences for these IPR under the TRIPS Agreement (Sucker and Kugler, 2022). Therefore, while suspending patent protection goes far, it does not guarantee access to a specific medical product if it is covered by other IPR that are *not* subject to the TRIPS flexibilities.

Compulsory licences are often issued by countries for domestic public health emergencies. These licenses are regularly issued by countries to authorise the production of medical products that are owned by mainly Western pharmaceutical companies. These transactions rarely involve the home state of the pharmaceutical company (Feldman, 2009; Epstein and Kieff, 2011; Moser and Voena, 2012; Urias and Ramani, 2020). In contrast, the WTO's compulsory licensing regime has, thus far, only been used once. This regime was established under Paragraph 6 of the 2001 Doha Declaration on the TRIPS Agreement and Public Health and was subsequently incorporated into the TRIPS Annex under its paragraphs 2(a) and 2(c).

The single time the 'Paragraph 6' procedures were used was when a Canadian firm, Apotex, wished to export an anti-retroviral (Apo-TriAvir) to Rwanda (Epstein and Kieff, 2011; Correa, 2019). This initiative was initiated by Doctors Without

Borders to test the Paragraph 6 mechanism and the suitability of the Canadian legislation, the Canadian Access to Medicines Regime, which was adopted in 2004 to implement Paragraph 6. One of the challenges was that the active ingredients of Apo-TriAvir were protected under a patent held by Canadian companies Boehringer Ingelheim (Canada) Ltd and GlaxoSmithKline Inc., Canada. Thus, Apotex had to first request a voluntary licence from these companies. It is reported that the company lost USD 3–4 million by offering a lower price to win Rwanda's tender to compete with lower-cost products from other countries, including India. Apotex initiated the process in December 2005. However, the first batch of Apo-TriAvir was shipped to Rwanda in September 2008, almost three years after the process began (Correa, 2019). To underscore the scepticism with which WTO Members (especially developing countries) regard the TRIPS Annex paragraphs 2(a) and 2(c) procedures, even with the massive health crisis that the entire world faced during the COVID-19 pandemic, only Bolivia submitted a notification to use the system in May 2021 (WTO, 2021).

Another issue plaguing the compulsory licensing procedures under the TRIPS Agreement is the fact that, currently, only twenty-five WTO Members have notified their national implementing legislation to facilitate these procedures (WTO, 2022a). Noticeably absent from this list is the US, which has a large pharmaceutical industry and even South Africa, which, with India, was the original co-sponsor of the WTO's COVID-19 TRIPS Waiver (WTO, 2022b). The waiver, which was adopted at the WTO's 12th Ministerial Conference in June 2022, establishes a special temporary regime for WTO Members to produce COVID-19 vaccines without the permission of the patent holder. A major advantage of the waiver is that countries that have not adopted the requisite national implementing legislation can access the TRIPS Agreement flexibilities that allow them to participate as exporting or importing countries, respectively.

The counterarguments provided against the use of the WTO's compulsory licensing mechanism have largely been centred around the possible negative effects of using compulsory licences in general. Commentators argue that these instruments discourage innovation in the pharmaceutical sector. They further posit that the frequent use of compulsory licenses will lead to more global health suffering because pharmaceutical companies will be disincentivised from innovating, as they will not be able to recover returns on their investments. Moreover, they argue that pharmaceutical companies will invest less in developing countries because they know that developing country firms will just obtain the right to produce generics of their medical products through compulsory licences. It is moreover argued that economic growth will decline in traditional knowledge economies that rely on strong IPR protection (like the US) (Feldman, 2009). Another argument is that other mechanisms, like price negotiations and voluntary licences, are more effective in facilitating access to medication than compulsory licenses (Beall et al., 2015; Raju, 2017; Ramani and Urias, 2018).

Some have also argued that the current IP regime has sufficient flexibility to allow countries in need to access medical products. Hence, the problem is not high IPR protection but rather the supply of the products (including key ingredients) (Ozili and Arun, 2020; WTO, 2022a) and logistics, infrastructure, and manufacturing capacity, the latter three being attributed to developing countries themselves (Organisation for Economic Co-operation and Development (OECD), 2021, Sucker and Kugler, 2022). Indeed, the lead-up to the adoption of the WTO's COVID-19 TRIPS Waiver garnered international attention and captured the global imagination because it was framed in the popular media as a David versus Goliath issue (Cviticanin, 2021; Das, 2021): the 'suffering' developing countries that do not have pharmaceutical IPR versus the 'evil' developed countries that have those rights and are denying the poorer countries access to, inter alia, critical COVID-19 vaccines. Essentially, the debate was focused on the barriers that IPR created for equitable access to medicines and medical products. However, a less sensationalised issue was the fact that most developing countries do not have the capacity to manufacture medical products and face severe infrastructural and technical skills shortages – even if the IPR were waived (Sucker and Kugler, 2022).

The above sketches a polemic global debate on the balance of IPR and access to essential medicines in pandemics and other public health crises. This conversation has become even more relevant because global pandemics have been projected to increase in number and frequency in the future (Marani et al., 2021). Due to the current impasse at the WTO, it is unlikely that the multilateral legal framework will change – this presents an opportunity for PTAs to cover the regulatory shortfall.

Currently, most concluded PTAs, including those that were concluded recently, only reinforce the WTO legal framework on TRIPS and public health (EU–UK TCA, Article 250; EU–New Zealand FTA, Article 18.71; RCEP, Article 11.8; and India–UAE CEPA, Article 11.6). Some recognise that the parties are not prevented from taking measures to protect public health (CPTPP, Article 18.6; India–UAE CEPA, Article 11.6; RCEP, Article 11.8). The China–New Zealand FTA Upgrade Agreement (2021) contains few substantive commitments. However, a provision has been included on cooperation and capacity building, where the parties undertake to encourage and facilitate 'cooperation between their respective government agencies, educational institutions and other organizations with an interest in the field of intellectual property rights' (Article 164(2)). It is anticipated that countries might use provisions like this to address access to medical products in public health crises.

We consider that future PTAs might include undertakings, in the form of non-binding provisions or, more likely, side letters or memoranda of understanding on facilitating PPPs. Through this, cooperation between the government, research-based industries, and civil society organisations (CSOs) steps in where market forces are insufficient to bring about adequate supplies and care to those in need (de Vries and Yehoue 2013). These undertakings seek to strengthen medicine and medical product-related manufacturing capacity in less resourced countries so that they can be less reliant on imports from better-resourced countries in global medical emergencies, while protecting IPR held by mainly developed country firms.

Indeed, there are already global PPP initiatives like the COVID-19 Vaccines Global Access (COVAX) Facility, Gavi (the Vaccine Alliance), and the World Health Organization's mRNA technology transfer hub and its COVID-19 Technology Access Pool (C-TAP). Resources are pooled to support the research, development, and distribution of COVID-19 vaccines, and their prices are negotiated (Berkley, 2020). Moreover, trusted platforms are provided for the developers of COVID-19 medical products to share their IP, knowledge, and data with high-quality manufacturers in countries that require affordable access to medical products through transparent, voluntary, and non-exclusive licences. These platforms also facilitate technology transfer agreements. Ultimately, through voluntary licensing and patent pooling, IP holders can reach new markets and increase production by using the untapped capacity of manufacturers around the world, while securing appropriate royalties. Simultaneously, the World Health Organization (WHO) and its partners provide capacity-building and technical assistance to more manufacturers to produce high-quality essential COVID-19 medical products, while increasing access and affordability of those products (Bosch, n.d.; WHO/Bosch, n.d.).

We thus submit that in the context of bilateral or even plurilateral PTAs, provisions could be included that obligate countries that are strong in pharmaceutical R&D and wish to protect their IPR to enter into PPPs with their pharmaceutical industries, government, and respective NGOs. These partnerships, under the auspices of the PTA, will allow the development of cooperation between research-based industries, local institutions, government agencies, and CSOs. It will enable bringing about knowledge and technology transfer by means of publicly funded voluntary licensing to local producers and securing adequate distribution and administration of medicines in the health system. This model directly addresses the weakness of domestic productive capacity in some developing countries and efforts to improve it, while maintaining IPR protection for the pharmaceutical industry.

More concretely, this type of provision could be included in already existing sections on the TRIPS Agreement and Public Health that are included in the IP chapters of most PTAs. Alternatively, a section on Cooperation During Public Health Crises can be added to the IP chapter. We propose to include the following provisions:

- The supporting state party would undertake to conclude PPPs with its pharmaceutical companies and CSOs to provide jointly funded technical assistance to pharmaceutical manufacturers in countries needing support to produce and disseminate medical products.
- The supporting country and industry will collaborate with the beneficiary government to identify the industry beneficiaries, health institutions, and

CSOs that will participate in the technical assistance and capacity-building and dissemination efforts.

- The supporting industry will permit the manufacture of the medical products under jointly funded voluntary licenses and share the requisite data, information, and know-how required to manufacture these products.
- The beneficiary government will protect the IPR of the supporting government and industry, and the beneficiary industry will not act in any manner to contravene IP laws or any confidentiality agreement they conclude.
- A Medical Product Knowledge Transfer Working Group will be established, which will comprise all the partners (and interested parties, including civil society and academia). They will meet periodically and review the efficacy of the cooperation.

5.2.2 *Diffusion of Sustainable Technologies and Knowledge*

As the discussion of PPPs in the health sector indicates, fundamental questions relating to access to technology have not been properly addressed in WTO law and have not been adequately addressed in PTAs (Brewer and Falke, 2012; Brewer, 2016). They are of particular importance in the context of trade and climate change (Delimatsis, 2016). While the framework for technology diffusion by means of voluntary licensing is workable for commercial transactions and is successful among industrialised and emerging economies, it fails to address the needs of lower-income countries short of finance and funding and a private sector able to engage forcefully by means of commercial acquisition of technology (Lybecker and Lohnse, 2015; Barton 2017; Zhuang, 2017). Low-income countries depend on concessionary aid and development cooperation which in turn depends on budgetary allocations of scarce funds in industrialised countries. At least in policy areas recognised as a common concern of humankind, such as climate change, loss of biodiversity, or health (Cottier 2021a, 2021b), this should change. Proper tools are needed to compensate for market failures as all share a common interest in effectively addressing these common concerns around the globe. It is no longer a matter of concessionary aid. It is a matter of effectively implementing and realising shared policy goals of equal interest to developed and developing countries alike.

Achieving these policy goals increasingly depends on the adoption of modern and sustainable modes and processes of production. These methods, in return, depend on access to advanced technologies. Access to such technologies thus moves centre stage in the process of shifting product standards to standards of process and production methods (PPMs) (Conrad, 2011; Holzer, 2014). Developing countries are more likely to accept PPMs, perceived as non-tariff barriers to their exports, if state-of-the-art technology for producing these exports in a sustainable manner is made available. In this process, IPR are important (Ockwell et al., 2010; Ockwell and Mallet, 2012).

Two types of measures should be contemplated in a new generation of PTAs with developing countries, next to concessionary aid support programmes and PPPs. Based on WTO law, they contribute to the common law of international trade (Cottier, 2015) as all WTO Members arguably will be entitled to benefit, as discussed above, from the benefits of such IPR-related measures due to the application of MFN (Cottier, 2022). PTAs could serve to develop and spearhead a set of ideas as discussed next.

5.2.2.1 Tax Rebates for Technology Dissemination

Commitments and pledges on the transfer of knowledge and technology in international agreements ignore that governments rarely have access to the technology that the private sector has. Article 66:2 of the TRIPS Agreement obliges developed members 'to provide incentives to enterprises and institutions in their territories for the purpose of promoting and encouraging technology transfer to least-developed countries in order to enable them to create a sound and viable technological base'. This provision has largely remained a dead letter, and special and differential treatment (SDT) here has remained an empty promise. This is because most governments making such promises do not legally have the technology (Cottier, 2017a). It is in the hands of companies and the private sector. Governments, however, should explore the possibility of financial incentives to foster technology transfer to developing countries.

It is submitted that industries engaging in low-income countries by investment or trade in the fields of healthcare, climate change mitigation, and adaption should benefit from domestic tax reductions in the exporting country and home state, in order to offset financial risks and difficulties encountered in the country of destination. This idea, introduced by Hoekman et al. (2005), still awaits implementation. Climate change is an excellent field, as such rebates can account for abatement measures abroad, contributing to globally agreed targets. There is a shared interest in making available the best IP-protected technologies in reducing climate change as a common concern of humankind. The same applies to the supply of medicines and medical services in combating pandemics under the WHO International Health Regulations, as all share a common interest in containing diseases. The approach can also apply to other fields recognised as a common concern of humankind, such as the protection of biodiversity or cultural diversity. A similar scheme could even be extended to developing countries in general.

The problem we face in trade is that financial incentives may be qualified as export subsidies beyond export credits and thus be contrary to the Agreement on Subsidies and Countervailing Measures (SCM Agreement) (Ahmad 2021a, 2021b). Tax reductions in technology-exporting countries would possibly require appropriate adaptation revisions in the SCM Agreement and a return to the category of non-actionable subsidies (Condon, 2009, 2017). This makes the adoption of unilateral policies more difficult in trade, compared, for example, to investment law, where no comparable problems exist. However, new and specific rules in PTAs could lawfully provide the foundations of such schemes in trade regulation and help to get them off the ground. They would exist independently of current WTO obligations and could spearhead future multilateral disciplines in the field. As they benefit all WTO Members alike due to the MFN clause of the TRIPS Agreement, implementing measures are unlikely to be challenged in WTO dispute settlement by developing countries seeking access to modern technology. Industrialised countries could avoid potential, but unlikely, disputes on the distortion of competition among themselves by moving forward the scheme in parallel, perhaps coordinated by the work in the OECD and subsequently in the WTO. The dialectical relationship between PTAs and multilateral rules (Cottier et al., 2015) may work again in creating shared foundations for tax rebates and adjustments of the SCM Agreement.

5.2.2.2 Tax and Tariff Revenues for Technology Dissemination

A second avenue to foster the transfer of sustainable technologies to developing countries in line with obligations under the 1992 United Nations Framework Convention on Climate Change (UNFCCC) and the 2015 Paris Accord and subsequent Conference of the Parties (COP) decisions is to earmark revenues generated from carbon tariffs and revenues from border tax adjustment measures, such as the 2023 EU Carbon Border Adjustment Mechanism (CBAM) regulation.[7] Tax revenues generated from import carbon tariffs and border tax adjustments should not be allocated to the general household. Instead, they should be used and earmarked to fund technology dissemination to low-and lower-income country producers with the aim of meeting sustainable production standards and thus avoiding further import restrictions. These funds could be accountable to abatement goals agreed upon by countries imposing tariffs and import restrictions in addressing climate change. Developing countries are entitled to such compensation for Carbon Border Tax Adjustment Measures under the UNFCCC and the Paris Agreement. In addition, part of such income could be used to fund international programmes supporting lower-income countries in readjusting to sustainable production standards beyond climate change.

PTAs are well placed to operationalise such cooperation and support in adjusting structures of industries to sustainable modes of production. Disciplines on refunding carbon tariff and border tax adjustment revenues could be mandatorily linked to sustainable and renewable energy and adaption technology dissemination and

[7] Regulation (EU) 2023/956 of the European Parliament and of the Council of 10 May 2023 establishing a carbon border adjustment mechanism.

transfer. They are thus linked to privileged access to IPR, earmarking and making revenues available for the acquisition and licensing of appropriate technologies on the market, independently of the origin of the technology. Such disciplines could amend chapters on IPR or be developed in a new chapter on technology transfer, squaring IP and climate change and possibly further policy areas. Implementing legislation and practices affecting privileged access to IP-protected technology will arguably apply to all eligible WTO Members alike under the MFN clause of the TRIPS Agreement (Cottier, 2022). The proliferation of such schemes could thus again serve as a template for future rules on IP funding and licensing for developing countries in plurilateral agreements and in the WTO as a matter of SDT.

5.2.3 *Trade Secrets and the Digital Economy*

The third twenty-first century challenge that we tackle in this chapter is the digital economy. We do so by examining one IPR in particular: trade secrets. The relationship between trade secrets and the digital economy is of growing importance, in part because trade secrets may be more easily available to protect important aspects of the digital economy, such as artificial intelligence (AI) algorithms, and data, than other IPR (Aplin, 2017). This draws from the relatively lower threshold for trade secret protection. According to Article 39 of the TRIPS Agreement, to be protected as a trade secret, certain information must be secret, have commercial value, and be subject to measures ('reasonable steps under the circumstances') to keep it secret. In contrast to this moderately low threshold for trade secret protection, other IPR require the fulfilment of more conditions. For instance, patent protection, according to Article 27 of the TRIPS Agreement, is conditional on the determination of a novelty (the invention must not already exist), inventive step or non-obviousness, and the capability of industrial application. In addition, recent case law arising in some jurisdictions showcases that patent protection may not be available for AI inventions, on the grounds that AI is not a 'natural person', and hence it cannot be considered an inventor (Kim, 2022). This has been more clearly exemplified by the recent US Federal Circuit decision in *Thaler v. Vidal*,[8] in which the US Federal Circuit confirmed that an AI software system ('DABUS') cannot be listed as the inventor on a patent application under US patent statutes. The importance of trade secret protection in international trade is also relevant to technological sectors beyond AI, all of them of critical importance to the digital economy. Linton (2016) explains that trade secret protection plays a key role in the computer and electronics, as well as information service sectors.

[8] *Thaler v. Vidal*, No. 2021-2347 (Fed. Cir. 2022).

Until recently, PTAs did not incorporate fully fledged provisions on trade secret protection,[9] in part because the main *demandeurs* for this right did not have the relevant statutes in their home countries. Only in 2016 did the US and the EU adopt specific and comprehensive trade secret legal frameworks.[10] However, the increased importance of trade secrets in strategic sectors (including high-end technology) and emerging concerns of trade secret theft, have led to the incorporation of TRIPS-plus trade secret provisions in certain PTAs. The Economic and Trade Agreement between the Government of the United States of America and the Government of the People's Republic of China , signed on 15 January 2020, is a case in point (Upreti and Vásquez Callo-Müller, 2020), but also other agreements, such as the CPTPP, contain detailed provisions going beyond multilateral standards.

Regarding the digital economy, and AI in particular, heightened standards for trade secret protection may impact emerging AI regulations promoting trust, fairness, and accountability of AI systems. Such regulations require the disclosure of algorithms or data necessary for the verification of the functionality of AI systems before these are deployed. For instance, the EU AI Act[11] requests that high-risk AI systems should be subject to more rigorous examination, which may include disclosure of algorithms or training data. However, the same Act provides that the disclosure requirements should be without prejudice of confidential business information or trade secrets.[12]

Some PTAs do not prevent these types of regulatory disclosures. At least the USMCA and the Economic and Trade Agreement between the Government of the United States of America and the Government of the People's Republic of China acknowledge that trade secrets may be submitted during regulatory proceedings, but the confidentiality of such information should be protected against unauthorised disclosure.[13]

Notably, certain PTAs extend the protection afforded to trade secrets to any other confidential information. The definition of trade secrets in Article 1 of the US–China Phase One Trade Agreement exemplifies this point. The object of protection is defined as broadly as:

9 In the case of US PTAs, trade secret protection is only included in the USMCA and the US–China Trade Deal. As for EU PTAs, specific trade secret provisions going beyond TRIPS standards are only included in two PTAs: the EU–Japan PTA and the EU–UK PTA. Finally, in the case of Asia-Pacific PTAs, trade secret protection is included, to different degrees, in the CPTPP and RCEP, the largest two mega-regional PTAs.

10 See: US Defend Trade Secrets Act (DTSA) of 2016; Directive (EU) 2016/943 of the European Parliament and of the Council of 8 June 2016 on the protection of undisclosed know-how and business information (trade secrets) against their unlawful acquisition, use, and disclosure.

11 Regulation (EU) 2024/1689 of the European Parliament and of the Council of 13 June 2024 laying down harmonised rules on artificial intelligence and amending Regulations (EC) No 300/2008, (EU) No 167/2013, (EU) No 168/2013, (EU) 2018/858, (EU) 2018/1139 and (EU) 2019/2144 and Directives 2014/90/EU, (EU) 2016/797 and (EU) 2020/1828 (Artificial Intelligence Act).

12 Ibid., Article 70.

13 See: USMCA, Article 20 (77), US–China Phase One Trade Agreement 1(9).

> [c]oncerns or relates to the trade secrets, processes, operations, style of works, or apparatus, or to the production, business transactions, or logistics, customer information, inventories, or amount or source of any income, profits, losses, or expenditures of any person, natural or legal, *or other information of commercial value, the disclosure of which is likely to have the effect of causing substantial harm to the competitive position of such person from which the information was obtained.* (emphasis added)

As more AI regulations will be adopted worldwide, and as TRIPS-plus standards of trade secret protection will increasingly be adopted in PTAs, the boundaries regarding what is a legitimate disclosure of a trade secret will become blurred. In this context, it is still unclear whether PTAs can – or should – provide additional safeguards enabling regulatory oversight. After all, the threshold of protection included in the TRIPS Agreement provides sufficient leeway for governments to adopt a different type of exceptions for trade secret protection at the domestic level. As Rowe and Sandeen put it, while '[a]rticle 39 [of the TRIPS Agreement] may seem onerous ... [i]n reality, it provides WTO member countries significant leeway in defining the parameters of trade secret law' (Rowe and Sandeen, 2015). Yet, PTA practice denotes that countries may also be willing to elucidate the scope of protection for trade secrets by clarifying the exceptions to protection. For instance, the USMCA provides that reverse engineering of a trade secret does not constitute misappropriation.[14]

Nonetheless, in seeking a balanced approach to IPR and obligations, as explained above, it is possible to contend that expansive trade secret protection in PTAs, should, at least, be coupled with sufficient flexibilities. As the digital economy evolves rapidly, governments require the necessary policy space to regulate AI and other cutting-edge technologies. It is thus important to observe and review how limitations and exceptions to trade secrets are being incorporated, especially under new TRIPS-plus agreements, and how such limitations and exceptions can ensure that while innovation in digital technologies is promoted, other societal considerations are also taken into consideration.

5.3 CONCLUSION

The issue of IPR provisions in PTAs remains a highly debated topic, highlighting once again the need to balance investment incentives with the safeguarding of other public interests. We propose incorporating a more balanced approach to IPR in PTAs by adding flexibilities and exceptions to match higher IPR protection standards. This approach can be customised to address specific challenges and types of IPR. In this chapter, we suggest three types of balanced IPR provisions to tackle the

[14] See: USMCA, Article 20(72).

three main challenges of the twenty-first century identified by WIPO: global public health pandemics, climate change, and the evolution of digital technologies.

For global pandemics, we found that medical products are protected by various types of IPR, not all of which are subject to compulsory licensing. As such, compulsory licensing may not be a viable solution to address inequalities in global access to medical products. Instead, we suggest exploring the potential for establishing PPPs as part of PTAs to promote collaboration among international stakeholders such as global businesses, governments, and CSOs.

Moreover, in the context of climate change, technology transfer has for a long time relied on voluntary licensing. This has, however, mainly benefitted industrialised and emerging economies. We have argued that an alternative approach would be to set up schemes in PTAs incentivising lower taxation of low-carbon technology exports to low-income countries. In the context of the increasing interest in mechanisms such as carbon border adjustment or import carbon tariffs, another possibility would be to leverage the gains derived from such mechanisms to fund technology transfer to low- and lower-income producers, thus promoting the adoption of sustainable production standards and avoiding further restrictions.

Lastly, as the digital economy continues to expand, the ever-increasing trade secret protection standards may have adverse effects on other important societal objectives, such as algorithm transparency. In order to address these concerns, it may be beneficial to implement regulatory checks on the functionality of AI systems. To achieve this, we suggest that limitations and exceptions to trade secrets should be included in PTAs alongside TRIPS-plus provisions.

REFERENCES

Abbott, F. M., T. Cottier and F. Gurry 2019. *International Intellectual Property in an Integrated World Economy*, 4th ed., Alphen aan den Rijn: Wolters Kluwer.

Ahmad, Z. 2021a. *WTO Law and Trade Policy Reform for Low-Carbon Technology Diffusion: Common Concern of Humankind, Carbon Pricing, and Export Subsidy Support*. Leiden/Boston: Brill 2021.

2021b. 'Trade Related Measures to spread Low Carbon Technologies: A Common Concern Based Approach', in T. Cottier (ed.), *The Prospects of Common Concern of Humankind in International Law*. Cambridge: Cambridge University Press.

Aplin, T. 2017. 'Trading Data in the Digital Economy: Trade Secrets Perspective', in S. Lohsse, R. Schulze and D. Staudenmayer (eds.), *Trading Data in the Digital Economy: Legal Concepts and Tools: Münster Colloquia on EU Law and the Digital Economy III*, 1st ed. Baden-Baden: Nomos Verlagsgesellschaft.

Australian Government Department of Foreign Affairs and Trade 2019. 'CPTPP: Intellectual Property', January, www.dfat.gov.au/trade/agreements/in-force/cptpp/outcomes-documents/Pages/cptpp-intellectual-property, accessed on 25 April 2023.

Baccini, L., A. Dür and M. Elsig 2015. 'The Politics of Trade Agreement Design: Revisiting the Depth-Flexibility Nexus', *International Studies Quarterly* 59(4): 765–775.

Barton, J. H. 2017. *Intellectual Property and Access to Clean Technologies in Developing Countries*. Geneva: ICTSD.

Beall, R., R. Kuhn and A. Attaran 2015. 'Compulsory Licensing Often Did Not Produce Lower Prices for Antiretrovirals Compared to International Procurement', *Health Affairs* 34(3): 493–501.

Berkley, S. 2020. 'COVAX Explained', 11 September, www.gavi.org/vaccineswork/covax-explained, accessed on 25 January 2023.

Bollyky, T. and C. Bown 2020. 'The Tragedy of Vaccine Nationalism: Only Cooperation Can End the Pandemic', *Foreign Affairs* 99(5): 96–108.

Bosch, R. (n.d.). 'The mRNA Vaccine Technology Transfer Hub', www.who.int/initiatives/the-mrna-vaccine-technology-transfer-hub, accessed on 25 January 2023.

Brewer, T. 2016. 'International Technology Diffusion in a Sustainable Energy Trade Agreement', in G. C. Hufbauer, R. Melendez-Ortiz and R. Samans (eds.), *The Law and Economics of a Sustainable Energy Trade Agreement*. Cambridge: Cambridge University Press.

Brewer, T. and A. Falke 2012. 'International Transfers of Climate Friendly Technologies: How the World Trade System Matters', in D. Ockwell and A. Mallet (eds.), *Low Carbon Transfer: From Rhetoric to Reality*. London: Routledge.

Center for International Environmental Law – CIEL 2008. 'Intellectual Property in European Union Economic Partnership Agreements with the African, Caribbean and Pacific Countries: What Way Forward after the Cariforum EPA and the Interim EPAs?' April 2008, www.ciel.org/Publications/Oxfam_TechnicalBrief_5May08.pdf, accessed on 30 January 2023.

Chander, A. 2015. 'How Law Has Made the Silicon Valley', *Emory Law Journal* 63: 639–694.

Chen, Y. and T. Puttitanun 2005. 'Intellectual Property Rights and Innovation in Developing Countries', *Journal of Development Economics* 78(2): 474–493.

Chu, A. C., G. Cozzi and S. Galli. 2014. 'Stage-Dependent Intellectual Property Rights', *Journal of Development Economics* 106(C): 239–249.

Condon, B. J. 2009. 'Climate Change and Unresolved Issues for Climate Change in WTO Law', *Journal of International Economic Law* 12(4): 895–926.

2017. 'Disciplining Clean Energy Subsidies to Speed the Transition to a Low Carbon World', *Journal of World Trade* 51(4): 675–690.

Conrad, C. R. 2011. *Processes and Production Methods (PPMs) in WTO Law: Interfacing Trade and Social Goals*. Cambridge: Cambridge University Press.

Correa, C. 2019. 'Will the Amendment to the TRIPS Agreement Enhance Access to Medicines?' South Centre Policy Brief 57, January, www.southcentre.int/wp-content/uploads/2019/01/PB57_Will-the-Amendment-to-the-TRIPS-Agreement-Enhance-Access-to-Medicines_EN-1.pdf, accessed on 25 January 2023.

Cottier, T. 2015. 'The Common Law of International Trade and the Future of the World Trade Organization', *Journal of International Economic Law* 18: 3–20.

2017a. 'Technology and the Law of International Trade Regulation', in R. Brownsword et al. (eds.), *The Oxford Handbook of Law, Regulation and Technology*. Oxford: Oxford University Press.

2017b. 'Intellectual Property and Mega-Regional Trade Agreements: Progress and Opportunities Missed', in S. Griller et al (eds.), *Mega-Regional Trade Agreements: CETA, TTIP and TiSA: New Orientations for EU External Economic Relations*. Oxford: Oxford University Press.

ed. 2021a. *The Prospects of Common Concern of Humankind in International Law*. Cambridge: Cambridge University Press.

2021b. 'The Principle of Common Concern of Humankind', in T. Cottier (ed.), *The Prospects of Common Concern of Humankind in International Law*. Cambridge: Cambridge University Press.

2022. 'Commentary TRIPs Agreement, Art. 4 (Most-favoured nation treatment)', in C. Ryffel (ed.), P. T. Stoll and H. P. Hestermayer (general eds.), *The TRIPs Agreement*, 2nd rev. ed., vol 6. Leiden: Brill Nijhoff.

Cottier, T., 2023. 'Tax Incentives for Technology Dissemination in Trade and Investment by Exporting and Home States', available at SSRN' https://papers.ssrn.com/sol3/papers.cfm?abstract_id=4857136

Cottier, T., D. Jost and M. Schupp 2017. 'The Prospects of TRIPS-plus Provisions in Future Megaregionals', in T. Reismann (ed.), *Megaregional Trade Agreements*. Cham: Springer.

Cottier, T., C. Sieber-Gasser and G. Wermelinger 2015. 'The Dialectical Relationship of Preferential and Multilateral Trade Agreements', in A. Dür and M. Elsig (eds.), *Trade Cooperation: The Purpose, Design and Effects of Preferential Trade Agreements*. Cambridge: Cambridge University Press.

Cviticanin, D. 2021. 'Cuban Vaccine Sovereignty: Brave David Confronting the Bully Goliath', International Public Policy Review, 1 May, https://ippr-journal.com/2021/05/01/cuban-vaccine-sovereignty-brave-david-confronting-the-bully-goliath/, accessed on 25 January 2023.

Das, A. 2021. 'David vs Goliath on Vaccine Development: Are Warm Vaccines Being Left Behind?' *The Business Standard*, 24 May, www.tbsnews.net/feature/panorama/david-vs-goliath-vaccine-development-are-warm-vaccines-being-left-behind-250021, accessed on 25 January 2023.

De Vries, P. and E. B. Yehoue 2013. *The Routledge Companion to Public-Private Partnerships*. London: Routledge.

Delimatsis, P. 2016. *Research Handbook on Climate Change and Trade Law*. Cheltenham: Edward Elgar.

Dinwoodie, G. B. and R. C. Dreyfuss 2012. *A Neofederalist Vision of TRIPS: The Resilience of the International Intellectual Property Regime*. New York: Oxford University Press.

Drahos, P. 1998. 'The Universality of Intellectual Property Rights: Origins and Development', WIPO-UNHCHR/IP/PNL/98/1, www.wipo.int/edocs/mdocs/tk/en/wipo_unhchr_ip_pnl_98/wipo_unhchr_ip_pnl_98_1.pdf, accessed on 15 May 2023.

Epstein, R. and F. Kieff 2011. 'Questioning the Frequency and Wisdom of Compulsory Licensing for Pharmaceutical Patents', *The University of Chicago Law Review* 78(1): 71–93.

Erixon, F., O. Guinea, E. van der Marel and P. Lamprecht 2022. 'The Benefits of Intellectual Property Rights in EU Free Trade Agreements: Full Report', ECIPE Occasional Paper, January, https://ecipe.org/wp-content/uploads/2022/01/Study-final.pdf, accessed on 30 January 2023.

European Union 2019. 'Guide to Geographical Indications in Canada: A Practical Business Guide', Publications Office of European Union, April, https://op.europa.eu/en/publication-detail/-/publication/847c1cd9-e007–11e9–9c4e-01aa75ed71a1/language-en/format-PDF, accessed on 30 January 2023.

Ezell, S. and N. Cory 2019. 'The Way Forward for Intellectual Property Internationally', Information Technology and Innovation Foundation (ITIF), 25 April, https://itif.org/publications/2019/04/25/way-forward-intellectual-property-internationally/, accessed on 30 January 2023.

Feldman, J. 2009. 'Compulsory Licenses: The Dangers behind the Current Practice', *Journal of International Business and Law* 8(1): 137–168.

Government of India (Ministry of Commerce and Industry, Department of Commerce) (n.d.). https://commerce.gov.in/international-trade/trade-agreements, accessed on 6 June 2023.

Hoekman, B., M. Maskus and K. E. Saggi 2005. 'Transfer of Technology to Developing Countries: Unilateral and Multilateral Policy Options', *World Development* 33(1587): 1593–1594.

Holzer, K. 2014. *Carbon-Related Border Adjustment and WTO Law*. Cheltenham: Edward Elgar.
House of Commons Canada 2012. 'Negotiations towards a Comprehensive Economic and Trade Agreement (CETA) Between Canada and the European Union: Report of the Standing Committee on International Trade', March, www.ourcommons.ca/Content/Committee/411/CIIT/Reports/RP5431905/CIITrp01/ciitrp01-e.pdf, accessed on 30 January 2023.
Joseph, S. and G. Dore 2022. 'Vaccine Apartheid: A Human Rights Analysis of COVID-19 Vaccine Inequity', *Journal of Transnational Law and Policy* 31: 145–190.
Kelly, B., D. Papanikolaou, A. Seru and M. Taddy 2021. 'Measuring Technological Innovation over the Long Run', *American Economic Review: Insights* 3(3): 303–320.
Kim, D. 2022. 'The Paradox of the DABUS Judgment of the German Federal Patent Court', *GRUR International* 71(12): 1162–1166.
Lall, S. 2003. 'Indicators of the Relative Importance of IPR in Developing Countries', *Research Policy* 32(9): 1657–1680.
Linton, K. 2016. 'The Importance of Trade Secrets: New Directions in International Trade Policy Making and Empirical Research'. https://papers.ssrn.com/sol3/papers.cfm?abstract_id = 2893319.
Liz, J. 2022. 'To Make Live and Let Die', in S. Navarro and S. Hernandez (eds.), *The Color of COVID-19: The Racial Inequality of Marginalized Communities*. London: Routledge.
Lybecker, K. M., and S. Lohnse 2015. *Innovation and Diffusion of Green Technologies: The Role of Intellectual Property and other Enabling Factors*. Geneva: WIPO Global Challenges Report.
Marani, M. et al. 2021. 'Intensity and Frequency of Extreme Novel Epidemics', *PNAS* 118(35): 1–4, https://doi.org/10.1073/pnas.2105482118.
Maskus, K. E. 2000. *Intellectual Property Rights in the Global Economy*. Washington, DC: Institute for International Economics.
2022. 'The International Intellectual Property System from an Economist's Perspective', in H. Grosse Ruse-Khan and A. Metzger (eds.), *Intellectual Property Ordering Beyond Borders*. Cambridge: Cambridge University Press.
Maskus, K. E. and W. Ridley 2017. 'Intellectual Property-Related Preferential Trade Agreements and the Composition of Trade', *Robert Schuman Centre for Advanced Studies Research Paper* (2016/35).
2021. 'Trade Impacts of Intellectual-Property-Related PTAs. Evidence from Using the World Bank Deep Trade Agreements Database', World Bank Policy Research Working Paper 9659.
Mohamad, J. and C. Cheng 2020. 'The Regional Comprehensive Economic Partnership (RCEP): What this means for ASEAN and Malaysia', ISIS Policy Brief, 17 November, www.isis.org.my/wp-content/uploads/2020/11/RCEP-POLICY-BRIEF-REV-3.pdf, accessed on 30 January 2023.
Morin, J.-F. and J. Surbeck 2019. 'Mapping the New Frontier of International IP Law: Introducing a TRIPS-plus Dataset', *World Trade Review* 19(1): 109–122.
Moser, P. and A. Voena 2012. 'Compulsory Licensing: Evidence from the Trading with the Enemy Act', *American Economic Review* 102(1): 396–427.
Neves, P., O. Afonso, D. Silva and E. Sochirca 2021. 'The Link between Intellectual Property Rights, Innovation, and Growth: A Meta-Analysis', *Economic Modelling* 97: 196–209.
Ockwell, D. and A. Mallett 2012. *Low Caron Technology Transfer: From Rhetoric to Reality*. London: Routledge.

Ockwell, D., R. Haum, A. Mallett and J. Watson 2010. 'Intellectual Property Rights and Low Carbon Technology Transfer: Conflicting Discourses of Diffusion and Development', *Global Environmental Change* 20: 729–738.

OECD 2021. 'Coronavirus (COVID-19) Vaccines for Developing Countries: An Equal Shot at Recovery', OECD Policy Responses to Coronavirus (COVID-19), 4 February, available at www.oecd.org/coronavirus/policy-responses/coronavirus-covid-19-vaccines-for-developing-countries-an-equal-shot-at-recovery-6b0771e6/, accessed on 25 January 2023.

Ozili, P. and T. Arun 2020. 'Spillover of COVID-19: Impact on the Global Economy', Munich Personal RePEc Archive, https://mpra.ub.uni-muenchen.de/99317/1/MPRA_paper_99317.pdf, accessed on 25 January 2023.

Raju, K. 2017. 'Compulsory v Voluntary Licensing: A Legitimate way to Enhance Access to Essential Medicines in Developing Countries', *Journal of Intellectual Property Rights* 22: 23–31.

Ramani, S. and E. Urias 2018. 'When Access to Drugs Meets Catch-Up: Insights from the Use of CL Threats to Improve Access to ARV Drugs in Brazil', *Research Policy* 47(8): 1538–1552.

Ricketson, S. 2018. 'The Emergence and Development of the International Intellectual Property System', in R. Dreyfuss and J. Pila (eds.), *The Oxford Handbook of Intellectual Property Law*. Oxford: Oxford University Press.

Rowe, E. A. and S. K. Sandeen 2015. *Trade Secrecy and International Transactions: Law and Practice. Elgar Intellectual Property Law and Practice*. Cheltenham, UK: Edward Elgar Publishing.

Sag, M. 2019. 'The New Legal Landscape for Text Mining and Machine Learning', *Journal of the Copyright Society of the USA* 66: 291–367.

Shadlen, K. C., A. Schrank and M. J. Kurtz 2005. 'The Political Economy of Intellectual Property Protection: The Case of Software', *International Studies Quarterly* 49(1): 45–71.

Shaffer, G. and H. Gao 2021. 'A New Chinese Economic Law Order?' in G. Shaffer (ed.), *Emerging Powers and the World Trading System: The Past and Future of International Economic Law*. Cambridge: Cambridge University Press.

Snorrason, S. T. 2012. 'The Theory of Trade Agreements, Economic Integration, Size of Economies, Trade Costs and Welfare', in S. T. Snorrason (ed.), *Asymmetric Economic Integration. Size Characteristics of Economies, Trade Costs and Welfare*. Heidelberg: Physica-Verlag.

Spence, M. 2009. 'Negotiating Trade, Innovation and Intellectual Property: Lessons from the CARIFORUM EPA Experience from a Negotiator's Perspective', UNCTAD Policy Brief, 4 September, https://unctad.org/system/files/official-document/IPR_pb20094_en.pdf, accessed on 30 January 2023.

Sucker, F. and K. Kugler 2022. 'The Proposed Covid-19 TRIPS Waiver: Not a Silver Bullet but Part of a Solution for Africa's Covid-19 Health Crisis', *Manchester Journal of International Economic Law* 19(1): 37–64.

Suzuki, M. and S. Yang 2022. 'Political Economy of Vaccine Diplomacy: Explaining Varying Strategies of China, India, and Russia's COVID-19 Vaccine Diplomacy', *Review of International Political Economy* 1–26.

Tatar, M. et al. 2021. 'International COVID-19 Vaccine Inequality Amid the Pandemic: Perpetuating a Global Crisis?' *Journal of Global Health* 11(03086): 1–3.

Townsend, B., D. Gleeson and R. Lopert 2016. 'The Regional Comprehensive Economic Partnership, Intellectual Property Protection, and Access to Medicines', *Asia Pacific Journal of Public Health* 28(8): 682–693.

Trimble, M. 2022. 'Unjustly Vilified TRIPS-Plus?: Intellectual Property Law in Free Trade Agreements', *American University Law Review*, 71, 1449.

Upreti, P. N. 2022. *Intellectual Property Objectives in International Investment Agreements.* Elgar Intellectual Property and Global Development Series. Cheltenham, UK: Edward Elgar Publishing.

Upreti, P. N. and M. Callo-Müller 2020. 'Phase One US–China Trade Deal: What Does It Mean for Intellectual Property?' *GRUR International* 69(4): 389–393.

Urias, E. and S. Ramani 2020. 'Access to Medicines After TRIPS: Is Compulsory Licensing an Effective Mechanism to Lower Drug Prices? A Review of the Existing Evidence', *Journal of International Business Policy* 3: 367–384.

Vásquez Callo-Müller, M. 2023. 'FTAs' Contribution Towards a More Flexible Copyright Space: Possibilities and Limits', *American University International Law Review* 38(1): 159–195.

Viju, C., M. T. Yeung and W. A. Kerr 2013. 'Geographical Indications, Conflicted Preferential Agreements, and Market Access', *Journal of International Economic Law* 16(2): 409–437.

WHO/Bosch, R. (n.d.). 'WHO COVID-19 Technology Access Pool', www.who.int/initiatives/covid-19-technology-access-pool, accessed on 25 January 2023.

WIPO 2022. *World Intellectual Property Report 2022: The Direction of Innovation*. Geneva: WIPO.

2021. Council for Trade-Related Aspects of Intellectual Property Rights. 'Notification under the Amended TRIPS Agreement: Notification of Need to Import Pharmaceutical Products Under the Special Compulsory Licensing System', IP/N/9/BOL/1, 11 May, https://docs.wto.org/dol2fe/Pages/SS/directdoc.aspx?filename = q:/IP/N/9BOL1.pdf& Open = True, accessed on 25 January 2023.

WTO 2022a. 'Members' Laws Implementing the "Paragraph 6" System', www.wto.org/english/tratop_e/trips_e/par6laws_e.htm, accessed on 25 January 2023.

2022b. 'Ministerial Decision on The TRIPS Agreement Adopted on 17 June 2022', WT/MIN(22)/30, WT/L/1141, 22 June.

Yu, P. K. 2019. 'Building Intellectual Property Infrastructure Along China's Belt and Road', *University of Pennsylvania Asian Law Review* 14: 280–284.

Zhuang, W. 2017. *Intellectual Property Rights and Climate Change: Interpreting the TRIPS Agreement for Environmentally Sound Technologies.* Cambridge: Cambridge University Press.

6

Government Procurement in Twenty-First Century PTAs

Maria Anna Corvaglia and Anirudh Shingal

6.1 INTRODUCTION

Preferential trade agreements (PTAs) have become the main vehicle to extend procurement rules to non-signatories of the WTO's Agreement on Government Procurement (GPA) (Hoekman, 2015). Preferential trade agreements with provisions on government procurement (preferential procurement agreements, PPAs, following Rickard and Kono 2014) include commitments to open access to procurement contracts on a bilateral/regional basis and explicit prohibition of procurement practices that discriminate against foreign suppliers. Preferential procurement agreements also tend to prohibit price discrimination and a range of other policies, such as local-content requirements, that favour domestic firms.

International rules on government procurement are required because the state has considerable influence over the allocation of resources in market economies through government procurement. Trionfetti (2000) estimates that contestable government procurement markets account for 7–9 per cent of GDP in developed countries, while estimates by the OECD (2002) suggest that government procurement accounts for between 9 and 20 per cent of GDP in developing countries.

A prominent aspect of distortive procurement practices is the preference for domestic over foreign firms in the award of public contracts despite cost and quality considerations. This 'home bias' in public purchase decisions has non-trivial efficiency effects. It can reduce trade flows and influence international specialisation, especially in sectors where public demand is large relative to domestic output and which are characterised by monopolistic competition and increasing returns to scale (Trionfetti, 2000).

Preferential trade agreements vary greatly in their scope and coverage of procurement provisions – some either reflect existing procurement policies of signatories or limit commitments to best endeavour, non-binding, non-enforceable clauses. However, many of the more recent PTAs include extensive procurement commitments and are also more enforceable, including through domestic bid challenge mechanisms. In fact, PTAs with 'deep' procurement provisions (deep procurement agreements, DPAs) have grown more popular over time, with the majority entering into effect since the turn of this millennium (Shingal and Ereshchenko, 2020).

In this chapter, we discuss and examine the coverage of government procurement in recently concluded PTAs with a view to examining their relationship with the World Trade Organization (WTO). We also assess potential gaps in their coverage and point to new areas that are likely to gain prominence as preferential procurement provisions in the near future. The chapter also suggests ways and mechanisms by which PTAs can incorporate these new issues.

6.2 STYLISED FACTS

Preferential trade agreements can be classified into three groups according to their coverage of government procurement: (a) no coverage at all ('no_prov'); (b) provisions on government procurement exist but are not detailed ('shallow_prov'); and (c) detailed provisions on government procurement are included in the agreement ('deep_prov'). Before the year 2000, most PTAs did not include any provisions on public procurement (Figure 6.1, left panel). The first decade of this millennium saw almost an equal number of PTAs with shallow and deep provisions on government procurement. The last ten years have clearly witnessed a proliferation of DPAs – with the exception of 2011, at least half of all new PTAs negotiated every year during the 2010–2019 period include deep provisions on government procurement (Figure 6.1, right panel).

A majority of the DPAs have been concluded among high-income country partners or involve at least one high-income country. The cohort of shallow-procurement agreements is dominated by PTAs in which one partner is a high-income country (or trade bloc) and the other partner is an upper-middle-income country. In contrast, the group of agreements with no procurement coverage exhibits a greater involvement of lower-middle-income countries. This is also the only cohort that includes agreements involving low-income countries.

6.3 ATTRIBUTES OF RECENT DPAS

Most DPAs negotiated between 2010 and 2019 include provisions on national treatment and transparency and also provide substantive coverage in terms of procuring entities and goods and services (Figure 6.2). Shingal and Ereshchenko (2020) provide a detailed analysis of the ingredients of the non-discrimination, coverage, transparency, dispute resolution, and procedural disciplines associated with DPAs entered into effect up until March 2017. Their analysis shows that, within non-discrimination, the most frequently included provisions pertain to national

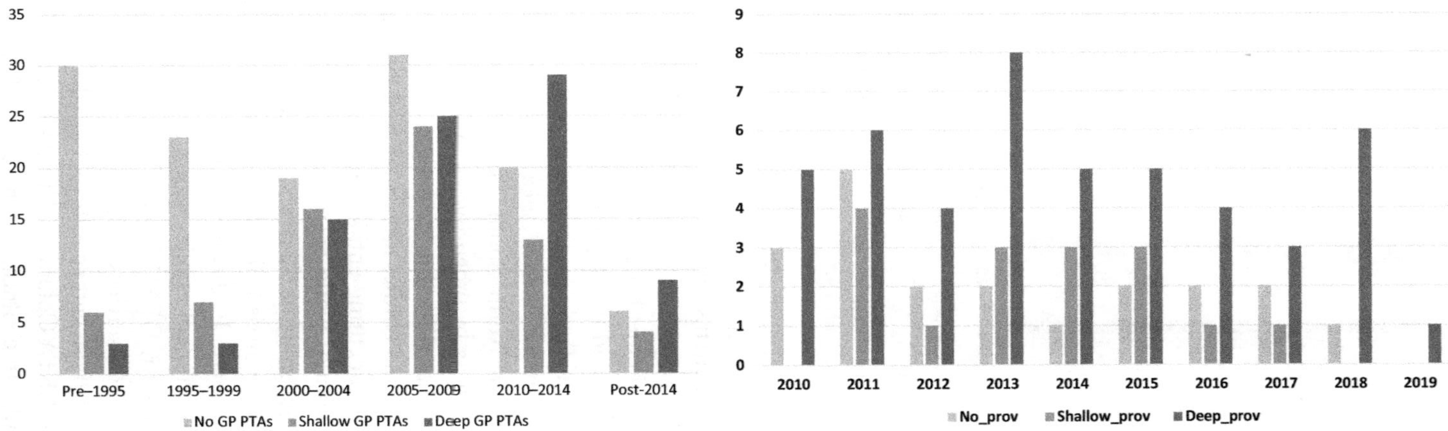

FIGURE 6.1 Evolution of PTA groups by government procurement coverage over time.
Sources: Dür et al. (2014); Shingal and Ereshchenko (2020); authors' own calculations

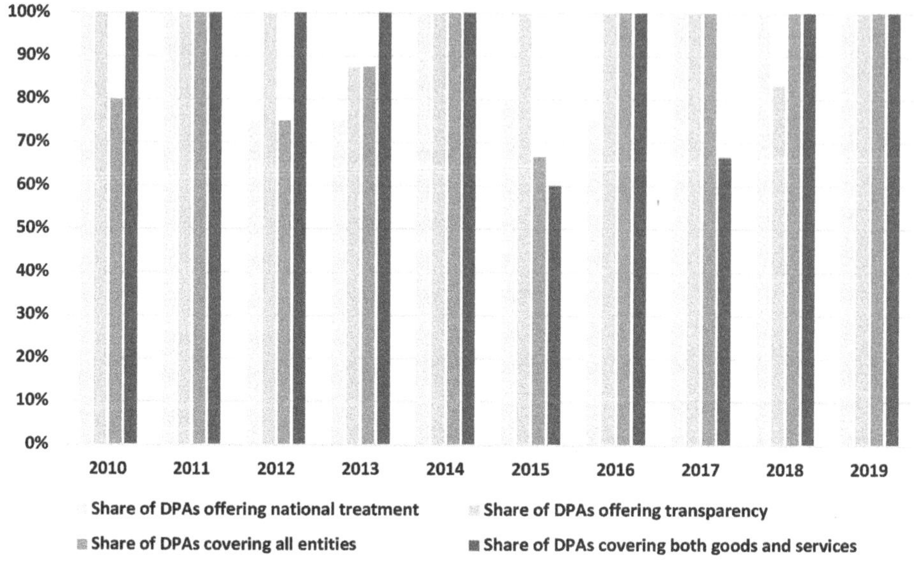

FIGURE 6.2 Attributes of recent DPAs.
Source: Dür et al. (2014); authors' own calculations

treatment, prohibition of offsets, and requiring rules of origin to be not different from those in the normal course of trade (Figure 6.3, top panel).

Deep procurement agreements with relatively high coverage of non-discrimination issues include the Comprehensive and Progressive Trans-Pacific Partnership (CPTPP) and agreements signed between the European Union (EU) and Central America, the EU and the Republic of Moldova, the EU and Ukraine, followed by the European Free Trade Association (EFTA)–Central America (Costa Rica and Panama) trade agreement. Notably, all agreements with extensive coverage of non-discrimination issues are North–South agreements.

In terms of coverage of DPAs by procuring entity, the analysis by Shingal and Ereshchenko (2020) shows that while the majority of the DPAs (forty-four agreements) until March 2017 covered entities listed under all three annexes (i.e. central and sub-central government procuring entities and utilities), fifteen DPAs covered only central government entities while twenty agreements covered both central (Annex 1) and sub-central government (Annex 2) entities.

Another dimension of the analysis is the threshold above which procurement is covered under a trade agreement. In this regard, thresholds for goods and services procurement by central government entities were *not found to be higher* than the GPA-stipulated thresholds for any DPA. Meanwhile, twenty-three DPAs had thresholds equal to the GPA in goods, services, and construction services covered under Annexes 1, 2, and 3. Most of these agreements include the EFTA countries or the EU as a party, for example EFTA-Colombia, EFTA–Korea, EU–Central America, EU–Ukraine, and EU–Chile. In contrast, twenty-seven DPAs have lower-than-GPA

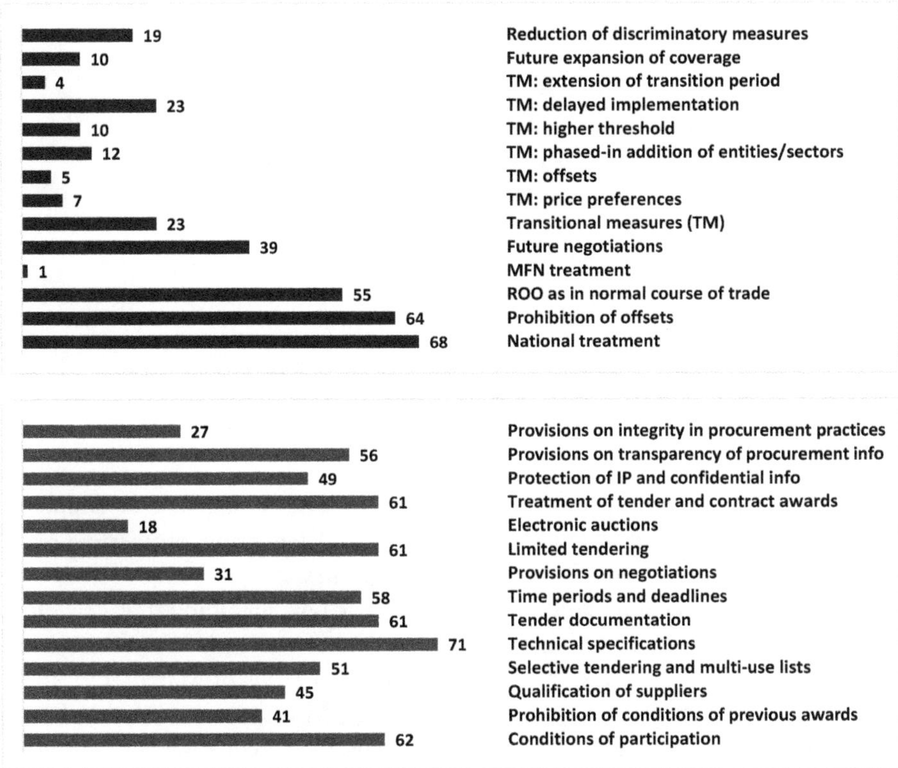

FIGURE 6.3 Snapshot of non-discrimination (first) and procedural (second) disciplines in DPAs.
Source: Shingal and Ereshchenko (2020)

threshold values in at least one area. Notably, in seven of these agreements, the threshold values are lower than the GPA in all measured aspects, that is, goods, services, and construction services under Annexes 1–3. Six of these DPAs have the United States (US) as a party (US–Morocco, US–Panama, US–Peru, US–Chile, US–Singapore, and the Central America Free Trade Agreement–Dominican Republic). The seventh is the EU–Georgia Agreement.

Deep procurement agreements also vary considerably in their coverage of procedural disciplines (Figure 6.3, bottom panel). Two agreements – EFTA–Peru and EFTA–Colombia – cover the highest number of procedural disciplines (twenty-three among the twenty-six classified as procedural disciplines by Shingal and Ereshchenko, 2020), followed by six DPAs that cover twenty-two procedural disciplines (these include EU–Korea, EFTA–Hong Kong, and EFTA–Ukraine). Most DPAs with high coverage of procedural disciplines include North–South or North–North countries. The most frequently covered procedural disciplines provisions (found in over 80 per cent of DPAs analysed by Shingal and Ereshchenko, 2020)

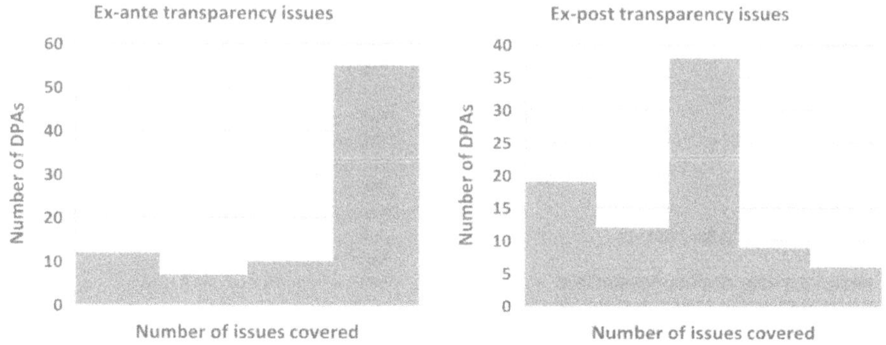

FIGURE 6.4 (a) Ex ante and (b) ex post transparency in DPAs.
Source: Shingal and Ereshchenko (2020)

include those on technical specifications, conditions of participation of suppliers, treatment of tenders and award of contracts, limited tendering, requirements for tender documentation, and time periods and deadlines.

Transparency is an important attribute of deep PTAs, including those covering government procurement. Shingal and Ereshchenko (2020) classify provisions as providing ex ante and ex post transparency (Figure 6.4). As of March 2017, there were only five DPAs that covered all transparency issues; these included South Korea's agreements with Canada and the EU. The most frequently covered provisions (found in 90 per cent of DPAs analysed by Shingal and Ereshchenko, 2020) include those on the requirement to publish a notice on intended/planned procurement and information provided to bidders (results and reasons for non-selection). In contrast, only a fifth of the DPAs studied by Shingal and Ereshchenko (2020) included provisions for the collection and reporting of statistics.

Thus, a critical element of ex post transparency is largely ignored by signatories that otherwise negotiate deep commitments on government procurement in their PTAs.[1]

An assessment of dispute resolution within DPAs includes an assessment of domestic review procedures and their consistency with Article XVIII of the WTO's Revised GPA (RGPA 2012), as well as that of provisions on dispute settlement and their consistency with Article XX of the RGPA. More than 70 per cent of the seventy-three DPAs studied by Shingal and Ereshchenko (2020) covered all four issues related to dispute resolution, including domestic review procedures and dispute settlement, and the consistency of those provisions with the GPA. More specifically, provisions on dispute settlement are found to be reflected in all DPAs except for Korea–Singapore, Japan–Switzerland, and Panama–El Salvador. The Korea–Singapore

[1] A similar lack of statistical reporting by GPA signatories is documented in Shingal 2011, 2012, 2015.

Agreement lists the particular chapters to which dispute settlement procedures apply, but the government procurement chapter is not among them. The Japan–Switzerland Agreement also excludes government procurement from dispute settlement. In contrast, the Korea–Canada Agreement specifically applies dispute settlement to government procurement provisions.

A number of disciplines have emerged in recent agreements that cover 'new' issues, including those on e-procurement, sustainable procurement, small and medium-sized enterprises (SMEs) participation, adoption of safety standards, and (as in the CPTPP) cooperation between the parties on matters of public procurement. As of March 2017, no agreement covered all five of the new issues. Meanwhile, provisions facilitating e-procurement were found in 60 per cent of DPAs; clauses facilitating SMEs participation were reflected in one-half of all DPAs; provisions on cooperation were observed in 40 per cent of DPAs; provisions on facilitation of safety standards were incorporated in only one agreement (US–Korea); and provisions on sustainable procurement were not found in any agreement as of March 2017.

6.4 ASSESSMENT OF THE RECENT PREFERENTIALISM IN GOVERNMENT PROCUREMENT

Despite the proliferation of DPAs in the last decade, procurement coverage in PTAs was found to be WTO+ in only three DPAs (US–Australia, US–Chile, and US–Peru), while in the majority the coverage was less than or equal to that in the WTO (Shingal and Ereshchenko, 2020). Several non-discrimination attributes are popular in recent DPAs, but very few agreements include provisions on most-favoured-nation (MFN) treatment suggesting that procurement liberalisation is still a 'restricted members-only club', signalling signatories' lack of comfort with open regionalism in a domain where political economy interests are generally protectionist.

Similarly, despite the recognised importance and need for transparency in the international economic order, only about a fifth of all DPAs have included provisions for collecting and reporting statistical data. Thus, a significant facet of ex post transparency is largely ignored by DPA signatories, which is not difficult to explain given that the availability of data on the subject enables a ready assessment of procurement practices. Again, despite the inclusion of new issues, provisions on green and labour-sensitive procurement, as well as those facilitating regulatory cooperation and SME participation, are less popular among DPA signatories.

These are all significant gaps in preferential rulemaking in this area, which future agreements may like to address. Such uptake is also likely to be fast-tracked in e-procurement (given the COVID-19-induced spurt in digitalisation), sustainable procurement (given the much needed realisation and growing impetus being given to climate change initiatives), and SMEs participation (given the growing need to facilitate their involvement in global trade and promote inclusive development).

New and upcoming PTAs can take up these selected issues, learning from the experiences of recent, cross-regional, North–South, deep PTAs and ensuring high levels of enforceability marked by binding obligations with some form of dispute settlement. We inform this discussion in the following section by looking at preferential rulemaking in government procurement in a few recent comprehensive trade agreements such as the CPTPP, the Regional Comprehensive Economic Partnership (RCEP), EU–Canada Comprehensive Economic and Trade Agreement (CETA), EU–Japan Economic Partnership Agreement, and the United Kingdom (UK)–EU Trade and Cooperation Agreement.

6.5 EMERGING MODELS OF PROCUREMENT REGULATIONS IN RECENTLY NEGOTIATED PTAS

As shown in the overview so far, various countries have negotiated procurement chapters in PTAs following different regulatory objectives and various negotiating approaches. Overall, the literature has so far identified two prominent models of procurement regulation within bilateral trade agreements: a US and EU model (Corvaglia, 2017).

The US has traditionally used the negotiation of PTAs to push the liberalisation of the procurement sector, parallel to the plurilateral negotiations of the GPA. However, this strategy was not pursued after 2012 and in the negotiation of PTAs under the Bush Presidency. In negotiating these previous agreements, the US adopted a 'one size fits all' approach, extending practically identical transparency and procedural requirements (Heilman Grier, 2022). The recent renegotiation of the North American Free Trade Agreement (NAFTA) consolidated in the United States–Mexico–Canada Agreement (USMCA) has represented a major backward step in US bilateral regulation and liberalisation of procurement, with the complete exclusion of Canada from the USMCA procurement provisions, leaving it only subjected to GPA provisions (Yukins, 2018).

In the landscape of the PTAs, as portrayed before, the EU approach to negotiating preferential regulation of public procurement seems to emerge as the indisputably influential regulatory model. Contrary to the US monolithic approach to negotiating and regulating public procurement in PTAs, the EU has adopted a more tailored approach in its more recent agreements, differentiating between GPA partners and non-GPA partners. On the one hand, EU PTAs with GPA partners (Canada, Japan, South Korea, and the UK) mirror the GPA provisions, even including some WTO+ requirements and exceeding GPA coverage in the market access offers. On the other hand, with middle- and low-income countries outside the GPA, the EU accepted GPA commitments focused on ensuring transparency in the conduct of the covered procurement contracts. Of the agreements signed with GPA parties, CETA and the UK–EU Trade and Cooperation Agreement are particularly relevant for our analysis as they include innovative provisions in the procurement chapter that exceed GPA commitments.

While CETA considerably expands procurement market access commitments beyond the GPA coverage of the CETA parties (including the MASH sector covering municipalities, academic institutions, schools and hospitals and Canada's all provinces and additional central government entities on both parties), the text of the agreement seems to replicate GPA procurement commitments. Chapter 19 of CETA includes general principles of non-discrimination and transparency (Article 19.5), together with specific procedural rules applicable to covered procurement contracts largely based on the procedural rules of the GPA. However, departing from the GPA's regulatory template, the CETA strengthens its national treatment commitments, prohibiting the inclusion in the tender documentation of a requirement of prior work experience in the country's territory. Similar provisions are also included in the EU–Korea and EU–Singapore PTAs, together with the EU–Japan Economic Partnership Agreement. Moreover, as new GPA+ procurement issues, CETA parties highlight the importance of using environmental, social, and labour-related criteria in procurement tenders (e.g. the obligation to comply with collective agreements), as not discriminatory and not constituting an unnecessary obstacle to international trade. The recognition of the importance of the use of procurement for socio-environmental purposes is also present in the text of the EU–Singapore PTA, including the possibility of using eco-labels or green labels in the technical specifications.

The EU–UK Trade and Cooperation Agreement consolidates the most innovative procurement commitments included in previous PTAs with GPA parties. Title VI of Heading One of Part Two covers public procurement in the framework of the EU–UK Free Trade Agreement (FTA) and is largely based on the GPA, but adds several innovative regulatory features present in other EU PTAs with non-GPA parties. First, like EU PTAs with Canada, Japan, and Singapore, an explicit prohibition from imposing prior work experience requirements in the country strengthens the application of the principle of non-discrimination in procurement contracts. Second, each party shall ensure that its procuring entities conduct covered procurement by electronic means to the widest extent practicable (Article 278). Moreover, additional GPA+ procedural rules focus on the inclusion of labour, social, and environmental considerations along the entire procurement process. And finally, the possibility for procuring authorities to review tenders with abnormally low prices is clearly allowed, to verify if it could constitute a grant of subsidy as this represents a possible regulatory overlap (similar to EU PTAs with Japan and Singapore).

6.6 THE SIGNIFICANCE OF PROCUREMENT CHAPTERS IN COMPREHENSIVE TRADE AGREEMENTS: CPTPP AND RCEP

Outside the procurement regulatory approaches followed in bilateral PTAs, where the US and the EU have traditionally been the most prominent actors, comprehensive trade agreements offer a different and more flexible regulatory approach. Under pressure to negotiate procurement obligations suitable for a larger membership, including GPA and non-GPA parties, different regulatory patterns shaped around transitional measures and GPA+ commitments seem to have emerged.

A special place in this analysis is reserved for Chapter 15 of the CPTPP, which incorporates the original Trans-Pacific Partnership (TPP) rules and annexes and contains government procurement regulations for goods and services. As highlighted in the first part of this chapter, the CPTPP provides an in-depth regulatory framework for the regulation of transparency and non-discrimination in the covered procurement activities of its Members and offers an extensive regulation of procurement practices and tendering procedures.

More precisely, the CPTPP regulation of public procurement aims to establish the principle of non-discrimination among parties to the agreement and ensure national treatment by explicitly prohibiting preferences for domestic goods, services, and suppliers in procurement activities conducted under the agreement (Article 15.4). The fundamental principle of national treatment is further strengthened by the prohibition of offsets and the attention to rules of origin in the procurement of goods, similar to GPA Article IV. Moreover, the entire conduct of the procurement process is also carefully regulated, considering the principles of non-discrimination and transparency, from technical specifications to the qualification of suppliers to conditions of participation and award criteria (Articles 15.12 5 to 15.17). Detailed provisions also focus on the publication of procurement information and time periods for different procurement methods (Articles 15.6 through 15.11).

Even if most of the CPTPP procurement provisions mirror the GPA text when it comes to transparency and non-discrimination, Chapter 15 offers innovative and ambitious GPA+ provisions addressing new and innovative regulatory features of procurement regulation. For example, one of the most original provisions is Article 15.18, requiring each party to ensure *integrity* in covered procurement practices. Special attention is also paid to the support of SMEs in Article 15.21, ensuring, to the extent possible, transparency and availability of information to facilitate the participation of SMEs in procurement and considering '*the size, design and structure of the procurement, including the use of subcontracting by SMEs*'. Regulatory attention to the procurement access of SMEs is also reflected in the market access negotiations. Several CPTPP parties excluded set-asides and domestic preferences for SMEs from their commitments, which is contrary to their position in the GPA Schedule, as in the most notable example of the US.

Finally, in terms of the emergence of innovative regulatory features, what is particularly interesting in the CPTPP procurement regulation is the inclusion of transitional and special measures to accommodate the market access needs of its parties in its extended membership. While Mexico replicated its transitional measures already achieved under the USMCA and its agreement with the EU, Malaysia and Viet Nam shaped their procurement regulation and market access commitments on the basis of extensive transitional measures. Various types of transitional measures have been included to help both Malaysia and Viet Nam implement the procurement chapter of the agreement. The key transitional measures in Malaysia's and Viet Nam's procurement commitments include higher thresholds during the transitional period (spanning from twenty to twenty-five years), and the possibility of imposing offsets or price preferences for a certain period after the implementation (again between twenty and twenty-five years).

In addition to these transitional measures common to both, the two countries added specific flexibilities in sensitive areas. On the one hand, Viet Nam was able to secure special measures for the protection of the purchase of pharmaceutical products, applying even higher thresholds, reserving extensive set-asides, and excluding distribution services from its commitments. On the other hand, Malaysia protected the possibility of continuing its traditional and well-established use of public procurement as a strategic instrument in support of the Bhumiputra minority under the CPTPP (McCrudden, 2006). To support the economic participation of this ethnic minority and shield it from the impact that the CPTPP could have, Malaysia was able to negotiate and ensure the application of permanent set-asides, price preferences, and higher thresholds. For all these reasons, the CPTPP has been described in this emerging literature as an example of '*how an FTA can facilitate the first-opening of procurement of developing countries*' (Heilman Grier, 2022).

The regulatory influence and relevance of the CPTPP become particularly visible in the procurement chapter of the RCEP, another comprehensive trade agreement with an extended membership combining GPA and non-GPA countries. Only five of the fifteen RCEP Members are GPA signatories (Australia, Japan, New Zealand, Singapore, and South Korea) while another six are 'Observers' to the GPA – China (2002), Indonesia (2012), Malaysia (2012), Philippines (2019), Thailand (2015), and Viet Nam (2012) – with China negotiating GPA accession since 2007. Notably, existing PTAs among RCEP Members cover government procurement and some even include deep provisions such as the CPTPP, and the Australia–South Korea, South Korea–New Zealand, and South Korea–Singapore trade agreements. Several RCEP Members' PTAs with third countries include deep procurement provisions, especially those of Korea and Singapore, but the influence of these agreements on the RCEP is limited.

Government procurement is covered under Chapter 16 of the RCEP Agreement. Regional Comprehensive Economic Partnership Members recognise the importance of promoting the transparency of laws, regulations, and procedures, and developing cooperation among themselves in matters of government procurement. They appreciate the role of government procurement in furthering the economic integration of the region and in promoting growth and employment. Provisions under the procurement chapter only apply to central government procuring entities (as notified by RCEP Members). The chapter also provides for derogation from transparency and cooperation obligations for RCEP least developed countries (LDCs) Members (Cambodia, Laos, Myanmar) though they can benefit from cooperation between other Members. Internationally competitive procurement by member countries are governed by generally accepted procurement principles. Members are also required to publish information on laws, regulations, and procedures (including on tender opportunities and by electronic means, if possible and in English) with the chapter annex specifying the means (paper or electronic) utilised by Members to publish procurement information.

The novelty of the RCEP procurement chapter lies in its provisions on the forms of cooperation that include information exchange on laws and procedures; training, technical assistance, and capacity building; sharing information on best practices, including with respect to micro-, small, and medium enterprises (MSMEs); sharing information on e-procurement systems; and designation of contact points to facilitate cooperation and information sharing. The agreement also provides for a review article aimed at improving the chapter in the future to facilitate government procurement. However, there is no recourse to dispute settlement under the RCEP Agreement for any matter arising under the procurement chapter.

On the whole, the level of ambition of the RCEP procurement chapter is low as it only focuses on transparency and cooperation, which are soft issues. Even on transparency, the chapter includes no obligation to report information on public purchases à la Article XVI: 4 of the RGPA. There is no explicit mention of market access or national treatment and no recourse to dispute settlement or provisions for a bid challenge mechanism. In that, RCEP falls way short of the GPA or procurement provisions in RCEP Members' PTAs with third countries and among themselves.

That said, there are similarities between the RCEP and the CPTPP, even if the latter's regulatory provisions addressing public procurement are significantly more detailed and its market access commitments more ambitious. Note that absent from the opening of RCEP negotiations in 2013, the procurement commitments were only added in 2017 and consolidated in 2018. Instead of aiming at regulating the sector, the RCEP procurement chapter thus aims at ensuring transparency and cooperation among the parties, to develop a greater and mutual understanding of each other's procurement systems. For this reason, the regulatory focus is on diffusing minimum transparency standards and ensuring that information is publicly available. Even if it does not offer deep procurement commitments, the RCEP has been praised as a '*step forward*' for the advancement of preferential procurement regulation in the Association of Southeast Asian Nations (ASEAN) region, where PTAs were traditionally excluding procurement commitments (Heilman Grier, 2022).

6.7 CONCLUDING REMARKS AND FUTURE REGULATORY PATTERNS

In the preceding sections of the analysis, we provided a quantitative and qualitative overview of the regulatory patterns in government procurement that have emerged in PTAs negotiated or ratified over the past decade. So far our focus has been on the current regulatory landscape of preferential regulation of public procurement, highlighting the emergence of deep procurement commitments. We specifically examined the incorporation of provisions such as non-discrimination and offsets, coverage and thresholds, procedural disciplines, ex ante and ex post transparency, dispute resolution, domestic review, as well as newer regulatory concerns like sustainability, safety standards, SMEs, integrity, and e-procurement. Throughout our analysis, we paid close attention to the membership of these preferential agreements, highlighting the increasing participation of high-income countries and signatories of the GPA as the key drivers behind these deeper regulatory trends.

Based on this analysis, we will now try to construct future scenarios and anticipate regulatory trends. In section 5, we explained how two models of preferential regulation of procurement emerged so far. In contrast to the US' standardised approach to regulating and liberalising public procurement in PTAs, the EU has adopted a more tailored strategy in its recent agreements, distinguishing between negotiations with GPA partners and with those who are not. Based on the trade strategies recently published by both actors, we expect to see the EU's model of preferential regulation of public procurement standing out as the one more influential in the future.

The European Commission's trade strategy for the coming years, based on the concept of open strategic autonomy, envisages the negotiation of future trade agreements focusing '*on strengthening bilateral partnerships; creating the conditions to support the security, resilience, and stability of supply chains; creating new opportunities for businesses through diversification of imports, exports and investments; and supporting sustainable development*' (WTO, 2023 European Union Trade Policy Review). The EU's future trade will be shaped on the basis of these strategic interests and values, alongside the more traditional EU's market access agenda, of which public procurement is a crucial pillar. Consistent with this, public procurement is a vital component of the EU's ongoing negotiations with Australia, India, Indonesia, and Malaysia. Moreover, the EU vision of an open and strategic trade agenda confirms the pattern of including strong sustainability clauses in the preferential regulation of public procurement.

Moreover, in the context of its future trade liberalisation agenda, a new EU International Procurement Instrument (IPI) is aimed at strengthening the international negotiating position of the EU in the area of government procurement. This influential instrument, adopted in 2022, enforces limitations on the participation of suppliers from countries outside the EU that have implemented measures to restrict EU suppliers' access to their own government procurement market. The primary focus of the 2022 IPI strategy is clearly aimed at third countries, outside the GPA reciprocity commitments, that do not currently have any established public procurement agreements with the EU, functioning more as a political platform for future negotiations (Dawar, 2023).

While the EU appears to be the more influential driver behind the preferential regulation of procurement, the US seems to set itself in a different direction. While the Trump Administration was even considering the possibility of withdrawing from the GPA (Anderson and Yukins, 2020), the current US administration seems to have adopted a 'light touch' approach to trade negotiations, marking a clear departure from past administrations. As shown in the critical minerals agreement[2] signed by the United States Trade Representative with Japan in March 2023, trade cooperation among the parties is advocated through the use of aspirational language. The US current administration seems to aim at building its future trade strategy on agreements lacking substantial market access commitments and enforceable obligations, similar to the case of the Indo-Pacific Economic Framework for Prosperity and contrary to traditionally negotiated US trade agreements (US, 2023 Trade Policy Agenda and 2022 Annual Report of the President of the United States on the Trade Agreements Program). The US seems to be oriented toward a shallower regulatory approach to government procurement, if included at all, in its strategic trade vision for the future.

Outside the influence of specific actors, in the previous analysis we saw how the liberalisation and regulation of procurement in DPAs have also followed specific designs of procurement commitments, shaped by the influence of commitments of GPA Members. Several DPAs include provisions based on and often mirroring those in the GPA, particularly those relating to non-discrimination, transparency, the conduct of the procurement process, and dispute settlement. That said, only five new parties have acceded to the GPA in the last decade, suggesting that the future procurement regulatory scenario is more likely to be driven by PTAs, in particular those led by the EU. It is undeniable that the GPA so far has provided a flexible regulatory baseline for the negotiations of DPAs, thanks to its flexible architecture of core harmonised commitments and additional flexibility in terms of coverage (Sanchez-Graells, 2022). However, some more recent agreements, like the UK–Australia FTA and UK–New Zealand FTA, have also started to show some emerging deviations in terms of the national treatment obligations and the requirements of domestic review procedures. This seems to indicate the possibility of moving in the future from a GPA= to a deeper GPA+ scenario in the preferential procurement regulation among GPA parties and particularly when it comes to the coverage of their DPAs.

At the same time, cross-regional agreements have also shown the possibility of transferring emerging regulatory patterns to lower-middle-income countries outside GPA membership. The most important and influential example in this regard, the CPTPP, shows a possible way forward outside the GPA template by offering transitional flexible measures in the form of price preferences, offsets and higher

[2] Agreement Between the Government of Japan and the Government of the United States of America on Strengthening Critical Minerals Supply Chains available at https://ustr.gov/sites/default/files/2023-03/US%20Japan%20Critical%20Minerals%20Agreement%202023%2003%2028.pdf.

thresholds, and coverage of emerging issues like the support of SMEs, inclusion of social and environmental consideration and reference to integrity and anti-corruption provisions. Patterns of graduation of commitments and flexibility of coverage could represent the way forward for a progressive integration of lower-middle-income countries in the preferential regulation of government procurement, a field that for too long has remained a club for high-income countries only.

REFERENCES

Anderson, R. D. and C. R. Yukins 2020. 'Withdrawing the United States from the WTO Government Procurement Agreement (GPA): Assessing Potential Damage to the U.S. and Its Contracting Community', GWU Legal Studies Research Paper No. 2020-08.

Corvaglia, M. A. 2017. 'Government Procurement in Preferential Trade Agreements', in T. Cottier and K. Nadakavukaren Schefer (eds.), *Elgar Encyclopedia of International Economic Law*. London, UK: Edward Elgar Publishing.

Dawar, K. 2023. 'The EU 2022 International Procurement Regulation Enters into Force Reciprocity', *Journal of World Trade* 57(1): 139–156.

Dür, A., L. Baccini and M. Elsig 2014. 'The Design of International Trade Agreements: Introducing a New Dataset', *Review of International Organizations* 9(3): 353–375.

Heilman Grier, J. 2022. *The International Procurement System: Liberalization and Protectionism*. London, UK: Dalston Press.

Hoekman, B. 2015. 'International Cooperation on Public Procurement Regulation', EUI Working Paper RSCAS 2015/88.

McCrudden, C. and S. G. Gross 2006. 'WTO Government Procurement Rules and the Local Dynamics of Procurement Policies: A Malaysian Case Study', *European Journal of International Law* 17(1): 151–185.

OECD 2002. *The Size of Government Procurement Markets*. Paris: OECD

Rickard, S. and D. Kono 2014. 'Think Globally, Buy Locally: International Agreements and Government Procurement', *Review of International Organizations* 9(3): 333–352.

Sanchez-Graells, A. 2022. 'The Growing Thicket of Multi-layered Procurement Liberalization Between WTO GPA Parties, as Evidenced in Post-Brexit UK', *Legal Issues of Economic Integration* 49(3): 247–268.

Shingal, A. 2011. 'Services Procurement under the WTO's Agreement on Government Procurement: Whither Market Access?' *World Trade Review* 10(4): 1–23.

2012. 'Estimating Market Access in Non-GPA Countries: A Suggested Methodology', NCCR-Trade Working Paper 2012/06.

2015. 'Econometric Analyses of Home-Bias in Government Procurement', *Review of International Economics* 23(1): 188–219.

Shingal, A. and V. Ereshchenko 2020. 'Public Procurement' in A. Mattoo, M. Ruta and N. Rocha (eds.), *Handbook of Deep Trade Agreements*. Washington, DC: World Bank.

Trionfetti, F. 2000. 'Discriminatory Public Procurement and International Trade', *The World Economy* 23: 57–76.

Yukins, C. R. 2018. 'The U.S.-Mexico-Canada Agreement (USMCA): Some Surprising Outcomes in Procurement', GWU Law School Public Law Research Paper No. 2018-45, GWU Legal Studies Research Paper No. 2018-45.

7

Digital Trade

New Design Elements in Preferential Trade Agreements

Mira Burri[*]

7.1 INTRODUCTION

'Digital trade'[1] can be said to be a relatively well-established topic in international economic rulemaking, if one considers that soon after the completion of the Uruguay Round, the Information Technology Agreement (ITA) (WTO 1996)[2] as a plurilateral arrangement aiming at zero tariffs for information technology (IT) products was adopted in 1996 and two years later the membership of the World Trade Organization (WTO) launched the Work Programme on Electronic Commerce (WTO 1998). The latter initiative sought to address the implications of the Internet that could potentially lead to adjustments in the existing rules for trade in goods, trade in services, and intellectual property (IP) rights protection. Interestingly, for those wishing to understand the broader context of emerging Internet governance, this was also the time when John Perry Barlow penned his declaration on the independence of cyberspace, claiming, in essence, that neither states nor companies will be able to control this new space of freedom (Barlow 1996). Since then, the perception that states should and can regulate online activities became a reality, and a flurry of regulations were adopted around the

* The support of the European Research Council under Consolidator Grant 101003216 is gratefully acknowledged.

1 The Organisation for Economic Co-operation and Development (OECD) has pointed out that, while there is no single recognised and accepted definition of digital trade, there is a growing consensus that it encompasses digitally enabled transactions of trade in goods and services that can either be digitally or physically delivered and that involve consumers, firms, and governments. Critical is that the movement of data underpins contemporary digital trade and can also itself be traded as an asset and a means through which global value chains (GVCs) are organised and services delivered (López González and Jouanjean 2017; López-González et al. 2022).

2 On the negotiating history of the ITA, see Fliess and Sauvé (1998). On the relevance of the ITA in regulatory landscape of digital trade, see Burri (2015).

world that targeted commercial transactions, personal data protection, online gambling, and other types of illegal activity online.[3] The WTO Work Programme on Electronic Commerce could not keep up with these developments and stalled for a variety of reasons, ultimately rendering WTO law dated in many aspects (Wunsch-Vincent and Hold 2012).

In the meantime, digital trade as practice and as a subject of regulation did substantially transform. On the one hand, this has been spurred by the progressively advancing digitisation of economies and societies as a whole with a number of palpable new trends in trade, such as the emergence of global value chains (GVCs) and increased servicification (Burri 2019; WTO 2019c), as well as by the more recently emerged critical importance of data (Manyika et al. 2011; Mayer-Schönberger and Cukier 2013; Henke et al. 2016; WTO 2018). On the other hand, the surge in digital trade rulemaking, which in this chapter covers both hard and soft rules creation (Abbott and Snidal 2000: 421–456; Shaffer and Pollack 2010), can be linked to the multiple new issues that the data-driven economy has raised. Some of them, such as those in the area of personal data protection, demand urgent regulatory responses (Burri 2021a; Chander and Schwartz 2023).

The chapter is set against this background and seeks to provide a better understanding and contextualisation of the highly dynamic field of digital trade rulemaking driven by preferential trade agreements (PTAs). The new rules found in bilateral and regional PTAs not only compensate for the lack of developments in the multilateral forum of the WTO (at least so far)[4] but effectively create a comprehensive, albeit fragmented, governance framework for the data-driven economy. The chapter's analytical lens is directed in particular towards the more recent and advanced models of digital trade rulemaking, such as those under the Comprehensive and Progressive Agreement for Trans-Pacific Partnership (CPTPP) and the United States (US)–Mexico–Canada Agreement (USMCA), as well as those endorsed by dedicated digital economy agreements (DEAs). The chapter then covers the European Union's (EU) new generation of trade deals, particularly the post-Brexit Agreement with the United Kingdom (UK), the agreement with New Zealand, and the currently negotiated deals with Australia and Tunisia. It looks at the Regional Comprehensive Economic Partnership (RCEP), as the first agreement with digital trade provisions that includes China, to give a sense of the dynamic governance environment on digital trade issues.

With the help of these enquiries, it is the chapter's objective to identify new design elements found in PTAs and to trace how these have diffused, especially in recent years, and to what extent one can observe convergence or divergence across regulatory templates and issues in the digital trade domain.

[3] For a great review of the theories on cyberspace regulation, their evolution over time, and review of the literature, see Eichensehr (2015: 313–334).

[4] For an analysis of the WTO relevance to digital trade, see Burri and Cottier (2012); Burri (2015).

7.2 THE PTA LANDSCAPE OF DIGITAL TRADE RULEMAKING

7.2.1 *Overview*

As earlier noted, since the WTO law did not undergo any adaptation in the past two decades, the regulatory environment for digital trade has been shaped exclusively by developments in PTAs. Out of the 432 PTAs entered into between 2000 and 2023, 214 contain provisions relevant to digital trade and 122 have dedicated electronic commerce chapters.[5] While it is true that the pertinent rules are very heterogeneous and differ as to issues covered, the scope and level of commitments, and their binding nature, it is apparent that the trend towards more detailed provisions on digital trade has intensified significantly over the years.[6] This regulatory push in the digital trade domain can be explained by the increased importance of the issue over the years, as noted earlier, and the role played by the US as a legal entrepreneur (Elsig and Klotz 2021).

The US has, over the years, endorsed its 'Digital Agenda' (US Congress 2001; Wunsch-Vincent 2003; Gao 2018) through the PTA channel. The agreements reached since 2002 with Australia, Bahrain, Chile, Morocco, Oman, Peru, Singapore, the Central American countries,[7] Panama, Colombia, and South Korea all contain important, albeit with different depths of commitment, provisions in the broader field of digital trade. However, it should be highlighted that the US is not a sole actor any longer, as the dynamic of digital trade rulemaking has changed over time. On the one hand, it is noteworthy that the US template is not limited to US agreements (Elsig and Klotz 2021) and has been replicated in a number of other PTAs as well, such as Singapore–Australia, Thailand–Australia, New Zealand–Singapore, Japan–Singapore, and South Korea–Singapore. On the other hand, it ought to be pointed out that smaller countries, in particular Singapore and New Zealand, have become the most innovative and bold rule-makers in the area of digital trade (Burri, Vasquez Callo-Müller and Kugler 2024). Although reckoned as a major actor in international economic law and policy, the EU has been, in comparison, a latecomer into the digital trade rulemaking domain, as the chapter reveals below.

The relevant aspects of digital trade governance can be found in: (1) the specifically dedicated electronic commerce PTA chapters; (2) the chapters on cross-border supply of services (with particular relevance of the telecommunications, computer

5 This analysis is based on a data set of all digital trade relevant norms in trade agreements (Trade Agreement Provisions on Electronic-commerce and Data, TAPED) (Burri and Polanco 2020; Burri, Vasquez Callo-Müller and Kugler 2024). For all data, as well as updates of the data set, see https://unilu.ch/taped.

6 For an overview of the PTA developments, see Burri (2021b).

7 Costa Rica, the Dominican Republic, El Salvador, Guatemala, Honduras, and Nicaragua as part of the Dominican Republic–Central America Free Trade Agreement (CAFTA-DR).

and related, audiovisual, and financial service sectors); and (3) the IP chapters.[8] This chapter focuses exclusively on the electronic commerce/digital trade chapters, as well as on the specific DEAs, which have become the critical source of new rulemaking in the area of digital trade and are also indicative of the novel legal design.

The electronic commerce/digital trade chapters play a dual role in terms of rule creation. For one, they represent an attempt to compensate for the lack of progress in the WTO and address many of the questions of the WTO Work Programme on Electronic Commerce that have been discussed but not resolved (Wunsch-Vincent 2006). For instance, a majority of the chapters recognise the applicability of WTO rules to electronic commerce (e.g. US–Singapore FTA, Article 14.1; US–Australia FTA, Article 16.1) and establish an express and permanent duty-free moratorium on electronic transmissions (e.g. US–Singapore FTA, Article 14.3, paragraph 1; US–Chile FTA, Article 15.3).[9] In most of the templates tailored along the US model, the chapters also include a definition of 'digital products', which treats products delivered offline as equally as those delivered online (e.g. US–Singapore FTA, Article 14.3; US–Australia FTA, Article 16.4), so that technological neutrality is ensured and some of the classification dilemmas under the General Agreement on Trade in Services (GATS) are cast aside (in particular when combined with negative committing for services).[10] In this context, one can observe some new design elements that essentially connect the multilateral discussions on e-commerce with actual rulemaking in the preferential forums. The level of legal certainty is increased for PTA partners even on some 'older' issues, such as the moratorium on customs duties on electronic transmissions, normally extended at the WTO Ministerial Conferences (MC), but the acceptance of which may be waning among WTO Members.[11]

The electronic commerce/digital trade chapters also include novel regulatory questions that have not been treated in the WTO context – the so-called 'WTO-extra' issues that have become increasingly important in the data-driven economy. One can group these rules into two categories: (1) rules that seek to facilitate digital trade, by tackling distinct issues, such as paperless trading, electronic contracts, and electronic authentication, as well as by increasing business and consumer trust; and (2) rules that address data governance, in particular cross-border data flows, and new data economy issues that can be of various natures. It should be noted that as to the

8 For analysis of all relevant chapters, see Burri (2017).

9 For a discussion of the variety of rules on the moratorium, see Burri and Polanco (2020).

10 The negative committing is different from the conventional opt-in committing for service sectors under the GATS and covers all sectors except for those explicitly excluded (Horn et al. 2009; Adlung and Mamdouh 2013; Burri 2017).

11 As the MC12 and MC13 proved. During these latest WTO Ministerial Conferences the scope and application of the moratorium were heavily contested, with, in particular, India and South Africa arguing against its extension (WTO 2021).

first cluster of issues on the facilitation of digital trade, the number of PTAs containing such rules is often substantial,[12] and one can observe some convergence regarding treaty language. Only a few agreements still include rules on data, and the data flow conditionalities may differ substantially.[13]

7.2.2 *Emerging Templates for Digital Trade and Stakeholders' Positioning*

In the following sections, the chapter looks at the new rules created in recent agreements through a detailed analysis of the most advanced electronic commerce/digital trade chapters thus far – those of the CPTPP, the USMCA, and the dedicated DEAs. We complement this analysis with an enquiry into the EU treaties, the EU's repositioning on data flows in particular, and into the RCEP as the first agreement with digital trade provisions to include China. The purpose is twofold: on the one hand, to highlight legal innovation in these treaties and, on the other, to give a sense of the positions of the major stakeholders.

7.2.2.1 The CPTPP

The Comprehensive and Progressive Agreement for Trans-Pacific Partnership was agreed upon in 2017 between eleven countries in the Pacific Rim[14] and entered into force on 30 December 2018. Beyond the economic significance of the agreement (Torrey 2018) and the new approach of a 'mega-regional' PTA (Kingsbury et al. 2019a, 2019b), the CPTPP chapter on electronic commerce created at that time the most comprehensive template in the landscape of PTAs. Despite the US having dropped out from the Trans-Pacific Partnership Agreement (TPP) with the start of the Trump Administration, the CPTPP chapter reflects the US efforts under its updated 'Digital 2 Dozen' agenda[15] to secure obligations on digital trade[16] and is a verbatim reiteration of the TPP chapter. A closer look at the CPTPP electronic commerce chapter is, therefore, well-deserved.

In the first part, and not unusually for US-led and other PTAs, the CPTPP electronic commerce chapter clarifies that it applies 'to measures adopted or maintained by a party that affect trade by electronic means' (Article 14.2(2) CPTPP). But it excludes from this broad scope (1) government procurement and (2) information held or processed by or on behalf of a party, or measures related to such information,

[12] So, for instance, 100 PTAs have rules on e-signatures; ninety-four PTAs have rules on paperless trading; and eighty-five PTAs contain a provision on electronic transactions frameworks.

[13] Forty-nine PTAs have rules on data flows; thirty-two PTAs have a ban on data localisation.

[14] Australia, Brunei, Canada, Chile, Japan, Malaysia, Mexico, New Zealand, Peru, Singapore, and Viet Nam.

[15] The 'Digital 2 Dozen' agenda sought to promote the digital economy through a free and open Internet and commerce without borders and defined twenty-four objectives, including free data flows, to this effect see https://ustr.gov/sites/default/files/Digital-2-Dozen-Final.pdf.

[16] See also in this sense New Zealand's Waitangi Tribunal (2021: 72 and passim).

including measures related to its collection (Article 14.2(3) CPTPP).[17] The following provisions address, again as customarily, some of the leftovers of the WTO Work Programme on Electronic Commerce and provide for the facilitation of online commerce. In this sense, Article 14.3 CPTPP bans the imposition of customs duties on electronic transmissions, including content transmitted electronically, and Article 14.4 endorses the non-discriminatory treatment of digital products,[18] which are defined broadly pursuant to Article 14.1 CPTPP.

With regard to digital trade facilitation, a number of provisions should be mentioned: Article 14.5 CPTPP is meant to shape the domestic electronic transactions framework by including binding obligations for the parties to follow the principles of the UNCITRAL Model Law on Electronic Commerce 1996 or the UN Convention on the Use of Electronic Communications in International Contracts. Parties must endeavour to (1) avoid any unnecessary regulatory burden on electronic transactions and (2) facilitate input by interested persons in the development of its legal framework for electronic transactions (Article 14.5(2) CPTPP). The provisions on paperless trading (Article 14.9 CPTPP) and electronic authentication and electronic signatures (Article 14.6 CPTPP) complement this by securing the equivalence of electronic and physical forms.

The remainder of the provisions found in the CPTPP electronic commerce chapter can be said to belong to the second and more innovative category of rulemaking that tackles the emergent issues of the data-driven economy. Most importantly, in this context, the CPTPP seeks to curb data protectionism. First, it does so through an explicit ban on the use of data localisation measures. Article 14.13 (2) prohibits the parties from requiring a 'covered person to use or locate computing facilities in that party's territory as a condition for conducting business in that territory'. Second, the CPTPP includes a hard rule on data flows: '[e]ach Party shall allow the cross-border transfer of information by electronic means, including personal information, when this activity is for the conduct of the business of a covered person' (Article 14.11(2) CPTPP). The rule has a broad scope and most data transferred over the Internet is likely to be covered.

Measures restricting digital flows or implementing localisation requirements are permitted only if they do not amount to 'arbitrary or unjustifiable discrimination or a disguised restriction on trade' and do not 'impose restrictions on transfers of information greater than are required to achieve the objective' (Article 14.11(3) CPTPP). These non-discriminatory conditions are similar to the strict test formulated by

[17] For greater certainty, measures affecting the supply of a service delivered or performed electronically are subject to the obligations contained in the relevant provisions on investment and services (Article 14.2(4) CPTPP) and some additional exceptions are also specified (Article 14.2(5) and (6) CPTPP).

[18] The obligation does not apply to subsidies or grants, including government-supported loans, guarantees, and insurance, nor to broadcasting. It can also be limited through the rights and obligations specified in the IP chapter. Article 14.2(3) CPTPP.

Article XIV GATS and Article XX General Agreement on Tariffs and Trade (GATT) 1994 – a test that is intended to balance trade and non-trade interests by 'excusing' certain violations but that is also extremely hard to pass, as the WTO jurisprudence has thus far revealed (Andersen 2015). The CPTPP test differs from the WTO norms in two significant elements: (1) while there is a list of public policy objectives in the GATT 1994 and the GATS, the CPTPP provides no such enumeration and simply refers to a 'legitimate public policy objective' (Article 14.11(3) CPTPP); and (2) in the chapeau-like reiteration of 'arbitrary or unjustifiable discrimination', there is no GATT- or GATS-like qualification of 'between countries where like conditions prevail'. The scope of the exception is thus unclear – it can be linked to legal uncertainty, as well as to potentially unworkable safeguards for domestic constituencies.[19] Lastly, it should be noted that the ban on localisation measures is softened on financial services and institutions;[20] government procurement is also excluded (Article 14.8(3) CPTPP).

The CPTPP addresses other novel issues as well – one of them is source code. Pursuant to Article 14.17, a CPTPP Member may not require the transfer of, or access to, source code of software owned by a person of another party as a condition for the import, distribution, sale, or use of such software, or of products containing such software, in its territory. The prohibition applies only to mass-market software or products containing such software (Article 14.17(2) CPTPP), which means that tailor-made products, as well as the software used for critical infrastructure and in commercially negotiated contracts, are excluded (Article 14.17(2) CPTPP).[21] This ban on forced technological transfer aims to protect IT companies and address their concerns about loss of IP or cracks in the security of their proprietary code. It may also be seen as a reaction to China's demands to access source code from software producers selling in its market (Joint Statement on Trilateral Meeting of the Trade Ministers of the United States, Japan, and the European Union 2020).

These provisions illustrate an important development in the PTA rulemaking in that they do not merely seek the reduction in trade barriers but effectively shape the regulatory space domestically. Particularly critical in this context are also the rules in the area of data protection. Article 14.8(2) requires every CPTPP party to 'adopt or maintain a legal framework that provides for the protection of the personal information of the users of electronic commerce'. Yet, there are no standards or benchmarks for the legal framework specified, except for a general requirement that CPTPP parties 'take into account principles or guidelines of relevant international bodies' (Article 14.8(2) CPTPP). A footnote provides some clarification in saying that: '... a Party may comply with the obligation in this paragraph by adopting or

[19] See, for example, in this sense New Zealand's Waitangi Tribunal (2021: 132–142). See also Burri and Kugler (2024).

[20] See the definition of 'a covered person' (Article 14.1 CPTPP), which excludes a 'financial institution' and a 'cross-border financial service supplier'.

[21] On the possible interpretations of the provision and difference to including algorithms, see New Zealand's Waitangi Tribunal (2021: 104–112).

maintaining measures such as a comprehensive privacy, personal information or personal data protection laws, sector-specific laws covering privacy, or laws that provide for the enforcement of voluntary undertakings by enterprises relating to privacy' (Article 14.8(2) CPTPP, at footnote 6). These norms can be interpreted as a prioritisation of trade over privacy rights. This has been pushed by the US during the TPP negotiations, as the US subscribes to a relatively weak and patchy protection of privacy (Whitman 2004; Schwartz and Solove 2014; Burri 2021a), which, among other things, means that the US has encountered difficulties in securing unhindered transatlantic data transfers (Burri 2021a; Chander and Schwartz 2023).

Next to the data protection provisions, the CPTPP also includes norms on consumer protection (Article 14.17 CPTPP), spam control (Article 14.14 CPTPP), and net neutrality (Article 14.10 CPTPP), as well as rules on cybersecurity cooperation (Article 14.16 CPTPP). The provisions are of soft law nature but are nonetheless important in trying to provide interoperability between domestic regimes and enhance business trust.

The accession of the UK to the CPTPP and recent requests for accession by China, Costa Rica, Taiwan and other countries (US Congressional Research Service 2021) will potentially expand this agreement's commercial reach and geopolitical dimension. Next to these possibilities for an enlarged CPTPP membership, it should also be pointed out that the CPTPP model has diffused in a substantial number of other agreements, such as the 2016 Chile–Uruguay FTA, the 2016 updated Singapore–Australia FTA (SAFTA), the 2017 Argentina–Chile FTA, the 2018 Singapore–Sri Lanka FTA, the 2018 Australia–Peru FTA, the 2019 Brazil–Chile FTA, the 2019 Australia–Indonesia FTA, the 2018 USMCA, the 2019 Japan–US Digital Trade Agreement (DTA), as well as a number of DEAs. The chapter discusses first the USMCA and then looks at selected DEAs.

7.2.2.2 The USMCA

After the US withdrew from the TPP, there was some uncertainty about the direction the US would take on matters of digital trade. The renegotiated North American Free Trade Agreement (NAFTA), now referred to as the 'USMCA', provides a useful confirmation of the US approach. The USMCA has a comprehensive 'Digital Trade' chapter that follows all critical lines of the CPTPP and creates an even more ambitious template. With regard to replicating the CPTPP model, the USMCA follows the same broad scope of application (Article 19.2 USMCA), bans customs duties on electronic transmissions (Article 19.3 USMCA), and binds the parties to non-discriminatory treatment of digital products (Article 19.4 USMCA). Furthermore, it provides for a domestic regulatory framework that facilitates online trade by enabling electronic contracts (Article 19.5 USMCA), electronic authentication and signatures (Article 19.6 USMCA), and paperless trading (Article 19.9 USMCA).

The USMCA replicates the CPTPP model also with regard to data issues and ensures the free flow of data through a clear ban on data localisation (Article 19.12 USMCA) and a hard rule on free information flows (Article 19.11 USMCA). Article 19.11 specifies further that parties can adopt or maintain a measure inconsistent with the free flow of data provision, if this is necessary to achieve a legitimate public policy objective, provided that there is no arbitrary or unjustifiable discrimination nor a disguised restriction on trade; and the restrictions on transfers of information are not greater than necessary to achieve the objective (Article 19.11(2) USMCA).[22]

Beyond these similarities, the USMCA introduces some novelties. The first is that the USMCA departs from the standard US approach and signals abiding by some data protection principles and guidelines of relevant international bodies. In this sense, Article 19.8 USMCA requires the parties to 'adopt or maintain a legal framework that provides for the protection of the personal information of the users of digital trade. In the development of its legal framework for the protection of personal information, each Party should take into account principles, and guidelines of relevant international bodies, such as the APEC Privacy Framework and the OECD Recommendation of the Council concerning Guidelines governing the Protection of Privacy and Transborder Flows of Personal Data (2013)' (Article 19.8(2) USMCA). The parties also recognise key data protection principles, including: limitation on collection, choice, data quality, purpose specification, use limitation, security safeguards, transparency, individual participation, and accountability (Article 19.8(3) USMCA), and aim to provide remedies for any violations (Article 19.8(4) and (5) USMCA). This is interesting because it may go beyond what the US has in its national laws on data protection (at least so far) (Chander and Schwartz 2023). Also it reflects some of the privacy protection principles the EU has advocated for, not only within the Union boundaries, but also under the Council of Europe. One can ponder whether this is a development caused by the so-called 'Brussels effect', whereby the EU 'exports' its own domestic standards and they become global (Bradford 2012, 2020), or whether a shift in the US privacy protection regime is underway (Chander et al. 2021).

Beyond data protection, three further innovations of the USMCA may be mentioned. The first refers to the inclusion of 'algorithms', the meaning of which is 'a defined sequence of steps, taken to solve a problem or obtain a result' (Article 19.1 USMCA), and has become part of the ban on requirements for the transfer or access to source code in Article 19.16.[23] The second novum refers to the recognition of 'interactive computer services' as particularly vital to the growth of digital trade.

[22] There is a footnote attached, which clarifies: 'A measure does not meet the conditions of this paragraph if it accords different treatment to data transfers solely on the basis that they are cross-border in a manner that modifies the conditions of competition to the detriment of service suppliers of another Party.' The footnote does not appear in the CPTPP treaty text.

[23] On the expansion of the scope of the source code provision, see New Zealand's Waitangi Tribunal (2021: 104–112).

Parties pledge in this sense not to 'adopt or maintain measures that treat a supplier or user of an interactive computer service as an information content provider in determining liability for harms related to information stored, processed, transmitted, distributed, or made available by the service, except to the extent the supplier or user has, in whole or in part, created, or developed the information' (Article 19.17(2) USMCA).[24] This provision is important, as it seeks to clarify the liability of intermediaries and delineate it from the liability of host providers with regard to infringement of IP rights. It also secures the application of Section 230 of the US Communications Decency Act,[25] which insulates platforms from liability (Goldman 2019; Goldman 2020; Bone 2021) but has been recently under attack in many jurisdictions in the face of fake news and other negative developments related to platforms' power (Feine 2020; Burri 2022).

The third and rather liberal commitment of the USMCA parties is with regard to open government data. This is truly innovative and very relevant in the domain of domestic regimes for data governance. In Article 19.18, the parties recognise that facilitating public access to and use of government information fosters economic and social development, competitiveness, and innovation. 'To the extent that a Party chooses to make government information, including data, available to the public, it shall endeavour to ensure that the information is in a machine-readable and open format and can be searched, retrieved, used, reused, and redistributed' (Article 19.18 (2) USMCA). There is in addition an endeavour to cooperate, so as to 'expand access to and use of government information, including data, that the Party has made public, with a view to enhancing and generating business opportunities, especially for small and medium-sized enterprises' (Article 19.8(3) USMCA). Finally, it can be mentioned that the cooperation provision of the USMCA goes beyond the CPTPP[26] and envisages an institutional setting to enable this cooperation, 'or any other matter pertaining to the operation of this chapter' (Article 19.14 (2) USMCA).

The US approach towards digital trade issues has been confirmed by the recent US–Japan DTA, signed on 7 October 2019, alongside the US–Japan Trade

[24] Annex 19-A creates specific rules with the regard to the application of Article 19.17 for Mexico, in essence postponing its implementation for three years. There is also a footnote to the provision, which specifies that a party may comply through 'application of existing legal doctrines as applied through judicial decisions'. For the argument that Canada's policy space has remained intact (Wolfe 2019: s78).

[25] Section 230 reads: 'No provider or user of an interactive computer service shall be treated as the publisher or speaker of any information provided by another information content provider' and in essence protects online intermediaries that host or republish speech.

[26] The provision envisages, among other things linked to enabling global digital trade, exchange of information and experience on personal information protection, particularly with the view to strengthening existing international mechanisms for cooperation in the enforcement of laws protecting privacy, and cooperation on the promotion and development of mechanisms, including the APEC Cross-Border Privacy Rules, that further global interoperability of privacy regimes (Article 19.14(1) USMCA, at paras. (a)(i) and (b) respectively).

Agreement.[27] The US–Japan DTA replicates almost all provisions of the USMCA and the CPTPP,[28] including the rules on open government data (Article 20 US–Japan DTA), source code (Article 17 US–Japan DTA), and interactive computer services (Article 18 US–Japan DTA)[29] but notably covering also financial and insurance services as part of the scope of the agreement. In the current WTO negotiations on electronic commerce, the US endorsed for a number of years an ambitious template, which was essentially a compilation of the USMCA and the DTA (WTO US Communication 2019a, 2019b). Yet, in October 2023, the United States rather surprisingly announced that it would not further pursue provisions on data flows, data localisation and source code, so as to safeguard 'policy space' for a digital trade rethink.[30]

7.2.2.3 DEAs

The increased preoccupation of policymakers with digital trade issues can be perhaps best exemplified by the new generation of the so-called digital economy agreements. This is a relatively new phenomenon in the trade rulemaking landscape and so far only six such treaties have been adopted – the aforementioned US–Japan DTA; the 2019 ASEAN Agreement on Electronic Commerce (within the context of ASEAN); the 2020 Singapore–Australia Digital Economy Agreement (SADEA); the 2020 Digital Economy Partnership Agreement (DEPA) between Chile, New Zealand, and Singapore; the 2021 Korea–Singapore DEA; and the 2022 UK–Singapore DEA. What is important to mention at the outset is that these agreements can be adopted as standalone initiatives, such as the DEPA, or as part of existing or new trade agreements, such as the ones between Singapore and Australia, and the UK and Singapore. The DEAs may also differ in scope and the extent to which they include new items on the regulation of the data-driven economy. So, while, for instance, the US–Japan DTA still very much resembles a conventional, albeit extended, digital trade chapter, the ASDEA, the DEPA, and the UK–Singapore DEA go beyond this and engage in entirely new areas of regulatory cooperation, including a mixed set of hard and soft law provisions. This section looks more closely

[27] For the text of the agreements, see: https://ustr.gov/countries-regions/japan-korea-apec/japan/us-japan-trade-agreement-negotiations/us-japan-digital-trade-agreement-text.

[28] Article 7: Customs Duties; Article 8: Non-Discriminatory Treatment of Digital Products; Article 9: Domestic Electronic Transactions Framework; Article 10: Electronic Authentication and Electronic Signatures; Article 14: Online Consumer Protection; Article 11: Cross-Border Transfer of Information; Article 12: Location of Computing Facilities; Article 16: Unsolicited Commercial Electronic Messages; Article 19: Cybersecurity US–Japan DTA.

[29] A side letter recognises the differences between the US and Japan's systems governing the liability of interactive computer services suppliers and parties agree that Japan need not change its existing legal system to comply with Article 18.

[30] See Inside US Trade, 'US to End Support for WTO E-commerce Proposals, Wants "Policy Space" for Digital Trade Rethink', 24 October 2023.

at the DEPA as a representative of this latter category and a model of innovative digital trade rulemaking.

The 2020 DEPA between Chile, New Zealand, and Singapore,[31] all parties also to the CPTPP, is, as noted earlier, not conceptualised as a pure trade agreement but one that is meant to address the broader issues of the digital economy. In this sense, its scope is wide, open, and flexible and covers several emergent issues, such as those in the areas of artificial intelligence (AI) and digital inclusion. The agreement is also not a closed deal, but one that is open to other countries (Article 16.2 DEPA) and the DEPA is meant to complement the WTO negotiations on electronic commerce and build upon the digital economy work underway within Asia-Pacific Economic Cooperation (APEC), the OECD, and other international forums. To enable flexibility and cover a wide range of issues, the DEPA follows a modular approach that provides countries with more options to pick and choose from and is very different from the 'all-or-nothing' approach of conventional trade treaties (Bacchus 2021: 8). After Module 1, specifying general definitions and initial provisions, Module 2 focuses on 'Business and Trade Facilitation'; Module 3 'Treatment of Digital Products and Related Issues'; Module 4 'Data Issues'; Module 5 'Wider Trust Environment'; Module 6 'Business and Consumer Trust'; Module 7 'Digital Identities'; Module 8 'Emerging Trends and Technologies'; Module 9 'Innovation and the Digital Economy'; Module 10 'Small and Medium Enterprises Cooperation'; and Module 11 'Digital Inclusion'. The rest of the modules deal with the operationalisation and implementation of the DEPA and cover common institutions (Module 12); exceptions (Module 13); transparency (Module 14); dispute settlement (Module 15); and some final provisions on amendments, entry into force, accession, and withdrawal (Module 16).

The type of rules varies across the different modules. On the one hand, all rules of the CPTPP are replicated; some of the USMCA rules, such as the one on open government data (Article 9.4 DEPA) (but not source code), and some of the US–Japan DTA provisions, such as the one on information and communication technology (ICT) goods using cryptography (Article 3.4 DEPA),[32] have been included too. On the other hand, there are many other rules – so far unknown to trade agreements – that try to facilitate the functioning of the digital economy and enhance cooperation on key issues. So, for instance, Module 2 on business and trade facilitation includes, next to the standard CPTPP-like norms,[33] additional efforts 'to establish or maintain a seamless, trusted, high-availability and secure interconnection of each Party's single window to facilitate the exchange of data

[31] For details and the text of the DEPA, see: www.mfat.govt.nz/en/trade/free-trade-agreements/free-trade-agreements-concluded-but-not-in-force/digital-economy-partnership-agreement/; for a comparison of the DEPA with existing PTAs, see Soprana (2021).

[32] The Article also provides detailed definitions of cryptography, encryption, and cryptographic algorithm and cipher.

[33] Article 2.2: Paperless Trading; Article 2.3: Domestic Electronic Transactions Framework.

relating to trade administration documents, which may include: (a) sanitary and phytosanitary certificates and (b) import and export data' (Article 2.2(5) DEPA).[34] Parties have also touched upon other important issues around digital trade facilitation, such as electronic invoicing (Article 2.5), express shipments and clearance times (Article 2.6), logistics (Article 2.4), and electronic payments (Article 2.7). Module 8 on emerging trends and technologies is also particularly interesting to mention, as it highlights a range of key topics that demand attention from policymakers, such as in the areas of fintech and AI. In the latter domain, the parties agree to promote the adoption of ethical and governance frameworks that support the trusted, safe, and responsible use of AI technologies, and in adopting these AI Governance Frameworks, parties would seek to follow internationally recognised principles or guidelines, including explainability, transparency, fairness, and human-centred values (Article 8.2(2) and (3) DEPA). The DEPA parties also recognise the interfaces between the digital economy, government procurement, and broader competition policy and agree to actively cooperate on these issues (Articles 8.3 and 8.4 DEPA). Along this line of covering broader policy matters in order to create an enabling environment that is also not solely focused on and driven by economic interests, DEPA deals with the importance of a rich and accessible public domain (Article 9.2 DEPA) and digital inclusion, which can cover enhancing cultural and people-to-people links, including between Indigenous peoples, as well as improving access for women, rural populations, and low socio-economic groups (Article 11.2 DEPA).

Overall, the DEAs are a new phenomenon in international trade law with the distinct objective of reflecting the broad range of issues the digital economy impinges upon. Digital economy agreements offer a good basis for harmonisation and interoperability of domestic frameworks and international cooperation that adequately takes into account the complex challenges of contemporary data governance that has essential trade but also non-trade elements. The appeal of the DEAs as a form of enhanced, but also flexible, cooperation on issues of the data-driven economy has been confirmed by South Korea's accession to the treaty in 2024 and Canada's (Government of Canada 2021) interest in joining the DEPA. Another example is the follow-up UK–Singapore DEA, which goes in some aspects beyond the DEPA and covers issues, such as lawtech cooperation and decent work for workers in the digital sector.

7.2.2.4 EU's Approach to Digital Trade

The EU has been a relatively late mover on digital trade issues and, for a long time, did not develop a distinct strategy. Although EU's PTAs did include provisions on

[34] 'Single window' is defined as a facility that allows parties involved in a trade transaction to electronically lodge data and documents with a single entry point to fulfil all import, export, and transit regulatory requirements (Article 2.1 DEPA).

electronic commerce, such as the 2002 agreement with Chile, the language tended to be cautious, with commitments not exceeding GATS levels, and limited to soft cooperation pledges in the services chapter (Article 102 EU–Chile FTA)[35] and in the fields of IT, information society, and telecommunications (Article 37 EU–Chile FTA). In more recent agreements, such as the EU–South Korea FTA (signed in 2009), the first EU Agreement with a dedicated electronic commerce chapter, the language is more concrete and binding, imitating some of the US template provisions, for instance, by confirming the applicability of the WTO agreements to measures affecting electronic commerce and subscribing to a permanent duty-free moratorium on electronic transmissions. Cooperation is also increasingly framed in more concrete terms and includes mutual recognition of electronic signature certificates, coordination on Internet service providers' liability, consumer protection, and paperless trading (Article 7.49 EU–South Korea FTA). As particularly insistent on data protection policies, the EU has also sought commitments from its PTA partners that the development of electronic commerce must be fully compatible with the international data protection standards (Article 7.48 EU–South Korea FTA).

The 2016 EU Agreement with Canada – the Comprehensive Economic and Trade Agreement (CETA) – goes a step further. The CETA provisions concern commitments ensuring (a) clarity, transparency, and predictability in their domestic regulatory frameworks; (b) interoperability, innovation, and competition in facilitating electronic commerce; as well as (c) facilitating the use of electronic commerce by small and medium-sized enterprises (Article 16.5 CETA). The EU succeeded in deepening the privacy commitments as the CETA has a specific norm on trust and confidence in electronic commerce, which obliges the parties to adopt or maintain laws, regulations, or administrative measures for the protection of personal information of users engaged in electronic commerce in consideration of international data protection standards (Article 16.4 CETA). Yet, there are no deep commitments on digital trade, or any rules on data and data flows (Wolfe 2019).

It is only very recently that the EU took up a more modern, CPTPP-comparable, approach towards the regulation of digital trade. Some indications for this turn were given by the 2018 EU–Japan Economic Partnership Agreement (EPA) (Article 8.81 EU–Japan EPA) and the modernisation of the trade part of the EU–Mexico Global Agreement. In these agreements, data flows were mentioned for the first time but still cautiously, as the parties only committed to 'reassess' within three years of the agreement's entry into force. The new EU approach towards the issue of cross-border data is now fully endorsed in the EU's currently negotiated deals with Australia and Tunisia, the 2020 post-Brexit Trade and Cooperation Agreement

[35] The agreement states that '[t]he inclusion of this provision in this Chapter is made without prejudice of the Chilean position on the question of whether or not electronic commerce should be considered as a supply of services'.

(TCA) with the UK,[36] as well as the 2022 Agreement with New Zealand. These PTAs' digital trade chapters include norms on the free flow of data and data localisation bans. However, this repositioning and newer commitments are also linked with high levels of data protection (European Commission 2018).

The EU wishes to permit data flows only if coupled with the high standards of its General Data Protection Regulation (GDPR)[37] and endorses a distinct model of privacy as a fundamental right. While the EU and its partners seek to permit the flow of data, these commitments are conditioned: first, by a dedicated article on data protection, which clearly states that: 'Each Party recognises that the protection of personal data and privacy is a *fundamental right* and that high standards in this regard contribute to trust in the digital economy and to the development of trade' (e.g. Article 6(1) draft EU–Australia FTA (emphasis added)),[38] followed by a paragraph on data sovereignty: 'Each Party may adopt and maintain the safeguards it deems appropriate to ensure the protection of personal data and privacy, including through the adoption and application of rules for the cross-border transfer of personal data. Nothing in this agreement shall affect the protection of personal data and privacy afforded by the Parties' respective safeguards' (e.g. Article 202(2) TCA).[39] The EU also wishes to retain the right to see how the implementation of the provisions on data flows impacts the conditions of privacy protection, so there is a review possibility within three years of the entry into force of the agreement, and parties remain free to propose to review the list of restrictions at any time (e.g. Article 201(2) TCA).[40] In addition, there is a broad carve-out, in the sense that: 'The Parties reaffirm the right to regulate within their territories to achieve legitimate policy objectives, such as the protection of public health, social services, public education, safety, the environment including climate change, public morals, social or consumer protection, privacy and data protection, or the promotion and protection of cultural diversity' (e.g. Article 198 TCA).[41] The EU thus reserves ample regulatory

[36] Trade and Cooperation Agreement between the EU and the European Atomic Energy Community, of the one part, and the United Kingdom of Great Britain and Northern Ireland, of the other part, OJ L [2020] 444/14.

[37] Regulation 2016/679 of the European Parliament and of the Council of 27 April 2016 on the protection of natural persons with regard to the processing of personal data and on the free movement of such data, and repealing Directive 95/46/EC (GDPR), OJ 2016 L 119/1.

[38] The same wording is found in the EU–New Zealand and the draft EU–Tunisia FTA. Interestingly, the TCA does not explicitly mention data protection as a fundamental right. This can be, however, presumed, since the UK incorporates the European Convention on Human Rights (ECHR) through the Human Rights Act of 1998 into its domestic law (Irion and Burri 2022).

[39] The same wording is found in the EU–New Zealand and the draft EU–Tunisia FTA, as well as in the amended in 2023 Article 8.81 EU–Japan FTA.

[40] The same wording is found in the EU–New Zealand and the draft EU–Tunisia FTA, as well as in the amended in 2023 EU–Japan FTA.

[41] The same wording is found in the EU–New Zealand and the draft EU–Tunisia FTA, as well as in the amended in 2023 EU–Japan FTA.

leeway for its current and future data protection (and other) measures. The exceptions are also fundamentally different than the objective necessity test under the CPTPP and the USMCA, or that under WTO law, because it is subjective and safeguards the EU's right to regulate (Yakovleva 2020: 496; Burri and Kugler 2024).

Beyond the topic of data flows and its interface with data protection, it should be noted that the rest of the EU digital trade template includes the issues covered by the CPTPP/USMCA model, such as software source code (Article 207 TCA),[42] facilitation of electronic commerce (Articles 205 and 206 TCA), online consumer protection (Article 208 TCA), spam (Article 209 TCA), and open government data (Article 210 TCA). However, provisions on non-discrimination of digital products are missing and audiovisual services are excluded from the scope of application of the digital trade chapter (Article 197(2) TCA).

7.2.2.5 The RCEP

An interesting and much-anticipated development against the backdrop of the diverging, at least on data flows, EU and US positions has been the RCEP, signed on 15 November 2020 between the ASEAN Members,[43] China, Japan, South Korea, Australia, and New Zealand. The RCEP has been in force since 1 January 2022.[44]

Chapter 12 of the RCEP includes the relevant electronic commerce rules. In a similar fashion to the CPTPP, it clarifies its application 'to measures adopted or maintained by a Party that affect trade by electronic means' but excludes from this broad scope (1) government procurement and (2) information held or processed by or on behalf of a party, or measures related to such information, including measures related to its collection. Regarding trade facilitation, the RCEP includes provisions on paperless trading, electronic authentication, and electronic signatures (Article 12.6 RCEP). On paperless trading, the RCEP Members avoid entering into binding commitments. They, instead, commit to 'work toward', 'endeavour', or 'cooperate' (Article 12.5 RCEP). The norms on accepting the validity of electronic signatures are

[42] Again with notable safeguards, specified in paragraphs 2 and 3 of Article 207, including the general exceptions, security exceptions, and prudential carve-out in the context of a certification procedure; voluntary transfer of source code on a commercial basis, a requirement by a court or administrative tribunal, or a requirement by a competition authority pursuant to a party's competition law to prevent or remedy a restriction or a distortion of competition; a requirement by a regulatory body pursuant to a party's laws or regulations related to the protection of public safety with regard to users online; the protection and enforcement of IP; and government-procurement-related measures.

[43] Brunei, Cambodia, Indonesia, Laos, Malaysia, Myanmar, Philippines, Singapore, Thailand, and Viet Nam.

[44] The RCEP entered into force on 1 January 2022 for ten original parties: Australia, New Zealand, Brunei Darussalam, Cambodia, China, Japan, Laos, Singapore, Thailand, and Viet Nam. The RCEP entered into force for the Republic of Korea on 1 February 2022 and for Malaysia on 18 March 2022. For the details and the text of the RCEP, see https://rcepsec.org/legal-text/.

more binding but, in contrast to the CPTPP and USMCA, permit domestic laws and regulations to provide otherwise and prevail in case of inconsistency.

Regarding commitments to create a conducive environment for electronic commerce, the inclusion of provisions on online personal information protection (Article 12.8 RCEP) and cybersecurity (Article 12.13 RCEP) is remarkable. On the former, RCEP Members establish that they shall adopt or maintain a legal framework that ensures personal information protection. Unsurprisingly, the RCEP is not prescriptive as to how parties may comply with this obligation. As for the latter aspect of cybersecurity, the parties do not establish a binding provision but recognise the importance of building capabilities and using existing collaboration mechanisms to cooperate. The RCEP Members also commit to adopt or maintain laws or regulations regarding online consumer protection (Article 12.7 RCEP), unsolicited commercial electronic messages (Article 12.9 RCEP), and a framework governing electronic transactions that take into account international instruments (Article 12.10 RCEP), as well as commit to transparency (Article 12.12 RCEP).

Concerning data flows, in essence, and similar to the EU PTAs, the RCEP provides only for conditional data flows, while preserving room for domestic policies, which may be of a data-protectionist nature. So, while the RCEP electronic commerce chapter includes a ban on localisation measures (Article 12.14 RCEP), as well as a commitment to free data flows (Article 12.15 RCEP), there are clarifications that give RCEP Members a lot of policy space and essentially undermine the impact of the made commitments. In this line, there is an exception possible for legitimate public policies and a footnote to Article 12.14.3(a), which says that: 'For the purposes of this subparagraph, the Parties affirm that the *necessity* behind the implementation of such legitimate public policy *shall be decided* by the implementing Party.'[45] This essentially goes against any exceptions assessment, as we know it under WTO law, and triggers a self-judging mechanism. In addition, subparagraph (b) of Article 12.14.3 says that the provision does not prevent a party from taking 'any measure that it considers necessary for the protection of its *essential security interests*. Such measures shall not be disputed by other Parties'.[46] Article 12.15 RCEP on cross-border transfer of information follows the same language and thus secures plenty of policy space, for countries like China or Viet Nam, to control data flows without further justification.

Noteworthy are also some things missing from the RCEP: in comparison to the CPTPP, the RCEP does not include provisions on customs duties, non-discriminatory treatment of digital products, source code, principles on access to and use of the Internet for electronic commerce, and Internet interconnection charge sharing. It is finally interesting to observe that the RCEP did not, at least

[45] Emphasis added.

[46] Emphasis added. The 'essential security interest' language has been endorsed by China also in the framework of the WTO electronic commerce negotiations.

initially, reflect China's position in the WTO negotiations, where China was more cautious and somewhat fuzzy in its demands. For instance, at the WTO, China subscribed to a very narrow definition of digital trade, arguing that the negotiations should focus on the discussion of cross-border trade *in goods* enabled by the Internet, together with relevant payment and logistics services, while paying attention to the digitisation trend of trade in services (WTO China Communication 2019: paragraph 2.5), and not engaging in commitments on data flows. This did change in later stages of the negotiations on the Joint Statement Initiative on Electronic Commerce, where China became more open to committing on digital trade issues, particularly those that facilitate it. This can be seen as a shift in China's position that now views a more open data economy as a key contributor to growth and can also be linked to China's wish to join the CPTPP.

7.3 THE NEW DESIGN ELEMENTS ON DIGITAL TRADE IN PTAS: CONCLUDING REMARKS

The above analysis of the developments in PTAs reveals the critical importance of digital trade as a negotiation topic and the substantial efforts made, particularly in recent years, to address it and create an adequate rule framework that goes beyond conventional trade liberalisation efforts. The achievements made by some PTAs and the dedicated DEAs are quite impressive. New and innovative approaches seek to address not only the 'old' issues raised under the 1998 WTO Work Programme on Electronic Commerce but also the contemporary issues in the context of a global data-driven economy. However, the new set of regulatory questions is not neatly defined and encompasses miscellaneous subject matters – from electronic contracts through source code to open government data. The question of free data flows and how to balance these against demands of digital sovereignty has become critical in recent years (Burri and Kugler 2024). In this context, the topic of personal data protection, typically one of fundamental rights' protection, has become a new preoccupation for trade negotiators (Burri 2021a; Chander and Schwartz 2023). The latter development attests to the fact that datafication has extended the scope of trade-related issues and that the electronic commerce/digital trade chapters have turned into centres of gravity to regulate all these.

One can also observe convergence on certain issues, in particular in the area of digital trade facilitation, but also divergence, in particular with regard to permitting and/or conditioning cross-border data flows, as this impacts on the sovereignty of states and their ability to protect the interests of their citizenry. This complex interface between domestic and international data governance regimes can be linked to crafting new reconciliation mechanisms in trade agreements but also to radical shifts and disengagement on data issues, as exemplified by the change in the US position from one of a legal *demandeur* to a more conservative stance (at least for now).

Finally, in terms of the overall evolution of international economic law, it is apparent that PTAs can serve as regulatory laboratories – testing new approaches as to scope, depth, different treaty language, and even new treaty forms, such as the DEAs. However, the political economy of this legal experimentation is complex, as it is linked to the formation of geopolitical blocks with overlaps that may lead to potential contestations and uncertainties as to the impact of the agreements on the ground. In this context, we see, for instance, that New Zealand is a member of the CPTPP, the RCEP, and the DEPA and also has an agreement with the EU; similarly, the UK has a deal with the EU, while also entering into ambitious digital trade commitments under DEAs and the CPTPP.

Overall, the landscape of digital trade rulemaking is likely to remain highly dynamic. We are bound to see the development of even newer design elements in PTAs as technology advances and as countries continue to position themselves – in particular in the area of AI regulation. The coming years will test the willingness for international cooperation in the domain of digital trade regulation and to what extent achievements made in the PTA venues can be translated to the multilateral forum of the WTO (Burri 2023a, 2023c). It would also test to what extent the digital trade agreements will be able to take up the new slew of issues that the data-driven economy affects – such as those around sustainability, platform power, and the protection of fundamental rights that are not solely focused on privacy (Burri 2023b). There are certain challenges intrinsic to these developments that would demand that treaty language adequately reflects the often precarious balance between economic and non-economic objectives, between domestic regulatory efforts and their external trade aspect. Moreover, digital trade rulemaking ought to become more inclusive and take the interests of developing and least developed countries on board.

REFERENCES

Abbott, K. W. and D. Snidal 2000. 'Hard and Soft Law in International Governance', *International Organization* 54(3): 421–456.

Adlung, R. and H. Mamdouh 2013. 'How to Design Trade Agreements in Services: Top Down or Bottom Up?' WTO Staff Working Paper 8.

Andersen, H. 2015. 'Protection of Non-Trade Values in WTO Appellate Body Jurisprudence: Exceptions, Economic Arguments, and Eluding Questions', *Journal of International Economic Law* 18(2): 383–405.

Bacchus, J. 2021. *The Digital Decide: How to Agree on WTO Rules for Digital Trade.* Special Report. Waterloo, ON: Centre for International Governance Innovation.

Barlow, J. P. 1996. 'A Declaration of the Independence of Cyberspace, 8 February 1996', www.eff.org/cyberspace-independence.

Bone, T. 2021. 'How Content Moderation May Expose Social Media Companies to Greater Defamation Liability', *Washington University Law Review* 98(3): 937–963.

Bradford, A. 2012. 'The Brussels Effect', *Northwestern University Law Review* 107(1): 1–68.

2020. *The Brussels Effect: How the European Union Rules the World*. Oxford: Oxford University Press.

Burri, M. 2015. 'The International Economic Law Framework for Digital Trade', *Zeitschrift für Schweizerisches Recht* 135(2): 10–72.

2017. 'The Regulation of Data Flows in Trade Agreements', *Georgetown Journal of International Law* 48(1): 408–448.

2019. 'Understanding and Shaping Trade Rules for the Digital Era', in M. Elsig, M. Hahn and G. Spilker (eds.), *The Shifting Landscape of Global Trade Governance*. Cambridge: Cambridge University Press.

2021a. 'Interfacing Privacy and Trade', *Case Western Journal of International Law* 53(1): 35–88.

2021b. 'Data Flows and Global Trade Law', in M. Burri (ed.), *Big Data and Global Trade Law*. Cambridge: Cambridge University Press.

2022. 'Fake News in Times of Pandemic and Beyond: An Enquiry into the Rationales for Regulating Information Platforms', in K. Mathis and A. Tor (eds.), *Law and Economics of the Coronavirus Crisis*. Berlin: Springer.

2023a. 'A WTO Agreement on Electronic Commerce: An Enquiry into its Substance and Viability', *Georgetown Journal of International Law* 53(4): 565–625.

2023b. 'Digital Trade Law and Human Rights', *AJIL Unbound* 117: 110–115.

2023c. 'Trade Law 4.0: Are We There Yet?' *Journal of International Economic Law* 26(1): 90–100.

Burri, M. and T. Cottier (eds.) 2012. *Trade Governance in the Digital Age*. Cambridge: Cambridge University Press.

Burri, M. and R. Polanco 2020. 'Digital Trade Provisions in Preferential Trade Agreements: Introducing a New Dataset', *Journal of International Economic Law* 23(1): 187–220.

Burri, M., M. Vasquez Callo-Müller and K. Kugler 2024. 'The Evolution of Digital Trade Law: Insights from TAPED', *World Trade Review* 22(1): 1–18, https://doi.org/10.1017/S1474745623000472.

Chander, A. and P. M. Schwartz 2023. 'Privacy and/or Trade', *University of Chicago Law Review* 90(1): 50–135.

Chander, A., M. E. Kaminski and W. McGeveran 2021. 'Catalyzing Privacy Law', *Minnesota Law Review* 105(4): 1733–1802.

Eichensehr, K. E. 2015. 'The Cyber-Law of Nations', *The Georgetown Law Journal* 103(6): 317–380.

Elsig, M. and S. Klotz 2021. 'Data Flow-Related Provisions in Preferential Trade Agreements: Trends and Patterns of Diffusion', in M. Burri (ed.), *Big Data and Global Trade Law*. Cambridge: Cambridge University Press.

European Commission 2018. 'Horizontal Provisions for Cross-Border Data Flows and for Personal Data Protection in EU Trade and Investment Agreements', https://trade.ec.europa.eu/doclib/docs/2018/may/tradoc_156884.pdf.

Feine, L. 2020. 'Big Tech's Favorite Law Is under Fire', CNBC. (19 February 2020) www.cnbc.com/2020/02/19/what-is-section-230-and-why-do-some-people-want-to-change-it.html.

Fliess, B. and P. Sauvé 1998. *Of Chips, Floppy Disks and Great Timing: Assessing the WTO Information Technology Agreement*. Paris: Institut Français des Relations Internationales.

Gao, H. 2018. 'Regulation of Digital Trade in US Free Trade Agreements: From Trade Regulation to Digital Regulation', *Legal Issues of Economic Integration* 45(1): 47–70.

Goldman, E. 2019. 'Why Section 230 Is Better Than the First Amendment', *Notre Dame Law Review Reflection* 95(1): 33–46.

2020. 'An Overview of the United States' Section 230 Internet Immunity', in: G. Frosio (ed.), *The Oxford Handbook of Online Intermediary Liability*. Oxford: Oxford University Press.

Government of Canada 2021. 'Global Affairs, Background: Canada's Possible Accession to the Digital Economy Partnership Agreement', www.international.gc.ca/trade-commerce/consultations/depa-apen/background-information.aspx?lang = eng.

Henke, N. et al. 2016. *The Age of Analytics: Competing in a Data-Driven World*. Washington, DC: McKinsey Global Institute.

Horn, H., P. C. Mavroidis and A. Sapir 2009. *Beyond the WTO? An Anatomy of EU and US Preferential Trade Agreements*. Brussels: Bruegel Print.

Irion, K. and M. Burri 2022. 'Digitaler Handel (Commentary of the Digital Trade Title of the EU–UK Trade and Cooperation Agreement)', in G. Kübek et al. (eds.), *Handels- und Kooperationsvertrag EU/GB Handbuch*. Baden-Baden: Nomos.

Joint Statement on Trilateral Meeting of the Trade Ministers of the United States, Japan, and the European Union. 2020. Washington, DC, https://trade.ec.europa.eu/doclib/docs/2020/january/tradoc_158567.pdf.

Kingsbury, B. et al. (eds.) 2019b. *Megaregulation Contested: Global Economic Ordering after TPP*. Oxford: Oxford University Press.

Kingsbury, B., P. Mertenskötter, R. B. Stewart and T. Streinz 2019a. 'The Trans-Pacific Partnership as Megaregulation', IILJ Working Paper 2019/2.

López-González, J. and M. Jouanjean 2017. 'Digital Trade: Developing a Framework for Analysis', OECD Trade Policy Papers 205.

López-González, J., F. Casalini and T. Nemoto 2022. 'Mapping Approaches to Cross-Border Data Flows', in I. Borchert and L. A. Winters (eds.), *Addressing Impediments to Digital Trade*. Brussels: CEPR Press.

Manyika, J. et al. 2011. *Big Data: The Next Frontier for Innovation, Competition, and Productivity*. Washington, DC: McKinsey Global Institute.

Mayer-Schönberger, V. and K. Cukier 2013. *Big Data: A Revolution That Will Transform How We Live, Work, and Think*. New York: Eamon Dolan/Houghton Mifflin Harcourt.

New Zealand's Waitangi Tribunal 2021. 'Report on the Comprehensive and Progressive Agreement for Trans-Pacific Partnership'. (19 November 2021) https://forms.justice.govt.nz/search/Documents/WT/wt_DOC_195473606/Report%20on%20the%20CPTPP%20W.pdf.

Schwartz, P. M. and D. J. Solove 2014. 'Reconciling Personal Information in the United States and European Union', *California Law Review* 102(4): 877–916.

Shaffer, G. C. and M. A. Pollack 2010. 'Hard vs. Soft Law: Alternatives, Complements, and Antagonists in International Governance', *Minnesota Law Review* 94(3): 706–799.

Soprana, M. 2021. 'The Digital Economy Partnership Agreement (DEPA): Assessing the Significance of the New Trade Agreement on the Block', *Trade, Law and Development* 13(1): 143–169.

Torrey, Z. 2018. 'TPP 2.0: The Deal without the US: What's New about the CPTPP and What Do the Changes Mean?' *The Diplomat*. (03 February 2018) https://thediplomat.com/2018/02/tpp-2-0-the-deal-without-the-us/.

US Congress 2001. 'Bipartisan Trade Promotion Authority Act of 2001', H.R. 3005.

US Congressional Research Service 2021. 'China and Taiwan Both Seek to Join the CPTPP', https://crsreports.congress.gov/product/pdf/IN/IN11760.

Whitman, J. Q. 2004. 'The Two Western Cultures of Privacy: Dignity versus Liberty', *The Yale Law Journal* 113(6): 1151–1221.

Wolfe, R. 2019. 'Learning about Digital Trade: Privacy and E-Commerce in CETA and TPP', *World Trade Review* 18(S1): s63–s84.

WTO 1996. 'Ministerial Declaration on Trade in Information Technology Products', WT/MIN(96)/16.
1998. 'Work Programme on Electronic Commerce', WT/L/274.
2018. *World Trade Report 2018: The Future of World Trade: How Digital Technologies Are Transforming Global Commerce*. Geneva: World Trade Organization.
WTO China Communication 2019. 'Joint Statement on Electronic Commerce, Communication from China', INF/ECOM/19.
WTO 2019a. 'Joint Statement on Electronic Commerce, Communication from the United States', INF/ECOM/5.
2019b. 'Joint Statement on Electronic Commerce, Communication from the United States', INF/ECOM/23.
2019c. *World Trade Report 2019: The Future of Services Trade*. Geneva: WTO.
2021. 'Work Programme on Electronic Commerce: The Moratorium on Custom Duties on Electronic Transmissions: Need for Clarity on its Scope and Impact', WT/GC/W/833.
Wunsch-Vincent, S. 2003. 'The Digital Trade Agenda of the US', *Aussenwirtschaft* 58(1): 7–46.
2006. *The WTO, the Internet and Digital Products: EC and US Perspectives*. Oxford: Hart.
Wunsch-Vincent, S. and A. Hold 2012. 'Towards Coherent Rules for Digital Trade: Building on Efforts in Multilateral versus Preferential Trade Negotiations', in M. Burri and T. Cottier (eds.), *Trade Governance in the Digital Age*. Cambridge: Cambridge University Press.
Yakovleva, S. 2020. 'Privacy Protection(ism): The Latest Wave of Trade Constraints on Regulatory Autonomy', *University of Miami Law Review* 74(2): 416–519.
Yonhap News Agency 2021. 'South Korea Starts Process to Join DEPA', https://en.yna.co.kr/view/PYH20211006124000325.

8

Recent Trends and Future Developments with Regard to Foreign Investment in PTAs

Federico Ortino

8.1 INTRODUCTION

The evolution of investment disciplines in preferential trade agreements (PTAs) is linked closely with the evolution of the wider world of international investment agreements (IIAs), in particular, bilateral investment treaties (BITs), that have been at the centre of the numerous and controversial disputes between foreign investors and host states brought before international arbitral tribunals in the last twenty years. The link is certainly stronger with regard to the core areas, including investment protection, investment liberalisation, and investor–state dispute settlement (ISDS). However, some of the more interesting innovations with regard to investment at the international level appear to have taken place in particular in the context of recent PTAs, as these have included a growing number of novel issues (at times found in distinct chapters) such as 'trade and development', 'regulatory coherence', 'corporate social responsibility' (CSR), and 'investment facilitation'. These novel issues have important implications for foreign investment and demonstrate a willingness to explore new ways to achieve more traditional objectives (such as promoting greater investment flows) as well as to pursue additional objectives (such as 'sustainable' development). As investment is still only marginally covered by the World Trade Organization (WTO), particularly in the Agreement on Trade-Related Investment Measures (TRIMs) and the General Agreement on Trade in Services (GATS), PTAs thus offer a window on possible interesting developments regarding investment policymaking at the international level.

This chapter starts with an analysis of recent (i.e. last fifteen years) trends in the investment chapters of PTAs focusing in particular on some of the traditional investment disciplines such as protection, liberalisation, and dispute settlement (Section 8.1). The analysis then moves on to address a few specific issues with regard to each of the three traditional sets of investment disciplines that are likely to become central in future PTAs (Section 8.2). Finally, the chapter focuses on novel approaches aimed at strengthening investment flows in terms of both quantity and quality (Section 8.3).

8.2 RECENT TRENDS IN PTAS WITH REGARD TO FOREIGN INVESTMENT

The first PTA with an investment chapter is the North American Free Trade Agreement (NAFTA), signed in 1992. Writing in the aftermath of its conclusion, Dan Price, former United States NAFTA Investment chapter negotiator, identified 'protection', 'liberalisation', and 'dispute settlement' as the three key objectives of NAFTA Chapter 11 on investment.[1] This chapter would set a standard for further multilateral and bilateral investment accords in the hemisphere. Most PTAs signed since the NAFTA with an investment chapter adopted the core disciplines contained in Chapter 11.[2] However, twenty years of interpretation and application of IIAs in the context of several hundred investor–state arbitrations have led to some changes with regard to investment disciplines in PTAs. In this section, I focus on a few key recent (i.e. in the last fifteen years) trends concerning the traditional features of investment chapters in PTAs.[3]

8.2.1 *Scope of Application*

Like traditional BITs, investment chapters in PTAs have historically adopted a broad scope of application, as reflected in particular in the definitions of key terms such as 'investment' and 'investor'. Following the wave of investor–state disputes, many states have, to some extent, narrowed the scope of investment provisions. With regard to the definition of 'investment', recent treaties have required that protected investments need to meet certain typical 'characteristics' such as 'a certain duration', 'the commitment of capital or other resources', 'the expectation of gain or profit', or 'the assumption of risk'; the list of express characteristics of investment is often illustrative.

Similarly, recent treaties exclude certain specific investments from their scope, such as 'claims to money that arise solely from commercial contracts for the sale of

[1] 'The investment chapter [in NAFTA] has three objectives: establish a secure investment environment through the elaboration of clear rules of fair treatment of foreign investment and investors; remove barriers to investment by eliminating or liberalizing existing restrictions; and provide an effective means for the resolution of disputes between an investor and the host government.' (Price 1993).

[2] See Crawford and Kotschwar (2018) analysing a data set on the content of investment provisions in PTAs including a total of 111 PTAs that entered into force between 1960 and 2017 and include distinct investment provisions.

[3] I rely on the United Nations Conference on Trade and Development (UNCTAD) database (investmentpolicy.unctad.org), the WTO database (rtais.wto.org), and the Electronic Database of Investment Treaties (EDIT) database (edit.wti.org).

goods or services' or 'any order, judgment, or arbitral award related to such claims' (Article 8.1 of the 2016 European Union (EU)–Canada CETA). Exceptionally, a few treaties have also opted to expressly exclude 'portfolio investment' from the scope of the investment chapter (see Article 8.1 of the 2018 Brazil–Chile Free Trade Agreement, FTA).

With regard to the definition of 'investor', recent PTAs have also limited the legal persons who qualify as 'nationals' of one of the contracting parties and are thus protected by the investment chapter. Contrary to many earlier treaties, being incorporated in the home state is not enough to benefit from the protection granted by the treaty. Recent treaties require, in addition, that such legal persons have 'substantial business operations' in the country of incorporation (2022 United Kingdom (UK) –Australia; 2019 China–Mauritius). Comparing all PTAs concluded between 1990 and 2004 (147), only 18 per cent contained the additional condition of 'substantial business activities', while among those concluded between 2005 and 2020, the percentage of investment chapters including such condition is thirty. This stricter approach appears to have been adopted to address the practice of so-called mailbox companies, owned or controlled by nationals or companies not intended to be protected by the underlying agreement and having no real connection with the country concerned, to benefit from the protection offered by the agreement itself ('nationality planning' practice).[4]

8.2.2 *Investment Protection*

Like older BITs, investment chapters in PTAs focus on providing certain protection guarantees to foreign investments, for example, by setting conditions for the expropriation of assets by the host state, or by requiring the host state to treat foreign investments in a fair, non-discriminatory, and reasonable manner. Recent PTAs have mainly focused on (a) clarifying traditional investment protection standards and, at the same time, (b) narrowing the extent of the protections offered by such standards to foreign investment. For example, in the last fifteen years, most investment chapters have included a more detailed definition of 'indirect expropriation' (often included in a separate annex on Expropriation), emphasising that a determination of whether a measure or series of measures constitute an indirect expropriation requires a case-by-case, fact-based inquiry that considers various factors including both the 'economic impact' of the government action and the 'character' of the government action (including its object, context, and intent).

Similarly, many recent PTAs have clarified and narrowed some of the key standards of protection, such as 'fair and equitable treatment' (FET) and 'full

[4] It should be pointed out that several older BITs adopted a similar, stricter approach to German and Swiss BITs, for example the Hungary-Switzerland BIT (1988).

protection and security' (FPS). The most common approach has been that of limiting both concepts by referring to the international customary minimum standard of treatment, which has historically provided for a more limited set of guarantees. For example, in line with United States and Canadian practice since the early 2000s, Article 14.6.1 of the United States–Mexico–Canada Agreement (USMCA) provides that 'Each Party shall accord to covered investments treatment in accordance with customary international law, including fair and equitable treatment and full protection and security' and that '[t]he concepts of "fair and equitable treatment" and "full protection and security" do not require treatment in addition to or beyond that which is required by that standard, and do not create additional substantive rights'.

A second approach, in particular with regard to FET, is to identify an exhaustive list of conducts that are in breach of the FET standard, without any express reference to customary law. For example, Article 8.10.2 of the 2016 Comprehensive and Economic Trade Agreement (CETA) between the EU and Canada identifies the following as constituting a violation of the FET obligation: '(a) denial of justice in criminal, civil or administrative proceedings; (b) fundamental breach of due process, including a fundamental breach of transparency, in judicial and administrative proceedings; (c) manifest arbitrariness; (d) targeted discrimination on manifestly wrongful grounds, such as gender, race or religious belief; (e) abusive treatment of investors, such as coercion, duress and harassment'. Furthermore, while the list does not refer to the frustration of investor's legitimate expectations, which has represented one of the key claims by investors based on FET, Article 8.10.4 does permit a tribunal, when applying the FET obligation, to 'take into account whether a Party made a specific representation to an investor to induce a covered investment, that created a legitimate expectation, and upon which the investor relied in deciding to make or maintain the covered investment'.

Interestingly, the difference between the two approaches may only be in form rather than in substance. While there is no express reference to customary law in Article 8.10 CETA, it can be argued that such provision does provide a list of the kinds of conduct that would be in breach of the customary minimum standard of treatment.[5] Even the reference to legitimate expectations appears to be in line with the way some investment tribunals have understood the customary minimum

[5] See *Waste Management Inc v. Mexico (II)*, ICSID Case No. ARB(AF)00/3, Award, 30 April 2004, para 98 ('the minimum standard of treatment of fair and equitable treatment is infringed by conduct attributable to the State and harmful to the claimant if the conduct is arbitrary, grossly unfair, unjust or idiosyncratic, is discriminatory and exposes the claimant to sectional or racial prejudice, or involves a lack of due process leading to an outcome which offends judicial propriety – as might be the case with a manifest failure of natural justice in judicial proceedings or a complete lack of transparency and candour in an administrative process'). See (Newcombe and Paradell 2009, pp. 235–253).

standard of treatment (particularly as referred to in Article 1105 NAFTA).[6] However, compared with the approach adopted in USMCA, the exhaustive list found in Article 8.10 of the CETA formulation may be said to bring greater (but not absolute) clarity with regard to the scope of FET as the interpreter has much less leeway in identifying the contours of the applicable standard (as it may have when the treaty simply refers to the unwritten concept of the customary minimum standard of treatment).

Beyond FET and FPS, in recent years, the inclusion of provisions in investment treaties aimed at protecting the host state's contractual commitments through so-called umbrella clauses has increasingly dwindled. An UNCTAD survey of publicly available investment treaties concluded between 2011 and 2015 has found that out of seventy-two treaties, only seventeen contain an umbrella clause (and thirteen of those seventeen treaties involved Japan as one of the contracting parties)(UNCTAD 2016). This roughly adds up to three in every four new treaties that do not contain an umbrella clause and contrasts with the pre-2004 treaties statistic of one in every two treaties (Gill et al. 2004; Pereira de Souza Fleury 2015, 2017). Even United States' PTAs have, since 2004, omitted the umbrella clause. However, it should also be noted that United States' investment treaties often adopt a wide jurisdictional clause, including the investor's right to submit to arbitration a claim that the respondent has breached an 'investment authorisation' or an 'investment agreement'.[7] Interestingly, the EU's position on umbrella clauses appears more nuanced. While the agreement with Canada does not contain any umbrella clause (and no broad jurisdictional clause), the 2015 EU draft proposal, in the context of the negotiation with the United States for the Transatlantic Trade and Investment Partnership (TTIP),[8] did contain an umbrella clause. The wording was, however, different from the traditional umbrella clauses as it attempted to clarify the various issues that had led to several controversies in arbitral practice.[9]

[6] For example, having identified the conduct that will infringe the minimum standard of treatment, the tribunal in Waste *Management v. Mexico* famously stated that '[i]n applying this standard it is relevant that the treatment is in breach of representations made by the host State which were reasonably relied on by the claimant'. *Waste Management v Mexico II*, Award, 30 April 2004, para 98.

[7] See, for example, Article 11.16.1 of the 2007 US–Korea FTA.

[8] European Commission, Transatlantic Trade and Investment Partnership (TTIP) – Documents <https://policy.trade.ec.europa.eu/eu-trade-relationships-country-and-region/countries-and-regions/united-states/eu-negotiating-texts-ttip_en> accessed 21 March 2023.

[9] Article 7 of the Chapter on Investment in the EU's draft proposal made public on 12 November 2015 reads as follows: 'Article 7 Observance of written commitments: Where a Party either itself or through any entity mentioned in Article X [Definition of 'measures adopted or maintained by a Party'] has entered into any contractual written commitment with investors of the other Party or with their covered investments, that Party shall not, either itself or through any such entity breach the said commitment through the exercise of governmental authority.' A footnote clarifies the meaning of 'contractual written commitment' as follows: 'For the purposes of this paragraph, a "contractual written commitment" means an agreement in writing, entered into by a Party, itself or through any entity mentioned in Article X [Definition

Furthermore, recent PTAs with investment protection have attempted to strengthen the contracting parties' right to regulate in the public interest in various ways. First, some recent treaties have excluded either expressly or implicitly the possibility of interpreting any of the traditional investment protection provisions (including the FET standard) as a guarantee of regulatory stability in the strict sense, which is perceived by several host states as representing a serious restraint on their ability to regulate. For an example of an implicit exclusion, the preamble of the 2015 Australia–China FTA refers to the 'rights of [the] governments to regulate in order to meet national policy objectives, and to preserve their flexibility to safeguard public welfare'. Arguably, reading an FET provision to include a guarantee of regulatory stability would contrast with an interpretation based on the customary rules of treaty interpretation that, in addition to the 'text', rely on the 'context' and 'object and purpose' of the treaty (Giannakopoulos 2019).

An example of an express, broad exclusion of legal stability *stricto sensu* is Article 8.9 CETA. While paragraph 1 reaffirms the contracting parties' 'right to regulate … to achieve legitimate policy objectives', paragraph 2 expressly clarifies that the host State's regulation negatively affecting an investment or interfering with an investor's expectations is not per se prohibited by the investment treaty.

A second approach to strengthen the right to regulate has been to include 'general exception' clauses often styled on the basis of the general exception provision in Article XX of the General Agreement on Tariffs and Trade (GATT), which are meant to vest on contracting parties a margin of regulatory discretion in order to act in the public interest (see Sabanogullari 2018). For example, several Canadian PTAs concluded in the last fifteen years include broad general exception provisions.[10]

8.2.3 *Investment Liberalisation*

While traditional investment treaties focused on investment protection, recent treaties, including, in particular, PTAs, include liberalisation obligations or market access commitments with regard to foreign investment. These obligations include, first of all, non-discrimination obligations (national treatment and most-favoured-nation, MFN), which apply to the pre-establishment phase of the investment. Accordingly, any restriction/condition of entry needs to apply in a non-discriminatory manner so that domestic investors (national treatment) and

of "measures adopted or maintained by a Party"], with an investor or a covered investment, whether in a single instrument or multiple instruments, that creates an exchange of rights and obligations, binding on both Parties.'

10 See, for example, 2008 Canada–Columbia and 2008 Canada–Peru FTAs. However, Canada's position seems to have changed as in its latest Model BIT, Canada has excluded the applicability of general exception clauses to traditional standards of investment protection. See 2021 Canada Model BIT.

third-party investors (MFN) in like circumstances are not treated more favourably than the foreign investors protected by the underlying treaty.[11]

In addition to such commitments, recent PTAs concluded by the EU include 'market access' commitments drafted on the basis of a similar provision included in the GATS (Article XVI), which expressly prohibits any measure that 'restricts or requires specific types of legal entity or joint venture through which an enterprise may carry out an economic activity' or that 'imposes limitations on:

- the number of enterprises that may carry out a specific economic activity whether in the form of numerical quotas, monopolies, exclusive suppliers or the requirement of an economic needs test;
- the total value of transactions or assets in the form of numerical quotas or the requirement of an economic needs test;
- the total number of operations or the total quantity of output expressed in terms of designated numerical units in the form of quotas or the requirement of an economic needs test;
- the participation of foreign capital in terms of maximum percentage limit on foreign shareholding or the total value of individual or aggregate foreign investment; or
- the total number of natural persons that may be employed in a particular sector or that an enterprise may employ and who are necessary for, and directly related to, the performance of economic activity in the form of numerical quotas or the requirement of an economic needs test'.[12]

Furthermore, the investment chapters in several recent PTAs include provisions prohibiting so-called performance requirements: domestic provisions that condition the ability of foreign investors to make an investment only if they undertake various acts such as exporting a given amount of goods or services or using a certain amount of domestic goods or services in their investments. Preferential trade agreements concluded, for example by the United States, Canada, Chile, Japan, Singapore, Korea, and recently the EU, include such performance requirements disciplines, sometimes mirroring the commitments found in the WTO TRIMs Agreement (see India–Singapore Comprehensive Economic Cooperation Agreement, CECA) and sometimes going beyond the TRIMs Agreement, for example applying to services and adding additional limitations such as on forced technology transfer, the hiring of

[11] See Article 14.4: National Treatment, USMCA: '1. Each Party shall accord to investors of another Party treatment no less favourable than that it accords, in like circumstances, to its own investors with respect to the establishment, acquisition, expansion, management, conduct, operation, and sale or other disposition of investments in its territory.' Article 14.5: Most-Favored-Nation Treatment: '1. Each Party shall accord to investors of another Party treatment no less favorable than the treatment it accords, in like circumstances, to investors of any other Party or of any non-Party with respect to the establishment, acquisition, expansion, management, conduct, operation, and sale or other disposition of investments in its territory.'

[12] Article 8.4.1 EU-Canada CETA.

a certain number or percentage of nationals, or acting as the exclusive supplier of the goods or services produced (for TRIMs+ examples, see US–Chile, US–Australia, the Dominican Republic–Central America FTA (CAFTA-DR), Korea–Chile, and Japan–Singapore).

All these liberalisation provisions in PTAs are subject to various exemptions, included in various annexes to the PTA, often on the basis of a negative-list approach, with regard to specific 'non-conforming measures' (and 'future measures') and 'excluded sectors'.

8.2.4 *ISDS*

In terms of dispute settlement, most recent PTAs with an investment chapter continue to include the ability of a protected investor to bring a claim directly against the host state before an ad hoc international arbitral tribunal (so-called investor–state dispute settlement). However, many of these most recent PTAs with ISDS specify in detail the arbitration procedures to be followed by an arbitral tribunal, including provisions on consolidation of claims, procedural mechanisms to avoid frivolous claims, transparency requirements, the appointment of experts, and the right of the tribunal to accept amicus briefs (Meltzer 2016).[13]

It is worth noting that a few recent PTAs have excluded ISDS altogether. See, for example, the 2018 USMCA, except between Mexico and the United States, and, in part, the 2018 Comprehensive and Progressive Agreement for Trans-Pacific Partnership (CPTPP) (with regard to Australia and New Zealand). Other agreements have provided for a permanent dispute settlement structure including both a first-instance tribunal and an appellate tribunal (see various recent PTAs and investment protection agreements concluded by the EU, e.g. with Canada, Viet Nam, and Singapore).

8.3 FUTURE CHALLENGES WITH REGARD TO MORE TRADITIONAL INVESTMENT DISCIPLINES IN PTAS

Looking ahead, future PTAs may need to address further issues when it comes to the three more traditional sets of investment disciplines: protection, liberalisation, and dispute settlement.

Regarding investment protection, two key issues will likely become more important in future policymaking/treaty-making: standards of review and available remedies.

To preserve the host state's right to regulate in the public interest, the current trend is to favour protection standards that consider the reasonableness (whether procedural or substantive) of the host state's conduct. This can be seen in the more

[13] See also Gáspár-Szilágyi and Usynin (2020).

detailed definition of an 'indirect expropriation' or in the reformulation of the FET standard. However, what has not yet been clarified, whether in the arbitral practice or recent investment treaties, is the nature and intensity of the review, which investment tribunals are called on to perform. For example, what is the nature of the case-by-case inquiry prescribed to determine the existence of an indirect expropriation in recent investment treaties? What relevance should be given to each of the various factors expressly identified in the recent annexes on expropriation? What kind of balancing does such inquiry require? These questions are linked with the concept of 'deference', which is 'a parameter of the relationship between international and domestic law and protects a state's domestic policy space against control by international law and international tribunals' (Schill 2012).

The second issue revolves around the question of the remedies that are available to a foreign investor in case the host state has breached any of the investment protection guarantees. Traditionally, investment treaties, including investment chapters in PTAs, do not specify what the available remedies (except for the case of a lawful expropriation) are. Only a few recent treaties (e.g. concluded by the United States and Canada) specify the applicable remedies (usually 'damages' and 'material restitution'). For example, Article 14.D.13 of USMCA specifies that 'the tribunal may award, separately or in combination, only: (a) monetary damages and any applicable interest; and (b) restitution of property, in which case the award shall provide that the respondent may pay monetary damages and any applicable interest in lieu of restitution'. Where the treaty is silent on the issue of remedies, arbitral practice shows that the award of damages is the typical form of remedy for violations of investment treaties, despite the fact that under general international law, various forms of restitution are also, in principle, available (Sabahi 2011). Policymakers may, in the future, want to consider providing more detailed rules on what should be the available remedies, in part to ensure that the remedy granted by a tribunal is in the best interest of the host state (and not just the foreign investor). In some situations, the 'restoration of the legal situation at the *status quo ante*' or 'specific performance' may represent a better remedy (at least from the perspective of the host state) compared to the payment of compensation. Does it always make sense to pay billions in damages to a foreign investor for the unlawful termination of its oil concession (often calculated on the basis of the investor's lost future profits) when the host state will nevertheless have 'to pay for' extracting the same oil from the ground?

When it comes to investment liberalisation, the future key challenge will be to strengthen the effectiveness of these disciplines. While the demand for greater investment liberalisation is certainly there (from foreign investors and certain capital-exporting countries), there are several issues that need to be addressed to increase investment liberalisation in PTAs.

First, liberalisation commitments in PTAs tend to be limited to what countries have already managed to liberalise unilaterally. In other words, the level of ambition in liberalising investment flows may need to be improved. Furthermore, in those countries that have traditionally been very open to inward foreign investment (such as developed economies), there seems to be a growing trend in subjecting foreign investors to a greater number of restrictions.[14] As a consequence, there is a greater use of self-judging 'national security' or 'essential security' exceptions in PTAs. Article 17.13 of the EU–Viet Nam FTA provides for a general 'security exception', which provides that '[n]othing in this Agreement shall be construed as: ... (b) preventing either Party from taking any action which it considers necessary for the protection of its essential security interests: (iv) taken in time of war or other emergency in international relations'. At times these exceptions are specific to the obligations in the investment chapter. For example, Article 10.15 RCEP provides that 'nothing in this Chapter [on Investment] shall be construed to: ... (b) preclude a Party from applying measures that it considers necessary for: ... (ii) the protection of its own essential security interests'. In light of the increased number of claims attempting to justify various restrictions on the entry of FDI on the basis of national security, there will be a greater need to identify clearer limits on the use (and possible abuse) of such exception provisions, which appear to particularly affect investment liberalisation commitments.

Second, to fully appreciate the level of liberalisation commitments that have actually been undertaken in PTAs is often a complex operation. This is so whether the scheduling has occurred on the basis of a positive-list approach (identifying the sectors where the liberalisation commitments have been undertaken) or a negative-list approach (identifying the sectors or measures falling outside such commitments). Understanding which sectors or subsectors are included or excluded and which specific non-conforming measure is allowed or not allowed often entails quite a difficult assessment. For example, ratchet clauses are sometimes included in PTAs to ensure that any investment liberalisation taking place unilaterally is 'locked in', and thus there can be no step backwards. On paper, this is an instrument to increase the level of investment liberalisation in the context of a PTA. However, the operation of such clauses in practice is not always straightforward, and there appears to be little empirical evidence to show its liberalising effects in practice.

When it comes to ISDS, the key question in future policymaking/treaty-making will be whether to keep it centred on arbitration, to opt for a more permanent, institutionalised (quasi-judicial) structure, or to omit ISDS altogether. All these options are being explored in the context of the discussion in the United Nations Commission on International Trade Law (UNCITRAL) Working Group III and reflect the variety of positions expressed by participating states and various stakeholders in those discussions. Professor Anthea Roberts has captured these different

[14] See Regulation (EU) 2019/452 of the European Parliament and of the Council of 19 March 2019 establishing a framework for the screening of foreign direct investments (FDIs) into the Union.

positions by suggesting the following three camps: incrementalists, systemic reformers, and paradigm shifters (Roberts 2018, pp. 410–432). According to the former camp, criticisms of the current system are overall overblown; investor–state arbitration remains the best option available to settle disputes, although modest reforms will deal with many of the various concerns raised in the last ten years. On the other hand, the second camp views investor–state arbitration as seriously flawed, but they do want to retain investors' direct claims to an international tribunal. This group champions more significant and systemic reforms, in particular the establishment of a permanent international tribunal or at least a multilateral appellate mechanism. Lastly, the paradigm shifters believe that the existing system is irrevocably flawed and reject the utility of investors making international claims against states. This camp embraces a variety of alternatives, such as a greater reliance on domestic courts, ombudsmen, and state–state dispute settlement, rather than ISDS.

Future PTAs will definitely be influenced by the outcome of the UNCITRAL ISDS reform discussion, which is hoped to reach a conclusion in the next two to three years. While it is difficult to predict the outcome of the UNCITRAL discussions, at the moment, it is perhaps fair to predict that changes will be rather on the 'incrementalist' end of the reformers' spectrum. Despite the heavy criticism or backlash against ISDS over the last fifteen years, the level of actual change of ISDS has been so far very minimal (Ortino 2023). One area where one can predict consensus, and which is likely to influence future investment PTAs, is around identifying certain principles and provisions strengthening the independence and impartiality of arbitrators as well as the integrity, fairness, and efficiency of proceedings.[15]

8.4 NOVEL APPROACHES TO INVESTMENT DISCIPLINES IN FUTURE PTAS: THE TURN TO INVESTMENT FACILITATION

The push towards finding better approaches to promote foreign investment in IIAs, including PTAs, is growing, and not only with regard to reforms of ISDS. In this section, I want to highlight four specific features that have slowly been developed in the last decade in the context of IIAs, including PTAs: (1) streamlining administrative procedures, (2) regulatory coherence (or good regulatory practices), (3) dispute prevention, and (4) responsible business conduct (RBC).

Interestingly, many of these new features are also part of a new agreement that has been concluded among a large group of WTO Members on Investment Facilitation for Development (IFD).[16] Unsurprisingly, the IFD Agreement has expressly

[15] See the draft 'Code of Conduct for Adjudicators in International Investment Disputes' elaborated jointly by the International Centre for Settlement of Investment Disputes (ICSID) and UNCITRAL Secretariats (icsid.worldbank.org/resources/code-of-conduct).

[16] See Agreement on Investment Facilitation for Development, contained in Communication from Members Parties to the Investment Facilitation for Development Agreement (IFDA),

excluded from its scope the more traditional (and controversial) disciplines of investment protection, investment liberalisation, and ISDS (Article 2.2 IFDA).

8.4.1 *Streamlining Administrative Procedures*

First, a few recent PTAs include provisions focusing on enhancing the streamlining of administrative procedures to facilitate foreign investment. These provisions tend to be general and programmatic in nature, thus requiring further work by the contracting parties. For example, Article 10.17 of the 2020 Regional Comprehensive Economic Partnership (RCEP) provides that '[s]ubject to their laws and regulations, the Parties shall cooperate to facilitate investment amongst China and ASEAN through, among others: ... (b) simplifying procedures for investment applications and approvals; ...'.[17] These PTAs often specify that such work will be led by a new institutional structure provided for as part of the underlying PTAs. For example, Article 8.26 of the 2018 Brazil–Chile FTA specifies that a 'Joint Committee will develop and discuss an Agenda for Cooperation and Investment Facilitation in relevant issues for the promotion of bilateral investment'.[18]

A more detailed set of obligations has been included in the WTO IFD Agreement under Section III on 'Streamlining and speeding up administrative procedures'. For example, Article 14 sets out 'General Principles for Authorisation Procedures', which provides as follows:

> 14.1. Each Party shall ensure that authorisation procedures it adopts or maintains do not unduly complicate or delay investment activities.
> 14.2. If a Party adopts or maintains measures relating to the authorisation for an investment, the Party shall ensure that:
> a. such measures are based on objective and transparent criteria;
> b. the procedures are impartial, and that the procedures are adequate for applicants to demonstrate whether they meet the requirements, where such requirements exist; and
> c. the procedures do not in themselves unjustifiably prevent the fulfilment of requirements.
> 14.3. The assessment by a Party's relevant competent authorities of an application for authorisation shall be made on the basis of criteria set out in a measure in accordance with the Party's legal system.

requesting incorporation of IFDA into Annex 4 of the WTO Agreement, 8 March 2024, WT/GC/W/927.

17 See also 2018 Agreement on Investment of the Framework Agreement on Comprehensive Economic Cooperation Between China and ASEAN (Article 21).

18 This follows Brazil's new approach with regard to investment treaties. See (Choer Moraes and Hees 2018).

To streamline 'authorisation procedures', the IFD Agreement sets out several specific parameters with regard to 'application periods', 'acceptance of authenticated copies', 'processing of applications', 'treatment of incomplete applications', and 'rejection of applications' (Article 15). Further provisions include the following obligations:

(1) 'Each Party shall, to the extent practicable, avoid requiring an applicant to approach more than one competent authority for each application for authorisation' (Article 16.1)
(2) 'If a Party requires authorisation for an investment, its competent authorities, taking into account their competing priorities and resource constraints, shall endeavour to accept electronic submission of applications, including in electronic format' (Article 18.1)
(3) 'If a Party adopts or maintains a measure relating to the authorisation for an investment, the Party shall ensure that the competent authority reaches and administers its decisions in a manner independent from any enterprise carrying out the economic activity for which authorisation is required' (Article 19.1).

While some of these obligations are not drafted as strictly binding commitments, their level of specificity is rarely seen in investment chapters of PTAs. Thus, this (for the moment, plurilateral) agreement represents a key step forward in terms of achieving greater foreign investment promotion without focusing on the more traditional strategies revolving around investment protection, liberalisation, and ISDS. As such, it will likely influence further developments in future PTAs with investment chapters.

8.4.2 *Regulatory Coherence*

Second, there is a growing trend in PTAs to rely on 'regulatory coherence' or 'good regulatory practices' to address 'behind-the-border' measures affecting international trade and investment.[19] While its exact definition is debated, 'regulatory coherence' disciplines in PTAs are principally aimed at improving the quality and effectiveness of regulatory measures of general application by identifying and encouraging best practices 'in the process of planning, designing, issuing, implementing and reviewing regulatory measures' (CPTPP, Article 25.2). Accordingly, rather than imposing general standards on the content of domestic regulation, these PTAs prescribe the regulatory processes that should be undertaken in developing regulation. In other words, rather than relying on content-based (or output-oriented) standards, these PTAs demonstrate a turn to process-based (or input-oriented) standards.[20]

[19] See also Chapter 17, Polanco 2024.
[20] See generally (Lin and Liu 2018).

Building on the work on 'regulatory reform' carried out by intergovernmental organisations, such as the Organisation for Economic Co-operation and Development (OECD), Asia-Pacific Economic Cooperation (APEC), and the World Bank,[21] the recent reliance on 'regulatory coherence' or 'good regulatory practices' may be observed in the 2016 CPTPP and 2018 USMCA. While Chapter 25 CPTPP is titled 'Regulatory Coherence' and Chapter 28 USMCA is titled 'Good Regulatory Practices', these two chapters are very much similar in terms of content and provide for several good regulatory practices. For example, Article 25.4 CPTPP on 'Coordination and Review Processes or Mechanisms' encourages each CPTPP party to establish internal processes or mechanisms to facilitate the effective inter-agency coordination and review of proposed regulatory measures. These processes and mechanisms should generally have the ability to (a) review proposed covered regulatory measures to determine the extent to which the development of such measures adheres to good regulatory practices and (b) strengthen consultation and cooperation among domestic agencies so as to identify potential overlap and duplication (Article 25.4, paragraph 2).

Moreover, Article 25.5 CPTPP on 'Implementation of Core Good Regulatory Practices' is aimed particularly at encouraging relevant regulatory agencies to conduct regulatory impact assessments when developing proposed regulatory measures. These impact assessments should, among other things, (a) assess the need for a regulatory proposal, (b) examine feasible alternatives, (c) explain the grounds for selecting a specific alternative, and (d) rely on the best reasonably obtainable existing information (Article 25.5, paragraph 2). Article 25.5 specifies other good regulatory practices, such as ensuring that:

(i) regulations are clearly and concisely written;
(ii) the public has access to information on new regulatory measures, if possible online;
(iii) existing regulatory measures are periodically reviewed to determine if they remain the most effective means of achieving the desired objective; and
(iv) CPTPP governments provide public notice annually of all regulatory measures they expect to take the following year. (Article 25.5, paragraphs 4–7).[22]

[21] See, for example, OECD *Recommendation of the Council on Regulatory Policy and Governance* (OECD 2012); World Bank *Regulatory Assessment Toolkit* (Molinuevo and Sáez 2014); APEC *2016 Final Report on Good Regulatory Practices in APEC Economies* (APEC 2017).

[22] Chapter 28 of USMCA includes many of the same good regulatory practices found in the CPTPP, including (1) adopting internal processes or mechanisms providing for consultation, coordination, and review in the development of regulations (Article 28.4 USMCA), (2) encouraging the use of regulatory impact assessments when developing proposed regulations

These disciplines are often found in separate chapters (not in the investment one) and apply to any 'measure of general application related to any matter covered by' the PTA, including trade in goods, services, and investment.[23] Despite this broad scope in principle, these chapters do provide for certain limitations. For example, Chapter 25 of CPTPP only applies to 'covered regulatory measures', which each party will notify no later than one year after the date of entry into force of the agreement (Ortino and Lydgate 2019).

The WTO Investment Facilitation Agreement includes a provision on 'Domestic regulatory coherence'. It encourages each member to carry out impact assessments when preparing major regulatory measures within the scope of the agreement, and offer reasonable opportunities for any interested person, on a non-discriminatory basis, to provide comments and take into consideration the potential impact of the proposed regulation on investors, including micro-, small, and medium enterprises (MSMEs) (Article 23).

8.4.3 *Dispute Prevention*

Third, some recent IIAs, including PTAs, attempt to provide for mechanisms capable of preventing investor–state disputes. Brazil has been at the forefront of strengthening dispute prevention through the inclusion of a number of institutions and procedures aimed at preventing differences between a foreign investor and the host state from escalating into litigious disputes (Bonnitcha and Williams 2022; Echandi 2013; Levashova 2020).

In addition to the establishment of Joint Committees (a political decision-making treaty organ, composed of both parties to the treaty acting jointly and responsible for administering the relevant agreement),[24] key institutions included in IIAs whose functions include dispute prevention are national 'focal points' (or 'ombudsman'). Focal points are inspired by the positive experience of South Korea's Office of the Foreign Investment Ombudsman (OFIO), which provides post-investment services for foreign investors and on-site consultations regarding issues of finance, taxation, accounting, intellectual property rights, construction issues, and labour issues. For example, Article 8.19 of the Brazil–Chile FTA requires each party to designate a National Focal Point, which shall have as its main responsibility the support for investors from the other party in its territory (in Brazil, a such focal point will be in the Chamber of Foreign Trade – CAMEX). Among other responsibilities, the

(Article 28.11), and (3) ensuring that those regulations are clear, concise, and easy for the public to understand (Article 28.8).

[23] See, for example, the 2022 UK–Australia FTA (Chapter 26 Good Regulatory Practices).

[24] See Article 8.18 'Joint Committee for the administration of the chapter' of the Brazil–Chile FTA. See also Article 815 of the 2008 Canada–Colombia FTA establishing the Committee on Investment.

National Focal Point will (i) manage inquiries from the other party or from investors of the other party, with the competent entities, and inform the interested parties about the results of their negotiations; (ii) evaluate, in dialogue with the competent government authorities, suggestions and claims received from the other party or from investors of the other party and recommend, when appropriate, actions to improve the environment of investments; (iii) seek to prevent investment disputes in collaboration with the government authorities and the competent private entities; and (iv) provide timely and useful information on investment regulation issues, in general, or on specific projects, when requested (Article 8.19.4).

These recent PTAs also provide a more formal dispute prevention procedure between the two contracting parties within the Joint Committee. Article 8.24 of the Brazil–Chile FTA provides a detailed procedure for this purpose, with specific strict deadlines (120 days from the date of the first meeting, extendable by mutual agreement, to evaluate the submission presented and to prepare a report) and the possibility of inviting any affected foreign investors as well as other stakeholders, including interested NGOs.

The WTO Investment Facilitation for Development Agreement also includes the establishment of one or more focal points or appropriate mechanisms in order to respond to enquiries from investors or persons seeking to invest regarding the measures covered by the agreement and assist investors or persons seeking to invest in obtaining relevant information from competent authorities (Article 22.1).

8.4.4 *Responsible Business Conduct (RBC)*

Fourth, a growing number of IIAs, including PTAs, include 'responsible business conduct' or 'corporate social responsibility' provisions. Responsible business conduct (RBC) can be defined as corporate practices making a positive contribution to economic, environmental, and social progress with a view to achieving sustainable development and avoiding and addressing adverse impacts related to an enterprise's direct and indirect operations, products, or services.[25] In international investment law and policy, RBC is used interchangeably with 'corporate social responsibility', which refers to the enterprise's responsibility 'to put in place a process to integrate social, environmental, ethical, human rights and consumer concerns into their business operations and core strategy in close collaboration with their stakeholders' (European Commission 2011). The growing emphasis on RBC or CSR in IIAs is linked with the growing realisation that the host state's policy goal should be 'sustainable development'. Accordingly, the focus of these international disciplines should not simply be maximising economic

[25] See the definition provided by the OECD, for example, in the context of its work on Responsible Business Conduct and the Sustainable Development Goals (available at mneguidelines.oecd.org).

development, but rather to ensure a wider set of parameters such as environmental protection and social development.

Most recent PTAs with an investment chapter include RBC or CSR provisions requiring contracting parties to encourage (foreign) investors to incorporate into their business practices and internal policies internationally recognised principles, standards, and guidelines of RBC, such as the 1976 OECD Guidelines for Multinational Enterprises, the 1978 International Labour Organization (ILO) Tripartite Declaration of Principles Concerning Multinational Enterprises and Social Policy, and the 2011 United Nations (UN) Guiding Principles on Business and Human Rights.[26] For example, Article 9.17 on Corporate Social Responsibility of the 2018 CPTPP provides as follows: 'The Parties reaffirm the importance of each Party encouraging enterprises operating within its territory or subject to its jurisdiction to voluntarily incorporate into their internal policies those internationally recognised standards, guidelines and principles of corporate social responsibility that have been endorsed or are supported by that Party.'[27]

The WTO Investment Facilitation for Development (IFD) Agreement also contains an RBC provision. As the long-term objective of facilitating FDI flows is to foster sustainable development, one of the key components of promoting sustainable investment is RBC. The RBC provision in the WTO IFD Agreement focuses on three specific aspects. First, it requires parties to encourage investors operating within their territory to voluntarily incorporate into their business practices internationally recognised principles, standards, and guidelines of RBC, such as those referred to in international instruments like the UN Guiding Principles on Business and Human Rights and the OECD Guidelines for Multinational Enterprises and related Due Diligence guidance. These principles, standards, and guidelines address areas such as labour, environment, gender equality, human rights, community relations, and the rights of Indigenous peoples. Second, the RBC provision in the WTO IFD Agreement also requires parties to undertake due diligence in order to identify and address adverse impacts, such as on the environment and labour conditions, in their operations, their supply chains, and other business relationships. Third, it requires parties to undertake and maintain meaningful engagement and dialogue with Indigenous peoples, traditional communities, and local communities.

26 'Since 2016, the number of RTAs with CSR-related provisions and the average number of CSR-related provisions in those agreements have increased significantly.' (Monteiro 2021)

27 See also Article 7.18 on Corporate Social Responsibility of the 2020 Indonesia–Korea Comprehensive Economic Partnership Agreement (CEPA): 'Each Party reaffirms the importance of encouraging enterprises operating within its territory to voluntarily incorporate into their internal policies those internationally recognized standards, guidelines, and principles of corporate social responsibility that have been endorsed or are supported by that Party.' See also Article 16.5 on *Trade and investment favouring sustainable development* of the 2018 EU–Japan Economic Partnership Agreement (EPA). However, the 2020 RCEP does not contain any reference or provision on RBC/CSR. See Romanin Jacur (2018, pp. 465–483).

8.5 CONCLUDING REMARKS

When it comes to IIAs, including investment chapters in PTAs, there are many challenges facing policymakers. On the one hand, the need to reform, or at least fine-tune, traditional disciplines on investment protection, investment liberalisation, and ISDS is increasingly growing. Continuing claims brought by foreign investors against both developed and developing states, as well as the need to ensure that international investment obligations do not restrain states' ability to address various emergencies, such as climate change, are increasing pressures on states to act.

On the other hand, scepticism (at least in some quarters) about the effectiveness of any such reform is also growing to leave two equally unsatisfactory options on the table: keeping the status quo or exiting the system altogether. One possible way out of the conundrum is to move the focus away from traditional investment disciplines and explore other mechanisms to encourage greater investment flows and maximise foreign investment's contribution to sustainable development. Streamlining administrative procedures, regulatory coherence, dispute prevention, and responsible business practices are some of the novel mechanisms that are currently being explored, in particular in the context of PTAs. These mechanisms are also reflected in the WTO Agreement on IFD.

Different from traditional investment disciplines, these various mechanisms require serious engagement (including technical and financial resources) from states to ensure their fruition. Has any of these mechanisms actually borne any fruit so far? If not, will any of them bear any fruit in the future? Empirical research is needed to shed light on these questions.

REFERENCES

APEC 2017. '2016 Final Report on Good Regulatory Practices in APEC Economies', August. Retrieved 21 March 2023, from www.apec.org/publications/2017/08/2016-final-report-on-good-regulatory-practices-in-apec-economies

Bonnitcha, J. and Z. Williams 2022. 'Investment Dispute Prevention and Management Agencies. Toward a More Informed Policy Discussion', 28 January. Retrieved 21 March 2023, from www.iisd.org/publications/investment-dispute-prevention-and-management-agencies

Choer Moraes, H. and F. Hees 2018. 'Breaking the BIT Mold: Brazil's Pioneering Approach to Investment Agreements', *AJIL Unbound* 112: 197–201.

Crawford, J.-A. and B. Kotschwar 2018. 'Investment Provisions in Preferential Trade Agreements: Evolution and Current Trends', WTO Working Papers 14(14).

Echandi, R. 2013. 'Complementing Investor-State Dispute Resolution: A Conceptual Framework for Investor-State Conflict Management', in R. Echandi and P. Sauvé (eds.), *Prospects in International Investment Law and Policy*. Cambridge: Cambridge University Press.

European Commission 2011. 'Communication from the Commission to the European Parliament, the Council, the European Economic and Social Committee and the

Committee of the Regions a Renewed Eu Strategy 2011–14 for Corporate Social Responsibility 2011'. Retrieved on 23 March 2023, from https://eur-lex.europa.eu/legal-content/EN/TXT/?uri = celex%3A52011DC0681

Gáspár-Szilágyi, S. and M. Usynin 2020. 'Investment Chapters in PTAs and Their Impact on Adjudicative Convergence', in D. Behn, M. Langford and S. Gáspár-Szilágyi (eds.), *Adjudicating Trade and Investment Disputes: Convergence or Divergence?* Cambridge: Cambridge University Press.

Giannakopoulos, C. 2019. 'The Right to Regulate in International Investment Law and the Law of State Responsibility: A Hohfeldian Approach', in P. Pazartzis and P. Merkouris (eds.), *Permutations of Responsibility in Internatioanl Law* Leiden: Brill Nijhoff.

Gill, J., M. Gearing and G. Birt 2004. 'Contractual Claims and Bilateral Investment Treaties', *Journal of International Arbitration* 21(5): 397.

Levashova, Y. 2020. 'Prevention of ISDS Disputes: From Early Resolution to Limited Access', in J. Chaisse, L. Choukroune, and S. Jusoh (eds.), *Handbook of International Investment Law and Policy*, Singapore: Springer.

Lin, C.-F. and H.-W. Liu 2018. 'Regulatory Rationalisation Clauses in FTAs: A Complete Survey of the US, EU, and China', *Melbourne Journal of International Law* 19(1): 1–29.

Meltzer, J. P. 2016. 'Investment', in B. Mercurio, L. Bartels, and S. Lester (eds.), *Bilateral and Regional Trade Agreements: Commentary and Analysis*. Cambridge: Cambridge University Press.

Molinuevo, M. and S. Sáez 2014. *Regulatory Assessment Toolkit: A Practical Methodology for Assessing Regulation on Trade and Investment in Services*, Washington, DC: The World Bank.

Monteiro, J. A. 2021. 'Buena Vista Social Corporate Responsibility Provisions in Regional Trade Agreements (WTO Working Papers 11(11)'. Retrieved 21 March 2023, from www.wto-ilibrary.org/economic-research-and-trade-policy-analysis/buena-vista-social-corporate-responsibility-provisions-in-regional-trade-agreements_26222a15-en

Newcombe, A. and L. Paradell 2009. *Law and Practice of Investment Treaties: Standards of Treatment*, The Netherlands: Kluwer Law International.

OECD 2012. 'Recommendation of the Council on Regulatory Policy and Governance'. 22 March. Retrieved 5 January 2023, from www.oecd.org/gov/regulatory-policy/2012-recommendation.htm

Ortino, F. 2023. 'ISDS and Its Transformations', *Journal of International Economic Law* 26(1): 177–187.

Ortino, F. and E. Lydgate 2019. 'Addressing Domestic Regulation Affecting Trade in Services in CETA, CPTPP, and USMCA: Revolution or Timid Steps?' *The Journal of World Investment and Trade* 20(5): 680–704.

Pereira de Souza Fleury, R. 2015. 'Umbrella Clauses: A Trend Towards Its Elimination', *Arbitration International* 31(4): 679–691.

2017. 'Closing the Umbrella: A Dark Future for Umbrella Clauses?' 13 October. Retrieved 21 March 2023, from https://arbitrationblog.kluwerarbitration.com/2017/10/13/closing-umbrella-dark-future-umbrella-clauses/

Price, D. 1993. 'An Overview of the NAFTA Investment Chapter: Substantive Rules and Investor-State Dispute Settlement', *The International Lawyer* 27(3): 727–736.

Roberts, A. 2018. 'Incremental, Systemic, and Paradigmatic Reform of Investor-State Arbitration', *American Journal of International Law* 112(3): 410–432.

Romanin Jacur, F. 2018. 'Corporate Social Responsibility in Recent Bilateral and Regional Free Trade Agreements: An Early Assessment', *European Foreign Affairs Review* 23(4): 465–483.

Sabahi, B. 2011. *Compensation and Restitution in Investor-State Arbitration: Principles and Practice*, Oxford: Oxford University Press.

Sabanogullari, L. 2018. *General Exception Clauses in International Investment Law: The Recalibration of Investment Agreements via WTO-Based Flexibilities*, Baden-Baden: Nomos Verlagsgesellschaft.

Schill, S. W. 2012. 'Deference in Investment Treaty Arbitration: Re-conceptualizing the Standard of Review', *Journal of International Dispute Settlement* 3(3): 577–607.

UNCTAD 2016. 'Taking Stock of IIA Reform'. IIA Issues Note, 1. Retrieved 23 March 2023, from www.tralac.org/images/docs/9186/taking-stock-of-iia-reform-unctad-march-2016.pdf

9

Subsidies and Future PTAs

From Market Distortions to Legitimate Policy Goals?

*Leopoldo Biffi, Yuliia Kucheriava, and Shailja Singh**

9.1 INTRODUCTION

Subsidies regulation is one of the most contentious and complicated issues in international trade. There are various reasons for that. Subsidies are extraordinarily complex in the sense that they are extremely difficult to evaluate and quantify. Another important factor is their political sensitivity. Above all, the debate over subsidies puts in stark contrast the national spending required to attain public policy goals and international rules founded on a free trade ideology. Striking a balance between these two objectives is as crucial as it is challenging in a world in which, on the one hand, market integration has unbundled production across multiple regions and, on the other hand, the climate crisis and a global pandemic call for an increasingly active role of the state at home.

A growing number of frictions around subsidies have been playing out both at the domestic level in the form of countervailing duty (CVD) investigations and at the international level, as evidenced by the number of subsidy-related disputes taken to the World Trade Organization (WTO). Between 1 January 1995 and 30 June 2022, governments initiated 669 CVD investigations (WTO 2023a), with at least one CVD investigation per week being launched in 2018–2020 (Evenett and Fritz 2021: 12). At the multilateral level, WTO Members invoked the WTO Agreement on Subsidies and Countervailing Measures (ASCM) as many as 130 times in disputes from 1995 to 2021.[1]

* Views expressed are personal.

[1] This is only slightly behind the Anti-Dumping Agreement (AD Agreement) with 142 and the General Agreement on Tariffs and Trade (GATT 1994) that appears in 511 of the 607 disputes initiated over the same period (WTO 2023b). Interestingly, however, as of 25 October 2022, only thirty-eight Members had notified that they maintain subsidies in accordance with Article 25.1 of the Agreement and Article XVI of GATT 1994, and ten Members had notified that they did not maintain any notifiable subsidies. See the 'Report (2022) of The Committee on Subsidies

Against this background, the chapter argues that a future-proof subsidies regulation in trade can only result from a paradigm shift in how these policy measures are evaluated, and therefore sanctioned or permitted. Such a shift would be concretised by moving away from singular assessments of a subsidy's trade-distortive potential to a balancing test that weighs any possible trade distortions against the benefits that subsidies pursuing legitimate policy objectives create. The latter crucially includes economic recovery, public health, and environmental protection – all objectives whose urgency and legitimacy cannot simply be undermined by a trade distortion benchmark. This approach would entail introducing a balancing test to 'legitimate' subsidies assessment, strengthening the transparency rules as well as expanding the list of prohibited subsidies, along with the requisite exceptions, to attain a more nuanced, practical, and balanced outcome. In elaborating on this argument, we look at preferential trade agreements (PTAs) as the most feasible institutional framework in which such a focal point shift can occur. Preliminary evidence already points in this direction. For instance, the European Union (EU) has incorporated into its recent PTAs a notion of 'state aid' with a wide scope and public policy focus that grants parties greater leeway in subsidy implementation than the current framework provided in the ASCM (Rubini and Hoekman 2022).

This chapter is structured as follows. First, we provide an overview of the state of the art of countries' resort to subsidies, discussing figures from advanced capitalist economies in the G7 (Section 9.2). Second, we conceptualise and discuss the hybrid and ambivalent policy nature of subsidies, which are caught between the pursuit of legitimate public policy objectives and the market distortions they might generate (Section 9.3). Third, we explain why and how PTAs are the right platform for introducing changes to subsidies regulation for the twenty-first century (Section 9.4). Fourth, we briefly conclude (Section 9.5).

9.2 THE STATE OF THE ART OF SUBSIDIES IN INTERNATIONAL TRADE

The ASCM is the primary legal framework governing subsidies regulation at the multilateral level. The ASCM deems a subsidy to exist if there is a 'financial contribution' by a government or any public body or if there is any form of 'income or price support' and a benefit is thereby conferred.[2] It broadly tackles the issue of subsidisation from two perspectives. First, it regulates the provision of subsidies by WTO Members, and second, it governs the use of countervailing measures to offset the adverse trade effects caused by subsidised imports. The ASCM disciplines two kinds of subsidies – prohibited and actionable subsidies (Part II and III of the

and Countervailing Measures', adopted on 28 October 2022 (Committee on Subsidies and Countervailing Measures 2022).

[2] See Article 1.1 of the ASCM.

ASCM, respectively). While the prohibition applies to local content and export-contingent subsidies that are deemed to be specific,[3] actionable subsidies are those specific subsidies that can be subject to challenge in the WTO or by resorting to countervailing measures at the national level.

As mentioned, the most significant controversy that revolves around the question of subsidisation is its *ambivalence*. Subsidies have been frequently seen as undermining the effects of market access prerogatives that result from tariffs and other trade concessions (Horlick and Clarke 2016: 8–9). However, there is increasing recognition that subsidies can and, in fact, do produce positive effects and pursue legitimate goals (Heyl et al. 2022: 9).

In this latter case, subsidies can, indeed, correct the market process at least as much as they may distort it (Schwartz and Harper 1972: 833). This section relaxes the assumption that subsidies are necessarily an expression of anti-competitive behaviour by anti-liberal countries challenging the tenets of the free market. Far from wanting to make a normative statement as to what is trade-distortive or not, we argue here that resorting to subsidies is a policy practice that can coexist with both an open economy and a political commitment to trade liberalisation. The multilateral legal framework has so far failed to properly take into account the positive externalities that subsidies may produce. Rather, it focuses on a trade distortion benchmark in assessing the effects of a particular subsidy scheme. Subsidy codification at the multilateral level also does not meet the level of detail and flexibility that such widespread and varied use of these policy tools would require.

The relationship between subsidies and trade law speaks directly to political economy debates assessing the role of the state within increasingly globalised and interconnected market economies. In this context, the 'retreat of the state' paradigm, which has populated political economy literature since the 1990s, has implied a mutual exclusivity between globalisation and market integration on one side, and an active role of the state in public and welfare policies on the other. Scholars like Strange (1996) argue that, as globalisation advances, the ability of the state to manage and regulate the market shrinks (see also Streeck and Crouch 1997). Similar arguments are in line with the idea that the need to counter trade distortions is hierarchically prior to and largely incompatible with the need for states to deliver public and welfare policies.

We suggest here, however, that thinking of future-proof subsidy rules in twenty-first century trade is best served by arguments that see globalisation and widespread market liberalisation as going hand in hand with a resilient, if not, growing role of the state at home. This phenomenon was famously captured by Ruggie (1982), who juxtaposed a notion of 'embedded liberalism' to neoliberal paradigms calling for an unconstrained role of markets, like the Washington Consensus (see also Cameron 1978; Rodrik 1998). The essence of embedded liberalism lies in seeking to strike a balance between

[3] In particular, see Article 3 of the ASCM.

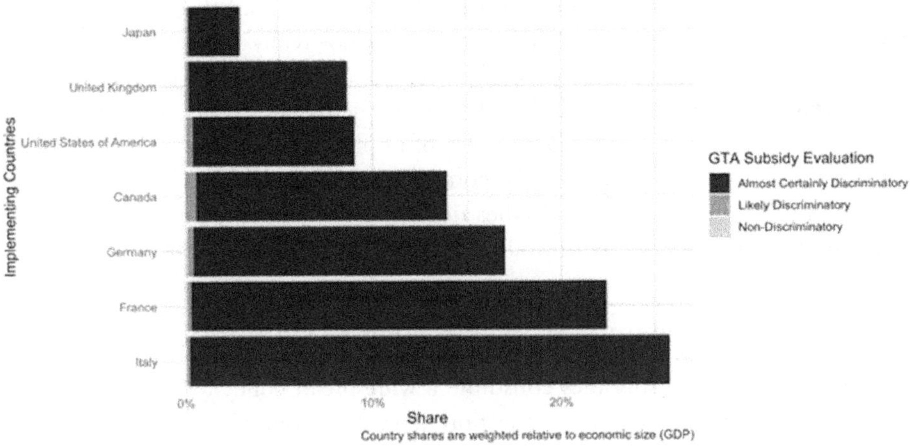

FIGURE 9.1 G7 country shares of subsidy measures implemented since 2008 (GTA data).

domestic demands for an active role of the state in the economy and the fact of remaining a globally integrated market. In this sense, the relationship between domestic subsidies and free trade poses a paradox for liberal democracies, understood in terms of states' 'political mandate … to pursue the political economic interests of their citizenry under conditions of complex economic, legal and regulatory interdependence where large parts of economic governance are no longer exclusively within their control' (Crouch 2008, as quoted in Clift and Woll 2012: 308; Clift 2013).

Figure 9.1 suggests that subsidies are a common feature of highly developed and economically integrated liberal democracies. The plot is based on the Global Trade Alert (GTA) database (Evenett and Fritz 2020) and displays the share of subsidies and state aid measures implemented by G7 countries since the 2008 financial crisis, relative to the economic size of each (measured in average GDP). It categorises them based on their estimated trade-distortive potential.

Figure 9.1 indicates that the main divide amid G7 economies is one of quantity, rather than quality. While Italy accounts for the largest share of implemented subsidy measures proportional to its economic size, all G7 Members predominantly resort to subsidies which, albeit with varying magnitude, go in the direction of creating distortions in foreign markets – according to GTA evaluations. That is, subsidy and state aid policies implemented by globally integrated liberal economies like G7 ones are unlikely to have effects that are limited to their home markets. Considering the political economy drivers of subsidisation, the fact of resorting to these policies also seems to go beyond the 'Varieties of Capitalism' (VoC) divide between liberal market economies (LMEs) and coordinated market economies (CMEs) (Hall and Soskice 2001). The VoC framework suggests subsidies would be utilised differently in deregulated political economies (LMEs) than they would in more regulated and welfare-oriented ones (CMEs). Yet, at least at a macro-level, the above figures indicate that the VoC intuition is not really reflected by the data. Proportionally to their economic size, both LMEs and CMEs rely on subsidisation extensively. Specifically, two LMEs like the United States (US) and the United Kingdom (UK) score higher in their share of implemented measures than a CME like Japan, and an LME like Canada scores closer to a CME like Germany than to the US and the UK. Overall, subsidies qualify as a ubiquitous policy tool, which becomes particularly prominent in the aftermath of shocks and crises.

9.3 SUBSIDIES AS HYBRID POLICY INSTRUMENTS

Having discussed how subsidies constitute a widespread policy tool in even highly integrated capitalist economies, this section moves to consider how the hybrid policy nature of subsidies and their specific politico-economic effects are at odds with existing subsidy rules at the WTO level.

Specifically, we contend that the ASCM has yet to cover existing gaps in multilateral subsidies regulation. The reason for that is that subsidies are ambiguous and ambivalent in nature, in that the same policy measure can pursue certain legitimate goals and be classified as actionable or prohibited under the ASCM at the same time.

A first challenge in regulating the issue of subsidies multilaterally lies precisely in the difficulty in accounting for overlaps between 'good' and 'bad' subsidies within the same policy measure (Hoekman and Kostecki 2009). We contend here that the reason for that lies in the ASCM's one-sided focus on the adverse trade effects of the subsidy in question as opposed to a balanced analysis of both its negative and positive effects.

Subsidies are often the most immediate, readily available, and politically invoked public policy measures for governments to pursue given public objectives. Yet, subsidies can also be pushed for by vested interests of import-competing groups. In this latter case, subsidies may qualify as trade-distortive measures invoked by given industrial sectors in view of enhancing their market competitiveness at the expense of foreign exporters. The recent US Inflation Reduction Act (IRA), which introduces subsidies supporting the electric vehicle sector, alongside a local content requirement limiting the provision of government transfers to American manufacturers (United States Congress 2022), is an example of how a measure targeting desirable public policy objectives (i.e. climate change mitigation) can likewise have a trade-distortive potential.

Another example is the EU Green Deal Industrial Plan, as announced in January 2023 by Commission President Von der Leyen. While it entails 'simplified' state aid rules aimed at pursuing legitimate public policy objectives, including targeted aid for R&D in green technologies (WEF 2023), its trade-distortive potential may not be excluded.

The ASCM category of *non-actionable subsidy* contained in its Part IV lapsed in 2000, which means WTO law currently fails to define a category of subsidies *de jure* considered to be legitimate on the ground of attaining goals such as climate change mitigation, environmental protection, public health, or economic recovery, both nationally and globally.[4] The main implication of this legal void is that the specific subsidy evaluation at the level of international trade law is currently possible only through the *prohibited* and *actionable* categories.

Therefore, the key limitation of the ASCM framework lies in the absence of a coherent 'test' to assess the dual nature of any given subsidy: its alleged trade-distortive potential (as either a prohibited or an actionable subsidy) on the one hand, and its sustainable non-actionable component on the other. More deeply, the ASCM also lacks the case specificity to measure the specific nature of spillovers generated by a given subsidy for foreign markets, at least without initiating a dispute settlement process under WTO rules.

9.4 PTAS: PAVING THE WAY FOR TRADE AND SUBSIDY REFORM

Having discussed the ubiquity of subsidies and how challenging it is to devise recommendations for allowing or proscribing them, we now move on to arguing why and how PTAs are a good place to start for future-proof subsidies regulation. We argue here that PTAs can serve as helpful institutional 'laboratories' for subsidies regulation. PTAs have the potential to enact subsidy provisions built around a 'balancing test' focal point, while strengthening related transparency obligations between two or more parties.

While objectives pursued by subsidies do matter, so does the design of the system. Subsection 9.4.1 below discusses how PTAs can ensure greater governance specificity to address subsidy spillovers along global value chains (GVCs). We understand GVCs as consisting of industries spread globally and each contributing to different segments of the production of a single good. In subsection 9.4.2 below, we propose that subsidies pursuing legitimate objectives should be guided by a set of principles, which are by their very nature more conceptual than prescriptive. It goes without saying that in order to make the notion of 'subsidies to attain a legitimate objective' operational, a lot of questions about their precise boundaries and treatment are yet to be answered. Nevertheless, we believe that incorporating principles as opposed to directly applicable rules to regulate them is the best approach currently available. It is flexible enough to apply to a wide set of all possible scenarios but, at the same time, stringent in the sense that it provides clear indications on how to practically

4 As per Article 1.2 of the ASCM, the agreement only applies to subsidies that are 'specific' within the meaning of Article 2; non-specific subsidies continue to be non-actionable as per the WTO framework.

determine what is covered and what is not covered, when a subsidy creates a positive spillover and when it does not.

Another necessary means to further reinforce the PTAs' potential to address current deficiencies in subsidies regulation is to improve the way they regulate transparency, which we discuss in subsection 9.4.3. Information is the key towards a constant improvement, and ensuring there is timely and sufficient information on subsidies is absolutely critical to creating a better and more effective subsidies regulation in the future.

Lastly, in subsection 9.4.4, we explain why and how PTAs are an appropriate avenue to expand the notion of 'prohibited subsidies' pending WTO deadlock. It is noteworthy that, unlike some other aspects of subsidies regulation, this is least likely to create a conflict with the WTO rules and could indeed be in the nature of a typical 'WTO-plus' obligation found in PTAs.[5] Future PTAs can develop a robust mechanism for governing newer types of extremely trade-distortive subsidies by including them within the definition of 'prohibited subsidies' and weighing their distortive potential against the stated domestic policy goal.

9.4.1 *PTAs and Value-chain Specificity*

The added value of PTAs in subsidies regulation is not only due to the limitations of the ASCM. It is also ascribable to the specificity of both the political economy drivers and effects of subsidisation across integrated markets, and more specifically GVCs. The effects – both positive and negative, and both market and non-market ones – of a given subsidy along a GVC are a function of a specific array of variables. These include the degree of subsidised goods' access to a given foreign market, the weight of a subsidised sector in a country's own export or import, as well as the specific politico-economic drivers leading to a subsidy in the first place.

Overall, the specificity of subsidy spillovers along GVCs qualifies PTAs as targeted institutional tools capable of prescribing and proscribing given policies in line with broader WTO rules. Paradoxically, the legitimacy of a subsidy cannot be measured separately from the market effects it yields on country B or C if implemented in country A, or vice versa (Hoekman and Nelson 2020). For instance, a subsidy implemented in final-good production by country B can expand the industrial base by multiplying intermediary inputs in country A (Baldwin and Venables 2015; Hoekman 2016). But intra-GVC subsidisation can also yield opposite effects. Biesebroek and Sturgeon (2010) argue that subsidisation of large downstream car manufacturers can damage upstream producers when downstream car producers are the largest purchaser of these intermediary products, hence controlling their market (see also Blonigen 2016). Against this background, another type of externality that

[5] A potential conflict may, however, arise to the extent that there are additional exceptions to the WTO-recognised prohibited subsidies incorporated in the PTA text.

could be envisioned has to do with 'free riding', and specifically with the problem of who is bearing the costs of subsidies generating *positive* spillovers along a GVC. Take, for instance, the implementation of a subsidy within a country (country A) sustaining the production of more innovative and energy-efficient microchips and bringing innovation also to the downstream semiconductors industry in country B, without requiring substantial technology adjustment in the latter. The subsidising government in country A would paradoxically be the one bearing the highest financial and political costs *vis-à-vis* taxpayers in terms of investment in new technologies, while country B would simply benefit from the positive spillover of a subsidy implemented elsewhere.

We argue here that PTAs qualify as viable institutions to govern the specificity of similar issues. For example, assuming that the intra-GVC externalities from subsidies were controlled for, a PTA would allow institutionalising processes of even burden-sharing for subsidies deemed to benefit the entire GVC. Let us go back to the semiconductors example, where intermediary-level innovation would positively impact also on downstream producers. A PTA would allow GVC Members to design forms of collective contributions, such as institutionalised shared funds, under the auspices of the agreement, from which subsidies with envisioned positive GVC spillovers would be disbursed. Contributions would be made on the basis of respective market size, or based on the extent to which a state's national industry is expected to benefit from the subsidy in question, and would be limited to sectors where subsidisation is expected to benefit *all* PTA Members. Similar arrangements could be reviewed periodically by an *ad hoc* PTA committee, as is the case for various policy domains in twenty-first century agreements (like sustainable development or data protection). That would guarantee sufficient flexibility to channel shared investments to a defined set of sectors having 'value-chain relevance', adjusting the magnitude and direction of investments based on the evolving priorities of the preferential partners.

Overall, we acknowledge that countries that are part of a GVC may not be members of the same PTA. Furthermore, subsidy spillovers may extend well beyond members of a PTA. Yet, it is reasonable to assume that countries in a GVC would be comparatively more incentivised to enter a PTA (if not having one already in place), as preferential agreements have witnessed faster tariff cuts on intermediate goods, whose flow is essential for the existence of GVCs (Baccini et al. 2018). Lower market barriers, in turn, would, all else being equal, make subsidy GVC spillovers (both positive and negative) more pronounced, and their impact assessment and regulation even more pressing.

9.4.2 *'Legitimate' Subsidies: A Balancing Test*

Subsidies granted to provide public services, provide regional aid, or ensure environmental protection have been frequently incorporated into PTAs as a part of sustainability chapters or provisions. These are frequently referred to as 'legitimate' subsidies (Rubini 2020) and would have belonged to the *non-actionable* category referred to above in Section 9.3, unless lapsed.

The EU has so far been a champion in promoting such provisions in PTAs with its trading partners, particularly in its 'new generation' PTAs (e.g. the EU–Korea FTA; EU–UK Trade and Cooperation Agreement (TCA). However, these PTAs differ significantly in what they consider a legitimate objective, be it greening the economy or providing support to underdeveloped regions.

While there cannot be a one-size-fits-all approach, we argue that in the multilateral or regional context, it is insufficient that a subsidy merely pursues a legitimate objective. It is critical that such a legitimate subsidy generates benefits that are at least regional or, preferably, global in nature.

As we have explained above, subsidies, even those that have the most commendable objectives, such as environmental stewardship, could either incidentally or intentionally improve the competitive outlook or performance of the respective domestic industry in the subsidising country. One example would be local content requirements introduced by the US in the IRA. The introduction of a balancing test between negative trade-distortive and positive (e.g. public good creation) effects of a subsidy is, therefore, necessary for a comprehensive and fair assessment of the real impact of the subsidy in question. Despite their prominence and variability, as of today, no PTA would contain such guidance and, thus, give an understanding of how to draft, incorporate, and enforce an effective mechanism to regulate legitimate subsidies, serving not only a subsidising country's interest but also of the peer countries'. The introduction of a balancing test that may allow assessing the effect of a particular legitimate subsidy taking into account its potential to bring about positive changes on a broader-than-national scale might, thus, act as a game changer in effective subsidies regulation.

We suggest that the focal point shift should take place in this context and along these lines.

Based on the best practices of the selected set of PTAs, as well as general economic and legal concepts, we draw up guiding principles and interpretation notes thereto (where relevant) that may serve as a basis for an efficient balancing mechanism for future PTAs.

This subsection, therefore, proceeds as follows. It suggests a respective principle to be incorporated, elaborates on its potential content and form, and discusses various settings where its application may be relevant.

The first principle is the *adequacy* of a subsidy in question to attain or otherwise promote the achievement of a legitimate objective. The critical question to be answered in this respect is how and why a subsidy may or may not be an adequate means to achieve a stated objective.

To answer this question, the respective competent authority in the granting country shall consider whether the potential beneficiary is capable of providing a business plan and/or investment strategy linked to a project with a detailed explanation of why that subsidy type is needed and its amount is necessary to achieve the stated objective.

The second principle is the *effectiveness* of a subsidy in attaining a legitimate objective. Effectiveness differs from adequacy in that while adequacy assesses whether a subsidy is the best instrument to pursue the stated objectives, effectiveness assesses the extent to which stated objectives are attained. Thus, the focus of effectiveness is on targeting the correct actions and completing them in a timely manner.

Here the test should be more stringent than a mere declaration that a subsidy is 'not incapable of' achieving the stated objective.[6] Instead, due regard must be given to the particular circumstances surrounding the granting of a subsidy.

These circumstances may include the effect of the policies already in place in the particular country and their contribution to the attainment of the stated legitimate objective (e.g. policies to promote renewables, tax cuts for 'green' production processes, etc.) akin to the 'non-attribution' test under the ASCM.[7]

In other words, the subsidy in question should be the main and genuine contributor to the attainment of the stated legitimate objective. The need for such a causal-link analysis stems from the necessity to eliminate double support in cases where the stated objective would be achieved nonetheless. For instance, consider the French government's EUR 7 billion bailout of Air France, which came with conditions for the airline to become 'the most environmentally friendly airline on the planet'. This ambitious goal was pegged to three conditions: (i) halving overall emissions from domestic flights by 2024; (ii) sourcing 2 per cent of its fuel from 'sustainable' sources by 2025; and (iii) reducing carbon intensity by 50 per cent by 2030 over 2005 levels (Alderman 2020). However, every other airline that neither received support from the government nor did commit to 'extra' obligations to protect the environment is bound to reduce emissions and switch to renewable energy sources[8] under the EU's Green Deal and the EU's commitments under the Paris Agreement. Also, the third condition attached to the Air France bailout is no more than a simple reaffirmation of a commitment that the airline made as part of its Horizon 2030 Initiative (AF 2019: 3).

The effectiveness of a subsidy to attain a legitimate objective may also be assessed as a part of the 'benefit' analysis. This could be done by introducing an additional pillar to the 'better off' test, namely, whether there are positive spillovers and whether these are the effect of the subsidy in question.[9]

6 Appellate Body Report, *Colombia – Textiles*, WT/DS461/AB/R, paras 5.67–5.70. See also Panel Report, *US – Tariff Measures*, WT/DS543/R, para 7.125.

7 See Article 15.5 ASCM.

8 Conditions i and ii under the Air France bailout.

9 The standard 'benefit' test under Article 1.1(b) of the SCM Agreement seeks to identify whether the financial contribution has made 'the recipient "better off" than it would otherwise have

On top of that, PTAs may introduce a supervision mechanism that would allow control over a subsidy's amount and allocation. This may include granting a subsidy incrementally, such as, for instance, every month/year based on the milestones achieved and/or actions undertaken at a particular stage of the project. A sunset clause may reinforce this obligation even further by making a payment of a subsidy feasible only insofar as it produces the incentive effect (Rubini 2015).

Introducing a yearly obligation of the beneficiary to provide a detailed status report on the progress achieved and on the particular items of expenditure is another instrument against opportunistic behaviour. Thus, in cases where resources were spent on purposes other than the stated objective (e.g. the delivery of a particular public good) and if the beneficiary failed to prove the opposite, a subsidy due for the next milestone should be reduced by this 'off-label' amount.

The third principle is the *enforceability* of the particular obligations attached to a subsidy to ensure the attainment of a legitimate objective.

There are several aspects that must be examined in this respect.

First is the enforceability of the transparency obligations, which will be discussed in more detail in the next subsection.

Second is the existence of an enforcement body, responsible for overseeing whether subsidies are being used for the intended purpose. This enforcement body may be either a separate and independent body or a division of the Subsidies Committee (or any similar body created by the parties to the PTA).

Third is the enforceability of the 'strings' attached to subsidies. One example is 'green strings' attached to subsidies granted to ailing undertakings in times of emergency.

The green stimulus has recently become a typical feature of state aid, even though it still comprises only a small chunk of the total stimulus packages. According to some estimations, as of February 2021, the world's leading economies have announced economic stimulus packages worth approximately USD 4.6 trillion directly into sectors that have a large and lasting impact on carbon emissions and nature, namely agriculture, industry, waste, energy, and transport, but less than USD 1.8 trillion has been allocated for green initiatives (GSI 2021). There are various reasons for such a disparity, including the lack of regulatory oversight on environmentally intensive sectors, and conflicting priorities, such as boosting economic performance during the crisis (as was the case during the COVID-19 crisis) versus environmental stewardship.

Therefore, attaching enforceable green conditions to the recovery packages is absolutely critical. This should be done, however, in a way that does not preclude the achievement of the primary growth-enhancing goals of such emergency-assistance packages, thus making them redundant. Instead, the main requirement

been, absent that contribution'. See Appellate Body Report, *US – Large Civil Aircraft (2nd complaint)*, WT/DS353/AB/R, paras 635–636, 662, and 690.

for such green commitments should be a precautionary 'do no harm' requirement obliging the respective undertakings to ensure that no harm is done to the environment as a result of the increased economic performance. Additional green commitments (beyond the status quo) may come into play as the recovery gains momentum.

9.4.3 *Transparency*

Transparency has become all the more important when it comes to subsidies schemes. In order to facilitate a discussion on government support and to develop effective disciplines to cover existing and potential new support, information on the nature and scale of government support would be very useful, if not indispensable. Yet, such information remains limited (WTO 2021). There are several explanations for that: first, the difficult technical nature of subsidies; second, the political sensitivity of state aid measures; third, the fact that subsidies are diffuse, namely granted by various departments and levels of government. Attempts to address the lack of transparency on the multilateral level by 'naming and shaming' serial defaulters at the WTO in 2019 were harshly criticised[10] and the proposal did not see the light of day. Addressing this concern at the level of PTAs may, therefore, be a feasible solution. Currently, many PTAs already include WTO+ obligations on transparency on subsidies (Mattoo et al. 2020). The Association of Southeast Asian Nations (ASEAN) Free Trade Area (AFTA), for example, contains requirements to create repositories on laws and measures. Preferential trade agreements of the EU with countries like Montenegro, Bosnia and Herzegovina, Serbia, and Ukraine provide for an inventory of all aid schemes. Another example is the PTA between Guatemala and Taiwan and China which contains the requirement to carry out studies.

However, more should be done.

Better information, objective analysis, and regular dialogue are key parameters that must be taken into account while elaborating a transparency chapter on subsidies in the model twenty-first century PTAs (IMF, OECD, World Bank and WTO 2022).

Keeping in mind these key pillars and based on the current best practices at the WTO (such as Technical Barriers to Trade (TBT)/Sanitary and Phytosanitary (SPS) Committees) as well as minimum standards elaborated by the Organisation for Economic Co-operation and Development (OECD) in the context of disclosed requirements, this subsection provides few recommendations that may underpin the transparency provisions in future PTAs.

10 The African Group, Cuba, and India stressed the capacity constraints of developing members, thus strongly opposing any transparency obligations that go beyond existing ones. See Communication from African Group, Cuba and India (Revision) 'An Inclusive Approach to Transparency and Notification Requirements in the WTO' (WTO 2019).

These recommendations seek a balance between the need for early and complete information on subsidy schemes with a requirement that notifications and disclosures are timely, complete, and enforceable and avoid placing an undue compliance burden on the respective party.

The first recommendation is *differentiated reporting obligations*. Reporting may contemplate different degrees of detail and/or different formats and/or content. For instance, reporting requirements may be a mere notification of a particular subsidy being granted when the subsidy is below the respective threshold value[11] Such an approach would be consistent with the EU's State Aid regime and potentially increase the mechanism's efficiency by attributing more resources (e.g. person-hours) to cases contemplating significant public spending.[12] These notifications, however, should be subject to review on a yearly basis to ensure that this flexibility is not being abused.

At the same time, when the subsidy scheme involves significant state aid, its notification should follow the pre-assessment procedure of the dedicated unit of the Subsidies Committee (or any similar body created by the parties to the PTA). Such a committee could incorporate best practices that currently exist at the WTO TBT/SPS Committees, namely discussion of 'specific trade concerns' (STC), annual reviews on implementation of transparency provisions (notifications), as well as the introduction of information management systems.

The second recommendation is obtaining the *high-quality data on subsidisation* that would allow measuring the fiscal, economic, and positive global spillover effects of subsidy schemes and carrying out respective assessments and/or audits. The data should be complete, comprehensive, verifiable, and accessible. For instance, the UK Department for Business Energy and Industrial Strategy (BEIS)[13] developed a subsidy transparency database where comprehensive information on subsidies can be uploaded and viewed. This database may be used as an example of good practice and used as a starting point in elaborating on the subsidies' data set template in future PTAs (BEIS 2022).

The third and last recommendation is the *enforceability* of transparency requirements. In particular, we suggest the application of non-monetary penalties such as

[11] For the purposes of this contribution, referred to as 'insignificant' while aid that exceeds this threshold is referred to as 'significant'.

[12] In particular, under the EU State aid control there are a few exceptions to mandatory notification, including de minimis aid that, among others, does not exceed €200,000 per undertaking over any period of three fiscal years. See Commission Regulation (EU) No 1407/2013 of 18 December 2013 on the application of Articles 107 and 108 of the Treaty on the Functioning of the European Union to de minimis aid (OJ L 352, 24.12.2013).

[13] Since 2023, the database has been maintained by the Department for Business and Trade (DBT) – one of the three departments, together with the Department for Energy Security and Net Zero (DESNZ) and the Department for Science, Innovation and Technology (DSIT) that BEIS was split into.

temporary revocation of benefits or concessions granted by the PTA in cases of non-compliance with transparency obligations.

9.4.4 *Prohibited Subsidies: A Future of Expansion?*

Over the years, the predominant approach in international subsidies regulation has centred around disciplining different kinds of trade-distortive subsidies depending upon the level of distortion caused.[14] This stems from the fact that the outcome of the ASCM negotiations prioritised the 'impact on competing producer interests' over the possible welfare effects from certain subsidies (Zhou and Fang 2021: 484). Arguably, prohibited subsidies, as envisaged under the ASCM, are the most trade-distortive of the lot. In fact, they are to be withdrawn immediately in case of a positive finding in a WTO dispute.[15]

While this chapter argues for a focal point shift from a trade distortion to a balancing approach for regulating subsidies in the PTAs (as elaborated in subsection 9.4.2 above), it does not propose to completely abandon the existing tenets of international subsidies regulations in these agreements, such as those surrounding prohibited subsidies. Indeed, the balancing test would assist in categorising a given assistance as prohibited, by assessing its trade-distortive effects over any potential positive effects. However, the outcome of the test may change in an exceptional situation, such as a financial emergency. This subsection hence proposes an update of the existing list of prohibited subsidies, counterbalanced by an expanded exceptions framework in future PTAs. In essence, this chapter argues for a yin–yang approach where modern twenty-first century PTA rules on subsidies adopt a well-balanced mechanism for both promoting and disciplining subsidies, depending upon their typology and effect. To this end, this subsection evaluates the current state and future prospects for disciplining the most trade-distortive subsidies in the PTAs with specific recommendations.

At present, the WTO rules explicitly prohibit two kinds of subsidies, namely the export subsidies and the import-substitution subsidies, under ASCM Article 3.1. While the former refers to subsidies contingent upon export performance,[16] the latter deals with subsidies contingent upon the use of imported over local products.[17] These kinds of subsidies are also presumed to be specific without any requirement to demonstrate adverse effects under the WTO rules (IMF, OECD, World Bank and WTO 2022; Rubini 2021).[18]

[14] Since the non-actionable subsidy category under the ASCM is now lapsed.

[15] See Article 3, ASCM. In case a WTO Member is found to have granted or maintained a prohibited subsidy through a dispute, it is to 'withdraw the subsidy without delay' as per Article 4.7, ASCM.

[16] See also Appellate Body Report, *Canada – Aircraft*, WT/DS70/AB/R, para 167.

[17] Appellate Body Report, *Canada – Renewable Energy*, WT/DS412/AB/R, para 5.6.

[18] See Article 2.3, ASCM regarding the deemed specificity of prohibited subsidies.

However, in recent times there has been a resurgence of discontent from certain quarters with respect to the narrow range of subsidies that are treated as prohibited under the WTO rules and, by extension, subject to the most stringent disciplines. The genesis of this can primarily be traced to the perceived inability of WTO rules to tackle trade-distorting subsidisation in the state-led economic model seen in countries such as China (McDonagh and Draper 2020).

Primarily led by the EU, two recent initiatives in this regard stand out. These are the Joint Statement of the Trilateral Meeting of the Trade Ministers of Japan, the United States and the EU (USTR 2020), and the EU's concept paper for WTO Modernisation (European Commission 2018). The primary thrust of these proposals is upon the need for expanding the current rules governing the most trade-distortive subsidies and going beyond prohibited subsidies.

The Trilateral Statement, for instance, proposes a trifold approach for updating the WTO disciplines since they are perceived to be inadequate to tackle market and trade-distorting subsidies in certain countries (USTR 2020). First, it argues for expanding the list of 'new' unconditionally prohibited subsidies based on what the proponents consider to be extremely trade-distortive. These could include unlimited guarantees, subsidies to ailing or insolvent enterprises without a credible restructuring plan, subsidies to enterprises operating in sectors or industries in overcapacity that cannot obtain long-term financing from independent commercial sources, etc. Second, the Trilateral Statement argues for a shift of the burden of proof on the subsidising country to demonstrate that its subsidy is not causing negative trade or capacity effects, for example, in the case of excessively large subsidies. Arguably, this approach could also be relevant in the context of GVCs. Finally, it argues for the direct linking of the concept of 'serious prejudice' under Article 6.3 to capacity.[19] The EU Concept Paper also provides the additional option of creating a rebuttable presumption of serious prejudice for these kinds of subsidies (as opposed to categorising them as prohibited subsidies).

Given the sweeping nature of changes to WTO rules proposed, both these initiatives are, however, surprisingly short on details or justifications. Concerns have also been raised regarding the lack of clarity on how the expanded notion of prohibited subsidies will interact with the developmental objectives of developing and least developed countries (Bhatnagar and Arora 2020).

With the WTO system already under considerable stress at the moment, an emerging consensus could very well be elusive on these issues, at least in the short

[19] For more details on the link between subsidies and overcapacity, see the submission from the European Union, Japan, Mexico and the United States, 'The Contribution of the WTO to the G20 Call for Action to Address Certain Measures Contributing to Overcapacity' (Committee on Subsidies and Countervailing Measures 2016); and the Communication from Canada, European Union and the United States, 'Role of Subsidies in Creating Overcapacity and Options for Addressing this Issue in the Agreement on Subsidies and Countervailing Measures' (Committee on Subsidies and Countervailing Measures 2017).

to medium term. Predictably, these proposals have failed to yet attract enough traction at the WTO. The PTAs are, hence, poised to emerge as a more viable platform for any future rulemaking in this field. They have the potential to serve as laboratories for the future, feeding into any future developments at the multilateral level.

Subsidies regulations in PTAs have largely remained underdeveloped beyond the transparency, dispute settlement, and countervailing duties frameworks for a large number of countries. While many PTAs do include disciplines on prohibited subsidies, very often these are a reiteration of the WTO position (Rubini 2020). However, this does not apply to the EU-, UK-, and US-led PTAs, particularly the recent ones (Sekine 2020). A limited expansion of the prohibited subsidies list is observed in these PTAs, primarily through the inclusion of unlimited guarantees and subsidies to insolvent or ailing enterprises without a credible restructuring plan within the ambit (e.g. EU–Japan Economic Partnership Agreement (EPA), EU–Singapore Free Trade Agreement (FTA), United States–Mexico–Canada Agreement (USMCA), UK–New Zealand FTA). This is considerably smaller in scope, compared to the proposed prohibited subsidies list in the Trilateral Statement at the WTO. Other major PTAs, such as the Regional Comprehensive Economic Partnership Agreement (RCEP) and the African Continental Free Trade Agreement (AfCFTA), do not include an expanded list of prohibited subsidies.

There is also a variance observed in the approaches of the EU and the US. While the EU-led PTAs tackle the issues of prohibited subsidies as part of the larger subsidies' disciplines, not much different to the WTO template, the US addresses this in the context of state-owned enterprises (SOEs). For instance, the USMCA prohibits non-commercial assistance provided by a party or its state enterprise or SOE to another SOE in case of insolvency without a credible restructuring plan.[20] At its core, the concept of non-commercial assistance is not very different to that of a subsidy, allowing for the above comparison.[21] As Siqi and Rubini (2021) note, the issue of state enterprises is largely a subsidy issue. This provides an avenue for streamlining the rules on the two issues. In sum, while limited strides have been made in the prohibited subsidies disciplines under PTAs by some countries, there is scope for developing these further in the coming times.

Any proposal for a future design of a PTA cannot be oblivious to its accompanying context, geopolitics, and global developments. When the world is only now bracing up to experience the full impact of COVID-19 on international trade and the global economy, the use of subsidies as a regulatory tool by governments to overcome the situation cannot be ruled out, and, indeed, can already be observed (IMF 2021). Against this background and building upon the existing rules and proposals, this

[20] See Article 22.6(b) of the USMCA.

[21] For the definition of a non-commercial assistance, see Article 22.1 of the USMCA.

subsection lays down an array of recommendations based on certain broad principles for tackling the issue of prohibited subsidies through future PTAs.

First, an overarching principle behind any future disciplining of prohibited subsidies must be viewed through the prism of maintaining a balance of the rights and obligations (Low et al. 2018) of the parties to the PTA. Rules that are skewed in favour of only expanding the list of prohibited subsidies, without accounting for the accompanying exemptions or flexibilities that may be needed – particularly to deal with exceptional situations – may not be a tenable proposition in the long run. For instance, the EU–Japan EPA exemption from the prohibited subsidies rules for subsidies granted temporarily to respond to a national or global economic emergency may serve as an effective precedent.[22] Despite their not very successful track record at the WTO, horizontal exceptions along the lines of Article XX of GATT 1994 and Article XIV of GATS can also be made available to the subsidies discipline under PTAs.[23] Further, going forward, PTAs should also be designed to provide the necessary flexibility from the prohibited subsidies disciplines in case of a pandemic or post-pandemic recovery or other kinds of health emergencies.

Second, there is a need for undertaking a robust assessment through the balancing test before any expansion of the prohibited subsidies list. As mentioned earlier, the Trilateral Statement and the EU Concept Paper list potential subsidies that could be included in the prohibited subsidies list in the context of the WTO. However, PTA parties should examine the economic/trade distortion effects of the subsidies in question before including these in their agreements (Bown and Hillman 2019). Further, the proposed treatment of the subsidies in question should be proportionate to their effects. It is prudent not to repeat the mistakes made in the past, particularly at the WTO. Sykes, for instance, argues the WTO rules on subsidies are indefensible from an economic perspective, and they fail to identify the types of subsidisation in any meaningful way (Sykes 2010).

Third, any negotiated outcome on prohibited subsidies would require preempting legal loopholes by accurately capturing the understanding of the parties on specific new terms used in the new PTA rules. For instance, there is yet to be any global consensus on what would constitute an industrial 'overcapacity' in relation to subsidies (Bown and Hillman 2019). This will, thus, need to be resolved in a future PTA, in the event the parties agree to include the related subsidies in the expanded ambit of prohibited subsidies.

Finally, future PTA rules on prohibited subsidies could be designed to make subsidies and the state-owned enterprise (SOE) approaches for tackling prohibited subsidies converge, given the conceptual overlap between the two subjects. At their core, both broadly target the issue of distortive subsidisation by public bodies/SOEs that escape the WTO disciplines through the PTA route. As mentioned earlier, the

[22] See Article 12.3.6 of the EU–Japan EPA.

[23] See, for instance, Article 12.9 of the EU–Japan EPA.

US deals with some of the subsidies-related issues in the chapter on SOEs in PTAs such as the erstwhile Trans-Pacific Partnership Agreement (TPPA) and the USMCA. This allows it the flexibility to define SOEs in broader terms, compared to the 'public body' definition under WTO. This chapter builds upon the ASCM Article 1.1 definition of a 'subsidy' as a basis for its analysis and recommendations. As per the ASCM, a subsidy is deemed to exist if there is a financial contribution by a government or any public body within the territory of a Member and a benefit is thereby conferred.

While the notion of 'public body' has not been defined under the ASCM, Appellate Body rulings have elaborated the meaning and scope of the term. For instance, in the *US – Antidumping Countervailing Duties (China)*, the Appellate Body concluded that a 'public body' 'must be an entity that possesses, exercises or is vested with governmental authority'.[24] According to the Appellate Body, the precise contours of a public body will vary from entity to entity, state to state, and case to case.[25] Thus, the Appellate Body interpretation appears to give precedence to governmental authority and control over governmental ownership of an entity. This would imply that the determination of whether an SOE is a public body would also vary on a case-by-case basis, despite both the terms being similar to some extent.

This interpretation has attracted much criticism, especially from the US, which argues that it is too narrow.[26] Thus, it is not surprising to see the US PTAs defining an SOE in clear terms, with ownership being an independent criterion front and centre of the definition.[27] The Trilateral Statement also states that the interpretation of the 'public body' by the WTO Appellate Body in several reports undermines the effectiveness of WTO subsidy rules, without proposing any specific modifications.

Future PTAs could be designed to include additional clarifications on what constitutes governmental authority or control in the context of a public body. While using ownership as an independent determinant may be easy to establish from publicly available resources, it may be unsuited to accurately capture the different shades of public bodies seen across the globe (OECD 2018) – for the specific purpose of prohibited subsidies. This approach can also be said to have contributed to a large number of exclusions sought and agreed upon with respect to SOEs in recent PTAs (Willemyns 2016). Hence, it is recommended that future PTAs further evolve the case-by-case analysis approach of the Appellate Body by laying down additional grounds for clarity and consistency. The enjoyment of monopolistic or dominant market positions by the SOE on account of

24 Appellate Body Report, *US – Antidumping Countervailing Duties (China)*, para 317.

25 Ibid.

26 Statement by the US at the 25 March 2011 meeting of the Dispute Settlement Body (United States Mission in Geneva 2011).

27 See the USMCA definition of SOE in Article 22.1. It defines an SOE, inter alia, to mean an enterprise that is principally engaged in commercial activities, and in which a party: (a) directly or indirectly owns more than 50 per cent of the share capital.

government-conferred advantages could be one such additional criterion to examine (Wu 2019).

In conclusion, the WTO and PTA experiences with prohibited subsidies, along with some of the reform proposals, provide the groundwork needed to tailor a modern twenty-first century PTA design for prohibited subsidies. The recommendations above attempt to weave together different stands of the prohibited subsidies discourse to form a coherent strategy for the future.

9.5 CONCLUSION

Subsidies are one of the most widely used instruments to pursue public policy objectives, be it support of ailing undertakings, export promotion, or green transition.

World Trade Organization subsidy disciplines do not prohibit subsidies per se. They do prohibit, however, subsidies that are distortive to international trade. Distortion is measured by economic indicators such as increased market share or revenue of the subsidised industry to the detriment of exporters that might have competed equally.

Therefore, the current regime's notion is that all prohibited or actionable subsidies are intrinsically harmful irrespective of oftentimes legitimate objectives they strive to pursue and their positive effects on the economy. We argue that this is one of the most critical omissions of the system, and where we see the need for a 'focal point' shift: from the system that fights against trade distortions to a system that would protect and shelter subsidies granted to attain legitimate objectives. We do not suggest that this system should bluntly exclude such subsidies from the ASCM regime. Neither do we suggest that one should turn a blind eye to subsidies with high distortive potential, such as unlimited guarantees, or subsidies to undertakings without a solid restructuring plan. We are also cognisant that the proposed approach may suit the interests of some countries more than others depending upon their level of development and capacity to subsidise.

Instead, we suggest introducing a set of guiding principles against which to assess not only the detrimental but also the positive effects of a particular subsidy. The Agreement on Subsidies and Countervailing Measures, in its current iteration, is incapable of fulfilling this task. That is where PTAs may serve as a game changer, first on the bilateral or regional and, later, on the multilateral level by gradually paving the way towards new and improved subsidies regulation for the twenty-first century.

REFERENCES

Aggarwal, V. K. and Evenett, S. J. 2010. 'Financial Crisis, "New" Industrial Policy, and the Bite of Multilateral Trade Rules', *Asian Economic Policy Review* 5: 221–224.

Air France (AF) 2019. 'Air France Horizon 2030', *Air France Corporate Communications Division*, pp. 3–11, https://corporate.airfrance.com/sites/default/files/air_france_horizon_2030_aftakescare_dossier_presse_eng.pdf, accessed on 30 January 2023.

Alderman, L. 2020. 'Europe Hands Air France-KLM a $10.8 Billion Lifeline', 26 April 2020, Section A, p. 22: *The New York Times*, New York edition, www.nytimes.com/2020/04/25/business/air-france-klm-bailout.html, accessed on 30 January 2023.

Baccini, L., Dür, A. and Elsig, M. 2018. 'Intra-Industry Trade, Global Value Chains, and Preferential Tariff Liberalization', *International Studies Quarterly* 62(2): 329–340.

Baldwin, R. and Venables, A. J. 2015. 'Trade Policy and Industrialisation When Backward and Forward Linkages Matter', *Research in Economics* 69(2): 123–131.

BEIS 2022. 'Subsidy Transparency Database', https://searchforuksubsidies.beis.gov.uk, accessed on 28 September 2022.

Bhatnagar, M. and Arora, P. 2020. 'Industrial Subsidies' Reform: The Developmental State under Siege', August, Centre for WTO Studies Working Paper, https://wtocentre.iift.ac.in/workingpaper/Industrial%20Subsidies.pdf, accessed on 30 January 2023.

Blonigen, B. A. 2016. 'Industrial Policy and Downstream Export Performance', *The Economic Journal* 126(595): 1635–1659.

Bown, C. and Hillman, J. 2019. 'WTO'ing a Resolution to the China Subsidy Problem', October, Peterson Institute for International Economics Working Paper, www.piie.com/sites/default/files/documents/wp19-17.pdf, accessed on 30 January 2023.

Busch, M. L. 1999. *Trade Warriors. States, Firms, and Strategic-Trade Policy in High-Technology Competition.* Cambridge: Cambridge University Press.

Cameron, D.R. 1978. 'The Expansion of the Public Economy: A Comparative Analysis', *American Political Science Review* 72(4): 1243–1261.

Clift, B. 2013. 'Economic Patriotism, the Clash of Capitalisms, and State Aid in the European Union', *Journal of Industry, Competition and Trade* 13(1): 101–117.

Clift, B. and Woll, C. 2012. 'Economic Patriotism: Reinventing Control Over Open Markets', *Journal of European Public Policy* 19(3): 307–323.

Committee on Subsidies and Countervailing Measures 2016. 'The Contribution of the WTO to the G20 Call for Action to Address Certain Measures Contributing to Overcapacity', Communication from the European Union, Japan, Mexico and the United States, 14 October, https://docs.wto.org/dol2fe/Pages/SS/directdoc.aspx?filename = q:/G/SCM/W569.pdf and Open = True, accessed on 29 August 2023.

2017. 'Role of Subsidies in Creating Overcapacity and Options for Addressing this Issue in the Agreement on Subsidies and Countervailing Measures', 13 April, Communication from Canada, the European Union, and the United States, https://docs.wto.org/dol2fe/Pages/FE_Search/FE_S_S009-DP.aspx?language = E&CatalogueIdList = 239757,239584,236014,235895,235880,235672,235491,235439,232337,231889&CurrentCatalogueIdIndex = 5&FullTextHash = &HasEnglishRecord = True&HasFrenchRecord = True&HasSpanishRecord = True, accessed on 29 August 2023.

2022. 'Report (2022) of the Committee on Subsidies and Countervailing Measures,' G/L/1438 G/SCM/161, www.wto.org/english/tratop_e/scm_e/scm_e.htm, accessed on 29 August 2023.

Crouch, C. 2008. 'Economic Patriotism and the Paradox of Neo-liberal Democracy,' Paper presented at the first *Economic Patriotism Workshop*, Warwick University, 13–14 February.

European Commission 2018. 'EU Concept Paper on WTO Modernisation,' 18 September, https://trade.ec.europa.eu/doclib/docs/2018/september/tradoc_157331.pdf, accessed on 30 January 2023.

2022. 'EU-New Zealand: Text of the Agreement – Chapter 16: Subsidies', 7 July, https://circabc.europa.eu/ui/group/09242a36-a438–40fd-a7af-fe32e36cbdoe/library/4dcdc64a-9f5b-415a-9087-b7befiboc2e4/details, accessed on 29 September 2022.

Evenett, S. and Fritz, J. 2020. *The Global Trade Alert Database Handbook*. Manuscript, 21 October 2022.

2021. 'Subsidies and Market Access: Towards an Inventory of Corporate Subsidies by China, the European Union and the United States', *The 28th Global Trade Alert Report*. London: CEPR Press, pp. 1–151.

Greenness of Stimulus Index (GSI) 2021. 'Finance for Biodiversity Initiative', www.google.com/url?sa = i&rct = j&q = &esrc = s&source = web&cd = &cad = rja&uact = 8&ved = 0CAMQw7AJahcKEwiot_vKsLf6AhUAAAAAHQAAAAAQAg&url = https%3A%2F%2Fwww.vivideconomics.com%2Fwp-content%2Fuploads%2F2021%2F01%2F201214-GSI-report_December-release.pdf&psig = AOvVaw2S8Hh98LYIKRSaTiGq9e59&ust = 1664450806551982, accessed on 28 September 2022.

Hall, P. and Soskice, D. 2001. *Varieties of Capitalism: The Institutional Foundations of Comparative Advantage*. Oxford: Oxford University Press.

Heyl, K., Ekardt, F., Sund, L. and Roos, P. 2022. 'Potentials and Limitations of Subsidies in Sustainability Governance: The Example of Agriculture', *Sustainability* 14(23): 15859. doi:10.3390/su142315859.

Hoekman, B. M. 2016. 'Subsidies, Spillovers and WTO Rules in a Value-chain World', *Global Policy* 7(3): 351–359.

Hoekman, B. M. and Kostecki, M. M. 2009. *The Political Economy of the World Trading System: The WTO and beyond*. Oxford: Oxford University Press.

Hoekman, B. M. and Nelson D. 2020. 'Rethinking International Subsidy Rules', *The World Economy* 43(12): 3104–3132.

Horlick, G. and Clarke, P. 2016. 'Rethinking Subsidy Disciplines for the Future. E15 Task Force on Rethinking International Disciplines – Policy Options Paper', *E15Initiative*. Geneva: International Centre for Trade and Sustainable Development (ICTSD) and World Economic Forum.

International Monetary Fund (IMF) 2021. 'Policy Responses to Covid 19', 1 July, www.imf.org/en/Topics/imf-and-covid19/Policy-Responses-to-COVID-19, accessed on 30 January 2023.

International Monetary Fund (IMF), Organisation for Economic Co-operation and Development (OECD), World Bank, and World Trade Organisation (WTO) 2022. 'Subsidies, Trade, and International Cooperation', 22 April, www.wto.org/english/news_e/news22_e/igo_22apr22_e.pdf, accessed on 28 September 2022.

Low, P., Mamdouh, M. and Rogerson, E. 2018. 'Balancing Rights and Obligations in the WTO – A Shared Responsibility', Government Offices of Sweden, www.swedenabroad.se, accessed on 30 September 2022.

Maskus, K. 2015. 'Research and Development Subsidies: A Need for WTO Disciplines?' The E15 Initiative, International Centre for Trade and Sustainable Development (ICTSD), World Economic Forum, pp. 1–10, https://e15initiative.org/publications/research-and-development-subsidies-a-need-for-wto-disciplines/, accessed on 30 January 2023.

Mattoo, A., Rocha, N. and Ruta, M. 2020. *Handbook of Deep Trade Agreements*. Washington, DC: World Bank.

McDonagh, N. and Draper, P. 2020. 'Industrial Subsidies, State-Owned Enterprises and WTO Reform: Prospects for Cooperation?' July. *Institute of International Trade Policy Brief 08*, https://iit.adelaide.edu.au/ua/media/783/mcdonagh-draper-2020-industrial-subsidies-soes-and-wto-reform_0.pdf, accessed on 30 January 2023.

Ministry of Foreign Affairs of Japan 2018. 'Japan–EU Economic Partnership Agreement (EPA)', 18 February 2021, www.mofa.go.jp/files/000382106.pdf, accessed on 29 September 2022.
Office of the United States Trade Representative (USTR) 2020. 'Joint Statement of the Trilateral Meeting of the Trade Ministers of Japan, the United States and the European Union', 14 January, https://ustr.gov/about-us/policy-offices/press-office/press-releases/2020/january/joint-statement-trilateral-meeting-trade-ministers-japan-united-states-and-european-union, accessed on 30 January 2023.
Organisation for Economic Co-operation and Development (OECD) 2018. 'Ownership and Governance of State-Owned Enterprises: A Compendium of National Practices', www.oecd.org, accessed on 30 September 2022.
Rodrik, D. 1998. 'Why Do More Open Economies Have Bigger Governments?' *Journal of Political Economy* 106(5): 997–1032.
Rosendorff, P. and Milner, H. 2001. 'The Optimal Design of International Trade Institutions: Uncertainty and Escape', *International Organization* 55(4): 829–857.
Rubini, L. 2015. 'Rethinking International Subsidies Disciplines: Rationale and Possible Avenues for Reform', E15Initiative. Geneva: International Centre for Trade and Sustainable Development (ICTSD) and World Economic Forum, 2015, https://cadmus.eui.eu/handle/1814/39404, accessed on 28 August 2023.
2020. 'Subsidies', in A. Mattoo, N. Rocha and M. Ruta (eds.), *Handbook of Deep Trade Agreements*. Washington, DC: World Bank, pp. 427–461.
2021. 'State Aid and International Trade Law', in L. Hancher and J. López (eds.), *Research Handbook on European State Aid Law*. Cheltenham: Edward Elgar Publishing Limited, pp. 103–133.
Rubini, L. and Hoekman, B. 2022. 'Transcending Territoriality: Expanding EU State Aid Control Through Consensus and Coercion', Robert Schuman Centre for Advanced Studies Research Paper No. RSC_33.
Ruggie, J. G. 1982. 'International Regimes, Transactions, and Change: Embedded Liberalism in the Postwar Economic Order', *International Organisation* 36(2): 379–415.
Schwartz, W. and Harper, E. 1972. 'The Regulation of Subsidies Affecting International Trade', *Michigan Law Review* 7: 833.
Sekine, T. 2020. 'Possibility of Developing and Expanding the Regulation of Subsidies Through Free Trade Agreements (FTAs): Analysis Focusing on a Trend in FTAs Concluded by the EU', *Public Policy Review* 16(5): 1–33.
Siqi, L. and Rubini, L. 2021. 'About Knowledge and Rule-Making: Reforming WTO Rules on Subsidies', in B. Hoekman, T. Xinquan and W. Dong (eds.), *Rebooting Multilateral Trade Cooperation: Perspectives from China and Europe*. London: CEPR Press.
Strange, S. 1996. *The Retreat of the State: The Diffusion of Power in the World Economy*. Cambridge: Cambridge University Press.
Streeck, W. and Crouch, C. 1997. 'Political Economy of Modern Capitalism', Political Economy of Modern Capitalism.
Sykes, A. O. 2010. 'The Questionable Case for Subsidies Regulation: A Comparative Perspective', *Journal of Legal Analysis* 2(2): 473–523.
United States Congress 2022. 'H.R.5376 – Inflation Reduction Act of 2022, 117th Congress (2021–2022)', the US Government Publishing Office, www.congress.gov/bill/117th-congress/house-bill/5376/text, accessed on 30 January 2023.
United States Mission in Geneva 2011. 'Statements by the United States at the March 25, 2011 DSB Meeting', 25 March 2011, https://geneva.usmission.gov/2011/03/28/mar-25-2011-dsb-meeting/, accessed on 29 August 2023.

Van Biesebroeck, J. and Sturgeon, T. 2010. 'Effects of the 2008–09 Crisis on the Automotive Industry in Developing Countries: A Global Value Chain Perspective', in O. Cattaneo, G. Gereffi and C. Staritz (eds.), *Global Value Chains in a Post-Crisis World: A Development Perspective*. Washington, DC: World Bank, pp. 209–244.

Willemyns, I. 2016. 'Disciplines on State-Owned Enterprises in International Economic Law: Are We Moving in the Right Direction?' *Journal of International Economic Law* 19(3): 657–668.

World Economic Forum (WEF) 2023. 'Davos 23: Special Address by Ursula von der Leyen, President of the European Commission', Davos, 17 January 2023, www.weforum.org/agenda/2023/01/davos-23-special-address-by-ursula-von-der-leyen-president-of-the-european-commission/, accessed on 30 January 2023.

World Trade Organization (WTO) 2019. 'An Inclusive Approach to Transparency and Notification Requirements in the WTO', Communication from African Group, Cuba and India (Revision), 11 July, https://docs.wto.org/dol2fe/Pages/FE_Search/FE_S_S006.aspx?MetaCollection = WTO&SymbolList = %22JOB/GC/218%22+OR+%22JOB/GC/218/*%22&Serial = &IssuingDateFrom = &IssuingDateTo = &CATTITLE = &ConcernedCountryList = &OtherCountryList = &SubjectList = &TypeList = &FullTextHash = 371857150&ProductList = &BodyList = &OrganizationList = &ArticleList = &Contents = &CollectionList = &RestrictionTypeName = &PostingDateFrom = &PostingDateTo = &DerestrictionDateFrom = &DerestrictionDateTo = &ReferenceList = &Language = ENGLISH&SearchPage = FE_S_S001&ActiveTabIndex = 0&languageUIChanged = true, accessed on 29 August 2023.

2021. 'World Trade Report 2021. Economic Resilience and Trade', Geneva: WTO www.wto.org/english/res_e/booksp_e/wtr21_e/00_wtr21_e.pdf, accessed on 28 September 2022.

2023a. 'Countervailing Initiations by Reporting Member 01/01/1995–31/12/2022', www.wto.org/english/tratop_e/scm_e/scm_e.htm, accessed on 29 August 2023.

2023b. 'Disputes by Agreement', www.wto.org/english/tratop_e/dispu_e/dispu_agreements_index_e.htm, accessed on 29 August 2023.

Wu, Y. 2019. 'Reforming WTO Rules on State-Owned Enterprises: SOEs and Financial Advantages', *Northwestern Journal of International Law and Business* 39(3): 275–308.

Zhou, W. and Fang, M. 2021. 'Subsidizing Technology Competition: China's Evolving Practices and International Trade Regulation', *Washington International Law Journal* 30(30): 470–544.

10

The Concept Design of International Rules on State Intervention in the Economy

Luca Rubini

10.1 MOTIVATION

Taking stock of the *acquis* in regulating subsidies and state enterprises in the World Trade Organization (WTO) and in preferential trade agreements (PTAs), this chapter aims to develop a conceptual framework to help thinking about new rules.

Regulating subsidies and state enterprises is a challenging exercise since, arguably, no other area touches more directly on state intervention in the economy and on the various ideas and interests surrounding it.[1] Talking about subsidies and state enterprises means referring to the various public policy objectives governments pursue (in some cases in the attempt to protect their own domestic industries) and to the role of markets. The topic of subsidies evokes the use of taxation and expenditure prerogatives to create incentives (and disincentives) for certain activities. State enterprises (broadly intended as any entity controlled by governments and operating in the market) constitute the economic arm of governments in the economy. Quite often, the two (subsidies and state enterprises) go hand in hand. Governments rely on direct participation in the economy through enterprises, and the same inevitably receive financial support from the public coffer in various forms. To a large extent, then, the issue of state enterprises is a subsidy issue. This factor alone would justify their joint analysis.

If the main goal of the chapter is to help readers in thinking afresh about the issue of how to regulate subsidies and state enterprises at the international level, this exercise does necessarily need to build up on an assessment – albeit cursory – of the status quo. Do PTAs regulate subsidies and state enterprises? If so, how? Are there common denominators among these PTAs? Are there any differences? Why? What works and what does not work in the current regulation? And, what can the 'zeroth

[1] For a recent take on this debate, see Orford (2023). For subsidies, see also Biffi et al. (2024).

level' of regulation, that is, the WTO rule book, say about subsidies and state enterprises? Does it constitute an 'efficient' standard? If not, why?

This exercise provides a useful diagnosis of the problem and enables us to offer a better prognosis for the 'out-of-the-box' thinking which aims to constitute the original contribution of the chapter. The chapter is thus organised as follows. After assessing the multilateral regulatory standard, represented by WTO rules, Section 10.3 will take stock of the chapters on subsidies and state enterprises in the PTAs currently in force. Section 10.4 invites the readers to think about the various issues in conceptual terms, using the notions of principles, standards, and rules. Sections 10.5 and 10.6 will then apply these conceptual 'bricks' to subsidies and state enterprises, respectively. Section 10.7 will conclude by moving from the substance of new rules to the process necessary to produce such rules.

10.2 WTO RULES ON STATE INTERVENTION: THE (NOW) INEFFICIENT MULTILATERAL STANDARD

Not many learned observers will be surprised by the statement that WTO subsidy disciplines do not really work. Nor that state enterprises, especially in their more troublesome activities, are virtually unregulated at the multilateral level.

As regards subsidies, the structure of the WTO Agreement on Subsidies and Countervailing Measures (ASCM) is fairly straightforward. The ASCM defines subsidies (Article 1) and provides that, in order to be regulated, they need to be specific to certain enterprises and industries (Article 2). The regulation was then used to divide these subsidies into three categories (under Articles 8, 5, and 3, respectively) – expressly permitted, potentially actionable, and expressly prohibited (the first category is now expired).[2] The original version of the ASCM (under Article 6.1) also provided that, for certain more troublesome subsidies, the serious prejudice triggering actionability should have been presumed (the rule that has too expired).[3] Building on the Tokyo Round Subsidy Code, the ASCM also includes important rules regulating the investigations and imposition of countervailing duties. Importantly, Members should have duly notified their subsidies to the relevant WTO Committee to enable peer control and discussion (see Articles 25 and 26 of the ASCM). Interestingly, this Committee could have set up auxiliary bodies, as appropriate (Article 24.2) – which has never happened – and could have been aided by an Expert Group (Article 24.3).[4] Equally subject to transparency were

[2] The provisions on 'non-actionable subsidies' were initially in force for five years only. Since WTO Members could not find an agreement to keep them, the relevant category expired at the end of 1999.

[3] Article 6.1, which included the presumption of serious prejudice, represented the counterbalance of 'non-actionable subsidies' provisions which presumptively permitted certain good subsidies.

[4] In fact, while established, the Expert Group was never consulted or utilised.

countervailing duty measures which the ASCM strictly regulated to ensure that they could not be captured by protectionist tendencies.

The Agreement on Agriculture offered a partly different approach based on baskets and scheduling. While the idea that subsidies within a certain given cap should be permitted (together with certain non-distorting laudable subsidies) remains (see Annex II, the so-called Green Box), the idea that certain other subsidies should be prohibited (notably export subsidies) has now taken grip of the agriculture regulation too (see Article 9 and 'Nairobi' Ministerial Decision on 'Export Competition').[5]

This brief overview gives a rough idea of the regulatory scheme for subsidies introduced by the WTO. That being said, the main indicator of the inefficient level of regulation is the limited number of measures of support that have been challenged before the WTO dispute settlement system since 1995. To be sure, this system has very often been confronted with subsidy issues (at the time of writing, for example, complaints on the ASCM account for 22 per cent of all the disputes filed with the WTO dispute settlement)[6] but, as far as domestic subsidies are concerned, complaints have been extremely rare (representing only 5 per cent of all consultations requests).[7] More crucially, however, 'actionable subsidies' claims have been pushed through by complainants and accepted by the adjudicating bodies in less than five cases! The measures that have been consistently condemned, in the form of export or local content requirement subsidies, are commonly held to be protectionist and are hence strictly prohibited.

The argument that the multilateral dispute settlement mechanism has, in fact, been used in a fairly limited way can be better appreciated if one considers the massive use of public budgets to face the numerous financial and economic crises that have confronted the world since the WTO was created. It is quite simply not possible that the several instances of this ubiquitous and massive governmental support cannot be configurated as domestic subsidies distorting international trade flows. Against this scenario, the increasing use of trade remedies (and in particular countervailing duties) has been the only significant constraint on foreign subsidisation. This is understandable since trade remedies have always been resorted to and truly represent the final protection of the inner citadel of the domestic industry.

Leaving litigation aside, it is very difficult to determine whether multilateral subsidy disciplines have really constrained the granting of distorting subsidies.[8]

5 'Export Competition', Ministerial Decision of 19 December 2015, Nairobi, WT/MIN(15)/45 WT/L/980.

6 One hundred and thirty-six out of a total of 616 registered disputes, www.wto.org/english/tratop_e/dispu_e/dispu_agreements_index_e.htm, accessed on 9 May 2023.

7 Thirty-two out of 136 requests for consultations based on the ASCM, https://www.wto.org/english/tratop_e/dispu_e/dispu_agreements_index_e.htm, accessed on 9 May 2023.

8 The answer to this question is by necessity empirical, very much like the one to whether litigating parties have really complied with the Dispute Settlement Body's rulings and recommendations; see Mavroidis (2019).

One further legal observation can be made in support of the claim that the current disciplines are probably under-inclusive overall and thus do not constitute a big disincentive against distorting financial support. This refers to the increasingly high legal standards that have to be met in order to win a subsidy claim. One of the reasons why there have not been many *successful* actionable subsidy claims in Geneva is that the 'serious prejudice' standard under Article 6.3 of the ASCM is very high. Similarly, with time, the Appellate Body has made the legal standard for de facto contingency in prohibited subsidies in Article 3 higher and higher.[9] The gate is so narrow that very few will get through. Crucially, it may well be that such a narrow scope was not what the negotiating parties had originally in mind. However, this is what has come out from the prevailing judicial interpretation (Rubini 2019; Crivelli and Rubini 2020).

Equally, current WTO subsidy disciplines do not include a single iota espousing the fact that subsidies may be legitimate if they pursue, certainly under given conditions, public policy goals. Accordingly, it would be difficult to argue that WTO subsidy disciplines provide an express and clear affirmation of countries' policy space. If this is ensured, it is done indirectly and implicitly (Rubini 2017). But the boundaries between what is legal and what is not are far from clear – and this happens at all levels, from the definition to the specificity test[10] up to the determination of adverse effects. Legal certainty is elusive (Rubini 2012).

Importantly, one of the sore points of the WTO subsidy regime is the poor transparency on subsidies. This can be explained by various factors, very often linked to the nature of subsidies themselves (Collins-Williams and Wolfe 2010). The fact remains that this is an area of gross inefficiency of the system. Without information on the measures supposed to be regulated, no real governance and regulation are possible.

A final, important gloss is that this assessment of WTO subsidy rules does not intend to constitute a critique of the work of the Uruguay Round negotiators and drafters. Being largely constituted of flexible norms, within a fairly flexible institutional setting, different interpretations and different directions could have been taken. Members' practice and WTO jurisprudence have given WTO subsidy rules their own life. However, the path that has been followed has essentially deactivated the potential of these important rules.

Moving now to state enterprises, it is pretty accurate to conclude that the current regulation is fairly limited (Mavroidis and Janow 2017). The WTO has not really managed to go beyond the non-discrimination standard, which has emerged, through dispute settlement clarifications, as the main (arguably the exclusive)

[9] Article 3 of the ASCM prohibits subsidies that are contingent, that is, conditional, on exports or the use of local products. This contingency can be explicit in the law (*de jure*) or come out from the factual circumstances (*de facto*).

[10] As noted above, Article 2 of the ASCM provides that subsidies should be specific to certain enterprises or certain industries.

applicable rule to these enterprises.[11] Once again, a different direction could have partly been taken if, for example, the provisions of the General Agreement on Tariffs and Trade (GATT) Article XVII[12] had each been given distinct dignity by recognising both an obligation of equal treatment and an obligation of commercial practice (Mavroidis and Janow 2017; Mavroidis and Sapir 2021).

The General Agreement on Trade in Services (GATS) simply added a non-circumvention provision for monopolies and exclusive service suppliers (Article VIII),[13] not really changing the general picture. Individual scheduling of market access and national treatment commitments can help address some of the concerns state enterprises raise,[14] but, by definition, scheduling implies an approach which is individualised and hence liable to create fragmentation and less legal certainty than a generalised approach would entail.

Moreover, since nowadays the issue with state enterprises is largely a subsidy issue, the above assessment of subsidy disciplines can be made for state enterprises too. The current rules do not manage to clearly capture the concerns raised by state enterprises operating in international trade nor to recognise the specific missions some of them might have (Li and Rubini 2021).

In conclusion, there are several indicators that the current WTO rule book on subsidies is – at the time of writing – 'inefficient' insofar as it does not achieve its main purpose of regulating troublesome subsidies while explicitly recognising which subsidies are legitimate.[15] Equally unsatisfactory is the discipline of state enterprises which has recently emerged as one of the most troublesome areas in international trade relations.

10.3 TAKING STOCK OF THE EXISTING PREFERENTIAL STANDARD: COMMON GROUND AND UNRESOLVED ISSUES

The review of the PTAs currently in force bears significant results. Recent research carried out by the World Bank in the context of their 'deep integration' research agenda has reviewed 283 PTAs, signed between 1956 and early 2016 and all currently in force (see Rubini 2020; Rubini and Wang 2020). What has emerged is that provisions on subsidies and state enterprises are particularly common in PTAs. In particular, while subsidy chapters were present in 94 per cent of the reviewed

[11] See Appellate Body, *Canada – Wheat Exports and Grain Imports*, WT/DS276/AB/R.

[12] Article XVII of the GATT is the provision applicable to 'State Trading Enterprises'.

[13] Paragraph 1 of Article VIII of the GATS provides that Members should ensure that monopoly suppliers do not act in a manner inconsistent with their obligations under the GATS. In a word, you cannot use other entities in your jurisdiction to avoid complying with your commitments.

[14] A Member may, for example, accept that certain educational services can be provided by any type of legal entity (and not only public establishments). It can equally commit to giving subsidies to any supplier of health services operating in the territory.

[15] On a similar score, see also Biffi et al. (2024).

PTAs, rules on state enterprises were present in 77 per cent. While subsidy provisions have consistently featured in PTAs across time, state enterprise disciplines were rare before 1991 and have really become frequent from 2012 onwards.

With respect to subsidies, the most common rules are those on transparency (78%), followed by those on countervailing duties (74%) and those that regulate export subsidies (55%) and subsidies distorting trade and competition (48%). Interestingly, 75% of the PTAs that include subsidy disciplines are enforceable inasmuch as they are subject to binding dispute settlement.

As far as state enterprises are concerned, the most common rules include those that prohibit anti-competitive behaviour (87%), that regulate subsidies (71.5%), and that prohibit discrimination (64%). Importantly, though both competition and subsidy disciplines are, in principle, applicable to any enterprise, state enterprises are not specifically mentioned. Rules confirming the neutrality of the parties vis-à-vis property regimes and liberalisation decisions were found in half of the PTAs with state enterprises provisions. Relatively less common were provisions committing parties to ensure that state enterprises or monopolies do not act in a manner contrary to the commitments accepted by the parties (38%) or that ask state enterprises to act in accordance with commercial considerations (29%). Importantly, only thirty-six PTAs included transparency rules and only twenty-four included corporate governance requirements.

How does all this compare with the WTO standard? If subsidy chapters are considered, the large majority is essentially in line with the WTO benchmark. WTO-plus provisions, in particular the prohibition of export subsidies to agricultural products between the parties (which often anticipated the 'Nairobi' Ministerial Decision), were rare. Occasionally, additional transparency obligations between the parties were provided for. Furthermore, while PTAs concluded by the United States are usually centred around CVDs only, European Union (EU) PTAs, the major player in preferential deals, are more complex. In particular, the closer the trade partner to the EU is, the closer subsidy disciplines are to internal EU state aid laws (see Rubini 2021). This is obviously the case for those countries that are in line to enter the EU. But even outside this relatively knit, and deep, European network, there are many other more recent PTAs that do arguably include the 'key principles' of EU state aid law and policy.[16]

What are these 'common' elements? They certainly include the definition of subsidy/state aid; what that covers (which encompasses both goods and services); the stricter regime for certain more troublesome subsidies; the highlighting of the importance of public interest goals pursued through subsidies; the introduction of exceptions for certain legitimate subsidies (which, in some cases, reproduce EU law

[16] The Negotiating Guidelines of the EU Commission often include the mandate to incorporate the 'standards and principles on State aid' in the prospective trade agreement. See, for example, Council of the European Union (2018).

verbatim); and the strengthening of transparency mechanisms. This comes out especially in some (though not all) so-called second-generation trade agreements concluded by the EU. See, for example, EU–Korea (2010), EU–Moldova (2014), EU–Ukraine (2014), EU–Mexico (2019), EU–Japan (2018), EU–Singapore (2019), EU–Viet Nam (2020).[17] are much closer to the WTO baseline.

Against the presence of common elements in many PTAs, and with so many interesting precedents, which extend to negotiations with countries as economically, politically, and geographically diverse as the United Kingdom (UK), Viet Nam, Singapore, and Japan, one wonders whether the normative process collectively emerging reflects the development of a 'common law' of subsidies. Apart from the inevitable variations that can be explained given the specific circumstances of the respective trade relations, if the analysis is maintained at the level of general principles regulating subsidies, a 'European common law' is indeed emerging (Rubini 2023).

The provisions on state enterprises, by contrast, are more composite, at times reflecting key EU law principles (such as the protection of public services), and at times interestingly following a mixed model, based on both EU provisions and US-led provisions.[18] While transparency and corporate governance provisions are limited, and binding dispute settlement is provided for in only two-thirds of the PTAs, EU PTAs often include an express recognition that state enterprises pursue public services or other legitimate public policy objectives. With time, we also notice longer and increasingly detailed provisions.

For example, the provisions of the *EU–Canada PTA* (2016) show various origins. While some provisions elaborate the GATT (and in particular Article XVII), clearly separating and distinguishing non-discrimination from commercial considerations, and others echo the NAFTA, some show an interesting common ground between European and Canadian sensitivities with respect to public policy goals. Thus, the PTA provides for limitations and exceptions to the application of commercial considerations that would hinder the fulfilment of public service or regional development obligations or the specific public mission assigned to state enterprises. Finally, and importantly, the chapter on state enterprises is subject to binding dispute settlement.

But for language, the *EU–UK* PTA (2020) clearly bears numerous resemblances to the EU state aid rules, which, for level-playing-field considerations, is fully understandable. While many provisions are extremely interesting and may provide useful guidance for law reform (the extensive chapter on tax incentives probably

[17] See also the EU–Chile PTA for which negotiations were concluded on 9 December 2022.

[18] By 'US-led provisions' I refer to rules initially developed in the context of the North American Free Trade Agreement (NAFTA) (1994) and then in the Trans-Pacific Partnership (TPP) (2016), then Comprehensive and Progressive Agreement for Trans-Pacific Partnership (CPTPP) (2018), and the United States–Mexico–Canada Agreement (USMCA) (2018).

provides the best example), this PTA is *sui generis* (being the expression of a disintegration – and not integration – process).

It is time for a few conclusive remarks. What does this brief overview of PTA practice suggest? First, the content and ambition of PTAs clearly depend on the objectives pursued by the parties and on the relative negotiating powers of the same. Second, while many PTAs simply replicate the WTO standard, there are increasingly numerous examples of innovative provisions, quite often finding origin in 'domestic' legal systems or in other PTAs. But these are not simply 'cut and paste' exercises. By contrast, what can be seen are interesting changes, specifications, omissions, etc. – in a word: variations.[19]

The time is probably ripe for digging deep into all these PTAs and provisions and learning what they have to say about countries' preferences on trade and other issues.

10.4 THINKING AFRESH: LEGAL-CONCEPTUAL BRICKS

When thinking afresh about a new regulatory framework, it is useful to consider the very basic legal-conceptual bricks that may be used in treaties.

10.4.1 *Principles, Standards, and Rules*

First, one needs to think about 'principles', 'standards', and 'rules'.

'Principles' express political, economic, and/or legal ideas, for example, that certain subsidies are overall so negative for the system that they should be automatically prohibited or that state and private enterprises should be treated equally or that there should be transparency on state action in the market. A good example of the use of principles can be traced back to the Tokyo Round Subsidies Code, where Article 11, paragraph 1 highlighted that:

> Signatories recognize that subsidies other than export subsidies are widely used as important instruments for the promotion of social and economic policy objectives and do not intend to restrict the right of signatories to use such subsidies to achieve these and other important policy objectives which they consider desirable.

Principles elucidate points of general importance for the design of treaties. They are thus often included in preambles. While principles guide negotiations and the drafting of new disciplines (and, if becoming embedded into a system, can take the nature of 'paradigms'), the specific legal bricks that are used to build the substantive norms of treaties are 'standards' and 'rules'.

[19] Space does not allow a more exhaustive analysis. For a more comprehensive and detailed analysis of subsidy and state aid provisions in EU PTAs, see (Rubini 2021). See also (Dür and Elsig 2015).

Differently from overarching principles, 'standards' and 'rules' are norms that can already guide the behaviour of operators.[20] This is particularly true for 'rules' that aim to define a specific situation with precision, with the result that operators who have to apply them are normally left without any significant doubt of what has to be done.[21] By contrast, to be operative, 'standards' need to be specified into 'rules'. In other words, while the prescriptive content of rules is determined beforehand, when the same rules are created, the content of standards is intentionally left vague so that it can be shaped when its application becomes necessary. Using economic language, while 'rules' are usually linked to *nearly* complete contracts,[22] 'standards' are the best example of incomplete contracts. Negotiators and drafters may decide it is not desirable, or even possible, to agree on the specific content of a norm and may thus simply adopt a standard that will need to be given more specific content when it needs to be applied in practice.[23]

Continuing with the use of economic concepts, and using a principal-agent framework, while with rules principals determine (at least) the key elements of the norm and leave to agents their simple implementation, with standards principals essentially delegate the normative act to agents.[24] One interesting form of delegation, which may involve more technical issues, would involve continuous or regular expert discussions and deliberations to develop or codify best practices.

It should be noted that, in practical terms, the agent may always be required to determine the content of the norm, the difference between rules and standards, thus becoming a matter of *degree* of definition and delegation. If the essential content of the norm/behaviour is already defined by the principal, we have a rule; if not, we have a standard. The use of a few examples taken from the WTO ASCM can illuminate this distinction.

Article 1.1(a)(2) of the ASCM reads that, for a subsidy to be deemed to exist, there must be a 'benefit'. This is a 'standard' which needs to be specified each and every time it has to be applied. Hence, the case law made it clear that the term 'benefit' implies a 'comparison' and that the best, the only logical comparator is the 'market'. This does not solve any issue since it is then necessary to identify the precise 'market

[20] These two notions are common currency in law and economics discussions; see, for example, Kaplow (1992).

[21] With the big caveat that any legal provision – be it a rule or a standard – has to be interpreted. No one can escape this level of uncertainty.

[22] The adverb 'nearly' signals that it may be difficult to have something as a fully complete contract. The issue should thus be looked at as a continuum where full completeness and incompleteness are the two (probably unreachable) ends.

[23] Borrowing from Kaplow (1992): 'Achieving complete and proper assessments is usually infeasible and, even if possible, unwise due to the cost involved.'

[24] Which is not necessarily a *carte blanche*. In these cases, what is crucial is to determine whether there are any specific limits to the activity of the agent, deriving from the specific act of delegation or from the nature of the legal system itself. For the sake of completeness, agents can be enforcers, adjudicators, or delegated lawmakers.

benchmarks' applicable to the financial contribution and the circumstances at hand.

By contrast, Article 14 of the ASCM, on the 'calculation of the benefit', already outlines various 'rules' to the interpreter and, in particular, various 'market benchmarks' to use. Thus, for example, a provision of equity capital shall not be considered as conferring a benefit if the investment is in line with the usual investment practice of private investors (Article 14 (a) of the ASCM). This reference is certainly more precise than a general indication that there must be a benefit. That said, it is clear that those delegated to apply the rule will have to carry out an assessment. A more precise rule could be found in the now-expired Article 8.2 (a). Assistance for research activities was permitted if it covered no more than 75 per cent of the costs of industrial research or 50 per cent of the costs of pre-competitive development actions. Footnotes specified the meaning of industrial research and pre-competitive development actions.

10.4.2 *Institutions, Procedures, and Remedies*

Importantly, norms, whether they are principles, standards, or rules, do not live in a vacuum. They are made operational within 'institutional frameworks', following certain 'procedures'. And, crucially, their breach ensues certain 'remedies'. Thinking about new rules on subsidies and state enterprises at the multilateral level will thus require considering this important level of regulation too. One cannot think about reforming the rules governing subsidisation or state enterprises' action without also considering where, how, and by whom these rules should be applied, enforced, monitored, and reviewed.

For example, subsidies are ambivalent measures where design is key to achieving the stated objectives while keeping international spillovers at bay. Their success often depends on tackling new challenges, which in turn is based on the proper assessment of policies and their effects. The same holds true for ensuring that they are designed in such a way that across-the-border distortions are kept to the minimum. The 'institutional' structure of subsidy governance should thus duly reflect this fundamental need for information and assessment, by encompassing bodies of new knowledge, on how best practices and suggestions for law reform are generated. Crucially, serious thinking should be directed at how information should be channelled into this process, how assessment and deliberation should take place, and how any output should be made available. These are essential 'procedural' issues.

10.5 NEW RULES FOR SUBSIDIES

Subsidies may distort international trade and competition – hence we regulate them internationally – but they may also be the first best to tackle market failures and pursue other important societal objectives.[25] Unfortunately, one does not exclude the other, and, at least theoretically, the final worth of a subsidy should be the result of a balancing of the negatives with the positives. This balancing involves difficult trade-offs between different interests, a process which may be certainly more difficult if it has to be performed across different jurisdictions (Rubini 2017). That being said, while more complex balancing scenarios necessarily require the existence of a very deep level of economic and political integration (see the EU), what can certainly be done in any international discipline regulating subsidies is to identify more clear-cut welfare situations and to regulate them.

It is also known that the design of subsidies is key, not only to achieve public policy goals, but also to avoid negative spillovers. It is, therefore, clear that any new rule should take into due consideration significant design elements.

Prohibitions should focus only on those subsidies that are more likely to produce a more negative impact on trade or that include discriminatory or protectionist elements. Other subsidies, which do not necessarily involve a negative impact on trade, should be objected to only if a requisite legal standard is satisfied. Crucially, however, if disciplines aim to be meaningful, this standard cannot be exceedingly difficult to satisfy. Governments can also decide that certain subsidies, pursuing laudable objectives and satisfying certain conditions of neutrality and non-discrimination, should be accepted. Variations on these themes are certainly possible with further sub-categories between the various types of subsidies depending on their expected distortedness (or otherwise) and their design. For example, governments can also decide to follow another approach, perhaps with those subsidies which, though troublesome, are difficult to remove from the statute book immediately or should deserve protection. They can negotiate caps on them and envisage only progressive reductions/phase-outs.

The reader will have surely realised by now that these suggestions do not depart dramatically from some of the main features of the trade law *acquis* resulting from the multilateral rule book (especially as it was originally devised) and many PTAs. To a large extent, there is no need to reinvent the wheel but to build up on the status quo – which, importantly, already reflects the common agreement of many governments.

One area where rules at the multilateral level have shown a high degree of deficiency is remedies. Following the GATT/WTO law mantra that remedies can only be prospective, and in derogation from the prevailing rule in general international law,[26] remedial action for subsidies granted in contravention of trade laws

[25] A good start for any new disciplines would thus explicitly recognise these two 'principles': subsidies may distort trade but may also mend market operation. Interestingly, many recent PTAs do include these two principles.

[26] Famously expressed in Permanent Court of International Justice, *Chorzów Factory*, Judgment of 13 September 1928.

has often lacked teeth.[27] Clearly, the strength – or lack of strength – of remedies is a key consideration that may be connected to the degree of ambition of a legal system. Accepting that trade law remedies are retrospective would be considered a Copernican revolution in trade circles. This does not exclude, however, that, against the prevailing standard of public international law, toothless remedies are a legal and political oddity.

Arguably, the area where more progress should be made – and could be more difficult to achieve – is transparency. Subsidies are complex, and there inherently is a great degree of uncertainty in their definition, classification, and evaluation (see Collins-Williams and Wolfe 2010; Hoekman and Nelson 2000a, 2000b). Furthermore, and leaving aside all these inherent difficulties, the issue is that the incentives are simply not there for being transparent. The only real solution to the question of transparency would be to go beyond the simple governmental channel. Data and information on public expenditure at the disposal of all international organisations (such as the International Monetary Fund (IMF), World Bank, International Energy Agency, and Organisation for Economic Co-operation and Development (OECD)) should be linked and harmonised if necessary. Moreover, any interested party – including individuals, companies, and trade associations – should be put in a position to inform the WTO of relevant subsidy measures. Any information should, of course, be subject to verification and comments by the relevant government; see Casier et al. (2014).

This liberation of information should be coupled with a suitable institutional framework where important knowledge-generating activities should take place in addition to the traditional peer-review function. In other words, the first best institutional governance of subsidies cannot accept ignorance of measures and their effects, due to the inherently difficult nature of subsidies and the opaque stance of governments. Knowledge on subsidies should be considered a 'public good', for the benefit of all. Not only may this help in reducing distorting practices, to the benefit of all, but it may also generate positive spillovers for the domestic governance of subsidies, which should be particularly welcome in an era of increasing budgetary constraints and vital common challenges like the fight against climate change.

All these substantive and governance principles can then be translated into 'rules' or 'standards'. The choice of one or the other should mainly be dependent on design considerations linked to the objective and nature of the activity that has to be carried out.

10.6 NEW RULES FOR STATE ENTERPRISES

There is obviously no need to reiterate that the most prevailing principle currently applying to state enterprises – that of non-discrimination – should feature

[27] Mavroidis (2016) offers an explanation.

prominently in any new disciplines. But prospective disciplines on state enterprises cannot certainly be centred around non-discrimination norms (be they standards or rules) only.

On the one hand, the issue is not just to preclude possible unjustified differential treatment between domestic and imported products, services, and players. What any discipline should entrench is a more general principle of 'competitive neutrality', whereby, in principle, governments commit not to favour the public sector or state enterprises to the detriment of the private sector and private enterprises (OECD 2021; Piernaz-Lopez 2023).

One key expression of this 'competitive neutrality' would be the principle that state enterprises should conduct themselves 'according to prevailing commercial practices' and/or to subject them expressly to competition laws.[28] What is, in particular, necessary is a clear separation of this principle (and emancipation from) the principle of non-discrimination. This would be overturning the WTO Appellate Body's jurisprudence, and aligning future disciplines to what most modern PTAs have done already (see Chapter 17 of the CPTTP). Benchmarking state enterprises' actions to commercial practice would, by necessity, avoid distortions to trade and competition. More specific rules and standards can then be introduced that are informed by this principle.

Compliance with 'competitive neutrality' and 'commercial considerations' can also be ensured by inserting a reference to prevailing 'corporate governance' principles which may, for example, introduce separation of functions and organs, accounting requirements, and transparency principles (OECD 2015).

By the same token, should the use of state enterprises be necessary to pursue legitimate public policy goals, such as the performance of public service obligations, this should be properly and expressly recognised in treaty language. Many EU PTAs represent a good model in this respect.

At the same time, while the market needs should be properly balanced with public needs, it would go too far to specifically require governments to liberalise sectors or privatise their enterprises. Future disciplines should thus include a principle of neutrality with respect to the organisation of the economy and the regimes of property. These are truly sovereign decisions that should be left to the preferences of each society and, crucially, are not needed in order to ensure that fundamental tenets of 'competitive neutrality' and 'commercial action' are safeguarded. Of course, this does not mean that we cannot envisage state enterprises disciplines which provide for liberalisation or privatisation processes. This is certainly one option but has to be placed in the context of a deeper integration contract that also pursues other distinct economic policy objectives (this is, for example, clear in the many association agreements that the EU concluded with would-be Members).

[28] On the important role that competition laws can play in regulating state enterprises, see Fox and Healey (2014) and Fox (2021).

As hinted at, transparency is of the essence and largely state enterprises' concerns are raised by the lack of transparency, in particular with respect to their decision-making and state financing. Requirements enabling more transparency with respect to these aspects would go very far in making the previous principle credible and also in facilitating any scrutiny of subsidy disciplines.

10.7 HOW TO CREATE NEW RULES: FOSTERING AN 'EPISTEMIC COMMUNITY' AND CREATING KNOWLEDGE

At the time of writing, it is extremely difficult – even audacious! – to speculate about what political factors could trigger countries to convene, spend part of their political capital, and amend the laws. Unlike in the Tokyo or Uruguay Rounds, there is no 'K group' anymore (Odell 2015; Koulen 2016). More fundamentally, however, the current geopolitical climate seems to be averse to any grand collective negotiating effort.[29]

Even assuming a real appetite for negotiating and changing the law did exist, the very preliminary step of any law-reform process would be to create the conditions for the creation of an 'epistemic community' or 'community of practice' that develops common understandings and, through the creation of a process of mutual trust, creates the conditions for deliberation and negotiations (Adler 2005; Koulen 2016). Along the same vein, the gathering of expertise must be based on data, and good data. This may require linking up various sources of knowledge in competition agencies and international organisations with expertise in subsidies and state enterprises (Hoekman and Nelson 2020a, 2020b).[30]

One interesting signal in this respect has been sent from the secretariats of the four key international organisations with an interest in subsidies (and state enterprises) with the joint publication of a momentous and most interesting report in the spring of 2022 (IMF, OECD, World Bank, WTO 2022) and, even more promising, the launch of a 'Subsidy Platform' making information on subsidies publicly available in one website (www.subsidydata.org) in May 2023. A ray of hope in gloomy times – where confrontation, subsidy wars, and 'new' massive industrial policies are on the rise.

REFERENCES

Adler, E. 2005. *Communitarian International Relations: The Epistemic Foundations of International Relations.* London and New York: Routledge.

[29] This does not mean that there are no meaningful discussions such as the US, EU, Japan 'Trilateral'. But much more is required to talk about a really consequential and sufficiently sponsored initiative.

[30] While Hoekman and Nelson (2020a, 2000b) make this point with respect to subsidies, the same is equally true for state enterprises; see Li and Rubini (2021).

Biffi, L., Y. Kucheriava and S. Singh 2024. 'Subsidies and Future PTAs: From Market Distortions to Legitimate Public Policy Goals?' in K. Claussen, M. Elsig and R. Polanco (eds.), *The Concept Design of 21st Century Trade Agreements*. Cambridge: Cambridge University Press.

Casier L., R. Fraseer, M. Halle and R. Wolfe 2014. 'Shining a Light on Fossil-Fuel Subsidies at the WTO: How NGOs Can Contribute to WTO Notification and Surveillance', *World Trade Review* 13(4): 603–632.

Collins-Williams, T. and R. Wolfe 2010. 'Transparency as a Trade Policy Tool: The WTO's Cloudy Windows', *World Trade Review* 9(4): 551–581.

Council of the European Union 2018. Negotiating Directives for a Free Trade Agreement with Australia, Brussels, 8 May 2018.

Crivelli, P. and L. Rubini 2020. '"Flying High in a Plane" – Appellate Body Report, European Communities and Certain Member States – Measures Affecting Trade in Civil Aircraft', *World Trade Review* 19(2): 316–340.

Dür, A. and M. Elsig 2015. *Trade Cooperation – The Purpose, Design and Effects of Preferential Trade Agreements*. Cambridge: Cambridge University Press.

Fox, E. 2021. 'The Promotion of Competitive Neutrality by Competition Authorities – Attacking State Restraints and Assuring Competitive Neutrality', OECD, DAF/COMP/GF(2021)10, 8 December 2021.

Fox, E. and D. Healey 2014. 'When the State Harms Competition', *Antitrust Law Journal* 79: 769–820.

Hoekman, B. and D. Nelson 2020a. 'Subsidies, Spillovers, and Multilateral Cooperation', Robert Schuman Centre for Advanced Studies Research Paper No RSCAS 2020/12.

2020b. 'Rethinking International Subsidy Disciplines', *The World Economy* 43(12): 3104–3132.

IMF, OECD, World Bank and WTO 2022. Subsidies, Trade, and International Cooperation, 2022/001.

Kaplow, L. 1992. 'Rules and Standards: An Economic Analysis', *Duke Law Journal* 42(3): 557–629.

Koulen, M. 2016. 'Reflections on the SCM Agreement', in L. Rubini and J. Hawkins (eds.), *What Shapes the Law? Reflections on the History, Law, Politics and Economics of International and European Subsidy Disciplines*. Florence: European University Institute.

Li, S. and L. Rubini 2021. 'About Knowledge and Rulemaking: Reforming WTO Rules on Subsidies', in B. Hoekman, X. Tu and D. Wang (eds.), *Rebooting Multilateral Trade Cooperation: Perspectives from China and Europe*. London: CEPR.

Mavroidis, P. C. 2016. 'Dispute Settlement in the WTO: Mind Over Matter', Robert Schuman School of Advanced Legal Studies Research Paper, No RSCAS 2016/04, European University Institute.

2019. 'A Little Less Conversation and a Little More Action (Property and Liability Rules in the DSU Review of the WTO)', in P. Pazartzis and P. Merkouris (eds.), *Permutations of Responsibility in International Law*. Leiden: Brill.

Mavroidis, P. C. and M. E. Janow 2017. 'Free Markets, State Involvement, and the WTO: Chinese State-Owned Enterprises in the Ring', *World Trade Review* 16(4): 571–581.

Mavroidis, P. C. and A. Sapir 2021. *China and the WTO: Why Multilateralism still Matters*. Princeton: Princeton University Press.

Odell, J. 2015. 'How Should the WTO Launch and Negotiate a Future Round?' *World Trade Review* 14(1): 117–133.

OECD 2015. Guidelines on Corporate Governance of State-Owned Enterprises.

2021. Council Recommendation on Competitive Neutrality, OECD/LEGAL/0462, 31 May 2021.

Orford, A. 2023. 'How to Think about the Battle for the State at the WTO', *German Law Journal* 24: 45–71.

Piernaz-Lopez, J. J. 2023. 'The Principle of Competitive Neutrality and the External Reach of EU State Aid Law and Policy', in L. Hancher, J. J. Piernaz-Lopez and L. Rubini (eds.), *The Future of EU State Aid Law and Policy: Consolidation and Expansion*. Madrid: EU Law Live Press.

Rubini, L. 2012. '*Ain't Wastin' Time No More*: Subsidies for Renewable Energy, The SCM Agreement, Policy Space, and Law Reform', *Journal of International Economic Law* 15 (2): 525–579.

2017. 'ASCM Disciplines and Recent WTO Case Law Developments: What Space for "Green" Subsidies?' in T. Cottier and I. Espa (eds.), *International Trade in Sustainable Electricity – Regulatory Challenges in International Economic Law*. Cambridge: Cambridge University Press.

2019. 'The Never Ending Story: The Puzzle of Subsidies', in: M. Crowley (ed.), *Trade War: The Clash of Economic Systems Endangering Global Prosperity*. London: CEPR.

2020. 'Subsidies', in A. Mattoo, N. Rocha and M. Ruta (eds.), *Handbook of Deep Trade Agreements*. Washington, DC: World Bank.

2021. 'Gli accordi di nuova generazione dell'Unione Europea e le innovazioni in materia di aiuti di Stato e imprese pubbliche', in G. Adinolfi (ed.), *Gli accordi preferenziali di nuova generazione dell'Unione Europea*. Torino: Giappichelli.

2023. 'Transcending Territoriality: Expanding EU State Aid Control through Consensus and Coercion', in L. Hancher, J. J. Piernaz-Lopez and L. Rubini (eds.), *The Future of EU State Aid Law and Policy: Consolidation and Expansion*. Madrid: EU Law Live Press.

Rubini, L. and T. Wang 2020. 'State-owned enterprises', in A. Mattoo, N. Rocha and M. Ruta (eds.), *Handbook of Deep Trade Agreements*. Washington, DC: World Bank.

11

Global Value Chains

The Road to Resilience

Selina Hauser, Israel Gutiérrez, and Christian Winkler

11.1 INTRODUCTION

Global value chains (GVCs) are a key pillar of the trade environment today. During the last decades, trade in intermediates, trade in value-added, and trade network complexity have significantly increased. Nowadays, goods and services often cross multiple borders, go through various stages of production, and are subject to different standards and taxes before reaching the final consumer. Today, about 70 per cent of trade in goods and services involves GVCs, according to the Organisation for Economic Co-operation and Development (OECD 2022a). While the rise of GVCs has long been associated with productivity- and welfare-boosting effects, recent events have exposed the vulnerability of globalised production networks. The 2008 Global Financial Crisis, the COVID-19 pandemic, and the Russian invasion of Ukraine have disrupted many GVCs and led to acute shortages of critical products such as pharmaceuticals, energy, or food in many countries around the world. As a response, various governments have taken initiatives to make their supply chains more resilient.[1]

In general, two different approaches to GVCs' resilience have emerged: First, national, bilateral, and multilateral incentives often summarised under the label of 'friend-shoring' or 'ally-shoring', which are set to strengthen the relationships with like-minded partners and to increase the strategic autonomy of countries; and second, attempts to promote supply chain diversification by putting in incentives

[1] Examples of such government initiatives include the United States (US)–Japan Critical Minerals Agreement, the European Union's (EU) Important Projects of Common European Interest (IPCEI) programme, or the plurilateral Supply Chain Resilience Initiative by Australia, India, and Japan. Moreover, resilient and secure supply chains feature prominently in various government reports, for instance, the European Commission's Strategic Foresight Report 2022, EU Commission's Report on Strategic Dependencies and Capabilities, or the US's Executive Order on America's Supply Chains.

to increase international cooperation and risk-sharing. This chapter focuses on the second approach to GVCs' resilience and explores which role international cooperation, and, in particular, preferential trade agreements (PTAs), can play in making GVCs more resilient.

The chapter is structured as follows. First, we give a brief historical perspective on the evolution of GVCs and elaborate on some recent shocks to GVCs and how they caused shortages and disruptions in the globalised production network. Second, we outline different strategies to make GVCs more resilient and discuss the theoretical justification for government involvement. Third, we discuss the relationship between PTAs and GVCs by providing a detailed analysis of the existing channels through which PTAs can enhance the resilience of supply chains. Fourth, we propose three additional approaches that could further increase GVCs' resilience and inform the future design of PTAs. Finally, we conclude the chapter by summarising our findings, while pointing to further research avenues on the link between PTAs and GVCs' resilience.

11.2 HISTORICAL CONTEXT OF GVCS

The development of GVCs can be understood as a natural result of globalisation: the main drivers of GVCs have been a lowering of trade costs and advances in transportation and transmission. Baldwin (2012) proposes looking at globalisation as two major unbundlings. The first unbundling roughly took place around the 1830s with the Industrial Revolution and its accompanying increase in steam power. Before the start of globalisation, each village would mostly consume what it produced. Propelled by the Industrial Revolution, the Global North (North America, Europe, Japan) industrialised while the Global South (China and India) staggered behind. At the same time, the steam revolution, with its impact on steamships and railroads, lowered transportation costs causing trade to explode during this period, but it mostly took place between countries of the Global North. This pattern of increased trade and industrialisation and lower costs continued roughly until the 1930s with the onset of the Great Depression, the Smoot–Hawley Tariff Act, and later World War II.

The second unbundling took place around the 1990s with the information and communication technology (ICT) revolution, and this is where GVCs started to emerge. The great technological advances and the reduction in communication costs made it possible for firms to coordinate complex processes at a distance and shift from just trading in goods to also trading in components and services. The big gap in wages between the developing and developed countries made this fragmentation in production profitable. The era of GVCs started when ICT made it possible to combine developed-country technology with developing-country labour. This period also coincided with significant changes in trade liberalisation. The World Trade Organization (WTO) was created; developing countries suddenly embraced

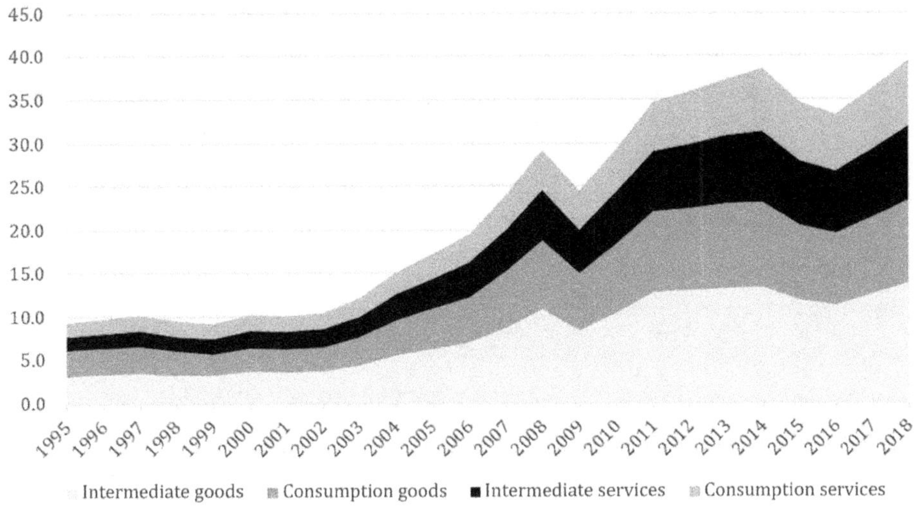

FIGURE 11.1 Decomposition of OECD gross exports, USD trillion.
Source: Created by the authors using OECD TiVA data

market openness facilitating production across countries; and along with this, there was a boom in the signing of bilateral investment treaties (BITs) and PTAs.

While GVCs undoubtedly play a central role in today's global economy, quantifying the exact extent to which GVCs dominate international trade is not trivial. In its simplest form, GVCs could be measured as the amount of imports embedded in a country's exports. It is, therefore, strongly associated with intra-industry trade. In Figure 11.1, which uses data from the OECD's Trade in Value Added (TiVA) Database and focuses on the period 1995–2018, we can see a clear increase in exports of intermediate goods and services, implying an absolute increase in GVCs. The 2008–2009 financial crisis explains the dip we see in the pattern.

Similar patterns can be observed when we focus on particular industries, as is the case for the automobile industry, which is illustrated in Figure 11.2. Here we present the foreign value-added (FVA)[2] share in the final output for six countries with different levels of integration. A prime example of the consequences of disruptions in GVCs is the recent global semiconductor chip shortage. Semiconductor chips are essential components of almost every electronic device, from cell phones to household appliances, medical devices, computers, and vehicles. Chip manufacturing is a multibillion-dollar industry which requires very specialised design and technology (Alicke and Luchtenberg 2021). However, the chip industry and its customers found themselves in a crisis during the 2020–2023 global shortage. Chip supply chains were under pressure due to the ramifications of the COVID-19

[2] We calculate FVA according to the OECD TiVA methodology. FVA = (value of foreign components in exports) / (value of exports).

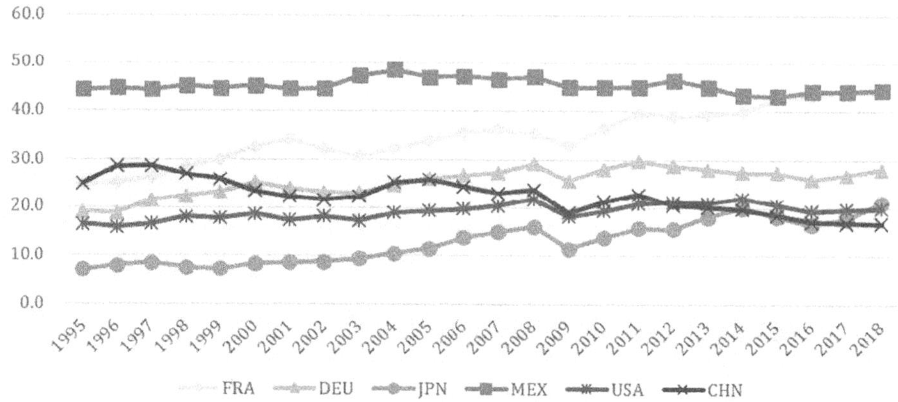

FIGURE 11.2 Foreign value-added share in the automotive sector.
Source: Created by the authors using OECD TiVA data

pandemic and the intensified geopolitical tensions between the US and China. For instance, the Biden Administration restricted exports of certain equipment and services to Chinese semiconductor companies and prompted allies to do the same. As a result, global demand for chips far exceeds global supply, a situation which has affected over 169 industries (Howley 2021). The consequence is major price increases, shortage queues, and bantering for chips between different industries. However, it is considered that the shortage started in the automobile sector during the COVID-19 pandemic before gradually affecting other industries (Wu et al. 2021).

At the beginning of the COVID-19 crisis, the auto industry faced a significant drop in demand. The automakers did not, therefore, increase the semiconductor orders. At the same time, due to confinement and remote work, there was a strong increase in demand for electronic products, such as computers and other devices heavily dependent on semiconductors. The semiconductor industry shifted its production to meet this new demand. By the time the auto sector made its recovery at the end of 2020 its demand for semiconductors could no longer be met. This chip shortage soon expanded to many other industries (Alicke and Luchtenberg 2021). Another problem concerns the lack of sourcing options, with world production depending almost exclusively on Taiwan. For instance, China relies on Taiwan for 70 per cent of the semiconductors it needs for its electronic industry (Cronin 2022). Taiwan Semiconductor Manufacturing Company (TSMC) alone has a worldwide market share of 92 per cent of advanced chips and a 53 per cent market share for the global foundry market (factories contracted to make chips designed in other countries). This dependence on Taiwan for semiconductors has been called a 'silicon shield' against a Chinese attack. However, a range of geopolitically motivated trade restrictions, such as the US Chips and Science Act, have played an important role in perpetuating the crisis further.

11.3 HOW TO MAKE GVCS RESILIENT

Global value chains are the backbone of today's global trade. However, recent events have led to a shift in the narrative of globalised production. While the discourse in the 1990s to the mid-2010s was dominated by widespread optimism about the merits and virtues of globalisation and, in particular, the productivity- and welfare-boosting effects of international production networks, the debate has changed dramatically in recent years. Against the background of rising economic and geopolitical uncertainty, the narrative surrounding GVCs has moved to emphasise the risks and vulnerabilities associated with geographically dispersed production (Bown 2021; Bade 2022; Posen 2022). This section will take a closer look at the various policy initiatives targeted at making GVCs more resilient such as 'friend-shoring' or supply chain diversification, outline the main approaches at the firm, domestic, and international levels, and elaborate on the role PTAs could play in this context.

11.3.1 *The Rise of 'Friend-shoring'*

Rising geopolitical tensions and domestic public pressure to protect markets from international competition have led many governments to rethink their approach to GVCs. In particular, making GVCs more resilient is high on the agenda of many policymakers around the world. Yet, what policymakers and experts understand by 'resilience' varies. While the International Monetary Fund (IMF) defines GVCs' resilience as 'the ability of supply chains to continue to operate even when hit by shocks' (see IMF 2022), the management literature has traditionally distinguished between the concept of supply chain resilience, which focuses on the ability to rebound and recover after a disruption, and robustness, which emphasises the ability to continue production during a crisis (Brandon-Jones et al. 2014; Brunnermeier 2021). While there is no common definition of GVCs' resilience (Khanna et al. 2022), for the purpose of this chapter, we follow the broader definition of the Brookings Institution, which incorporates both the notion of resilience and robustness. In particular, we define resilience as 'the ability of a given supply chain to prepare for and adapt to unexpected events; to quickly adjust to sudden disruptive changes that negatively affect supply-chain performance; to continue functioning during a disruption (sometimes referred to as "robustness"); and to recover quickly to its pre-disruption state or a more desirable state' (Brookings Institution 2020).

In the political discourse, one of the most prominent policy proposals to increase GVCs' resilience is the concept of 'friend-shoring'.[3] As US Secretary Janet Yellen elaborated, 'working with allies and partners through "friend-shoring" is an

[3] Similar approaches to 'friend-shoring' with slightly different meanings are 'near-shoring' and 're-shoring'. While the former concept encompasses policy initiatives that focus on the relocation of production to a geographically close region, the latter concept describes approaches that aim to bring once-outsourced production back into the territorial boundaries of a state.

important element of strengthening economic resilience while sustaining the dynamism and productivity growth that comes with economic integration' (CNBC 2022). The Biden Administration has championed this new approach to GVCs and senior policymakers of other countries have started to follow. For instance, Canadian Treasury Secretary Chrystia Freeland views friend-shoring as a 'new norm' (Financial Post 2022). Likewise, the concept of 'secure trade' features prominently in the European Commission's Strategic Foresight Report 2022, calling into question the open trading system of the post-Cold War period.[4]

The new narrative is also reflected in a range of unilateral, bilateral, and multilateral policy initiatives in a variety of countries. In the US, a mix of executive and legislative actions have been taken, which include the Chips and Science Act aimed at encouraging the onshoring of semiconductor production; the Defense Production Act, which restricts funding for sourcing minerals in foreign countries; and the Inflation Reduction Act, which in parts promotes 'friend-shoring' of manufacturing processes. Moreover, a range of bi- and multilateral incentives aimed at enhancing economic relationships with 'friendly' countries and allies are taking shape, such as the Indo-Pacific Economic Framework for Prosperity (IPEF) and the US–EU Trade and Technology Council (TTC). In Europe, the European Commission launched the IPCEI programme to strengthen the continent's 'strategic autonomy' and the European Chips Act, which aims at relocating and setting up semiconductor production capacities in Europe. Such initiatives have also been taken or are underway in other parts of the world. For example, China is pursuing its Dual Circulation Strategy, and Japan has set up a fund to relocate factories from China back home or to neighbouring countries.

While it seems apparent that 'friend-shoring' has become part of the foreign economic policy zeitgeist (Harput 2022), some see this new policy strategy as a dangerous retreat to protectionism and the fragmentation of global trade. For instance, Ngozi Okonjo-Iweala, Director General of the WTO, voiced concerns about the current trend of 'friend-shoring', highlighting that fragmentation might not only be costly but hinder the multilateral cooperation necessary for tackling global problems such as climate change (WTO 2022). Moreover, it remains unclear whether those policy initiatives will achieve the desired goal of making GVCs more resilient. Recent studies raise questions about the effectiveness of 'friend-shoring' and whether GVC disruptions are a market failure best fixed by policy interventions (Grossman et al. 2021; Peiris et al. 2021). For one thing, firms themselves have incentives to manage the risks in their supply chains and make them more resilient (Christopher and Peck 2004). For another thing, diversification – instead of

[4] The European Commission's 'Secure Trade' approach focuses mainly on integrating EU interests into trade and investment policies, for instance in export controls or foreign investment screening mechanisms, as well as on working with so-called like-minded partners in protecting GVCs from geopolitical risks and securing access to critical raw materials (EU Commission 2022).

'friend-shoring' – might be the socially more desirable and economically more efficient policy option (Grossman et al. 2021).

11.3.2 *Alternative Paths to GVCs Resilience*

In general, one can distinguish between different paths on the road to resilient GVCs. 'Friend-shoring' and related policy initiatives are one path that has gained prominence in the current political environment. However, as outlined above, these initiatives also carry significant risks, as they may be neither the most efficient nor the most politically sensitive strategy to increase the resilience of GVCs in the context of growing geopolitical tensions. A second path to resilient GVCs focuses on promoting the diversification of supply chains by putting more emphasis on international cooperation and risk-sharing. Here, PTAs could play an important role as a tool to make GVCs more resilient. Yet, before elaborating on how exactly PTAs could improve GVCs' resilience, it makes sense to recall what exactly the policy objective of resilient GVCs entails.

Various risks are associated with GVCs depending on the sector, geographical location, production characteristics, business models, and firms' strategies (Cattaneo et al. 2010). In general, the risks firms face in GVCs can be distinguished between supply shocks, demand shocks, and transportation disruptions. Examples of supply shocks include disruptions caused by natural disasters, cyberattacks, workers' strikes, or broader economic and political instabilities. Demand shocks are, for instance, new competitors, reputational damages, bankruptcy, etc. Transportation disruptions examples are the Suez Canal Blockage in 2021 or disruption in port logistics (see Miroudot 2020a). While many shocks to GVCs in the past have been geographically limited, such as the 2011 Tohoku earthquake in Japan (Carvalho et al. 2021), more recent shocks, such as the COVID-19 pandemic or the Russian invasion of Ukraine, have led to more widespread disruptions.

Against this background, firms operating in international production networks have developed various tools to increase the resilience of GVCs. These tools range from supply chain reengineering, collaboration, agility, and supply chain risk management (Christopher and Peck 2004) to specific pro-resilience strategies, including the promotion of interchangeability of inputs or the boosting of inventories (Alicke and Luchtenberg 2021; WEF 2021). The crucial question remains, whether there is a need for policy intervention to guarantee resilient GVCs. A useful conceptualisation of this question is provided by Baldwin and Freeman (2022), who argue that state action might be desirable if there is a Pigouvian wedge between the private assessment of the trade-off between risks and rewards associated with GVCs and the social evaluation of this trade-off (see Figure 11.3). If the public has a lower risk tolerance, illustrated by point X, than the private sector, illustrated by point Y, then state intervention may be justified. Whether this scenario applies to reality is an empirical question. However, as pointed out by the authors, in sectors

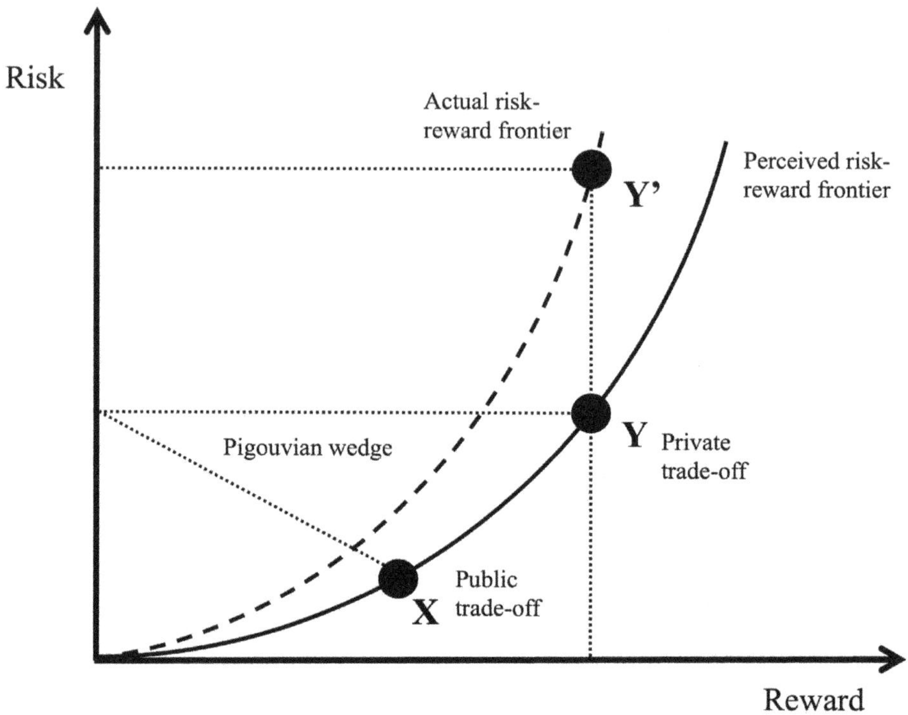

FIGURE 11.3 Illustration of the public–private wedge analysis of GVC risks.
Source: Created by the authors

such as banking, food production, or defence, the public–private risk wedge has traditionally justified government measures (Baldwin and Freeman 2022).

Policy interventions aiming at promoting GVCs' resilience might be legitimate in sectors critical to economic or national security, such as semiconductors, pharmaceuticals, or energy. While careful attention is required to ensure that the designation of 'security-related' measures to particular sectors is not exploited by special interests seeking to extract rents from state intervention, it seems obvious that in light of current events, some sectors are of fundamental national interest. Indeed, many recent policy initiatives aimed at enhancing GVCs' resilience are targeted at sectors regarded as crucial for national security. The remaining question is, therefore, what policies effectively increase the resilience of GVCs. In general, we argue that substantial improvements in the resilience of GVCs are only possible through an interplay of public and private initiatives. As Figure 11.4 shows, targeted measures at all levels of GVCs governance are needed.

For example, at the company level, these initiatives include building and maintaining higher inventory levels, digitising the supply chain, or investing in risk management capabilities. Indeed, recent evidence suggests that companies have been increasing their inventories and improving their warehousing in reaction to

Firm level	
• Increase in inventory	• Digitalisation
• Investment in GVC risk management	• Diversifying suppliers
Domestic level	
• Infrastructure development and increase of transport capacity, such as ports, railway networks, etc.	• Regulatory flexibility, temporary lifting of regulatory requirements such as import licences, custom duties, etc.
International level	
• International agreements such as PTAs, cooperation initiatives, etc.	• International regulatory cooperation

FIGURE 11.4 Tackling GVCs' resilience at different levels.
Source: Created by the authors

recent shocks to supply chains (Zhang and Doan 2023). At the domestic level, improved logistics infrastructure, such as port capacity and rail networks, as well as more flexible regulation and better supply management, can contribute to the greater resilience of GVCs. Finally, at the global level, international cooperation and information sharing, particularly improved pluri- and multilateral international agreements and cooperation initiatives, as well as regulatory cooperation, can increase the resilience of GVCs.

11.3.3 *An Example of the Multilevel Approach in the Case of Trade in Services*

The multilevel approach to GVCs' resilience discussed previously illustrated its potential for yielding the desired outcome in the case of trade in services. During the COVID-19 pandemic, trade in goods was not directly targeted by pandemic policies, except for export bans and restrictions on specific medical supplies and medicines. However, policies limiting the movement of people or reinforcing border controls led to disruptions in trade. For instance, the transport industry demonstrated how goods trade could be affected through services (Miroudot 2022). Restrictions on the movement of people negatively impacted international transportation networks, as demonstrated by the decline in passenger flights, which, in turn, adversely affected the air cargo services supply. Additionally, road transport was impacted by quarantine and sanitary measures at borders, and maritime transport was significantly disrupted by bottlenecks in ports and the reluctance of shipping companies to adapt to the recovery (Miroudot 2020b).

Furthermore, lockdown policies resulted in a decrease in output and a shift in demand, for example heightened demand for goods needed for home offices. Services activities are heterogeneous, so different service sectors were impacted differently by the pandemic, depending on the mode of provisions and the shifting demand. Pandemic policies more severely affected service sectors that involved consumer or producer movement than service sectors that could be supplied digitally or through commercial presence within a country (Shingal 2021). For instance, service sectors involving jobs that could be performed from home (Dingel and Neiman 2020) or service sectors such as e-commerce, computer services, and health services, which benefited from the shift in demand, suffered less (WTO 2022). In contrast, transport and travel services, which account for about one-third of total export services in the G20 countries, suffered the most from pandemic policies. These sectors recovered slowly compared to the other service sectors, such as financial services, telecommunications and information services, and other business services.

To make trade in services more resilient in the future, measures at the firm, domestic, and international levels were necessary. Resilience was primarily built by firms employing dynamic capabilities like agility, flexibility, cooperation with other firms, and visibility in the supply chain (Kamalahmadi and Parast 2016). It was, therefore, crucial for firms to invest in these capabilities and to build effective risk management strategies. However, service firms often operated in highly regulated environments, where governments played an important role; thus, accompanying government policies at the domestic and international level were necessary to facilitate and support firms in building more resilient GVCs. Hence, at the domestic and international levels, rule setting and standards encouraged firms to build risk management strategies to comply with necessary capacities. For example, air and maritime transport, severely impacted by COVID-19 and having indirect but crucial effects on the functioning of product markets, was also subject to high trade restrictions, creating bottlenecks and emphasising disruptions (OECD 2022b). Sectors like these held high potential by introducing reforms that improved capacity, flexibility, and transparency to foster the ability to adjust to demand shifts and ensure supply continuity.

Moreover, during the crisis, the focus lay on maintaining the operation of essential GVCs and increasing supply. This was achieved by facilitating trade and investment to foster supply, prioritising shipments of essential goods, and adapting the rules for the movement of key personnel. An open trade and investment environment was needed to reduce the recovery time. This included supporting micro-, small, and medium enterprises (MSMEs) and addressing financial and other issues of firms that might delay the recovery. In this context, creating a stable regulatory environment, introducing standard and certification procedures, including risk awareness, and reviewing transport and customs regulations to better absorb disruptions could promote resilient GVCs in the long term. To make GVCs more robust during the crisis, policies aimed to maintain the operations of essential GVCs and scale up the production of key products while promoting international cooperation (Miroudot 2020b).

In addition, policies aimed at enhancing information exchange, namely investment in infrastructure, could reduce bottlenecks and add capacity for services firms to deal with an increase in demand. This was done by increasing collaboration to guarantee the supply reliability of critical products during the crisis, and by incentivising information exchange and transparency across internal departments and suppliers. As proposed previously, by setting standards, control towers, and cross-functional supply chain management hubs, efficient infrastructure might have helped firms adapt to disruptions by efficiently reorganising their activities. In addition, policies fostered regulatory flexibility that allowed firms to continue to operate during a crisis. COVID-19 demonstrated how crucial the movement of people across borders was to supply services. Further cooperation at the international level could have helped to develop common rules and harmonised measures. The following section discusses the role PTAs could play in this context as a specific form of international cooperation.

11.4 WHAT ROLE PTAS ALREADY PLAY

Over the past decades, PTAs have grown more complex, expanding to cover a broader range of policy areas and increasing in detail (see Figure 11.5). Recent studies have shown that diversification of GVCs among foreign suppliers can promote resilience as

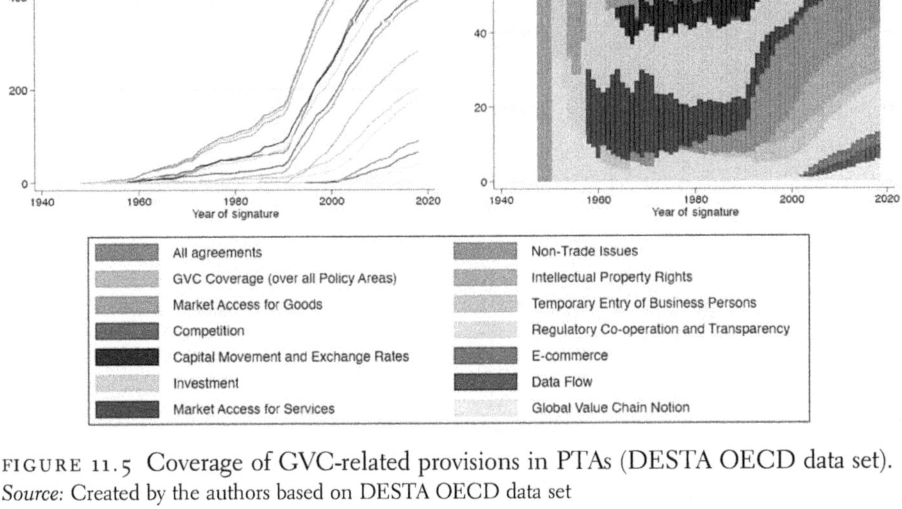

FIGURE 11.5 Coverage of GVC-related provisions in PTAs (DESTA OECD data set).
Source: Created by the authors based on DESTA OECD data set

the exposure to single countries is reduced (Bank of England 2021). One way to facilitate diversification is through the conclusion of PTAs. In recent decades, PTAs have become one of the main instruments of global trade governance (Mansfield and Milner 1999; Dür et al. 2014; Baccini 2019). Their existence and design shape the nature of GVCs. A rich body of literature has shown that GVCs and PTAs are closely linked. Global value chains play a substantial role in the diffusion of PTAs. For example, large and productive firms involved in foreign direct investments and offshoring activities facilitate the conclusion of PTAs and their design (Chase 2005; Manger 2009; Blanchard and Matschke 2015; Baccini et al. 2018). However, the relationship between GVCs and PTAs is not one-directional. Preferential trade agreements influence the shape and nature of regional and global production networks. For instance, the North American Free Trade Agreement (NAFTA) substantially impacted the geographic distribution of production in the automotive sector in North America (Wall, 2002; Klier 2017). To further explore the role of PTAs in the development of GVCs and their resilience, we first describe the existing channels through which GVCs are managed in PTAs. Second, we present some new approaches to regulating GVCs more comprehensively.

11.4.1 *Promote Long-term Relationships with Trading Partners*

Preferential trade agreements have the potential to promote GVCs' resilience by diversifying input sources and promoting long-term partnerships. We identified seven groups of provisions which are especially promising to build trust among trading partners. Our analysis is based on the updated Design of Trade Agreements (DESTA OECD) data set, which covers GVC-related provisions. The following seven groups of provisions support the functioning of GVCs and include potential instruments for managing GVCs' resilience. These are: direct references to GVC management, the specific investment definition, the application of dispute settlement mechanisms (DSMs), competition rules, rules of origin (RoOs), transport, and regulatory cooperation. In the following sections, we explain the channels through which obligations in the various groups might affect GVCs' resilience. These obligations might serve as complements or substitutes among each other, and the list discussed below is by far not complete. Also, the channels through which the obligations impact GVCs' resilience might have contradicting intentions and outcomes.

11.4.2 *Direct References to GVC Management*

This group of provisions covers whether a PTA includes terms like supply chain, production network, or value chain. These terms are only part of PTAs signed in the last decade. This shows that the terminology around GVCs slowly starts to be part of the government's negotiation process and reflects how negotiators have become aware of the growing role of GVCs.

11.4.3 *Investment Definition*

Several studies have already observed that deep PTAs foster GVC operations (Laget et al. 2020). The impact of deep PTAs is higher on trade in value added in intermediates rather than value-added trade in final goods and services. Preferences of international firms may differ in terms of the design of deep PTAs depending on how firms have organised their value chains (Eckhardt and Lee, 2018). Further, signing a deep PTA with investment provisions has a higher impact on trade in value added compared to signing a shallow PTA and a BIT (Boffa et al. 2019). This is a recently observed trend towards regulating investment in deep PTAs rather than in BITs. Since investment enables GVCs' expansion and development in different dimensions, we assume that certain investment provisions of deep PTAs have an impact on GVCs' resilience. When firms serve foreign markets or organise their GVCs, there is no binary choice between trade and investment, that is, between working with independent firms or with subsidiaries owned by the parent company. In between, different types of relationships involve some form of alliance or control but are not based on equity or ownership. As with trade and investment, these strategic partnerships can complement or be substitutes for other corporate relationships. The data set takes seven specific types of these non-equity modes (NEMs) or strategic partnerships into account, namely contract manufacturing and services outsourcing, contract farming, licensing, franchising, management contracts, concessions, and strategic alliances and contractual joint ventures. Thus, investment chapters typically contain a definition of what qualifies as an investment and who qualifies as an investor. The enterprise-based definition of investment with a closed list of what is considered as investment was featured in the NAFTA and several Canadian PTAs. Since then, the investment definition has evolved to an open-ended asset-based list.

Moreover, many investment chapters include a provision on the denial of benefits (DoB), specifying that only investors or investments with substantial business activities (SBA) are entitled to the PTAs' benefits. The chapter on trade in services contains similar provisions for service providers. These clauses can be seen as RoOs for goods which lay down under which conditions goods qualify as originating from the PTA Members.

In the context of GVCs with widespread production fragmentation, RoOs (see Section *RoOs*) can create significant distortions in firms' strategic decisions on the location of production and supply relationships. Since multinationals closely integrate trade in goods, services, and investment in the operation of GVCs, clarity and consistency between these rules are important (see Section *Regulatory Cooperation*). Coherence is necessary to ensure neutrality between different trade and investment decisions and avoid distortions.

11.4.4 *DSMs*

Preferential trade agreements typically offer relative and absolute standards of protection to foreign investors, often backed by an investor–state DSM. The possibility of settling disputes between states and states and investors helps to prevent the adverse effects of unresolved trade conflicts. They also mitigate the imbalances between stronger and weaker players by settling disputes based on rules rather than having the power to determine the outcome. Two types of DSMs are often included in PTAs *State-to-State Dispute Settlement (SSDS)* and in PTAs with investment chapters also *Investor–State Dispute Settlement (ISDS)*. In theory, both mechanisms can be used to cover regulations and institutional arrangements addressing the divergence of private and social returns that arise with the inadequate appropriation, either between the states (SSDS) or for investors by the host state (ISDS). They cover rights recognised in the PTA, such as national treatment, most-favoured-nation (MFN) treatment, fair and equitable treatment (FET), and full protection and/or security (FPS). Some PTAs further distinguish two situations (UNCTAD 2012): first, direct expropriation, in which an investment is wholly or partially nationalised or otherwise directly expropriated through formal transfer of title or outright seizure; and second, indirect expropriation, in which a party's action or series of actions have an effect equivalent to direct expropriation without formal transfer of title or outright seizure (*Direct Expropriation and Indirect Expropriation*). In addition, provisions regulating compensation for losses in case of strife are also considered (*Compensation: Expropriation and Strife*)

11.4.5 *Competition*

Another group of provisions we identified as having a crucial impact on managing GVCs is the consistency in global competition law. Anti-competitive behaviour impacts GVCs in many ways. Generally, a cartel raises prices downstream while a buyer's cartel depresses prices upstream. Firms with monopolistic roles can also abuse their market power to exclude competitors when they try to extend their activities to other levels of GVCs or refuse to deal with firms other than their affiliates. Mergers also affect market positions. Horizontally they create market power, and vertically they create incentives for abusing a dominant position. Thus, gaps between regional enforcement of competition policy can be a problem.

However, the literature proposes that competition law is not a good instrument for the reallocation of added value among various stakeholders within the chain or for changing the country's position at the production chain stages (Davies 2018). Existing domestic competition legislation does not explicitly favour particular firms, as the maximisation of production efficiency is conceived to benefit all parties universally. Consequently, governments address distributional apprehensions through alternative policy channels. Nevertheless, the strategic application of international competition law can contribute towards achieving distributional goals by preserving competition within and between GVCs, eliminating entry barriers, and facilitating shifts in the production stage position, given that the firms can compete with existing entities. Governments naturally prioritise the welfare of their own producers over consumers in foreign countries. Additionally, disadvantaged producers, who are marginalised by larger downstream firms, are unlikely to receive compensation from the benefiting consumers (Geradin 2009). Therefore, strengthening international competition law is essential for addressing distributional issues in the context of GVC management.

The DESTA OECD data set covers several competition provisions. The principle of non-distortion of competition, a well-established and early incorporated doctrine, is included in most PTAs. Subsequently, the competition policy area was reaffirmed as a fundamental pillar along GVCs, leading to the inclusion of a competition-focused chapter in approximately one out of every four PTAs. Figure 11.6 *Panel d*

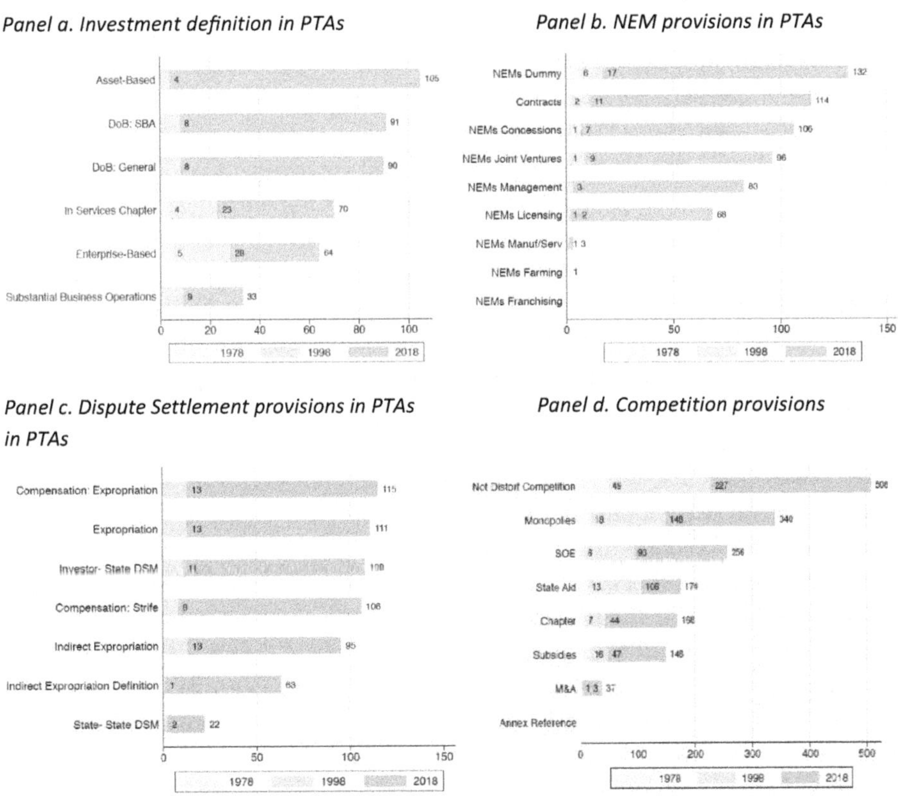

FIGURE 11.6 Provisions in PTAs I.

Note: DoB: SBA = denial of benefits: substantial business activities; DoB: General = denial of benefits: general NEM; Contracts: contracts are included in the definition of investment; NEMs Dummy: PTA covers at least one of the seven NEMs and/or allows for contracts being part of the investment definition; DSM = dispute settlement mechanism; SOE = state-owned enterprises; M&A = mergers and acquisitions; FET = fair and equitable treatment; FPS = full protection and/or security.

Source: Created by the authors based on DESTA OECD data set

indicates that competition commitments are more exhaustive in PTAs signed recently compared to those signed prior to 2000. More recent PTAs also encompass provisions related to specific competition-related topics such as monopolies and cartels (*Monopolies*), mergers and acquisitions (*M&A*), state-owned enterprises (*SOE*), state aid (*State Aid*), and subsidies (*Subsidies*).

11.4.6 *RoOs*

Rules of origin are an inherent part of any PTA. They define the conditions a good must comply with to be considered an 'originating good' and, therefore, eligible to be exported at the preferential tariff rate. The primary purpose of the RoOs is to avoid trade deflection making sure that the non-signatories of the PTA do not take advantage of it without signing it. The most common rules either define the specific transformation that goods must undergo to be considered originating (change in tariff classification) or determine what percentage of the product's final value (regional value content) needs to have been sourced in the preferential trade area of the agreement.

Rules of origin can naturally shape GVCs, and conversely, GVCs can affect the RoOs being negotiated. From a firm perspective, signing a trade agreement means gaining preferential access to a new market, and potentially using economies of scale to service the current and the new markets (Eckhardt and Lee 2018). Firms sourcing mostly domestic inputs (e.g. a juice company) might prefer to have more restrictive RoOs (a higher percentage of originating goods to benefit from the agreement) to conquer a larger part of the market and avoid competition from firms that might consider sourcing their inputs (e.g. fruits) from abroad. Firms relying primarily on foreign inputs (e.g. an electronics company) might prefer to have laxer RoOs (lower percentages of originating goods required to benefit from the agreement) to obtain their inputs from the most competitive suppliers. Consequently, more flexible RoOs not only improve economic competition but also, in the event of a negative external shock, GVCs are less likely to be disrupted if firms can readily supply themselves with inputs from other countries.

An illustration of the substantial nexus between RoOs and GVCs is that the world's biggest international manufacturing clusters, for example, Factory North America, Factory Europe, and Factory Asia (Baldwin and Lopez-Gonzales 2013), coincide with the most comprehensive PTAs worldwide: the NAFTA, Treaty on European Union, and Association of Southeast Asian Nations (ASEAN). The RoOs and related provisions in these PTAs are often key determinants of the dynamics of the integrated industries in the region.

11.4.7 *Transport Services*

Another highly interconnected set of provisions regarding the management of GVCs are services provisions. Service supply chains are generally more resilient to shocks than manufacturing value chains. On the one hand, services value chains are more branched (Baldwin and Venables 2013; Davies and Markusen 2021). They have fewer production stages because their production usually coincides with their consumption. Interestingly, just-in-time production strategies have been criticised as being more prone to shocks due to low inventory, but in the case of services, it is the opposite. According to Netland (2020), the most resilient firms rely on lean production to react better to demand shocks. Not being subject to inventory adjustments is an advantage for services (Ariu 2016) because they cannot be overproduced and the producers instantly know the change in demand (Miroudot 2020b).

On the other hand, services involve long-term arrangements that mitigate the impact of fluctuations in demand. These arrangements are used in uncertain environments to respond to risks (Amann and Marin 1990; Swinney and Netessine 2009). But they do not offer full protection against shifts in demand, as seen in the increased shipping time. The ocean timeliness indicator (OTI) measures how long it takes from pickup in Asia to final delivery in North America or Europe. Before the pandemic, it was 50 days; in late 2020, 70 days; and since late 2021, up to today, 100 days (Flexport research). Different factors drive this increase: on the supply side, fixed capacities (ports and boats), people on sick leave (in not automated ports), and truck driver shortage. On the demand side, unpredictable consumer spending patterns, and large consumer durables (space on the logistic network per dollar spent).

Since the production of goods is highly dependent on transport services, we see this indirect impact through increased shipping times having a significant effect on the functioning of GVCs. The literature on transport restrictions shows that international transport services play an important role in influencing international trade flows (Andriamananjara 2004). For example, a substantial welfare gain could be obtained by letting foreign shipping companies operate on domestic routes in the US (Francois et al. 1996). The fact that certain transport service sectors are included in or excluded from the services and/or investment chapter of PTAs might have an impact on the functioning of GVCs. The DESTA OECD data set covers this in different dimensions: on the one hand, it differs between air, land, and maritime transport service sectors, and on the other, it differs between domestic and international services, asking explicitly whether these sectors are excluded from the service sector of the PTA (see Figure 11.7 *Panel a*).

11.4.8 *Regulatory Cooperation*

We split the group into three dimensions: coherence, transparency, and the introduction of new regulations. The first dimension covers regulations with other PTAs that might contain overlapping and contradicting provisions. Many countries have been rethinking, revising, and evolving their BITs, occasionally including market access commitments. Likewise, investment treaties potentially overlap with PTAs

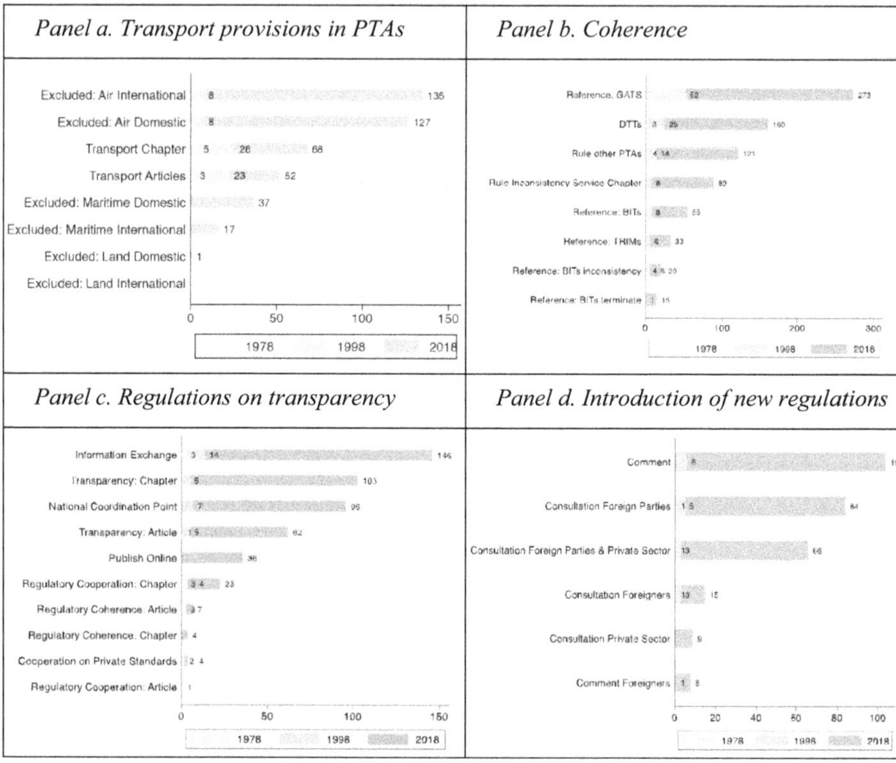

FIGURE 11.7 Provisions in PTAs II.
Notes: GATS = General Agreement on Trade in Services; DTTs = double taxation treaties; PTAs = preferential trade agreements; BITs = bilateral investment treaties; TRIMs = Trade Related Investment Measures.
Source: Created by the authors based on DESTA OECD data set

with investment protection provisions. But potential overlaps and complementarities appear not only in BITs and other PTAs, but also in double taxation treaties (DTTs) with complementary measures that affect investment decisions. This coherence requires specific rules, for example, in terms of which agreement prevails in the case of inconsistency.

The second dimension covers regulations on transparency. They include a broad spectrum of provisions from consultations and exchanges of information to mutual recognition and harmonisation. They cover any provision aimed at reducing the impact of divergences in regulatory approaches among the parties to the agreement. Figure 11.7 shows that information exchange provisions are widespread (146 PTAs include an information exchange regulation covering all sectors and policy areas). Also, the organisation and regulation of transparency in PTAs can vary substantially. We find commitments on the online publication of regulations (*Publish Online*), the establishment of national contact points for regulatory coordination (*National*

Coordination Point), and references to information exchange (*Information Exchange*) and private standards in the agreement (*Cooperation on Private Standards*).

The third dimension covers provisions for the introduction of new regulations. Two variables capture *comment* mechanisms, and four variables capture *consultation* mechanisms. Consultations require action from the state, asking the relevant stakeholders (legal community, civil society, businesses) what they think about a proposed regulation. Although these stakeholders are not obliged to give their comments, if they do, the state needs to react to these comments. Comments are more passive because the state (or state agencies) receive the inputs from stakeholders without explicitly asking for these comments.

11.5 WHAT ROLE PTAS COULD PLAY IN THE FUTURE

The previous section has elaborated on various provisions already part of many PTAs meant to enhance supply chain resilience. This section outlines three additional approaches that could further promote the resilience of GVCs and inform the future design of PTAs. Thus, in contrast to the already existing provisions that indirectly affect GVCs' resilience, we propose additional design features that aim at directly addressing the management of GVCs. First, we suggest that PTAs can play an important role in enhancing GVCs' resilience by making it easier and cheaper for corporations and authorities to develop and manage inventories for critical products. Second, we argue that RoO provisions in PTAs could be leveraged to increase GVCs' resilience. Finally, we propose that developing and including new minimum resilience standards for GVCs in PTAs can further protect supply chains from shocks and increase their resilience. Resilience refers to the process of successfully adapting to difficult situations. It relates to attributes such as strength, flexibility, and adaptability. Accordingly, these same attributes are reflected in the proposed strategy: firstly, larger common inventories make firms stronger. Additionally, less restrictive and more homogeneous RoOs provide firms with additional flexibility in supplying their inputs; and lastly, the minimum industry standards would permit firms to adapt to future shocks quickly.

11.5.1 *Common Inventories*

Future PTAs could include provisions related to the development, management, and accessibility of pooled inventories for critical products. The build-up of stockpiles can be an effective part of a broader strategy to increase GVCs' resilience (OECD 2022c). While forming PTAs can already make it easier and cheaper for companies and authorities to build up stocks by encouraging supplier diversification and reducing costs, the impact of PTAs could be further enhanced by incentivising contracting parties to engage in regional stockpiling of critical products. The basic idea is to add a provision to a PTA regulating the pooling and sharing of inventories. For instance, two countries could agree within the framework of a PTA to build up stockpiles of different critical products, for example, medical products, food, energy, etc., which, in case of an external shock, will be deployed to the country in crisis. Such a new provision would therefore have to define clear rules regarding the pooled stockpile's development, maintenance, and deployment. For instance, this provision could set legally binding obligations when it comes to sharing the pooled stockpiles. While common inventory provisions might be more feasible for regional PTAs, for example, PTAs whose members are in geographically close proximity, falling transportation and logistical costs make the relocation and distribution of resources across long distances increasingly manageable. How common inventory provisions might work in practice can be illustrated by the case of pharmaceutical supplies during the COVID-19 pandemic.

When the first wave of COVID-19 infections hit the US at the beginning of 2020, over 100 drugs were already in shortage (FDA 2020). The disruption of supply chains following various pandemic-related policy measures led to severe shortages of various essential medical devices, pharmaceutical products, and personal protective equipment (Lupkin 2020; Perrone and Johnson 2020). This was the case because the production of pharmaceutical products is highly internationalised (Baldwin and Evenett 2020). Against this background, policy measures ranging from lockdowns to travel and export bans further aggravated the situation. For instance, travel restrictions constrained health authorities' capacities to inspect overseas drug manufacturing facilities, reducing their ability to approve new sources of drugs (Socal et al. 2021), while export bans prevented the distribution of essential medical supplies (Evenett 2020). Hence, the pandemic shed light on a significant long-term weakness of many health systems worldwide, which could not supply the pharmaceutical products needed to meet the rapid rise in demand.

One major cause of the poor response to the COVID-19 pandemic was the initial low level of stockpiles (Bhaskar et al. 2020). For instance, during the 2009 H1N1 Swine flu pandemic, the US had a national strategic stockpile of 100 million masks, but when COVID-19 hit, the US did not have even half of that number at its disposal (Queen 2020). The very low levels of stock of critical medical equipment in the US limited not only the capabilities of the health system to respond adequately to the crisis, but the following drastic rise in demand for medical products from the US and other rich countries led to price surges and shortages as countries simultaneously tried to build up their stocks. Preferential trade agreements can not only play an essential role in facilitating global trade and the functioning of supply chains during times of crisis by promoting trust and legal predictability, but they can also help societies build a sufficient stockpile of essential medical supplies *before* a crisis hits.

Modern healthcare systems rely heavily on the effective management of pharmaceutical inventory. The management of pharmaceutical inventory is a complex process involving developing, sustaining, and re-evaluating the stock of pharmaceutical products against financial constraints and technological advances (Management Sciences for Health 2012). Generally, one can distinguish between the basic stock, for example the level of stock held to meet average demand, and the safety stock, for example the additional amount of inventory held to compensate for potential fluctuations in demand (NCPA 2021). Effective management of pharmaceutical inventory is a balancing act between limiting the stock level to reduce pharmaceutical wastage, inventory holding costs, and ultimately financial loss, and maintaining a high stockpile as protection against uncertainties in demand or as a buffer in case of disrupted supply chains.

In most countries, domestic regulation requires hospitals and other healthcare providers to have a particular stock of specific pharmaceutical products. However, the healthcare sector was not immune to the general trend of just-in-time production, which fundamentally transformed production relations in recent decades. The basic idea of just-in-time production is that companies can increase their efficiency by sourcing products in smaller numbers and more frequently, which reduces the costs of holding large inventories (Ohno 1988). This management philosophy contributed to the decline in inventory levels in many sectors, including the health and pharmaceutical industry. While just-in-time production is associated with an increase in a firm's profitability, it is also correlated with higher volatility caused by external events (Ortis 2021). Hence, in cases of natural catastrophes such as hurricanes, storms, or pandemics, the low inventory levels linked to just-in-time production might bear severe consequences for human well-being and safety. In this context, PTAs can be one channel through which the stockpiling of critical products can be facilitated.

Generally, building up buffer stocks can be achieved through three channels. First, the government can build up strategic national reserves of critical supplies, which will be developed and sustained by national health authorities. Second, the government can incentivise healthcare providers, such as hospitals, and producers of pharmaceutical products, to find a better balance between inventory management strategies based on a just-in-time philosophy to a just-in-case approach. Indeed, a recent study by Lafrogne-Joussier et al. (2022) shows that effective inventory management can help firms to weather shocks better. And third, countries can engage in regional stockpiling of critical products. Regional stockpiling entails that countries share the burden of building up resistance levels of critical medical inventories. For instance, the EU Commission has initiated the creation of a strategic stockpile of medical equipment based in nine Member States which can be accessed by other Members participating in the EU Civil Protection Mechanism (EU Commission 2021).

In this context, PTAs can play a key role in supporting the stockpiling of critical products by making it easier and cheaper for companies and government agencies to store them. For one thing, PTAs can promote the diversification of supply for critical medical products by increasing the regulatory convergence of standards for medical products between different countries. Regulatory convergence or 'regulatory cooperation' is a prominent feature of modern PTAs (Polanco, Lazo and Sauvé 2018). In pharmaceutical products and medical practices, greater regulatory harmonisation can be one building block of making national healthcare systems more resilient. More harmonisation not only promotes the exchange and transfer of medical goods across borders in times of crisis, but also makes it easier for corporations and authorities to increase stockpiles as they can choose from a broader range of suppliers. For another, PTAs can decrease the price of sourcing critical medical products, making it easier for corporations and authorities to build up and manage inventory. Preferential trade agreements can reduce the costs associated with non-tariff measures as harmonisation and mutual recognition reduce compliance costs for firms (Cadot and Gourdon 2016). As a result, the decrease in sourcing costs can offset part of the costs associated with holding large inventories.

11.5.2 *Rule of Origin Provisions*

Rule of origin provisions in PTAs could be leveraged to increase GVCs' resilience. The previous section illustrated the strong nexus between RoOs and GVCs. Firm surveys have indicated that burdensome RoOs can be a significant detriment to making use of a trade agreement limiting the sourcing options available to the firms if they wish to export at a preferential rate. The problem with the spaghetti bowl syndrome presented below is that firms might have to adjust their production depending on what country they are trading with, despite having PTAs with either of them, to comply with the different RoOs. Against this background, we provide three suggestions related to RoOs that may help make GVCs more resilient:

1. *Less restrictive RoOs:* With more flexible RoOs, a firm could supply its foreign inputs from more countries. It would also create more economic competition, given that more firms could comply with the rules and service both the domestic and foreign markets while providing more alternatives and lower consumer prices. Finally, more flexible RoOs mean that if a negative shock hits a particular country or firm, it could readily supply inputs from another competitor, rendering the supply chain more resilient.
2. *More homogeneous RoOs across PTAs*: Having more homogeneous RoOs would help dampen the problems with the spaghetti bowl syndrome. Firms would not need to drastically alter their production process when exporting to different countries if the RoOs required to trade preferentially are similar to all the trading partners. Under the Pan-European preference system, for example, all PTAs signed by the EU include essentially the same RoOs and use the same EUR.1 certificate of

origin, with all its trading partners, lessening the administrative burden for the traders.

3. *Wider cumulation schemes*: Cumulation rules basically determine if the countries that count towards accumulating 'origin' for a good are only the signatories of the agreement or if certain third countries can also join. The cumulation scheme would determine not only where the inputs can be provided from but also what processes are permitted for these third countries. A wider cumulation scheme, namely, going from a bilateral towards a diagonal or a full cumulation scheme, can effectively have the same impact as relaxing product-specific RoOs or homogenising them across PTAs.

The problems arising from the lack of proper management of RoOs are best exemplified by the 'spaghetti bowl' phenomenon which has been exacerbated in the past few decades due to the proliferation of PTAs. Initially coined by Bhagwati (1995) in the context of a potential Asia-Pacific Economic Cooperation (APEC) PTA following the NAFTA, the 'spaghetti bowl' problem describes the accumulation of criss-crossing RoOs included in the various PTAs with different partners which require other activities and inputs to be considered. This results in high transactions and administrative costs for industries and distorted trade and investment decisions by firms, which in turn can have a negative impact on the smooth functioning of GVCs (Bhagwati et al. 1998). Interestingly, the boom of PTAs in Asia during the 2000s prompted the Asian Development Bank's President Haruhiko Kuroda to warn about the Asian noodle bowl effect and its challenges to regional and global integration. Figure 11.8 illustrates the 'spaghetti bowl' problem by mapping the distribution of RoOs in a sample of PTAs.

If a firm wishes to export a product without paying a tariff, it will have to incur the costs necessary to satisfy the RoOs requirements determined in the trade agreement it wishes to use. 'The costs include managerial costs for redesigning their production networks, transaction costs for searching new vendors of intermediate goods, physical costs for setting up a new facility if necessary, as well as documentation costs for obtaining a certificate of origin.' (Kimura et al. 2006). However, given the significant costs associated with complying with the various RoOs, companies often choose not to use the preferential access granted under the trade agreement and pay the non-preferential tariff instead. For instance, for the predecessor to the NAFTA, the US–Central America Free Trade Agreement (US-CAFTA), Krueger (1999) reports that some Canadian firms preferred to pay the tariff instead of having to comply with the burdensome RoOs of the agreement. Similarly, Kawai et al. (2009) find that in a series of surveys of South Asian firms, 42% of giant firms, 26% of large firms, and 25% of small and medium enterprises (SMEs) indicate that having multiple RoOs across PTAs represents a significant business cost. In this context, an empirical study of 132 countries using a gravity model framework finds a positive bilateral relationship

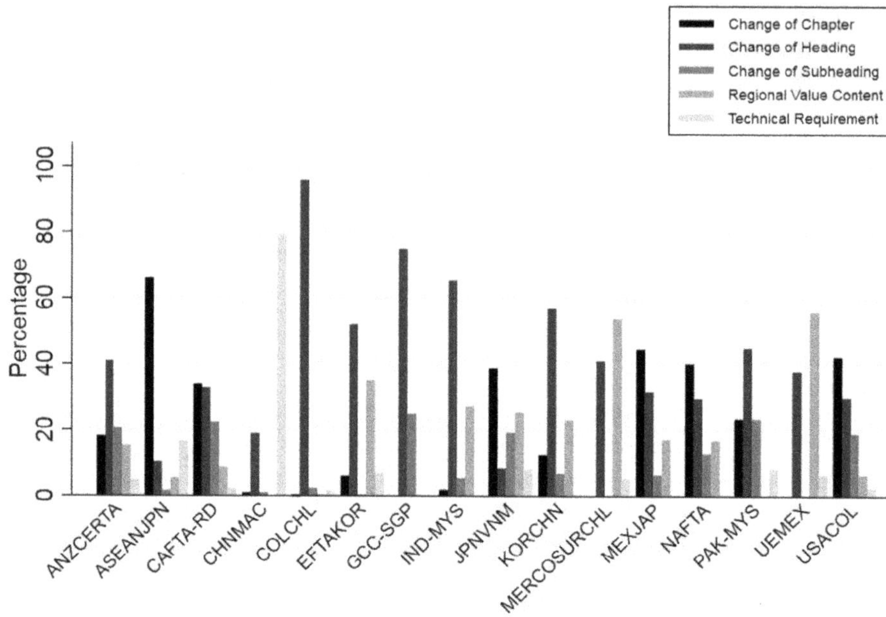

FIGURE 11.8 RoOs across PTAs.
Note: The signatories of these PTAs are the following: ANZCERTA (Australia, New Zealand); ASEANJP (ASEAN, Japan); CAFTA-DR (Costa Rica, El Salvador, Guatemala, Honduras, Nicaragua, Dominican Republic, the US); CHNMAC (China, Macau); COLCHL (Colombia, Chile); EFTAKOR (European Free Trade Association countries, Korea); GCCSGP (Gulf Cooperation Council countries, Singapore); MERCOSURCHL (Mercado Común del Sur countries, Chile).

between trade and having a trade agreement, but a negative agreement between trade and the amount of other PTAs, indicating the existence of the spaghetti bowl phenomenon (Kimura et al. 2006).

Given this phenomenon, a greater emphasis on the role of PTAs in homogenising RoOs and reducing their restrictiveness can help to address the 'spaghetti bowl' problem. As indicated by firm surveys and econometric studies, the harmonisation of RoOs would reduce both the administrative and operative costs for firms and allow them to source their inputs from a larger number of countries, ensuring the smooth functioning of supply chains. Related to this, more lax cumulated provisions should be attached to the RoOs. Depending on the agreement's cumulation framework, this would allow the countries to either cumulate origin just with the parties of the PTA or include third parties, effectively making the RoOs easier to comply with.

11.5.3 *Standard on GVC Resilience*

Finally, we propose to develop a standard (control tower) that on one side allows making informed decisions to improvise effective solutions and on the other side is

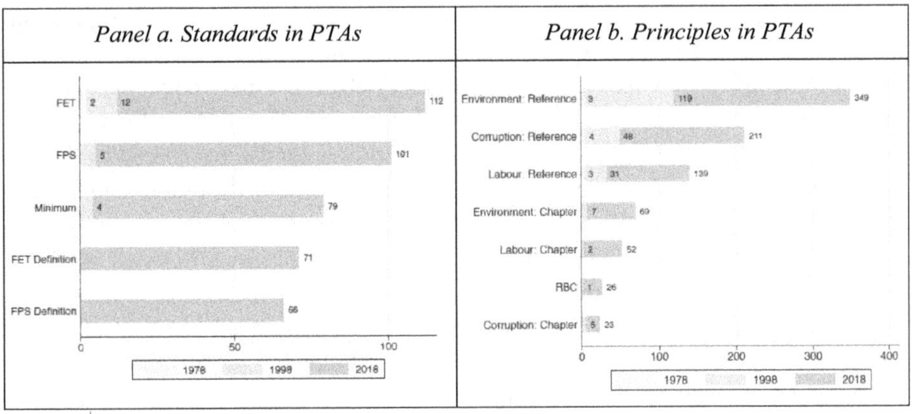

FIGURE 11.9 Provisions in PTAs III.
Note: FET = fair and equitable treatment; FPS = full protection and/or security; RBC = responsible business conduct.
Source: Created by the authors based on DESTA OECD data set

accepted among all parties (states, firms, and customers). In the following paragraphs, we explain the existing approaches for standards in PTAs. We first present FET and FPS and differentiate between absolute and relative standards. Then we explain corporate social responsibility (CSR) and responsible business conduct (RBC) and briefly show the emergence of non-binding principles on labour, corruption, human rights, and environment. Finally, and inspired by the different designs of the above-mentioned standards, we propose the control tower approach.

Figure 11.9 shows the coverage of different standards and principles in PTAs. In contrast to national treatment and MFN treatment, which are relative standards based on the discriminatory treatment afforded to other groups of investors, in most recent PTAs FET and FPS standards are absolute standards drawn from customary international law. Fair and equitable treatment and FPS have, to this day, no international consensus on their definition and have been given an ample interpretation in ISDS cases, transposed differently depending on national context. But also, companies express interest in provisions guaranteeing that trade and investment operations follow high standards and that societal concerns are considered. For these concerns, CSR and RBC were developed. Responsible business conduct is defined as a set of standards and business ethics promoted by governments for companies that invest to integrate environmental and social issues within core business activities, throughout supply chains and business relationships, while CSR is considered less comprehensive and integral to core business (Bule and Tebar Less, 2016). As an example, the OECD adopted the 'Guidelines for Multinational Enterprises' as part of the Declaration on International Investment and Multinational Enterprises in 1976. Since then, the guidelines have been updated five times and today constitute the most comprehensive set of government-backed recommendations on RBC in existence. More recent PTAs also cover different principles in areas such as labour, environment, human rights, and/or anti-corruption. But these provisions are mainly non-binding. Responsible business conduct encourages companies to commit themselves to international standards in these areas and to engage with stakeholders. This is quite different from the previously mentioned FET and FPS standards, which are binding standards enforced by the law and governments. In this sense, FET and FPS are enforceable through ISDS, while CSR and RBC are mainly 'best efforts' and do not trigger ISDS.

The literature mentions different approaches to such standards in terms of GVCs' resilience. In the case where suppliers are not meeting increasing demand, the implementation of cross-functional control towers is discussed (Atali et al. 2022). We explain this approach with an example in the following paragraph.

The previous example of semiconductors showed how digitisation across industries and a widespread move to a home office environment, in combination with panic purchasing, supplier shutdowns in Asia, and political instabilities, have induced a shortage in supply and a collapse of the market in several industries. Stops in production and damage to growth ambitions and performance have led to an unfavourable environment for crisis management. What might help in this situation is an instrument that allows making informed decisions to improvise effective solutions. To achieve this, one possible answer might be a control tower, or supply chain management hub, that enables centralised data sharing, bridging the information gap between internal departments and suppliers. Inspired by the already existing and previously explained standards and principles, these control towers can have different designs in terms of enforceability, bindingness, and implementation. On the international level, incentives can be set by promoting standards and certification procedures that include risk awareness either by using absolute standards drawn from international law such as FET and FPS, or by introducing voluntary standards such as RBC. The focus when introducing such a standard should be put on information management across functions, departments, and suppliers.

Such an instrument can set priorities according to conditions and product categories. It can automate communication and guarantee transparency by informing about product recovery time, plant utilisation, and inventory level of product lines. Predictive forecast models can solve complex allocation decisions to reconfigure geographical priorities and resource allocation. Decision-making platforms allow implementing decisions rapidly across multiple departments, all while assessing performance indicators. Such a flexible and straightforward structure lowers uncertainty but also costs. Whether these structures will prevail in the future depends on how sustainably demand will exceed supply.

11.6 CONCLUSION

In this chapter, we elaborated on the role of PTAs in making GVCs more resilient. Historically, GVCs are seen as a product of the same technological and socio-economic dynamics that have shaped globalisation. Lower trade costs caused by revolutionary advances in shipping and information and communication technologies have led to an increasingly complex trade network. New regulations are needed to ensure the smooth and equitable functioning of supply chains. At best, these regulations prevent the formation of monopoly positions of countries, sectors, and firms, cushion economic and geopolitical uncertainties, and ensure regulatory transparency and flexibility. However, increasing economic and geopolitical uncertainty has increased the vulnerability of widely dispersed and poorly regulated production networks and put the resilience of GVCs on the agenda of many policymakers worldwide. In this context, one can distinguish between two different approaches to GVCs' resilience: The first approach, often referred to as 'friend-shoring' or 'ally-shoring', focuses on strengthening relationships with like-minded partners, while the second approach emphasises the role of international cooperation and risk-sharing to promote supply chain diversification. This chapter has focused on the second approach and explored the role that PTAs can play in increasing the resilience of GVCs.

To assess the role of PTAs within the orchestra of public and private initiatives at the firm, domestic, and international levels, we examined different channels through which international regulations can apply incentives to increase GVCs' resilience sustainably. First, we identified seven groups of provisions that already exist in PTAs and impact the functioning of the trade network. Second, we described three new approaches to increasing GVCs' resilience directly. These are common inventories, a synchronised RoOs strategy, and introducing a GVCs' resilience standard. Yet, the link between PTAs, their design, and the resilience of GVCs is still an understudied field. Global value chains have only recently started to feature in PTAs, and little is known about the complex relationship between PTA provisions and their effect on GVCs' resilience. Which provisions in PTAs have an actual impact on GVCs' resilience? What are the legal implications of national legislation on supply chain resilience on PTAs? How do 'friend-shoring' initiatives aimed at GVCs' resilience impact the global trading system? These and further research questions will require a more comprehensive and detailed investigation than the scope of this chapter. However, we hope our explorative analysis of the link between PTA design and GVCs' resilience can serve as a basis for further research in this area.

REFERENCES

Alicke, K. and D. Luchtenberg 2021. 'Supply-Chain Resilience: Is there a Holy Grail?' www.mckinsey.com/capabilities/operations/our-insights/supply-chain-resilience-is-there-a-holy-grail, accessed November 2022.

Amann, E. and D. Marin 1990. 'Long-Term Contracts in International Trade'. CEPR Discussion Papers.

Andriamananjara, S. 2004. 'Trade and International Transport Services: an Analytical Framework'. *Journal of Economic Integration*, 19(3): 604–625.
Ariu, A. 2016. 'Crisis-Proof Services: Why Trade in Services Did Not Suffer during the 2008–2009 Collapse', *Journal of International Economics*, 98: 138–149.
Atali, A., S. Fuchs and A. Sankur 2022. 'The Cross-Functional Solution to the Semiconductor Chip Shortage: A Control-tower Case Study', www.mckinsey.com/capabilities/operations/our-insights/navigating-the-semiconductor-chip-shortage-a-control-tower-case-study, accessed September 2022.
Baccini, L. 2019. 'The Economics and Politics of Preferential Trade Agreements', *Annual Review of Political Science*, 22: 75–92.
Baccini, L., A. Dür and M. Elsig, M. 2018. 'Intra-Industry Trade, Global Value Chains, and Preferential Tariff Liberalization', *International Studies Quarterly*, 62(2): 329–340.
Bade, G. 2022. 'Biden's Trade Team: RIP Globalization'. POLITICO.
Baldwin, R. 2012. 'Global Supply Chains: Why They Emerged, Why They Matter, And Where They Are Going', Working Paper FGI-2012-1.
Baldwin, R. and S. Evenett 2020. 'COVID-19 and Trade Policy: Why Turning Inward Won't Work'. Centre for Economic Policy Research.
Baldwin, R. and R. Freeman 2022. 'Risks and Global Supply Chains: What We Know and What We Need to Know', *Bank of England*, 14(1): 153–180.
Baldwin, R. and J. Lopez-Gonzales 2013. 'Supply-Chain Trade: A Portrait of Global Patterns', CEPR Discussion Paper, 9421.
Baldwin, R. and A. J. Venables 2013. 'Spiders and Snakes: Offshoring and Agglomeration in the Global Economy', *Journal of International Economics*, 90(2): 245–254.
Bank of England 2021. 'Global Value Chains', www.bankofengland.co.uk, accessed August 2022.
Bhagwati, J. N. 1995. 'US Trade Policy: The Infatuation with FTAs', Discussion Paper Series, No. 726.
Bhagwati, J., D. Greenaway and A. Panagariya 1998. 'Trading Preferentially: Theory and Policy', *The Economic Journal*, 108(449): 1128–1148.
Bhaskar, S., J. Tan, M. L. A. M. Bogers, T. Minssen, H. Badaruddin, S. Israeli-Korn and H. Chesbrough 2020. 'At the Epicenter of COVID-19–the Tragic Failure of the Global Supply Chain for Medical Supplies', *Frontier in Public Health* 8, 562882.
Blanchard, E. and X. Matschke 2015. 'US Multinationals and Preferential Market Access', *The Review of Economics and Statistics*, 97(4): 839–854.
Boffa, M., M. Jansen and O. Solleder 2019. 'Do We Need Deeper Trade Agreements for GVCs or Just a BIT?' *The World Economy*, 42(6): 1713–1739.
Borchert, I. and A. Mattoo 2010. 'The Crisis-Resilience of Services Trade', *The Service Industries Journal*, 30(13): 2115–2136.
Bown, C. P. 2021. 'How COVID-19 Medical Supply Shortages Led to Extraordinary Trade and Industrial Policy', CEPR Discussion Paper, No 16359.
Brandon-Jones, E., B. Squire, C. W. Autry and J. K. Petersen 2014. 'A Contingent Resource-Based Perspective of Supply Chain Resilience and Robustness', *Journal of Supply Chain Management*, 50(3): 55–73.
Brookings Institution. 2020. How to build more secure, resilient, next-gen U.S. supply chains, www.brookings.edu/articles/how-to-build-more-secure-resilient-next-gen-u-s-supply-chains/, accessed June 2022.
Brunnermeier, M. K. 2021. *Die resiliente Gesellschaft: Wie wir künftige Krisen besser meistern können-Gewinner des Deutschen Wirtschaftsbuchpreises 2021*. Aufbau Digital.

Bule, T. and C. Tebar Less 2016. Promoting Sustainable Development through Responsible Business Conduct. OECD Development Co-operation Report 2016.
Burkacky, O. and J. Deichmann 2022. 'Semiconductor Shortage: How the Automotive Industry Can Succeed'. Semiconductor, www.mckinsey.com/industries/semiconductors/our-insights/semiconductor-shortage-how-the-automotive-industry-can-succeed#, accessed October 2022.
Cadot, O. and J. Gourdon 2016. 'Non-Tariff Measures, Preferential Trade Agreements, and Prices: New Evidence', *Review of World Economics*, 152(2): 227–249.
Carvalho, V. M., M. Nirei, Y. U. Saito and A. Tahbaz-Salehi 2021. 'Supply Chain Disruptions: Evidence from the Great East Japan Earthquake', *The Quarterly Journal of Economics*, 136(2): 1255–1321.
Cattaneo, O., G. Gere and C. Staritz 2010. *Global Value Chains in a Postcrisis World: A Development Perspective*. World Bank Publications.
Chase, K. A. 2005. *Trading Blocs: States, Firms, and Regions in the World Economy*. Ann Arbor: University of Michigan Press.
Christopher, M. and H. Peck 2004. 'Building the Resilient Supply Chain', *International Journal of Logistics Management*, 15(2): 1–13.
CNBC 2022. Yellen Says the U.S. and Its Allies should Use 'Friend-Shoring' to Give Supply Chains a Boost, by Su-Lin Tan, www.cnbc.com/2022/07/19/us-treasury-secretary-on-supply-chain-resilience-use-friend-shoring.html, accessed August 2022.
Cronin, R. 2022. *Semiconductors and Taiwan's 'Silicon Shield'*. Stimson Research, 16.
Davies, J. 2018. *Global Value Chain Policy Series: Competition*. World Economy Forum, 12.
Davies, R. B. and J. R. Markusen 2021. 'What Do Multinationals Do? The Structure of Multinational Firms' International Activities', *The World Economy*, 44(12): 3444–3481.
Dingel, J. I. and B. Neiman 2020. 'How Many Jobs Can Be Done at Home?' *Journal of Public Economics*, 189: 104–235.
Dür, A., L. Baccini and M. Elsig 2014. 'The Design of International Trade Agreements: Introducing a New Dataset', *The Review of International Organizations*, 9(3): 353–375.
Eckhardt, J. and K. Lee. 2018. 'Global Value Chains, Firm Preferences and the Design of Preferential Trade Agreements', *Global Policy* 9: 58–66.
EU Commission 2021. Strategic Dependencies and Capacities. Commission Staff Working Document, SWD (2021) 352.
2022. 2022 Strategic Foresight Report. Twinning the Green and Digital Transitions in the New Geopolitical Context. COM (2022) 289 final.
Evenett, Simon. 2020. Sickening thy neighbour: Export restraints on medical supplies during a pandemic. VoxEU Column, https://cepr.org/voxeu/columns/sickening-thy-neighbour-export-restraints-medical-supplies-during-pandemic, accessed August 2022.
FDA. 2020. Drug Shortages for Calendar Year 2020. 8th Annual Report to Congress, www.fda.gov/media/150409/download.
Financial Post 2022. Friends Today May Be Foes Tomorrow: Freeland's Embrace of Friend-Shoring Is Fraught with Problems. By Marisa Coulton, https://financialpost.com/news/economy/chrystia-freeland-embrace-friend-shoring-fraught-problems, accessed August 2022.
Francois, J. F., H. M. Arce, K. A. Reinert and J. E. Flynn. 1996. 'Commercial Policy and the Domestic Carrying Trade', *Canadian Journal of Economics*, 29(1): 181–198.
Geradin, D. 2009. 'The Perils of Antitrust Proliferation: The Globalization of Antitrust and the Risks of Overregulation of Competitive Behavior', *Chicago Journal of International Law*, 10: 189.

Grossman, G. M., E. Helpman and H. Lhuillier 2021. 'Supply Chain Resilience: Should Policy Promote Diversification or Reshoring?" Working Paper, 61.

Harput, H. 2022. 'What do the Friends of Friend-shoring Think Its Rationale Is?' *ZEITGEIST SERIES*.

Howley, D. 2021. 'These 169 Industries Are Being Hit By the Global Chip Shortage', https://news.yahoo.com/these-industries-are-hit-hardest-by-the-global-chip-shortage-122854251, accessed September 2022.

IMF 2022. 'The Stretch of Supply Chains. Finance and Development', www.imf.org/en/Publications/fandd/issues/2022/06/the-stretch-of-supply-chains-BB, accessed June 2022.

Kamalahmadi, M. and M. Mellat Parast 2016. 'A Review of the Literature on the Principles of Enterprise and Supply Chain Resilience: Major Findings and Directions for Future Research', *International Journal of Production Economics*, 171: 116–133.

Kawai, M. and G. Wignaraja 2009. 'The Asian "Noodle Bowl": Is It Serious for Business?' Asian Development Bank Institute (ADBI) Working Paper Series No. 136.

Khanna, G., N. Morales, and N. Pandalai-Nayar 2022. Supply Chain Resilience: Evidence from Indian Firms. NBER Working Paper Series, No. 30689.

Kimura, F., A. Kuno and K. Hayakawa 2006. *Does the Number of RTAs Matter? Empirical Analysis on the Spaghetti Bowl Phenomenon*. Keio University.

Klier, Thomas and James M. Rubenstein. 2017. 'Mexico's Growing Role in the Auto Industry Under NAFTA: Who Makes What and What Goes Where', *Economic Perspectives*, 6: 1–29.

Krueger, A. O. 1999. 'Are Preferential Trading Arrangements Trade-Liberalizing or Protectionist?' *Journal of Economic Perspectives*, 13(4): 105–124.

Lafrogne-Joussier, R., J. Martin and J. Mejean 2022. 'Supply Shocks in Supply Chains: Evidence from the Early Lockdown in China', Working paper.

Laget, E., A. Osnago, N. Rocha, and M. Ruta. 2020. 'Deep Trade Agreements and Global Value Chains', *Review of Industrial Organization*, 57(2): 379–410.

Lupkin, S. 2020. 'How Coronavirus Is Affecting the US Pharmaceutical Supply', www.kcur.org/2020-03-12/how-coronavirus-is-affecting-the-u-s-pharmaceutical-supply, accessed November 2022.

Management Sciences for Health. 2012. *MDS-3: Managing Access to Medicines and Health Technologies*. Arlington, VA: Management Sciences for Health.

Manger, M. 2009. *Investing in Protection: The Politics of Preferential Trade Agreements between North and South*. Cambridge, UK: Cambridge University Press.

Mansfield, E. D. and H. V. Milner. 1999. The New Wave of Regionalism. *International Organization*, 53(3): 589–627. https://doi.org/10.1162/002081899551002.

Miroudot, S. 2020a. 'Reshaping the Policy Debate on the Implications of COVID-19 for Global Supply Chains', *Journal of International Business Policy*, 3(4): 430–442.

2020b. Resilience versus Robustness in Global Value Chains: Some Policy Implications. COVID-19 and Trade Policy: Why Turning Inward Won't Work, VoxEU Column, 117–130.

2022. 'Resilience in Services Value Chains. Council on Economic Policies', www.cepweb.org/resilience-in-services-value-chains/, accessed September 2022.

NCPA 2021. 'Managing the Pharmacy Inventory', www.bccpharmacytech.wee bly.com/uploads/7/5/0/4/7504847/ownership-managinginventory.pdf, accessed November 2022.

Netland, T. 2020. 'Lean and the Corona Pandemic: A Clarification. Better Operations', https://better-operations.com/2020/12/28/lean-and-the-corona-pandemic-a-clarification/, accessed September 2022.

No Author. 2012. 'Managing Medicines Selection', Managing Access to Medicines and Health Technologies, Geneva Bd. 26(1): 44.
OECD 2022a. 'Global Value Chains and Trade', www.oecd.org/trade/topics/global-value-chains-and-trade/#:~:text = In%20reality%2C%20about%2070%25%20of,consumers%20all%20over%20the%20world, accessed October 2022.
2022b. 'OECD Services Trade Restrictiveness Index: Policy Trends up to 2022', www.oecd.org/trade/topics/services-trade/, accessed September 2022.
2022c. 'Keys to Resilient Supply Chains. Policy Tools for Preparedness and Responsiveness', www.oecd.org/trade/resilient-supply-chains/, accessed February 2023.
Ohno, T. 1988. *Toyota Production System: Beyond Large Scale Production*. New York: Productivity Press.
Ortiz, Julio. 2021. Spread too thin: The impact of lean inventories. VoxEU Column, https://cepr.org/voxeu/columns/spread-too-thin-impact-lean-inventories, accessed August 2022.
Peiris, S., D. Muir, R. Mano, D. Cerdeiro and J. Eugster 2021. 'Sizing Up the Effects of Technological Decoupling'. IMF Working Papers 2021(069), 1.
Perrone & Johnson 2020. 'US Reports First Drug Shortage Tied to Virus Outbreak', www.google.com/search?client = safari&rls = en&q = US+Reports+First+Drug+Shortage+Tied+To+Virus+Outbreak&ie = UTF-8&oe = UTF-8, accessed February 2023.
Polanco Lazo, R. and P. Sauvé 2018. 'The Treatment of Regulatory Convergence in Preferential Trade Agreements', *World Trade Review*, 17(4): 575–607.
Posen, A. S. 2022. 'The End of Globalization?', www.foreignaffairs.com/articles/world/2022-03-17/end-globalization, accessed October 2022.
Queen, K. 2020. 'What Supply Chain Players are Learning from the Pandemic', SME, www.sme.org/technologies/articles/2020/march/what-supply-chain-players-are-learning-from-the-pandemic/, accessed July 2022.
Shingal, A. 2021. The COVID-19 Shock and Services Trade: Explaining the Heterogeneous Decline. Robert Schuman Centre for Advanced Studies Research, Paper No. RSC 85.
Socal, M. P., J. M. Sharfstein and J.A. Greene 2021. 'The Pandemic and the Supply Chain: Gaps', *American Journal of Public Health*, 111(4): 635–639.
Swinney, R. and S. Netessine 2009. 'Long-Term Contracts under the Threat of Supplier Default', *Manufacturing and Service Operations Management*, 11(1): 109–127.
UNCTAD 2012. 'UNCTAD Series on Issues in International Investment Agreements II', https://unctad.org/system/files/official-document/unctaddiaeia2011d7_en.pdf, accessed September 2022.
Wall, Howard J. 2002. NAFTA and the geography of North American trade, Working Papers 2000-017, Federal Reserve Bank of St. Louis.
WEF 2021. 'The Resiliency Compass: Navigating Global Value Chain Disruption in an Age of Uncertainty', www.weforum.org/whitepapers/the-resiliency-compass-navigating-global-value-chain-disruption-in-an-age-of-uncertainty/, accessed November 2022.
WTO 2022. 'National Foreign Trade Council: Strengthening the WTO and the Global Trading System', Remarks by DG Okonjo-Iweala, www.wto.org/english/news_e/spno_e/spno25_e.htm, accessed October 2022.
Wu, X., C. Zhang, C. and W. Du 2021. 'An Analysis on The Crisis Of "Chips Shortage" In Automobile Industry: Based on the Double Influence of COVID-19 and Trade Friction', *Journal of Physics Conference Series*, 1971: 1.
Zhang, Hongyong and Thi Thanh Ha Doan. 2023. Global Sourcing and Firm Inventory during the Pandemic, RIETI Discussion Paper 23-E-018.

12

Mode 4 'On the Move'

Towards a Migrantification of the Temporary Movement of Persons in Preferential Trade Agreements?

Marion Panizzon and Amanda Bisong

12.1 INTRODUCTION

In 2021 there were an estimated 281 million international migrants, including 169 million migrant workers. This number has risen from 164 million in 2017 (IOM World Migration Report 2022). Sixty-two per cent of those were concentrated in the service sector (ILO 2021). Seasonal labour, including agricultural work, construction, and agri-food, remained stable during the pandemic alongisde care work and rose again in 2021 (OECD 2022a). Other forms of temporary labour, including those falling under the General Agreement on Trade in Services (GATS) and preferential trade agreements (PTAs) categories, such as intra-corporate transfers, dipped in relation to the COVID-19 pandemic between 2020 and 2021, by 52% and 47%, respectively, while for graduate trainees, numbers decreased by 69% and for working holidaymakers numbers fell sharply in 2020 by 59% and in 2021 by 47% (OECD 2022). Preferential trade agreements have diversified the subsectors and categories of GATS mode 4, and have thus contributed to increasing commercial opportunities for servicing consumers by natural persons (UNCTAD 2016). At the same time, migrant host states are increasingly keen on concluding bilateral labour migration agreements (BLMAs) to serve the double purpose of stilling labour shortage while containing migration considered unauthorized according to their national laws. Whereas the two sets of agreements, the PTAs and BLMAs differ from one another in ambition and ambit, their overlap is widening, either because the trade venue features fewer restrictions, or because other trading rights in the production or sale of goods, e.g. the lowering of customs duties, tariffication of border barriers, regulatory cooperation over sanitary or technical barriers diversifies and widens the field for negotiating the mutual understanding, which paves the way for sending and hosting states to cooperate on human mobility. As has been researched by trade and migration study scholars alike, the temporary movement of natural persons is an essentiality for the trade regime, as persons' movement abroad is an essential ingredient – to production, construction, maintenance, instruction – and a key accessory for uninterrupted global value chains (Panizzon 2010). Hence, this chapter starts an inquiry into what appears to be a migrantification of PTAs, by discussing the different add-ons, which have been uploaded onto mode 4 services delivery in trade agreements. In so doing, this chapter draws on the different data sets developed to understand the uptake of mobility provisions in PTAs, including the MITA (Lavenex et al. 2024) and the Bilateral Labour Agreement (BLA) data set (Chilton and Woda 2022). Conversely to directly comparing the BLAs with PTAs, this chapter takes the perspective of mode 4 GATS as a starting point. It sets out with the state-of-play on what the Uruguay Round trade negotiators had in mind when conceiving of the temporary movement of natural persons (TMNP) conceived as 'GATS mode 4'.

After surveying the the two-tiered definition which GATS offers for the personal scope of mode 4, the approaches to scheduling mode 4 commitments (horizontal, sectoral, full, partial), the immigration law caveat in the GATS Annex on the Temporary Movement of Natural Persons (TMNP) and some specifics in the market access, national treatment, and additional commitments, a cross-comparison to mode 4 in different PTAs and select mega regionals is undertaken. Whereas we do not systematically map PTAs, as Pauwelyn et al. (2020), Gootiiz et al. (2020), and Lavenex et al. (2024), have done for their data sets, we draw on some of their findings to highlight a few legal challenges surrounding the mode 4 design features, which are usually quite constraining and thus often prove inadequate for adjusting to global challenges, as in the COVID-19 pandemic, interrupted production chains, and drying out of the pool of skilled workers in ageing societies.

From our sample of the European Union (EU), African, American, and Asian PTAs, we extract those provisions, which improve over the multilateral GATS Mode 4 commitments in terms of regulatory design (e.g. standardising timelines and procedures for visa/work permit applications, improved access to and portability of social security, skill transfer) or which, increase the movement of persons (e.g. by adding categories (instructors, trainees, installers, and maintainers), by creating subsectors and finally, by removing admission quotas, work permit requirements or economic needs tests – ENTs). In this context, our chapter discusses how PTAs have altered the architecture for incentivising liberalised TMNP (GATS-extra). Here, we highlight the relationship of GATS to visa and border management (screening, biometric data collection) and to wider immigration law, including return clauses. Finally, we discuss how the global health pandemic impacted mode 4 workers as 'essential workers' and what responsibilities accrue to states under GATS and PTAs for service provision in key sectors, which is a topic moving GATS and PTAs into the spotlight of the

Global Compacts for Migration and for Refugees, as well to BLMAs, which we also discuss.

12.2 WHAT IS MODE 4? DEFINITIONS AND CONCEPTS

Mode 4 refers to the fourth mode of supply of services trade, which is the supply of services through the 'presence of natural persons'. Whereas Article 1:2(d) GATS defines mode 4, as the 'service supplied ... by a service supplier of one Member, through the presence of natural persons of a Member in the territory of any other Member', the Annex MNP paragraph 1 uses a narrower definition which implies that employees must be of a foreign firm, as opposed to a national firm, in a host country. On the one hand, the International Labour Organization (ILO)'s Conventions 97 and 143 relate to 'migration for employment', and Article 2 of the International Convention on the Protection of the Rights of All Migrant Workers and Members of Their Families (ICRMW) covers those who migrate for a 'remunerated activity', and thus excludes freelance or independent professionals; these categories, are on the other hand covered by the GATS, as it extends to those who supply a service on their own account. What remains unclear, from the GATS viewpoint, minuscule persons working irregularly as independent professionals or service suppliers are, like in the ICRMW, included or not in the scope of GATS (Ryan 2013).

Nonetheless, mode 4 cannot be entirely separated from issues around direct labour market competition between foreign service providers and local workers (Jacobsson 2015). Best practice from GATS/PTA commitments informs that the temporary nature ranges from ninety days/three months (typically applied to maintainers, installers, and service people) to five years and, in the case of the New Zealand–Malaysia Free Trade Agreement (FTA), even ten years (Schott et al. 2012). It is usually higher for workers in the information and communications technology (ICT) sector than for the rest of the categories and is both shorter and longer than the ILO's 1932 definition of 'temporary worker', which was for stays up to one year.

Another separator is that mode 4 uses highly technical language and liberalising the movement of different categories of persons, where 'political debates about the potentially negative effects of labour migration on wages, labour conditions or welfare states are excluded ...' (Lavenex et al. 2024). Finally, mode 4, incidentally the only type of service delivery which requires an additional annex, formulates some key red lines, applicable to all of mode 4 trade. Excluded are persons seeking employment, residence, citizenship, and naturalisation. Annex MNP further narrows the scope to natural persons employed by foreign (as opposed to local) firms in another Member, to carefully prevent mode 4 trade from intervening in or becoming a labour migration issue (Bast 2008). Yet, certain PTAs operate a dual definition of TMNP, a narrow one limited to the mode 4 definition of the GATS, which can be complemented by a broader definition including investors and persons moving internationally to produce or manufacture goods, as discussed below.

12.2.1 *Measuring Mode 4 Trade in GATS and PTAs*

Mode 4 trade is more challenging 'to capture' than for the other three modes of service supply (South Centre 2007), because, as the United Nations (UN) Technical Sub-Group on the Movement of Persons – Mode 4 (TSG) highlights, one needs to consider two interrelated variables. First, the value of services supplied and, second, the number of persons present and crossing borders. According to the United Nations Conference on Trade and Development (UNCTAD 2006), it is the least 'liberal' of the modes of supply, because most offers are in horizontal commitments. The exact share of services supplied across modes is not well known (Khachaturian and Oliver 2021).

This is made more complicated because sector-specific characteristics or regulations may affect how services are delivered. Also, modal compositions of services trade vary across sectors, countries, and types of trade flow (Khachaturian and Oliver 2021), making it difficult to have realistic and comparable data on mode 4 trade flows. For example, some states count seasonal labour in the subsectors of care, construction, or agri-food business as seasonal labour, as for seasonal agricultural labour, so that service supply in those categories is not counted towards services trade and does not enter those statistics.

Services exports, including through mode 4, remain an important export for several countries. United Nations Conference on Trade and Development notes that in 2020, global services exports were valued at USD 5 trillion, representing 5.9 per cent of the world GDP (UNCTAD 2021). Although trade in services declined due to the COVID-19 pandemic, in some countries services exports accounted for more than 10 per cent of their GDP. But, mode 4 still remains the least utilised mode of service delivery, having some of the highest trade costs and being the most restricted form of services trade across several sectors (OECD 2020; Shingal 2022) at and beyond the border.

In 2020, the Organisation for Economic Co-operation and Development (OECD)'s Service Trade Restrictiveness Index (STRI) noted a 30 per cent increase in trade-restrictive measures across most service sectors among OECD countries between 2018 and 2019 (OECD 2020). Many of these restrictive measures were adopted in mode 4 trade, affecting the TMNP. Some policies applied horizontally across all or several service sectors and included the introduction of quotas for all or some categories of service suppliers (OECD 2020). In 2021, more liberalisations in mode 4 commitments and changes in national policies reduced the restrictions in mode 4 trade (OECD 2022). These included new visa categories introduced by the United Kingdom (UK) and a reduction in the number of forms required for service suppliers in Australia (OECD 2022).

12.3 IMPLICATIONS OF FRAMING MOBILITY AS 'SERVICES TRADE' OR AS TEMPORARY MOVEMENT OF PERSONS?

The drafters of GATS mode 4 faced several challenges, one of which was to maintain the appearance and ensure in the law that the TMNP to be liberalised by World Trade Organization (WTO) Members' individual commitments in services did not amount to labour migration, since neither industrialised countries nor trade unions wanted to see that happening. Current negotiators still face this challenge, so the need to try to distinguish mode 4 commitments from labour migration has contributed to its unique architecture and framing.

12.3.1 *Categories of Persons and Skill Levels*

In theory, GATS covers the entire skill range, but in practice, Members' commitments remain clustered around the highly skilled and formally trained (executive, manager, and specialist (EMS) category as well as graduate trainees). These are commonly called 'professionals', a fact that transpires from the credential requirements in Members' additional commitments as well as from spousal working rights. In WTO/GATS, 80 per cent of mode 4 commitments have been made for skilled work (which includes doctors and nurses and higher managerial and executive staff) as opposed to 20 per cent for low-skilled work (Chaudhuri et al. 2004). Developing countries have opened up to foreign workers in around 50–60 services, while least developed countries (LDCs) have done so in just around 25 sectors on average (Adlung and Roy 2005).

Most services PTAs replicate the specific wording and scope of the GATS mode 4 definitions. Still, some have improved the clarity or enhanced the scope to cover services supplied in relation to goods production or investment, for example, Chapter 9 of the Australia–India Economic Cooperation and Trade Agreement (ECTA).[1] These former TMNP provisions are labelled by Lavenex et al. (2024) as 'mobility provisions', as they encompass the movement of persons in sectors in a broader way than mode 4. As Carzaniga and Sharma (2022: 4) find, many PTAs operate a mode 4 schedule of commitments in the services chapter complemented by an additional TMNP annex, section, or chapter, liberalising the cross-border movement of business persons 'irrespective of the sector of activity'. Through the inclusion of such a, mobility' annex, the thus mode 4 definition includes internationally mobile professionals supplying services, but is not limited to that. Hence, mode 4 and TMNP should not be used interchangeably, but, in practice, are often deemed co-equal and substitutes (Bhatnagar 2014: 3).

[1] See: 'this Chapter shall apply, as set out in each Party's Schedule in Annex 9A (Schedules of Specific Commitments on Temporary Movement of Natural Persons), to measures by that Party affecting the movement of natural persons of a Party into the territory of the other Party, where such *persons are engaged in trade in goods, the supply of services, or the conduct of investment*' (italics added).

In PTAs, mode 4 trade generally draws on the GATS mode 4. But there are examples of treaties expanding this narrow category to include other commercial activities of persons moving across borders to produce goods and services. They include subcontracting (service sellers), consultants and employees of international organisations, foreign students and graduate/occupational trainees, persons in exchange programmes, investors, and pensioners (UN Stats).[2] For example, several Australian PTAs include categories that do not exist in GATS, like, instructors and working holidaymakers. Moreover, PTAs have broadened a sector by adding a subsector, 'storage and warehouse services', which has a broader scope than in the original GATS schedule, and even include more services than in the W-120 classification (UNCTAD 2016). Therefore, PTAs contribute to 'expanding and diversifying' regular pathways, which is a goalpost to which the 153 states committed under Objective 16 of the Global Compact for Safe, Orderly and Regular Migration (GCM).

12.3.2 *Multimodal Service Delivery versus Clustering*

Besides the categories of persons, what distinguishes cross-border movement of persons from how states liberalise and facilitate mobility of services in the other three modes, is that mode 4 is 'bundled' with or 'supports' another mode of supply (Chanda 2018). For example, it often supports Mode 3, which involves establishing a commercial presence abroad and requiring the mobility of high-level personnel to the site, or Mode 1, the execution of a service contract, which requires the mobility of high-level professionals to the client's site abroad. (Chanda 2018). In PTAs, foreign tour guides may be restricted to serving only tourists from the same country as the tour guide (Indian tour operators catering to Indians, at the exclusion of Swiss or other foreign tourist groups in Switzerland).

Multimodal supply is inherently produced by the temporary, part time nature of mode 4, which permits a person to engage simultaneously in care work while pursuing an education or training. In mode 4, multimodality means to enhance the efficacy of acquiring new skills. When mode 4 is linked to mode 3, the latter is financial collateral against the risk of foreign professionals relying on the host country's social services or entering the labour market and accessing essential services (Panizzon 2010). Thus, a mode 3 reservation on national treatment, for example, limiting the number of foreign nationals allowed to be on a company's governing board, may also affect mode 4 (Adlung and Roy 2005). Graduate or occupational trainees, a category introduced by the EU–Caribbean Forum (CARIFORUM) 2006 Economic Partnership Agreements (EPAs), is narrowly seen as a non-commercial category and thus technically outside mode 4. But at the same

2 The EU–Japan EPA TMNP is extended to spouses and dependents; see Annex III B Article 11 to Annex 8B.

time, they may consume educational services through mode 2 (Sauvé and Ward 2009). Beyond education services (Sauvé 2004), the mode 4–mode 2 nexus prevails in service sectors such as heritage, sports, music/concert and film festival tourism, health, sports, and leisure.

Multimodal supply must not always be working against developing countries and LDCs; 'clustering' can be more beneficial to them than if market access is limited to a single mode of delivery. For many small and medium enterprises, administrative, logistical, and technical communications are often tied tightly together in a single business transaction abroad. Hence, it is advisable for states to open up market access in all modes (UNCTAD 2016: 20).

Since the pandemic, a new type of mode 4-specific multimodal supply emerged when states recognised remittances as 'essential services', to the effect that a mode 4 worker would not only deliver a cross-border service, but in addition transfer the payment received via a mode 1 financial transaction, or remittances flow.[3]

12.3.3 Embedding Service Provision into the Production of Goods and The Shift to Permanent Status of Essential Workers

A variation of multimodal delivery is the practice of embedding services into the production of goods (Chanda 2018) or transportation of goods. For example, it is often unclear if a truck driver bringing farmed goods across a border is covered by trade in services or not (Bisong 2022). Likewise, repair work is increasingly part of mode 4 schedules in PTAs.

In food processing and other labour-intensive work areas with agricultural goods, such as meat, dairy, oils, rice, and sugar, separating between providing a service and working for the industrial production of a good is not always clear. To Cheong et al. (2013), a benchmark could be the proximity to the consumer.[4] But, there are food security and rural development policy considerations that work against considering harvest workers as service providers. One health pandemic outcome is that essential services in key sectors qualify in Europe and the United States as 'services' workers falling under the category liberalised in a trade agreement. At the same time, they obtain a regularisation of status, an extension or renewal of permits of stay or visa, and fast-tracked access to permanent status. France treated them as 'non-confinable'

[3] At the initiative of Great Britain, Northern Ireland, and Switzerland, thirty-three countries joined a 'remittance in crisis' group, which conceptualized remittances as an essential service; Kenya and others had already unilaterally called for such a move for cash-based and digital remittance-related services.

[4] For instance, should a fruit picker be seen as a person supplying services incidental to agriculture (fruit picking services) or as an agricultural worker? This, of course, depends on how Members define the GNS/W/120 category 'Services incidental to agriculture, hunting and forestry'. The same applies to other categories of the breakdown of item 'Other business services' of the GNS/W/120 such as services incidental to mining, manufacturing, etc.

(Odasso and Fornalè 2022). Portugal[5] granted status to any undocumented foreign national, regardless of occupation or employment, as long as the person had applied for status by 18 March 2020 (state of emergency declaration),[6] and the Italian Relaunch Decree of 13 May 2020 applying to employees in agriculture, fishery, caretaking, or domestic work who entered before 8 March 2020 and can show proof of sponsorship by an employer.[7]

These examples showcase a trend towards de-temporalization of mode 4 service supply during the health crisis. Conversely, certain areas of service delivery are exempted from the professional activity of the foreign service supplier. For example, traditional Chinese medicine and therapy or Ayurvedic medicine and therapy might be accounted towards the subsector of 'beauty and physical well-being services' under section 972 of the Classic Product Classification (CPC) list, version 2.1,[8] instead of subsumed under the CPC entry 973 for 'human health and social services', which features (Western) medical services, including for restoring health, and for medical or rehabilitation purposes. In addition, there is a protectionist intention to relegate a health-related service to the CPC category of physical well-being services, as it prevents the patient/consumer from redeeming the cost of the service through their health insurance which produces the intended effect of excluding the foreign service supplier from generating an income guaranteed by the consumer's mandatory health insurance and thus keeps the foreign service provider effectively out (Jansen and Piermartini 2004). This is how the Sino-Swiss FTA of 1 July 2014 is treating traditional Chinese medicine, namely, not as an entry in the Swiss Schedule of Services commitments, which would allow TCM health professionals from China to supply their services in Switzerland, but rather, as the side letter suggests as an area of 'further cooperation', implying that for China, the starting point of the discussion must be that TCM professionals from China can issue the same billing towards their Swiss/other patients which is to get reimbursed by the patients' compulsory health insurance.[9]

5 Despacho n.° 3863-B/2020 de 27 de março [Order no. 3863-B/2020], https://dre.pt/dre/detalhe/despacho/3863-b-2020-130835082 (Portugal).

6 In Portugal, third-country nationals 'only need to prove that they have a pending case at SEF as of 18 March 2020'. This proof works to safeguard their stay in Portugal as one of being legal during the period of 27 March until 30 June 2020, 'and can be presented in the various public services to access the relevant rights'.

7 Decreto legge 19 maggio 2020, n.34, G.U. 19 May 2020, n.128 (Italy)

8 Central Product Classification List, UN DESA (2015) UN Document ST/ESA/STAT/SER.M/77/Ver.2.1, available at: https://unstats.un.org/unsd/classifications/Econ/Download/In%20Text/CPCv2.1_complete(PDF)_English.pdf, accessed 13 May 2024.

9 Sino-Swiss Free Trade Agreement of 1 July 2014, Annex XI Reimbursement of TCM under the Health System, available at: https://www.seco.admin.ch/seco/en/home/Aussenwirtschaftspolitik_Wirtschaftliche_Zusammenarbeit/Wirtschaftsbeziehungen/handel_mit_dienstleistungen/freihandelsabkommen/china.html ; for more information: Switzerland Global Enterprise, https://www.swisscham.org/shanghai/wp-content/uploads/2018/08/SBH%20The%20Sino-Swiss%20FTA_EN.pdf, accessed 13 May 2024.

A feature of mode 4 is the potential for substitution with other modes of supply (cross-modality), especially when entry regulations make it difficult for a service provider to access the domestic market, hence a switch to remote modes of service delivery (mode 1 and mode 3) (Khachaturian and Oliver 2021). But this substitution is not possible in all sectors.

12.4 GATS-PLUS IN PTAS: ADDING CATEGORIES OF PERSONS THROUGH CREATIVE LAW-MAKING?

Services trade distinguishes three types of schedulings of commitments: the positive list (GATS-type), the negative list (NAFTA-type,[10] used in CPTPP 2018[11]), and the hybrid approach (RCEP 2022[12], and the EU–UK TCA 2020[13]). In 2021, a study found that out of 183 PTAs notified to the WTO, 100 of those had a chapter or annex on TMNP (Carzaniga and Sharma 2022:3). Out of 119 PTAs in 2019 with mode 4 chapters, 80 per cent used positive listing[14] and 76 per cent used negative listing.[15] Hence, it comes as no big surprise that the propensity for more ambitious liberalisation steps in mode 4 is higher in the negative listing, which features more advanced acceleration of visa and work permit procedures as well as deeper transparency obligations (Carzaniga et al. 2019).

Many PTAs have diverged from the GATS mode 4 negative scheduling to either positive scheduling or a hybrid approach. The more diverse the membership of a PTA, the more likely it is that the political sensitivities over mode 4 and labour mobility will diverge, where mode 4 scheduling of entry and stay of professionals will is hybrid and the levels of liberalisation, and the harvest over GATS-plus/GATS-extra are very limited (e.g. RCEP).[16] In mode 4 the EU–UK TCA adopts a mix of positive and negative listings: contractual service suppliers (CSS), independent professionals, and short-term business visitors must fall into one of the sectors listed in the annexes. In contrast, business visitors for establishment purposes and intra-corporate transferees are not subject to sectoral limitations.

[10] North American Free Trade Agreement.

[11] Comprehensive and Progressive Agreement for Trans-Pacific Partnership.

[12] Regional Comprehensive Economic Partnership.

[13] EU–UK Trade and Cooperation Agreement (TCA).

[14] Positive listing: 'All sectors and subsectors where market access and national treatment commitments are made must be listed. All exceptions or conditions to the listed commitments must be clearly stated.'

[15] Negative listing: 'Unless otherwise indicated in the lists of reservations, all services are deemed liberalized. All measures and sectors are considered to be liberalized unless there is a reservation indicated that these may include existing and future non-conforming measures. All sectors not listed are considered open to foreign service suppliers.'

[16] The GATS-*plus* concept corresponds with provisions that come under the current mandate of the WTO/GATS, while the GATS-*extra* category implies measures and regulatory features that fall outside the current WTO/GATS mandate.

However, all categories of mode 4 service suppliers in the EU–UK TCA are subject to country-specific reservations. What this means in practice for service providers is highly variegated, by type of mobility, destination, member state, and service sector. Family members' rights (for families that may travel with a service provider) can go as far as including working rights' for spouses, for example in the EFTA-India TEPA. However, such working rights apply to partners, children, and family members of ICTs only.

Hybrid scheduling is used for implementing variable speeds of liberalisation across modes (and sectors). Hybridity means, first, that members are free to choose positive scheduling at first and to waive after a three-year transition period into negative scheduling (twelve years for LDCs) (Zhang and Sasanabanchakul 2022). It also means that market access is scheduled differently (positive listing) than national treatment obligations (negative listing) (Sauvé 2014). In mode 4 even the 'traditional' GATS-style services chapters invert that architecture by oftentimes limiting any openings made in mode 4 to horizontal commitments without specifying any additional opening in the specific commitments (Stephenson 2015).

In PTAs using positive scheduling, mode 4 is treated like the other modes, meaning there might be a list for exempting future, non-conforming measures. In the positive scheduling scenario, the horizontal section must be read with the sector-specific schedule and, in addition, most-favoured-nation (MFN) exemptions, the former of which might inform that a country is liberalising the movement of professionals through bilateral labour migration agreements (e.g. France in GATS and Bulgaria, Jordan, and the Dominican Republic for health workers; see Carzaniga et al. 2019). In the negatively scheduled mode 4 commitments, mode 4 is presumed fully liberalised, unless otherwise specified. The limitations, conditions, and reservations appear in annexes, one being a standstill, for example, preventing governments from making the sector more restrictive, or introducing new non-confirming measures, and another providing full regulatory freedom to governments to exclude entire sectors or introducing new measures.

Whereas mode 4 features in services chapters in many PTAs, mainly those operating positive scheduling like the CPTPP, mode 4 is liberalised outside the trade in services chapter. The CPTPP has a Chapter 10 Cross-Border Trade in Services and a Chapter 12 on the Temporary Entry for Business Persons. The former refers to a separate labour chapter, Chapter 19 and the non-conforming measures in Annexes I and II. Oftentimes, a combination of both is used with a 'pure' mode 4 in a services chapter (Carzaniga and Sharma 2022) and an annex or separate chapter on the international movement of professionals.

In regional integration agreements such as the Association of Southeast Asian Nations (ASEAN) or the African Continental Free Trade Area (AfCFTA), there is a self-standing agreement on the movement of natural persons (MNP). These agreements use a dual strategy to liberalise the MNP, one on mode 4 and another protocol on the broader, free movement of persons (Zanker and Bisong 2022). Perhaps the oldest example is how the ASEAN Agreement on the Movement of

Natural Persons (AAMNP) 2012 and mode 4 in the ASEAN Trade in Services Agreement (ATiSA) (2020) came out of the ASEAN Framework Agreement on Services (AFAS) of 1995 (Natanael and Verico 2019). Another example is Article 27(3) of the Protocol on Trade in Services (TiS) in AfCFTA and the concomitant track of liberalising the movement of persons through a Protocol Relating to Free Movement of Persons, Right of Residence and Right of Establishment also concluded under the umbrella of the AfCFTA, albeit possibly, endorsed at a later stage by the African Union (AU) Member States (Apiko et al. 2021: 17).

At the same time, a comparison between mode 4 in Chapter 12 of the CPTPP (2018) and Chapter 9 of the RCEP (2022) reveals that the RCEP pledges to engage in cooperation on facilitating more TMNP (ADP Economics Working Paper Series No. 639, 2021: 4).[17] Otherwise, RCEP mode 4 is similar to the ASEAN–Australia–New Zealand Free Trade Agreement (AANZFTA) (Chapter 9) and the AFAS (Kimura et al. 2022).

The Indonesia–Australia Comprehensive Economic Cooperation Agreement (IA-CEPA, in force since 5 July 2020) reaffirms in Article 12.5 the commitment to the Asia-Pacific Economic Cooperation (APEC) Business Travel Card programme, but, otherwise, is a step further than the AANZFTA in the sense of adding a skill transfer obligation to benefit Indonesian lawyers[18] and adding an IA-CEPA Skills Development Exchange Pilot Project. Yet, the IA-CEPA has not as far-reaching cooperation over border security, biometrics, and travel data provision as the Peru–Australia FTA (PAFTA) in force since 11 February 2020. The PAFTA also has mutual recognition of professions, and, to some extent, even harmonises the educational and professional pathway and accreditation for engineers and architects, lawyers, and other business persons (Annex 9-A) and therefore has installed a standing professional services working group. Even if the projected Australia–India Comprehensive Economic Cooperation Agreement (ECTA, in force since 29 December 2022) uses positive scheduling, it is advanced in the sense that Australia grants two types of visas to India, the work holiday visa and post-study work visa, both of which are not typical mode 4-type service deliveries, but rather cover broader labour migration and training-type mobility (see below).

Beyond the above-mentioned progress on facilitating mode 4 mobility, there are also emerging impediments to mode 4 trade, which seem motivated by political economic constraints of the host country labour actors, including trade unions, employer associations, and professional boards (medicine, architects, law), which

[17] See www.adb.org/sites/default/files/publication/740991/ewp-639-regional-comprehensive-economic-partnership.pdf

[18] See Annex 12-A: Indonesia's Schedule of Movement of Natural Persons Commitments: 'Foreign lawyers (advocates) are: 1) Subject to recommendation from the Advocate Association; 2) Obliged to transfer legal knowledge and professional capabilities to Indonesian lawyers; and 3) Obliged to transfer knowledge to education, legal research or government institutions for at least 10 hours each month free of charge.'

use their power to oppose the accreditation necessary for an independent service supply, including recognition of the credentials for opening a private practice. The first such inflexibility seems to be the non-recognition by the host country's compulsory health insurance of the traditional medicine and acupuncture services, brought by 'health specialists', notably from Asian countries, for example, traditional complementary medicine (TCM) practitioners, who are not always accredited in the host country as medical doctors. For that reason, China, in its PTAs (ChAFTA[19] side letter on TCM (2015), China–Switzerland FTA (2015), Annex XI on TCM (2014), is insisting on a side letter where the partner country seeks to engage in best efforts to include TCM in its public health insurance plan. In this way, TCM doctors and practitioners are not discriminated against by medical staff and doctors trained in Western medicine, and patients are not led by financial considerations when choosing their treatment plan.[20] This would include supervised or co-supervised activity for TCM practitioners in a practice owned by a domestic medical doctor.

In the Comprehensive Economic and Trade Agreement (CETA) between the EU and Canada, there is no automatic mutual recognition of professional qualifications, but a call for separate agreements by professional bodies. The CETA leaves it to the relevant authorities or professional bodies in both the EU and Canada to negotiate a proposal on so-called mutual recognition that can then be integrated into the CETA. Also, there are sectoral carve-outs, for example the financial sector, with a separate chapter in the agreement, including implications for mode 4.[21]

12.5 GATS-EXTRA: VISA, BORDER MANAGEMENT, RETURN, AND COOPERATION ON LABOUR

Comparing mode 4 trade in GATS to the movement of persons in PTAs, there are 'improvements on mode 4 . . . and downsides to services PTAs' (Marchetti and Lim 2007). Pauwelyn et al. 2020 find that due to the rise of regional economic communities (RECs), PTAs no longer see the necessity to regulate visa, border control, immigration, and asylum issues. Similarly, Lavenex et al. (2024) and Carzaniga and Sharma (2022) report that most GATS-*extra* advances in PTAs have occurred over transparency and information duties within certain timelines, including a duty to report about relevant changes in immigration laws, (ninety days in Article 8 AANZFTA), as well as expedited visa, travel documentation, and work permit application procedures within certain timelines (e.g. 160 days for CETA, Chapter 10). Most far-reaching is the duty to establish a contact point, which is a feature that merges visa application with information duties in a single administrative entity

[19] China–Australia Free Trade Agreement.

[20] China–Switzerland FTA (2014), Annex XI, Reimbursement of Traditional Chinese Medicine under the Health System.

[21] See CETA, Annex 10-A–F.

(Switzerland–China FTA Articles 13.5 and 13.8; and CETA Annex 10-A and Article 10.5 – list of contact points of the EU Member States and Canada, respectively).

Yet, as Pauwelyn et al. (2020) noted, the 'need for the harmonisation of border procedures and travel documentation to facilitate the entry of travellers and address irregular migration and cross-border mobility' is reserved for RECs. Conversely, PTAs like COMESA, which are concluded exclusively and essentially for cross-border business and trade, will never want to reach these levels of harmonisation. The same applies to the treatment of vulnerable traders and other mode 4 service suppliers, the screening and inspecting against human trafficking and smuggling, and the detection of cross-border movement, which is determined by humanitarian motives. This is also because member states within certain RECs, like the Economic Community of West African States (ECOWAS) or Common Market for Eastern and Southern Africa (COMESA), are bound by a common human rights charter. This is the African Charter on Human and People's Rights and Duties (Banjul Chapter) of 1981, also binding for the AfCFTA. Conversely, neither Pacific and East Asian countries united under the Asia-Pacific Trade Agreement (APTA) nor the RCEP or the CPTPP has a similar common human rights treaty in place, against which screening or related border measures intruding on fundamental rights, including the right to leave one's country, the right to (private) life, and the right to health could be reviewed.

However, for border screening motivated by public health grounds in a post-COVID-19 environment, some PTAs might likely include provisions similar to those in REC settings, by having measures such as screening at the border (hitherto reserved for goods through sanitary and phytosanitary (SPS) measures), designating border crossings, surveillance, detection and outbreak capacities, and public health emergency contingency plans (IOM and COMESA 2020: 29).

12.5.1 *Return Obligations in PTAs: Trade as a Venue to Control Immigration?*

Furthermore, several PTAs contribute to combatting irregular migration by including voluntary and forced return obligations or provisions on cooperating or sharing experience over integrated border management. For example, Chapter 9 of the Malaysia–India Comprehensive Economic Cooperation Agreement (MICECA) of 1 July 2011 'recognizes the need to ensure border security' (Article 9.1),[22] while the

[22] Article 9.1 MICECA reads: 'The objectives of this Chapter are: (a) to provide for rights and obligations additional to those set out in Chapters 8 (Trade in Services) and 10 (Investment) in relation to the movement of natural persons between the Parties while *recognizing the need to ensure border security*; (b) to enhance and facilitate the movement of natural persons engaged in the conduct of trade in services, goods and investment between the Parties; and (c) to *establish simplified streamlined and transparent procedures for immigration formalities* for the temporary entry of natural persons to whom this Chapter applies' (italics added).

PAFTA of 11 February 2020 goes much further in the suggestion that 'cooperation' Article 11.6 leads to a 'sharing of experiences':

> (C) *consider mutually agreed cooperation* activities, subject to available resources, including by *sharing experiences* with regulations and the implementation of programs and technology related to . . . the use of biometric technology, advanced passenger information systems, frequent passenger programs and security in travel documents. (italics added).

As has been extensively reported in policy circles and scholarship (Panizzon 2010; Naiki 2015), the Japan–Philippines EPA Annex 8 requires nurses and caregivers who fail the national board examination (NBE) in Japan to return to the Philippines. Indonesia and Viet Nam have similar EPAs with Japan. Even the EU–Japan EPA in Annex 17 provides:

> The Parties acknowledge that the enhanced movement of natural persons following from paragraphs 1 to 6 *requires full cooperation on return and readmission* of natural persons staying in the territory of a Party in contravention of its rules for entry and temporary stay (*italics added*).

Among twenty-three nurse candidates and twenty-two caregivers returning to the Philippines in 2011 due to the dissolution of their contracts because of 'dissatisfaction' with the workplace (Ohno 2012), only half continued working as caregivers in the Philippines (Takahashi 2018). The Japanese model of recruiting lower-skilled TMNP through trade agreements is considered a 'failure' by the public, the press, and some academics (Naiki 2015). The costs for the employers, for example hospitals and medical institutions, of hiring foreign nurses and caregivers without having Japanese-language training taking place at home were too high and the risk of deskilling and brain drain for these 'EPA nurses' too costly (Takahashi 2018; Hirano et al. 2020).[23] Others evaluate the success–failure of Japan's EPA nurses in a more nuanced way. They suggest that if the trading partner puts efforts into language training (Indonesians learn 32 per cent more Japanese than Filipinos) and a positive attitude among the younger population about working in Japan, the success rate is higher (Ohno 2012).

Again, this result shows that in GATS-extra categories, there is little leverage from the GATS/WTO to tie a trading partner to cooperate on border management, return, and combatting irregular migration. As a result, the efforts must come from both trading partners' close cooperation and sharing of experience, as the PAFTA suggests. Without legal guarantees in a PTA over GATS-extra or soft recommendations, a PTA might choose to limit the extent of GATS-extra regulation, thus restricting the categories of persons within a sector or subsector, so as

[23] Hirano et al. 2020: 'As of January 2019, only 136 foreign registered nurses remained in Japan, which is merely 10.5% of the 1300 EPA nurse candidates who had entered Japan since 2008.'

not to liberalise in categories of persons, where irregular migration might become an issue.

Many PTAs, including those by the European Free Trade Association (EFTA), limit the independent professional category to those holding 'occupations with cultural, ethnic, national characteristics'. For example, the ChAFTA opens to 'occupations with Chinese characteristics', like traditional Chinese medicine practitioners, Mandarin language teachers, Chinese chefs, and Wushu martial arts coaches.[24] But by embedding these occupations into the independent professionals (IP) category, as opposed to CSS, Australia could recoup the potential costs of the training or the risk of unemployment to the self-employed person themself.

12.5.2 *Knowledge Transfer Obligation: Token for Political Acceptance?*

In the Asian context, governments have pushed for more sectoral openings in leisure, sports, and cultural service supply (Lavenex and Jurje 2021). These include adding the new category of 'instructors' of yoga, cuisine, boxing, martial arts (ChAFTA), traditional music, medicine, and healing (India–Australia ECTA, 2022).[25]

These are sectors without much domestic competition, culturally or ethnically defined, also referred to in the literature as an 'ethnic enclave economy' (Portes and Shafer 2007), and fall into the 'others' sector under the CPC classification. They can be used to explore the niches where domestic labour is not a competition, increasing the political acceptance of mode 4 workers.

The labour-services trade issues are often not clear-cut and increasingly blur or become permeable, as in the ChAFTA and IA-ECTA. Australia has granted China (ChAFTA) and India (IA-ECTA) quotas in its Work-Holiday Maker Visa Scheme, thus preferring Indians and Chinese over other foreign nationals by reserving a share of its global quota for nationals from these two countries. Even though the WTO Secretariat discourages using quotas in mode 4, visa practices are excluded from GATS through a footnote in Annex MNP. Thus, such practices might be considered as visas rather than quotas, regardless of whether the holiday work falls under the scope of service supply or not.

12.5.3 *Labour Standards and Foreign Credential Recognition (FCR)*

Another key feature of labour provisions in PTAs is the so-called cooperation provisions, including sustainabale agriculture, industrial cooperation in particular

[24] See China, MOFCOM, Interpretation for the ChAFTA, http://english.mofcom.gov.cn/article/policyrelease/Cocoon/201510/20151001144954.shtml.

[25] See Australia–India ECTA (2022): 'Temporary entry and temporary stay shall be granted for up to a combined total of 1,800 per year of qualified, professional Indian traditional chefs and yoga instructors entering as Contractual Service Suppliers of India.'

for small and medium-size enterprises, product safety, and in relation to mode 4/ TMNP flows, the one with the closest link, labour standards. These provisions call on both parties to regularly monitor labour issues (working conditions, remuneration, labour inspection, forced labour, youth/child, gender, occupational health, and corporate social responsibility – CSR). To what extent do such cooperation clauses incorporate and replicate the ILO standards, expressly refer to the relevant ILO norm or defer to monitoring by the ILO and other stakeholders, and what themes they cover, is where the diversification among trade agreements lies, for example Article 18.7 PAFTA or Article 19.10 CPTPP:

> ... Subject to the agreement of the Parties involved, cooperative activities may occur through bilateral or plurilateral engagement and may involve relevant regional or international organisations, such as the ILO, and non-Parties.

According to ILO LP Hub, 68 per cent of all PTAs from 1994 to 2021 used labour-restrictive provisions, which prevent the trading partner from using labour laws to create unfair trade advantage or protectionist trade. However, this feature is missing from most PTAs initiated by African and Arab countries (ILO 2022: 11).

Whereas the ILO and the Economic and Social Council (ECOSOC) are specialised UN agencies, the WTO is not, but is an observer in ILO. Conversely, the ILO and ECOSOC (the latter in charge through the Committee on Economic, Social and Cultural Rights (CESCR) of monitoring the implementation of the International Covenant on Economic, Social and Cultural Rights (ICESCR)) lack standing in the WTO. Hence, aligning trade law to adherence to international labour standards without those becoming a protectionist barrier to trade, has been an ongoing issue of debate since the Singapore 1996 Ministerial, which extends to PTAs.[26]

The ICESCR guarantees a right to work for non-resident populations (Article 6 and Article 7.2). Yet, so far, no international obligation compels states to admit migrant workers into the labour market, except for the ICRMW.[27] Coming closest to multilaterally opening up a work-related pathway is the GATS and its mode 4 of service delivery (Howse and Teitel 2009).[28]

Unlike GATS, the ICRMW posits that states have a positive obligation to ensure that residents and workers may 'achieve the full realization of this right', which 'shall include technical and vocational guidance and training programs, policies and techniques to achieve steady ... development and full and productive employment'. The ILO and WTO have worked jointly on skills development, but have failed to recommend a specific design for scheduling mode 4 commitments. General

26 See WTO, www.wto.org/english/thewto_e/whatis_e/tif_e/bey5_e.htm.

27 International Convention on the Protection of the Rights of All Migrant Workers and Members of Their Families, 2220 UNTS 3, 18 December 1990

28 General Agreement on Trade in Services (GATS), 1869 UNTS 183, 15 April 1994 (entry into force: 1 January 1995).

Comment 18 to ICESCR, deepens in paragraph 27, by restating that the 'right to work requires States parties, to take positive measures to enable and assist individuals to enjoy the right to work and to implement technical and vocational education plans to facilitate access to employment'. Article 52 of the ICRMW enshrines a sovereign prerogative of states to:

> 'restrict free choice of remunerated activity ... concerning recognition of occupational qualifications acquired outside its territory', states 'shall endeavour to provide for ... the assessment, certification and recognition of foreign (professional) formal and informal qualifications'.

One key embodiment of this best-efforts clause is embodied in Article VII GATS, which calls on states to remove obstacles to the recognition of foreign credentials. These are similar to product conformity assessments and embody a behind-the-border barrier to services trade and mobility of persons. Whereas Article VII GATS encourages the conclusion of mutual recognition agreements for an across-the-board, horizontal recognition of qualifications, that can even break away from the MFN obligation under Article II GATS, but not from non-discriminatory treatment among WTO Members, more recent PTAs, including the CPTPP, go for a sectoral recognition broken down by trades or professions, including engineers and architects. The RCEP even has a temporary mutual recognition possibility for states to temporarily agree to recognise each other's qualifications limited to the duration of a specific joint project. In the CETA, there is no automatic, horizontal mutual recognition. Instead, professional bodies are encouraged to conclude sectoral agreements to be later integrated into the CETA.

12.6 FLEXIBILITIES: DEVELOPMENT-FRIENDLY, GENDER-SENSITIVE MODE 4

In the Doha Development Agenda (DDA), which is the negotiations package that was launched by the WTO's fourth Ministerial meeting in Doha, Qatar, in November 2001, developing countries requested more openings in mode 4: adding new categories, lifting sectoral limitations, and de-coupling mode 4 from being held hostage to mode 3 (75 per cent of mode 4 commitments remain coupled to mode 3, UNCTAD 2006). In 2005, the Hong Kong Ministerial Declaration, the Plurilateral Request, and the LDCs' request expressly called for the de-coupling and added new categories. In 2011, trade negotiators adopted the so-called LDC waiver, which is an LDC-specific 'Enabling Clause for services' (UNCTAD 2016). It allows industrialised Members to deviate from their MFN obligation to grant preferential treatment on services to all WTO Members when they wish to benefit from service provision from an LDC. At the Bali 2013 Ministerial, efforts were made to 'operationalise' this LDC waiver through the LDC collective request, and in 2015 at the Nairobi Ministerial, the LDC waiver was extended until 2030.

Another issue is the gendered impact of mode 4. Here, the concern is that temporary mobility poses a high risk for women, who experience 'prolonged family separation' and uncertain social security (Hennebry et al. 2022). At the same time, trade has been shown to deliver advantages for women's empowerment and produce gains in terms of equalising opportunities. The WTO provides a database on gender provisions in regional trade agreements (RTAs), which could be the basis for designing more gender-responsive PTAs.[29] At the same time, the category of instructors, healers, and health workers in mode 4 should be liberalised as this is where the feminisation of migrant labour takes place most often. However, in these sectors, female labour is usually at higher risk of being exposed to trade disruption, for example social distancing measures and travel bans during COVID-19. Thus, even if access to information technology (IT) skills should be available to all, the transferability to online or hybrid service provision is often more challenging for women with less access to adequate IT supply (WTO and World Bank 2020: 118–119).

In 2016 the European Parliament found that there is little data on the gender effects of liberalising trade in services, except for some studies in tourism and communication. However, what is evident is that more mode 4 openings in healthcare could offer female healthcare professionals from low-income countries the opportunity to gain experience and earn higher wages working for healthcare facilities in higher-income countries. Hence, PTAs like the Japan–Philippines EPA, liberalising mode 4 for nurses and caregivers, have charted a new pathway in mode 4 liberalisation, despite restrictive language and training pre-employment requirements (European Parliament 2016: 26).[30]

Another way gender equality concerns can be mainstreamed into trade agreements is to open up the graduate trainee pathway within the ICT category and broadly define the former. A WTO and OECD study shows that internationally active companies trading cross-border employ more women than companies doing commerce domestically (WTO and OECD, 2017). European Union PTAs have recently included graduate trainees (CARIFORUM), installers, and maintainers. By liberalising graduate trainees, the host country might defer the cost of opening its mode 4 in a development-friendly way to the international company, a feature that the Swiss migration partnership with Nigeria opted for when Nestlé Nigeria agreed to train Nigerian workers (Losada 2023). By upskilling the workers, a know-how transfer occurs, which Article 6(2) ICESCR encourages. However, for such a transfer to benefit the sending country and the worker or trainee, a solid private

29 WTO, www.wto.org/english/tratop_e/womenandtrade_e/gender_responsive_trade_agreement_db_e.htm

30 Speech by WTO DDG Ellard on 17 December 2021: 'DDG Ellard: WTO is taking action to make trade work for women: women account for 33% of the workforce of exporting businesses, compared with 24% of non-exporting firms. Moreover, women constitute 36% of the workforce of firms involved in global value chains and 38% of the workforce of foreign-owned firms', available at: www.wto.org/english/news_e/news21_e/ddgae_17dec21_e.htm.

partnership is required, as paragraph d of Objective 18 GCM suggests, without providing for indicators on how to measure such partnerships and by which standards. It seems that similarily, EU (pilot) talent or skills partnerships defer to the private sector for identifying the demand for the skills on which they are prepared to offer training offered. These include Towards a Holistic Approach to Labour Migration Governance and Labour Mobility in North Africa (THAMM) and the Project Addressing Labour Shortages Through Innovative Labour Migration Models (PALIM) initiated under the EU Talent Partnership. They also include India's Skills and Mobility Partnerships with the UK, which might be read as complementing mode 4 commitments in PTAs.

12.7 BILATERAL LABOUR AGREEMENTS AND MODE 4: SYNERGY OR SUBSTITUTES?

Mobility as part of global value chains (GVCs) has also been observed in countries where mobility commitments are undertaken to ensure the supply of labour, combined with mode 3 commitments granted to investors in specific sectors, especially in manufacturing. In this case, the mobility of low-skilled workers is liberalised under another visa scheme or covered by bilateral labour agreements (BLA) and not covered by mode 4 although their presence stems from the existence of the PTAs. A central feature of all these forms of temporary mobility is the failure to address the welfare and protection of workers' rights, resulting in a less-than-favourable working environment and de facto slavery employment conditions for these workers (Gordon 2022).

Bilateral labour agreements have been used over the years to regulate the temporary migration of people (Chilton and Woda 2022). Dawson (2013) argued that BLAs are in a 'synergetic' relationship with GATS mode 4 since states can experiment in smaller, flexible units that could later be multilateralised. Such a view, reminiscent of the 2017 Sutherland Report 'making migration work for all', and the idea of a mini-multilateralism among like-minded groups of states, is not shared by sending countries. They fear that conditionalities between trade and irregular migration will be costly for them, and, inversely, host countries are opposed to lock-in liberalisation of labour market demand for foreign workers in GATS.

Nonetheless, PTAs are being used to replace BLAs – or certain parts of them – either to restrict the entry of specific categories of persons or to facilitate the mobility of workers and other persons. The India–Malaysia CEPA, the NZ–China FTA, and the ChAFTA foresee a holidaymaker visa and the India–Malaysia CEPA a post-study work visa, which are categories BLAs traditionally covered or opened unilaterally through national immigration legislation. This trend of PTAs absorbing categories of work, is evidence by the increased permeability between the silos of cross-border mobility.

Another area of convergence between BLAs and PTAs offer skills training or transfer opportunities, such as occurs when the former the Indonesia–Australia Skills

Development Exchange Pilot Project, which relies on private companies. Another example is the New Zealand–China PTA that offers a New Zealand–China Doctoral Research Scholarships programme, a type of cooperation traditionally found in bilateral stagiaire or internship agreements, which China is now bringing into trade agreements. Similarly, India and China are pursuing a strategy to have their trading partners include their work holiday visas in PTAs instead of having them be unilaterally offered.

In contrast to trade agreements, some BLAs codify the protection of the human rights and labour rights of migrant workers sent abroad. In particular, if both countries are signatories of the ICRMW.[31] In contrast, others minimally relate to the ILO Convention 189 on domestic workers, which enshrines the right to collective bargaining and freedom of association for domestic workers. Bilateral labour migration agreements concluded between the Gulf and Asian countries tie the migrant worker to the employer, for example the Kafala system. In the GATS context, we question whether this element of contract law, which de jure prohibits job switching and prevents upskilling or undoing of an exploitative labour situation, constitutes an implicit barrier to services trade because workers supply inefficiently if their rights are not protected (ITU 2017).[32]

Safe routes for regular migration and orderly return, screening, and identification, as well as standard operating procedures against smuggling and trafficking, are additional reasons why sending countries, including Pakistan, Myanmar, Vanuatu, Mongolia, Nepal, Sri Lanka, but also Gambia or Guinea, sign and implement bilateral plans, policies, and agreements. If trade agreements could deliver that safety and anti-smuggling/trafficking effort, countries would no longer need that doubled-up effort. For example, Nepal has nine Memorandum of Understanding (MoUs) with Jordan, and Vanuatu, and labour (in particular seasonal) mobility schemes with Australia, New Zealand, the Republic of Korea, and Japan (Chilton and Woda 2022).

Bilateral labour migration agreements regulate irregular migration through a panoply of measures, including return obligations, border management, and joint capacity building, which are all more developed than in PTAs. The Uzbekistan–Bahrain and Philippines–Bahrain bilateral schemes offer free return air tickets, alongside border management tools, like pre-arrival screening.[33] Unlike trade agreements, an advantage

[31] UN OHCHR (Office of the High Commissioner of Human Rights). 1990. International Convention on the Protection of the Rights of All Migrant Workers and Members of Their Families. Adopted by General Assembly resolution 45/158 of 18 December 1990. New York. Available at: www.ohchr.org/en/professionalinterest/pages/cmw.aspx.

[32] Bilateral labour migration agreements were reported to have been concluded by the following destination and sending countries in Asia: Indonesia, Kazakhstan, Mongolia, Myanmar, Nepal, Pakistan, the Philippines, the Republic of Korea, the Russian Federation, Tonga, Turkmenistan, Uzbekistan, Vanuatu, and Viet Nam.

[33] ESCAP, Implementing the Global Compact for Safe, Orderly and Regular Migration: a synthesis of voluntary Global Compact reviews in Asia and the Pacific, 20 February 2021, UN Document ESCAP/GCM/2021/CRP.1.

TABLE 12.1 *Advanced* GATS-plus *and* GATS-extra *mode 4 categories in PTAs*

Trade Agreement	Sector	Category	Impact on Skills
Japan EPA • Philippines • Indonesia • Viet Nam	1. Nurses 2. Caregivers	1. CSS 2. employees	De-skilling due to failed linguistic and societal integration & unsuccessfully planned return
1. China–Switzerland[34] 2. ChAFTA 3. IA-ECTA	1. TCM & acupuncture[35] 2. music, cuisine, sport, Mandarin language instructors 3. yoga instructors and chefs	1. Specialists/IP (medical doctors with a qualification in TCM/ acupuncture) China–Switzerland FTA 2. Instructors (ChAFTA) 3. Specialist within CSS (IA-ECTA)	De-skilling and underemployment if state bodies do not recognise the profession; professional boards or services cannot be reimbursed by a compulsory health insurance plan
EU EPA	Horizontal commitment	1. Graduate trainee 2. Graduate trainee within ICT	Upskilling
IA-ECTA, ChAFTA	Side letter	1. Post-study work visa 2. Work holiday visa	Upskilling

Source: Created by the authors.

over them is that certain provisions in BLAs tend to be sufficiently precise enough to grant individual rights, which the worker can invoke before judicial or administrative bodies. For example, under France's agreements with West and North African countries, workers can get their removal orders or denial of work permits judicially reviewed before France's administrative courts of appeal (Panizzon 2022) (Table 12.1).

12.8 FUTURE TRENDS: DIGITAL NOMADS, ESSENTIAL WORKERS, AND THE GLOBAL COMPACTS

Since the COVID-19 pandemic challenged lawmakers and policymakers to regulate the evolving transformation of the world of work, with remote models figuring as

[34] Annex VI, Section IV Article 14 Traditional Chinese Medicine Services.

[35] Sometimes also included under services provided by midwives, nurses, physiotherapists, and paramedical personnel (CPC 93191).

the key pandemic response of workers and employers to halt contagion, today, these at-a-distance service deliveries are seemingly an asset here to stay. At the same time, the adoption of the two Global Compacts in 2019 for refugees and migrants has also changed some policy paradigms about refugee employment and strengthened the call for regular and complementary pathways. The three features for future issues are dealt with below.

12.8.1 *Moving COVID-19 Essential Workers into Mode 4 Trade: A Win–Win Scenario?*

The COVID-19 pandemic contributed to drastic labour shortages across sectors and supply chain disruptions. These labour supply shortages are being felt mainly in the manufacturing sector and other sectors which require close contact with people, such as food and beverages, hospitality, accommodation, and tourism (Causa et al. 2022; Odasso and Fornalè 2022).

In response to the shortages in key sectors, states introduced short-term visas for categories of workers, especially in transportation and healthcare. Mode 4 commitments could offer a more sustainable way of ensuring labour supply in these sectors, mostly lower-skilled. But most low-skilled categories are not liberalised in GATS or PTAs.

Measures to liberalise mode 4 services, even if limited to only PTA Member States, would have far-reaching effects on the economy (OECD 2020). Liberalisation measures can be restricted to specific sectors with the most acute shortages. More so, using mode 4 commitments to address these shortages will include lower-skilled categories in trade agreements, especially those essential workers on the front line during the pandemic.

The COVID-19 pandemic also revealed the fate of service providers, particularly independent professionals, who fell outside the scope of social welfare measures and were left to navigate the pandemic and resultant economic difficulties without any state support. During the pandemic, most foreign nationals fell through the cracks and were not addressed by any government policies or safety nets, not from their home countries or host countries. More so, issues relating to social welfare and workers' rights and protection are not covered by trade agreements, thus creating a lacuna, which is difficult for workers who operate solely within the purview (scope) of PTAs or similar trade agreements.

Temporary workers/ service providers faced several difficulties during the pandemic, including difficulty in transferring remittances, wage theft, and abandonment by their employers. As mentioned, due to the pandemic, remittances have been labelled as 'essential services' by a group of thirty-three countries led by the UK, Northern Ireland, and Switzerland. According to the UN Secretary-General Report on the Global Compact for Migration (2021), the format of 'essential services' seems not to have yet benefitted from a similar distinction and WTO/GATS. More so, PTAs are not prepared to single out 'essential service providers' from other services and the potential risk of discrimination. Additionally, the issue of responsibility in trade agreements has not been researched fully (Bisong et al. 2020).

12.8.2 *Digital Nomads – Depicting the Future of Work in Mode 4*

Globalisation, digital transformation, the evolution of work, and, most recently, the COVID-19 pandemic have also impacted trade in services and modes of delivery, blurring the lines between modes of service delivery.

The International Labour Organization estimates that the number of workers working from home rose from about 260 million before the pandemic to 558 million by the second quarter of 2020 (Soares et al. 2021). The COVID-19 pandemic fast-tracked the emerging evolving work patterns towards remote work and teleworking.

In response to the evolving world of work and also to aid struggling economies by reducing tourist revenues, among other factors (OECD 2022), many countries introduced digital nomad visas (DNVs). These visas allow digital nomads (DNs) to live and work in countries under several conditions. As of September 2022, over forty-six countries have introduced some type of DNVs for categories of professionals with varying degrees of requirements. These visas allow remote workers to legally work from a specific country for a period of time (ranging from ninety days to 3/5 years, with a possibility of extending in some countries). Digital nomads are excluded from taxes or provided with generous rebates (as high as 50 per cent in Greece) or tax holidays for several years. In addition, they require valid health insurance for the duration of their stay. Remote work generally raises questions regarding tax requirements, entitlement to social welfare, and other HR requirements for employers. For employees, DNVs have raised issues around workers' protection, double taxation, competition, and which employment laws are applicable (Hooper and Brenton 2022; OECD 2022).

More and more employees, freelancers, and self-employed entrepreneurs choose remote work to combine global travel and online careers and business. Although digital-intensive sectors, such as marketing, design, IT, writing, media, tutoring, and consulting, are the most represented, a wide range of activities and occupations are compatible with digital nomadism.

While DNVs may have implications for labour migration, the holders are strictly precluded from being involved in the domestic labour market by ensuring that they are working for foreign employers or foreign clients, if they are self-employed.

The implication of DNs for trade in services is ambivalent, as specific commitments may not apply to DNs. Whereas DNs previously travelled under tourist or business categories, and these would fall under mode 1 trade/supply, the new visas are similar to mode 4 means of supply. The similarities are the temporary nature of mode 4 and the DNVs, and they may be restricted in some countries to specific regulations or sectors. Also, these categories of visas are highly regulated. The DNs need to show an intent to depart, thus ensuring that this is a temporary visa and not leading to permanence. However, Latvia offers a possibility for permanent residency after two years on a DNV.

Digital nomads are a hybrid between labour migration and mode 4. The complementarity of these schemes with mode 4 commitments is yet to be tested. For example, what will happen when service providers can move under DNVs in sectors restricted under mode 4 commitments and provide services within the territory of a member state? Does this amount to a unilateral liberalisation of a state? Will states be liable for breaching their commitments under mode 4 or MFN, especially if other member states are excluded from DNVs? (Some states specify the countries of origin for potential DNV applicants.)

Digital nomads may fit into the categories defined by GATS and most PTAs, for example the CSS and the self-employed persons. Persons employed by foreign companies may be intra-corporate transferees choosing to work remotely from another location (this may be a third location which is neither the office nor their country of origin).

Digital nomad visas raise further questions for mode 4 trade because of the temporary presence of the individuals in the territory of another member state. A motivation for further study of the implication of DNVs on services trade may be whether DNVs can serve as a precursor for GATS visas.

Also, due to the COVID-19 pandemic, it was clear that workers were not within the scope of welfare protection. For example, independent workers moving within the confines of mode 4 were excluded from welfare packages offered by states to workers living in these states. This situation exposed the gap between commitments in trade agreements and the welfare of workers who move under these agreements. The question, therefore, remains where these gaps can be addressed to protect the rights of service suppliers who may be self-employed or employed by companies. The challenge exists less where the service suppliers are employed and more when they are independent. Several workers fall within this category, across low- and highly skilled jobs.

12.8.3 *More Responsibilities for Mode 4 under the Global Compacts for Migration and Refugees*

The Global Compact for Safe, Orderly and Regular Migration, endorsed by a large majority of UN Member States (152) on 19 December 2018,[36] has been advertised as a collective fact-finding effort to map the law and fill gaps in international migration law and policymaking (Panizzon and van Riemsdijk 2019).

[36] See Global Compact for Safe, Orderly and Regular Migration (A/RES/73/195).

Yet, trade agreements go unmentioned in the twenty-three intergovernmental objectives and intergovernmental commitments to create more pathways. Objective 5, which calls on states to develop 'regional and multilateral labour mobility agreements',[37] fails to mention trade agreements when listing the types of possible such agreements. One reason for this might be the fear of developing, migrant-sending countries becoming caught in a conditionality scheme that would request cooperation over irregular migration in exchange for obtaining trade preferences or commitments facilitating the movement of professionals (Bisong 2023).

As Lavenex et al. (2024) argue, trade agreements would carry a significant representational gain over bilateral labour migration and other non-trade cooperation formats on labour migration. In trade, the bargaining space is usually wider than in BLAs, where trade-offs occur over remittance transfer costs and tax exemptions, traineeships, and upskilling labour rights (Bauböck and Ruhs 2022).

12.9 CONCLUSION

When negotiators, policymakers, and academics address mode 4, the many limitations, caveats, carve-outs, and preferences surrounding this mode of service delivery seem so daunting that it drives away any desire to use mode 4 as a commercial tool or labour market measure. Unsurprisingly then, boundary work is necessary for a field like mode 4, which stands and falls with national and regional borders and their temporary crossings. Logically, any legal treatment of the temporarily moved natural persons touches upon those disciplines applicable at the border and governing the national sovereignty over admissions, work permits, and credential recognition. Any employee or self-employed foreign service provider, which GATS labels as a cross-border worker, will be subject to more rules and regulations than just WTO/GATS. These range from international labour standards, regional border management, biometric and other data collection and screening, visa and travel documentation, permit processing fees, timelines, administrative procedures, portability of social security, and wage parity. Usually, these regulatory issues pose no conflict with WTO/GATS or PTA law, because the points of convergence and divergence have been made clear. General Agreement on Trade in Services Annex MNP exempts Members from applying for a visa or travel documentation requirements. It possibly includes nowadays biometric screening and other artificial intelligence (AI) tools, from the scope of the MFN obligation (Article II GATS), such that visa relaxation or elimination applied to some, but not all, WTO or PTA membership is not deemed per se a violation of the MFN principle.

[37] See Objective 5 GCM lists: '(f)acilitate regional and cross-regional labour mobility through international and bilateral cooperation arrangements, such as free movement regimes, visa liberalization or multiple-country visas, and labour mobility cooperation frameworks, to review and revise existing pathways, to develop temporary, seasonal circulation and fast-track programs in the areas of labor shortage'.

The more delicate issues come in from a different angle. On the one hand, mode 4 keeps being bundled into mode 3, thus impeding LDCs and developing countries from deploying meaningful service-providing units into more developed states, because mode 3 would, in each case, require a foreign investment in that country of mode 4 residents. Several production processes require a close alignment to mode 4 service provision, including truck drivers, repair work, and food and beverage logistical services. Such multimodal or delivery involving trade in goods remains within the ambit of WTO/trade law and poses a legal challenge confined to the right to regulate within the WTO.

Another issue is when PTAs make GATS-extra advances by including return obligations for mode 4 and therefore mingle trade with immigration legislations, in particular efforts at curbing irregular migration. It is clear that the drafters of the GATS did not intend Mode 4 to become a catalyst for better management of irregular and risky migration, as would be the case if trade openings were made conditional on the partner country's cooperation in taking back its citizens who are in an irregular situation. Neither did GATS negotiators intend for the temporary movement of service providers to become interchangeable with temporary migrant labour, as the convoluted definitional quandaries between Article I:2(d) GATS and the Annex MNP show. Hence, labour standards and issues related to permanent stay, citizenship, and employment, as per Annex MNP replicated by many PTAs, in theory, are outside the scope of trade law.

Yet, the COVID-19 pandemic and the need for essential workers in key sectors, many of which were face-to-face and online service providers, falling under the GATS definition, showed that separating the world of trade and labour is an artificial undertaking. The reality check in the form of the pandemic shows that GATS and PTAs need to take workers' rights more seriously. World Trade Organization Members should commit mandatorily to open market access and to provide national treatment for essential services (water, health, sanitation, education) for mode 4 beneficiaries. Such a responsibility could be derived from Objectives 15 and 16 of the Global Compact for Migration, as well as from Article 43 of the UN Migrant Workers' Convention (MWC).

We would even go so far as to argue that signatories to the MWC need to ensure better coherence between their national treatment obligations on mode 4 in PTAs and in GATS and Article 43 of that Convention. It would require a national treatment in mode 4 that deviates from the one in modes 1–3, because it would limit the discretionary space these countries have concerning national treatment in mode 4, since the former would necessarily have to be identical to Article 43 MWC.

Beyond the institutional and conflict-of-laws issues, we observe quite a few takeaways in terms of liberalisation and regulatory add-ons: categories of service suppliers have diversified, in particular in Asia, visa restrictions have fallen or special pathways created, and the indivisibility of services trade and labour migration has increased.

In PTAs, the commitments/rules regarding the temporary movement of persons have changed from a one-way, linear, and temporary 'moving' of service suppliers across borders to an additional 'transfer' of skills. For example, in the Indonesia–Australia Comprehensive Economic Partnership (IA-CEPA), mode 4 is reciprocal and part of a skills development package, whereby Australian providers of technical and vocational education and training (TVET) are given the opportunity to establish training facilities (up to 68 per cent ownership by Australia) for providing, on a face-to-face basis, Indonesians with new skills – the self-proclaimed first TVET scheme in a PTA – while at the same time, the skills package offers a work holiday scheme to young Indonesians to work in Australia, a workplace skills training programme for Indonesians in certain sectors in Australia, and a reciprocal skills exchange programme.[38] Such regulated upskilling efforts amount to more circular mobility, which aligns more with Agenda 2030's 'build back better'. Inversely, the medium-skilled category of nurses and caregivers introduced by Japan's EPAs with Indonesia, the Philippines, and Viet Nam has failed to bring the expected returns.

A convergence over categories of service workers between PTAs and BLAs is a further phenomenon. Australia's ECTAs with India and China introduced a post-study and a work holiday visa category based on numerical quotas, which in the past had been a preferential pathway to Australia's labour market, which had been reserved for BLAMs. This is the case even if such visas, including some e-business visas, are increasingly populating different PTAs (Pauwelyn et al. 2020), and even if applying to natural persons, who are less than directly or not at all involved in the supply of a service as per the Article 1:2(d) GATS mode 4 definition, like the working holiday makers or the interns and trainees. Through the import of visa provisions into PTAs, the plain meaning of the Article 1:2(d) GATS definition of TMNP is diversifying and acquiring a new object and purpose, which is to expand the scope of TMNP to persons who are being admitted on a country's services cum labour market, even if showcasing little, none or a hybrid affiliation with services trade (trainees or interns, who consume education services while working for a foreign or domestic service provider or in production). In the sense that PTAs ingest visa provisions and procedures to obtain visas are harmonized in terms of timelines, fees, availability of inquiry points and judicial review, and transparency obligations, there is a certain migrantification of mode 4, which used to be shielded off from border and visa issues as per the Annex TMNP caveat. Yet, an even more striking migrantification is taking place when PTAs harmonize visa categories, which is a development changing the clientele of mode 4 workers by diversifying the categories of persons whose movement abroad is to be facilitated, to categories blending the goods and services distinction (maintainers, installers) and those oscillating between different modes of services supply, e.g. trainees, post-study workers, interns, and instructors.

38 www.dfat.gov.au/trade/agreements/in-force/iacepa/outcomes-documents/outcomes-skills-development.

Among the challenges preventing PTAs from venturing beyond current levels of GATS mode 4 commitments, is regulatory fragmentation and the low level of compliance and cooperation among the involved authorities: if immigration, trade, and labour ministries were to operate under a 'whole of government approach', as also the GCM mandates in paragraph 15, it would mean a step forward for migrants and employers and one for which trade facilitation under the WTO is already available (Gillson et al. 2020).

Finally, the COVID-19 pandemic has revealed further weaknesses in facilitating TMNP within the pathway of trade agreements. First, the trade format lacks the different regulatory components to ensure that essential workers in key service sectors are not discriminated against in terms of their access to health, housing, and education rights and services. Second, the health crisis also revealed the expanding dimension of digital nomads, a category which would have traditionally been considered a mode 1 delivery of services. However, due to several governments' attempts to create a DNV, it could also be qualified as mode 4, an ambivalence which requires more research and policy work.

In terms of convergence, greater agility among the categories of workers appears to be linking temporary labour being liberalised in BLAs and the TMNP being facilitated in PTAs, thus suggesting the label of a 'migrantification' of PTAs. Incidentally, it is at the regional levels where most advances in GATS-extra are being made in terms of new categories of persons. Conversely, conglomerate PTAs, or mega-regionals, like the RCEP or the CPTPP, feature weaker mode 4 advances, mostly limited to the right to work for spouses and dependents, which implies that the spouse or dependant acquire the right to actually enter the foreign labour market, which turns out to carve out an even deeper entry than that of the service supplying, first permit holder. Furthermore, in terms of information, inquiry points, expedited visa and authorisation procedures and transparency obligations, the mega-regionals mirror the lowest common denominator. In a situation of tighter public resources, skill transfer, upskilling through occupational internships, and other forms of skill circulation where the costs are carried by the multinational enterprise or the self-employed individual will continue to use the trade venue, as it caters directly to private sector business and enterprises, and often protects their investments.

Inversely, attempts to attract lower-skilled workers to move within government-sponsored schemes in a trade setting, like the Japanese EPA nurses and caregiver systems, will likely fall out of use, precisely because trade agreements, as seen during the pandemic with essential workers, shy away from taking on immigration policy responsibilities, including for welfare in the host country and return home, for the persons moving across borders.

As PTAs are driven by commercial interests, much of what migrantification entails will not materialize for mode 4 worker mobility. Rather, only select immigration and labour market integration features, such as visa harmonization, occupational upskilling and on-the-job training schemes could become transplanted into PTAs. Instead, BLMAs, which are much quicker to set up to stopgap the human resource consequences of a health, humanitarian, climate crisis, will continue to embody the larger part of the policy response which the ongoing migrantification of the world of work requires.

REFERENCES

Adlung, R. and M. Roy 2005. 'Turning Hills into Mountains? Current Commitments under the GATS', Staff Working Paper no. ERSD-2005-01, WTO.

Apiko, Ph., A. Bisong and B. Byiers 2021. 'Connecting African Markets and People: Streamlining Regional Trade and Free Movement Protocols', ECDPM Discussion Paper 311, Maastricht.

Bast, J. 2008. 'Max Planck Commentaries on Word Trade Law Vol. 6) 2008, Annex on Movement of Natural Persons', in *WTO – Trade in Services, Leiden*, R. Wolfrum, P.-T. Stoll, C. Feinäugle (eds.), Den Haag: Martinus Nijhoff Publishers.

Bauböck, R. and M. Ruhs 2022. 'The Elusive Triple Win: Addressing Temporary Labour Migration Dilemmas through Fair Representation', *Migration Studies*, pp. 1–25, https://doi.org/10.1093/migration/mnac021.

Bhatnagar, P. 2014. 'GATS Mode 4: Movement of Natural Persons and Protection of Migrant Workers' Rights', Geneva: ILO.

Bisong, A. 2022. Labour mobility as a key element of the AfCFTA: What role for the AU's free movement protocol? ECDPM Brief16 December 2022, https://ecdpm.org/work/labour-mobility-key-element-afcfta-role-au-free-movement-protocol

2023. 'Trade Conditionalities in Migration Cooperation with African Countries', LinkedIn post. 13 February 2023.

Bisong, A., P. E. Ahairwe and E. Njoroge 2020. 'The Impact of COVID-19 on Remittances for Development in Africa', European Center for Development Policy Management Discussion Paper No. 269, Maastricht.

Carzaniga, A. and S. Sharma 2022. 'Regulatory Disciplines on the Mobility of Service Professionals – Lessons from Regional Trade Agreements', WTO Staff Working Paper ERSD-2022-12 17.

Carzaniga, A., I. S. Dhillon, J. Magdeleine and L. Xu 2019. 'International Health Worker Mobility and Trade in Services', WTO Staff Working Paper, No. ERSD-2019-13, World Trade Organization (WTO), Geneva, https://doi.org/10.30875/9ba2dfed-en.

Causa, O., et al. 2022. 'The Post-COVID-19 Rise in Labour Shortages', OECD Economics Department Working Papers, No. 1721, OECD Publishing, Paris, https://doi.org/10.1787/e60c2d1c-en.

Chanda, R. 2018. 'The Case for Mode 4: Recognizing the Gains and Addressing the Challenges', RBI Chair Professor of Economics Indian Institute of Management Bangalore WTO, Geneva.

Chaudhuri, S., A. Mattoo and R. Self 2004. 'Moving People to Deliver Services: How Can the WTO Help?' Policy Research Working Paper; No. 3238. Washington, DC: The World Bank. Available at: https://openknowledge.worldbank.org/handle/10986/15618.

Cheong, D., M. Jansen and R. Peters 2013. '*Shared Harvests: Agriculture, Trade, and Employment*', Geneva: ILO and UNCTAD.

Chilton, A. and B. Woda 2022. 'The Expanding Universe of Bilateral Labor Agreements', *Theoretical Inquiries in Law* 23(2): 1–64, https://doi.org/10.1515/til-2022-0010

Ciuriak, D., A. Dadkhah and D. Lysenko 2019. 'The Effect of Binding Commitments on Services Trade', *World Trade Review* 19(3): 365–378.

Dawson, L.R. 2013. 'Labour Mobility and the WTO: The Limits of GATS Mode 4', *International Migration* 51: 1–23.

European Commission 2021. 'European Business Statistics Compilers Guide for European Statistics on International Supply of Services by Mode of Supply', Luxembourg: Publications Office of the European Union. Available at: https://ec.europa.eu/eurostat/documents/3859598/13985649/KS-GQ-21-025-EN-N.pdf/d99b42c1–2dfa-2660-d200–50a4887a41e4t=1639751283517

European Parliament 2016. Gender Equality in Trade Agreements. Study for the FEMM Committee, Directorate General For Internal Policies, Policy Department C: Citizens' Rights And Constitutional Affairs, Women's Rights and Gender Equality, www.europarl.europa.eu/RegData/etudes/STUD/2016/571388/IPOL_STU(2016)571388_EN.pdf

Gillson, I., M. Molinuevo and S. Saez 2020. 'Trade Facilitation in Services: A Conceptual and Empirical Analysis', World Bank Policy Research Working Paper No. 9233. Available at SSRN: https://ssrn.com/abstract=3595766.

Gordon, J. 2022. 'In the Zone – Work at the Intersection of Trade and Migration', *Theoretical Inquiries in Law* 23(2), 111–142.

Gootiiz, B., G. Jonetzko, J. Magdeleine and J. Marchetti 2020. 'Services', in A. Mattoo, N. Rocha and M. Ruta (eds.), *Handbook of Deep Trade Agreements*. Washington, DC: The World Bank.

Hennebry, J., N. Piper, K. C. Hari and K. Williams 2022. 'Bilateral Labor Agreements as Migration Governance Tools: An Analysis from a Gender Lens', *Theoretical Inquiries in Law* 23(2): 184–205.

Hirano, Y. O., K. Tsubota and S. Ohno 2020. 'Factors Associated with the Recruitment of Foreign Nurses in Japan: A Nationwide Study of Hospitals', *Human Resource Health* 18: 88, https://doi.org/10.1186/s12960–020-00532-5.

Hooper, K. and M. Benton 2022. 'The Future of Remote Work: Digital Nomads and the Implications for Immigration Systems', Migration Policy Institute, June 2022. Available at www.migrationpolicy.org/sites/default/files/publications/mpi-remote-work-2022_final.pdf.

Howse, R. and R. Teitel 2009. 'Beyond the Divide: The International Covenant on Economic, Social and Political Rights and the World Trade Organization', in S. Joseph, D. Kinley, J. Waincymer (eds.), *The World Trade Organization and Human Rights*. Cheltenham: Edward Elgar Publishing.

ILO 2021. *ILO Global Estimates on International Migrant Workers – Results and Methodology*, Third edition. Geneva: International Labour Office.

2022. *A Multi-Faceted Typology of Labour Provisions in Trade Agreements: Overview, Methodology and Trends*. Geneva: ILO.

India–Australia Economic Cooperation and Trade Agreement (ECTA). 2022, www.dfat.gov.au/trade/agreements/in-force/australia-india-ecta/australia-india-ecta-official-text

IOM World Migration Report 2022. International Organization for Migration (IOM), Geneva.

IOM and COMESA 2020. Making the Case to Integrate Human Mobility into Cross-Border Trade and Trade Facilitation, Geneva: IOM. https://publications.iom.int/system/files/pdf/making-the-case-to-integrate-human-mobility.pdf

ITU. 2017. Measuring the Information Society Report 2017 Volume 1, ITU, Genève.

Jacobsson, J. 2015. 'GATS Mode 4 and Labour Mobility: The Significance of Employment Market Access', in M. Panizzon, G. Zürcher, E. Fornalé (eds.), *The Palgrave Handbook of International Labour Migration*. London: Palgrave Macmillan.

Jansen, M. and R. Piermartini 2004. 'The Impact of Mode 4 on Trade in Goods and Services', WTO Staff Working Paper 7/2004, World Trade Organization: Geneva.

Khachaturian, F. and S. Oliver 2021. The Role of 'Mode Switching' in Services Trade Tamar Khachaturian and Sarah Oliver Office of Industries U.S. International Trade Commission (USITC) February 2021, USITC Working Paper, ID-071.

Kimura, F., Sh. Thangavelu and D. Narioko 2022. 'Regional Comprehensive Economic Partnership (RCEP): Implications, Challenges, and Future Growth of East Asia and ASEAN'. (Economic Research Institute for ASEAN and East Asia (ERIA) and Ministry of Commerce of Cambodia), www.eria.org/uploads/media/Books/2022-RCEP-Book1/RCEP-Implications-Challenges-Future-Growth.pdf

Lavenex, S. and F. Jurje 2021. 'Opening-up Labor Mobility? Rising Powers' Rulemaking in Trade Agreements', *Regulation and Governance* 15: 598–615.

Lavenex, S., P. Lutz and P. Hoffmeyer-Zlotnik 2024. 'Migration Governance through Trade Agreements: Insights from the MITA Dataset', *Review in International Organisation* 19: 147–173, https://doi.org/10.1007/s11558-023-09493-5

Losada, R. 2023. *Die Internationale Zusammenarbeit im Migrationsrecht der Schweiz*. Bern: Stämpfli Verlag, 308.

Marchetti J. A. and H. Lim 2007. Services liberalization in the new generation of preferential trade agreements (PTAs): How much further than the GATS? *World Trade Review* 6(2): 155–192.

Marchetti, J. A. and M. Roy 2014. 'The TISA Initiative: An Overview of Market Access Issues', *Journal of World Trade* 48(4): 683–728.

Naiki, Y. 2015. 'Labour Migration under the Japan–Philippines and Japan–Indonesia Economic Partnership Agreements', in M. Panizzon, G. Zürcher, E. Fornalé (eds.), *The Palgrave Handbook of International Labour Migration*. London: Palgrave Macmillan.

Natanael, Y. and K. Verico 2019. 'The Impact Analysis of ASEAN Movement of Natural Persons in ASEAN-5 Countries Skilled Workers Mobility to Indonesia', *International Journal of Economic Policy in Emerging Economies* 12(6): 523–541.

Odasso, L. and E. Fornalè 2022. 'The "inconfinables" or the Creation of Superfluous Life in Time of Crisis', *Migration Letters* 19(6): 739–749.

OECD 2019. 'International Migration Outlook'. Available at www.oecd-ilibrary.org/sites/c13aecc1-en/index.html?itemId = /content/component/c13aecc1-en.

2020. 'The OECD Services Trade Restrictiveness Index: Policy Trends up to 2020', www.oecd.org/trade/topics/services-trade/documents/oecd-stri-policy-trends-up-to-2020.pdf.

2022a. 'International Migration Outlook'. Available at www.oecd-ilibrary.org/sites/30fe16d2-en/1/2/2/index.html?itemId = /content/publication/30fe16d2-en&_csp_ = 97175d429ae5e4e04cd3cccbbfc84945&itemIGO = oecd&itemContentType = book.

2022b. 'Should OECD Countries Develop New Digital Nomad Visas?' *Migration Policy Debates* No. 27.

Ohno, S. 2012. 'Southeast Asian Nurses and Caregiving Workers Transcending the National Boundaries: An Overview of Indonesian and Filipino Workers in Japan and Abroad', *Southeast Asian Studies* 49(4): 541–569.

Panizzon, M. 2010. 'Trade and Labor Migration GATS Mode 4 and Migration Agreements', Friedrich-Ebert-Stiftung, Occasional Dialogue on Globalization N° 47/January 2010.

2022. 'Adjudicating Labor Mobility under France's Agreements on the Joint Management of Migration Flows: How Courts Politicize Bilateral Migration Diplomacy', *Theoretical Inquiries in Law* 23(2): 326–373.

Panizzon, M. and M. van Riemsdijk 2019. 'Introduction to Special Issue: "Migration Governance in an Era of Large Movements: A Multi-Level Approach', *Journal of Ethnic and Migration Studies* 45(8): 1225–1241. Available at https://doi.org/10.1080/1369183X.2018.1441600

Pauwelyn, J., T. Nguyen and K. Kamal 2020. 'Visa and Asylum', in M. Ruta, N. Rocha, A. Mattoo (eds.), *Handbook of Deep Trade Agreements.* Washington, DC: The World Bank.

Portes, A. and S. Shafer 2007. 'Revisiting the Enclave Hypothesis: Miami Twenty-Five Years later. The Sociology of Entrepreneurship', *Research in the Sociology of Organizations* 25: 175–190.

Raess, D. and D. Sari 2020. 'Labour Market Regulations', in A. Mattoo et al. (eds.), *Handbook of Deep Trade Agreements.* The World Bank. Available at https://elibrary.worldbank.org/doi/pdf/10.1596/978-1-4648-1539-3_ch19.

Riccardi, L. and G. Riccardi 2020. 'ASEAN Agreement on the Movement of Natural Persons', in: Invest in ASEAN. Springer, Singapore, https://doi.org/10.1007/978-981-15-5378-3_13

Roy, M., J. Marchetti and H. Lim 2007. 'Services Liberalization in the New Generation of Preferential Trade Agreements (PTAs): How Much Further Than the GATS?' *World Trade Review* 6(2): 155–192.

Ryan, B. 2013. 'In Defence of the Migrant Workers Convention: Standard-Setting for Contemporary Migration', in S. S. Juss (ed.), *The Ashgate Research Companion to Migration Law, Theory and Policy.* London: Routledge, pp. 491–515

Sauvé, P. 2004. 'Trade, Education and the GATS: What's In, What's Out, What's All The Fuss About?' *Higher Education Management and Policy* 14(3): 47–76.

2014. 'Towards a Plurilateral Trade in Services Agreement (TISA): Challenges and Prospects', *Journal of International Commerce, Economics and Policy* 15(1): 1440006-1 to 1440006-16 (it's an electronic journal), www.wti.org/media/filer_public/ec/20/ec20a4d2-1a02-4461-b7e1-1224798dfe10/s1793993314400067.pdf.

Sauvé, P. and N. Ward 2009. 'The EC-Cariforum Economic Partnership Agreement: Assessing the Outcome on Services and Investment', European Centre for International Political Economy, Brussels.

Schmieg, E. 2019. 'Connections between Trade Policy and Migration, a Sphere of Action for the EU', SWP Research Paper 2019/RP 15.

Schott, J., M. Lee and J. Muir 2012. 'Prospects for Services Trade Negotiations, Peterson Institute for International Economics', Working Paper No. 12–17.

Shingal, A. 2022. 'Mode 4 Restrictiveness and Services Trade', *Review of World Economics* 159: 757–786.

Soares, S., F. Bonnet, J. Berg and R. Labouriau 2021. 'From Potential to Practice: Preliminary Findings on the Numbers of Workers Working from Home during the COVID-19 Pandemic', ILO policy brief, Geneva: ILO.

South Centre 2007. Why Inclusion of Services in the EPAS is Problematic: Legal and Development Implications. South Center, Policy Brief no. 10, 2007, www.southcentre.int/policy-brief-10-august-2007/

Stephenson, S. 2015. 'Overview of the TISA Negotiations Training Workshop on Trade in Services Negotiations for AU-CFTA Negotiators', 24–28 August 2015, Nairobi, Kenya. Available at https://unctad.org/system/files/non-official-document/ditc-ted-Nairobi-24082015-USAID-stephenson-2.pdf.

Takahashi, Kazu 2018. 'Japan's Immigration Policy and the EPA between the Philippines and Japan, Yamagata University Faculty of Humanities and Social', *Sciences Annual Research Report* 15: 161–170.

UN, Report of the UN Secretary-General 2021. 'The Global Compact for Safe, Regular and Orderly Migration', 21 February 2021, UN Document A/76/642.

UNCTAD 2007. Challenging Conventional Wisdom: Development Implications of Trade in Services Liberalization', Luis Abugattas Majluf and Simonetta Zarrilli UNCTAD/DITC/TAB/POV/2006/1.

2016. 'The LDC Services Waiver – Operationalized? A First Look at Preferences Granted, Constraints Persisting, and Early Conclusions to be Drawn'. Available at https://unctad.org/system/files/official-document/ditc-05072016-LDCWaiver-AssessmentPaper.pdf.
WTO, Presence of Natural Persons (Mode 4) 2009. 'Background Note by the Secretariat', WTO Document S/C/W/301, 15 September 2009.
WTO and OECD 2017. 'Aid for Trade at a Glance 2017: Promoting Trade, Inclusiveness and Connectivity for Sustainable Development', WTO. Available at www.wto.org/english/res_e/booksp_e/aid4trade17_fore_e.pdf
WTO and World Bank 2020. 'Women and Trade: The Role of Trade in Promoting Gender Equality', W.TO Report.
Zanker, F. and A. Bisong 2022. 'Free Movement in West Africa: the Culture of Mobility still Matters despite Challenges', in The Conversation (24 August 2022), https://theconversation.com/free-movement-in-west-africa-the-culture-of-mobility-still-matters-despite-challenges-188607
Zhang, R. and C. Sasanabanchakul 2022. 'Means of Liberalization and beyond: Understanding Scheduling Approaches in Services Trade Agreements', WTO Staff Working Paper ERSD-2022-13.

13

The Trade and Labour Nexus

Envisioning the Design and Implementation of Future Labour Chapters in Preferential Trade Agreements

Gregory Felder, Kirthana Ganeson, Martin Jehli, and Patrick Wagner

13.1 INTRODUCTION

Since the 1990s, preferential trade agreements (PTAs) have proliferated, increasing international market access and reducing trade barriers. Stasis at the World Trade Organisation (WTO) following the collapse of the Doha Development Round in 2001 has only amplified this trend, contributing to a marked shift away from multilateralism towards regionalism. Preferential trade agreements are now a principal supranational forum through which countries engage in trade and, in recent years, have evolved to include a wide range of non-traditional trade issues.

This chapter focuses on labour provisions in PTAs. Trade and labour have an inherent tension due to the mixed effects that trade can potentially have on the domestic labour market. On the one hand, exports can create new job opportunities, increase wages, and improve working conditions. On the other hand, import competition can lead to job losses in competing industries and put downward pressure on wages and working conditions, particularly for low-skilled workers. Additionally, globalisation and increased competition from foreign workers can lead to a race to the bottom in terms of labour standards, as companies look to cut costs and increase profits. Ultimately, the impact of trade on labour depends on several factors, including the specific sectors and countries involved, labour market flexibility, the state of the global economy, and the presence or absence of strong and enforced domestic labour regulations. Given these complex dynamics, investigating the impact of trade agreements on labour standards and the optimal formulation of labour provisions in order to improve the status quo are important areas of enquiry that warrant attention.

This chapter is structured as follows. The first section starts with a general mapping of trends in labour provisions in PTAs on two levels: internationally and regionally. On the international level, it examines the role of international organisations such as the General Agreement on Tariffs and Trade (GATT), WTO, and, in particular, the International Labour Organization (ILO), in relation to labour provisions in PTAs. On the regional level, we examine how different regions approach the issue of trade and labour in their design of PTAs and how they differ in significant ways. After taking stock of the current state of play, the second section evaluates the successes or failures of past practices, focusing on four main points: i) enforcement mechanisms of labour provisions in PTAs, ii) a textual interpretation issue concerning the phrase 'manner affecting trade', iii) the possibility of the expansion of labour rights in PTAs to accommodate future trends in labour, and iv) the different approaches between developed and developing countries in their inclusion of labour provisions in PTAs. The chapter then concludes with recommendations for labour provisions in future PTAs, in both formulation and compliance.

13.2 CURRENT STATE OF PLAY

Advocates of free trade often claim that it allows individuals and workers to benefit from a system that offers a greater choice of goods for cheaper prices. This stems from the principle of comparative advantage famously posited by David Ricardo, where maximum efficiency can be obtained when countries of differing factor abundance use their comparative advantage to trade goods that utilise their abundant factors (Ricardo 1817). Since economies will be open to more competition, this creates a plethora of other benefits, such as a dynamic business climate, increased investments, knowledge transfer from foreign companies, and job creation. Indeed, several studies have shown that trade does in fact encourage economic growth (e.g. Edwards 1993; Krueger 1998; Frankel and Romer 1999). Regarding PTAs in particular, Baier et al. (2014) note that PTAs can have a positive effect on increasing trade flows between member countries but note that the overall impact on trade and economic growth varies depending on size, distance, and level of development of the countries involved.

However, recent research also points to the increasing costs of trade. Inequality within countries has been found to increase with the expansion of trade (Ghose 2001; Helpman 2016; Pavcnik 2017), and unsatisfactory labour conditions in developing countries have been linked to trade liberalisation via the well-known concept of the 'race to the bottom' enabled by international trade and foreign investment (Davies and Vadlamanatti 2013; Anner 2018; Wang 2018).

Given that trade is an issue that transcends borders and involves power asymmetries among private and public actors between trading partners, the debate concerning whether trade is ultimately beneficial or harmful raises interesting questions that must be addressed when considering future labour provisions. Which (if any) international institutions are the proper forum to protect labour rights and ensure a more equitable global economy? Should PTAs include labour provisions, or should those remain strictly under the purview of the ILO? Are labour provisions in PTAs consistent with other international rules? Additionally, what has worked and what has not worked in labour chapter templates and what are the potential avenues for improvement or expansion of labour provisions in PTAs?

13.2.1 *Developments on the International Level (GATT, WTO, and ILO) and Their Relationship with Labour Provisions in PTAs*

Preferential trade agreements are not the only treaties dealing with labour issues. The most prominent international organisations with an interest in labour issues are the WTO and the ILO. This section outlines the role of these two organisations and highlights the ways in which they are compatible in advancing workers' rights in trade.

The United States (US) and the former European Economic Community/ European Community sought to include labour standards in both the GATT and the WTO agreements. In 1953, for instance, the US State Department proposed an 'unfair labour clause' to the GATT, but the member countries could not reach a consensus on its definition (Cottier and Caplazi 1998). In 1994, the European Parliament proposed to broaden Article XX(e) of the GATT by including child labour as well as the infringement of the principle of freedom of association and collective bargaining (FACB) (Waer 1996).

However, these attempts failed mainly due to the opposition of India and other developing countries, who opposed the inclusion of labour clauses at the WTO on the grounds that they represent 'protectionism in its new garb' (Kolben 2006: 237; see also Hepple 2005: 130; Bhagwati 1995; Staiger 2003; McCrudden and Davies 2000). India's government, business interests, and even labour and civil society organisations actively worked against including or expanding labour clauses, organising opposition among developing nations. Moreover, scholars have criticised the inclusion of non-trade issues (NTIs) at the WTO and in PTAs (and the agreements themselves, generally) as tools of neocolonialism and a means for enforcing foreign, Western norms on other parties to the agreements (Bhala 2007; Villalta Puig and Ohiocheoya 2011).

At the 1996 Singapore Ministerial Conference, WTO Members formally conferred on the ILO authority over labour standards in its Declaration: 'We renew our commitment to the observance of internationally recognized core labour standards. The International Labour Organization (ILO) is the competent body to set and deal with these standards, and we affirm our support for its work in promoting them … We reject the use of labour standards for protectionist purposes, and agree that the comparative advantage of countries, particularly low-wage developing countries, must in no way be put into question…'. (WTO 1996).

Again in 1999, leading up to the third WTO Ministerial Conference in Seattle, both the US and the European Communities proposed a joint ILO/WTO working forum (WTO 1999a, 1999b). This forum would serve as a formal mechanism within the WTO to foster dialogue and research on labour issues and strengthen the ILO by granting it observer status at the WTO.

However, despite the proposed forum, labour unions and antiglobalisation protesters expressed concerns about the negative impacts of globalisation on workers' rights, the environment, and human rights. The widespread protests were a turning point in the global debate on trade and globalisation and brought attention to growing public opposition to unfettered free trade, to the degree that the protests surrounding this conference were dubbed the 'Battle in Seattle'. Since then, there has been little sustained effort to bring labour issues into the WTO agenda.

The ILO figures prominently in the relationship between trade and labour given that its internationally recognised labour standards are often integrated into trade agreements. Most labour provisions in PTAs refer to the 1998 ILO Declaration on Fundamental Principles and Rights at Work and its follow-up, the '1998 ILO Declaration', or the eight fundamental conventions and the ILO Decent Work Agenda (Velut et al. 2022: 84). The 1998 ILO Declaration contains four fundamental principles regarding labour (ILO 1998):

1. Freedom of association and the effective recognition of the right to collective bargaining.
2. The elimination of all forms of forced or compulsory labour.
3. The effective abolition of child labour.
4. The elimination of discrimination in respect of employment and occupation.

There are various manners in which ILO commitments are referenced in PTAs. Sometimes, parties only reaffirm their ILO-related obligations entailing no further legal obligations or choose to incorporate ILO commitments directly into PTAs, either through 'best endeavours' clauses or by directly requiring parties to implement those standards in their domestic legislation (Agustí-Panareda et al. 2014). In principle, it is possible that a country binds itself by incorporating ILO conventions that it has not yet ratified into a PTA, and thus expands its obligations through the signing of the PTA. However, this has not happened so far, as countries have only included ILO treaties which they previously ratified.

While PTA labour provisions usually mirror the ILO-related obligations of a country, some PTAs require the parties to 'make continued and sustained efforts towards ratifying and effectively implementing the fundamental ILO conventions'. Through this approach, countries with higher ambition on labour standards use PTAs to put additional pressure on a partner country to ratify the ILO conventions. This is especially common in North–South agreements. Moreover, as the ILO does not have a legally binding enforcement mechanism for non-compliance through their conventions, dispute settlement mechanisms in PTAs can help to close that gap. Allowing a party to take trade sanctions to offset the violation of a treaty provision has potential to be a stringent and efficient way to enforce ILO commitments (Melo Araujo 2018).

On the implementation front, the role of ILO is less pronounced (Peels and Fino 2015: 197). While the ILO is not so present as an actor in the domestic space, many agreements still specify ILO assistance in technical cooperation activities, monitoring, and capacity building (Agustí-Panareda et al. 2014: 20). For example, in the European Union (EU)–Caribbean Forum (CARIFORUM) and EU–Canada Comprehensive Economic and Trade Agreement (CETA) , the ILO is named in a provision on advice for best practices and the use of effective policy tools in addressing labour rights challenges. In the US–Colombia agreement, the ILO is explicitly stated as a supporting pillar for national contact points in capacity-building work. The ILO is also involved in a consultative capacity for disputes in some instances. In the case of EU–Singapore, the PTA specifies that 'parties may seek the views of [the ILO] in order to fully examine the matter' in the case of labour disputes.

In addition to the link through the ILO or PTAs, labour standards and trade are connected via the Generalised System of Preferences (GSP). Based on what is commonly referred to as the enabling clause under WTO law, WTO Members can deviate from the 'most-favoured-nation' principle and accord more favourable treatment to developing countries. The US and the EU made use of this mechanism by establishing their respective domestic GSPs, where benefits such as preferential tariff treatment can be granted if a developing country meets certain criteria. However, preferences under GSP programmes may be suspended in case of violations of ILO core labour standards (Siroën 2013). Thus, these schemes provide for the unilateral trade suspension of benefits against developing countries that are independent from the suspension of concessions that may be used based on a PTA.

13.2.2 *Variation of Labour Provisions PTAs by Region*

As of 2022, 113 out of 354 PTAs included labour provisions, half of which were ratified over the last decade (ILO 2022). Although labour provisions tend to be concentrated in North–South trade agreements, there is an increasing trend to integrate labour provisions into trade agreements among developing countries, or South–South trade agreements.

Figure 13.1 depicts the cumulative number of trade agreements that include labour provisions. We observe a very strong trend in the early 2000s of including labour provisions in North–South trade agreements. This indicates that countries in the North possibly use PTAs as a conditionality tool to grant market access in return for improvements in domestic labour standards within Southern counterparties. Interestingly, we find a smaller trend among South–South and North–North partner countries, which indicates that these governments may attach lesser importance to including provisions among partners with similar labour standards.

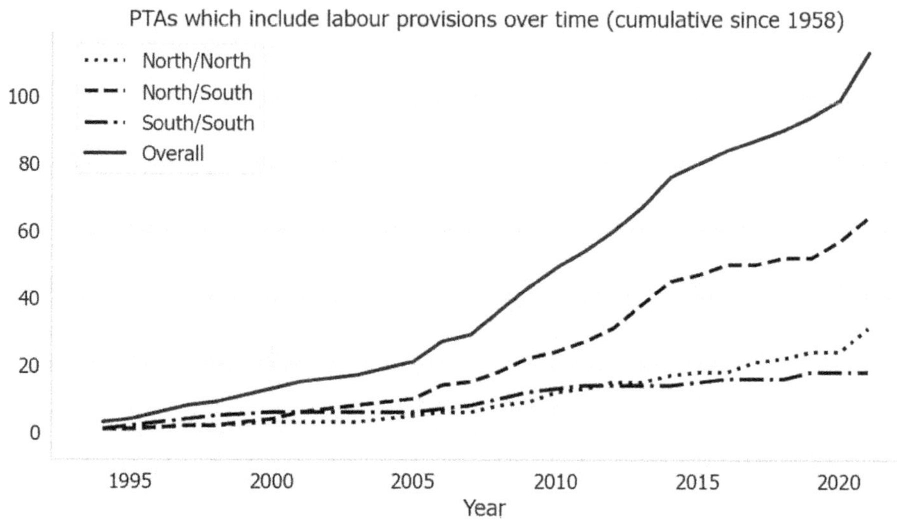

FIGURE 13.1 Labour provisions over time.
Source: Data taken from the ILO LP Hub (ILO 2022). Own classification and depiction

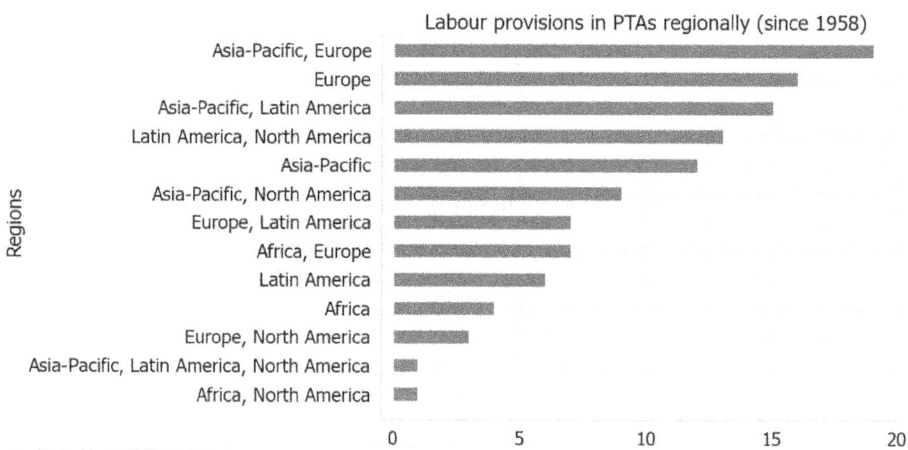

FIGURE 13.2 Labour provisions by region.
Source: Data taken from the ILO LP Hub (ILO 2022). Own classification and depiction

A similar picture is shown when we look at the variation of labour provisions in PTAs through a regional lens. Figure 13.2 depicts the number of PTAs with labour provisions by region. Most agreements of this sort have been concluded extra-regionally between European states and countries in the Asia-Pacific region. Sixteen agreements of this sort have been concluded within Europe, and another dozen within Asia-Pacific countries. To date, approximately ten agreements have been concluded that contain labour provisions in African countries.

As Figure 13.2 illustrates, labour provisions are especially present in North–South agreements since the labour standards of members of North–North and South–South treaties are often homogeneous. Due to the different levels of ambition, there exists variation in the scope, enforcement mechanisms, and compliance.

We categorise these various approaches into two broad schools of thought – enforcement or managerial (Tallberg 2002). The enforcement school is rooted in the political economy theory of collective action and assumes that states are rational actors. It emphasises that labour laws must be strictly enforced through penalties, fines, and other legal sanctions to ensure that states and companies comply with the law. This approach is based on the idea that some actors may not comply with the law unless there is a strong deterrent in place.

The managerial school, on the other hand, emphasises that actors, both states and companies, should be encouraged to voluntarily comply with labour laws and regulations through cooperation, mutual capacity building, and technical assistance. This approach relies on the idea that companies inherently want to comply with the law, but may need help understanding their obligations, especially if the language leaves room to be interpreted broadly.

Most parties adopt a mixed approach, which is a combination of both the enforcement and managerial. In this section, we take account of the different approaches taken by countries over time.

Since its first venture of including labour in its PTAs, the US has always adopted an enforcement approach in its PTA design. The US often requires its negotiating partners to make changes to domestic labour laws prior to the agreement's entry into force.

A side agreement to the North American Free Trade Agreement (NAFTA), which entered into force in 1994, was the first time the US introduced binding labour provisions in connection with a trade agreement. The North American Agreement on Labour Cooperation (NAALC) contained clear obligations imposed on the contracting parties, such as an obligation to provide for high standards with reference to eleven labour principles, as well as obligations concerning the enforcement of domestic labour laws (Article 2 and Annex 1, NAALC). The agreement established domestic institutions called the National Administrative Offices (NAOs) to take on the role of acting as contact points between partners for information exchange and to oversee implementation.

The NAFTA also included a general dispute settlement mechanism that could be applied to labour issues. In the case of a labour law abuse, a committee of independent experts is convened if the issue is not resolved after rounds of consultations. A persistent pattern of failure to enforce the labour provisions, namely child labour, lack of minimum wage standards, and occupational safety and health risks could lead to the issue being escalated to an arbitral panel (Arestoff-Izzo et al. 2008). In the event the panel ruled against a country, the penalties could include a monetary assessment and temporary suspension of trade benefits outlined in the main text.

In these ways, the US' strong enforcement approach was a way to signal to partners the importance it ascribes to high labour standards and fair competition.

Following the NAFTA, the US signed an agreement with Cambodia in 1999 (US–Cambodia Textile and Apparel Trade Agreement [UCTA]) that limited labour standard provisions to the textile industry and conditioned market access on Cambodia demonstrating compliance with specific labour standards (Wells 2007). In 2001, the US–Jordan PTA's labour clause reflected a commitment by both parties to not waiving or derogating from their labour laws in their pursuit of encouraging trade, as well as effective enforcement of domestic labour laws. Subsequent agreements led by the US also followed suit, such as bilateral PTAs with Chile, Morocco, Australia, Singapore, Bahrain, Oman, and Peru as well as multilateral agreements, most notably the Central American Free Trade Agreement (CAFTA).

Given that the US was the first mover on high-ambition labour provisions, the language in US labour chapters has spilled over into other agreements as well. The labour obligations in the Trans-Pacific Partnership (TPP) form part of the Canada–EU CETA concluded in 2016. They also appear in the recently concluded EU–Viet Nam Free Trade Agreement, in the sustainable development chapter (Claussen 2021).

Similar language can also be found in certain agreements signed by Asian countries. However, the main difference is that none of these agreements has a sanction mechanism in case of non-compliance. Hence, they embody the managerial approach as opposed to the enforcement tactic. Latin American countries do not include labour provisions in their PTAs – both Mercosur and the Pacific Alliance do not include any labour references in their PTAs.

The US has strengthened its approach towards enforcement of labour provisions in recent times. In 2020, the US along with Mexico and Canada reached a consensus on the United States–Mexico–Canada Agreement (USMCA), which is considered to be a modernised, high-standard reinvention of the now-defunct NAFTA. The revision was due to growing criticisms that the NAFTA no longer addressed the present-day issues, and the USMCA was designed to account for changes in the global economy and to address issues such as intellectual property protection, digital trade, labour rights, and environmental standards. Interest groups also raised concerns that the NAALC provided insufficient means for the parties to enforce its obligations, leading to concerns regarding a 'race to the bottom' regarding working conditions and standards.

The USMCA was designed with a prominent emphasis on labour standards, and those standards are found directly in the main text as opposed to being delineated in a side agreement. Moreover, the USMCA also includes novel mechanisms to enforce labour standards. The key achievements of the USMCA include commitments by Mexico to change domestic law to provide effective recognition of the right to collective bargaining, new provisions prohibiting imports of goods produced by forced labour, addressing violence against workers, and protection of migrant workers. The agreement also includes new trade rules of origin to push for higher wages by requiring that 40–45 per cent of auto content be made by workers earning at least USD 16 per hour. Finally, and possibly most notable, is the novel dispute settlement mechanism called the Rapid Response Mechanism (RRM) that ensures expedited enforcement of labour rights to ensure effective implementation (USTR 2016). The RRM will be expanded upon in a later part of this chapter.

Even though it relied almost entirely on legally non-enforceable labour provisions, Europe was also a pioneer with its inclusion of labour provisions in PTAs in the 1990s (Raess et al. 2018). With the expansion of the EU over time and trade linkages being formed outside of the region, many scholars have characterised the bloc's approach to labour provisions as advancing a 'values-based trade agenda'.

Manners (2002) conceptualised the EU as a normative power that works mainly through ideas and values using trade relations and instruments such as PTAs as a viable channel rather than military force. Normative power is not typically exerted with force, but instead through deliberation. The underlying rationale of this 'norm-diffusion' stems from a more social and human rights perspective, in which labour provisions can be used to improve labour conditions in countries that otherwise would lack the political will or implementing capacity. Hence, labour provisions are viewed as a means of ensuring respect for labour-related human rights that reflect values universally accepted by the international community (European Commission 2018). Labour rights in signatory countries to EU PTAs are impacted ex post rather than ex ante, which differs from the US. The EU also does not include sanctions as a remedy for failure to enforce labour standards. Hence, the EU approach has been characterised as more consultative and managerial.

However, this approach has led to criticism that the EU policy on labour in trade is not assertive enough (Nissen 2022). Coincidentally, in the wake of these criticisms, the EU has undergone institutional changes in its decision-making process. With the enactment of the Treaty of Lisbon, elected members in the EU Parliament (EP) now have an enhanced role in trade policy, and they advocate for heightened focus towards having obligations for investors and partners, such as adhering to environmental and labour standards to maintain public support for trade (Orbie et al. 2016).

Following this shift, EU PTAs since 2015 have included more comprehensive labour provisions within a broader sustainable development chapter that is made legally binding using the dispute settlement mechanism. It also confers a pronounced role for civil society in the monitoring process (Orbie et al. 2016), by establishing Domestic Advisory Groups (DAGs) and Civil Society Dialogues. In 2022, the European Commission released a communication after its annual trade policy review that proposes new legal instruments that will inter alia include trade sanctions for material breaches of trade and sustainable development (TSD) provisions in PTAs (European Commission 2022).

One would be hard-pressed to categorically assert which of these two approaches – enforcement or managerial – is better. Consulting the literature, Hafner-Burton

(2005) argues that PTAs with hard human rights standards can rely on coercion (instead of reputational effects) to influence their treaty members towards establishing and adhering to high human rights standards. On the other hand, Spilker and Böhmelt (2013) counter this by illustrating that countries sign PTAs with hard human rights standards only if they are certain they can comply. As such, there might exist an inherent selection bias in which only countries with a good human rights record would be willing to add a hard human rights clause, and so paradoxically, the inclusion of hard human rights standards would primarily occur in those cases in which they are hardly necessary.

The Comprehensive and Progressive Agreement for a Trans-Pacific Partnership (CPTPP) is one good example of the enforcement approach and has been lauded as a significant improvement to the approach to labour rights in PTAs. The TPP labour chapter had specific and well-defined labour rights in the main text and side agreements, cooperative labour dialogue, and the participation of the public and any interested or involved groups, including organised labour and business. However, it also had notable shortcomings outlined by politicians (e.g. Warren 2016), trade unions (e.g. LAC 2015), and international non-governmental organisations (INGOs) (e.g. ITUC 2015). In future PTAs, providing relevant civil society groups (NGOs, INGOs, labour unions) with a larger role in negotiations could help prevent such shortcomings while also improving the acceptability of labour provisions in the agreements. A potential model of how to define what constitutes acceptable (and improved) labour rights above former PTAs is to begin with the rights outlined in the ILO's core conventions as a minimum and build country-specific rights obligations up from there.

However, as with the inclusion of labour clauses at the WTO, countries have vocally opposed the inclusion of labour provisions in PTAs. Developing countries are most likely to oppose the inclusion of labour rights in PTAs on the grounds that they are 1) disguised protectionism, 2) that they would penalise countries for their stage-of-development, or 3) that they represent the imposition of Western norms on unwilling parties, representing neocolonial attitudes. At its core, these countries fear loss of their comparative advantage in labour-intensive industries and argue that improvements in labour rights will follow from economic growth and development. And yet, other voices from the developing world, like Sujata Gothoskar of the Workers Solidarity Centre, argue that such a view means that 'every struggle by the workers for a better life may be argued as eroding the competitive advantage of [their] country' (cited in Hensman 2000 and Fields 2003). Export-related economic growth is often associated with increasing inequality, growing informality, and structural barriers that can impede widespread improvements in labour standards (Paz 2014; Das et al. 2017). Labour provisions in trade agreements arguably can help rectify market failures, and adhering to core labour standards promotes a framework for inclusive growth (Martin and Maskus 2001; ILO 2016). Balancing the protection of workers' rights within global value chains (GVCs) and export-oriented sectors with developing countries' desire to pursue economic growth and their own developmental path requires including local, national, and international actors in the negotiation and enforcement of labour provisions in PTAs.

The mixed results of labour conditionalities in PTAs have also fuelled the debate further. In a study comparing the effects of human rights agreements (HRA) and PTAs, Hafner-Burton (2005) found that when benefits of trade are conditional to human rights standards through legally binding and enforceable provisions, change in behaviour is more apparent. On the flip side, PTAs that use 'soft' standards that are only vaguely tied to market access reflect no difference in the actions of parties with regard to increasing human rights standards. On labour clauses specifically, Carrère et al. (2022) found that including such clauses in PTAs has on average no impact on bilateral trade flows. However, in North–South agreements, the impact of labour clauses is higher when there is more cooperation among parties. Carrère et al also found that strong enforcement mechanisms only reflect marginal improvements on compliance. Nonetheless, with the rise of PTAs, countries that prioritise countries that prioritise extensive labour rights have engaged on a bilateral basis to push for the inclusion of labour provisions in trade agreements.

In examining these patterns in past PTAs empirically, we can evaluate the instances where some approaches worked better than others. First, the coverage and level of ambition with regard to labour rights in PTAs exhibit a lack of consistency. Second, low legalisation – in the precision, obligations, and enforcement – of labour provisions presents as a problem in adhering to these standards in actualisation. As such, future PTAs should move towards more effective legalisation of labour provisions. Finally, on the enforcement of these labour provisions, the numbers are – at first glance – very disappointing: up until 2020, only two cases had been solved under the dispute settlement mechanisms of these PTAs, which implies that the impact of having labour provisions enforced under PTA dispute settlement is limited. Bearing in mind that enforcement does not exclusively include the formal settlement of disputes, the enforcement of labour conditions could improve if dispute settlement procedures were more accessible, and potentially more inclusive towards civil society groups and labour organisations. In fact, some provisions could have been enforced on a political level by these actors.

The lack of a stringent enforcement mechanism at the ILO was one of the main motives for including labour provisions in PTAs. Thus, PTAs and dispute settlement mechanisms might be an avenue to ensure labour provisions can be properly enforced.

13.3 FUTURE TRENDS AND RECOMMENDATIONS

Having mapped past practices and institutional interaction, the next section puts forward key recommendations on the design, enforcement, and compliance mechanisms of labour provisions in future PTAs.

13.3.1 *Expansion of Labour Rights*

Labour rights are often divided into two categories: collective and individual (sometimes called substantial) rights. The former refers to FACB rights, that is, the right of workers to act collectively and negotiate as a collective in their own best interest. The latter category of rights is less well-defined but overlaps to a large degree with the components of the ILO and UN's concept of decent work, that is, formal work contracts, humane work hours, adequate earnings, occupational safety and health, non-remuneration benefits, and social security (ILO 2009). While unions may be viewed as a threat in developing countries for political (regime stability) and economic reasons (disruption of production and higher negotiated wages, etc.), allowing workers the right to organise does not imply higher labour costs, per se. Employers in developing countries can (and often do) refuse to negotiate in good faith with workers' legitimate representatives and will even find ways to circumvent laws pertaining to FACB rights by, for example, installing 'yellow' or employer-friendly unions. Collective labour rights, therefore, represent a relatively inexpensive way of signalling labour upgrading to (potential or current) trading partners without losing price advantage as an exporter (Wang 2020; Messerschmidt and Janz 2023). Individual rights, on the other hand, can be very costly to implement. Upgrading workplace safety, reducing excessive hours or paying overtime, providing non-wage benefits, providing formal employment contracts, and paying into pension schemes all are associated with higher labour and therefore production costs which is perceived as a loss in competitiveness in export markets, especially for countries whose comparative advantage is in low-skill production.

For these reasons, labour provisions in trade agreements have primarily focused on enforcement of domestic laws (Raess and Sari 2018). Doing so avoids the projection of exogenous standards (i.e. from the Global North) on developing (or otherwise low-standard) countries and pre-empts opposition based on claims that trade-related labour provisions are little more than disguised protectionism. However, while substantive commitments to enforcing domestic laws are widespread, they are largely ineffective in improving the working conditions on the ground. Partner countries are unlikely to trigger dispute settlement regarding violations, and enforcement within a violating country is more likely to occur as a means of signalling suitability as a potential future partner in PTAs, rather than to stop abuses (Kolben 2013; Van Roozendaal 2015; Vogt 2015).

When labour provisions do mention protection of specific rights, they tend to focus on two things, both derived from the ILO 1998 Declaration: FACB rights and prohibitions on the worst forms of labour abuses, namely, child and forced (i.e. slave) labour. After this, several individual rights are specifically referenced in a steadily declining percentage of agreements as substantive commitments. Elimination of discrimination and equal remuneration are included in ~40% of PTAs, followed by health and safety (~30%), working conditions and wages (in ~20%), and decent work and working time, which can be found in only about 15% of agreements. Freedom of association and collective bargaining labour rights are frequently included in trade agreements because they are considered the cheapest option (i.e. they do not incur increased labour costs), second only to references to upholding domestic laws, and because proponents of their inclusion argue that FACB rights can lead to improvements in working conditions and individual labour rights. However, while signatory countries often improve their collective labour laws, they do little to improve de facto enforcement, leading to no improvement or sometimes even worsening conditions (Raess et al. 2018).

Expanding the types of labour rights in PTAs has the potential to lead to improvements in on-the-ground conditions that have remained elusive thus far, particularly when paired with the other advancements that we recommend. Inhumane working hours, unsafe working conditions, and informal employment are endemic in developing countries and in global supply chains, in particular (Beliner et al. 2015). So far, state-centred approaches in labour provisions have proven ineffective in alleviating these violations (Vogt 2015; Brown 2016). In tandem with targeted sanctions and empowerment of local civil society, more clearly defined and expanded labour rights would make improved working conditions a more attainable and enforceable goal (Brown 2016). We can also envision an expansion of protected rights to those of migrant workers, a group whose relevance continues to grow, as many regions in the world grapple with climate change and conflict-exacerbated migration flows. As an example, the draft TPP, which made many progressive steps regarding protection of labour rights, included 'Labor Consistency Plans' (LCPs) for some potential signatories. One of these was an LCP for Malaysia, which called on the country to stop withholding migrant workers' passports and provide them with formal contracts (Dong 2016). Although the US ultimately withdrew from the TPP and it has since been replaced by the CPTPP, many of the advances made during the negotiations are being held up as an indication of shifting political will among parties as well as examples of what is possible when negotiating far-reaching trade agreements. Of course, defining the acceptable floor for labour rights in such a way as to avoid the perception (or reality) of disguised protectionism or projection of standards from one country to another will require involvement of not only state representatives, but relevant societal actors from each party. By involving labour representatives or other civil society actors, inclusion and enforcement of labour rights in PTAs can avoid sanctioning countries simply due to their stage-of-development (Fields 2003).

13.3.2 *The 'Manner Affecting Trade' Issue*

Another key issue observed in past dispute cases regarding labour rights violation is the 'manner affecting trade' term. According to Article 16.2.1(a) of the Dominican Republic–Central America FTA (CAFTA-DR), 'A Party shall not fail to effectively enforce its labour laws, through a sustained or recurring course of action or inaction, in a manner affecting trade between the parties, after the date of entry into force of this Agreement.' In order to establish a labour violation, two conditions must be met. First, the claimant must prove a persistent pattern of violations of labour laws. Second, this lack of enforcement must have affected trade between the Members of the PTA (Paiement 2018). This term is a key feature from the May 10 template from the US that appears in several agreements (Cimino-Isaacs 2020). To demonstrate the complications brought upon by this term, this section unpacks the dispute between the US and Guatemala over Article 16.2.1(a) of the CAFTA-DR agreement.

The CAFTA-DR includes a state-to-state mechanism that allows for a complaint of labour violations to be brought for dispute under the arbitration mechanisms of the agreement. In 2008, the US government raised a dispute under this mechanism against Guatemala, claiming that they violated commitments to enforce labour laws outlined in the CAFTA-DR PTA. This was after the American Federation of Labour and Congress of Industrial Organizations (AFL-CIO) and six Guatemalan labour unions filed complaints. Formal labour consultations between the two nations failed to yield results, and the United States Trade Representative (USTR) filed for arbitration under the CAFTA-DR dispute resolution chapter in 2011. Nine years after the complaint was submitted, the panel put forth its decision in 2017, finding that the US had not shown that Guatemala breached the agreement in relation to labour rights.

During the proceedings, both countries came forth to explain their interpretation of the language in the agreement. The US submitted that 'in a manner affecting trade' means that a violation 'has a bearing on, influences or changes cross-border economic activity, including influencing conditions of competition within and among the CAFTA-DR Parties'. Conversely, Guatemala submitted that Article 16.2.1(a) requires an 'unambiguous showing that the challenged conduct has an effect on trade between the Parties'.

However, the panel had differing interpretations. The panel interpreted the notion of 'sustained or recurring course of action or inaction' in Article 16.2.1 (a) of CAFTA-DR as either '(i) a repeated behaviour which displays sufficient similarity' or '(ii) prolonged behaviour in which there is sufficient consistency in sustained acts or omissions as to constitute a line of connected behaviour by a labour law enforcement institution, rather than isolated or disconnected instances of action or inaction'. The panel acknowledged that 'in a manner affecting trade between the Parties' only applies if it provides a competitive edge to an employer or employers involved in trade between the parties. They explained further how this can be proven – by first demonstrating that the business is engaged in markets or competes with imports of CAFTA-DR Parties and identifying that a failure to enforce labour obligations is sufficient to cause 'some competitive advantage' on said enterprise.

The panel's interpretation faced significant criticism. They conclusively determined that Guatemala did not uphold its labour laws according to Article 16.2.1(a) of the CAFTA-DR, as evident from violations affecting 74 workers at eight different locations. Though this appeared to be a straightforward win for the US, two key criteria remained: the persistence of the violations and their impact on trade. The panel firmly concluded that even though Guatemala consistently neglected its labour laws, this neglect did not impact trade. Additionally, in the single instance where trade was affected, the violation was neither sustained nor recurring. Essentially, according to the panel, one of the conditions of Article 16.2.1(a) was always unmet, leading them to rule in favour of Guatemala and against the US.

Given that this was the first labour enforcement case brought to dispute settlement under a PTA, the expectations on whether this mechanism can be evoked to protect workers' rights were high. The fact that the panel did not find a breach was met with disappointment from stakeholders, including from the Office of US Trade Representative (USTR 2014). The results raised questions of whether labour chapters act as safeguards for workers in the way they are currently formulated (Claussen 2020).

Hence, the main recommendation of this section regarding 'manner affecting trade' is that this term should be rephrased with unambiguous language, encompassing strong legal obligations and sharper precision (Abbott et al. 2000). We suggest this change on two grounds. First, the term 'manner affecting trade' should be phrased in a clearer way that does not allow for narrow interpretations by arbitration panels that primarily adopt a perspective of trade considerations as opposed to worker's rights, and instead be inclusive to the voices and submissions of civil society. Second, labour rights violations should not only be considered when they are predicated upon whether the violation affects trade. The central goal of including labour provisions should be to protect workers' rights in traded sectors, not to protect workers' rights only if labour law violations distort competition in ways that negatively affect trade. Moreover, the combined conditionality of 'sustained or recurring course of action' sets a high requirement that worker groups and unions might not be able to prove or reach. Overall, these recommendations can prevent possibilities of interpretations that have adverse effects on the welfare of the workers and instead prioritise labour rights-based considerations.

13.3.3 *Enforcement Mechanisms*

A main criticism of labour provisions in PTAs is that even if they are included in the agreement, enforcement is weak. Using the USMCA's enforcement mechanisms as the current gold standard, we make three broad recommendations on how enforcement can be strengthened in future PTAs to fully unlock the potential of these provisions that have been painstakingly negotiated and advocated for.

13.3.3.1 USMCA's Rapid Response Mechanism

When contemplating novel enforcement mechanisms in PTAs for the future, parties ought to look at the USMCA, since its enforcement mechanisms have been praised as a 'significant innovation' (Corvaglia 2021: 664) and as 'forging a path toward a third generation' (Polaski et al. 2022: 149) of enforcement possibilities for labour provisions. While the USMCA will serve as the baseline, we will provide additional ideas and concepts regarding the enforcement of labour provisions in PTAs.

The enforcement regime of the USMCA's labour chapter consists of three main pillars: first, there is the pre-ratification conditionality regarding worker representation in collective bargaining in Mexico (Annex 23-A USMCA). It focuses on domestic provision of collective bargaining rights in Mexico and the establishment of independent entities and courts for the registration of unions and the adjudication of labour disputes. To ensure compliance with these provisions, the entry into force of the entire PTA was made dependent on the implementation of such legislation by Mexico (Annex 23.A (3.) USMCA). The US has regularly made use of its bargaining leverage to push for labour reforms by inserting such preconditions into its PTAs. The second pillar addresses the effectiveness of collective bargaining rights in Mexico after the ratification of the PTA by establishing an innovative adjudicatory mechanism called 'Facility-Specific Rapid Response Labour Mechanism' (hereinafter: 'RRM'). The mechanism applies whenever a party believes that 'workers at a Covered Facility are being denied the right of free association and collective bargaining' (Article 31-A.2 USMCA). Thus, while the parties to these disputes are still the respective countries, it is specific to a particular denial of rights at a specific facility. After an on-site review by the respondent party of whether a denial of rights exists, the complainant party may request the establishment of a panel if an agreement on the matter cannot be reached. The short duration of the procedure is where a first advantage of the RRM lies: it can be expected to last only 120 days from the initial request for a review to the implementation of a remedy (Claussen 2021: 356). In all five occasions in which the RRM has been used so far, an agreement was found after around two months without the need to establish a panel. The second major innovation can be seen in the facility specificity of not only the investigation of the denial of rights, but also the remedies provided by Article 31-A.10 (2.) USMCA. These remedies include the suspension of preferential tariff treatment or the imposition of penalties specifically against the goods from a particular factory found guilty of the denial of rights. Third, in addition to the settlement of disputes concerning the denial of rights via the RRM, the USMCA also features a traditional dispute settlement mechanism under which all labour disputes not concerning the denial of collective bargaining rights are adjudicated (Article 31.2 USMCA).

Clearly, this approach also has a few drawbacks of its own. First, there is the issue of extraterritorial application and enforcement of domestic law, which results in the loss of sovereignty for the contracting party; we address this issue in our recommendation for the dispute settlement mechanism below. Second, it is evident that the further apart working conditions and domestic labour laws are for the two (or more) countries under a PTA, the more difficult it will be to implement such a system: for example, the interpretation of collective labour rights is a concept very specific to Western countries. The implementation of it might work well between the US and Mexico. In a PTA between two countries of the Global South, this might not be as easy. However, we consider the design of the enforcement mechanisms in the USMCA a step in the right direction, especially given that the RRM has been a success, with five cases already having been resolved in the two and a half years since its entry into force. Inspired by this, we suggest that enforcement in future PTAs should focus on the three aspects explained in more detail below.

13.3.3.2 Targeted Sanctions

One of the main innovations of the RRM is the implementation of sanctions targeted at specific worksites. We consider this facility specificity a step in the right direction and a necessity for future PTAs for two different reasons. First, it increases accountability on a company level. Companies that do not comply with labour rights will see their goods being charged additionally and hence sustain a disadvantage with respect to their law-abiding competitors. This should serve as a deterrent against violations. Second, since preferential tariff rates keep being applied on goods from other facilities, trade flows are not hampered the same way they would be if these higher tariff rates were applied to an entire sector or even additional sectors as well. With the negative effect on the most vulnerable stakeholders being the main point of criticism against the traditional sanction mechanisms (Orbie 2021: 200), targeted sanctions would be much more effective. However, there are certain aspects that need to be considered when designing targeted sanctions for future PTAs. First, such enforcement schemes would have to make sure that companies in the territory of all parties face enforcement in case of a denial of rights at their facility. Under the USMCA, limiting the scope of possible action under the RRM concerning facilities in the US (LeClercq 2021) has led to a very one-sided application so far. Second, due process rights for affected companies must be guaranteed. This is not an easy undertaking, since a lot of cases are solved on a political level before the establishment of an independent panel. However, not only panel decisions have to be open for judicial review, but there is also a need to give companies the possibility to challenge the legality of the actions of state actors in the context of their accusations.

13.3.3.3 Private Arbitration

A concept that has already been proposed by other scholars but has faced criticism due to political feasibility concerns (Claussen 2021: 366) is the establishment of mixed arbitration for dispute settlement concerning labour rights issues. The idea would be to have an adjudicative body comparable to an investor–state arbitration tribunal where trade unions, NGOs, or even individuals could make claims regarding the violation of labour rights in the PTA. Such an advancement would be paramount for the enforcement potential of labour chapters, as various scholars have attributed their underperformance to the lack of non-governmental actors involved (Gött 2020: 151; Dombois et al. 2004: 267, Kolben 2017). An independent panel made up of labour experts could review the claim and issue a decision, including its reasoning. With more cases being brought forward by trade unions and NGOs, panels could – taking into consideration the input of the ILO and its experts – develop lines of jurisprudence and thus breathe life into the often rather vaguely phrased labour provisions in PTAs. Admittedly, this would mark a huge shift in the approach taken towards enforcing PTA provisions and countries are wary of giving away even the slightest degree of sovereignty when it comes to PTAs. This could be countered by leaving the enforcement action in the hands of the parties. If a company violating labour rights were to receive a monetary fine instead of the suspension of tariff benefits, the party where said company is located would be competent to enforce this fine. This approach would include all the above-mentioned benefits while leaving the ultimate say to the parties of the PTA. Moreover, it could foster the legitimacy of PTAs and increase public approval, which in times of increased scepticism towards free trade and calls for deglobalisation could become a good hard to come by. Another possible solution to assuage fears over loss of sovereignty is to implement the so-called pyramid model proposed by Kolben (2007: 248). In such a model, an overall council organises numerous local-level councils built of stakeholders who can shape how the standards in a labour provision are implemented and can monitor compliance, making information available regarding plants' compliance (or lack thereof). This model would function similarly to Better Factories in Cambodia, which has received positive feedback regarding its effectiveness at improving working conditions as a result of included and empowered local actors.

13.3.3.4 Certification System

An idea we consider worth exploring is the inclusion of a certification system for factories and companies that adhere to certain labour standards. For that matter, we take inspiration from the European Free Trade Association (EFTA)–Indonesia Comprehensive Economic Partnership Agreement (CEPA): in its Annex V, Switzerland limits preferential tariff treatment for palm oil conditional on meeting the sustainability objectives as set out in Article 8.10 in the main text of the PTA, which requires parties inter alia to 'ensure that [palm oil] traded between the Parties [is] produced in accordance with the sustainability objectives referred to in subparagraph (a)'. Switzerland implemented this provision by enacting the so-called palm oil regulation, pursuant to which only palm oil certified under an approved certification system (Article 3 of the palm oil regulation) enjoys preferential tariff treatment. If this is possible for certified palm oil, why would it not be possible for goods produced at a certified worksite? Admittedly, the search for an effective common certification standard might pose its challenges. However, given such certification systems might become a standard in future PTAs, even the involvement of the ILO together with existing private initiatives is conceivable. As for the compatibility of such preferential tariff schemes in PTAs with WTO law, research suggests that it is not whether tariff differentiation based exclusively on production and process methods (PPMs) violated WTO law per se, but rather how such a scheme is designed (Bürgi Bonanomi 2021: 373).

13.4 CONCLUSIONS

To conclude, there is no 'one size fits all' in terms of labour provisions. Countries must consider domestic capacities of their partner countries and widen the engagement of stakeholders when conceiving a labour chapter in a PTA. There currently exist some templates of labour chapters, which we loosely classify into managerial and enforcement approaches. The first part of this chapter has outlined the successes and failures of both these models, and the latter part includes some key recommendations on the design, enforcement, and compliance of labour provisions for the future.

On the design of labour provisions in future PTAs, we generally recommend continuing the current practice of using internationally recognised standards by the ILO. However, keeping in mind the domestic capacity gap of certain developing countries, we recommend that standards be determined on a case-by-case basis, which encourages flexibility in adopting some domestic standards as well, to account for the particularities of certain countries. This is also a good way to avoid sentiments of labour provisions being viewed as neocolonial by developing countries, especially if done in a consultative manner between negotiating parties, with stakeholder representation including unions, activists, and members of the civil society. Considerations regarding domestic capacity and stage-of-development must be balanced with the ultimate goal of mediating labour abuses and accounting for the preferences of labour and civil society groups. Expanding the types of labour rights incorporated in PTAs can help ensure that trade-related economic development is sustainable and equitable and that labour provisions are more effective.

Additionally, we recommend reforming the language regarding 'manner affecting trade', which is prevalent, especially in US-led labour chapters. There is a need to adapt new templates and language that embody higher levels of legalisation in the case of disputes. This will confine room for interpretation and make disputes fairly straightforward to adjudicate. Furthermore, future labour provisions in PTAs need to eschew this embeddedness of labour violations being considered only when they affect a traded sector. To maintain high standards in labour, worker's rights should be a standalone issue, regardless of whether violations substantially impact trade flows or not.

As for enforcement mechanisms, we think that the RRM in the USMCA displays a substantial step forward and will be copied into future PTAs. However, there needs to be higher ambition on the enforcement front. Whereas trade sanctions targeted at specific facilities limit the disturbance of trade flows and increase accountability for firms, we also pointed out several flaws of the RRM that will need to be addressed in future PTA negotiations. The inclusion of private arbitration mechanisms providing for a direct access for civil society organisations to dispute settlement, as well as the implementation of a certification system could help enhance the effectiveness of future labour chapters.

REFERENCES

Abbott, K. W., R. O. Keohane, A. Moravcsik, A.-M. Slaughter, and D. Snidal 2000. "The Concept of Legalization", *International Organization* 54(3): 401–419.

Agustí-Panareda, J., F. C Ebert, and D. Leclercq 2014. "Labour Provisions in Free Trade Agreements: Fostering Their Consistency with the ILO Standards System," International Labour Office Background Paper.

Alben, E. 2001. "GATT and the Fair Wage: A Historical Perspective on the Labor-Trade Link," *Columbia Law Review* 101(6): 1410–1447.

Anner, M. 2018. "Binding Power: The Sourcing Squeeze, Workers' Rights, and Building Safety in Bangladesh Since Rana Plaza," Center for Global Workers' Rights (CGWR) Research Report.

Arestoff-Izzo, F., R. Bazillier, C. Duc, and C. Granger-Sarrazin 2008. "The Use, Scope and Effectiveness of Labour and Social Provisions and Sustainable Development Aspects in Bilateral and Regional Free Trade Agreements: Final Report," Brussels: European Commission.

Bhagwati, J. 1995. "Trade liberalisation and 'fair trade' demands: Addressing the environmental and labour standards issues" *The World Economy* 18(6): 745–759.

Baier, S. L., J. H. Bergstrand, and R. Mariutto 2014. "Economic Determinants of Free Trade Agreements Revisited: Distinguishing Sources of Interdependence," *Review of International Economics* 22(1): 31–58.

Bhala, R. K., 2007. *International Trade Law: Interdisciplinary Theory and Practice*, 3rd ed. LexisNexis.

Berliner, D., A. Greenleaf, M. Lake, and J. Noveck 2015. "Building Capacity, Building Rights? State Capacity and Labor Rights in Developing Countries," *World Development* 72: 127–139.

Bolle, M. J. 2001. "Jordan–U.S. Free Trade Agreement: Labor Issues," Congressional Research Service for the United States Congress.

Brown, R. C. 2015. "Fostering Labor Rights in A Global Economy: The Efficacy of the Emergent US Model Trade and Investment Frameworks to Advance International Labor Standards in Bangladesh," *International Labour Review* 155(3): 383–406.

2016. "Labor Implications of TPP," Working Paper, East-West Center Workshop on Mega-Regionalism-New Challenges for Trade and Innovation.

Bürgi Bonanomi, T. 2021. "PPM-Based Trade Measures to Promote Sustainable Farming Systems? What the EU/EFTA-Mercosur Agreements Can Learn From the EFTA-Indonesian Agreement," in M. Bungenberg, M. Krajewski, C. J. Tams, J. P. Terhechte, and A. R. Ziegler (Eds.), *European Yearbook of International Economic Law 2020* Berlin: Springer 359–385.

Campling, L., J. Harrison, B. Richardson and A. Smith 2016. "Can Labour Provisions Work Beyond the Border? Evaluating the Effects of EU Free Trade Agreements," *International Labour Review* 155(3): 357–382.

Carrére, C., M. Olarreaga, D. Raess, 2022. "Labor Clauses in Trade Agreements: Hidden Protectionism?," *The Review of International Organizations* 17(3): 453–483.

Cimino-Isaacs, D. C. 2020. "Labor Enforcement Issues in U.S. FTAs," Congressional Research Service for the United States Congress.

Claussen, K. 2021. "Trade's Experimental Compliance Mechanisms," in M. Elsig, R. Polanco, and P. Van Den Bossche (Eds.), *International Economic Dispute Settlement: Demise or Transformation?* Cambridge: Cambridge University Press, pp. 350–370.

2020. "Reimagining trade-plus compliance: The labor story," *Journal of International Economic Law* 23(1): 25–43.

Corvaglia, M. 2021. "Labour Rights Protection and Its Enforcement Under the USMCA: Insights from a Comparative Legal Analysis," *World Trade Review* 20(5): 648–667.

Cottier, T., and A. Caplazi 1998. "Labour Standards and World Trade Law: Interfacing Legitimate Concerns," in T. Geiser, H. Schmid, and E. Walter-Busch (Eds.), *Arbeit in Der Schweiz Des 20. Jahrhunderts. Wirtschaftliche, Rechtliche Und Soziale Perspektiven.* Bern: Verlag Paul Haupt, pp. 469–508.

Das, S. B., R. Sen, and S. Srivastava 2017. "Labour Provisions in Trade Agreements with Developing Economies: The Case of TPPA and ASEAN Member Countries," https://openrepository.aut.ac.nz/bitstream/handle/10292/12331/iseas_ewp_2017-01.pdf?sequence=2&isallowed=y, accessed on August 29, 2023.

Davies, R. B., and K. C. Vadlamannati 2013. "A Race to the Bottom in Labor Standards? An Empirical Investigation," *Journal of Development Economics* 103: 1–14.

Dombois, R., E. Hornberger, and J. Winter. 2004. *Internationale Arbeitsteilung in Der Souveränitätsfalle. Das Lehrstück Des North American Agreement on Labor Cooperation Zwischen Den USA, Mexiko Und Kanada.* Politik, Gemeinschaft und Gesellschaft in einer globalisierten Welt, Vol. 2. Münster: LIT Verlag.

Dong, V. 2016. "Enforcing Labour Standards Under the Trans-Pacific Partnership," *On Labour*, https://onlabor.org/2016/02/29/enforcing-labor-standards-under-the-trans-pacific-partnership/, accessed on August 29, 2023.

Dür, A., L. Baccini, and M. Elsig 2014. "The Design of International Trade Agreements: Introducing a New Database," *Review of International Organizations* 9(3): 353–375.

Edwards, S. 1993. "Openness, Trade Liberalization, and Growth in Developing Countries," *Journal of Economic Literature* 31(3): 1358–1393.

European Commission 2018. "President Jean Claude Junker's State of the Union," September 12, https://ec.europa.eu/commission/presscorner/detail/en/SPEECH_18_5808, accessed on August 29, 2023.

2022. "Commission unveils new approach to trade agreements to promote green and just growth", June 22, https://ec.europa.eu/commission/presscorner/detail/en/IP_22_3921, accessed on August 29, 2023.

Fields, G. S. 2003. "International Labor Standards and Decent Work: Perspectives from the Developing World," in J. Robert, Y. Flanagan, and B. Williams (Eds.), *International Labor Standards: Globalization, Trade and Public Policy*. Stanford: Stanford University Press, pp. 61–80.

Frankel, J. A., and D. H. Romer 1999. "Does Trade Cause Growth?" *American Economic Review* 89(3): 379–399.
Ghose, A. K. 2001. "Global Economic Inequality and International Trade," Geneva: International Labour Organization.
Gött, H. 2020. Linkages of Trade, "Investment and Labour in Preferential Trade Agreements: Between Untapped Potential and Structural Insufficiencies," in M. Bungenberg, M. Krajewski, C. J. Tams, J. P. Terhechte, and A. R. Ziegler (Eds.), *European Yearbook of International Economic Law 2019*. Cham: Springer, pp. 133–165.
Hafner-Burton, E. M. 2005. "Trading Human Rights: How Preferential Trade Agreements Influence Government Repression," *International Organization* 59(3): 593–629.
Helpman, E. 2016. "Globalization and Wage Inequality," NBER Working Paper, (22944), www.nber.org/system/files/working_papers/w22944/w22944.pdf, accessed on August 29, 2023.
Hensman, R. 2000. "World Trade and Workers' Rights: To Link or Not to Link?" *Economic and Political Weekly* 35(3): 1247–1254.
Hepple, B. A. 2005. *Labour Laws and Global Trade* Oxford: Hart Publishing.
Horn, H., P. Mavroidis, and A. Sapir 2010. "Beyond the WTO? An Anatomy of EU and US Preferential Trade Agreements," *The World Economy* 33(11): 1565–1588.
ILO 1998. "ILO Declaration on Fundamental Principles and Rights at Work and its Follow-up," International Labour Office, www-preview.ilo.org/sites/default/files/2024-04/ILO_1998_Declaration_EN.pdf
2009. "World of Work Report 2009. The Global Jobs Crisis and Beyond," www.ilo.org/wcmsp5/groups/public/@dgreports/@dcomm/documents/publication/wcms_118384.pdf, accessed on August 29, 2023.
2016. "Assessment of Labor Provisions in Trade and Investment Agreements," www.ilo.org/wcmsp5/groups/public/—dgreports/—inst/documents/publication/wcms_498944.pdf, accessed on August 29, 2023.
2022. "ILO Labour Provisions in Trade Agreements Hub," www.ilo.org/lphub, accessed on August 29, 2023.
ITUC 2015. "Transpacific Partnership Labour Chapter Scorecard Fundamental Issues Remain Unaddressed," www.ituc-csi.org/img/pdf/trans_pacific.pdf, accessed on August 29, 2023.
Kolben, K. 2006. "The New Politics of Linkage: India's Opposition to the Workers' Rights Clause," *Industrial Journal of Global Legal Studies* 13: 225.
2007. "Integrative Linkage: Combining Public and Private Regulatory Approaches in the Design of Trade and Labor Regimes," *Harvard International Law Journal* 48: 203–256.
2013. "Trade, Development, and Migrant Garment Workers in Jordan," *Middle East Law and Governance* 5(1–2): 195–226.
2016. "A New Model for Trade and Labor: The Trans-Pacific Partnership's Labor Chapter and Beyond," *New York University Journal of International Law and Policy* 49: 1063.
2017. "A Supply Chain Approach to Trade and Labour Provisions," *Politics and Governance* 5(4): 60–68.
Krueger, A. O. 1998. "Why Trade Liberalisation Is Good for Growth," *The Economic Journal* 108(450): 1513–1522.
Labour Advisory Committee (USTR) 2015. "Report on the Impacts of the Trans-Pacific Partnership By the Labor Advisory Committee on Trade Negotiations and Trade Policy," https://ustr.gov/sites/default/files/labor-advisory-committee-for-trade-negotiations-and-trade-policy.pdf, accessed on August 29.

LAC (AFL-CIO) 2015. "Report on the Impacts of the Trans-Pacific Partnership," https://aflcio.org/sites/default/files/2017-11/LAC%20Report–Final%2012-2-15%20As%20Adopted.pdf, accessed on 12 May 2024.

Leclercq, D. 2021. "Biden's Worker-Centered Trade Policy: Whose Workers?" *International Economic Law and Policy Blog*, May 16, 2021.

Manners, I. 2002. "Normative Power Europe: A contradiction in terms?," *JCMS: Journal of Common Market Studies* 40(2): 235–258.

Martin, W., and K. E. Maskus 2001. "Core Labor Standards and Competitiveness: Implications for Global Trade Policy," *Review of International Economics* 9(2): 317–328.

McCrudden, C. and A. Davies 2000. "A Perspective on Trade and Labor Rights," *Journal of International Economic Law* 3(1): 43–62.

Melo Araujo, B. 2018. "Labour Provisions in EU and US Mega-Regional Trade Agreements: Rhetoric and Reality," *International and Comparative Law Quarterly* 67(1): 233–253.

Messerschmidt, L., and N. Janz 2023. "Unravelling the 'Race to the Bottom' Argument: Foreign Direct Investment and Different Types of Labour Rights," *World Development* 161.

Nissen, A. 2022. "Not That Assertive: The EU's Take on Enforcement of Labour Obligations in Its Free Trade Agreement with South Korea," *European Journal of International Law* 33(2): 607–630.

Orbie, J. 2021. "EU Trade Policy Meets Geopolitics: What About Trade Justice," *European Foreign Affairs Review* 26(2): 197–202.

Orbie, J., D. Martens, M. Oehri, and L. Van Den Putte 2016. "Promoting Sustainable Development or Legitimising Free Trade? Civil Society Mechanisms in EU Trade Agreements," *Third World Thematics: A TWQ Journal* 1(4): 526–546.

Ortino, F. 2021. "Trade and Labour Linkages and the US-Guatemala Panel Report Critical Assessment and Future Impact," ETUI Working Paper 11.

Paiement, P. 2018. "Leveraging Trade Agreements for Labor Law Enforcement: Drawing Lessons from the US–Guatemala CAFTA Dispute," *Georgetown Journal of International Law* 49(2): 675–692.

Pavcnik, N. 2017. "The Impact of Trade on Inequality in Developing Countries," NBER Working Paper (23878), www.nber.org/system/files/working_papers/w23878/w23878.pdf, accessed on August 29.

Paz, L. S. 2014. "The Impacts of Trade Liberalization on Informal Labor Markets: A Theoretical and Empirical Evaluation of the Brazilian Case," *Journal of International Economics* 92(2): 330–348.

Peels, R., and M. Fino 2015. "Pushed out the Door, back in through the Window: The Role of the ILO in EU and US Trade Agreements in Facilitating the Decent Work Agenda," *Global Labour Journal* 6(2): 189–202.

Polaski, S., K. A. Nolan Garcia, and M. Rioux 2022. "The USMCA: A 'New Model' for Labor Governance in North America?", in G. Gagne and M. Rioux (Eds.), *From the First NAFTA To the United States-Mexico-Canada Agreement*. London: Palgrave Macmillan, 139–156.

Raess, D., and D. Sari 2018. "Labor Provisions in Trade Agreements (LABPTA): Introducing a New Dataset," *Global Policy* 9(4): 451–466.

Raess, D., D. Sari, and D. Kucera 2016. "Do PTAs Including Labor Provisions Reduce Collective Labor Rights Violations? The Role of Labor Cooperation Provisions," Paper Prepared for Presentation At the 10th Annual Conference on the Political Economy of International Organizations, University of Bern, January 12–14, 2017.

Raess, D., A. Dür, and D. Sari 2018. "Protecting Labor Rights in Preferential Trade Agreements: The Role of Trade Unions, Left Governments, and Skilled Labor," *The Review of International Organizations* 13(2): 143–162.
Ricardo, D. 1817. *On the Principles of Political Economy, and Taxation*, London: John Murray.
Rogowsky, R. A., and E. Chyn 2007. "U.S. Trade Law and FTAs: A Survey of Labor Requirements," *Journal of International Commerce and Economics* 1(24): 113–137.
Siroën, J. M. 2013. "Labour Provisions in Preferential Trade Agreements: Current Practice and Outlook," *International Labour Review* 152: 85–106.
Spilker, G., and T. Böhmelt 2013. "The Impact of Preferential Trade Agreements on Governmental Repression Revisited," *The Review of International Organizations* 8(3): 343–361.
Staiger, R. W. 2003. A Role for the WTO. *International Labor Standards: History, Theory, and Policy Options*, pp. 272–308.
Tallberg, J. 2002. "Paths to Compliance: Enforcement, Management, and the European Union," *International Organization* 56(3): 609–643.USTR 2012. "Bilateral and Regional Trade Agreements," www.ustr.gov/issue-areas/labor/bilateral-and-regional-trade-agreements, accessed on August 29.
USTR 2014. "In the Matter of Guatemala – Issues Relating To the Obligations Under Article 16.2.1(A) of the CAFTA-DR," www.ustr.gov/issue-areas/labor/bilateral-and-regional-trade-agreements/guatemala-submission-under-cafta-dr, accessed on August 29.
2016. "United States–Mexico–Canada Trade Fact Sheet Modernizing NAFTA Into A 21st Century Trade Agreement," www.ustr.gov/trade-agreements/free-trade-agreements/united-states-mexico-canada-agreement/fact-sheets/modernizing, accessed on August 29.
Van Roozendaal, G. 2015. "The Diffusion of Labour Standards: The Case of the US and Guatemala," *Politics and Governance* 3(2): 18–33.
Velut, J., D. Baeza-Breinbauer, M. D. Bruijne, E. Garnizova, M. Jones, K. Kolben, L. Oules, V. Rouas, F. Tigere Pittet, and T. Zamparutti 2022. "Comparative Analysis of Trade and Sustainable Development Provisions in Free Trade Agreements," London School of Economics Policy Hub.
Villalta Puig, G., and O. Ohiocheoya 2011. "Regional Trade Agreements and the Neo-Colonialism of the United States of America and the European Union: A Review of the Principle of Competitive Imperialism," *Liverpool Law Review* 32(3): 225–235.
Vogt, J. S. 2015. "The Evolution of Labor Rights and Trade – A Transatlantic Comparison and Lessons for The Transatlantic Trade and Investment Partnership," *Journal of International Economic Law* 18(4): 827–860.
Waer, P. 1996. "Social Clauses in International Trade," *Journal of World Trade* 30(4): 25–42.
Wang, Z. 2018. "Economic Competition, Policy Interdependence, and Labour Rights," *New Political Economy* 23(6): 393–411.
2020. "Thinking Outside the Box: Globalization, Labor Rights, and the Making of Preferential Trade Agreements," *International Studies Quarterly* 64(2): 343–355.
Warren, S. E. 2016. "Senator Warren Floor Speech on the Trans-Pacific Partnership," www.warren.senate.gov/files/documents/2016-2-2_warren_tpp.pdf, accessed on August 29.
Wells, D. 2007. "'Best Practice' in the Regulation of International Labor Standards: Lessons of the U.S.–Cambodia Textile Agreement," *Comparative Labor Law and Policy Journal* 27(3): 357–376.
WTO 1996. "Singapore Ministerial Declaration, Para. 4, WT/MIN(96)/DEC/W," www.wto.org/english/thewto_e/minist_e/min96_e/wtodec_e.htm, accessed on August 29.

1999a. "Preparations For the 1999 Ministerial Conference 'WTO Forward Work Programme: Proposed Establishment of a Working Group on Trade and Labour': Communication from the United States," WT/GC/W/382, https://docs.wto.org/dol2fe/pages/ss/directdoc.aspx?filename = q:/wt/gc/w382.pdf&open = true, accessed on August 29.
1999b. "Preparations For the 1999 Ministerial Conference 'WTO Forward Work Programme: Proposed Establishment of a Working Group on Trade and Labour': Communication from the European Communities," WT/GC/W/383, https://docs.wto.org/dol2fe/pages/ss/directdoc.aspx?filename = q:/wt/gc/w383.pdf&open = true, accessed on August 29.
2001. "Doha 4th Ministerial – Ministerial Declaration WT/MIN(01)/DEC/1, November 20, 2001," www.wto.org/english/thewto_e/minist_e/min01_e/mindecl_e.html, accessed on August 29.

14

Taking Climate Change Seriously in the Design of Trade Agreements

Clara Brandi, Kateryna Holzer, Jean-Frédéric Morin, and Harro van Asselt

14.1 INTRODUCTION

The environmental implications of trade agreements have long been contested. Some analysts and activists have suggested that preferential trade agreements (PTAs) lead to environmental degradation. Ken Conca, for example, argued at the turn of the century that the trade regime dismantled 'decades of global environmental rule making' and sold 'important dimensions of the global commons' (Conca 2000: 492). Others have a more nuanced outlook. Tana Johnson, for instance, argues that the 'international trade regime offers various instruments by which states can pursue environmental policies, even at the expense of freer trade' (Johnson 2015: 207).

This debate echoes trade's multiple and conflicting effects on the environment. On the one hand, it is undeniable that increased trade has various negative impacts on the environment, including increased extraction of natural resources, the introduction of invasive species, and air pollution from the shipping sector. On the other hand, trade facilitates the diffusion of clean technologies, globalises environmental standards, and favours greater efficiency in resource consumption. These negative and positive impacts occur simultaneously. The question is not whether trade is inherently harmful or virtuous, but under what conditions trade's net effect is environmentally positive.

In answering this question, it is crucial to acknowledge that variations in the design of PTAs matter. In particular, recent research suggests that the inclusion of environmental provisions (EPs) in PTAs can make a significant difference in improving their environmental performance. Jinnah and Lindsay (2016) provide evidence that PTAs with EPs can favour the diffusion of environmental norms and increase compliance with multilateral environmental agreements. Brandi et al. (2019) show that PTAs with EPs promote environmental reforms at the domestic level, particularly in developing countries. In another study, Brandi et al. (2020) find that EPs can help reduce dirty exports and increase green exports from developing countries. Abman et al. (2021) observe that PTAs with EPs offer sufficient protection to offset the net increases in forest loss observed in other PTAs. Several studies find that PTAs with EPs are associated with lower emissions of greenhouse gas (GHGs) and atmospheric particulate matter than PTAs without such provisions (Baghdadi et al. 2013; Zhou et al. 2017; Martinez-Zarzoso and Oueslati 2018; Sorgho and Tharakan 2022).

That said, environmental chapters in PTAs have not reached their full potential. Several of their provisions are vague, weak, and unimaginative (Morin and Jinnah 2018). Yet, it remains unclear how to improve their design. Until now, the literature on the design of environmental chapters in PTAs has focused on enforcement mechanisms (Bastiaens and Postnikov 2017; Velut et al. 2022). Here, we take a different and complementary approach. We look at the design of climate-related provisions, as climate change is one of the most pressing and vital environmental issues (IPCC 2021).

This chapter is divided into two parts. The first part reviews existing trends and patterns in EPs of PTAs. To this end, we develop a typology of four different types of EPs. The second part focuses on four climate-related provisions, each associated with one of these four different types of EPs. We subsequently discuss various options to make these provisions stronger and more precise.

14.2 THE CURRENT DESIGN OF ENVIRONMENTAL PROVISIONS

This first part builds on an updated version of the TRade and ENvironment Database (TREND) data set (Morin et al. 2018) to review existing trends and patterns in the design of EPs in PTAs (for a recent overview, see also Brandi and Morin, 2023). This data set was built by borrowing the full text of 774 PTAs from the Design of Trade Agreements (DESTA) collection (Dür et al. 2014) and identifying in them the occurrence of 300 different types of EPs. These provisions are remarkably diverse. They include, for example, the polluter-pays principle, the exclusion of environmentally harmful inventions from patentability, the requirement to consult stakeholders when adopting domestic regulations, and the expression of support for an international moratorium on whaling.

As Figure 14.1 shows, the average number of EPs per PTA is increasing. In the last decade, not a single PTA was concluded without including at least a few EPs. In fact, several recent PTAs include more than 100 different EPs as documented by the TREND data set. The record for the PTA with the highest number of EPs is frequently broken. In 2018, the United States–Mexico–Canada Agreement (USMCA) included no fewer than 153 EPs, according to the TREND catalogue.

However, the number of EPs is not necessarily a good measure of how ‘green’ a PTA is. It is possible to fill the pages of an environmental chapter with meaningless provisions. To have a better sense of the types of provisions that are included in PTAs, we classify EPs along two dimensions: the first concerns EPs’ targeted subject

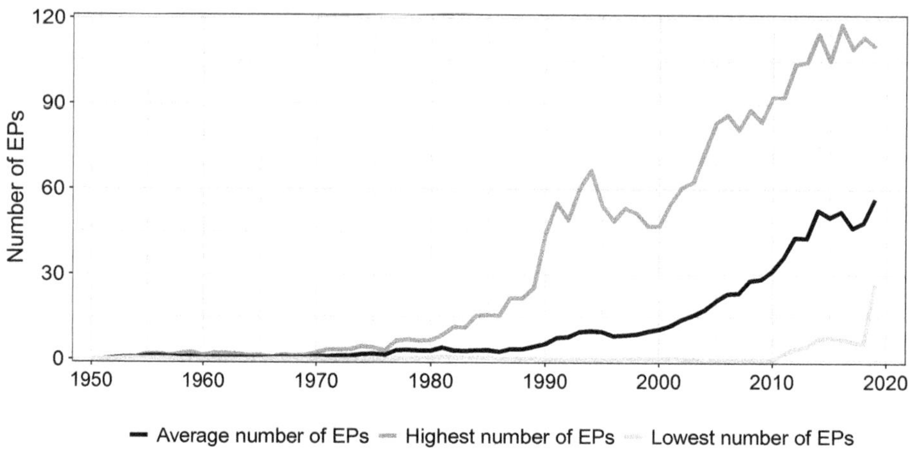

FIGURE 14.1 Growing number of EPs per year.
Source: authors' elaboration (based on Brandi and Morin 2023)

(the parties to the PTA) and the second concerns their targeted object (the environmental issue area). We discuss these two dimensions in turn.

14.2.1 *Defensive and Offensive Provisions*

The first dimension distinguishes provisions that states adopt to protect their own regulatory sovereignty on environmental matters from provisions that states adopt to change their partners' environmental regulations. We call the former 'defensive provisions' and the latter 'offensive provisions' (Blümer et al. 2020). A well-known example of defensive EPs is the exception to trade commitments for domestic measures necessary to protect the life and health of humans, animals, and plants. This exception, expressed most notably in Article XX(b) of the General Agreement on Tariffs and Trade (GATT), is found in at least 310 PTAs. Another example of a defensive provision is the precautionary principle, which protects parties' right to regulate even when there is a lack of scientific certainty over the negative externalities of the regulated subject matter.

By contrast, offensive provisions prescribe specific environmental rules, policies, or behaviours. Examples of offensive provisions include commitments to restrict exports of hazardous waste, to combat illegal fishing, and to ratify certain environmental agreements. States typically support offensive provisions to induce changes in their partners' policies or to make sure that these partners do not lower their level of environmental protection.

We do not make any claim regarding the true motivations underlying either defensive or offensive provisions. Arguably, both types can be driven primarily by economic considerations. Defensive provisions can shield domestic firms from foreign competitors, and offensive provisions can level the playing field with trade

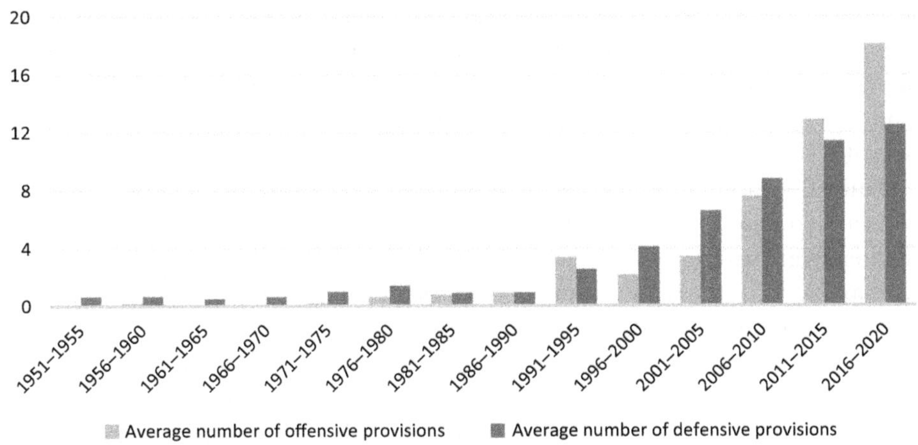

FIGURE 14.2 Average number of offensive and defensive provisions per PTA.
Source: authors' elaboration (based on Brandi and Morin 2023)

competitors. Nevertheless, from an environmental governance perspective, both types play an important role. One type is not intrinsically more valuable than the other. It is equally essential to protect the capacity of states to adopt ambitious environmental regulations and to encourage states to increase their level of protection.

The average number of defensive provisions per PTA grew substantially over the last thirty years (see Figure 14.2). This growth, in part, reflects the increasing depth of PTAs (Dür et al. 2014). Recent PTAs go well beyond the liberalisation of trade in goods and the reduction of tariff barriers. The range of trade issues covered in PTAs is constantly expanding and commonly includes issues such as intellectual property, services, public procurement, and agriculture. Since each of these new chapters includes new trade commitments, states agree on new (defensive) environmental exceptions to limit these commitments.

The growth in the average number of defensive provisions is also fuelled by controversial trade disputes related to domestic environmental regulations. In the 1990s, the tuna–dolphin and the shrimp–turtle cases convinced the United States (US) that it should better protect itself against future legal challenges over its environmental regulations. At the request of US negotiators, the North American Free Trade Agreement (NAFTA, now supplanted by the USMCA) included numerous provisions protecting regulatory sovereignty. The agreement specifically stated that each party may 'establish the level of protection it considers appropriate' (Article 904). The NAFTA also provided that certain multilateral environmental agreements should prevail over any trade commitments in case of inconsistency (Article 104).

Investor–state disputes also led to the design of new defensive provisions. In the last thirty years, several disputes opposed a foreign investor to a host state concerning environmental regulations. They include the *Metalclad*, *Ethyl*, *S.D. Myers*, *Methanex*,

Lone Pine, and *Vattenfall* cases. In response, defensive provisions were added in the investment chapter of recent PTAs. These provisions include a recognition of the parties' right to exercise discretion with respect to environmental matters (Gagné and Morin 2006). These additions have become common defensive provisions in recent PTAs.

Since the early 2000s, the average number of offensive provisions per PTA has grown even more rapidly than the number of defensive provisions (see Figure 14.2). Rather than treating environmental protection as merely an exception to trade commitments, an increasing number of states use PTAs as instruments for diffusing their environmental standards to other countries (Poletti and Sicurelli 2016; Morin and Rochette 2017; Cima 2018). Recent PTAs typically include a full-length chapter entirely devoted to environmental protection and full of offensive provisions. Some of these offensive provisions, such as those on whaling or the prevention of water pollution, have little trade implications but can contribute to addressing environmental challenges. The fact that there are ever more numerous and diverse offensive provisions suggests that PTAs have become a vehicle to negotiate a wide range of environmental commitments.

In principle, offensive provisions are more difficult to negotiate than defensive ones as they are typically more specific and prescriptive and often concern extraterritorial questions. By definition, they restrict rather than protect regulatory sovereignty. Nevertheless, PTAs provide a relatively favourable vehicle to negotiate offensive environmental commitments. Whereas multilateral environmental negotiations have often proved to be labourious and led to disappointing outcomes, PTAs have at least three features that facilitate the negotiation of offensive provisions. First, PTA negotiations involve just a limited number of like-minded partners. Second, PTA negotiations cover a wide range of issues that open the door for bargaining over trade-offs across issue areas. Third, PTAs offer opportunities for regulatory experimentation since several of them are concluded every year. These characteristics make PTAs a relatively favourable vector for the negotiation of offensive provisions compared to multilateral environmental negotiations.

Some offensive provisions of PTAs are more precise than similar provisions found in multilateral environmental agreements. The 2008 PTA between the US and Peru, for example, includes an eight-page-long annex entirely devoted to forest governance (Jinnah and Morin 2020). It includes prescriptive provisions regarding criminal penalties, inventories, export quotas, producers' audit, and chain of custody. This annex resulted from a US offensive strategy to change Peruvian norms and practices, deemed insufficient by the US government. The US–Peru agreement also includes a side letter on biodiversity and traditional knowledge, which reflects primarily the offensive interests of Peru. In it, the US government acknowledges the principles of prior informed consent and benefit sharing, which is a significant achievement for Peru, considering that the US remains one of the two states (alongside the Vatican) that has not ratified the Convention on Biological

Diversity (Morin and Gauquelin 2016). From this perspective, both the US and Peru successfully included unprecedented offensive provisions in their shared PTA.

14.2.2 *Generic and Specific Provisions*

The second dimension differentiates between generic and specific provisions. Generic provisions are applicable to any environmental issue. Specific provisions address particular issue areas.

The first generation of PTAs included only generic provisions. These early generic provisions included commitments to cooperate on environmental matters, provisions on environmental aid and assistance, the requirement to consider scientific evidence in environmental policymaking, and the acknowledgement that lowering environmental standards to attract foreign investment is inappropriate.

The average number of specific provisions has increased over time. Recent PTAs cover issues as diverse as fisheries, deforestation, toxic wastes, the ozone layer, migratory species, endocrine-disrupting chemicals, soil erosion, wetlands, invasive species, scenery preservation, mercury, heavy metals, and genetically modified organisms. European Union (EU) PTAs were among the first to address specific environmental issues, which varied according to the concerned partner. By contrast, the first generations of US PTAs included almost exclusively generic provisions, including in environmental side agreements that complemented some of these PTAs. Starting with the US–Peru agreement, however, recent US PTAs also include specific provisions, notably on issues such as energy, endangered species, forestry, and fisheries.

The most prevalent environmental issue areas in PTAs are waste, biodiversity, and water. Environmental provisions that focus on these issue areas frequently appear both in North–South and South–South PTAs. In recent years, PTAs have increasingly addressed climate change (Morin and Jinnah 2018; WTO 2022). The first PTA to mention the 'greenhouse effect' was the 1989 Lomé IV Agreement concluded between the European Economic Community and African, Caribbean, and Pacific countries, three years before the United Nations Framework Convention on Climate Change (UNFCCC) was concluded. Since then, an increasing number of PTAs have addressed climate adaptation, promoted renewable energy, favoured the harmonisation of climate regulations, or called for the ratification of climate treaties (see Figure 14.3). Yet, there are still many PTAs with detailed environmental chapters that do not address climate change specifically, or only do so superficially.

Considering the proliferation of issue-specific EPs in PTAs, it is surprising that so few PTAs address climate change directly. There are several possible reasons for this hesitancy. Arguably, countries are reluctant to include strong climate provisions in PTAs for the same reasons they are reluctant to accept them in multilateral forums: the costs of reducing GHG emissions are high and largely borne by politically influential actors, such as oil companies and their shareholders (Colgan et al. 2021). If more PTAs address biodiversity than climate change, it might be because

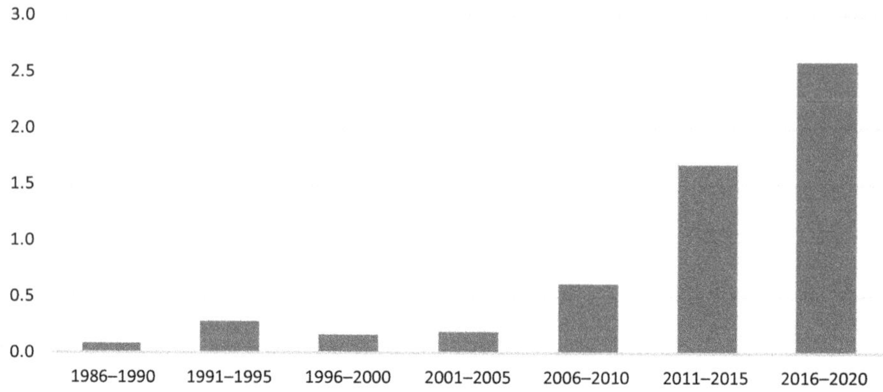

FIGURE 14.3 Average number of climate-related provisions in PTAs.
Source: authors' elaboration (based on Brandi and Morin 2023)

the costs of biodiversity conservation are largely borne by poorer countries. It is also possible that for biodiversity-rich countries, the benefits of market access outweigh the costs of conservation. Because trade negotiations tend to value utility in short-term economic gains, it is unlikely that the costs of climate mitigation would meet this bar (Morin and Jinnah 2018).

That said, several generic EPs that are not specifically related to climate change could nevertheless be useful in addressing it. For instance, environmental exceptions in the investment chapter could allow states to adopt the necessary measures for a clean energy transition. Another example is provisions on technical assistance and capacity building that can play an important role in the implementation of PTAs with climate-related provisions. As more diverse economies move into more leadership roles on climate change, it will be interesting to see if and how they incorporate climate issues into their future trade agreements.

14.2.3 A *Typology*

Combining the two dimensions introduced above results in a 2x2 typology. Environmental provisions in PTAs can be specific/offensive, generic/offensive, specific/defensive, generic/defensive. Table 14.1 presents a few examples for each of these four types. In the following paragraphs, we briefly discuss one example for each type (as underlined in Table 14.1).

An example of *specific/offensive* provisions is restrictions on fossil fuel subsidies. Such provisions focus on the specific issue of climate change (as opposed to environmental protection in general) and proscribe certain policies (instead of protecting regulatory sovereignty). Governments have made numerous voluntary commitments to phase out inefficient fossil fuel subsidies (including in the context of the G20, G7, Sustainable Development Goals (SDGs), UNFCCC, and Asia-

TABLE 14.1 *Typology of climate-related provisions.*

	Climate-specific provisions	Generic provisions
Offensive provisions	• Restrictions on fossil fuel subsidies • Requirement to ratify the Paris Agreement • Promotion of energy efficiency • Adopt/harmonise climate regulations	• Liberalisation of environmental goods and services • Requirement to provide environmental aid • Requirement to conduct impact assessments
Defensive provisions	• Exceptions allowing border carbon adjustment measures	• Environmental exceptions to the investment chapter • Certified goods are not similar to non-certified goods

Pacific Economic Cooperation (APEC)). Still, fossil fuel subsidies amounted to a staggering USD 697.2 billion in 2021 (OECD and IEA 2022), leading to a range of adverse environmental and socio-economic effects, including on climate change and air pollution (Skovgaard and van Asselt 2019). Fossil fuel subsidies do not only lead to GHG emissions and carbon lock-in, but they also distort international trade (Moerenhout and Irschlinger 2020). As a consequence, fossil fuel subsidy reform has also been discussed in the trade context, with several World Trade Organization (WTO) Members (including the EU) adopting a Ministerial Statement in 2021, in which they expressed their intention to 'advance discussion … aimed at achieving ambitious and effective disciplines' (WTO 2021: paragraph 8).

Although no multilateral rules on fossil fuel subsidies exist, a few PTAs have begun to include provisions on fossil fuel subsidies. In the 2018 agreement between the EU and Singapore, the parties 'recognise the need to ensure that, when developing public support systems for fossil fuels, proper account is taken of the need to reduce greenhouse gas emissions and of the need to limit distortions of trade as much as possible'. They also 'share the goal of progressively reducing subsidies for fossil fuels' (Article 12.11(3)). This vague formulation is not enforceable under the dispute settlement mechanism of the agreement. For its part, the 2021 agreement between the United Kingdom (UK), Iceland, Liechtenstein, and Norway provides that parties should cooperate on the 'global phase-out of inefficient fossil fuel subsidies' (Article 13.22(3)(h)). Similarly, the 2021 agreement between the EU and the Organisation of African, Caribbean and Pacific States provides that 'they shall phase out environmentally harmful fossil fuel subsidies' (Article 24.3). One of the most detailed provisions on fossil fuel subsidies in a PTA can be found in the 2022 UK–New Zealand Agreement, in which the parties commit to, among others, 'take steps to eliminate harmful fossil fuel subsidies where they exist, with limited exceptions in support of legitimate public policy objectives', 'ensure that information on fossil fuel support measures, including any subsidies, is published', and 'encourage non-parties to develop and undertake best practice approaches to fossil fuel subsidy reform' (Article 22.8). New Zealand is also involved in negotiating a new Agreement on Climate Change, Trade and Sustainability (ACCTS) with Costa Rica, Fiji, Iceland, Norway, and Switzerland, with the stated aim of developing new rules restricting fossil fuel subsidies.

An interesting example of *generic/offensive* provisions is commitments to liberalise environmental goods and services (EGS). While these commitments do not directly address climate change, they can greatly contribute to the diffusion of climate technologies, such as solar panels and wind turbines, making the uptake of these technologies cheaper and faster. More than seventy PTAs mention the benefits of liberalising EGS, but few of them include clear commitments in this regard. In most of the cases, these provisions are formulated in best endeavour language, where parties only 'recognise the importance' (USMCA 2019), 'resolve to make efforts' (CARIFORUM 2008), 'strive to facilitate' (European Free Trade Association (EFTA)–Turkey 2018), or 'pay special attention' (Comprehensive Economic and Trade Agreement (CETA) 2016) to the liberalisation of EGS. One of the most precise PTAs in relation to EGS is the 2013 agreement between New Zealand and Taiwan. It covers the elimination of all tariffs on 132 environmental goods immediately upon the entry into force of the agreement, as well as the movement of business persons involved in the supply of environmental services. The 2022 New Zealand–UK PTA goes even further by eliminating tariffs on 293 environmental goods, which is the largest list agreed upon in any PTA to date.[1]

While the proliferation of PTAs automatically contributes to the removal of tariffs on environmental goods, this is not enough, given that applied tariffs are relatively low (particularly in advanced economies) in multilateral (most-favoured-nation) trade, whereas non-tariff barriers (NTBs) are the main obstacle. Countries, therefore, attempt to address the issue of NTBs in PTAs as well.[2] Most common in this respect are provisions addressing technical barriers to trade (TBT), including the mutual recognition of technical regulations, standards, and conformity assessment procedures for the production, processing, or labelling of organic products (Comprehensive and Progressive Agreement for Trans-Pacific Partnership (CPTPP) 2018). Some PTAs also include provisions for the promotion of good regulatory practices in standard-setting. Particularly, they oblige the parties to use standards of specific international standard-setting bodies listed in the agreements when introducing domestic standards for specific environmental goods (EU–Singapore 2018; EU–Viet Nam 2019). Moreover, the EU strives to include in its PTAs provisions that commit parties to refrain from the use of local content

[1] These lists are living documents in that they can be adjusted to include new information about environmental goods and technologies.

[2] In the 2013 New Zealand–Taiwan PTA, parties agreed to endeavour to address any NTB identified by either party that impedes trade in environmental goods or services.

requirements or any other performance requirements that negatively influence the other party's products and services relevant for the promotion of renewable energy (EU–Singapore 2018; EU–Viet Nam 2019).

Some PTAs also contain commitments on environmental services that go beyond existing commitments in the General Agreement on Trade in Services (GATS). These 'GATS-plus' commitments in PTAs extend to all four environmental services' subsectors (6.A sewage, 6.B refuse disposal, 6.C sanitation, and 6.D other) and enhance market access and national treatment obligations. In some cases, liberalisation also concerns mode 4, which facilitates the movement of business persons for the sale and installation of environmental goods or the supply of environmental services (New Zealand–Taiwan 2013). Moreover, there are specific provisions in some PTAs on strengthening technology transfer and capacity building in the field of environment and sustainable development by means of grants, development funds, or other financial instruments.[3]

Environmental exceptions to commitments with respect to investment protection are examples of the *generic/defensive* type (Gagné and Morin 2006). They include general exceptions giving the host state the possibility to lawfully take action directed at environmental protection (112 PTAs), clarifications that regulatory action designed to protect the environment does not constitute indirect expropriation (64 PTAs), the explicit granting of the right to regulate investment in specific sectors (47 PTAs), and the exclusion of environmental measures from the scope of investor–state dispute settlement (ISDS) (six PTAs).

General exceptions applicable to commitments with respect to investment are incorporated *mutatis mutandis* or copied (sometimes with slight modifications) from the texts of the general exceptions of GATT Article XX and GATS Article XIV. They can be found in different parts of PTAs, including investment chapters (Japan–Singapore 2002; EFTA–Indonesia 2018) and chapters specifically dedicated to exceptions (New Zealand–China 2008; CETA 2016). While normally applying to provisions of the whole treaty, in some PTAs, general exceptions apply only to specific investment protection standards, which substantially limits the host state's flexibility to take environmental measures. For instance, in the EU–Canada CETA, general exceptions apply only to two subsections of the investment chapter – establishment of investment and non-discriminatory treatment. In this case, the risk of violation by the host state of other investment-related provisions, such as unlawful expropriation and fair and equitable treatment (FET), linked to the application of environmental measures is not mitigated through the general exceptions. Instead, possible violations are precluded by means of the interpretive language delimiting the scopes of application of these provisions (Sabanogullari 2015). For instance, in relation to indirect expropriation, one of the CETA provisions contained in Annex 8A stipulates that 'except in the rare circumstance when the impact of a measure …

3 See, for example, Chapter 9 on cooperation and capacity building of the 2019 EFTA–Indonesia PTA.

appears manifestly excessive, non-discriminatory measures of a Party that are designed and applied to protect legitimate public welfare objectives, such as health, safety and the environment, do not constitute indirect expropriations' (Annex 8A.3). Several PTAs incorporate similar language.

Moreover, some PTAs reaffirm the right of the host state to regulate. This is done either as a reference to the right in the preamble of a PTA (New Zealand–UK 2022), which, while not creating real rights for states, can play an important role in treaty interpretation by arbitrators, or as a provision in the investment chapter. For instance, Article 8.9 of CETA contains the explicit recognition of the right of each party 'to regulate in their territories to achieve legitimate policy objectives such as the protection of public health, safety, the environment' and explains that 'the mere fact that a Party regulates … in a manner which negatively affects an investment or interferes with an investor's expectations … does not amount to a breach of an obligation'. At the same time, provisions that carve out non-discriminatory measures with legitimate public policy objectives from ISDS claims (Colombia–Panama 2013; Australia–China 2015) are less common but very significant from the perspective of climate action, as they help to shield domestic climate policy measures.

Provisions that specifically allow for border carbon adjustment (BCA) would be examples of *specific/defensive* provisions. The idea of achieving more ambitious climate policy targets without energy-intensive sectors shifting their emissions abroad (carbon leakage) through imposing BCAs is no longer theoretical. In 2023, the EU introduced a carbon border adjustment mechanism (CBAM) to charge imported goods according to the CO_2 emitted during their production. While the CBAM is the first time such a measure is adopted, it will unlikely be the last, given that countries are implementing domestic climate policies at different speeds and with varying levels of ambition. Key questions in this context include how BCAs can be made compatible with international trade law and how cooperation and dialogue on issues such as pricing carbon and on carbon leakage can be furthered in light of the increasingly fragmented landscape at this interface of trade and climate policies.

At the moment, PTAs do not include specific/defensive provisions on BCAs. States have to rely on generic/defensive provisions, such as environmental exceptions that allow countries to restrict trade to protect human, animal, or plant life or health (311 PTAs), or conserve natural resources (386 PTAs), similar to those contained in the GATT (Article XX(b) and (g)). Some of these exceptions in PTAs are 'WTO-plus', as they provide useful clarifications on the scope of the exceptions clarifying that, for instance, GATT Article XX (g) covers the conservation of both living and non-living exhaustible natural resources.[4] The importance of

[4] For instance, the 2022 New Zealand–UK PTA states that the measures referred to in GATT Article XX(b) of and GATS Article XIV(b) of GATS include environmental measures necessary to protect human, animal, or plant life or health and measures necessary to mitigate climate change. Moreover, it specifies that Article XX(g) of GATT 1994 applies to measures relating to the conservation of living and non-living exhaustible natural resources, whereby 'non-living

clarifications of the GATT general exceptions becomes evident from the analysis of environment-related WTO jurisprudence, especially the gasoline and shrimp–turtle cases. These clarifications improve the chances of successfully defending a BCA measure in case of a dispute.

Other provisions relevant to BCAs include those on the promotion and cooperation of carbon markets.[5] These provisions address the challenge of fragmented domestic climate action at different speeds and different levels of ambition around the world. The 2020 PTA between the EU and the UK contains a separate article on carbon pricing obliging the parties to have in place an effective carbon pricing system embracing GHG emissions from electricity and heat generation, industry, and aviation. The parties also agreed 'to give serious consideration to linking their respective carbon pricing systems in a way that preserves the integrity of these systems and provides for the possibility to increase their effectiveness'.[6] Similarly, the 2022 UK–New Zealand Agreement contains a provision promoting carbon pricing as an effective policy tool for reducing GHG emissions, and a provision on cooperation on trade-related measures of climate policy, including those related to linking emissions trading systems and carbon leakage. The latter provision is closely related to the use of BCAs.

Another set of BCA-relevant provisions aims at facilitating dialogue on measures taken to comply with multilateral environmental agreements, such as the Paris Agreement, thus potentially also covering the use of trade measures, such as BCA. For example, Article 16.3.3 of the 2015 Korea–New Zealand Agreement states that '[i]n the event a Party proposes to take a measure to comply with its obligations under a multilateral environmental agreement that may directly and adversely affect the other Party's trade or investment, either Party may seek to engage in dialogue to resolve the matter'.

In the next part, we lay out options for the future that have the potential to strengthen climate protection via PTAs, focusing on these four types of provisions.

14.3 DESIGNING BETTER CLIMATE-RELATED PROVISIONS

14.3.1 *Fossil Fuel Subsidies*

With a few countries beginning to include provisions on fossil fuel subsidies in their PTAs, and new rules under negotiation in the ACCTS context (and, possibly in

exhaustible natural resources' include clean air and a global atmosphere with safe levels of greenhouse gases.

5 For instance, the 2015 South Korea–New Zealand Agreement focuses on 'co-operation on trade related aspects of the current and future international climate change regime, including issues relating to global carbon markets and ways to address adverse effects of trade on climate' (Annex 16-A). The 2019 EU–Viet Nam PTA agreed to exchange information and experience on designing, implementing, and operating mechanisms for pricing carbon (Article 13.6, para 2(a)).

6 See the 2020 Trade and Cooperation Agreement between the EU and the UK (2020), Article 392(6).

future, in the WTO context), the question arises of how trade negotiators can design such provisions in a way that can effectively (and fairly) contribute to climate protection. This question can be discussed with reference to: (1) the scope of the provisions, (2) the type of discipline, (3) provisions for special and differential treatment (SDT), and (4) procedural aspects (including notifications). These points will be discussed in turn.

In terms of the scope, there are ways to craft provisions that make them more specific. It is not difficult to think about vague and broad formulations. For instance, following the language of the voluntary G20 commitment (G20 2009), the scope could be limited to 'inefficient' fossil fuel subsidies that 'encourage wasteful consumption'. As there is no agreement on what these terms mean (OECD and IEA 2022), adding these qualifiers would make the scope of a provision less clear. Even without these terms, however, questions remain over what constitutes a 'fossil fuel subsidy', with different definitions being used in different contexts. For instance, the International Monetary Fund includes the non-internalisation of negative social and environmental externalities in its definition, leading to estimates that are an order of magnitude greater than the more conservative estimates by the Organisation for Economic Co-operation and Development (OECD) and the International Energy Agency (Parry et al. 2021).

To clarify the scope, negotiating parties can consider three options. First, they can adopt a standard definition of a 'subsidy', with the definition of Article 1 of the WTO Agreement on Subsidies and Countervailing Measures (SCM Agreement) being a prime candidate. They would also need to clearly define 'fossil fuels', for instance, following the definition put forward by the United Nations Environment Programme to help measure progress towards the SDGs (UNEP and IISD 2019). By doing so, the parties could decide only to cover fossil fuel subsidies that are 'specific' within the meaning of the SCM Agreement, they could omit the specificity requirement, leading to a broader coverage (including non-specific subsidies such as fixed fuel prices), or they could adopt an alternative specificity requirement. Second, rather than agreeing on a definition, parties could list specific types of targeted subsidies, such as those known to be particularly environmentally harmful (e.g. subsidies for new coal mines). Third, parties can alternatively self-select which subsidies they intend to subject to disciplines. Such discretion would, however, run the risk of no or only limited subsidies being put forward by parties.

In terms of the type of discipline, the provisions could include a prohibition of either all or a subset of fossil fuel subsidies, following the model of prohibited subsidies under the SCM Agreement and the 2022 WTO Agreement on Fisheries Subsidies. Likewise, following the example of the SCM Agreement's category of actionable subsidies, disciplines could be related to the assessment of the environmentally harmful effects of subsidies (e.g. on GHG emissions). However, establishing a causal link between an individual subsidy and specific environmental effects may be challenging (though not impossible; see Achakulwisut et al. 2021). Subsidy disciplines could also follow the model of the WTO Agreement on Agriculture by requiring the phasing down or out of fossil fuel subsidies over a given time period. This approach requires that parties have a good understanding – and agreement – of the overall size of fossil fuel subsidies, which would serve as the basis for reduction commitments. Another approach, discussed in the APEC context, is for countries to agree on a 'stand-still' obligation, under which they agree to not introduce any new fossil fuel subsidies.

Depending on the negotiating parties, the rules developed in a PTA could seek to accommodate SDT for developing countries. The rationale for such provisions would be the challenges faced by developing countries in shifting away from fossil fuel dependence. Such SDT could be applied to any developing country party in a PTA, or only to least developed countries. Provisions could be in the form of a (temporary) derogation from key disciplines, for instance, for fossil fuel subsidies provided to ensure energy access for the most vulnerable and poorest. Moreover, provisions could be put in place providing for technical and/or financial assistance and technology transfer to support the clean energy transition in developing countries.

Lastly, PTA parties could strengthen transparency around fossil fuel subsidies by providing for the notification of such subsidies by parties, counter-notification by other parties, or third-party notification by international organisations, thereby addressing one of the core challenges surrounding fossil fuel subsidies: a lack of transparency (Casier et al. 2014). Another model, building on the G20 and APEC experience, would be for countries to regularly report on their fossil fuel subsidies and progress made in their phase-out, with those reports being subject to a peer review by other parties. Depending on the type of disciplines and the placement of provisions on fossil fuel subsidies, they may also be subject to dispute settlement, allowing countries to challenge each other's inconsistent fossil fuel subsidies.

14.3.2 *Environmental Goods and Services*

Preferential trade agreement negotiations offer an alternative channel for promoting trade in EGS, in view of the failed multilateral and plurilateral negotiations on the liberalisation of trade in EGS.[7] The potential of PTAs to promote trade in EGS is underlined by the above-mentioned examples of the inclusion of lists of environmental goods for tariff elimination in PTAs. A major drawback of these PTA provisions setting commitments to eliminate tariffs on specific environmental goods

[7] An important step was made in 2012 when the twenty-one APEC Members agreed to reduce tariffs for a list of fifty-four environmental goods (Bellmann and Sugathan 2022; de Melo and Solleder 2022). Since then, however, momentum was lost. In 2016, the forty-six Members that were negotiating the Environmental Goods Agreement at the WTO put these negotiations on hold. At the same time, there is renewed discussion in the WTO on how governments can cooperate to promote trade in EGS.

is their lack of binding character. These provisions are part of chapters devoted to trade and sustainable development (TSD) or environmental protection, which are often not subject to dispute settlement under the agreements. To increase compliance with these provisions, they would need to be included in the chapters on trade in goods and services, to which dispute settlement provisions apply. Alternatively, PTA parties may consider the application of a PTA's general dispute settlement rules with remedies for non-compliance (including suspension of concessions) to the environmental or TSD chapter.[8] In fact, a move towards such a reform is currently underway in the EU. In 2022, the EU Commission announced that it wants to extend the PTA's general state-to-state dispute settlement mechanisms to their TSD chapters.[9]

A list-based approach to the liberalisation of environmental goods can also be supplemented with a preferential tariff rate approach following the example of the 2019 PTA between the EFTA (consisting of Iceland, Liechtenstein, Norway, Switzerland) and Indonesia. This agreement establishes preferential tariff-rate quota access for palm oil produced sustainably in Indonesia. Under this approach, countries may consider the introduction of sustainability criteria for tariff elimination or reduction (including within tariff quotas) under their PTAs. These sustainability criteria may favour certain low-carbon technologies for the production of specific goods and would incentivise producers from PTA partners to switch to production methods that are more climate-friendly. It would particularly work for goods with bound tariffs that are high enough to allow for differentiation at a scale sufficient to create an incentive for producers to convert to greener technologies.

Given that non-tariff measures (NTMs) present a major problem for EGS, it is especially important to focus in PTAs on the reduction of NTMs. Addressing NTMs cannot be effective without reducing the use of antidumping (AD) and countervailing duties (CVD), which undermines the elimination of tariffs. In many cases, AD and CVD imposed on imports of solar panels and wind turbines constitute 100 per cent of the value of the imported products (WTO 2022). Tackling the problem of trade remedies requires negotiating rules additional to those found in the WTO SCM Agreement. For example, PTAs can include mandatory public interest clauses that would oblige investigating authorities to consider the interests of different stakeholders and environmental externalities in the imposition of trade remedies (Espa and Marín Durán 2020). This would balance the benefits of trade remedies to the domestic industry against the costs for other economic operators and broader public policy objectives, including climate protection, thereby avoiding the imposition of AD and CVD harmful for the deployment of green technologies.

8 There is a risk, however, that the extension of general dispute settlement to environmental provisions will result in a non-binding best endeavour language of environmental provisions (i.e. a higher degree of delegation will be achieved at the expense of obligation and precision). This remains a debated question.

9 See https://ec.europa.eu/commission/presscorner/detail/en/ip_22_3921.

Environmental standards that are not harmonised or based on inadequate methodologies also constitute trade barriers for EGS. Preferential trade agreements provide the opportunity to negotiate the introduction and harmonisation of sound standards and certification schemes for particular environmental goods (Holzer and Cottier 2015). It is particularly in the interest of developing countries to join discussions to regulate standards and sustainability criteria, as they tend to face challenges with standard compliance. Promoting good regulatory practices and providing technical and financial assistance to developing countries and their producers to support compliance with TBT measures, as well as to ensure a well-functioning domestic quality infrastructure system, should therefore be part of PTA negotiations.

Another important driver of the diffusion of low-carbon or other environmental technologies is trade in environmental services. Inasmuch as environmental services are essential for the effective use of environmental goods, the potential benefits of simultaneously liberalising trade in environmental services and in environmental goods are much greater than liberalising trade in only one or the other. Future PTA negotiations should therefore seek to enable better trade in environmental services. Yet, this is a challenging task for at least two reasons. First, the liberalisation of environmental services is constrained by the natural monopoly character of many environmental services' provisions (sewage, waste disposal, etc.). Second, services negotiations usually follow different modalities than goods negotiations, which makes it even more difficult to agree on definitional and technical issues. However, negotiating environmental services in PTAs can make an agreement easier, especially with partners from developing countries where the supply of high-quality environmental services presents an acute problem. Practical approaches to the liberalisation of environmental services under PTAs include facilitating trade in services directly related to specific environmental goods and using 'ex-outs', or additional descriptions, within the service categories under the Central Product Classification to identify specific services relevant to the environment (Bellmann and Sugathan 2022).

Finally, as the experience at the WTO shows, negotiations on the liberalisation of trade in environmental goods can be facilitated by allowing for certain flexibilities for developing country parties. These flexibilities may include lower levels of tariff cuts for developing country parties, or cuts on fewer goods and over a longer time period, or different levels of liberalisation for different categories of environmental goods. In addition, there could be provisions on technology transfer and technical assistance that impact EGS production and export to make sure that developing countries can also derive substantial benefits from promoting trade in EGS via PTAs.

14.3.3 *Investment*

There is much discussion about how to improve the climate-friendliness of international investment agreements (IIAs), including PTAs, bilateral investment treaties

(BITs), and sectoral agreements such as the Energy Charter Treaty (ECT). Most active discussions revolve around the need to put restrictions on the application of ISDS to foreign investor claims regarding measures taken by governments to address climate change, or, conversely, creating more regulatory space for governments to protect the environment and the climate. The availability of ISDS results in multiple claims by investors against climate policy measures, potentially inflicting major losses on state budgets as a result of paid damages. Many analysts believe that this risk has a 'chilling effect' on climate policy measures (Tienhaara 2018). In this sense, general exceptions for public policy measures are likely to be a less effective safeguard of the host state's regulatory space compared to more precisely calibrated carve-outs, especially in areas where the potential for ISDS claims is high. Scepticism about general exceptions is based on the arguments that these exceptions will not provide more regulatory flexibility than what is already available in customary law or jurisprudence (Newcombe 2011). On the contrary, they may even limit existing flexibility due to their exhaustive lists of permissible objectives and allegedly overly rigid requirements (Gehring and Tokas 2022). Based on these discussions, several reform options regarding exceptions and carve-outs can be suggested in support of climate policy.

As a first option, PTA parties can develop a treaty-wide exception specifically for climate policy measures. To this end, general exceptions need to be updated and refined to make clear that they apply to measures taken with a climate protection objective. A specific reference in the exceptions to climate change is important because it is not entirely clear whether public policy exceptions modelled after the GATT and GATS general exceptions will necessarily be interpreted to cover measures addressing climate change. It is also important to ensure that taking climate policy-related measures is not only lawful but does not entail any compensation. This would avoid a situation like in *Eco Oro v. Colombia*, where the tribunal reached the conclusion that states remained liable to pay compensation for legitimate, non-discriminatory measures falling within the scope of the treaty's general environmental exception. To prevent similar findings, clarification can be added to the exception that no compensation needs to be paid for the application of climate policy measures falling under the exception.

Second, in addition, and in line with the first option, the right to regulate could be explicitly extended to climate policy measures, as foreseen in the 2021 Canadian Model BIT. To this end, the right to regulate in the investment chapter needs to be linked to a specific aim of addressing climate change. Moreover, parties to PTAs can go further and explicitly allow measures to be taken to implement their Paris Agreement commitments, following the example of the TSD chapter of the 2018 EU–Japan Economic Partnership Agreement.[10]

[10] See Article 16.4 and 16.5 of the EU–Japan Agreement.

Third, better use could be made of carve-outs and clarifications concerning the application of investment protection standards to climate policy measures (Polanco et al. 2017). Carve-outs from certain investment protection standards, such as non-discrimination and performance requirements, can be made for specific climate policy measures, such as subsidy schemes for renewable energy and government procurement. Investment provisions can also include a presumption of conformity of climate measures with indirect expropriation provisions. Additional provisions can provide clarifications and guidance to arbitrators on how to decide whether or not a government measure constitutes a violation of FET, which can also be supplemented with a closed list of measures that constitute a breach of FET.[11] Refining the host state commitments by clarifying and limiting the scope of any investment protection standard that could put climate protection goals at risk arguably offers a more systemic approach for climate policy-driven reform of the investment treaty regime than general exceptions or issue-by-issue carve-outs for climate policy measures (UNCTAD and IIED 2022).

Finally, climate policy measures can be protected from legal challenges through a carve-out from ISDS. In that case, climate policy measures would still be covered by the obligations under PTAs (and could potentially be in breach of those obligations), but the carve-out from ISDS would eliminate the risk of a successful challenge and award of damages to an investor (Paine 2022). A carve-out from ISDS for climate policy measures or for investments in the energy sector would enable ample regulatory flexibility necessary to take ambitious climate action. Although this looks like the most effective reform for climate protection purposes, very few existing PTAs include such a carve-out. One of the rare cases includes the 2000 PTA between Mexico and the Northern Triangle, which excludes from ISDS measures adopted by Honduras regarding health, national security, and the protection of the environment.[12] Trade negotiators should consider carve outs that are less contentious by excluding entire sectors or measures aimed at reducing GHGs.

Successful implementation of the above-mentioned reform options requires a thorough consideration of several cross-cutting issues. The first issue to be considered is whether exceptions and carve-outs would function as defences or permissions. The latter is preferable for climate policy objectives, as it would make a measure fall outside investment protection and place the burden of proof on the investor to demonstrate that the exception does not apply (Henckels 2022). Another important step is to define what measures should be protected by an exception. In other words, how should those measures be circumscribed? Should qualifiers such as 'necessary' or 'relating to' be used, or should the link to climate policy be made rather vague and formulated through the words 'designed and applied to' or 'appropriate to'? The experience with WTO disputes, where the term 'necessary' was

[11] See, for example, CETA Article 8.10.
[12] Mexico–Northern Triangle FTA, Article 14-41 and Annex 14-41.

interpreted as requiring the consideration of alternative, less restrictive measures, suggests a preference for a vaguer connection. Parties can also decide to include a condition that measures must be non-discriminatory to fall under the exception. For example, if domestic investors receive compensation for a climate policy measure that negatively impacts their business, foreign investors should be entitled to it as well. In that case, parties would also need to provide guidance on what is meant by 'non-discriminatory' (Paine 2022). Another important question is who should decide on whether a measure is covered or a subject exempted from ISDS when a dispute is initiated – arbitrators, parties, or an independent body with climate-related expertise. Given the absence of climate policy expertise and the high public interest in the matter, an investor–state arbitration tribunal is unlikely to be an appropriate body to decide. Instead, a climate-related carve-out from ISDS should better be governed by a multilateral body set up within the UNFCCC or by an independent panel of climate change experts (Paine 2022).

14.3.4 *Border Carbon Adjustments*

Preferential trade agreements offer a valuable avenue for negotiations on the use of BCAs. States are likely to be more willing to negotiate on BCAs under PTAs than in the WTO due to the wide coverage of issues that promise to bring economic benefits to PTA parties. This wide coverage offers a large scope for bargaining and trade-offs between economic and climate policy interests. In relation to BCAs, states have so far used PTAs in a defensive mode, primarily relying on environmental exceptions that could shield their prospective BCAs from legal claims of PTA partners. Today, as the use of BCAs has become imminent, countries can be more proactive on the issue of BCAs in their PTA negotiations. They can negotiate offensive provisions laying down rules for the application of BCAs.

If the PTA parties agree on the use of BCAs in their bilateral trade, they can include a provision on a BCA in the environmental or TSD chapter (for instance, in a subchapter on carbon markets, carbon pricing, and BCAs), which will regulate several important aspects essential for the design and implementation of a BCA measure. This provision could oblige the parties to ensure the implementation of a BCA in a transparent and non-discriminatory manner based on prior notification and consultation, fostering cooperation on BCA design and implementation with the other party. It could also require the parties to develop mutually accepted sector-based emission measuring, reporting, and verification systems and carbon footprint certification schemes and ensure a transparent mechanism of crediting for domestic carbon prices in the application of the BCA obligation. The latter option would be useful for a party seeking to reach an agreement on the comparability of climate policy measures for the purposes of the deduction of already paid emission costs from a BCA charge in case of importation. Crediting for domestic climate policies, and providing exemptions in general, is an important feature of BCA design that affects its legality and acceptance by trading partners (Espa and Holzer 2022). The EU and other countries intending to introduce BCA measures can therefore use their PTAs to negotiate criteria for the exclusion of imports, which paid emission reduction costs or bore the burden of non-pricing climate policy regulations in their countries of origin.

Like in the case of the inclusion of lists of environmental goods, the inclusion of a BCA provision in the environmental or TSD chapters raises the question about the legal bindingness of this provision, considering that these chapters are usually exempted from the application of dispute settlement provisions under PTAs. Yet, the case of BCA is different from the elimination of tariffs for environmental goods, and the non-application of dispute settlement provisions to BCA provisions under a PTA is not critical. Unlike the case of elimination of tariffs for environmental goods, which represents 'WTO-plus' provisions, the BCA provisions constitute 'WTO-minus' obligations, that is, those perceived to contradict certain WTO rules (Cosbey 2022).[13] Therefore, if a PTA party disagrees with the other party on any aspect of the application of a BCA in the implementation stage, it is likely to take the case straight to the WTO dispute settlement rather than adjudicate the issue under the PTA.

That said, PTA negotiations can still be useful for settling issues around the implementation of BCAs. In fact, dealing with BCAs under PTAs has a number of distinct advantages (Holzer and Shariff 2012). While PTA parties can still bring a legal claim against a BCA at the WTO, dealing with BCAs under PTAs would mitigate, to some extent, the risk of a legal challenge, as BCAs would be applied on conditions previously agreed upon among PTA parties.[14] Negotiations on BCAs under PTAs might also avoid trade retaliations because PTAs may provide a useful forum for negotiations with the largest trading partners. It can be useful to discuss the application of a BCA in PTA forums with the largest trading partners, even in a situation where the BCA is not applied in a bilateral agreement. Even where a BCA is applied in trade with all trading partners, it is the largest trading partners that are likely to have the greatest objection to the measure. Discussing the application of a BCA under a PTA could enable the state imposing the BCA to work out the design details to the satisfaction of its largest trading partner and potentially offer concessions to elicit acceptance of the BCA (Holzer and Shariff 2012). While this does not eliminate the risk of a legal challenge, it may substantially reduce it. Last but not

13 It should be noted that legal hurdles to the implementation of BCAs would remain even in the case of implementation through PTAs because except for the allowed derogation of the most-favoured-nation principle, all other WTO rules regulating the application of BCAs are supposed to be followed (Holzer and Shariff 2012).

14 The parties could even agree to refrain from using the WTO dispute settlement mechanism for BCAs that comply with certain conditions. While this PTA commitment might not have strong legal currency at the WTO, it would have political value.

least, such negotiations on a BCA under a PTA may also encourage the other party or parties to impose more stringent climate policies of their own.

14.4 CONCLUSION

Preferential trade agreements offer the opportunity to experiment on a limited scale with innovative ways to use trade policies to tackle environmental challenges. Several PTAs are concluded every year, and many of them introduce small variations to established templates. As a result, recent PTAs include an ever-increasing number of EPs.

Some of these experiments might prove disappointing or lead to unintended consequences. Others, however, might accelerate our transition towards greener economies. They can help protect states' regulatory capacity, incentivise ecological transition, and favour the diffusion of green technologies. Hopefully, these successful experiments are replicated in other PTAs and inspire multilateral negotiations at the WTO. The CPTPP, for example, already contained fisheries subsidies rules a few years before the Agreement on Fisheries Subsidies was concluded at the WTO.

At the same time, EPs in PTAs have not been designed in a way that lives up to their full potential. Many of them remain vague, weak, and not very innovative. This is particularly the case for EPs that address climate change. They are less frequent and less precise than provisions related to biodiversity. Where they exist, they are often excluded from the main dispute settlement mechanism and left without any monitoring system, such as stakeholder committees or periodic ex post impact assessment.

In light of the urgency to tackle the climate crisis, it is important to unlock the full potential of PTAs for climate governance. This chapter has shown how this could be done for four types of EPs: provisions on fossil fuel subsidies, EGS, environmental exceptions to investment protection rules, and exceptions for BCAs. We have identified clear options for more ambitious and enforceable provisions in each of these four types. In many cases, these provisions would help mitigate climate change without creating additional trade distortion. Looking ahead, this untapped potential of PTAs for climate governance should be leveraged much more strongly.

Introducing ambitious EPs in PTAs would not only enable trade negotiators to learn how to design greener trade agreements, but also create political and economic conditions for their widespread adoption. Ambitious EPs can strengthen environmental industries, weaken the influence of polluting firms, and create new benchmarks for future trade negotiations. Trade governance is a complex system with multiple self-reinforcing feedback loops (Morin et al. 2017; Morin and Gomez-Mera 2019). The key is to reach as soon as possible the tipping point when this system will really help accelerate our transition towards sustainability. It is crucial to reach this tipping point in the trade governance system before the Earth system reaches its own critical thresholds leading to large-scale new self-reinforcing dynamics.

REFERENCES

Abman, R., C. Lundberg and M. Ruta 2021. "The Effectiveness of Environmental Provisions in Regional Trade Agreements," Policy Research Working Paper No. 9601. Washington, DC: World Bank.

Achakulwisut, P., P. Erickson and D. Koplow 2021. "Effect of Subsidies and Regulatory Exemptions on 2020–2030 Oil and Gas Production and Profits in the United States," *Environmental Research Letters* 16: 084023.

Baghdadi, L., I. Martinez-Zarzoso and H. Zitouna 2013. "Are RTA Agreements with Environmental Provisions Reducing Emissions?" *Journal of International Economics* 90(2): 378–390.

Bastiaens, I. and E. Postnikov 2017. "Greening up: The Effects of Environmental Standards in EU and US Trade Agreements," *Environmental Politics* 26(5): 1–23.

Bättig, M. B. and T. Bernauer 2009. "National Institutions and Global Public Goods: Are Democracies More Cooperative in Climate Change Policy?" *International Organization* 63(2): 281–308.

Bellmann, C. and M. Sugathan 2022. "Promoting and Facilitating Trade in Environmental Goods and Services: Lessons from Regional Trade Agreements," Geneva; TESS Forum.

Blümer, D., J.-F. Morin, C. Brandi and A. Berger 2020. "Environmental Provisions in Trade Agreements: Defending Regulatory Space or Pursuing Offensive Interests?" *Environmental Politics* 29(5): 866–889.

Brandi, C. and J. F. Morin 2023. *Trade and the Environment: Drivers and Effects of Environmental Provisions in Trade Agreements*. Cambridge University Press.

Brandi, C., D. Blümer and J.-F. Morin 2019. "When Do International Agreements Matter for Domestic Environmental Legislation?" *Global Environmental Politics* 19(4): 14–44.

Brandi, C., J. Schwab, A. Berger and J.-F. Morin 2020. "Do Environmental Provisions in Trade Agreements Make Exports from Developing Countries Greener?" *World Development* 129: 104899.

Casier, L., R. Fraser, M. Halle and R. Wolfe 2014. "Shining a Light on Fossil Fuel Subsidies at the WTO: How NGOs Can Contribute to WTO Notification and Surveillance," *World Trade Review* 13(4): 603–632.

Cima, E. 2018. "Promoting Renewable Energy through FTAs? The Legal Implications of a New Generation of Trade Agreements," *Journal of World Trade* 52(4): 663–695.

Colgan, J.D., J. F. Green and T. N. Hale 2021. "Asset Revaluation and the Existential Politics of Climate Change," *International Organization* 75(2): 586–610.

Conca, K. 2000. "The WTO and the Undermining of Global Environmental Governance," *Review of International Political Economy* 7(3): 484–494.

Cosbey, A. 2022. "Trade and Climate Change: Working through the Conflicts and Synergies," in M. Jakob (Ed.), *Handbook on Trade Policy and Climate Change*. Cheltenham: Edward Elgar.

de Melo, J. and J. M. Solleder 2022. "Towards an Environmental Goods Agreement Style (EGAST) Agenda to Improve the Regime Complex for Climate Change," in M. Jakob (Ed.), *Handbook on Trade Policy and Climate Change*. Cheltenham: Edward Elgar.

Dür, A., L. Baccini and M. Elsig 2014. "The Design of International Trade Agreements: Introducing a New Database," *Review of International Organizations* 9(3): 353–375.

Espa, I. and K. Holzer 2022. "From Unilateral Border Carbon Adjustments to Cooperation in Climate Clubs: Rethinking Exclusion in light of Trade and Climate Law Constraints," *European Yearbook of International Economic Law* 13.

Espa, I. and G. Marín Durán 2020. "Promoting Green Energy Through EU Preferential Trade Agreements: Potential and Limitations," *Legal Issues of Economic Integration* 47(2): 115–150.

G20 2009. "G20 Leaders Statement: The Pittsburgh Summit," www.g20.utoronto.ca/2009/2009communique0925.html.

Gagné, G. and J.-F. Morin 2006. "The Evolving American Policy on Investment Protection: Evidence from Recent FTAs and the 2004 Model BIT," *Journal of International Economic Law* 9(2): 357–382.

Gehring M. and M. Tokas 2022. "Synergies and Approaches to Climate Change in International Investment Agreements: Comparative Analysis of Investment Liberalization and Investment Protection Provisions in European Union Agreements," *Journal of World Investment and Trade* 23(5–6): 778–812.

Henckels, C. 2022. "Submission: OECD Public Consultation on Investment Treaties and Climate Change," in OECD (Ed.), *Compilation of Submissions to OECD Public Consultation on Investment Treaties and Climate Change, January-March 2022*. Paris: OECD.

Holzer, K. and T. Cottier 2015. "Addressing Climate Change under Preferential Trade Agreements: Towards Alignment of Carbon Standards under the Transatlantic Trade and Investment Partnership," *Global Environmental Change* 35: 514–522.

Holzer, K. and N. Shariff 2012. "The Inclusion of Border Carbon Adjustments in Preferential Trade Agreements: Policy Implications," *Carbon and Climate Law Review* 6(3): 246–260.

IPCC 2021. "Summary for Policymakers," in V. Masson-Delmotte et al. (Eds.), *Climate Change 2021: The Physical Science Basis. Contribution of Working Group I to the Sixth Assessment Report of the Intergovernmental Panel on Climate Change*. Cambridge, UK: Cambridge University Press.

Jinnah, S. and A. Lindsay 2016. "Diffusion through Issue Linkage: Environmental Norms in US Trade Agreements," *Global Environmental Politics* 16(3): 41–61.

Jinnah, S., and Morin, J.-F. 2020. *Greening through Trade: How American Trade Policy is Linked to Environmental Protection Abroad*. Cambridge, MA: MIT Press.

Johnson, T. 2015. "Information Revelation and Structural Supremacy: The World Trade Organization's Incorporation of Environmental Policy," *The Review of International Organizations*, 10: 207–229.

Martínez-Zarzoso, I. and W. Oueslati 2018. "Do Deep and Comprehensive Regional Trade Agreements Help in Reducing Air Pollution?" *International Environmental Agreements: Politics, Law and Economics* 18(6): 743–777.

Milewicz, K., J. Hollway, C. Peacock and D. Snidal 2016. "Beyond Trade: The Expanding Scope of the Nontrade Agenda in Trade Agreements," *Journal of Conflict Resolution* 62(4): 743–773.

Moerenhout, T. and T. Irschlinger 2020. "Exploring the Trade Impacts of Fossil Fuel Subsidies," Geneva: International Institute for Sustainable Development, www.iisd.org/system/files/publications/trade-impacts-fossil-fuel-subsidies.pdf.

Morin, J.-F. and M. Gauquelin 2016. "Trade Agreements as Vectors for the Nagoya Protocol's Implementation," CIGI Paper no 115, www.cigionline.org/sites/default/files/documents/Paper%20no.115.pdf.

Morin, J.-F. and L. Gomez-Mera 2019. "The Evolution of Governance Systems: the Case of the Trade Regime," *International Studies Review* 22(4): 15–20.

Morin, J.-F. and S. Jinnah 2018. "The Untapped Potential of Preferential Trade Agreements for Climate Governance," *Environmental Politics* 27(3): 541–565.

Morin, J.-F. and M. Rochette 2017. "Transatlantic Convergence of PTAs' Environmental Clauses," *Business and Politics* 19(4): 621–658.
Morin, J.-F., J. Pauwelyn and J. Hollway 2017. "The Trade Regime as a Complex Adaptive System: Exploration and Exploitation of Environmental Norms in Trade Agreements," *Journal of International Economic Law* 20(2): 365–390.
Morin, J.-F., A. Dür and L. Lechner 2018. "Mapping the Trade and Environment Nexus: Insights from a New Data Set," *Global Environmental Politics* 18(1): 122–139.
Newcombe, A. 2011. "General Exceptions in International Investment Agreements," in M.-C. Cordonnier Segger, M. Gehring and A. Newcombe (Eds.), *Sustainable Development in World Investment Law*. The Hague: Kluwer Law International.
OECD and IEA 2022. "Support for Fossil Fuels Almost Doubled in 2021, Slowing Progress toward International Climate Goals, According to New Analysis from OECD and IEA," www.oecd.org/environment/support-for-fossil-fuels-almost-doubled-in-2021-slowing-progress-toward-international-climate-goals-according-to-new-analysis-from-oecd-and-iea.htm.
Paine, J. 2022. "Submission to OECD Public Consultation on Investment Treaties and Climate Change," in OECD (Ed.), *Compilation of Submissions to OECD Public Consultation on Investment Treaties and Climate Change, January–March 2022*. Paris: OECD.
Parry, I. W. H., S. Black and N. Vernon 2021. "Still Not Getting Energy Prices Right: A Global and Country Update of Fossil Fuel Subsidies," IMF Working Paper No. 2021/236. Washington, DC: International Monetary Fund.
Polanco, R., J. de Sepibus and K. Holzer 2017. "TTIP and Climate Change: How Real Are Race to the Bottom Concerns?" *Carbon and Climate Law Review* 11(3): 206–222.
Poletti, A. and D. Sicurelli 2016. "The European Union, Preferential Trade Agreements, and the International Regulation of Sustainable Biofuels," *Journal of Common Market Studies* 54(2): 249–266.
Sabanogullari, L. 2015. "The Merits and Limitations of General Exception Clauses in Contemporary Investment Treaty Practice," *IISD Investment Treaty News*, May 21, 2015.
Skovgaard, J. and H. van Asselt 2019. "The Politics of Fossil Fuel Subsidies and Their Reform: Implications for Climate Change Mitigation," *WIREs: Climate Change* 10(4): e581.
Sorgho, Z. and J. Tharakan 2022. "Do PTAs with Environmental Provisions Reduce GHG Emissions? Distinguishing the effectiveness of Climate-Related Provisions," *Environmental and Resource Economics* 83: 709–732.
Tienhaara, K. 2018. "Regulatory Chill in a Warming World: The Threat to Climate Policy Posed by Investor-State Dispute Settlement," *Transnational Environmental Law* 7(2): 229–250.
UNCTAD and IIED 2022. "International Investment Agreements and Climate Action," Policy Brief, https://investmentpolicy.unctad.org/news/hub/1684/20220124-register-now-webinar-on-iias-climate-%20act.
UNEP and IISD 2019. *Measuring Fossil Fuel Subsidies in the Context of the Sustainable Development Goals*, Nairobi, Kenya: UNEP.
Velut, J. B., D. Baeza-Breinbauer, M. De Bruijne, E. Garnizova, M. Jones, K. Kolben, L. Oules, V. Rouas, F. Tigere Pittet and T. Zamparutti 2022. "Comparative Analysis of Trade and Sustainable Development Provisions in Free Trade Agreements," London: LSE Trade Policy Hub, https://trade.ec.europa.eu/doclib/docs/2022/february/tradoc_160043.pdf.
WTO 2021. "Ministerial Statement on Fossil Fuel Subsidies," WT/MIN(21)/9/Rev.1, https://docs.wto.org/dol2fe/Pages/SS/directdoc.aspx?filename = q:/WT/MIN21/9r1.pdf&Open = True.
2022. "World Trade Report 2022: Climate Change and International Trade". Geneva: World Trade Organization.
Zhou, L., X. Tian and Z. Zhou 2017. "The Effects of Environmental Provisions in RTAs on PM2. 5 Air Pollution," *Applied Economics* 49(27): 2630–2641.

15

Gender Equality in Trade Agreements

The Old, the New, and the Future

Anoush der Boghossian, Amrita Bahri, and Lolita Laperle-Forget

15.1 INTRODUCTION

Over the past few decades, countries have increasingly negotiated and adopted gender provisions in preferential trade agreements (PTAs). While the first gender provision was included in the Treaty of Rome establishing the European Economic Community in 1957 (Ghailani 2013), the trend of integrating gender provisions in PTAs kicked off in Africa in the 1980s with the establishment of regional economic communities (Laperle-Forget 2022). The 'gender champions' of PTAs are now largely concentrated in Africa, Europe, Latin America, and North America. Yet, the most recent trends suggest their expansion worldwide (Lechner 2019) as even countries that still question the link between trade and gender in the World Trade Organization (WTO) have gone ahead and have now entered into PTA negotiations that include provisions and chapters on gender issues.[1] This marks a turning point in PTA negotiations which will very likely influence future WTO discussions on gender and women's economic empowerment.

But what is the advantage of introducing gender provisions in PTAs, and why do countries negotiate such commitments? In fact, governments increasingly recognise women's specific and determinant roles in the economy and their fundamental contribution to sustainable growth (der Boghossian 2023a). At the WTO 12th Ministerial Conference (MC12), the 164 Members of the WTO multilaterally and by consensus recognised the importance of women's economic empowerment and the work of the WTO in this field (WTO 2022b).

In addition, governments' concerns about gender equality are addressed in their national trade policies, not only as part of the objectives, but also as targeted measures to support women in trade and in the economy. Governments often adopt policies facilitating women's access to the workforce and jobs in export-oriented

[1] Authors' informal exchanges with trade negotiators, 2022.

sectors by creating women-favouring employment incentives for the private sector. Also, more and more, governments are adopting measures to foster female entrepreneurship (der Boghossian and Bahri 2023). While trade policies foster women's access to economic opportunities as part of a win–win partnership between governments and their female population, countries also consider that social issues, such as lack of mobility, unequal access to healthcare, or gender-based violence, are creating obstacles for women to take full advantage of opportunities created by trade policies, and these can be seen as new types of trade barriers. Therefore, some governments embed social issues in their trade policies or accompany them with socially oriented policies. Looking closely at trade policies and discussions at the WTO, some research shows that it is increasingly recognised that without social advancements, women's economic empowerment cannot be achieved, and without women's empowerment, economic efficiency and productivity cannot be developed fully (der Boghossian 2023a and 2023b).

Through PTAs, governments aim at establishing agreed tariff reductions for an easier access to parties' markets or at creating a set of harmonised rules to limit or eliminate technical barriers to trade, thereby creating legal commitments in these fields for governments that negotiate and adopt them.

As of 2022, about one-third of PTAs notified to the WTO contain commitments on gender equality, ranging from general non-discrimination objectives based on sex to targeted commitments such as access to training, employment, or finance (WTO 2022a). Governments also pursue these commitments in specific areas such as procurement, health, or services and focus on female workers and leaders, as well as women entrepreneurs and exporters (Bahri 2021a).

The range of gender commitments in existing PTAs is, therefore, wide and often goes beyond strictly defined trade issues.[2] This is not surprising, considering that the term 'gender' refers to the social roles, responsibilities, behaviours, and identities associated with men and women in society at large. These are constructed based on social, cultural, and historical factors. Therefore, provisions that address gender issues are bound to touch upon multiple wide-ranging issues. Owing to this reason, gender provisions in PTAs not only focus on levelling the trade playing field for women and eliminating the barriers they face in trade, but also addressing the ones existing in the economy and in the society at large. For this purpose, there is an intrinsic need to also integrate gender issues in trade policies even though they are not directly linked to economic growth.

Despite the fact that PTAs have the potential to effectively promote gender equality, as countries assume various commitments in their legal provisions, they lack essential elements for the implementation of promises that members assume

[2] As recognised by the Aid for Trade Task Force Recommendations in 2006 (WT/AFT/1), gender issues are cross-cutting, https://docsonline.wto.org/dol2fe/Pages/SS/directdoc.aspx?filename=Q:/WT/AFT/1.pdf&Open=True.

within these policy instruments. They also overlook some issues that are essential for women's economic empowerment and directly deal with the problems women face in accessing opportunities offered by trade. These elements are identified and analysed in this chapter and form the basis for prompting future design elements in PTAs related to gender.

In its first section, this chapter reviews how gender provisions are integrated in the existing PTAs. In particular, it will categorise these provisions in three generations evolving from binding provisions to including new gender-related issues. In the second section, the chapter looks at the commonalities between these gender provisions across regions, specifically outlining that some provisions focus on economic gains for women, while others target merely social issues. Going further, in the third section, this chapter establishes that gender provisions fall under both WTO-plus and WTO-extra commitment categories. It also explores how PTAs and gender provisions foster the implementation of other international commitments taken by governments in other instruments, notably the Convention on the Elimination of Discrimination against Women (CEDAW). In the fourth section, the chapter reviews what gender issues are not included in PTAs so far. It also looks at the reasons why they should be included and how they can be integrated in PTAs. This section also explores how some implementation and enforcement processes are missing from the gender provisions in existing PTAs, such as impact assessments, and it also analyses how transparency can be a powerful implementation process involving new actors, such as national parliaments, and establishing a link with the 2006 WTO Transparency Mechanism on Regional Trade Agreements (RTAs). On the basis of this analysis, the fifth section of the chapter defines a new model and roadmap for the concrete implementation of gender provisions contained in PTAs.

In conclusion, the chapter shows how strong implementation processes can support gender equality across the policy board.

15.2 GENDER PROVISIONS IN PTAS: A STATE OF PLAY

Over the past 65 years, gender provisions have evolved, revealing different trends across periods and regions. Looking at different phases in time, specific trends can be observed that help define and categorise gender equality provisions in three generations.

15.2.1 *Three Generations of Gender Provisions from 1957 to 2022*

The first generation of gender provisions is defined by the binding factor of the provisions. This set of initial provisions addressing gender issues in explicit terms[3]

[3] Gender provisions are the ones that include an explicit mention of gender, sex, women, girls, or related terminology, including the international instruments promoting women's rights,

was couched in binding language, and they provided for precise obligations on gender equality. For example, the very first gender provision in the Treaty of Rome formulates a binding and precise obligation for state parties to ensure and implement the principle of equal pay for men and women workers (Article 119). Similarly, twenty-six years later, the Treaty for the Establishment of the Economic Community of Central African States (ECCAS) also provided for a specific obligation for Member States to develop research and policies aimed at 'improving the economic, social and cultural status of women in urban and rural areas and increasing their integration in development activities' (Article 60). Other regional economic integration agreements concluded in the 1990s have also provided such binding language for gender equality, including the Treaty of the Southern African Development Community (SADC).

In 1993, the Treaty Establishing the Common Market for Eastern and Southern Africa (COMESA) was concluded with Chapter 24 on Women in Development and Business, the first chapter on trade and gender that was ever included in a PTA. This chapter recognises women's contribution to socio-economic development and provides for a set of binding obligations and actions to close gender gaps. Based on this chapter, parties committed to eliminating discriminatory laws, regulations, and customs against women, and those that prevent them from owning land or accessing credit. The COMESA Treaty also promotes the 'effective integration and participation of women at all levels of development especially at the decision-making levels' and for 'special programmes for women in small and medium-size enterprises' (Articles 154 and 155). These specific obligations have been similarly included in the Treaty establishing the East Africa Community (EAC) in 1999 (Articles 121 and 122). None of the mentioned provisions are excluded from the PTA's dispute settlement mechanism. During this period, PTAs did not treat gender equality obligations differently from any other provisions with regard to their enforcement potential.

Also, the first generation of gender provisions were mostly, if not only, included in the PTAs described above. In fact, these regional agreements go beyond reducing trade barriers between state parties. For example, many include environmental objectives. On average, in the 1990s, about seventy-six agreements included such objectives (OECD 2023). Similarly, these agreements included social and gender equality objectives. In particular, in the 1983 ECCAS, state parties committed to 'develop collective research by appropriate policies aimed at improving the economic, social and cultural status of women in urban and rural areas and increasing their integration in development activities'.[4] In 1992, the Maastricht Treaty of the

such as the CEDAW, the Beijing Declaration and Platform for Action for the Rights of Women and Girls, the Buenos Aires Declaration on Trade and Women's Economic Empowerment, or the UN Sustainable Development Goal 5 on gender equality.

4 Article 60 (Social Affairs).

European Union (EU) included a provision recognising 'equality between men and women with regard to labour market opportunities and treatment at work'.[5] EU Member States also committed to 'ensure equality between men and women with regard to labour market opportunities and treatment at work'.[6] The Treaty also encourages state parties to adopt measures providing advantages for women to ease their access to vocational activity or to address disadvantages in their professional careers. Similarly, during the same period, state parties of the North American Free Trade Agreement (NAFTA) addressed employment discrimination and equal pay between men and women (Monteiro 2021). The second generation of gender provisions merely addresses gender issues with a few references in PTAs and contains relatively low commitments reconciling gender equality with trade liberalisation. These gender provisions were included in PTAs around 1995 with agreements between the EU and developing countries. Between 1995 and 2002, eight PTAs with provisions addressing women's access to education and family-related issues were concluded. While only European and African countries have concluded the first generation of gender provisions,[7] the practice spread across the globe with the second generation. This is the 'propagation era', when the number of PTAs with gender provisions progressively increased, and new PTAs with gender provisions were concluded in the Middle East, North America, Latin America, the Caribbean, and Asia (WTO 2022a). With a few exceptions, the binding level of second-generation gender provisions has generally decreased compared to the first one. This period can also be described as the 'era of mitigated commitments'. Instead of binding provisions with precise obligations, the vast majority of the second-generation provisions address gender issues as part of cooperation activities and information-sharing or only include one reference to gender issues without addressing women's specific needs or interests.

In addition, the obligation to cooperate is often diluted with the inclusion of an indicative list of potential cooperation activities, thus leaving at the discretion of the parties which actions to take to address gender issues (as can be seen in the Chile–Viet Nam Free Trade Agreement (FTA) (Articles 9.3 and 9.4)). Also, gender considerations are often addressed along with several other issues in a list of potential areas of cooperation, thus depriving gender equality commitments of any tangible importance that they otherwise might have if they are frontloaded in an agreement (as can be seen in the Association Agreement between the European Union and the European Atomic Energy Community and their Member States, of the one part, and the Republic of Moldova, of the other part (Article 375)).

5 Article 2.1.

6 Article 6.1.

7 At the time of the first generation of gender provisions, only a few PTAs were concluded. The Regional Trade Agreements Database (World Trade Organisation 2022) maps forty-five RTAs in force in 1995; see also https://rtais.wto.org/UI/charts.aspx.

Interestingly, the first gender provision to be explicitly excluded from the dispute settlement chapter was concluded under Article 16.5 of the Dominican Republic–Central America–United States FTA (CAFTA-DR).[8] From this agreement onwards, the number of gender provisions that cannot be adjudicated or enforced through the agreements' dispute resolution mechanism has gradually increased.

However, the year 2016 has marked a turning point. The conclusion of the Chile–Uruguay FTA ushered in the third and current generation of gender provisions. In this agreement, gender issues are addressed in a more comprehensive manner through multiple provisions and chapters, including a standalone chapter on trade and gender. This contrasts with the previous practice of merely considering gender issues in PTAs. Among others, this PTA addresses in eight provisions various gender issues related to women's participation in the labour force, female entrepreneurship, women's access to education, health, and productive resources (Articles 11.9, 13.2, 13.3, 14.1, 14.2, 14.3, 14.4, and 14.5).

The Chile–Uruguay FTA served as a model for the negotiations of gender provisions and chapters in subsequent trade agreements. Not only have similar gender issues been addressed in recent PTAs, but the structure of the chapter on trade and gender in the Chile–Uruguay FTA has also been duplicated in eleven other subsequent trade agreements.[9]

Also, similar institutional arrangements and enforcement mechanisms applicable to gender provisions are provided in these PTAs. These FTAs, just like the

8 Article 16.5 provides for cooperation on gender issues and the elimination of discrimination in the workplace. Article 16.6 explicitly excludes Chapter 16 on labour from the application of the dispute settlement mechanism provided in the agreement.

9 Since the conclusion of the Acuerdo de Libre Comercio entre la República de Chile y la República Oriental del Uruguay (Chile–Uruguay) (signed 4 October 2016, enforced 13 December 2018), the chapters on trade and gender included in subsequent PTAs have followed a similar structure: they include general provisions stating the common objectives, a provision recalling international women's rights instruments, provisions listing area and activities for cooperation, and provisions on institutional arrangements. Preferential trade agreements with similar gender chapters or sections are: Acuerdo Comercial entre la República Argentina y la República de Chile (Chile–Argentina) (signed 2 November 2017, enforced 1 June 2019), Free Trade Agreement between the Government of Canada and the Government of the Republic of Chile (Canada–Chile) (signed 5 June 2017, enforced 5 February 2019), Canada–Israel Free Trade Agreement (signed 1 June 2018, enforced 1 September 2019), Free Trade Agreement between the Republic of Chile and the Federative Republic of Brazil (Chile–Brazil) (signed 21 November 2018, enforced 25 January 2022), Agreement between the United Kingdom of Great Britain and Northern Ireland and Japan for a Comprehensive Economic Partnership (UK–Japan) (signed 7 October, enforced 1 January 2020), Chile–Ecuador Acuerdo de Complementación Económica No. 75 (signed 13 August 2020, enforced 16 May 2022), Free Trade Agreement between Iceland, the Principality of Liechtenstein and the Kingdom of Norway and the United Kingdom of Great Britain and Northern Ireland (UK–Iceland, Liechtenstein, and Norway) (signed 8 July 2021), Acuerdo de Libre Comercio Chile–Paraguay (Chile–Paraguay) (signed 1 December 2021), Free Trade Agreement between the United Kingdom of Great Britain and Northern Ireland and Australia (UK–Australia) (signed 16 December 2021), and Pacific Alliance–Singapore FTA (signed 22 January 2022).

Chile–Uruguay FTA, also establish a technical body in charge of coordinating cooperation efforts and reviewing the implementation of the gender provisions, while all chapters on trade and gender in third-generation PTAs are explicitly excluded from the dispute settlement chapter – except for Chapter 13 in the Canada–Israel FTA.[10]

In third-generation PTAs, a new variety of gender issues is addressed, and new types of gender provisions are formulated. For example, recent PTAs address women's leadership and education in male-dominated sectors or the conciliation of professional and family responsibilities, as well as unpaid care work and sexual harassment in the workplace. These issues were not addressed in previous PTAs. Also, recent PTAs include provisions on public awareness of gender equality and equity laws, policies, and good practices. Additionally, they contain commitments on the parties' right to establish, modify, and monitor compliance with their gender laws and policies in accordance with their priorities. Some post-Brexit PTAs concluded by the United Kingdom (UK) also include novel gender provisions (Bahri, 2021b). For example, PTAs concluded with Japan, Australia, and New Zealand formulate one of the few trade rules on gender found in PTAs in the chapter on domestic services regulations, where parties are prohibited from adopting or maintaining qualification and certification measures and requirements that are discriminatory against women.[11] Interestingly, the UK–New Zealand FTA is also the first PTA to include a provision stipulating 'that it is inappropriate to waive, or otherwise derogate from, their gender equality laws to encourage trade or investment' (Article 25.3). This type of provision is usually found in environment and labour chapters and was not used for gender equality standards before.

15.2.2 *Gender Provisions in PTAs: Different Priorities across the Globe*

In addition to the different trends in gender equality provisions over time, topics addressed in gender-related provisions also vary from one region to the other. Some regions have included provisions on social and healthcare concerns of women, and others have grounded these provisions in purely economic and market-oriented interests. For example, the North American countries have treated gender-related

[10] The text of the agreement provides that parties can bring a dispute arising on a matter related to the chapter on trade and gender under the dispute settlement chapter, provided that both parties consent (Article 13.6).

[11] A few gender provisions in PTAs formulate trade or investment rules, as most provide for cooperation or laws or policies to promote gender equality at the domestic level. Another example of a rule is provided in the Comprehensive Economic and Trade Agreement (CETA) between Canada, of the one part, and the European Union and its Member States, of the other part (EU–Canada) (signed 30 October 2016, entry into force 21 September 2017), Article 8.10, in which non-discrimination on the basis of gender is included in the fair and equitable treatment of investors.

concerns from an economic and market access perspective[12] and negotiated provisions that mainly relate to labour standards, women's access to productive resources, markets, technology, and skill development, as seen in the United States–Mexico–Canada Agreement (USMCA, Articles 23 and 25). In this sense, they have essentially focused on women employees or entrepreneurs. The EU's approach is geared towards the inclusion of provisions that deal with gender equality, non-discrimination, labour standards, education and skill development, health and safety, and maternal care.[13] Hence, most of the agreements negotiated by the EU have explored women in their three different roles: as employees, social actors, and mothers.

Another contrast can be seen in the areas that countries in the Asia-Pacific region have explored in their trade agreements. Many of the inclusions are drafted as right-to-regulate provisions, wherein countries reserve the policy space to regulate specific areas that may impact women's health and maternal concerns, such as healthcare, child nutrition, childcare, and women's personal safety.[14] These inclusions depict that the countries in this region have mostly looked at women as mothers and caretakers, but not as employees or as business stakeholders, as depicted in the gender-explicit provisions accommodated in their trade agreements.

On the other end, South America's approach is similar to that of North America, but some agreements in this region include gender concerns with topics similar to those in the Asia-Pacific region as the provisions negotiated with Asia-Pacific countries focus exclusively and solely on health, childcare, and other maternity concerns.[15]

Lastly, the gender-explicit provisions found in agreements signed between African countries seek to integrate women into the region's development process by enhancing women's access to resources, promoting female entrepreneurship, and increasing women's representation and participation in political and decision-making positions.[16] In this sense, these countries have sought to employ their agreements

[12] Comprehensive and Progressive Agreement for Trans-Pacific Partnership (CPTPP) (signed 8 March 2018, effective 30 December 2018), Chapter 23: Development, Article 23(4); USMCA (signed 30 November 2018, effective 1 July 2020), Chapter 25: Small and Medium Sized Enterprises, Article 25(2).

[13] Agreement establishing an Association between the EU and its Member States on the one hand and the Central America on the other (EU–Central American Association Agreement) (signed 29 June 2012, enforced 2013), Articles 13, 32, 41, and 47; Stabilisation and Association Agreement between the European Communities and their Member States of the one part and the Republic of Albania of the other part (EU–Albania Stabilisation and Association Agreement) (signed 12 June 2006, entry into force (G) 1 December 2006, (S) 1 April 2009), Article 99.

[14] Australia–New Zealand Closer Economic Agreement (ANZCERTA) (Australia–New Zealand) (adopted 28 March 1983, entry into force (S) 1 January 1989), Annex II; Chile–South Korea Free Trade Agreement (adopted 21 July 2018), Article 10(2).

[15] Free Trade Agreement between the Republic of Korea and the Republic of Chile (signed 15 February 2003, enforced 1 April 2004), Article 10.2

[16] Economic Community of West African States (ECOWAS) (signed in 24 July 1993, enforced 23 August 1995), Articles 3, 63; COMESA (signed 5 November 1993, enforced 8 December 1994), Articles 154, 155.

to improve the conditions of women not only as social or cultural actors or contributors to economic development, but also as entrepreneurs, politicians, and decision-makers.

15.3 GENDER PROVISIONS: WTO-PLUS OR WTO-EXTRA?

Depending on their scope, some gender provisions fall under the 'WTO-plus' commitment category while others can be considered as 'WTO-extra' commitments. In addition, gender provisions are also closely linked with international commitments on gender equality beyond the WTO objectives.

15.3.1 *Gender Equality in WTO-plus and WTO-extra Commitment Categories*

15.3.1.1 Gender Equality in WTO-plus Provisions

Some gender commitments agreed by governments in PTAs come under the current mandate of the WTO, but they go beyond those adopted at the multilateral level. They can be categorised as WTO-plus commitments (Horn et al. 2010). Gender provisions intersect with topics considered in the WTO mandate, such as agriculture, fisheries, government procurement, and digital trade (Horn et al. 2010).[17] However, they go further than WTO agreements, which do not include explicit language on gender or women's economic empowerment and are therefore gender blind. Consequently, given their nature, these provisions automatically go beyond the WTO agreements and mandates.

In agriculture, some gender provisions in a trade agreement encourage data collection of women engaged in the agriculture sector.[18] They also promote cooperation activities and support the development of adequate policies to support the economic development of rural women in trade and investment and their inclusion in the economy.[19] Some also explicitly recognise the role of women in agriculture and how they contribute to economic development or how rural transformation is

[17] A new agreement was multilaterally adopted on fisheries subsidies at the 12th WTO Ministerial Conference: Agreement on Fisheries Subsidies, Ministerial Decision of 17 June 2022, WT/MIN(22)/33 and WT/L/1144. About public procurement, although a plurilateral agreement was adopted, it comes under the WTO mandate and has been identified as a WTO-plus commitment. Similarly, while WTO Members have established a joint initiative on e-commerce, leading to the negotiation of a plurilateral agreement on e-commerce, it is also part of the WTO multilateral agenda (WT/L/274 and WT/MIN(22)/32).

[18] Pacific Agreement on Closer Economic Relation Plus (PACER PLUS) (signed 14 June 2017, enforced 13 December 2020), attachment B.

[19] For example, ECCAS (signed 18 October 1983, enforced 18 December 1984), Article 77 (of the revised treaty); Chile–Paraguay FTA, Article 13.15.

ineffective without the full participation of women.[20] Other provisions promote the application of good practices in agriculture supported by a 'gender approach in development policies and strategies'[21] and address gender biases that influence the nature of farming systems.[22]

On fisheries, some PTAs promote building women's capacity in the sector and target women traders engaged in fishing and future fisherwomen.[23]

Similarly, in digital trade, most gender provisions focus on building women's digital skills and fostering their access to digital tools and technology.[24] Additionally, in a few PTAs, governments commit to collecting and developing data on the barriers women face in digital trade to inform their policies and monitor women's participation in digital trade.[25]

Some gender provisions also aim at facilitating and increasing women's participation in public procurement markets, either through cooperation[26] or preferential treatment.[27] Interestingly, one provision links women's digital skills enhancement and their access to digital tools and technology to improve their participation in government procurement markets.

15.3.1.2 Gender Equality in 'WTO-extra' Commitments

Some gender provisions address issues that are external to the strict and explicit WTO mandate and are thus considered to be 'WTO-extra' (WTO-X) commitments (Horn et al. 2010). Under this group, two types of provisions can be considered. The

[20] COMESA, Articles 154 and 155; EAC (signed 30 November 1999, enforced 7 July 2000), Article 122.

[21] Free Trade Agreement between the Government of the People's Republic of China and the Government of the Republic of Peru (signed 28 April 2009, enforced 1 March 2010), Article 164.

[22] Economic Partnership Agreement between the East African Community Partner States, of the one part, and the European Union and its Member States of the other part (signed September 2016), Article 83; UK–Kenya Economic Partnership Agreement (signed 8 December 2020), Article 83.

[23] For example, UK–Kenya, Article 89; Agreement Establishing An Economic Partnership Agreement between the Eastern and Southern Africa States and the United Kingdom of Great Britain and Northern Ireland (signed 31 January 2019, enforced 1 January 2021), Article 34; Economic Partnership Agreement between the Eastern and Southern Africa States, on the one part, and the European Community and its Member States, on the other part (signed August 2009, enforced 14 May 2012), Article 35.

[24] For example, Chile–Brazil FTA, Article 10.15.

[25] For example, UK–New Zealand, Article 15.20.

[26] For example, UK–New Zealand Articles 16.22 and 25.5; Chile–Paraguay, Article 13.5; UK–Australia, Articles 16.22 and 24.1.

[27] The United States (US) has included a reservation clause to the chapter on public procurement to allow a preferential treatment to women-owned businesses. For example, Free Trade Agreement between Peru and the United States of America (US–Peru) (signed 12 April 2006, enforced 1 February 2009); Free Trade Agreement between the United States and Morocco (signed 15 June 2004, enforced 1 January 2006), Annex 9-A-1.

first one includes provisions that are not trade issues by nature but are nonetheless directly related to trade. For example, several gender provisions focus on facilitating women's access to financing, capital, credit, and financial assistance and building their financial literacy and skills.[28] Interestingly, one provision addresses women's access to capital and credit through the development of their digital skills and access to digital tools and technology.[29] These issues, although not considered as trade issues, directly affect women's ability to participate in trade.

The second group includes those provisions that are not trade issues by nature and are not related to trade, but rather focus on women's roles and place in society. For example, provisions focusing on female leadership and women's participation in decision-making do not fall under the WTO mandate and are not directly or indirectly related to trade. Such provisions support or promote women's high-level positions in society and their contribution to decision-making in business or in the public sphere. In particular, some agreements include commitments to develop female leadership through training and experience sharing, foster female leadership networks in business and trade, and promote and facilitate equal participation of men and women in decision-making positions and in positions of authority.[30] Other commitments also aim at fostering women's leadership in technology, science, and innovation, where women are greatly underrepresented (OECD 2017).[31] The question is why countries have gone ahead to include such provisions in trade agreements if they are not directly impacting women's access to opportunities created by trade. In fact, evidence shows that when women lead companies, companies are more efficient, and therefore even these issues can be considered as ones that are indirectly related to trade interests (International Labour Organization 2019). Similarly, governments run by women can be more efficient, as demonstrated during the COVID-19 pandemic. Such countries were, in fact, better prepared and faced a lower death rate level due to COVID-19 because female political leaders had invested more in their countries' universal healthcare (Abras et al. 2021). Therefore, fostering female leadership could result in better policymaking, both in the public and private sectors.

15.3.2 *Gender Provisions Aligned with CEDAW*

In 1979, the United Nations adopted the CEDAW.[32] Currently, 189 state parties have ratified or acceded to CEDAW, and of these, 14 per cent have not signed any PTAs with gender provisions. Also, only 7.5 per cent have negotiated and adopted gender provisions in their PTAs. The Convention on the Elimination of Discrimination against Women is one of the most important and compelling

[28] For example, COMESA, Articles 154 and 155; EAC, Articles 121 and 122; UK–New Zealand, Article 25.5; Chile–Argentina, Article 15.3.

[29] UK–New Zealand, Article 15.20.

[30] For example, UK–Japan, Article 21.2; Chile–Uruguay, Article 14.3; CPTPP, Article 23.4.

[31] For example, Chile–Argentina, Article 15.3; Canada–Israel, Article 13.3; UK–Australia, Article 24.2.

[32] See text of the Convention, www.ohchr.org/en/instruments-mechanisms/instruments/convention-elimination-all-forms-discrimination-against-women, accessed on 6 October 2022.

international treaties addressing women's rights, gender equality, and gender-based discrimination. It goes beyond setting general objectives regarding gender equality and women's protection against discrimination. It outlines a set of specific commitments to address issues related to gender equality or discrimination against women in a targeted manner. Countries that ratified or acceded to the Convention are bound by these provisions. Additionally, CEDAW is often used by governments as a legal basis to pursue their development objectives. For example, Switzerland stated that CEDAW provides a legal basis for its Swiss Agency for Development and Cooperation (SDC) to elaborate 'partnership and policy dialogue with its partner countries on bilateral and multilateral level' (SDC 2017). All the articles contained in CEDAW are covered by gender provisions in PTAs, as outlined in Table 15.1 below.[33] Therefore, gender provisions directly support the implementation of the Convention and are aligned with its objectives and principles.

TABLE 15.1 *Gender provisions in PTAs implicitly support the implementation of the Convention*

Types of gender provisions in PTAs	Corresponding Articles in CEDAW
Gender inequality issues	Preamble, Article 1, Article 2, Article 3, Article 4, Article 5
Women's participation in economic and development activities • Women's participation in the workforce • Women's participation in business • Women's access to productive resources	Preamble, Article 10.a, Article 11, Article 13, Article 14.2.d, Article 14.2.e
Social issues and the role of women in social life • Women's access to education • Women's safety • Family-related issues • Social inclusion and vulnerability • Women's access to health and food security	Article 5.b, Article 6, Article 9, Article 10, Article 11.1.e, Article 11.1.f, Article 11.2, Article 12, Article 13.a, Article 13.c, Article 14, Article 16
Representation of women in decision-making roles and leadership and representation of women in politics	Article 5, Article 7b, Article 7.c, Articles 8
Role of women in cultural life and protection of cultural rights	Article 10.g, Article 13.c

Source: Authors' analysis based on WTO 2022 (Table 1).[34]

[33] The Convention on the Elimination of Discrimination against Women includes 30 Articles overall, classified in six parts. The provisions specifically related to gender discrimination issues are outlined in the Convention from Articles 1 to 16. Articles 17 to 30 focus on the enforcement and implementation mechanism. For the purpose of this chapter, Table 1 does not go beyond Article 16.

[34] INF/TGE/COM/4.

Moreover, 10 per cent of trade agreements that include gender provisions explicitly refer to this Convention. State parties of most of these agreements reaffirm or recall their commitments under CEDAW. Interestingly, one PTA makes an explicit link between the achievements of the gender equality goals of the trade agreement and the effective implementation of CEDAW.[35] Therefore, trade agreements can serve as an instrument for effective gender equality, not just in trade but across the policy spectrum.

15.4 GENDER PROVISIONS IN THE NEXT DECADE: HOW TO MOVE FORWARD?

As mentioned above, gender provisions have significantly evolved over time. However, one can observe several gaps in existing gender provisions to effectively support gender equality and women's participation in trade, either through the depth or rather shallowness of issues addressed in PTAs or through the lack of proper enforcement and transparency mechanisms.

15.4.1 *New Topics for Future Trade Negotiations*

Gender-related provisions vary from one region to the other, but a majority of them have focused so far on education and training,[36] representation of women in decision-making roles,[37] women's employment,[38] labour standards,[39] equality and

[35] European Union–Central American Association Agreement, Article 47.1.

[36] Euro-Mediterranean Agreement establishing an Association between the European Community and its Member States, of the one part, and the People's Democratic Republic of Algeria, of the other part (signed 22 April 2002, enforced 1 September 2005), Article 78; Euro-Mediterranean Agreement establishing an Association between the European Communities and their Member States, of the one part, and the Arab Republic of Egypt, of the other part (signed 25 June 2001, enforced 1 June 2004), Article 42.

[37] Agreement establishing an association between the European Community and its Member States, of the one part, and the Republic of Chile, of the other part (signed 18 November, enforced 1 March 2003), Article 45; Association Agreement between the European Union and its Member States, of the one part, and Ukraine, of the other part (signed 27 June 2014, enforced 23 April 2014), Article 420; Agreement for the Establishment of the Preferential Trade Area for Eastern and Southern Africa (signed December 1981, enforced 30 September 1982), Article 154.

[38] USMCA, Article 23.12; Canada–Jordan Free Trade Agreement (signed 28 June 2009, enforced 01 October 2012), Article 1.

[39] Free trade Agreement between the European Union and its Member States, of the one part, and the Republic of Korea, of the other part (EU–Korea, Republic of) (signed 16 September 2010, enforced 1 July 2011), Article 13.4; Free Trade Agreement between the European Union and the Socialist Republic of Viet Nam (signed 30 June 2019, enforced 1 August 2020), Article 13.4.

non-discrimination,[40] physical safety,[41] protection of maternity,[42] healthcare concerns,[43] and entrepreneurial capacity.[44] Yet, many crucial areas remain unexplored in current trade agreements, which, if included, can have the potential to enhance women's empowerment even further in international trade. Three such areas can be considered, as they can further improve the potential of trade agreements to help women overcome the barriers they currently face.

15.4.1.1 Going beyond Traditional Promises of Enhancing Access to Finance

Various countries in existing trade agreements committed to and recognised the need to enhance women's access to finance or financial inclusion,[45] but most of these agreements so far have not gone into the 'how' part, that is, 'how' countries can enhance women's access to finance. This depends on many factors, including access to basic financial services, trade finance instruments, affordable credit, and acceptable collaterals. Hence, what remains to be seen so far are concrete commitments and plans on how countries can put such provisions into action.

In particular, in future trade agreements, countries can agree on setting up strategies, developing better financial inclusion policies, and appropriate legislation to regulate these issues. Countries can also appoint a committee that may identify procedures to improve women businesses' access to finance and to financial and non-financial services, including through innovative mechanisms, as these mechanisms

[40] Dominican Republic–Central America–United States Free Trade Agreement (CAFTA-DR) (signed 5 August 2004, enforced 1 March 2007), Annex 16.5; United States–Colombia Trade Promotion Agreement (signed 22 November, enforced 15 May 2012), Annex 17.6; United States–Peru Free Trade Agreement (signed 1 February 2009), Annex 17.6; Free Trade Agreement between Canada and the Republic of Peru (Canada–Peru) (signed 29 May 2008, enforced 1 August 2009), Annex I; Canada–Ukraine Free Trade Agreement (signed 11 July 2016, enforced 1 August 2017), Annex 13-A; Treaty Establishing the European Community (signed in 1957, enforced in 1958), Article 3; Agreement on Trade, Development and Cooperation between the European Community and its Member States, of the one part, and The Republic of South Africa, of the other part (signed 11 October 1999, enforced 1 May 2004 2004), Article 86.

[41] Free Trade Agreement between Australia and the Republic of Peru (Australia–Peru) (signed 12 February 2018, enforced 11 February 2020), Article 20.2; Free Trade Agreement between the European Union and the Republic of Singapore (signed 15 October 2018, enforced in 2019), Appendix 8-B-1.

[42] Euro-Mediterranean Agreement establishing an Association between the European Communities and their Member States, of the one part, and the Republic of Tunisia, of the other part (signed 17 July 1995, enforced 1 March 1998), Article 65; Free Trade Agreement between New Zealand and the Republic of Korea (signed 23 March 2015, enforced 20 December 2015), Annex II.

[43] Free Trade Agreement between the Government of Malaysia and the Government of the Republic of Turkey (signed 17 April 2014, enforced 1 August 2015), Article 9.13; USMCA, Article 23.12

[44] EU–Canada, Article 8.10.

[45] For example, Australia–Peru, Article 22.4; Chile–Uruguay, Article 14.3

can, in particular, provide affordable credit to women entrepreneurs running small formal and informal businesses. Moreover, when countries assume commitments in relation to financial access, it is important for them to acknowledge that both public and private stakeholders play an important role in supporting private sectors' access to finance. Hence, to put such commitments into action, it is important for countries to develop transparent and predictable frameworks for collaborating with private stakeholders through public–private partnerships (PPP) or blended finance mechanisms (OECD n.d).

15.4.1.2 Provisions on Digital Inclusion and E-commerce

In an increasingly digitally enabled society, the significant challenge that remains is the digital inclusion of women. The global pandemic has made it clear that digital access is no longer a luxury but an absolute necessity. The existing trade agreements so far have not been that vocal about the need to enhance women's access to digital technologies and e-commerce opportunities; however, there are very few examples of recently concluded trade agreements where parties have acknowledged this barrier. Although a few FTAs deal with digital inclusion, the Digital Economy Partnership Agreement (DEPA)[46] between Chile, New Zealand, and Singapore (South Korea has just initiated the process of joining) is a leading example as it includes specific language that emphasises digital inclusion for marginalised groups including women. This is an Agreement wherein parties recognise 'the importance of expanding and facilitating digital economy opportunities by removing barriers' and cooperating 'on matters relating to digital inclusion'.[47] Other recent examples that feature similar provisions include CPTPP (Article 23.4) and the UK–Australia FTA (Articles 14.21, 24.1, 24.2, and 24.4).

These recent inclusions are a welcome step, but it is important to note that increasing women's participation in the digital economy and increasing their e-commerce entrepreneurial capacity require bringing together three related aspects, that is, (i) access to digital learning, (ii) access to digital infrastructure, and (iii) access to e-commerce platforms and opportunities (which is fostered by access to finance). In this sense, two problems can be seen with the existing inclusions.

First, the recent PTAs that mention the related concerns mainly focus on the need to enhance women businesses' access to digital learning or infrastructure, and they continue to remain silent on 'how' they might put these promises into action. Second, almost all PTAs in force so far have focused on access to digital learning or infrastructure, mostly leaving out of their scope the third component of increasing their businesses' access to e-commerce platforms and opportunities. As a result, most

[46] Digital Economy Partnership Agreement between Singapore, Chile, and New Zealand (signed 11 June, enforced 7 January 2021).

[47] Ibid., Article 11.1.

of the existing agreements do not integrate concrete commitments, including the means that countries may employ to enhance women's access to affordable and reliable digital infrastructure, digital financial wallets and e-banking, and e-commerce platforms, which could lead to an overall increase in women's participation in the economy and in trade. The use of digital platforms, for example, may offer women many additional opportunities, including the possibility to overcome challenges related to physical immobility, accessing new markets and knowledge, connecting with potential markets and customers, and enjoying flexible work hours and modes.

15.4.1.3 A Closer and More Explicit Consideration of Voluntary Sustainability Standards

Another innovative and comparatively unexplored way to integrate a gender equality discussion within the trade policy context is to include in trade agreements provisions on voluntary sustainability standards (VSS) (UNFSS 2012).[48] These are guidelines that encourage businesses to respect and accommodate within their operations different non-economic interests such as human rights, animal welfare, labour standards, environmental impacts, and gender equality considerations. Through these standards, countries can encourage or even require multinational enterprises (MNEs) operating within or subject to their jurisdiction to include gender equality concerns within their codes of conduct or in their contracts for the sale of goods and services. These standards can promote internal compliance (within a company with respect to owners and employees) and external compliance (with respect to their suppliers, sub-suppliers, and consumers (Mola and Poncibò 2021).

Voluntary sustainability standards can be used as a tool to articulate and encourage sustainable and inclusive practices in trade transactions and processes (Smith 2020). While most standards so far are not designed to promote gender equality, there is an increasing number of gender-focused VSS that are being developed within the trade policy space. Through the inclusion of corporate social responsibility (CSR) provisions in trade agreements, governments can push companies to include sustainability standards in their business plans and procedures (Smith 2020). This approach seems quite promising, as enterprises are the main players in international trade and the operation of trade agreements in particular. If PTAs can support companies' businesses through enhanced and frictionless market access, they can also encourage or require them to trade in an inclusive and sustainable manner (International Trade Centre 2019). Various agreements, such as the United

[48] Voluntary sustainability standards defined as 'standards specifying requirements that producers, traders, manufacturers, retailers or service providers may be asked to meet, relating to a wide range of sustainability metrics, including respect for basic human rights, worker health and safety, environmental impacts, community relations, land-use planning and others'.

States–Peru Trade Promotion Agreement (Article 17.6) and the EU–Georgia Association Agreement (Article 348), already contain provisions on CSR; however, these provisions do not explicitly mention gender equality concerns. Very few current agreements include gender-explicit CSR provisions.

One such PTA is the Canada–Israel agreement, wherein the parties seek to encourage their businesses to use CSR to address issues including labour, environment, and gender equality (Article 16.4); a similar provision also exists in the Canada–Chile agreement (Article G-14bis.). These examples show that policymakers can identify opportunities to engage with VSS initiatives as a means to deliver on gender equality commitments while also promoting trade liberalisation measures. Policymakers and trade negotiators should recognise the growing influence of VSS in global trade and the role of government in encouraging businesses to employ such inclusive policies that may help in reducing the barriers women employees currently face.

15.4.2 *Rethinking Enforcement and Implementation Mechanisms for Gender Provisions*

Gender issues are mostly addressed as part of cooperation efforts, often formulated with a mix of binding and permissive language, which narrows the precision of the obligations and their binding nature. This impacts how gender provisions can be enforced and monitored through PTA mechanisms, which are, in practice, very limited for two reasons.

First, the monitoring of gender provisions is deficient in many aspects. Although the vast majority of gender provisions are under the supervision of a monitoring institution, only a few PTAs provide for the establishment of a technical body on trade and gender, which is solely responsible for overseeing the implementation or impact of the gender provisions.[49] This body is usually composed of representatives of parties, and its primary function is to coordinate cooperation rather than conduct in-depth monitoring and evaluation activities on the impact of the provisions.

With the objective to increase the impact of gender provisions on the ground, future PTAs could consider establishing a technical body on trade and gender composed not only of party representatives but also of external stakeholders that can take on the monitoring and review exercise. The UK–New Zealand FTA can serve as an example. Although only composed of party representatives, the Inclusive

[49] The WTO Database on Gender Provisions in Regional Trade Agreements maps 252 gender provisions under the supervision of a monitoring institution (see www.wto.org). Among others, ninety-four are under the supervision of the institution in charge of the whole agreement, fifty under a technical cooperation body, and thirty-six under a technical body on trade and gender (e.g. the Canada–Chile establishes the Trade and Gender Committee (Article N bis-04) and the UK–Japan establishes the Working Group on Trade and Women's Economic Empowerment (Article 21.3)).

Trade Sub-Committee has the explicit mandate to conduct monitoring activities regarding the implementation of the chapter on trade and gender equality and determine activities to address remaining barriers that exist for women in trade.

During these activities, the Sub-Committee must consult with qualified experts on trade and gender and other stakeholders (Articles 25.6 and 30.8). This is a good example of a monitoring mechanism for gender provisions that can ensure parties' accountability and representation of women's interests in implementation efforts.

Other PTAs provide for ensuring a platform for individuals and organisations to share their views with the technical body on issues related to trade and gender and formulate, in binding language, the obligation for parties to provide a similar platform, at the domestic level.[50] These considerations should continue to be addressed in PTAs to allow experts, civil society, and women's associations to share their perspectives and experience to ensure that the state parties' efforts are oriented towards women's needs.

Another deficiency of the existing monitoring mechanisms applicable to gender equality provisions is the lack of accountability of the parties and the power of the institutions to issue recommendations.

On the one hand, except for a few PTAs, state parties do not have an obligation to report on how they have been implementing gender provisions.[51] In addition, in very few PTAs, parties have committed to monitoring the impact of the provisions and the whole agreement on women.[52] These two aspects could be addressed in future PTAs to increase parties' accountability for the implementation of the commitments they undertake on gender.

On the other hand, monitoring institutions are usually not entitled to make specific recommendations to parties on which areas should be addressed for the implementation of the commitments, as well as on how to accelerate the achievement of the objectives stated in gender provisions. Strengthening the role of the institutions and bodies could lead to a greater positive impact of gender provisions on women's economic empowerment by increasing parties' accountability.

Second, the enforcement of gender provisions through PTAs' dispute resolution mechanism is quite limited, although many PTAs do not treat gender provisions differently than the other commitments with regard to dispute resolution mechanisms.[53] However, even though gender provisions in some agreements are not

50 For example, Chile–Paraguay, Article 13.7; Chile–Ecuador, Article 18.6.

51 For example, Canada–Chile, Article N bis-04; Brazil–Chile, Article 18.4.

52 For example, Economic Partnership Agreement between the CARIFORUM States, of the one part, and the European Community and its Member States, of the other part (signed 15 July 2008, enforced 30 October 2008), Article 5. Other PTAs provide for gender impact assessment as part of cooperation activities, often in an indicative list of areas for cooperation. For example, European Union–Central American Association Agreement, Article 47; UK–Australia, Article 24.2.

53 The WTO Database on Gender Provisions in Regional Trade Agreements maps 168 gender provisions that are not explicitly excluded from the dispute settlement chapter.

explicitly excluded from the agreement's dispute settlement processes, gender provisions are often hardly enforceable given the permissive and low-level precision of their language.

In contrast, some PTAs provide a specific procedure in case of disputes on matters related to specific chapters. Hence, when a dispute arises on a gender obligation located in these specific chapters, parties usually have to engage in consultations before bringing the matter under the dispute settlement chapter.[54] Alternative mechanisms can be provided, such as an expert panel entitled to make non-binding recommendations on how to comply with the provisions.

These alternative procedures often exclude the possibility of suspending trade concessions as temporary remedy measures, thus outlining a hierarchy of remedies.[55] Nonetheless, there are advantages to opting for an expert panel to resolve certain issues, such as the short timeline for having a final decision.[56]

Other PTAs explicitly exclude gender provisions from applying any dispute settlement mechanism provided in the agreements. About one-quarter of the provisions, regardless of the scope of the obligation, cannot be adjudicated under the agreement's dispute settlement chapter. In case of conflict, parties can try to resolve the matter through consultations, dialogue, and cooperation, as seen in the Chile–Argentina FTA (Article 15.5). Rather than excluding trade and gender chapters from the application of dispute settlement chapters, future PTAs could explicitly replicate the mechanism of consultation and a panel of experts. This would increase the parties' accountability, as the panel of experts can closely assess compliance with the provisions and make recommendations accordingly. The responding party will then have to report after a certain period of time on which measures have been taken to implement the relevant provisions.

15.4.3 *Transparency as an Implementation Tool for Gender Equality Commitments*

Transparency guarantees the flow of accurate information, that is available publicly to all and can be assessed or commented on by any authority or the public at large. As such, transparency can help evaluate how provisions are being implemented. It is the cornerstone of any implementation and evaluation process and a key element in the enforceability of gender provisions.

54 For example, Chapter 23 on Labour of USMCA, Article 23.17.

55 For example, Economic Partnership Agreement between the CARIFORUM States, of the one part, and the United Kingdom of Great Britain and Northern Ireland, of the other part (UK–CARIFORUM) (signed 22 March 2019, enforced 20 October 2021), Articles 191, 212, and 213. The WTO Database on Gender Provisions in Regional Trade Agreements maps thirty-seven gender provisions bound to a specific procedure for dispute resolution.

56 For example, a panel of experts established under UK–CARIFORUM has 150 days to issue its report after the date of its establishment (Article 209).

15.4.3.1 Examples of Transparency Practices in Relation to PTAs' Implementation

Some PTAs include the principle of transparency as a general rule of effective implementation[57] and as contributing to the positive impact of trade and development policies. Governments also recognise that transparency is part of their PTAs' good governance package, along with the principles of accountability and gender equality. Lastly, they link transparency as a guiding principle for the PTAs' implementation and as a key objective in supporting the application of the agreement and, therefore, the gender provisions contained in it.

Governments have various ways of conducting transparency processes with the view to better implementing their PTA. For example, Australia has set up a transparency mechanism to communicate its PTAs. In 2018–2019, in addition to publishing its annual report, the Australian Trade and Investment Commission organised twenty-three workshops across the country, reaching more than 1,500 participants with the objective of promoting its PTAs, their economic opportunities, and benefits (Austrade 2018).

Similarly, in Switzerland, the government heavily involves the civil society at large in consultations and information meetings on its PTA implementation and trade negotiations. It also involves academia in the joint organisation of specialised and thematic discussions on trade-related matters. Switzerland also set up, twice a year, a 'Liaison Group WTO/FTA' to disseminate information on PTAs and their implementation and includes representatives from academia and research, the political community, business associations, and non-governmental organisations (NGOs) (SECO n.d).

In 2015, the US created a new role in the United States Trade Representative (USTR), to deal with transparency issues. The Chief Transparency Officer (CTO) is to 'engage with the public, advise the USTR and consult with the Congress on transparency policy, and coordinate transparency in trade negotiations', with the objective of 'improving transparency in the development of U.S. trade policy'. In addition to the CTO, USTR has released a new set of transparency principles to help the involvement of the public at large in the development and implementation of the US trade policy and PTAs (USTR 2021).

15.4.3.2 National Parliaments: The Forgotten Transparency and Implementation Partners

National parliaments can have three roles in fostering the implementation of gender provisions in PTAs. First, national parliaments ratify trade agreements. This is their

[57] Association of the overseas countries and territories with the European Union, Council Decision 2021/1764 (signed and enforced 5 October 2021); European Union–Central American Association Agreement, Article 24; UK–New Zealand (Article 11.11); EAC (Article 6).

main function with regard to PTAs. They arrive in the process almost at the end of the value chain. Often negotiators increase their communication and 'lobbying' towards parliaments after the agreement is finalised and approved between parties. With the exception of some WTO Members, such as the EU or the US, where parliaments participate in shaping the negotiation agenda, most of them are not involved in this process. But the role of parliaments is not limited to ratification. They also have the key responsibility of scrutinising governments' actions. Through this role, they can question governments specifically about how they are implementing gender provisions that are contained in PTAs. This is where transparency principles can play an important role and be used by parliaments to monitor the implementation of the PTA.

Second, as the legislative arm of the country, national parliaments can encourage governments to include gender provisions that are not yet the focus of current PTAs, as seen in Section 15.5 of this chapter.

Third, national parliaments could link to regional legislative assemblies, which are one of the PTAs' governing bodies. For example, the Treaty for the Establishment of the East African Community (EAC) created the East African Legislative Assembly (Article 9), where members are appointed by national parliaments. The Treaty also establishes an obligation for the Assembly to liaise with national parliaments to become involved in the implementation of the PTA (Article 49).

15.4.3.3 Links with the WTO's New Transparency Mechanism on RTAs

The WTO has established a notification process to circulate information on PTAs and evaluate them through the RTA Committee, which is responsible for carrying out 'the examination of agreements' and reviewing their impact on the multilateral trading system (WT/L/127).[58] Internal WTO reporting mechanisms can be a tool for sharing information on gender provisions among WTO Members and promoting their implementation through advanced transparency.

Articles 1.b and 1.c of the terms of reference of the RTA Committee (WT/L/127) offer room for reporting on specific provisions included in trade agreements both in form and format. These articles give space to the Committee to establish how to report on the operation of agreements and to develop dedicated processes with the objective of improving the analysis of agreements. Therefore, WTO Members are at liberty to proceed with the examination of an agreement as they see fit and could request notifications specifically focusing on gender provisions. Similarly, parties

[58] The General Council instructed this Committee to report back on PTAs to the relevant WTO bodies, including the Council for Trade in Goods, the Council for Trade in Services, and the Committee of Trade and Development, and to provide an annual report to the General Council.

could notify trade agreements and could communicate on their PTAs in a more targeted manner and therefore focus on gender provisions in their notifications.

This notification process has the potential to strengthen the implementation of gender provisions. Indeed, the RTA Committee is a platform to share information between Members, to present their agreements and to explore provisions in PTAs during committee meetings (in line with the Committee terms of reference). These discussions are contained in official WTO agreements that are, in the majority, available and accessible publicly.

So far, in the WTO RTA Committee, the issue of gender has been outlined in the questions-and-answer sessions when an agreement has been notified and examined and in some of the WTO Secretariat's factual presentation of notified agreements.[59] Gender provisions have not yet been specifically or precisely identified and notified independently from the entire agreement. One could argue that the mandate of the RTA Committee does not provide for the notification of targeted information regarding specific provisions. However, the new WTO RTA transparency mechanism, adopted by the WTO General Council in 2006 (WT/L/671), could serve as a basis for such specific notifications, therefore, enhancing PTAs' implementation through transparency. For example, the new transparency process creates an obligation for state parties to communicate 'any related schedules, annexes and protocols' (Section B, Notification, Article 4). Through this obligation, the gender protocol of the African Continental Free Trade Area (AfCFTA) currently being developed would have to be duly notified to the WTO.

This new mechanism gives the WTO Secretariat, responsible for drafting the factual presentation of notified PTAs, flexibility in using data beyond the information provided by parties, making the presentation more precise and accurate (Article 7.b. and Article 9).

Even if the new RTA mechanism provides an annex outlining which provisions, information, and data parties shall provide, this is just a basis on which Members can expand as they see fit. Therefore, nothing in the WTO RTA Committee terms of reference and the new transparency mechanism prevents the notification of gender provisions in RTA notifications to the WTO.

15.5 THE 'HIT' ROADMAP: A NEW PROCESS FOR CONCRETE IMPLEMENTATION OF GENDER PROVISIONS

The core objective of gender provisions is to change the status quo in favour of women, as they are usually facing higher obstacles than men in accessing economic opportunities, benefiting from trade, and acquiring social rights. Many governments

[59] For example, Factual Presentation Comprehensive and Progressive Agreement for Trans-Pacific Partnership (CPTPP) (Goods and Services), Report by the Secretariat, WT/REG395/1/Rev.1, 8 September 2021.

have engaged in achieving this goal through PTAs. But the main question remains: are they succeeding in levelling the playing field for women? With regard to gender provisions, the weakness of PTAs resides in their implementation process or the lack thereof. This is reinforced by the fact that PTAs do not identify concrete action points based on the provisions that could be monitored and assessed. The authors are therefore proposing a new roadmap to guide state parties towards their implementation goals. The new instrument, entitled 'HIT', includes three pillars.

The first pillar is 'How' to concretely implement gender provisions. Governments have not outlined specific and concrete action points to achieve their objectives beyond establishing capacity-building programmes. Identifying and defining concrete action points within PTAs are, therefore, the first step towards implementation of gender provisions, because they can be quantifiable and evaluated. For example, based on the overall commitment to make finance more accessible for women, or create special programmes for women entrepreneurs, as seen in PTAs, governments could agree to create a 'women's fund', making it easier for women to apply and receive guaranteed credits or secure quotas for businesswomen in financial schemes dedicated to small businesses. Going further, they could also identify policy instruments to execute these concrete action points, such as aid for trade programmes. Of course, several PTAs have established experience-sharing processes, training, and exchanges in dedicated workshops between parties as tools to implement gender provisions. However, this is clearly not enough, and the lack of transparency about these discussions and their concrete outcomes impairs adequate implementation.

The second pillar is 'Impact': it includes three combined processes: monitoring, evaluation, and enforcement. The monitoring exercise serves as a data collection and mapping tool outlining what measures have been taken based on the 'How' pillar. The evaluation process would explore the effectiveness of the concrete measures taken and assess the importance of changes made by PTAs on the ground. And the enforcement mechanism focuses on dispute resolution, making provisions binding.

The third one is 'Transparency', which is a process supporting the other two pillars. The tenets of this pillar are discussed in the previous subsection.

15.6 CONCLUSIONS

As this chapter depicts, trade agreements are not gender-neutral. Gender provisions go beyond market access and opening, as seen in the sections above. Therefore, the effective implementation of PTAs is even more important for women as they can be a game changer for their economic and social roles, and create economic and social environments that are gender equal and inclusive enough to allow women to fully benefit from trade opportunities offered by PTAs.

Preferential trade agreements can therefore be powerful instruments for achieving gender equality. But they have two main weaknesses that are currently preventing them from having a concrete and positive impact on women: the lack of concrete commitments and action points to achieve general and specific goals set up by gender provisions and the lack of dedicated and staged implementation processes. The next generation of gender provisions should address both weaknesses if PTAs are to work for women.

REFERENCES

Abras, A., A. C. Polato e Favo and M. Y. Kuwahara 2021. 'Women Heads of State and Covid-19 Policy Responses', *Feminist Economics* 27(1–2): 380–400.

Austrade 2018. Australian Trade and Investment Commission, Annual Report 2018-2019. www.transparency.gov.au/annual-reports/australian-trade-and-investment-commission/reporting-year/2018-2019-17

Bahri, A. 2021a. *Gender Mainstreaming in Free Trade Agreements: A Regional Analysis and Good Practice Examples*, Social Inclusion and Trade Knowledge Product Series.

2021b. 'Making Trade Agreements Work for Women Empowerment', *Latin American Journal of Trade Policy* 4: 11.

der Boghossian, A. 2023a. 'Gender-Responsive WTO: Making Trade Rules and Policies Work for Women', in *Handbook on Trade Policy and Gender Equality*, edited by Amrita Bahri, Dorotea López and Jan Yves Remy. Cambridge: Cambridge University Press. www.cambridge.org/core/books/trade-policy-and-gender-equality/EECD723F67B7555150C926A78A0DB439

2023b. 'Gender Social Norms: New Trade Barriers Addressed through Trade Policy', In *The Elgar Companion to the World Trade Organization*, edited by Julien Chaisse and Cristian Rodríguez-Chiffelle. Cheltenham: Edward Elgar. (December 2023). www.e-elgar.com/shop/gbp/the-elgar-companion-to-the-world-trade-organization-9781800882850.html Available at the WTO library

der Boghossian, A. and A. Bahri 2023. 'Finding Feet on Trade Agreements: Empowering Women Entrepreneurs Amidst a Pandemic', *Legal Issues of Economic Integration* 50(1): 13–40.

Ghailani, D. 2013. Gender Equality, from the Treaty of Rome to the Quota Debate: Between Myth and Reality. Social Developments in the European Union, ETUI.

Horn, H., P. Mavroidis and A. Sapir 2010. 'Beyond the WTO? An Anatomy of EU and US Preferential Trade Agreements', *The World Economy* 33(11):1565–1588.

International Labour Organization 2019. Women in Business and Management: The Business Case for Change, Bureau for Employers' Activities (ACT/EMP).

International Trade Centre 2019. *From Europe to the World: Understanding Challenges for European Businesswomen*. Geneva: ITC.

Laperle-Forget, L. 2022. 'Gender Provisions in African Trade Agreements: What Commitments are there for Reconciling Gender Equality and Trade?" Tralac Trade Report No. S22TR05/2022. Stellenbosch: tralac.

Lechner, L. 2019. 'The Trend to More and Stricter Non-Trade Issues in Preferential Trade Agreements', in M. Elsig, M. Hahn and G. Spilker (Eds.), *The Shifting Landscape of Global Trade Governance: World Trade Forum*. Cambridge: Cambridge University Press.

Mola, L. and C. Poncibò 2021. 'Trade and UN SDGs 2030: The Interplay between Public International Law and Contract Law', in A. Bahri, W. Zhou and D. Boklan (Eds.), *Rethinking, Repackaging, and Rescuing World Trade Law in the Post-Pandemic Era*. UK: Hart Publishing.

Monteiro. J. 2021. 'The Evolution of Gender-Related Provisions in Regional Trade Agreements', Staff Working Paper ERSD-2021-8, World Trade Organization, Geneva.
OECD 2017. The Pursuit of Gender Equality. An Uphill Battle, Chapter 7: The under-representation of women in STEM fields.
2023. OECD Work on Regional Trade Agreements and the Environment. Policy Perspectives. https://web-archive.oecd.org/temp/2023-03-30/413579-environment-and-regional-trade-agreements.htm
Smith, S. 2020. Advancing Gender Equality through Voluntary Standards for Trade', Gender, Social Inclusion and Trade Working Group. www.evidensia.eco/resources/1094/advancing-gender-equity-through-voluntary-sustainability-standards-for-trade/
Swiss Federal Department of Foreign Affairs FDFA, November 2017. Fact Sheet, 'The Convention on The Elimination of All Forms of Discrimination Against Women (CEDAW) – And Its Relevance For SDC'.
USTR 2021. 'USTR Releases Agency Transparency Principles', May 7, 2021. https://ustr.gov/about-us/policy-offices/press-office/press-releases/2021/may/ustr-releases-agency-transparency-principles
WTO 2022a. *Trade and Gender-Related Provisions in Regional Trade Agreements*. INF/TGE/COM/4. Geneva: World Trade Organization.
2022b. WTO Ministerial Conference Twelfth Session, (June 12–15, 2022), Geneva, WT/MIN(22)/24 WT/L/1135.

16

The Future of Trade Agreement Dispute Settlement Provisions

Kathleen Claussen

16.1 INTRODUCTION

The present generation of dispute settlement mechanisms (DSMs) in trade agreements is not hugely varied in terms of institutional design, but that consistency is beginning to change. Today, a core feature of comprehensive trade agreements is a set of enforcement provisions designed to ensure that governments comply with the obligations they have undertaken. Unlike other areas of international law, state-to-state DSMs are well accepted and widely implemented in trade agreements. The fact that we speak of them as 'mechanisms' already suggests the advancement of their institutional form. They are no longer sole provisions or short references; in many instances, they create standalone bodies and occupy entire chapters of text. Moreover, trade agreement DSMs from around the world have converged in recent years towards an ad hoc adjudicatory process heard by a neutral panel of adjudicators. When the panel identifies a violation of the agreement, the agreement typically provides a further process for trade sanctions to induce compliance where needed.

Despite the proliferation of hundreds of trade agreements with dispute settlement provisions of some type, states rarely have activated those provisions and the cumulative number of formal disputes has remained low for many decades. As disputes have now appeared with greater frequency in the last five years, in part as a result of the World Trade Organization's (WTO) own DSM decline, states are experimenting with new models of and approaches to dispute settlement, including some that empower other actors beyond the state in seeking to ensure compliance with trade agreement commitments. The moment is ripe to review the present evolution into new realms of disputes and to contemplate alternative designs to resolve conflict between states.

This chapter begins by briefly surveying DSMs that commonly appear in trade agreements. Many trade agreements include binding arbitration tools for the resolution of disputes among the parties, but not all commitments in the agreement may be subject to dispute settlement. Some trade agreements differ with respect to the legal result or outcome of the arbitration process. Agreements vary in the remedies they provide to the successful party. While a comprehensive study exceeds the bounds of this short chapter, reviewing the taxonomy is useful for understanding the landscape.[1] After mapping the terrain, the chapter then turns to the primary issues facing states and other stakeholders as they write new trade agreements and negotiate less orthodox mechanisms to address problems that arise in trade relationships. Finally, the chapter makes recommendations for future negotiations and for further research.

16.2 MAPPING TRENDS

Much ink in international law scholarship has been spilled on questions of institutional design surrounding dispute settlement. In trade, commentators over the last forty years have praised the concept of third-party dispute settlement as a great achievement in our long-time sovereigntist discipline of international law. These are typically state-to-state mechanisms, although not exclusively so. We focus on state behaviour because one of the primary goals of international law is to shape that behaviour. That is true likewise in trade: commitments made in trade agreements seek to install reciprocal behavioural constraints. The primary mechanism for holding states accountable in trade is, like elsewhere, third-party dispute settlement – whether in the form of arbitration or through a standing judicial body. The culmination of that exercise is licence to one state to impose economic penalties (often in the form of suspension of concessions) on the party that has acted in breach of the agreement. States invoke the dispute settlement chapter as a means by which to ensure that other states are complying – in effect, to enforce the agreement. As this chapter shows, that story is changing, but state-to-state dispute settlement continues to be the norm, for now.

Scholars have identified different reasons as to why strong state-to-state DSMs have developed and why they have become more prevalent. The chapter mentions these in context below. One common rationale is that DSMs gained importance with the heightened demands of deeper agreements with wider membership (Allee and Elsig 2015). Thus, more elaborate DSMs emerged as trade agreements themselves became more elaborate along multiple dimensions.

16.2.1 *Trends in Provisions*

Nearly all (87 per cent according to the Design of Trade Agreements (DESTA) data set; Allee and Elsig 2015) comprehensive trade agreements negotiated in the last

[1] Note that this chapter does not take account of trade remedies disputes or investor–state provisions. Those matters are covered elsewhere in this volume.

thirty years include some form of DSM.[2] Most modern trade agreements that contain binding and enforceable dispute settlement provisions, roughly half of the trade agreements overall, rely on ad hoc adjudication, similar to the WTO. But the institutional framework for dispute settlement is varied and the prevalence of arbitration is relatively new. This generation of trade agreements has been characterised by what I call 'forum proliferation': a shift in interpretive power from treaty parties to a plethora of ad hoc, independent panels unrestricted by precedent and unsupervised by any superior authority (Claussen 2018a). This section reviews the structural models across the cartography of trade agreements in brief and then turns to some recent highlights.

16.2.1.1 Common Taxonomies

There are several ways to categorise structural models of DSMs. Some scholars have undertaken to categorise them by region, while others have primarily organised them by type. Beginning in the early 2000s, political scientists and lawyers developed multiple taxonomies for this purpose. The WTO Secretariat reviewed the literature in 2013 (Chase et al. 2013). For purposes of our institutional design review, it makes sense as others have done to divide DSMs into three broad groups: (1) political or diplomatic dispute settlement, (2) systems based on a standing panel, and (3) referral to an ad hoc arbitral panel (Porges 2011). Of all the 727 trade agreements captured by the DESTA data set, 80 per cent have consultation mechanisms, 23 per cent have mediation mechanisms, 46 per cent have arbitration mechanisms, and 5 per cent have standing judicial bodies. But those total numbers are insufficient to understand the clear trend towards ad hoc arbitration processes in the last four decades of trade agreements.

Todd Allee and Manfred Elsig have captured not only this trend towards more ad hoc arbitration in trade agreement DSMs but also a tendency towards increased 'legalisation' through their textual analysis of DSMs (Allee and Elsig 2015). They consider stronger DSMs to exhibit greater legalisation which they measure along six dimensions. The first dimension tracks the Porges taxonomy and turns on the extent to which dispute settlement authority is delegated to a third party, legal body. On a three-tiered scale, the 'weakest' agreements are those lacking any provision for dispute settlement authority, the middle ground is those which rely primarily on ad hoc arbitration, and the 'strongest' are those that create a standing body. The other elements relied upon by Allee and Elsig include the presence of a choice of forum clause, the process for selection of the chair of the arbitral panel, time limits for dispute settlement, the availability of post-award sanctions, and the comprehensive scope of the dispute settlement provisions vis-à-vis the rest of

[2] See also www.designoftradeagreements.org, Dür et al. (2014).

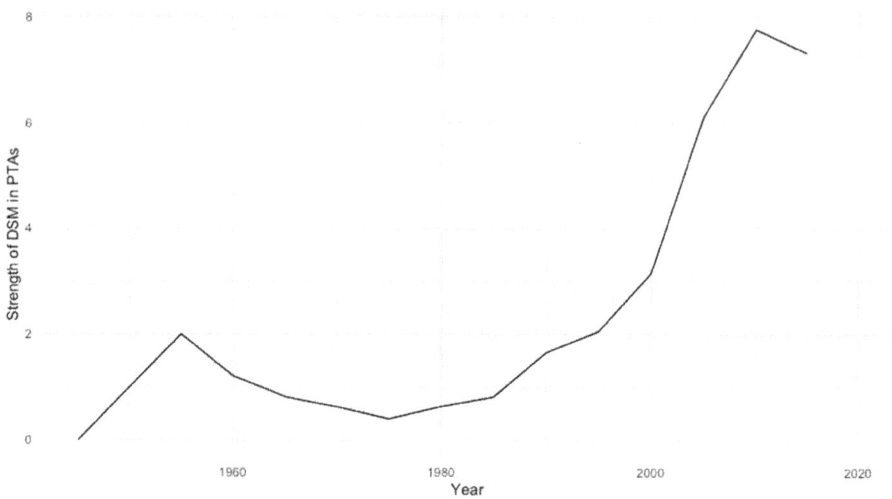

FIGURE 16.1 Strength of DSM over time.
Source: author's elaboration based on DESTA

the agreement. The following figures are drawn from the Allee and Elsig data as updated through 2023.[3]

First, the DESTA data show more robust DSMs over time, and particularly beginning in the 2000s, led by the United States (US) but not limited to it. As Figure 16.1 reflects, up until the 1990s, there were in fact very few DSMs apart from judicial-styled arrangements or consultative mechanisms, with heavy reliance on joint committees – committees of the parties' trade officials.

Past research provides evidence that the most important predictor for DSM strength is depth of the agreement (see Allee and Elsig 2015). Put differently, the more ambitious or comprehensive the agreement, the stronger or more legalistic the DSM is on average. Over time, as trade agreements have grown deeper also DSM has increased in strength (Figure 16.2). And, as I discuss further below, the enforcement of trade agreement provisions on issues of social and environmental sustainability has catalysed this shift just as it has followed it. States have incorporated more sustainability commitments and gradually made them enforceable through the same DSM as the commercial provisions of the agreement.

Both these trends can be seen also when disaggregating the type of DSM. The following Figure 16.3 shows the diminution in agreements with no DSM at all, and likewise the small numbers in modern agreements of DSMs that have only consultative or mediation procedures. As can be seen, arbitration becomes popular as a form of dispute settlement beginning in the 1980s.

[3] My thanks to Kirthana Ganeson for assistance with the figures.

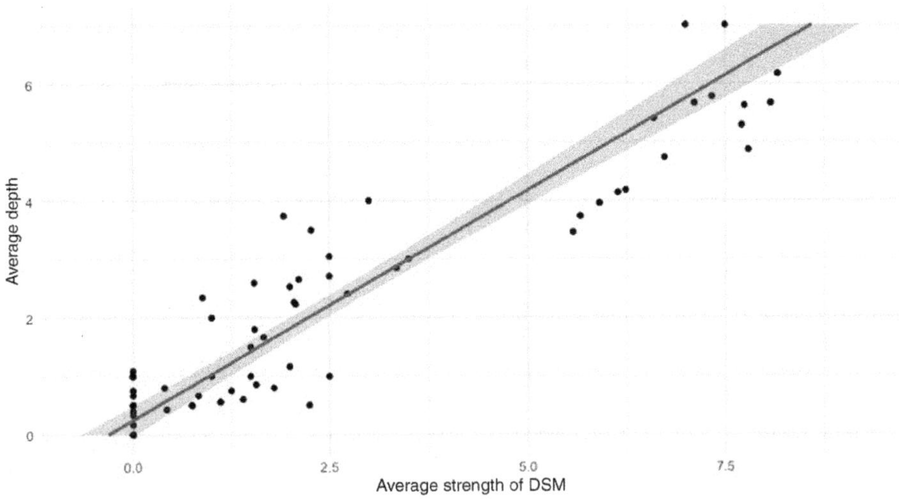

FIGURE 16.2 Depths of preferential trade agreements (PTAs) and strength of DSMs.
Source: author's elaboration based on DESTA

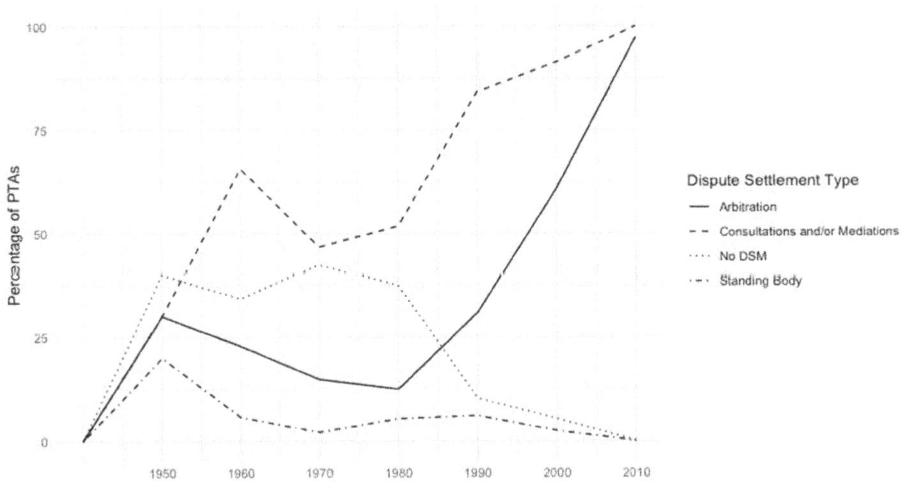

FIGURE 16.3 Types of DSM over time.
Source: author's elaboration based on DESTA

16.2.1.2 Regional Trends

Many trends in trade agreement design follow regional patterns as other contributions to this volume have shown. Dispute settlement is no different. The following Figure 16.4 shows the pathways towards arbitration across regions.

The DESTA data also show that on average intercontinental agreements have the highest degree of legalisation, followed by agreements in the Americas (Figure 16.5).

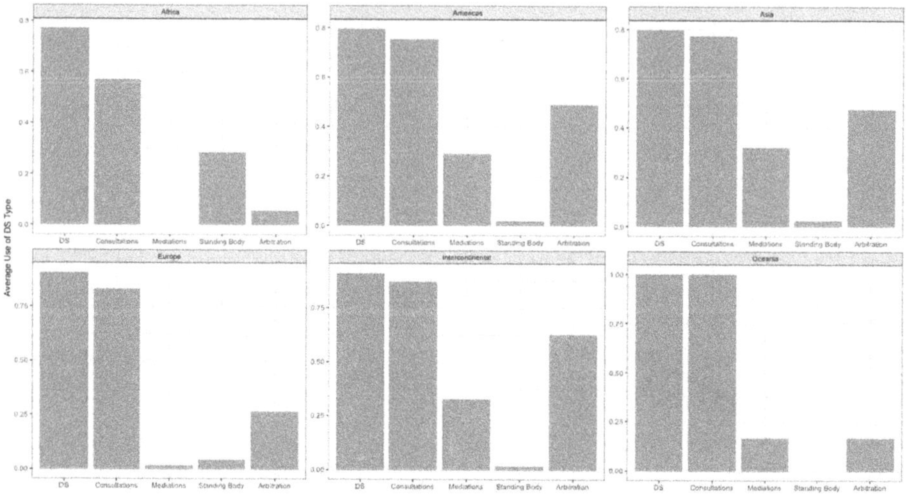

FIGURE 16.4 Types of DSM per region.
Source: author's elaboration based on DESTA

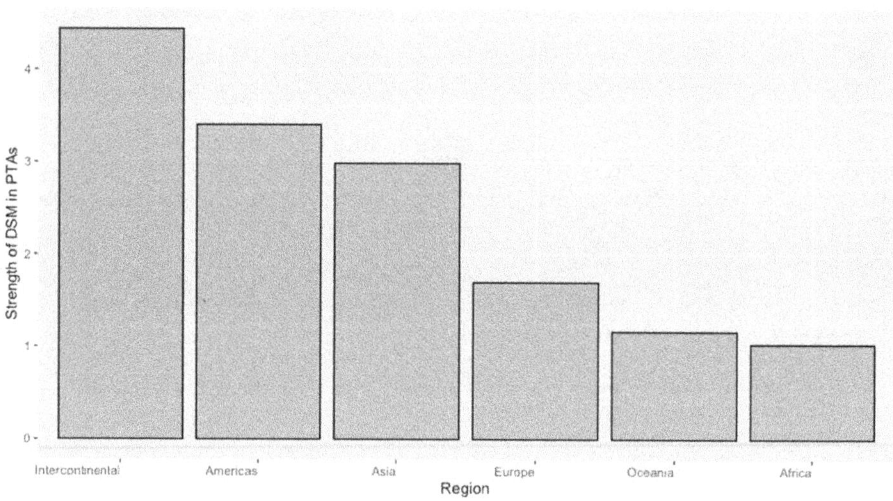

FIGURE 16.5 Strength of DSMs per region.
Source: author's elaboration based on DESTA

The US has led the way in making DSMs more legally elaborate. Nearly all US comprehensive trade agreements[4] presently in force provide for ad hoc arbitration. In their most basic terms, these sorts of DSMs work in panels composed of three or five panel members with each side picking an equal number of arbitrators and

[4] I use the term preferential trade agreements (PTAs) hereafter for consistency with the rest of the volume.

agreeing on the chair. The panel sets a timetable in consultation with the parties that provides for the submission of written pleadings and a hearing, which is open to the public. The panel then provides a report to the parties with a decision as to whether the panel finds the responding party to have acted inconsistently with the agreement. The offending party is expected to come into compliance with panel decisions. If not, compensation, suspension of benefits, or fines are possible remedies.

Compared to the US, European Union (EU) trade agreements are less legalised as defined by the DESTA data because most of the older agreements were not subject to arbitration, but they have changed dramatically in recent years. With the exception of the European Economic Area (EEA), all EU trade agreements from before 2000 are based on a diplomatic approach to dispute settlement in which consultations are the key mechanism (Garcia Bercero 2006). These consultations occur within the framework of a joint committee. The EEA is the only agreement that provided for judicial enforcement procedures, modelled on the European Court of Justice (ECJ). The other agreements concluded by the EU before 2000 permit adjudication only upon agreement of the parties. Most of those intend arbitration, but the Association Agreement with Turkey is exceptional in that it allows the parties to choose the ECJ for disputes. Another exception is the Cotonou Agreement in that it foresees the possibility of multi-party dispute, and arbitration following consultations.[5]

A fundamental shift in EU DSMs occurred in the conclusion of the agreements with Mexico (2000) and Chile (2001). This shift occurred in part at the urging of Mexico which had sought to adopt the North American Free Trade Agreement (NAFTA) model in its negotiations with the EU (Garcia Bercero 2006). These agreements use an arbitration model DSM, drawing heavily from the WTO Dispute Settlement Understanding (DSU). By this time, the EU was already a major player in the WTO DSM, and there was some growing dissatisfaction with the lack of effectiveness of the traditional diplomatic approach. Garcia Bercero explains that it was also during the negotiations with Mexico that leadership for the agreement within the Commission was allocated to the Directorate General for Trade, which was 'institutionally more inclined toward procedures that ensure a rapid solution of commercial disputes'. All EU agreements concluded since that time have included similar dispute settlement procedures. Most recently, the trend has been to expand the topical coverage of EU trade agreement DSMs. The European Commission's New Action Plan introduced a shift towards judicialisation of sustainability provisions in 2022. This model is being introduced for the first time in the EU–New Zealand free trade agreement (FTA).

5 Note that in April 2021, the EU and the Organisation of African, Caribbean, and Pacific States initialled an agreement on a new legal framework which is intended to replace the Cotonou Agreement and that agreement provides only for the possibility of consultations, and in some instances the involvement of a joint committee.

A similar evolution can be seen among the European Free Trade Association (EFTA) countries: Norway, Iceland, Liechtenstein, and Switzerland. The original EFTA Convention (1961) employed a consultation approach to disputes, although it incorporated the possibility for an examining committee to make recommendations to the EFTA Council. By the 1990s, however, sentiments towards dispute settlement had changed and an arbitration procedure was introduced in 2001 as a backup to bilateral consultations and negotiations (Ziegler 2006). Likewise, in the agreements concluded by the EFTA states with other countries, they sought to include arbitration clauses from the late 1990s forward, and even renegotiated some that did not include such clauses. Thus, many of the EFTA agreements today set out a path to consultation within a joint committee followed by mandatory arbitration.

The pattern continues with the story of Mercosur, the Southern Common Market. Mercosur has had a DSM since its inception, but introduced a panel system only in 1993. It included three stages: consultations, intervention by the Common Market Group, and arbitration before an ad hoc panel. In 2004, the parties introduced the Olivos Protocol, which added a permanent review panel to hear appeals from panels. Other trade agreements in the region follow a similar approach. For example, the Andean Community has a system which includes automatic third-party review and which grants treaty signatories and private actors the right to initiate disputes. Procedures to settle disputes among Member States over non-compliance with regional norms can be heard by a secretariat and ultimately by the Andean Panel of Justice.

Most Indian PTAs have followed the same trend from political DSMs to, by the early 2000s, arbitral models (Singh 2022). The latter seek to emulate the WTO DSU, following consultations or direct negotiations. Some Indian agreements permit a complaining party to initiate arbitration directly after consultations, while others require the party to first refer the dispute to a committee. Further, in some agreements the committee referral step is optional whereas in others it is mandatory.

As the DESTA data show, African agreements exhibit the least legalisation, together with agreements from Oceania, but this may be changing. An important feature of the recent African Continental Free Trade Area (AfCFTA) is its Protocol on Dispute Settlement. Unlike the majority of the African regional economic community courts that are modelled after the ECJ, the AfCFTA DSM tracks the WTO model.

Asian agreements reflect a high degree of legalisation, even if there have been no known adjudicated disputes among them. The Association of Southeast Asian Nations (ASEAN) agreements followed the same trajectory seen elsewhere. Initially, the ASEAN agreements provided for relatively informal dispute settlement, but by the late 1990s they had instituted a panel system with the possibility of appealing a decision to the ASEAN ministers. The ASEAN DSM covers all ASEAN economic agreements and the reports from panels and the Appellate Body are binding (Luo 2006). Even though Asian agreements include adjudicatory mechanisms, they often heavily emphasise cooperation and consultation may explain the lack of adjudication. For example, the Regional Comprehensive Economic Partnership (RCEP) chapter on dispute settlement promotes flexibility, consensus, and the avoidance of formal dispute. There is thus some initial evidence that for some Asian PTAs, legalisation has declined.

Not all Asian agreements have adopted legalistic mechanisms. Agreements from China are very much mixed – with some including complex dispute systems and some not. Indonesian agreements with other developing countries often have no formal DSM, which scholars have seen as reflective of a general reluctance among developing states to embrace legalistic institutions (Widiatedja 2020).

Several scholars have investigated the sources and consequences of the widespread move towards legalistic mechanisms for resolving disputes in international trade agreements. Gomez-Mera and Molinari (2014) sum up these reasons and note also some overarching trends. For example, they show that democracies are more likely than autocracies to prefer moderately strict DSMs. They also demonstrate that many countries have been motivated to formalise their systems given the perceived success of the WTO. Sometimes WTO disputes have prompted the inclusion of a formal DSM in a trade agreement, such as in the case of the trade agreement between Indonesia and Australia. In other circumstances, some legalised DSMs have been the result of colonial relationships. A further reason is the simple copy-paste, repetition effect that we have seen in the substantive commitments also (Claussen 2018b; Allee and Elsig 2019).

16.2.1.3 Additional Features

Formal disputes are 'not just the tip, but the tip of the tip of the iceberg' (Melillo 2019). Dispute settlement apparatuses can provide an extensive institutional architecture apart from the actual panel, or consultation, system. Trade agreement DSMs and other chapters typically establish multiple committees. Margherita Melillo has shown that trade agreements, especially those of the EU of the latest generation, have many subcommittees, and evidence suggests that parties are addressing potential dispute issues there (Melillo 2019).

Some agreements also exclude individual topics from their DSMs. Scholars have catalogued these exclusions and their evolution over time (e.g. Froese 2016). By one count, more than half of trade agreements with arbitration mechanisms exclude at least one subject from their DSMs (Chase et al. 2013). Most often excluded is competition, followed by trade in services, and then sanitary and phytosanitary (SPS) measures. Generally, however, states and civil society actors have pushed for bringing more topics into the main DSM rather than the other way around, at least until recently as discussed further below. While agreements have for many years provided special procedures for certain topics, and even for certain trading partners (Froese 2016), the broad shift towards including trade-plus commitments such as labour and environment provisions among the set of binding and enforceable obligations to which the DSM applies has begun to fade. Recent trade agreements have also diminished some of the offerings of past agreements or otherwise departed from the strict procedures of the WTO DSU in what they permit such as the RCEP mentioned above.

A further and often-discussed matter is the relationship between trade agreement DSMs and the WTO DSM. Some agreements include 'choice of forum' clauses permitting parties to choose, while others rely on exclusive jurisdiction clauses. Twenty-seven per cent of agreements in the DESTA data set include choice of forum-type provisions. For example, the NAFTA included a preference for NAFTA resolution of disputes involving environmental, SPS, or standard-related measures and even provided that a responding party may insist that a WTO complaint be withdrawn. But this provision of the NAFTA is rather exceptional. Other disputes under the NAFTA were subject to a choice of forum clause where the complaining party could elect whether to constitute a WTO panel or a PTA panel. That practice is more common: of the agreements that discuss forum choice, 97 per cent restrict the use of the other forum when one has been selected by the claimant or jointly. Other disputes under the NAFTA were subject to a choice of forum clause where the complaining party could elect whether to constitute a WTO panel or a PTA panel. In some instances, parties have sought review of the same measure under different agreements which has led to concern about re-litigation and an abuse of forum shopping privileges (Hillman 2009). Panel members have queried states about the option of consolidation in litigation, but no such mergers have yet occurred. Some agreements, such as the EU–Chile Agreement, include clauses that express a preference for using the WTO where the breach is 'equivalent in substance to a WTO obligation'.

16.2.2 *Trends in Litigation*

Scholars have queried why there have been so few disputes under trade agreements outside the WTO. Before 2020, fewer than twenty state-to-state disputes under trade agreements were known to have reached a final decision by an arbitral panel. Since 2020, however, more than a dozen cases have appeared on trade agreement dockets for a variety of reasons. One likely contributing factor is the WTO Appellate Body's effective suspension, but not all disputes that have been litigated under FTAs in the last three years could have been brought to the WTO. Some parties to these recent disputes are not WTO Members. More importantly, most of the disputes that have materialised have arisen under obligations that are unique to the trade agreement in question. For example, a case between the EU and Korea arose under the sustainable development chapter of their trade agreement. The several United States–Mexico–Canada Agreement (USMCA) cases now ongoing or recently concluded were the result of heightened rules or special disciplines found in the USMCA.

A further rationale for the increase in litigation is that of demonstrating strength among trade agreement enforcement. This is especially true in the US. In the absence of support for the WTO dispute settlement system, the US has actively pursued enforcement under the USMCA to demonstrate the utility of that system in the face of scepticism. Even those economies that continue to use the WTO dispute settlement system regularly recognise the limitations of that system in light of the absence of the Appellate Body. They have developed new means for carrying out enforcement and new ways to invigorate their trade agreement engagement. A good illustration is the institution of the EU single entry point which provides a means for members of the public to bring issues to the attention of the European Commission. Some commentators have also suggested that litigating under trade agreements outside the WTO may be more politically desirable. They may receive less public attention – although that has varied – and they may appear to be less confrontational outside the presence of all other WTO Members. Further, remedies may be especially crafted for the context of a trade agreement in ways not possible at the WTO.

The increase in litigation has begun to give rise to new forms of challenges that future designers will need to consider. One is the interpretive difficulty facing panels where certain language is repeated in other agreements and parties may urge panels to take account of other decisions interpreting the same language. Agreements may benefit from 'interpretation selection clauses' to guide the contours of interpretational jurisdiction for decision-makers, particularly with respect to the appearance of the same terms elsewhere. The EU–Canada Comprehensive Economic and Trade Agreement, for one, directs panels as to how to consider WTO case law. Even WTO-accommodating provisions can be subject to debate, however. These provisions do not offer guidance with respect to the decisions of other trade agreement panels – guidance that may soon be needed. Under current conditions, a panel may or may not seek to reach consistent outcomes and states have no way to predict how an individual panel will proceed in this respect. One useful option may be for states to develop rules like in conflict of laws to govern the relationship between different systems (Claussen 2018). The New Zealand–Brunei Side Agreement to the Comprehensive and Progressive Agreement for Trans-Pacific Partnership (CPTPP) expressly provides for how arbitrators should treat other decisions (saying other agreements with the same language should be interpreted consistently).

Whereas the other chapters in this book speak to normative development in areas of commitments made by states, DSMs raise the stakes still more by outsourcing that development to panels of adjudicators. More attention ought to be paid to the argumentation, the sources, the outcomes, and the impacts on other areas of trade law that will soon evolve. Many recent disputes are in the public eye, which makes them both politically important and also legally relevant in ways that may be undercounted as yet. This is partly due to the fact that scholars tend to segregate trade and trade disputes from other areas of international law, but it need not be that way. There are lessons to be learned in both directions and more cross-pollination would be beneficial.

16.3 NOVELTIES

This section turns to the recent specific advances in the development of trade agreement dispute settlement design. After some early experimentation, states have adopted, or considered, how to improve the dispute settlement experience – sometimes in response to popular pressure. Space does not permit a full review of novelties in individual agreements. Rather, I highlight a few movements with wide application. This section takes up six such areas of review: rules of procedure and evidence; transparency and accessibility; panel member requirements and selection; public participation; the role, if any, of a secretariat; and, means through which disputes end.

16.3.1 *Rules of Procedure and Evidence*

States in recent years have included rules of procedure in their dispute settlement chapter, or, more often, they have mandated the later development of such rules. These rules set out expectations regarding requirements for submission of pleadings, evidence and arguments, deadlines, conduct of hearings, language, translation and interpretation, among other topics. But the rules that parties have developed thus far sometimes have not covered all disputes, or all issues that have arisen in disputes. For example, arbitrators have on occasion noted that their disputes were underserviced by rules developed by the parties (Boisson de Chazournes and Lee 2022).

Scholars likewise have called for rules of evidence to help manoeuvre new types of documents and unusual-to-trade forms of exhibits (Claussen and Wu forthcoming 2019). In a dispute between the US and Guatemala, the panel highlighted the 'difficulty' of the task before it, given the absence of rules to provide for the handling of evidence, the appearance of witnesses, and the testing of evidence through examination. In the absence of those additional tools, the panel decided to attribute little to no weight to several redacted statements, concluding that they were not credible because they did not have sufficient 'indicia of reliability' that the panel developed. Thus, although the panel admitted the statements, in some cases, the panel did not attribute any weight to certain of them because they were not accompanied by corroborating evidence or had insufficient detail or lacked precision. In direct response to the outcome of this dispute, the US insisted on the inclusion of rules of evidence in the USMCA.

Rules of evidence and procedure become more important as trade disputes evolve to cover new areas of regulatory cooperation and social policies. Our trade systems to date do not yet present a vision for how to resolve disputes that may not lend themselves to ordinary evidentiary principles or obvious presentation. A live question for DSM designers is how to develop a system for resolving disputes about trade problems that cannot be easily proven (Claussen 2019). These are not new problems, but they will become increasingly acute as these new DSMs face their first legitimacy tests.

A further procedural innovation that scholars have highlighted but which has not yet received sufficient attention by parties is that of the purpose and opportunity presented by interim review. Most trade agreements with arbitration DSMs, and 20 per cent overall, include an interim report stage, in which an initial draft of the panel's report is presented to the parties prior to its publication. The parties comment on the initial report and the panel then pens a final report which is made public and serves as the ultimate decision and conclusion of the proceedings. But both in the WTO and in trade agreement disputes, states have given limited guidance to panels on the purpose of this intermediate stage, what changes the panel might make, and what the purpose of revision might be. Panellists and states have thus brought different approaches to bear on the interim process, and those divergences make the interim review ripe for further consideration and innovation in future designs.

16.3.2 *Transparency and Accessibility*

Trade agreements vary greatly in how much transparency is required by their DSMs. Since 1998, the US has pushed for much greater transparency in the WTO as well as in trade agreements, advocating that all panel submissions be available to the public and that panel hearings be open to public observation, except where there is a need to protect confidential business information. For example, the US has required all dispute documents to be made public within ten days of submission. In contrast, other economies like Canada or among ASEAN Members have authorised but not required their parties to make their own submissions public. US agreements also call for public hearings, though the degree of publicity has varied in the few disputes that have materialised. Some disputes have been webcasted via video livestream, whereas others offered a public hearing room in the building of the hearing, and still others provided an audio livestream. These provisions surrounding the public nature of the hearing and the location of the hearing, among others, are reflective of a general push towards greater transparency at least among some governments.

16.3.3 *Arbitrators and Their Selection*

Another area of recent innovation and of evolution is that of the arbitrator selection process in ad hoc arbitral dispute settlement. In nearly all instances, each of the two parties in a bilateral dispute appoints one arbitrator. Then agreements use at least four types of different appointment processes for the appointment of the chair: 5 per cent of trade agreements leave it to the parties to agree on the chair of the panel; 4 per cent leave it to the party-appointed arbitrators to select a chair; 18 per cent provide for selection of the chair by lot from a list; and 17 per cent provide for selection by an individual or organisation external to the dispute, usually a specific official of an intergovernmental organisation.[6]

Some early ad hoc arbitration mechanisms did not appropriately safeguard from the possibility of a responding state blocking the constitution of an arbitral panel. For example, the NAFTA suffered from this flaw and allowed the parties to halt the dispute settlement process entirely. From the late 1990s until its termination in 2020, no NAFTA panels were formed (Lester et al. 2019). By contrast, in WTO disputes, the Director-General makes appointments where the parties cannot agree on the panellists. Only 17 per cent of trade agreements outside the WTO provide a mechanism for a third party to appoint panellists in the absence of agreement by the parties. That third party may be the WTO Director-General, or in other instances, another prominent leader of an adjudicatory body such as the Secretary-General of the Permanent Court of Arbitration or the President of the International Court of Justice. The latter approach is common among investor–state dispute settlement, as well.

Among the DSMs that feature ad hoc arbitration, some trade agreements now include rosters of potential arbitrators who the parties consider to be qualified and willing to serve so that the dispute settlement process can commence as soon as it is required. The practice of maintaining rosters also facilitates a ready list of individuals with specialised expertise. For example, the EU maintains a specialised roster of individuals with backgrounds in sustainable development for potential sustainable development disputes. The creation of specialised rosters coincides with parties' insistence on specialised expertise for those types of disputes, a development that the US–Guatemala dispute precipitated (Claussen 2020). Generally, however, agreements that speak to qualifications of arbitrators typically limit those requirements to expertise in the relevant field and nationality, where they say anything at all.

These rosters can be either open, meaning that disputing parties may choose any panellists they wish including from the roster, or closed, meaning that the parties are constrained by the roster. The latter is rare – one example is the EU–Chile Agreement – but even among open lists, there is mixed practice among party choices. For example, in the USMCA disputes to date, all but one panel member was named from the roster. Additionally, most agreements prescribe rules to decide which panellists shall serve as an arbitrator. Apart from any requisite qualifications, several agreements constrain party choice on the basis of nationality (Chase et al. 2013).

6 Note that these numbers reflect the final option or outcome for selection; many chapters contemplate stages for selection with choosing by lot or relying on a third party as a last resort.

Agreements vary in the number of arbitrators that may serve on any given panel. All of the disputes except one that have resulted in a panel report since 2017 have involved three panel members. The dispute between Mexico, Canada, and the US concerning automotive parts under the USMCA involved five panel members, consistent with the requirements of the agreement which specifies that in case of three parties – two complainants, one respondent – five panellists are to be selected. In fact, under the USMCA, the default panel size for a bilateral dispute is also five unless the parties choose to have three panellists. Some PTAs, particularly Indian FTAs of recent years, provide for just one arbitrator, in case the second party refuses or is unable to nominate one (Singh 2022).

Panel members have included retired trade officials, adjudicators, lawyers in private practice, and academics. Most panel members serve in a part-time, hourly capacity for a particular dispute apart from their full-time jobs elsewhere. With the rise in the number of disputes, a legal community is developing both with respect to counsel and with the arbitrator pool. Likewise, industry counsel are now increasingly engaged in trade agreement disputes. In the near term, scholars ought to study these sociological developments more closely.

Finally, more work is needed to understand the codes of conduct and ethical rules that apply in the trade agreement space. Most DSMs with active disputes require panellists to sign and commit to a code of conduct which relies heavily on disclosures and confidentiality. No publicly known challenges to arbitrators' commitments have come to light, and this system appears to function with sufficient confidence from the parties. Most arbitral DSMs split panellist costs evenly among the parties to the dispute which also lends legitimacy to the arbitration arrangement just like nationality requirements do, although there are some notable exceptions (Chase et al. 2013). Under the RCEP, for instance, each party pays costs of the panellist that it appointed.

16.3.4 *Public Participation*

Some of the recently concluded trade agreements include novelties that alter in small and large ways the nature of litigation that could arise. For example, both the USMCA and the CPTPP provide the opportunity for non-governmental entities (NGEs) to apply to the panel for permission to provide a written submission in the proceedings. To be granted such permission, the NGE based in the territory of one of the parties must identify specific issues of fact and law that the NGE will address in its submission and explain how the submission would assist the panel in the determination of the factual or legal issue related to the dispute by bringing a perspective or knowledge different from that of the participating parties. Non-governmental entities have made submissions in several of the disputes heard by panels in the last three years. Most of these NGEs have been industry associations supporting the complaining party's position. Panels have granted leave liberally and permitted these NGEs to submit but they also have, in some instances, rejected an NGE's request.

Likewise, US agreements and now EU agreements, among others, include public submission opportunities to trigger a review by the government into non-compliance by a trading partner. For example, under the NAFTA and now under the USMCA, the governments of North America provide contact points for members of the public to provide information about the practices of the other North American parties in the areas of labour and environment. The US Department of Labor has received numerous such submissions, though none has led to a state-to-state dispute settlement proceeding, apart from the one petition submitted under the auspices of the FTA among Central America, the US, and the Dominican Republic (Claussen 2020).

16.3.5 *Secretariats*

Few trade agreements concluded in the last forty years make reference to any permanent institution for dispute management. Secretariats are typical only where agreements provide for a standing court. Those courts require legal and administrative support. One example is the Andean Court of Justice which is to be given 'all necessary facilities for proper fulfilment of its functions', and is required to 'appoint its necessary Secretary and the necessary personnel to perform its duties'. These agreements with standing bodies also will usually have a permanent budget process that involves substantial contributions by the parties.

Apart from standing bodies, only some trade agreements provide for the administration of state-to-state dispute settlement through a quasi-ad hoc secretariat with limited authority. These trade agreements require each party to maintain a government office, separate from the office representing the government in the dispute, to be ready to manage a case should one arise. In US trade agreements, the office of the responding party to the dispute picks up this role. The staff are charged with providing administrative assistance to the panel, serving as the panel's contact point, arranging payment, organising and coordinating logistics, and performing 'all other tasks' as established under the agreement, the rules, or by the parties. These tasks may include those of management of document exchanges and hearings; coordination of any roster; secretarial, translation, and interpretation services; provision or rental of a place to hold hearings; research and drafting assistance to panellists; payment of panellist fees and expenses; information services; and capacity building. A similar model establishes a standing secretariat comprised of national sections across the parties. The national sections collaborate and may cooperatively provide administrative assistance to panels. The 2004 ASEAN Protocol on Enhanced Dispute Settlement Mechanism provides a clearly defined role in dispute settlement for a secretariat and is similar to the Mercosur Administrative Secretariat in that way.

Other approaches to dispute settlement management include those that permit panellists to hire assistants to provide research assistance as a complement to a separate office that provides logistical support. In recent practice, panellists have not often hired assistants. Still, other dispute chapters are silent entirely on assistance to panels.

States generally remain reluctant about setting up a robust secretariat given the potentially heavy financial burden they create, particularly for bilateral trade agreements where the costs are shared by only two parties. Questions have arisen as to who bears the cost of the secretariat; this was a debated question in the Trans-Pacific Partnership Agreement negotiations, for instance. Likewise, where a trade agreement relies on the parties to manage the administrative functions of a panel, parties have debated whether the complaining party or the responding party should bear that burden. In US trade agreements, for example, the burden falls on the responding party.

To address these issues, in future agreements, states could consider setting up specialised secretariats or elaborating guidance for ad hoc staff. Such changes could (1) better facilitate the management of the dispute; (2) clarify and delineate roles and responsibilities; and (3) likely yield financial savings to the extent those staff can assist with management issues presently imposed upon the panel members with their high hourly rates. Another alternative is for parties to add to the agreement an option for them to use an existing institution, such as the Permanent Court of Arbitration in The Hague, as a case manager for the dispute, much like what is done in trade agreement investor–state dispute settlement chapters. Although relying on a professionalised secretariat to manage a dispute comes at a cost, some secretariats may be willing to lower their usual rates to accommodate state needs.

16.3.6 *The End of Disputes*

Trade agreement disputes also provide an opportunity to consider alternative endings for disputes rather than simply a panel report with a pronouncement on breach. It is too early to tell just how well traditional outcomes serve parties' interests, but we know that states are experimenting somewhat with their pathways to an outcome. After more disputes reach their conclusion, further research will be required to determine whether states are changing their measures in response or seeking alternative solutions.

Many agreements provide an option to the parties to agree to good offices, conciliation, and mediation anytime during the lifetime of the dispute. The DESTA data also tell us that as deeper agreements evolved, the parties also built in off-ramps. They made more references to mutually agreed solutions and made clear that they could stop litigation at any time they wished to solve the issue through negotiation (see Figure 16.6).

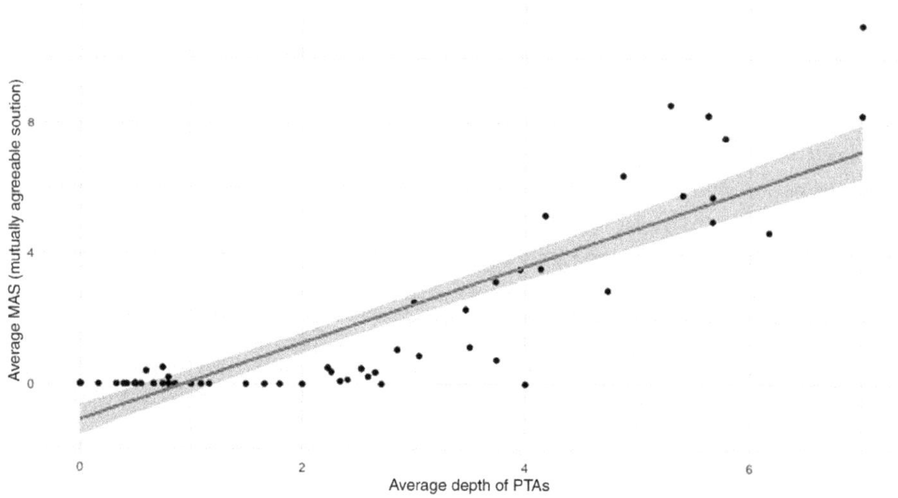

FIGURE 16.6 Strength of DSMs and references to MAS.
Source: author's elaboration based on DESTA

Another important feature of trade agreement DSMs is their short timeline. US agreements, for one, demand that a panel issue a final report within 150 days, or 120 days in the case of perishable goods, absent agreement by the parties. These timelines facilitate quick turnarounds on measures in question unseen in other fora.

I do not take up remedies and compliance with dispute settlement decisions here, but further research is urgently needed on that topic as trade agreements have begun to innovate in that area and many go beyond the WTO model. For example, some trade agreement DSMs provide for the possibility of provisional measures.[7] Some provide for financial compensation.[8] Approximately half of trade agreements in the DESTA data set provide for retaliation in case of non-implementation.

16.4 FUTURE

As this chapter has described, the trend of avoiding trade agreement disputes has waxed and waned. More topics in trade agreements have been made subject to DSMs – having been brought into the 'ordinary' process – just as more economies adopted a more legalistic procedure; yet, few disputes have been brought. Only in the last three years have trade agreement disputes begun to emerge with any consistency. Those disputes have yielded some positive outcomes in that states engaged with the reports and have worked within their contours, so far as public information depicts. The growing body of jurisprudence will soon form the foundation for disputes of the future, as this section takes up. The reports issued by panels

[7] See Chase et al., at footnote 9.
[8] Ibid.

in these early years have the potential to shape what will follow as states treat them as sources of authority or otherwise rely on them for their policy choices.

Ironically, with trade agreement dispute settlement now beginning to normalise, states have turned their attention to the extent of dispute settlement's reach, pushing the boundaries of what may be possible to ask a trade agreement to resolve. This section turns to the latest innovations in trade agreement dispute settlement: first, alternative styles of dealmaking, and sector-specific dispute designs; and second, disputes beyond the states, and specialised dispute tools.

16.4.1 *Next-generation Deals and Their Disputes*

The most important move by states in 2022–2023 has been the move away from comprehensive trade agreements entirely. In these US-led next-generation agreements, governments are unlikely to include binding commitments, and without binding commitments, enforcement mechanisms are unlikely. For example, more than a dozen countries are presently negotiating a new Indo-Pacific Economic Framework which will be 'self-enforcing and incentive-based' (Inside U.S. Trade 2022). This could mean 'unilateral' enforcement instead of traditional state-to-state dispute settlement, which, as some have noted, risks power plays and questions of durability (Lester 2022). This is not necessarily an aberration, but it remains to be seen if large club-like systems will replace comprehensive trade agreements in other parts of the world, with actors other than the US. In such systems, enforcement is likely to take on a softer form.

The US has also led the charge on sector-specific deals, including product-specific deals such as in the area of critical minerals. Again, this is not a new trend, but it is one that could pick up speed in upcoming decades as narratives about free trade falter. Governments have for many years negotiated smaller trade-related deals. The US has more than 1,200 trade-related agreements with more than 100 countries that regulate everything from cross-border tomatoes to trousers to titanium. These are not insignificant. So far, few of these deals maintain any sort of DSM, but that too could depend on their upcoming direction as well as their linkage to existing agreements. If future trade-related agreements are not about market access, or are limited to individual issue areas, even if they do lead to disputes, these might look different from the traditional sorts of disputes and, if so, they may require distinct sorts of mechanisms. We may see less arbitration and more expert determination, for example. Indeed, we already have.

In these times of institutional diversity, states may wish to consider incorporating into future trade agreements graduated menus of dispute settlement options. Some states have sought to do so, building in systems that offer several routes to get to a result in a dispute, such as the environmental provisions of the USMCA. There, parties may invoke the DSM, go to a committee, hold Ministerial consultations, proceed to a panel, and include public submissions, among still other options.

Diversification in DSMs is an appropriate way to manage diverse dealmaking. Governments ought to continue to think broadly about paths to resolution that are non-traditional and get the job done.

16.4.2 *Disputes beyond the States*

Another trend is now on the rise as states have turned attention to the potential for trade agreement DSMs to effectuate other goals beyond state-to-state compliance. Some of these innovative mechanisms for compliance have gained considerable public attention. They have garnered notice for their innovativeness as well as for their considerable reach and emphasis on 'trade plus' as seemingly more important than 'ordinary trade' matters, and they have altered the conversation on *who* or *what* is the target of our DSMs.

This trend is the increased attention to corporate accountability as subject to and part of trade agreement dispute settlement. The new tools in trade policing that most exemplify its corporate turn are those related to sustainability: both environmental and social sustainability. These are tools that US negotiators first developed and have recently implemented and deployed to ensure that companies are abiding by environmental and labour laws where they operate. Such instruments enable US bureaucrats to stop goods at the border that fail to meet these requirements.

A primary example is the USMCA Facility-Specific Rapid-Response Labor Mechanism (RRM, for short). The RRM is a bilateral annex to the dispute settlement chapter of the USMCA – between Canada and Mexico on the one hand, and separately between the US and Mexico on the other. It is designed to enable one of the governments to raise concerns about a denial of workers' rights at a factory on the territory of the other and ultimately to impose tariff penalties on the goods from that facility if the problem is not resolved. More concretely, the RRM permits US trade agencies to detain goods at the border if those goods come from a factory that is denying workers their collective bargaining rights, such as by tampering with a union voting process. For example, Customs can stop cars manufactured in Mexico at the Texas border and hold them there until the problematic labour issue at the General Motors factory from which they came is resolved to US trade officials' satisfaction. And it has done just that. General Motors was the first company to be subject to this tool. As of August 2023, the tool has been deployed a dozen times by the US against facilities in Mexico.

The point of the RRM is clear: it puts compliance responsibility not on the government but on companies. Rather than set up a panel to identify whether Mexico is at fault, the tool would allow a panel to make a determination as to whether there has been a violation of workers' rights at a workplace – effectively, bringing action against a company rather than against the Mexican government as would have been the case under most ordinary DSMs.

And the RRM is not unique. The US has used a similar approach in a forestry annex to the environmental chapter of its trade agreement with Peru, and other governments are now contemplating similar moves in their trade agreements (Claussen 2024). These tools are more akin to corporate social responsibility and corporate due diligence tools than they are to ordinary trade agreement DSMs, but they coexist and are squarely situated among the DSMs of these agreements.

Thus, these recent mechanisms have implications for how we think about DSMs – what counts as a dispute and what constitutes enforcement? These questions align also with questions about standing and actors. The new dispute settlement tools do not rely on either state-to-state settlement or domestic adjudication or entities that use force as we can see in other areas of government and international law.

16.5 CONCLUSION

The future is bright for trade agreement dispute settlement design. This is a moment of unusual experimentation. After thirty years of convergence towards state-to-state arbitration, trading partners are now re-evaluating the potential for trade agreement enforcement tools to achieve other aims. Bespoke designs are emerging for bilateral problems that target not states but other actors, including private actors and including for trade-plus matters. Designs are beginning to advance beyond boilerplate towards innovative and tailored tools.

Building on this potential will be important to keep enforcement efforts at the supranational level rather than slide into unilateral enforcement as recent pressures on governments to demonstrate that trade agreements are meaningful tools for positive social change have led to some questioning and some faltering. But the new tools, even if reciprocal on paper and agreed among parties, may not necessarily apply equally or be deployed consistently. The next several years will be a proving ground for innovative DSMs and their parties.

REFERENCES

Akinkugbe, O. 2020. 'Dispute Settlement under the African Continental Free Trade Area Agreement: A Preliminary Assessment', *African Journal of International Comparative Law* 28: 138–158.

Allee, T. and M. Elsig 2015. 'Why Do Some International Institutions Contain Strong Dispute Settlement Provisions? New Evidence from Preferential Trade Agreements', *The Review of International Organizations* 11(1): 89–120.

2019. 'Are the Contents of International Treaties Copied and Pasted? Evidence from Preferential Trade Agreements', *International Studies Quarterly* 63(3): 603–613.

Bercero, I. G. 2006. 'Dispute Settlement in European Union Free Trade Agreements: Lessons Learned?", in L. Bartels and F. Ortino (Eds.), *Regional Trade Agreements and the WTO Legal System*. Oxford: Oxford University Press, pp. 383–405.

Chase, C. et al. 2013. 'Mapping of Dispute Settlement Mechanisms in Regional Trade Agreements – Innovative or Variations on a Theme?' World Trade Organization: Economic Research and Statistics Division ERSD-2013-07.

Chazournes, L. and J. Lee 2022. 'The European Union–Korea Free Trade Agreement Sustainable Development Proceeding: Reflections on a Ground-Breaking Dispute', *Journal of World Investment and Trade* 23(3): 329–346.

Claussen, K. 2018a. 'Separation of Trade Law Powers', *Yale Journal of International Law* 43(2): 315–354.

2018b. 'Dispute Settlement Under the Next Generation of Free Trade Agreements', *Georgia Journal of International and Comparative Law* 46(3): 611–634.

2019. 'Forgotten Statutes: Trade Law's Domestic (Re)turn', *American Journal of International Law Unbound* 113: 40–44.

2020. 'Reimagining Trade-Plus Compliance: The Labor Story', *Journal of International Economic Law* 23(1): 25–43.

2023. 'Trade Policing', *Harvard International Law Journal* 65: 25–78.

Claussen, K. and M. Wu. forthcoming. 'Rules of Evidence under Free Trade Agreements', *Working Paper.*

Fortnam, B. 2022. 'IPEF Members Eye Incentive-Based, Self-Enforcing Commitments', *Inside US Trade.* (13 September 2022) https://insidetrade.com/daily-news/ipef-members-eye-incentive-based-self-enforcing-commitments

Froese, M. 2016. 'Mapping the Scope of Dispute Settlement in Regional Trade Agreements: Implications for the Multilateral Governance of Trade', *World Trade Review* 15(4): 563–585.

Gathii, J. 2019. 'Evaluating the Dispute Settlement Mechanism of the African Continental Free Trade Agreement', Afronomicslaw Blog, April 10, www.afronomicslaw.org/2019/04/10/evaluating-the-dispute-settlement-mechanism-of-the-african-continental-free-trade-agreement

Gastle, C. M. 1995. 'Policy Alternatives for Reform of the Free Trade Agreement of The Americas: Dispute Settlement Mechanisms', *Law and Policy in International Business* 26(3): 735–822.

Gomez-Mera, L. and A. Molinari 2014. 'Overlapping Institutions, Learning, and Dispute Initiation in Regional Trade Agreements: Evidence from South America', *International Studies Quarterly* 58: 269–281.

Hillman, J. 2009. 'Conflicts Between Dispute Settlement Mechanisms in Regional Trade Agreements and the WTO – What Should WTO Do?' *Cornell International Law Journal* 42: 193–208.

Jo, H. and H. Namgung 2012. 'Dispute Settlement Mechanisms in Preferential Trade Agreements: Democracy, Boilerplates, and the Multilateral Trade Regime', *Journal of Conflict Resolution* 56(6): 1041–1068.

Kwak, K. and G. Marceau 2003. 'Overlaps and Conflicts of Jurisdiction between the World Trade Organization and Regional Trade Agreements', in L. Bartels and F. Ortino (Eds.), *Regional Trade Agreements and the WTO Legal System.* Oxford: Oxford University Press, pp. 465–524.

Lester, S. 2022. 'Enforcing the IPEF: Unilateralism and Incentives vs. Adjudication', International Law and Policy Blog, September 19, www.WorldTradeLaw.net

Lester, S., I. Manak and A. Arpas 2019. 'Access to Trade Justice: Fixing NAFTA's Flawed State-to-State Dispute Settlement Process', *World Trade Review* 18(1): 63–79.

Luo, Y. 2006. 'Dispute Settlement in the Proposed East Asia Free Trade Agreement: Lessons Learned from the ASEAN, the NAFTA, and the EU', in L. Bartels and F. Ortino (Eds.),

Regional Trade Agreements and the WTO Legal System. Oxford: Oxford University Press, pp. 419–445.
Melillo, M. 2019. 'Informal Dispute Resolution in Preferential Trade Agreements', *Journal of World Trade* 53(1): 95–128.
Nedumpara, J. 2022. 'Dispute Settlement in International Trade Agreements: Prospective Pathways', *Global Trade and Customs Journal* 17(7&8): 261–265.
Porges, A. 2011. 'Dispute Settlement', in J. Chauffour and J. Maur (Eds.), *Preferential Trade Agreement Policies for Development: A Handbook*. Washington, DC: The World Bank, pp. 467–501.
Ray, R. and R. Meena 2022. 'Application of Dispute Settlement in Free Trade Agreements (FTAs): A Cross Country Analysis of Modern FTAs', *Global Trade and Customs Journal* 17(7&8): 317–324.
Schill, S. W. and G. Vidigal 2018. 'Reforming Dispute Settlement in Trade: The Contribution of Mega-Regionals', International Centre for Trade and Sustainable Development and the Inter-American Development Bank. https://dare.uva.nl/search?identifier=ec9307bf-8012-4bcf-9225-7d3ef51db51c
Schneider, A. K. 1999. 'Getting Along: The Evolution of Dispute Resolution Regimes in International Trade Organizations', *Michigan Journal of International Law* 20: 697–773.
Singh, S. 2022. 'Dispute Settlement in Indian FTAs: Shaping the Future with Lessons from the Past', *Global Trade and Customs Journal* 17(7&8): 304–309.
Smith, J. 'The Politics of Dispute Settlement Design: Explaining Legalism in Regional Trade Pacts', *International Organization* 54(1): 137–180.
Vidigal, G. 2017. 'Why Is There So Little Litigation under Free Trade Agreements? Retaliation and Adjudication in International Dispute Settlement', *Journal of International Economic Law* 20: 927–950.
2022. 'Regional Trade Adjudication and The Rise of Sustainability Disputes: *Korea – Labor Commitments and Ukraine – Wood Export Bans*," *American Journal of International Law* 116(3): 567–578.
Widiatedja, I. 2020. 'The Evolution of the Dispute Settlement Mechanism in Preferential Trade Agreements [PTAs]: The Case of Indonesia', *Asian Journal of Economic Law* 10: 346–374.
Zhao, J. and Y. Hu 2016. 'Formal or Informal? The Dispute Settlement Mechanisms of China's Free Trade Agreements', *Journal of Shanghai University (Science)* 21(1): 44–50.
Ziegler, A. 2006. 'Dispute Settlement in Bilateral Trade Agreements: The EFTA Experience', in L. Bartels and F. Ortino (Eds.), *Regional Trade Agreements and the WTO Legal System*. Oxford: Oxford University Press, pp. 407–417.

17

Regulatory Convergence in Preferential Trade Agreements

What Does the Future Hold?

Rodrigo Polanco

17.1 INTRODUCTION

In recent years, a new type of chapter has increasingly been included in preferential trade agreements (PTAs), under different monikers, like 'regulatory cooperation', 'regulatory improvement', 'regulatory coherence', and more commonly, 'good regulatory practices'. They represent a significant new development in trade governance.

Scholars generally use these concepts interchangeably with no agreed typology. Following the framework established in previous works (Polanco Lazo 2013; Polanco Lazo and Sauvé 2018), this chapter considers that these mechanisms should be viewed as forming part of the overarching notion of 'regulatory convergence', since they all aim to reduce unnecessary regulatory incompatibilities between countries.

Such a development raises important questions to which this chapter seeks answers: What are the main similarities and differences between these concepts? Do the different denominations matter? What are the guiding principles and objectives of such provisions? What are the challenges to implementing them? What are the possible future developments?

The chapter is organised as follows. Section 17.2 explores the foundations of the notion of regulatory convergence. Section 17.3 looks at its origins, while Sections 17.4 and 17.5 map and compare its different denominations, content, and meaning in early and recent PTAs. Section 17.6 examines the possible future developments of regulatory convergence in PTAs. The final section provides some brief conclusions.

17.2 REGULATORY DIVERGENCE AND REGULATORY CONVERGENCE

The law and political science literature has described several reasons why regulatory divergence might occur. First, the legal framework and social norms that countries have inherited create a strong path dependency that intrinsically limits the cross-country convergence of legal systems. Countries usually choose rules primarily consistent with their legal traditions (Glaeser and Shleifer 2002; La Porta et al. 2008). Second, regulatory divergence may result from different public policy choices, underlying objectives, and local preferences. Even if countries have the same choices, objectives, and preferences, regulators often adopt different approaches to reach them (e.g. more or less stringent environmental or health regulations), typically resulting in distinct compliance requirements (Basedow and Kauffmann 2016). Third, regulatory differences may also reflect information asymmetries between states (e.g. different access to relevant information) and network effects (e.g. sharing of information across regulators of different countries) (Chirico and Larouche 2013).

Regulatory divergence could be considered a trade barrier if it significantly increases trade costs that hinder cross-border exchanges. Non-tariff barriers have become a significant hurdle for businesses seeking enlarged access to other markets (Basedow and Kauffmann 2016; Chirico and Larouche 2013; Sheargold and Mitchell 2016). For example, they can lead to costly duplication in product development, manufacturing, and testing, affecting internationally active enterprises and especially small or medium-sized enterprises (SMEs), for which such costs can be a decisive factor in exporting (Malmström 2015).

By contrast, the literature highlights some factors that lead to regulatory convergence, based on the repeated interactions at the international level of policymakers, traders, and academics. Other causes of this phenomenon include the perceived need or pressure to comply with a dominant culture of regulatory hegemons, for example by using 'legal transplants' (Watson 1993). International law facilitates the dissemination of shared standards and underlying values or ideologies, and the adoption and implementation of uniform laws (Street 2013). Functional convergence among regulators may sometimes occur even as formal regulations diverge (Crettez et al. 2014).

Regulatory convergence and divergence are incomplete and dynamic processes for several reasons. Equal rules may mean different things in different legal systems or have distinct interpretations or applications, even in systems that share a legal culture. Tribunals typically accept a degree of divergence when applying laws (Chirico and Larouche 2013). The pace, form, and degree of convergence also differ over time, across sectors, and are affected by the costs and benefits of change, bureaucracy, and the cultural or social importance of the process (Crettez et al. 2014). Regulatory convergence involves actors with different 'regulatory capacity' and degrees of autonomy, and it requires coordination across ministries and regulators within a state (Young 2015). Furthermore, regulatory differences may evolve, fostering convergence or nurturing further divergence (Hoekman 2015).

Regulatory convergence can include substantive or procedural aspects that are aimed at two different types of regulatory outcomes. In the first type, regulatory convergence seeks to achieve *substantive* regulatory convergence (same or equivalent regulations). The second type considers the convergence of the processes by which regulations are developed, adopted, publicised, and implemented (same or equivalent regulatory procedures), or *procedural* regulatory convergence. In other words, those that address problems related to the quality of the regulations and their effects are mainly substantive, and those that address issues of design and implementation of regulations are primarily procedural (Sheargold and Mitchell 2016). With different denominations, both approaches are present in the PTAs examined in this chapter.

Regulatory convergence can be achieved through top-down or bottom-up processes (Chirico and Larouche 2013), like harmonisation at the international level (top-down) or exceptions in domestic law for regulatory measures of other countries (bottom-up). Preferential trade agreements consider several mechanisms for these purposes.

There are different typologies of these mechanisms. The Organisation for Economic Co-operation and Development (OECD) has identified eleven forms of 'international regulatory cooperation' (IRC), from the least to the most legally binding, including dialogues/ad hoc exchange of information, soft law, recognition/incorporation of international standards, unilateral convergence through good regulatory practices (GRPs), trans-governmental networks of regulators, mutual recognition agreements (MRAs), PTAs with regulatory provisions, joint standard-setting through intergovernmental organisations, formal regulatory cooperation partnerships, specific regulatory agreements between countries, and integration/harmonisation through supranational or joint institutions (Malyshev and Kauffmann 2015; OECD 2013). Good regulatory practices encompass regulatory impact assessments (RIAs), stakeholder engagement, and ex post evaluation (Basedow and Kauffmann 2016).

The distinctions among all these mechanisms are not always clear. Still, one can consider that some aim mainly for substantive convergence (e.g. MRAs, recognition of international standards, joint standard-setting) and others for procedural convergence (e.g. GRPs, exchange of information).

17.3 THE ROOTS OF REGULATORY CONVERGENCE

The roots of regulatory convergence are found in the evolution of the United States (US) administrative law after World War II. The philosophy that has governed American administrative law since then is mainly focused on what we have called procedural convergence, including, among others, transparency and public consultation, RIAs, inter-agency cooperation or coordination and compatibility, and judicial or administrative review. Other developed countries like Australia and New Zealand have also highlighted elements of regulatory convergence in their domestic settings (Lin and Liu 2018).

However, the idea of adopting measures to address regulatory divergence has also been present for a long time in the global arena. Examples include international organisations and forums like the World Trade Organization (WTO), the OECD, the Asia-Pacific Economic Cooperation (APEC), and transatlantic cooperation between the European Union (EU) and the US.

17.3.1 *WTO*

Since the establishment of the General Agreement on Tariffs and Trade (GATT), behind-the-border regulatory measures have raised concerns about diluting or nullifying the value of tariff bindings by discriminating against foreign products and thus affecting international trade (Sykes 1999). For that reason, drafters of the GATT included general substantive rules on 'national treatment' and 'most-favoured-nation treatment' (MFN) in GATT Articles III and I, respectively.[1] Similar provisions concerning services are enshrined in Articles XVII and II of the General Agreement on Trade in Services (GATS).[2]

But, regulatory discrimination often involves barriers that are not as easy to detect as tariffs or quotas applied at the border. Areas such as food inspection, product labelling, and safety guidelines are governed by internal health, safety, and technical regulations, all of which can be designed or implemented to raise costs for foreign firms in comparison with domestic ones, giving the latter an advantage in the home market (Fishbein and Trebilcock 2007). Over time, countries have recognised that implementing GRPs minimises unnecessary trade barriers (Bollyky 2012). In the WTO, the agreements addressing such measures are the Agreement on Technical Barriers to Trade[3] (TBT), concerning technical regulations, standards, and procedures for testing and certification, and the Agreement on Sanitary and Phytosanitary Measures[4] (SPS), regarding food safety and animal health. Both deal with substantive and regulatory convergence using tools such as transparency obligations, recognition of equivalence, MRAs, and treaty bodies to oversee treaty implementation.

But these agreements also further promote substantive regulatory convergence by encouraging members to use international standards and opting for least trade-restrictive ways to satisfy public policy objectives or minimise their adverse effects. Neither the TBT nor the SPS Agreements explicitly compel members to use international standards. However, if they adopt measures that depart from them,

1 Marrakesh Agreement Establishing the World Trade Organization, 15 April 1994, (in force 1 January 1995), Annex 1A, General Agreement on Tariffs and Trade (GATT) 1994, incorporates by reference the GATT 1947, www.wto.org/english/docs_e/legal_e/gatt47_01_e.htm (accessed 13 May 2024).

2 Marrakesh Agreement, Annex 1B, General Agreement on Trade in Services, www.wto.org/english/docs_e/legal_e/26-gats_01_e.htm (accessed 13 May 2024).

3 Marrakesh Agreement, Annex 1A, Agreement on Technical Barriers to Trade.

4 Marrakesh Agreement, Annex 1A, Agreement on the Application of Sanitary and Phytosanitary Measures.

they shift the burden of proof regarding the necessity of a measure to the country adopting any regulation that departs from the international standard.[5]

17.3.2 *OECD*

The notion of 'regulatory cooperation' emerged at the OECD in the mid-1990s. A study noted that building more integrated systems for rulemaking and implementation required institutional and procedural cooperation frameworks within national governments, sub-national governments, and the wider public, subject to the constraints of democratic values, such as accountability and openness (Jacobs 1994).

Members of the OECD were the first to consider concerted actions directed at improving the quality of their regulatory systems, particularly by using procedural convergence tools, like RIAs, which are defined as 'a process of systematically identifying and assessing the expected effects of regulatory proposals, using a consistent analytical method' (OECD 2008). A study noted that from a couple of countries using this tool in 1980, by 1996, more than half of OECD Members had adopted RIAs (Jacobs 1997). By 2009, RIAs were/became mainstream among OECD Members to improve the quality of regulatory decision-making and inform whether and how to regulate to achieve public policy goals (OECD 2009). In 2012, the OECD Council on Regulatory Policy and Governance issued a recommendation that explicitly promotes the integration of RIAs into the early stages of policy formulation (OECD 2012).

Regulatory impact assessments are comparative and ex ante in character. They determine the underlying regulatory objectives sought and identify all the policy interventions capable of achieving them, using risk analysis or, more often, cost–benefit analysis. The latter can be used as a mechanism of regulatory convergence on its own, without the comparative element of RIAs. Key aspects of RIAs include defining a regulatory problem, identifying different regulatory options (including no policy change), collecting data (from public consultations, interviews, questionnaires, surveys, focus groups, etc.), assessing alternative options, identifying preferred regulatory options, and communicating RIAs results (usually through websites) (Lemoine 2018).

Stakeholders are vital drivers of RIAs. They include groups concerned with the costs and impact of regulations on their business activity, with the promotion of specific values (like transparency and accountability), and with the effect of regulations, such as job creation or the environment (Jacobs 1997). To avoid 'capture' by

[5] Under TBT Agreement Article 2.4, WTO Members are required to use relevant international standards as a basis for their technical regulations except when they would be an ineffective or inappropriate means for the fulfilment of the legitimate objectives pursued. Likewise, under SPS Agreement Article 3.1, WTO Members are required to base their SPS measures on international standards or guidelines, but they may choose to depart from them if there is a scientific justification, or as a consequence of adopting a higher level of protection.

stakeholders, effective and transparent RIA processes are often conducted or overseen by a specialised government body that can provide regulators with high-quality, trusted, and impartial advice (Lemoine 2018).

17.3.3 *APEC*

In the 2000s, APEC economies[6] developed a work programme on regulatory reform as part of a joint initiative with the OECD, establishing the APEC–OECD Integrated Checklist on Regulatory Reform (the 'Checklist') (APEC and OECD 2005).

The Checklist is a voluntary tool that contains four pillars: regulatory policy, competition policy, market liberalisation policy, and regulatory reform. Concerning the latter, the Checklist comprises mechanisms that APEC economies may use to evaluate their process of development and implementation of regulatory policy, with flexibility in the methods applied, recognising the diversity of economic, social, and political environments and values of APEC economies (Polanco Lazo and Sauvé 2018).

The focus here is also primarily on procedural regulatory convergence, mainly through RIAs, allowing policy comparisons. However, as RIAs alone cannot build a regulatory policy, the Checklist also highlights the need to focus on an integrated system, involving all state sectors acting in coordination and mutual support. It is often difficult for regulators to reform due to close identification with outdated regulatory regimes, countervailing pressures from regulated sectors or different parts of society, as well as personal or bureaucratic interests. For that purpose, the Checklist proposes the creation of a central coordinating body and establishing a coordination mechanism. Additionally, it fosters the use of transparency measures. National and foreign stakeholders are considered in the creation of regulations, through appropriate and publicised procedures of public consultation, not only limited to affected businesses but also including other interested parties, such as trade unions, interest groups (e.g. consumer or environmental organisations), and other pertinent levels of government. Finally, the Checklist suggests a procedure for evaluating a proposed regulatory action's compliance with international obligations, like commitments under the WTO, PTAs, and international investment agreements (IIAs) (APEC and OECD 2005).

The Asia-Pacific Economic Cooperation developed a baseline study which reviewed the application of selected GRPs across the twenty-one APEC economies (APEC 2011). By 2016, these countries had made visible progress in three practices:

6 Asia-Pacific Economic Cooperation is an intergovernmental forum established in 1989, to promote free trade throughout the Asia-Pacific region. Members include Australia, Brunei, Canada, Chile, China, Hong Kong, Indonesia, Japan, South Korea, Malaysia, Mexico, New Zealand, Papua New Guinea, Peru, the Philippines, Russia, Singapore, Taiwan, Thailand, the US, and Viet Nam. APEC, https://www.apec.org/ (accessed 13 May 2024).

internal government coordination of rulemaking activity, public consultation mechanisms, and RIAs – with the latter becoming 'the norm' in the APEC region. However, as the implementation of the Checklist is voluntary, notable differences in regulatory processes remain (Jacobs 2017). Additionally, some have warned that a core tenet of RIAs – the need for 'clear evidence' that regulation is needed – could be dangerous/questionable if it is subordinated to free trade and investment. For them, reducing red tape has served primarily business and not society as a whole (Trade Union Advisory Committee 2016).

17.3.4 *Transatlantic Cooperation*

Historically, various initiatives have addressed regulatory divergence between the EU and the US.[7] Still, it was not until 2005, with the establishment of the EU–US High-Level Regulatory Cooperation Forum (HLRCF), that both parties decided to create a body to discuss these issues.

In 2007, the EU and the US renamed the HLRCF as the Transatlantic Economic Council (TEC), with the formal task of avoiding increased cross-border trade costs stemming from duplicative regulations and to 'oversee and accelerate government-to-government cooperation in furthering economic integration' (Posner and Wolff 2011). The TEC addressed the 'regulatory cooperation' issue by establishing a framework for fostering cooperation and reducing regulatory burdens.[8] To meet these objectives, the EU and the US established two kinds of cooperative efforts on substantive and procedural convergence. On the latter, the TEC promoted the exchange of experiences and information among regulators and developed a methodological framework allowing comparisons between RIAs, risk assessments, and cost–benefit analyses concerning regulations.[9] On substance, the TEC advanced regulatory convergence in specific sectors (cosmetics, medical devices, pharmaceuticals, automobiles, electrical equipment, and nano-materials)(Woolcock et al. 2015).

The TEC did not succeed in promoting regulatory convergence between the US and the EU and stumbled 'over efforts to resolve disputes involving sales of poultry, cosmetics, and electrical equipment' (Ahearn 2009). Obstacles to bilateral regulatory cooperation remained, particularly in food safety, the environment, and security,

7 Examples include the 1995 New Transatlantic Agenda, the 1997 Joint Statement on the Principles of Good Regulation, the 1998 Transatlantic Economic Partnership, the 1999 Joint Statement on Early Warning and Problem Prevention Mechanisms, the 2000 Consultative Forum on Biotechnology, the 2002 Guidelines for Regulatory Cooperation and Transparency, and the 2004–2005 Roadmaps for US–EU Regulatory Cooperation and Transparency, to name just a few (Lin and Liu 2018)

8 Framework for Advancing Transatlantic Economic Integration between the United States of America and the European Union (hereinafter 'TEC Framework'), 30 April 2007, https://2009-2017.state.gov/p/eur/rls/or/130772.htm (accessed 13 May 2024).

9 TEC Framework Annex 1.

where both parties have maintained diverging risk perceptions and regulatory philosophies (Mildner and Ziegler 2009). After five meetings, the TEC stopped functioning at the ministerial level in 2010, although cooperation was still being pursued at a technical level (European Commission 2015).

The EU and the US reignited transatlantic cooperation after a summit on 15 June 2021 in Brussels, establishing a Trade and Technology Council (TTC) to serve as a forum to coordinate approaches to key global trade, economic, and technology issues and to deepen transatlantic trade and economic relations (European Commission 2021). The EU and the US have established ten TTC Working Groups, respectively, focused on tech standards, climate and green tech, secure supply chains, information and communications technology and services (ICTS) security and competitiveness, data governance and tech platform regulation, misuse of technology threatening security and human rights, export controls, investment screening, promoting SME access to and use of digital technologies, and global trade challenges (US Department of Commerce 2023).

Up to now, the TTC focus largely seems to be on procedural convergence, as manifested in the initial functioning of its Working Groups on activities of cooperation and promotion. But a more substantive convergence is intended in at least two areas: joint standards in post-quantum encryption and cybersecurity of the internet of things, and extending MRAs on marine equipment and vaccines (European Commission 2022). It is too early to assess if the TEC will deliver. Swift regulatory alignment between the US and the EU is still unlikely, and initial effects have been mainly geopolitical (Ringhof 2022).

17.4 REGULATORY CONVERGENCE IN EARLY PTAS

Individual chapters on regulatory convergence are not found in most PTAs, but disciplines relating to some of its elements, like transparency, were common even before the notion of regulatory convergence appeared (Lin and Liu 2018).[10]

With different degrees of success, some regional PTAs were early movers, as questions about regulatory convergence matter for countries that trade a lot and have borders. In 1983, the Australia–New Zealand Closer Economic Relations Trade Agreements (ANZCERTA)[11] established joint institutions, including common regulatory agencies, to develop 'joint food standards, harmonised approaches to certification of quality management systems, and mutual recognition of product standards and occupational qualifications' (Steger 2012). Both countries

[10] See, for example, South Korea–US FTA, Peru–Singapore FTA, and China–New Zealand FTA.

[11] Australia–New Zealand Closer Economic Relations Trade Agreement, 28 March 1983, www.dfat.gov.au/trade/agreements/in-force/anzcerta/Pages/australia-new-zealand-closer-economic-relations-trade-agreement (accessed 13 May 2024).

established an MRA on product standards and professional qualifications in 1997,[12] and a common food standards code in 2003 issued by a joint agency, the Food Standards Australia New Zealand (FSANZ).[13]

Canada, Mexico, and the US concluded several ad hoc or informal cooperative arrangements outside the North American Free Trade Agreement (NAFTA), like the Security and Prosperity Partnership (SPP) of North America, the Mexico–US High-Level RCC (HLRCC), and the Canada–US Regulatory Cooperation Council (RCC). Besides some substantive regulatory convergence from the latter, in health products, energy efficiency, and motor vehicle safety rules, these initiatives have been largely unsuccessful (Manak 2022).

The Association of Southeast Asian Nations (ASEAN)[14] aims to align domestic norms with international standards and develop MRAs on conformity assessment and professional services (Steger 2012). So far, however, the extent of convergence has been limited. The Association of Southeast Asian Nations has a Consultative Committee on Standards and Quality (ACCSQ) with the goal of 'One Standard, One Test, Accepted Everywhere' (ASEAN 2014b), and a Framework Agreement on Mutual Recognition Arrangements (ASEAN 2014a). Using these tools, ASEAN Members have fostered substantive regulatory convergence through MRAs on medical services, architecture, accountancy, and tourism services, among other areas (Sheargold and Mitchell 2016).

Members of the Southern Common Market ('Mercado Común del Sur' – Mercosur)[15] established in 1992 a standardisation committee to elaborate voluntary standards, promote cooperation to facilitate harmonisation, align Members' regulations on international standards, promote training in standardisation and quality control, and encourage the development of certification systems and MRAs.[16] However, the Protocol of Ouro Preto in December 1994[17] suppressed the standardisation committee without providing reasons behind this decision.

The 2010 EU–South Korea Free Trade Agreement (FTA),[18] included a section on 'regulatory framework', in Chapter 7 on trade in services, investment, establishment, and electronic commerce, containing some tools of substantive regulatory

[12] Trans-Tasman Mutual Recognition Act 1997, www.legislation.gov.au/Details/C2015C00470 (accessed 13 May 2024).

[13] FSANZ, www.foodstandards.gov.au/code/pages/default.aspx (accessed 13 May 2024).

[14] ASEAN Declaration, Bangkok, 8 August 1967, https://agreement.asean.org/media/download/20140117154159.pdf (accessed 13 May 2024). ASEAN Members are Brunei, Cambodia, Indonesia, Laos, Malaysia, Myanmar, the Philippines, Singapore, Thailand, and Viet Nam.

[15] Treaty Establishing a Common Market between the Argentine Republic, the Federal Republic of Brazil, the Republic of Paraguay and the Eastern Republic of Uruguay, 26 March 1991, treaties.un.org/Pages/showDetails.aspx?objid = 0800000280 0a84a2 (accessed 13 May 2024).

[16] MERCOSUR/GMC/RES Nro. 02/92: Comité Mercosur de Normalización, normas.mercosur .int/public/normativas/2264 (accessed 13 May 2024).

[17] Protocol of Ouro Preto, 17 December 1994, treaties.un.org/Pages/showDetails.aspx?objid = 080000028008a9d6 (accessed 13 May 2024).

[18] Free Trade Agreement between the European Union and its Member States, of the one part, and the Republic of Korea, of the other part, 6 October 2010, eur-lex.europa.eu/legal-content/

convergence, like mutual recognition or harmonisation of minimum common standards, avoiding needless or unjustified differences in rulemaking. It also considers mechanisms of procedural regulatory convergence, such as dialogues and committees, exchange of information, experiences, and data, as well as through deepened scientific and technical cooperation (Laurenza and Mathis 2013). Under the guise of 'regulatory cooperation', parties adopted international standards in pharmaceutical goods, medical products,[19] and the automotive industry.[20]

17.5 REGULATORY CONVERGENCE IN RECENT PTAS

Regulatory convergence in PTAs has evolved from a relatively voluntary principle (e.g. OECD and APEC) to a more legalised treaty obligation (with some elements in early PTAs), to having dedicated chapters in this discipline, as explained in this section.[21]

17.5.1 *Transatlantic Trade and Investment Partnership*

In June 2013, the EU Member States mandated the European Commission (EC) to negotiate a Transatlantic Trade and Investment Partnership (TTIP) with the US. One of its objectives was to increase trade and investment through greater regulatory compatibility, setting the path for global standards.

According to the EU, the TTIP should include cross-cutting disciplines on 'regulatory coherence', featuring both substantive and procedural convergence. Some were not wholly new, like GRPs on transparency, early stakeholder consultations, periodic reviews of regulations, and RIAs. Novel mechanisms included focal points to facilitate information exchange between regulators or, if specific common interests were identified, recognition of equivalence or harmonisation of regulatory acts. A Regulatory Cooperation Body (RCB) would develop horizontal provisions on regulatory cooperation, complemented by commitments in nine specific sectors: automotive, chemicals, cosmetics, pharmaceuticals, information and communication technology, engineering, financial services, medical devices, and textiles. The

EN/TXT/?uri=CELEX%3A22011A0514%2801%29 (accessed 13 May 2024). Provisionally applied since 1 July 2011 and in force since 6 October 2010.

19 EU–South Korea FTA, Annex 2-D Pharmaceutical Products and Medical Devices, Article 5. They include those of the World Health Organization (WHO), the OECD, the International Conference on Harmonization of Technical Requirements for Registration of Pharmaceuticals for Human Use, the Global Harmonization Task Force, and the Pharmaceutical Inspection Convention and Pharmaceutical Inspection Cooperation Scheme.

20 EU–South Korea FTA, Annex 2-C Motor Vehicle and Parts, Articles 2 and 4. They recognise those of the World Forum for Harmonization of Vehicle Regulations, a working party of the Inland Transport Committee of the United Nations Economic Commission for Europe (UNECE).

21 Concerning the effects of these chapters on investment, see Federico Ortino's Chapter 8 of this book.

Regulatory Cooperation Body was not supposed to have regulatory competence *per se*, and both parties would continue to regulate following their domestic regulatory frameworks, procedures, and principles (European Commission 2013, 2015).

The US position concerning regulatory convergence in the TTIP was never publicly available. It was reported that a July 2014 proposal sought only to cover federal rulemaking on the US side but both community-level and Member States' legislation and regulations on the EU side. A negotiating draft leaked in 2016 included both procedural and substantive convergence. On the latter, it proposed a bilateral cooperation mechanism, information and regulatory exchanges, the promotion of regulatory compatibility and international cooperation, as well as the establishment of an RCB. The procedural part featured a section on GRPs, including RIAs, decision-making based on evidence, internal coordination of regulatory development, prior notification procedures, stakeholder consultations, transparency obligations, and the possibility of reviewing regulations. (Greenpeace Nederland 2016).

Transatlantic Trade and Investment Partnership negotiations were halted by the US during the Trump Administration, and on 15 April 2019, the EC declared them 'obsolete and no longer relevant' (Council of the European Union 2019).

17.5.2 *PTAs with Regulatory Convergence Chapters*

Several recent trade agreements include standalone chapters on regulatory convergence. According to the OECD, PTAs increasingly incorporate horizontal chapters on GRPs, IRCs, or both (Kauffmann and Saffirio 2021). We have found a total of twenty PTAs, including regulatory convergence chapters, which are detailed in Table 17.1 below.[22]

When negotiations of the Comprehensive Economic and Trade Agreement (CETA) between the EU and Canada concluded in August 2014, they included for the first time a chapter on 'regulatory cooperation' (Chapter 21). CETA focuses mainly on substantive convergence, including improving regulatory quality by avoiding or reducing unnecessary differences, identifying alternatives (like the recognition of equivalence), and minimising administrative costs.[23] It also has features of procedural convergence like RIAs, data collection and analysis, sharing regulatory proposals, joint high-level dialogue, and specific sectoral cooperation initiatives dealing with consumer safety, among others (Steger 2014).

The next milestone in incorporating regulatory convergence chapters in PTAs can be observed in the Pacific Alliance (PA). The PA Members (Chile, Colombia, Mexico, and Peru) aimed to deepen intra-regional trade, investment, and mobility,

[22] AIT–TECRO Trade Agreement, Chapter 3, https://ustr.gov/sites/default/files/2023-05/AIT-TECRO%20Trade%20Agreement%20May%202023.pdf (accessed 13 May 2024).

[23] CETA, Articles 21.2 and 21.3.

TABLE 17.1 *PTAs with regulatory convergence chapters*

	Name	Date of signature	Date of entry into force	Name	Chapter / Title
1	Pacific Alliance Additional Protocol (PAAP)	03.07.15	01.04.20	Regulatory Improvement	Ch. 15bis
2	Trans-Pacific Partnership (TPP)/ Comprehensive and Progressive Trans-Pacific Partnership (CPTPP)	04.02.2016 / 08.03.2018	30.12.2018	Regulatory Coherence	Ch. 25
3	Chile–Uruguay FTA (2016)	04.10.16	13.12.18	Regulatory Coherence	Ch. 15
4	Canada–EU Comprehensive Economic and Trade Agreement (CETA)	30.10.16	21.09.2017 (provisionally applied)	Regulatory Cooperation	Ch. 21
5	Australia–Peru FTA	12.02.18	11.02.20	Regulatory Coherence	Ch. 24
6	EU–Japan Economic Partnership Agreement (EPA)	17.07.18	01.02.19	Good Regulatory Practices and Regulatory Cooperation	Ch. 18
7	Brazil–Chile FTA	21.11.18	25.01.22	Good Regulatory Practices	Ch. 3
8	US–Mexico–Canada Agreement (USMCA)	30.11.18	01.07.20	Good Regulatory Practices	Ch. 28
9	Protocol to amend the Agreement between New Zealand and Singapore Comprehensive Economic Partnership Agreement (CEPA)	17.05.19	01.01.20	Regulatory Cooperation	Ch. 13
10	Japan–United Kingdom (UK) CEPA	23.10.20	01.01.21	Good Regulatory Practices and Regulatory Cooperation	Ch. 18
11	EU–UK and Cooperation Agreement	30.12.20	01.05.21	Good Regulatory Practices and Regulatory Cooperation	Part. II; Tit. X
12	Chile–Paraguay FTA	12.01.21	14.02.24	Good Regulatory Practices	Ch. 3
13	Iceland–Liechtenstein–Norway–UK FTA	08.07.21		Good Regulatory Practices and Regulatory Cooperation	Ch. 11
14	Australia–UK FTA	16.12.21		Good Regulatory Practices	Ch. 26

(*continued*)

TABLE 17.1 (*continued*)

	Name	Date of signature	Date of entry into force	Name	Chapter / Title
15	Pacific Alliance–Singapore FTA	26.01.22		Good Regulatory Practices	Ch. 20
16	New Zealand–UK FTA	28.02.22		Good Regulatory Practices	Ch. 21
17	Taiwan–US Trade Initiative	01.06.23		Good Regulatory Practices	Ch. 3
18	EU–New Zealand FTA	09.07.23	01.05.24	Good Regulatory Practices	Ch. 22
19	Canada–Ukraine Modernized Free Trade Agreement	22.09.2023		Good Regulatory Practices	Ch. 26
20	Chile–EU Interim Trade Agreement	13.12.2023		Good Regulatory Practices	Ch. 29

focusing on improving regulatory processes and their transparency (Ministerio de Comercio, Industria y Turismo de Colombia 2016). On 3 July 2015, Members signed a Protocol Amending the First Additional Protocol to the Framework Agreement of the Pacific Alliance (PAAP, in force since 1 May 2016), which includes (in its Annex 4) a new chapter on 'Regulatory Improvement'.[24] This chapter primarily focuses on procedural convergence, with Members affirming their desire to improve their regulatory performance through establishing and systematically implementing tools such as transparency and public consultation, review, and ex ante and ex post measurement of the impact of regulations, and the simplification of procedures.

On 4 February 2016, the TPP was signed by twelve countries. Although the chapter on 'Regulatory Coherence' was concluded after CETA and the PAAP, its negotiations predate both agreements. It primarily focuses on procedural convergence, improving regulatory practices, conducting regulatory processes more trade-facilitatively, eliminating redundancies in testing and certification, and increasing transparency and stakeholder engagement. It also aimed to make the regulatory systems of member countries more compatible, removing unnecessary barriers, reducing regional divergences in standards, and promoting cooperation on specific regulatory issues (Bollyky 2012). In the wake of the January 2017 decision of the US to withdraw from the agreement, a revised version of the treaty, now renamed CPTPP, was signed on 8 March 2018, keeping the same chapter on regulatory coherence as in the original TPP.

[24] Protocolo Adicional al Acuerdo Marco de la Alianza del Pacífico, 3 July 2015, alianzapacifico.net/en/download/protocolo-adicional-al-acuerdo-marco-de-la-alianza-del-pacifico/ (accessed 13 May 2024).

In both the PAAP and the CPTPP, emphasis is laid on the use of international GRPs in planning, drafting, promulgating, implementing, and reviewing regulatory measures, considering the input from interested stakeholders in their development.[25] The USMCA – an agreement that partially follows and expands this model – also encourages regulatory compatibility between the contracting parties.[26]

Subsequent agreements have primarily followed the template of the CETA and CPTPP/PAAP. A more detailed comparison of both models follows in the next section.

17.5.3 *Comparison of PTAs Models of Regulatory Convergence*

This section offers a comparative analysis of provisions in the PTAs that currently include regulatory convergence chapters. With some variations, we can detect two main models among these treaties: the CETA model (followed mainly in subsequent EU and UK agreements), and the CPTPP/PAAP model (followed by some countries of those trading blocs).

17.5.3.1 Definition

The chapter on regulatory cooperation in the CETA does not include a definition of such a discipline. The same happens in the EU–Japan EPA, the Japan–UK CEPA, the EU–UK TCA, Iceland–Liechtenstein–Norway–UK FTA, Australia–UK FTA, and New Zealand–UK FTA. Definitions help to identify the real focus of regulatory convergence, whether substantive, procedural, or both.

The definition of 'regulatory coherence' in the CPTPP is mainly about procedural convergence. It refers to the 'use of good regulatory practices in the process of planning, designing, issuing, implementing, and reviewing regulatory measures to facilitate achievement of domestic policy objectives, and in efforts across governments to enhance regulatory cooperation to further those objectives and promote international trade and investment, economic growth, and employment'.[27] Basically the same definition is included in the Chile–Uruguay FTA, Australia–Peru FTA, and PA–Singapore FTA (although the latter uses 'best practices' to define 'good regulatory practices').[28] The PAAP definition of 'regulatory improvement' is essentially identical to 'regulatory coherence' in the CPTPP, with one telling difference. While the CPTPP refers to the use of 'good regulatory practices', the PAAP refers to

[25] PAAP, Article 15 bis2; CPTPP, Article 25.2.
[26] USMCA, Article 28.17.
[27] CPTPP, Article 25.2.1.
[28] Chile–Uruguay FTA, Article 15.1; Australia–Peru FTA, Article 24.2.1; PA–Singapore FTA, Article 20.2.

'good *international* regulatory practices'.[29] This would appear to acknowledge that such good practices are most likely to be 'imported' and not generated by the PA Members.

A different definition, but also concerning procedural convergence, is found in the Chilean FTAs with Brazil and Paraguay, which define 'good regulatory practices' as the use of tools in the process of planning, drafting, adoption, implementation, review, and follow-up of regulatory measures.[30]

Broader definitions, including substantive and procedural convergence elements, are found in three PTAs following the CPTPP/PAAP model. The United States–Mexico–Canada Agreement and the Taiwan–US PTA define 'regulatory cooperation' as 'an effort between two or more Parties to prevent, reduce, or eliminate unnecessary regulatory differences to facilitate trade and promote economic growth, while maintaining or enhancing standards of public health and safety and environmental protection'.[31] The updated New Zealand–Singapore CEPA defines it as 'efforts between the Parties to enhance regulatory cooperation to further domestic policy objectives, improve the effectiveness of domestic regulation in the face of increased cross-border activity, and promote international trade and investment, economic growth, and employment'.[32]

17.5.3.2 Scope of Application

The regulatory cooperation chapter in the CETA considers the development, review, and methodological aspects of regulatory measures covered by WTO agreements: TBT, SPS, GATT, and GATS, all deemed incorporated in the treaty.[33] The parties may expand this scope of application by discussing regulatory policy issues of mutual interest, via consultations or in a treaty body (the Regulatory Cooperation Forum – RCF).

Other treaties following the CETA model have a broader scope. Regulatory convergence applies to all measures issued by the parties' regulatory authorities regarding any matter covered by the agreement, or when they are relevant to regulatory cooperation activities, such as guidelines, policy documents, or recommendations.[34] Yet, some

[29] PAAP, Article 15 bis2.1.

[30] Brazil–Chile FTA, Article 3.1; Chile–Paraguay FTA, Article 3.1.

[31] USMCA, Article 28.1; Taiwan–US Trade Agreement, Article 3.1.

[32] New Zealand–Singapore CEPA, Article 13.1.

[33] CETA, Articles 21.1 and 21.2.1. Article 21.1. The chapter also replaces the Framework on Regulatory Co-operation and Transparency between the Government of Canada and the European Commission done at Brussels on 21 December 2004 (European Commission, 2004), and covers the activities previously undertaken in the context of that framework (CETA, Article 21.2).

[34] EU–Japan EPA, Article 18.3; Japan–UK CEPA, Article 18.3; EU–UK TCA, Article 342.2.

PTAs consider exclusions to this rule (e.g. taxation, public procurement, and public financial assistance).[35]

In contrast, regulatory convergence in PTAs following the CPTPP/PAAP model applies only to 'covered measures'. These are measures of general application, with which compliance is mandatory, adopted, issued, or maintained by a regulatory authority. In determining the covered measures, each party should aim to achieve 'significant' coverage, promptly after the date of entry into force of the agreement: no later than one year (CPTPP, Brazil–Chile FTA), two years (PA–Singapore FTA), or three years (PAAP, Chile–Uruguay FTA) and make it publicly available.[36]

Some of these treaties briefly depart from the CPTPP/PAAP model, and have a larger scope, applying to all regulatory practices, not requiring to achieve significant coverage.[37] However, some of these PTAs include exceptions to this rule. The United States–Mexico–Canada Agreement excludes measures concerning military or defence, agency organisation, taxation (for Canada and Mexico), and financial services (for Mexico and the US).[38] Financial and military regulations are excluded from the Taiwan–US PTA.[39]

17.5.3.3 Guiding Principles and Objectives

Both the CETA and CPTPP/PAAP models of regulatory convergence share general principles, and more detailed objectives like the right to regulate and interstate cooperation.

17.5.3.3.1 GENERAL PRINCIPLES Some general principles are recurrent in PTAs with regulatory convergence chapters. Two are not entirely novel or specific to this discipline, namely facilitating increasing trade and investment between the parties,[40]

35 Iceland–Liechtenstein–Norway–UK FTA, Article 11.3 and Annex XXV; Australia–UK FTA, Article 26.1; New Zealand–UK FTA, Article 21.1. Chile-EU Interim Trade Agreement excludes the regulatory authorities and regulatory measures, practices or approaches of the Member States of the EU.

36 CPTPP, Articles 25.1 and 25.3; Chile–Uruguay FTA, Articles 15.1 and 15.3; PA–Singapore FTA, Articles 20.1 and 20.3; PAAP, Articles 15 bis.1 and 15 bis.3; Brazil–Chile FTA, Articles 3.1 and 3.3.

37 Chile–Paraguay FTA, Article 3.1.

38 USMCA, Article 28.2 and Annex 28-A.

39 Taiwan–US PTA, Article 3.1 and Annex 3-A.

40 PAAP, Article 15 bis.2.2 a); CPTPP, Article 25.2.2 a); CETA, Article 21.3 c); Chile–Uruguay FTA, Article 15.2 a); Australia–Peru FTA, Article 24.2.2 a); Brazil–Chile FTA, Article 3.4.1; USMCA, Article 28.2.1; Iceland–Liechtenstein–Norway–UK FTA, Article 11.1.1; Australia–UK FTA, Article 26.2.1; PA–Singapore FTA, Article 20.2.1; New Zealand–UK FTA, Article 21.11 a); New Zealand–Singapore CEPA, Article 13.2.2 a) (only concerning trade).

and reducing or removing potential regulatory barriers,[41] which are also generally found in other PTAs.

But PTAs with regulatory convergence chapters also include principles that are more specific to the domain, like having an effective, transparent, and predictable regulatory environment,[42] taking into account input from interested persons in developing regulatory measures,[43] and reducing or removing unnecessarily burdensome, duplicative, or divergent regulatory requirements.[44]

Other principles mentioned in a few PTAs include facilitating innovation, adopting new technologies,[45] and international models, norms, and rules.[46]

17.5.3.3.2 RIGHT TO REGULATE All regulatory convergence mechanisms can be seen as diminishing the regulatory autonomy of states, limiting their choices in how to pursue public policy objectives (Sheargold and Mitchell 2016). Probably for that reason, most PTAs address the relation of this discipline with the state's right to regulate either directly or indirectly, balancing more depth with flexibility.

The CETA explicitly upholds the right to regulate in its investment, labour, and environment chapters.[47] Other PTAs that follow the same model recognise that right in their chapters on trade and sustainable development,[48] labour,[49] or animal welfare.[50] One recognises it in services, investment, digital trade, competition, and sustainable development.[51] However, most of them do not explicitly recognise the right to regulate in pursuit of public policy objectives according to each party's legal system, in their regulatory cooperation chapter, except for three UK PTAs, where

41 CETA, Article 21.2.4 a); EU–Japan EPA, Article 18.1.1 b); USMCA, Article 28.2.1; New Zealand–Singapore CEPA, Article 13.2.2 c); Japan–UK CEPA, Articles 18.1.1 b) and 18.13 a); EU–UK TCA, Article 340.4; Australia–UK FTA, Article 26.2.1 b); PA–Singapore FTA, Article 20.3.a); New Zealand–UK FTA, Article 21.11 b); Taiwan–US PTA, Article 3.2.

42 CETA, Article 21.2.4 c); EU–Japan EPA, Article 18.1.1 a); Japan–UK CEPA, Article 18.1.1 a); Iceland–Liechtenstein–Norway–UK FTA, Article 11.1.1 a); Australia–UK FTA, Article 26.2.1 a). Certain PTAs include only some of these elements, for example, just effectiveness (New Zealand–UK FTA, Article 21.11) or just transparency (Chile–Paraguay FTA, Article 3.2; Brazil–Chile FTA, Article 3.2).

43 CETA, Article 21.8; PAAP, Articles 15 bis 2.2 e) and 15 bis.8; CPTPP, Articles 25.2.2 d) and 25.8; Chile–Uruguay FTA, Article 15.2 d); Australia–Peru FTA, Article 24.2.2 d); PA–Singapore FTA, Article 20.2.2.d).

44 CETA, Article 21.2.4 a); EU–Japan EPA, Article 18.1.1 b); USMCA, Article 28.2.1; New Zealand–Singapore CEPA, Article 13.2.2 c); Japan–UK CEPA, Articles 18.1.1 b) and 18.13 a); EU–UK TCA, Article 340.4; Australia–UK FTA, Article 26.2.1 b); PA–Singapore FTA, Article 20.3.a); New Zealand–UK FTA, Article 21.11 b); Taiwan–US PTA, Article 3.2.

45 New Zealand–UK FTA, Article 21.11.

46 New Zealand–Singapore CEPA, Article 13.2.2 b).

47 CETA, Article 8.9.

48 EU–Japan EPA, Article 16.2; Japan–UK CEPA, Article 16.2; Iceland–Liechtenstein–Norway–UK FTA, Article 13.3.

49 Australia–UK FTA, Article 21.2; New Zealand–UK FTA, Article 23.4.

50 New Zealand–UK FTA, Article 6.3.

51 EU–UK TCA, Articles 123, 198, 303, and 356.

parties are free to adopt regulatory measures to address their regulatory priorities to ensure the levels of protection they consider appropriate to achieve their public policy objective.[52] Likewise, some recognise the freedom of each party to determine its approach to GRPs in a manner consistent with its own legal framework, practice, procedures, and fundamental principles.[53]

Without explicitly mentioning the 'right to regulate', the CPTPP/PAAP model reaffirms the parties' sovereign right to establish regulations, identify their regulatory priorities, and implement measures to address them, at the scope and the levels they deem appropriate.[54]

Compared to the CPTPP/PAAP model, the CETA model clearly delineates its regulatory objectives. The CETA mentions the parties' commitment to ensuring high levels of protection for human, animal, and plant life, health, and the environment.[55] Similar PTAs explicitly include health, safety, and environmental goals as public policy objectives.[56] Some add occupational health and safety, labour conditions, climate change, consumer protection, social protection and social security, personal data and cybersecurity, cultural diversity, financial stability, and energy security.[57] The EU–UK TCA also adds money laundering.[58] In contrast, among the treaties following the CPTPP/PAAP model, only the USMCA and the Taiwan–US PTA explicitly mention public policy objectives like health, safety, and environmental or sustainable goals.[59]

17.5.3.3.3 INTER-STATE COOPERATION Both models promote cooperation activities between state parties to develop regulatory reform policies.[60] In some, these activities also include capacity building and strengthening in this field.[61] In most cases, the regulatory cooperation activities are voluntary or include hortatory language, although some agreements have binding commitments to cooperate.[62]

52 Iceland–Liechtenstein–Norway–UK FTA, Article 11.1; Australia–UK FTA, Article 26.2; New Zealand–UK FTA, Article 21.2.
53 EU–UK TCA, Article 340.1; EU–New Zealand FTA, Article 22.1; Chile–EU Interim Trade Agreement, Article 29.1.
54 PAAP, Article 15 bis.2; CPTPP, Article 25.2.2; Chile–Uruguay FTA, Article 15.2; Australia–Peru, Article 24.2.2; Brazil–Chile FTA, Article 3.4; USMCA, Article 28.2; PA–Singapore FTA, Article 20.2.
55 CETA, Article 21.2.2.
56 Australia–UK FTA, Article 26.2.3; New Zealand–UK FTA, Article 21.2.3.
57 EU–Japan EPA, Article 18.1.2; Japan–UK CEPA, Article 18.3.
58 EU–UK TCA, Article 340.3.
59 USMCA, Article 28.2.1; Taiwan–US PTA, Article 3.2.
60 CETA, Article 21.2; EU–Japan, Article 18.1; New Zealand–Singapore FTA, Article 13.4
61 PAAP, Article 15 bis 2; CPTPP, Article 25.2; Chile–Uruguay FTA, Article 15.2; Australia–Peru FTA, Article 24.2; EU–UK TCA, Article 351; New Zealand–UK, Article 21.9.
62 Chile–Uruguay FTA, Article 15.7; Brazil–Chile FTA, Article 3.7; New Zealand–Singapore FTA, Article 13.4; Chile–Paraguay FTA, Article 3.4; Australia–UK FTA, Article 26.10; PA–Singapore, Article 20.7; New Zealand–UK FTA, Article 21.8.

Several agreements include concrete cooperation activities, such as information exchange, dialogues, meetings between the parties, their regulatory authorities, and stakeholders; training programmes, seminars, and other technical assistance initiatives.[63] Certain PTAs add activities of data exchange, information and practices, including management, RIAs, cost–benefit analysis, ex post review, and public consultations.[64]

Most of these PTAs foresee cooperation exclusively between parties. The CETA considers it between 'relevant trading partners', and is open to others 'only if practicable and mutually beneficial'.[65] The CPTPP acknowledges cooperation between treaty partners, without any express limitation or exclusion of third parties.[66] However, some are explicitly open to IRC with non-parties,[67] or in international forums.[68] According to the PAAP, parties can consider *existing* measures of Member States or regional forums.[69] Likewise, the Brazil–Chile FTA encourages parties, when developing regulatory measures, to consider international and foreign references, to the extent appropriate and consistent with domestic law.[70]

17.5.3.4 Mechanisms of Regulatory Convergence

Preferential trade agreements with horizontal chapters on regulatory convergence promote several GRPs that we can classify as internal and external mechanisms. Internal mechanisms aim to build convergence starting from each state ('bottom-up'), which are then coordinated, implemented, and reviewed with other contracting parties. External mechanisms aim first to achieve convergence between contracting parties, a process that is later internalised ('top-down') (Polanco Lazo and Sauvé 2018).

a) **Internal mechanisms** refer to bottom-up processes which are generally binding, such as *RIAs*[71] (carry out and make public an analysis of

63 Chile–Uruguay FTA, Article 15.7; USMCA, Article 28.17; Japan–UK, Article 18.12; Iceland–Liechtenstein–Norway–UK FTA, Article 11.10; PA–Singapore, Article 20.7; Canada–Ukraine Modernized Free Trade Agreement, Article 26.12.

64 Chile–Paraguay FTA, Article 3.4; Australia–UK FTA, Article 26.10.3; Brazil–Chile FTA, Article 3.7.

65 CETA, Articles 21.2.3 and 21.7.

66 CPTPP, Article 25.7.

67 Japan–UK FTA, Article 18.13 b); New Zealand–UK FTA, Article 21.11.

68 Australia–UK FTA, Article 26.10.3 e); New Zealand–UK FTA, Article 21.9.1 c).

69 PAAP, Article 15 bis 7.

70 Brazil–Chile FTA, Article 3.6.4.

71 PAAP, Article 15 bis.5; CPTPP, Article 25.5; Chile–Uruguay FTA, Article 15.5; Australia–Peru FTA, Article 24.5; EU–Japan EPA, Article 18.8; Brazil–Chile FTA, Article 3.6.2; USMCA, Article 28.11; Japan–UK FTA, Article 18.8; EU–UK TCA, Article 347; Chile–Paraguay FTA, Article 3.3.2; Australia–UK FTA, Article 26.5; PA–Singapore FTA, Article 20.5; New Zealand–UK, Article 21.5; EU–New Zealand FTA, Article 22.8; Chile–EU Interim Trade Agreement, Article 29.8; Taiwan–US PTA, Article 3.11.

regulatory measures under preparation, considering the need of them, and any feasible and appropriate alternatives, including the option of not regulating);[72] *transparency* (including publication, free and searchable access to regulatory measures online through a 'regulatory register' or a dedicated website),[73] *stakeholder participation* (usually through public consultation),[74] and establishing *internal coordination and review processes and mechanisms*.[75] In addition, some PTAs recognise the important role of existing central regulatory coordination bodies (CRCBs) in the contracting parties,[76] or encourage its establishment.[77] Other less common internal mechanisms are the *periodic or retrospective review* or evaluation of regulatory measures,[78] determining whether they should be modified, streamlined, expanded, or repealed,[79] to reduce regulatory burden;[80] the *use of plain language* to ensure that new regulatory measures are clear, concise, well-organised, and easy to understand;[81] and *early information on planned regulatory measures*, at

72 Iceland–Liechtenstein–Norway–UK FTA, Article 11.7; USMCA, Article 28.11.

73 PAAP, Article 15 bis.5.6; CPTPP, Article 25.5.5; Chile–Uruguay FTA, Article 15.5.5; Australia–Peru FTA, Article 24.5.5; Brazil–Chile FTA, Article 3.6.6; USMCA, Article 28.12; EU–UK TCA, Article 349; Chile–Paraguay FTA, Article 3.3.5; PA–Singapore FTA, Article 20.5.6; Australia–UK FTA, Article 26.8; New Zealand–UK, Article 21.6; EU–New Zealand FTA, Articles 22.4 and 22.10; Chile–EU Interim Trade Agreement, Articles 29.5 and 29.10; Taiwan–US PTA, Articles 3.7, 3.9, and 3.12.

74 EU–Japan EPA, Article 18.7; Brazil–Chile FTA, Article 3.6.1; Japan–UK FTA, Article 18.7; EU–UK TCA, Article 346; Chile–Paraguay FTA, Article 3.3.1; Iceland–Liechtenstein–Norway–UK FTA, Article 11.6; Australia–UK FTA, Article 26.6; New Zealand–UK, Article 21.4; EU–New Zealand FTA, Article 22.7; Chile–EU Interim Trade Agreement, Article 29.7.

75 PAAP, Article 15 bis.4; CPTPP, Article 25.4; Chile–Uruguay FTA, Article 15.4; Australia–Peru FTA, Article 24.4; EU–Japan EPA, Article 18.4, Brazil–Chile FTA, Article 3.5; USMCA, Article 28.4; Japan–UK FTA, Article 18.4; EU–UK TCA, Article 343; Iceland–Liechtenstein–Norway–UK FTA, Article 11.4; Australia–UK FTA, Article 26.3; PA–Singapore FTA, Article 20.4; New Zealand–UK, Article 21.3; EU–New Zealand FTA, Article 22.5; Chile–EU Interim Trade Agreement, Article 29.4.

76 USMCA, Article 28.3.

77 PA–Singapore FTA, Article 20.8.2 a); Taiwan–US Trade Initiative, Article 3.3.

78 EU–Japan EPA, Article 18.9; Japan–UK FTA, Article 18.9; EU–UK TCA, Article 348; Iceland–Liechtenstein–Norway–UK FTA, Article 11.8; New Zealand–UK FTA, Article 21.7; EU–New Zealand FTA, Article 22.9; Chile–EU Interim Trade Agreement, Article 29.9; Taiwan–US PTA, Article 3.13; Canada–Ukraine Modernized Free Trade Agreement, Article 26.11.

79 PAAP, Article 15 bis.5.7; CPTPP, Article 25.5.6; Chile–Uruguay FTA, Article 15.5.6; Australia–Peru FTA, Article 24.5.6; Brazil–Chile FTA, Article 3.6.7; USMCA, Article 28.13; Chile–Paraguay FTA, Article 3.3.6; PA–Singapore FTA, Article 20.5.7.

80 Australia–UK FTA, Article 26.9.

81 PAAP, Article 15 bis.5.5; CPTPP, Article 25.5.4; Chile–Uruguay FTA, Article 15.5.4; Australia–Peru FTA, Article 24.5.4; Brazil–Chile FTA, Article 3.6.5; USMCA, Article 28.8; Chile–Paraguay FTA, Article 3.3.4; Australia–UK FTA, Article 26.7; PA–Singapore FTA, Article 20.5.5; Taiwan–US PTA, Article 3.8; Canada–Ukraine Modernized Free Trade Agreement, Article 26.8.

least on an annual basis, with a brief description of its scope and objectives, the estimated time for its adoption, and opportunities for public consultation.[82]

b) **External mechanisms** follow a top-down process, such as establishing *treaty bodies*,[83] *contact points*,[84] or specific cooperation activities between parties to the agreement, like exchanges of information on regulatory practices[85] in case of planned regulatory measures.[86] The New Zealand–UK FTA further details informal cooperation (including dialogues or meetings between policy officials), formal cooperation (including MRAs, equivalence, or harmonisation), and engaging with interested persons, including businesses and consumers.[87]

As we can see, PTAs largely favour procedural convergence. One of the few internal measures aimed at substantive convergence found in both models calls for a general 'consideration' of other treaty parties' regulatory measures. But such soft commitments leave plenty of room for divergence. In CETA and like agreements, parties undertake, *when appropriate*, to consider the regulatory measures or initiatives of the other party on the same or related topics. However, that does not prevent parties from adopting different approaches, including institutional and legislative set-ups, circumstances, values, or priorities.[88] In other PTAs following this model, when developing new or revising existing regulatory measures, parties shall consider, to the 'extent feasible', any regulatory approach by the other party, on the same or a related matter.[89]

[82] PAAP, Article 15 bis.5.8; CPTPP, Article 25.5.7; Chile–Uruguay FTA, Article 15.5.7; Australia–Peru FTA, Article 24.5.7; EU–Japan EPA, Article 18.6; USMCA, Article 28.6; Japan–UK FTA, Article 18.6; EU–UK TCA, Article 345; EU–New Zealand FTA, Article 22.6; Chile–EU Interim Trade Agreement, Article 29.6; Taiwan–US PTA, Article 3.6.

[83] A Committee on Good Regulatory Practices (Taiwan–US PTA, Article 3.17), a Trade Specialised Committee on Regulatory Cooperation (EU–UK TCA, Article 352); a Committee on Regulatory Cooperation (Japan–UK FTA, Article 18.14; EU–Japan FTA, Article 18.14); a Committee on Good Regulatory Practices (USMCA, Article 28.18); a Regulatory Coherence Committee (Chile–Uruguay FTA, Article 15.6; CPTPP, Article 25.6); a Regulatory Cooperation Forum (CETA, Article 21.6); or a Regulatory Improvement Committee (PAAP, Article 15 bis.6).

[84] CETA, Article 21.9; Australia–Peru FTA, Article 24.6; EU–Japan EPA, Article 18.15; Brazil–Chile FTA, Article 3.8; USMCA, Article 28.19; New Zealand–Singapore FTA, Article 13.3; Japan–UK FTA, Article 18.15; EU–UK TCA, Article 353; Chile–Paraguay FTA, Article 3.5; Iceland–Liechtenstein–Norway–UK FTA, Article 11.11; Australia–UK FTA, Article 26.11; PA–Singapore FTA, Article 20.6; New Zealand–UK, Article 21.10; EU–New Zealand FTA, Article 22.12; Chile–EU Interim Trade Agreement, Article 29.12; Taiwan–US PTA, Article 3.18.

[85] EU–Japan EPA, Article 18.11; Japan–UK FTA, Article 18.11; EU–UK TCA, Article 350; Chile–EU Interim Trade Agreement, Article 29.11.

[86] Japan–UK FTA, Article 18.16; Iceland–Liechtenstein–Norway–UK FTA, Articles 11.9 and 11.12.

[87] New Zealand–UK, Article 21.12.

[88] CETA, Article 21.5; Australia–UK FTA, Article 26.10.4.

[89] EU–Japan EPA, Article 18.12.5 c); Iceland–Liechtenstein–Norway–UK FTA, Article 11.10.3 c); Japan–UK FTA, Article 18.12.5 c); EU–UK TCA, Article 351.4 c).

In the CPTPP/PAAP model, each party should *encourage* its relevant regulatory agencies to consider regulatory measures in other parties, as well as relevant developments in international, regional, and other forums when planning covered regulatory measures, but only to the extent appropriate and consistent with its legal system.[90]

As we can see, most of the internal mechanisms of regulatory convergence included in existing PTAs are binding and aim to achieve procedural rather than substantive convergence. Provisions on substantive convergence are increasingly found, but their 'bindingness' is very small. We are still at the beginning when thinking about substantial commitments.

17.5.3.5 Implementation

For purposes of transparency and to serve as a basis for cooperation and capacity-building activities, several PTAs following the CPTPP/PAAP model undertake to issue a regular report on the implementation of their regulatory convergence chapters. In these agreements, each party shall submit a 'notification of implementation' to the free trade commission (FTC) through national contact points, describing the steps taken since the entry into force of the treaty and those intended to take in implementing the regulatory convergence chapter. The FTC will examine these notifications and ask questions or discuss specific aspects of the notification of that party.[91] In contrast, CETA and other PTAs following that model do not have explicit commitments concerning the implementation of regulatory convergence chapters.

In practice, this does not make much of a difference, as there is very little information about the implementation of these agreements in general. The CPTPP Committee on Regulatory Coherence just met for the first time in May 2021.[92] The EU–Japan Committee on Regulatory Cooperation has met three times in the past two years, with no concrete commitments.[93]

17.6 POSSIBLE FUTURE DEVELOPMENTS

17.6.1 *New Mechanisms of Internal Regulatory Convergence*

Recent PTAs expand the toolkit of regulatory convergence, particularly those we have identified as 'internal' mechanisms. Among them, we find:

[90] PAAP, Article 15 bis.5.4; CPTPP, Article 25.5.8; Chile–Uruguay FTA, Article 15.5.8; PA–Singapore FTA, Article 20.5.4; Australia–Peru FTA, Article 24.5.8.

[91] The periodicity of these reports varies, from an annual report (USMCA, Article 28.16), to every three years (PA–Singapore FTA, Article 208; Brazil–Chile FTA, Article 3.9; PAAP, Article 15 bis.9, although the latter considered an initial report two years after its entry into force), and four years (Chile–Uruguay FTA, Article 15.8; CPTPP, Article 25.9, although the initial report was due only after three).

[92] CPTPP Committee on Regulatory Coherence, https://www.cas.go.jp/jp/tpp/tppinfo/2021/session/pdf/210901_en_02.pdf (accessed 13 May 2024).

[93] Committee on Regulatory Cooperation: EU–Japan EPA, circabc.europa.eu/ui/group/09242a36-a438-40fd-a7af-fe32e36cbd0e/library/99bdf2d0-edad-42f8-8bf4-b38b51a2e6f7?p=1 (accessed 13 May 2024).

a) *Descriptions of regulatory processes and mechanisms*, including RIAs and other relevant GRPs.[94] Some add that these descriptions shall be freely and publicly available online.[95]
b) Provide any person with an *opportunity to submit comments for improvements of regulatory measures* in force, including suggestions for simplifying or reducing unnecessary burdens.[96]

Among the most recent PTAs, the USMCA and the Taiwan–US PTA include more of these new mechanisms. In addition to those referred to above, both treaties recognise the need for *regulations to be based on reliable information and of high quality* (including scientific, technical, economic, and other information relevant to the regulation). To that end, parties should adopt or maintain publicly available guidance or mechanisms that encourage regulatory authorities when developing a regulation to seek such information.[97] Likewise, they recognise that regulatory authorities may seek advice and recommendations to prepare or implement regulations from *expert advisory groups*, including those outside the government.[98]

Future PTAs dealing with regulatory convergence will probably expand and refine such mechanisms, based on the experience gained from their implementation. However, increasing internal regulatory convergence is likely to require more than that. One possible way forward would be actively promoting central regulatory coordinating bodies in each country, one of the few internal mechanisms of regulatory convergence found in PTAs that are not binding. The mandatory establishment of such bodies could be coupled with assistance (both technical and financial) from states with prior experience in this regard (like OIRA in the US,[99] or the Treasury Board in Canada),[100] to help this development in countries lacking such institutions, particularly developing countries. There are already some signs in that direction. A few Latin American countries have established CRCBs, including some of those that have negotiated PTAs with regulatory convergence chapters, like Chile, Mexico, Peru, and Colombia (as well as El Salvador).[101]

94 EU–Japan EPA, Article 18.5; USMCA, Article 28.9; Japan–UK FTA, Article 18.5; EU–UK TCA, Article 344.
95 USMCA, Articles 28.7 and 28.15; Iceland–Liechtenstein–Norway–UK FTA, Article 11.5; Australia–UK FTA, Article 26.4; Taiwan–US PTA, Article 3.15.
96 EU–Japan EPA, Article 18.10; USMCA, Article 28.14; Japan–UK FTA, Article 18.10; Taiwan–US PTA, Article 3.14.
97 USMCA, Article 28.5; Taiwan–US PTA, Article 3.5.
98 USMCA, Article 28.10; Taiwan–US PTA, Article 3.10.
99 Office of Management and Budget (OMB), Executive Office of the President, Office of Information and Regulatory Affairs (OIRA), www.whitehouse.gov/omb/information-regulatory-affairs/ (accessed 13 May 2024).
100 Treasury Board of Canada, www.canada.ca/en/treasury-board-secretariat.html (accessed 13 May 2024).
101 For a list of these CRCBs, see: www.interamericancoalition-medtech.org/regulatory-convergence/quick-links/central-regulatory-coordination-bodies/ (accessed 25 May 2023).

17.6.2 *More Substantive Regulatory Convergence?*

As we have seen, up to now, PTAs have primarily focused on procedural convergence. Still, another possible future development could be the increase of substantive regulatory convergence in general and specific sectors.

Some recent PTAs include glimpses in that direction. The EU–Japan EPA aims to promote common principles, guidelines, codes of conduct, and implementing tools.[102] In 2021, the PA agreed on common rules for eliminating technical barriers to food supplements, cosmetic products, household cleaning products, and medical devices, mostly on certificates and labelling.[103] Although the current CETA RCF work plan is mainly about information-sharing activities, since 2017, it has considered initiatives to align regulations between Canada and the EU in consumer product safety, pharmaceutical inspections, and animal welfare (started in 2021).[104]

Furthermore, outside PTAs, substantive regulatory convergence has increased in specific sectors, particularly at a regional level. For example, the Pan American Network for Drug Regulatory Harmonization (PANDRH), created in 1999, focuses on harmonising regulations for small molecule drugs in the Americas. The African Medicines Regulatory Harmonisation Initiative ('Zazibona Process') was launched in 2009 and involves cooperation between Zambia, Zimbabwe, Botswana, and Namibia, among others (Alvaro et al. 2019).

Among the different challenges posed by the COVID-19 pandemic, we found the recognition of vaccination certificates from other countries. Still, some convergence was partially achieved concerning WHO-approved vaccines – even though global vaccination coverage on this and other vaccines is lacking.[105] Harmonisation of regulatory guidelines of clinical trials is much needed (e.g. consent, handling of data, the equivalence of conclusions).[106]

Avoidance or reduction of regulatory divergence during the COVID-19 crisis was possible through cooperation and coordination across regulatory agencies, not only on vaccines and related issues, but also on other issues like food and refugees.[107] Inter-agency cooperation or coordination is a model for avoiding divergence in the

[102] EU–Japan EPA, Article 18.13.

[103] Alianza del Pacífico, Pacific Alliance countries define the same rules of the game for marketing medical devices, https://alianzapacifico.net/en/pacific-alliance-countries-define-the-same-rules-of-the-game-for-marketing-medical-devices/ (accessed 20 February 2023).

[104] Comprehensive Economic and Trade Agreement Regulatory Cooperation Forum – Work plan, www.international.gc.ca/trade-commerce/trade-agreements-accords-commerciaux/agr-acc/ceta-aecg/2023-01-03-work-travail-plan.aspx?lang = eng (accessed 13 May 2024).

[105] World Health Organization (WHO), Immunization Dashboard, https://immunizationdata.who.int/ (accessed 13 May 2024).

[106] OECD, Regulatory Policy and the COVID-19 Crisis, www.oecd.org/regreform/regulatory-policy/reg-covid-19-activities.htm (accessed 13 May 2024).

[107] See, for example, World Food Programme (WFP), Inter-Agency Humanitarian Response of the Covid-19 Humanitarian Response, www.wfp.org/publications/inter-agency-humanitarian-response-covid-19-humanitarian-response (accessed 13 May 2024); and UNHCR, COVID-19:

first place and can be used to achieve more substantive regulatory convergence in the future (although this is likely to happen only for specific topics).

17.6.3 *Increased Role of Private Actors*

The distinction between public and private regulations is not always clear, as there are different sources of regulations following the 'governance triangle' that includes state-led, private-led, and collaborative regulations (Abbott and Snidal 2010).

Future developments in regulatory convergence in PTAs may include an increasing role of private actors in developing regulations. As mentioned, one of the most common general principles found in agreements with regulatory convergence chapters is precisely to consider inputs from interested persons in developing regulatory measures.

As Vallejo points out, some private actors already have regulatory authority. However, such recognition is subject to formal and substantive conditions of validity that are not equivalent to those applicable to public agents (Vallejo Garretón 2021). Examples of these entities include the International Financing Reporting Standards (IFRS) Foundation,[108] which has become the focal point of transnational accounting standard-setting being endorsed by the WTO, the International Organization of Securities Commissions (IOSCO), the World Bank, the G7, and the Basel Committee (Vallejo Garretón 2020). Likewise, since its creation in 1990, the International Council for Harmonisation of Technical Requirements for Pharmaceuticals for Human Use (ICH) has brought together regulatory authorities and the pharmaceutical industry to discuss scientific and technical aspects of pharmaceuticals and develop guidelines to achieve greater harmonisation worldwide.[109]

However, an increasing role of these stakeholders may increase the risk of 'regulatory capture', without a clear delineation of how the public consultation processes should be conducted, and whether they should be opened to include other stakeholders and governments than the one planning to regulate. Some fear that as 'interested persons' or 'stakeholders' are not always clearly defined, that may lead to agenda capture by major corporations and business lobby groups (Kelsey 2011). However, it could also be the case that the influence of private standards could decrease trade costs and facilitate convergence, particularly in sectors where private standards are commonplace, as in the automotive industry (Costa and Jacoby 2014).

17.6.4 *Dispute Settlement*

A significant limitation of most treaties following the CPTPP/PAAP model is that they are not subject to dispute settlement provisions. This means that instances of

Inter-Agency Coordination, https://data.unhcr.org/en/working-group/251 (accessed 13 May 2024).

108 IFRSF, www.ifrs.org/ (accessed 13 May 2024).

109 ICH, www.ich.org/ (accessed 13 May 2024).

non-compliance with the chapter's obligations are not directly enforceable by the Member States.[110]

There is no explicit exclusion from the dispute settlement mechanism in CETA. However, the limitations inherent in the CETA approach make conflict unlikely, as the parties commitments are largely voluntary and do not limit their ability to carry out their regulatory, legislative, and policy measures.[111] Activities like conducting, comparing, and sharing post-implementation reviews are also only facultative. All other treaties following the CETA model have explicitly excluded their regulatory convergence chapters from the treaties' dispute settlement mechanism.[112]

A further significant limitation of the CPTPP/PAAP model is that in the event of any inconsistency between their respective chapters, and any other chapter of the agreement, the latter will prevail.[113] The CETA has no similar provisions, and neither treaties that follow its model except for the UK FTAs with Japan, Iceland–Liechtenstein–Norway, Australia, and New Zealand.[114]

However, current developments in both models open the possibility of dispute settlement concerning regulatory convergence commitments. A couple of recent agreements that largely follow the CETA model – the EU–Japan EPA and the Japan–UK CEPA – include a mechanism through which a party may submit to the other party a request to consider its concerns about a planned or existing regulatory measure. The requesting party shall identify the regulatory measure at issue, describe its concerns, and, where relevant, submit questions. The responding party shall, as soon as possible but, unless justified, no later than 60 days after the receipt of the request, provide written comments as regards the concerns raised by the requesting party. Even though there is no possibility of accessing the general dispute settlement mechanism, the requesting party may request consultations with the responding party, to address the concerns of the requesting party. This might include proposals for adjusting the regulatory measure or adopting a less trade- or investment-restrictive one. However, they do not require the responding party to achieve a particular regulatory outcome and shall not delay the adoption of a regulatory measure.[115] It is also noteworthy that in both agreements, no provision makes other chapters prevail in case of inconsistency with the regulatory convergence chapter.

[110] PAAP, Article 15 bis 11; CPTPP, Article 25.11; PA–Singapore FTA, Article 20.10.

[111] CETA, Article 21.2.

[112] EU–UK TCA, Article 354; Iceland–Liechtenstein–Norway–UK FTA, Article 11.13; Australia–UK FTA, Article 26.13; New Zealand–UK, Article 21.15; Japan–UK FTA, Article 18.19; EU–Japan FTA, Article 18.19.

[113] CPTPP, Article 25.10; PAAP Article 15 bis 10; Chile–Uruguay FTA, Article 15.9; Australia–Peru FTA, Article 24.8; Brazil–Chile FTA, Article 3.10, New Zealand–Singapore FTA, Article 13.5; Chile–Paraguay FTA, Article 3.6.

[114] Japan–UK FTA, Article 18.18.2; Iceland–Liechtenstein–Norway–UK FTA, Article 11.3; Australia–UK FTA, Article 26.12; and New Zealand–UK FTA, Article 21.14.

[115] Japan–UK FTA, Article 18.16; EU–Japan FTA, Article 18.16.

Most importantly, there is an explicit recourse to dispute settlement in the USMCA. Recognising that a mutually acceptable solution can often be found outside recourse to dispute settlement, a 'sustained or recurring course of action or inaction' that is inconsistent with a provision of the chapter on good regulatory practices is subject to dispute settlement. No other chapters of the agreement take precedence in case of inconsistency.[116] Therefore, it seems likely that future PTAs may include dispute settlement provisions – either general or special – concerning their regulatory convergence chapter. This could make a difference concerning the implementation of internal mechanisms, which are largely binding.

Another concern that might appear – although it seems highly unlikely in the current development of investment law – is that the breach of regulatory convergence commitments is used as a basis to start investor–state dispute settlement (ISDS), if the PTA has an investment chapter that considers such possibility. Several ISDS arbitral tribunals have interpreted the obligation to provide a 'predictable and transparent legal framework' as a source of investors' legitimate expectations as an element of the fair and equitable treatment (FET) or indirect expropriation standards, although the contours of these obligations are controversial (Henckels 2016). These tribunals have interpreted transparency obligations as requiring states to be forthcoming with information about intended changes in policy and regulations that may significantly affect investments so that the investor can adequately plan their investment and, if needed, engage the host state in dialogue about protecting their legitimate expectations.[117] Although the purpose of measures subject to RIAs may not be to expropriate or treat a foreign investor unfairly, it could be considered to do so if the assessment does not appropriately balance policy goals with science- or evidence-based information (Sheargold and Mitchell 2016).[118]

It is also important to note that regulatory convergence does not work in the same way as FET, or indirect expropriation provisions. While the latter usually requires an *ex post* establishment infringement of investment treaty rules, regulatory convergence usually implies an *ex ante* analysis of a potentially challenged measure even before its legal existence, without necessarily examining the measure's effects concerning foreign investors. Thus, even if a party undertakes an RIA and adopts a measure that has net benefits, such a measure could still be deemed inconsistent with investment treaty obligations if it disproportionately affects foreign entities (Polanco Lazo 2013).

[116] USMCA, Article 28.20.

[117] See Eskosol S.p.A. *in liquidazione v. Italian Republic*, ICSID Case No. ARB/15/50, Award, 4 September 2020, §416; *Electrabel S.A. v. Hungary*, ICSID Case No. ARB/07/19, Decision on Jurisdiction, Applicable Law and Liability, 30 November 2012, § 7.79.

[118] In particular with respect to their analysis of *Clatyon and Bilcon v. Canada* (Award on Jurisdiction and Liability), PCA Case No. 2009–04 (17 March 2015).

17.7 CONCLUSION

Under different names, the introduction of notions of regulatory cooperation, improvement, coherence, or, more commonly, GRPs have become a new frontier in PTA governance, primarily built on the roots of domestic and international rulemaking principles.

The distinction between these typologies is not really relevant, as all these concepts aim to increase regulatory convergence, whether substantive or procedural, through different internal ('bottom-up') and external ('top-down') tools. While early PTAs only included some provisions on regulatory convergence, recent agreements consider specially dedicated chapters on this discipline, which are applied horizontally.

Most PTAs having dedicated chapters to this new discipline focus on different internal mechanisms of procedural convergence, which are largely binding. Starting with RIAs, these tools have grown over the years, including commitments to transparency, inter-agency coordination, stakeholder participation, periodic or retrospective review or evaluation of regulatory measures, use of plain language, and early information on planned regulatory measures. Future design for these areas could include more detailed and transparent descriptions of RIAs, increased opportunities to suggest improvements of regulations, more access to scientific, technical, economic, and other information used as a basis to develop the regulation, and mandatory establishment of CRCBs.

The most common mechanisms envisaged to achieve substantive convergence in PTAs are establishing treaty bodies (up to now with somewhat limited or indirect regulatory powers) and a host of general and specific cooperation activities. But it still remains a *voluntary* undertaking under which neither party is obliged to enter into particular regulatory cooperation activities, nor where either party may refuse to cooperate or withdraw from ongoing cooperation initiatives.

The scope of these chapters has also grown over time, extending from some regulations to almost all regulations. These provisions are also increasingly less of a 'second-class' commitment – meaning that PTAs are less likely to include a provision where other chapters prevail in case of inconsistency with the regulatory convergence chapter. Yet, many provisions on regulatory convergence in PTAs are aspirational or 'best efforts'.

Up to now, the main drivers of this new discipline are the US, EU, the UK, and countries from the Asia-Pacific rim like Australia, Chile, Japan, New Zealand, and Singapore. China is conspicuously absent and probably hesitates to embrace international commitments on regulatory convergence for political reasons (Lin and Liu 2018).

The notion of regulatory convergence raises questions of influence and legitimacy. In a world of pronounced regulatory asymmetries, will the regulations of the most powerful actors not tend to prevail? Will this increase the tendency towards harmonising or adopting dominant regulatory standards issued by the small group of rulemaking nations with greater negotiating power ('regulatory hegemons')? (Kelsey 2011). Does it run the risk of resulting in the dissemination of 'the regulatory gospel' of 'regulation-exporting' states? (Slaughter 2005).

Developing countries may prefer to ascribe to substantive or regulatory convergence for other reasons, like participation in their development, as it has happened at the regional level with ASEAN and the PA. On the other hand, regulatory convergence by 'developed economies' may not lead to emerging markets automatically upgrading to higher standards, either because they were not part of the negotiation that created the standard or because they are simply unable to meet and implement them, in the absence of capacity-building provision for North–South agreements.

If the introduction of regulatory convergence disciplines in PTAs is successful, it is likely to inform the evolution of trade global norms and play a significant role in a wide range of subject areas subject to PTA disciplines, including TBTs, intellectual property rights, financial services, investment, competition policy, consumer rights, and the recognition of professional service qualifications (Stoler et al. 2014)

But the mere existence of regulatory divergence need not always be problematic. Alternative legal solutions adopted by countries might be neutral from an efficiency viewpoint (Mattei et al. 2000). Legitimate cross-country differences in collective preferences, attitudes to risk and uncertainty, legal traditions, etc., can also explain such differences (Chirico and Larouche 2013). Fostering deeper forms of regulatory convergence could generate high costs, particularly if enacted in asymmetrical North–South relations and agreements. Finally, addressing the competition-impairing effects of regulatory differences can be administratively and politically more challenging than eliminating traditional impediments to trade and investment.

REFERENCES

Abbott, K. W., and D. Snidal 2010. 'International Regulation without International Government: Improving IO Performance through Orchestration', *The Review of International Organizations* 5(3):315–344.

Ahearn, R. J. 2009. Transatlantic Regulatory Cooperation: Background and Analysis (Congressional Research Service). Retrieved 13 May 2024, from https://fas.org/sgp/crs/row/RL34717.pdf

Alvaro, D., C. A. Challener, and E. Branch 2019. From Regulatory Convergence to Global Regulatory Harmonization. Retrieved 13 May 2024, from www.pharmasalmanac.com/articles/from-regulatory-convergence-to-global-regulatory-harmonization

APEC 2011. Good Regulatory Practices in APEC Member Economies – Baseline Study. Retrieved 13 May 2024, from www.apec.org/publications/2011/11/good-regulatory-practices-in-apec-member-economies—baseline-study

APEC and OECD 2005. APEC–OECD Integrated Checklist on Regulatory Reform, APEC–OECD Co-operative Initiative on Regulatory Reform. Retrieved 13 May 2024, from www.oecd-ilibrary.org/governance/apec-oecd-integrated-checklist-on-regulatory-reform_9789264051652-en

ASEAN 2014a. ASEAN Framework Agreement on Mutual Recognition Arrangements. Retrieved 13 May 2024, from https://asean.org/asean-framework-agreement-on-mutual-recognition-arrangements/

2014b. Standards and Conformance. Retrieved 13 May 2024, from https://asean.org/our-communities/economic-community/standard-and-conformance/

Basedow, R., and C. Kauffmann 2016. International Trade and Good Regulatory Practices: Assessing the Trade Impacts of Regulation (OECD Regulatory Policy Working Papers No. 4), Vol. 4.

Bollyky, T. 2012. 'Regulatory Coherence in the TPP Talks'. In: C. L. Lim, D. K. Elms, and P. Low (Eds), *The Trans-Pacific Partnership: A Quest for a Twenty-first Century Trade Agreement*, Cambridge: Cambridge University Press, 171–186.

Chirico, F., and P. Larouche 2013. 'Convergence and Divergence, in Law and Economics and Comparative Law'. In: P. Larouche and P. Cserne (Eds), *National Legal Systems and Globalization*, The Hague, The Netherlands: T. M. C. Asser Press, 9–33.

Costa, M., and W. Jacoby 2014. 'Informal Drivers of Regional Regulatory Integration. The Auto Sector in Central Europe and Latin America'. In: L. Bruszt and G. A. McDermott (Eds), *Leveling the Playing Field: Transnational Regulatory Integration and Development*, Oxford: Oxford University Press, 183–204.

Council of the European Union 2019. Council Decision Authorising the Opening of Negotiations with the United States of America for an Agreement on the Elimination of Tariffs for Industrial Goods. 6052/19. Retrieved 13 May 2024, from www.consilium.europa.eu/media/39180/st06052-en19.pdf

Crettez, B., B. Deffains, and O. Musy 2014. 'Legal Convergence and Endogenous Preferences', *International Review of Law and Economics* 39: 20–27.

European Commission 2013. Directives for the negotiation on the Transatlantic Trade and Investment Partnership between the European Union and the United States of America. ST 11103/13 RESTREINT UE/EU RESTRICTED. Retrieved 13 May 2024, from https://data.consilium.europa.eu/doc/document/ST-11103-2013-DCL-1/en/pdf

2015. EU–US cooperation. Retrieved 13 May 2024, from http://ec.europa.eu/growth/industry/international-aspects/cooperation governments/eu-us/index_en.htm

2021. EU–US launch Trade and Technology Council. [Text]. Retrieved 13 May 2024, from https://ec.europa.eu/commission/presscorner/detail/en/IP_21_2990

2022. EU–US Trade and Technology Council – Third Ministerial Meeting. Retrieved 13 May 2024, from https://commission.europa.eu/strategy-and-policy/priorities-2019-2024/stronger-europe-world/eu-us-trade-and-technology-council_en

Fergusson, I. F., and B. Vaughn 2011. The Trans-Pacific Partnership Agreement (Congressional Research Service). Retrieved 13 May 2024, from www.fas.org/sgp/crs/row/R40502.pdf

Fishbein, M., and M. Trebilcock 2007. 'International Trade: Barriers to Trade'. In: A. T. Guzman and A. O. Sykes (Eds), *Research Handbook in International Economic Law*, Cheltenham, UK ; Northampton, MA: Edward Elgar Pub, 1–61.

Glaeser, E. L., and A. Shleifer 2002. 'Legal Origins', *The Quarterly Journal of Economics* 117(4): 1193–1229.

Greenpeace Nederland 2016. Regulatory Cooperation. Retrieved 13 May 2024, from https://trade-leaks.org/ttip/regulatory-cooperation/

Henckels, C. 2016. 'Protecting Regulatory Autonomy through Greater Precision in Investment Treaties: The TPP, CETA, and TTIP', *Journal of International Economic Law* 19(1): 27–50.

Hoekman, B. 2015. 'Fostering Transatlantic Regulatory Cooperation and Gradual Multilateralization', *Journal of International Economic Law* 18(3): 609–624.
Jacobs, S. H. 1994. 'Regulatory Co-Operation for an Interdependent World: Issues for Government'. In: Organisation for Economic Co-operation and Development (OECD), *Regulatory Co-operation for an Interdependent World*, Paris: Organisation for Economic Co-operation and Development. Retrieved 13 May 2024, from www.oecd-ilibrary.org/content/book/9789264062436-en
1997. An Overview of Regulatory Impact Analysis in OECD Countries. In: Organisation for Economic Co-operation and Development (OECD), *Regulatory Impact Analysis: Best Practices in OECD Countries*, Paris: Organisation for Economic Co-operation and Development, 13–32.
2017. 2016 Final Report on Good Regulatory Practices in APEC Economies. Retrieved 13 May 2024, from www.apec.org/publications/2017/08/2016-final-report-on-good-regulatory-practices-in-apec-economies
Kauffmann, C., and C. Saffirio 2021. *Good Regulatory Practices and Co-Operation in Trade Agreements: A Historical Perspective and Stocktaking*, Paris: OECD. Retrieved 13 May 2024, from www.oecd-ilibrary.org/governance/good-regulatory-practices-and-co-operation-in-trade-agreements_cf520646-en
Kelsey, J. 2011. Preliminary Analysis of the Draft TPP Chapter on Domestic Coherence. Retrieved 13 May 2024, from www.citizenstrade.org/ctc/wp-content/uploads/2011/10/TransPacific_RegCoherenceMemo.pdf
La Porta, R., F. Lopez-De-Silanes and A. Shleifer 2008. 'The Economic Consequences of Legal Origins', *Journal of Economic Literature* 46(2): 285–332.
Laurenza, E. C. and J. Mathis 2013. 'Regulatory Cooperation for Trade in Services in the EU and US Trade Agreements with the Republic of Korea: How Deep and How Compatible?' *Melbourne Journal of International Law* 14(1): 171–204.
Lemoine, J. 2018. Global Indicators of Regulatory Governance: Worldwide Practices of Regulatory Impact Assessments. Retrieved 13 May 2024, from https://documents.worldbank.org/en/publication/documents-reports/documentdetail/905611520284525814/Global-Indicators-of-Regulatory-Governance-Worldwide-Practices-of-Regulatory-Impact-Assessments
Lin, C.-F. and H.-W. Liu 2018. 'Regulatory Rationalisation Clauses in FTAs: A Complete Survey of the US, EU, and China', *Melbourne Journal of International Law* 19(1): 1–29.
Malmström, C. 2015. Trade in the 21st Century: The Challenge of Regulatory Convergence. Retrieved 13 May 2024, from www.podomatic.com/podcasts/friendsofeurope/episodes/2015-03-20T09_16_04-07_00
Malyshev, N., and C. Kauffmannn 2015. *International Regulatory Co-operation: The Menu of Approaches. E15 Task Force on Regulatory Systems Coherence Think Piece*, Geneva, Switzerland: International Centre for Trade and Sustainable Development (ICTSD) and World Economic Forum. Retrieved August 28, 2017, from http://e15initiative.org/wp-content/uploads/2015/09/E15-Regulatory-Coherence-Kauffmann-and-Malyshev-Final.pdf
Manak, I. 2022. 'Increasing North American Competitiveness through Regulatory Cooperation', *USMCA Briefs*, no. 5, Woodrow Wilson Center.
Mattei, U. A., L. Antoniolli, and A. Rossato 2000. 'Comparative Law and Economics'. In: B. Bouckaert and G. de Geest (Eds), *Encyclopedia of Law and Economics*, Cheltenham, UK; Northampton: Edward Elgar Publishing, 505–560.
Mildner, S., and O. Ziegler 2009. 'A Long and Thorny Road: Regulatory Cooperation under the Framework for Advancing Transatlantic Economic Integration', *Intereconomics* 44(1): 49–58.

Ministerio de Comercio, Industria y Turismo de Colombia 2016. 100 Preguntas de la Alianza del Pacífico. Retrieved 13 May 2024, from www.tlc.gov.co/preguntas-frecuentes/100-preguntas-de-la-alianza-del-pacifico

OECD 2008. *Introductory Handbook for Undertaking Regulatory Impact Analysis (RIA)*, Paris, France: OECD. Retrieved 13 May 2024, from www.oecd.org/mena/governance/41727566.pdf

2009. *Regulatory Impact Analysis*, Paris, France: OECD Publishing. Retrieved 13 May 2024, from www.oecd-ilibrary.org/governance/regulatory-impact-analysis_9789264067110-en

2012. Recommendation of the Council on Regulatory Policy and Governance. Retrieved 13 May 2024, from www.oecd.org/gov/regulatory-policy/2012-recommendation.htm

2013. *International Regulatory Co-operation*, Paris: Organisation for Economic Co-operation and Development. Retrieved 13 May 2024, from www.oecd-ilibrary.org/content/book/9789264200463-en

Polanco Lazo, R. 2013. 'The Trans-Pacific Partnership Agreement and Regulatory Coherence'. In: T. Voon (Ed.), *Trade Liberalisation and International Co-operation: A Legal Analysis of the Trans-Pacific Partnership Agreement*, Edward Elgar Publishing, 231–261.

Polanco Lazo, R., and P. Sauvé 2018. 'The Treatment of Regulatory Convergence in Preferential Trade Agreements', *World Trade Review* 17(4): 575–607.

Posner, T., and D. Wolff 2011. Making 'Regulatory Coherence' Coherent. Retrieved 13 May 2024, from www.crowell.com/en/insights/publications/making-regulatory-coherence-coherent

Ringhof, J. 2022. Setting the Tone: The Value of the EU–US Trade and Technology Council – European Council on Foreign Relations. Retrieved 13 May 2024, from https://ecfr.eu/article/setting-the-tone-the-value-of-the-eu-us-trade-and-technology-council/

Sheargold, E., and A. D. Mitchell 2016. 'The TPP and Good Regulatory Practices: An Opportunity for Regulatory Coherence to Promote Regulatory Autonomy?' *World Trade Review* 15(4): 587–612.

Slaughter, A.-M. 2005. *A New World Order*, Princeton, NJ: Princeton University Press.

Steger, D. 2012. 'Institutions for Regulatory Cooperation in "New Generation" Economic and Trade Agreements', *Legal Issues of Economic Integration*, 39(1): 109–126.

2014. CETA – A New Model for Regulatory Cooperation, Transparency and Coherence? Retrieved 13 May 2024, from https://dokumen.tips/documents/ceta-a-new-model-for-regulatory-cooperation-transparency-.html

Stoler, A. L., P. N. Pedersen, and S. Herreros 2014. 'Negotiating Trade Agreements for the 21st Century', *Comercio Internacional* 116, 1–40.

Street, A. W. 2013. The Art of Legal Convergence. Retrieved 13 May 2024, from www.yumpu.com/en/document/view/51650331/the-art-of-legal-convergence-by-alexander-w-seven-wentworth

Sykes, A. 1999. 'Regulatory Protectionism and the Law of International Trade', *The University of Chicago Law Review* 66(1): 1–46.

Trade Union Advisory Committee 2016. Regulatory Quality for Whom and for What? Retrieved 13 May 2024, from https://tuac.org/news/regulatory-quality-for-whom-and-for-what/

US Department of Commerce 2023. USEUTTC-Documents. Retrieved 13 May 2024, from www.trade.gov/useuttc-documents

Vallejo Garretón, R. 2020. 'The Law of Political Economy: Transformation in the Function of Law'. In: P. F. Kjaer (Ed.), *After Governance?: The Idea of a Private Administrative Law*, Cambridge: Cambridge University Press, 320–347.

2021. 'The Private Administrative Law of Technical Standardization', *Yearbook of European Law* 40: 172–229.

Watson, A. 1993. *Legal Transplants: An Approach to Comparative Law*. Athens: The University of Georgia Press.

Woolcock, S., B. Holzer, and P. Kusmu 2015. The Transatlantic Trade and Investment Partnership: Challenges and Opportunities for Consumer Protection (Paul H. Nitze School of Advanced International Studies, Center for Transatlantic Relations, and B. Centre for European Policy Studies (Brussels, Eds.), Vol. Paper No. 11 in the CEPS-CTR project 'TTIP in the Balance' and CEPS Special Report No. 115.

Young, A. R. 2015. 'Liberalizing Trade, Not Exporting Rules: The Limits to Regulatory Co-ordination in the EU's "New Generation" Preferential Trade Agreements', *Journal of European Public Policy* 22(9): 1253–1275.

Index